Features New To This Edition

This edition of *Teach Yourself Perl 5 in 21 Days* covers the following features, which have been introduced in version 5 of Perl. These new features are listed by the chapter in which they appear.

Day 3, "Understanding Scalar Values"

☐ The \Q escape character enables you to ignore special pattern characters in strings.

Day 4, "More Operators"

☐ Any expression containing an assignment operator can appear on the left side of another assignment operator.

☐ The conditional operator can appear on the left side of an assignment.

☐ not, and, or, and xor are logical operators with lower precedence than the &&, ¦¦, and ! logical operators.

Day 7, "Pattern Matching"

☐ The pos function tells you how much of a string has been searched by the pattern matcher when the g operator is specified.

☐ The m pattern-matching option tells the Perl interpreter that the string to be matched contains multiple lines of text.

☐ The s pattern-matching option specifies that the string to be matched is to be treated as a single line of text.

☐ The x pattern-matching option tells Perl to ignore white space when matching a pattern.

☐ The m and s options are defined for the substitution operator as well.

☐ Extended pattern-matching capabilities enable you to parenthesize subpatterns, embed options, look ahead before matching, and add comments to patterns.

Day 9, "Using Subroutines"

☐ You do not need to supply an & character when calling a subroutine if you have already defined the subroutine.

☐ The my statement defines variables that exist only inside a subroutine.

☐ The BEGIN subroutine, if defined, is called when your program starts running.

☐ The END subroutine, if defined, is called when your program terminates.

☐ The AUTOLOAD subroutine, if defined, is called when your program can't find a subroutine it is supposed to execute.

Day 10, "Associative Arrays"

☐ You can use either => or , to separate array subscripts and values when assigning a list to an associative array.

Day 13, "Process, String, and Mathematical Functions"

☐ The lc and uc functions convert strings to lowercase or uppercase.

- [ ] The `lcfirst` and `ucfirst` functions convert the first letter of a string to lowercase or uppercase.
- [ ] The `quotemeta` function places a backslash in front of every non-word character in a string.
- [ ] The `abs` function returns the absolute value of a number.

Day 14, "Scalar-Conversion and List-Manipulation Functions"

- [ ] The `chomp` function checks whether the last characters of a string or list of strings match the input line separator defined by the `$/` system variable.
- [ ] The `chr` function converts a number to its ASCII character equivalent.
- [ ] The `map` function enables you to use each of the elements of a list, in turn, as an operand in an expression.
- [ ] The `wantarray` function enables you to specify subroutine behavior that depends on whether it is dealing with scalar values or lists.
- [ ] The `exists` function enables you to determine whether a particular element of an associative array exists.

Day 15, "System Functions"

- [ ] The `dump` function enables you to generate a UNIX core dump from within your Perl program.

Day 16, "Command-Line Options"

- [ ] The `-F` option specifies the pattern to use when splitting input lines into words.
- [ ] The `-T` option specifies that data obtained from the outside world cannot be used in any command that modifies your file system.

Day 17, "System Variables"

- [ ] System variables now have alphabetic equivalents, which make them easier to understand.

Day 18, "References in Perl 5"

- [ ] See how to use references in Perl 5 to create complicated data structures and pointers to functions, and learn about subroutine parameter passing.

Day 19, "Object-Oriented Programming in Perl"

- [ ] Learn object-oriented fundamentals in Perl 5 to develop your own Perl classes and modules.

Day 20, "Miscellaneous Features of Perl"

- [ ] You can use a `require` statement to specify the version of Perl needed to run your program.
- [ ] If the value you assign to a `$#array` variable is less than the current maximum subscript, the leftover array values are destroyed.
- [ ] The `qw` string delimiter provides a convenient way of breaking a string into words.
- [ ] In Perl 5, the package name and variable name are separated by a pair of colons instead of a quotation mark.

teach
yourself
PERL 5

in 21 days,
second edition

teach yourself
PERL 5
in 21 days, second edition

David Till

PUBLISHING

201 West 103rd Street
Indianapolis, Indiana 46290

Trademarks

All terms mentioned in this book that are known to be trademarks or service marks have been appropriately capitalized. Sams Publishing cannot attest to the accuracy of this information. Use of a term in this book should not be regarded as affecting the validity of any trademark or service mark.

Acquisitions Editor
Chris Denny

Development Editors
Angelique Brittingham
Keith Davenport

Software Development Specialist
Steve Straiger

Production Editor
Tonya R. Simpson

Copy Editor
Kimberly K. Hannel

Technical Reviewer
Elliotte Rusty Harold

Editorial Coordinator
Bill Whitmer

Technical Edit Coordinator
Lynette Quinn

Formatter
Frank Sinclair

Editorial Assistants
Carol Ackerman
Andi Richter
Rhonda Tinch-Mize

Cover Designer
Tim Amrhein

Book Designer
Gary Adair

Copy Writer
Peter Fuller

Production Team Supervisor
Brad Chinn

Production
Michael Brumitt, Charlotte Clapp
Jason Hand, Sonja Hart
Louisa Klucznik, Ayanna Lacey
Clint Lahnen, Paula Lowell
Laura Robbins, Bobbi Satterfield
Carol Sheehan, Chris Wilcox

Publisher and President	Richard K. Swadley
Acquisitions Manager	Greg Wiegand
Development Manager	Dean Miller
Managing Editor	Cindy Morrow
Marketing Manager	John Pierce
Assistant Marketing Manager	Kristina Perry

Overview

Contents

7 Pattern Matching   199

Acknowledgments

I would like to thank the following people for their help:

- [ ] David Macklem at Sietec Open Systems for allowing me to take the time off to work on the first edition of this book
- [ ] Everyone at Sams Publishing, for their efforts and encouragement
- [ ] Jim Gardner, for telling the people at Sams Publishing about me

I'd also like to thank all those friends of mine (you know who you are) who tolerated my going stir-crazy as my deadlines approached.

About the Authors

David Till

David Till is a technical writer working in Toronto, Ontario, Canada. He holds a master's degree in computer science from the University of Waterloo; programming languages was his major field of study. He also has worked in compiler development and on version-control software. He lists his hobbies as "writing, comedy, walking, duplicate bridge, and fanatical support of the Toronto Blue Jays."

He can be reached via e-mail at am671@freenet.toronto.on.ca or davet@klg.com, or on the World Wide Web at http://www.interlog.com/~davet/.

Kamran Husain

Kamran Husain is a software consultant with experience in UNIX system programming. He has dabbled in all sorts of software for real-time systems applications, telecommunications, seismic data acquisition and navigation, X Window/Motif and Microsoft Windows applications. He refuses to divulge any more of his qualifications. Kamran offers consulting services and training classes through his company, MPS Inc., in Houston, Texas. He is an alumnus of the University of Texas at Austin.

You can reach Kamran through Sams Publishing or via e-mail at khusain@neosoft.com or mpsi@aol.com.

Introduction

This book is designed to teach you the Perl programming language in just 21 days. When you finish reading this book, you will have learned why Perl is growing rapidly in popularity: It is powerful enough to perform many useful, sophisticated programming tasks, yet it is easy to learn and use.

Who Should Read This Book?

No previous programming experience is required for you to learn everything you need to know about programming with Perl from this book. In particular, no knowledge of the C programming language is required. If you are familiar with other programming languages, learning Perl will be a snap. The only assumption this book does make is that you are familiar with the basics of using the UNIX operating system.

Special Features of This Book

This book contains some special elements that help you understand Perl features and concepts as they are introduced:

- ☐ Syntax boxes
- ☐ DO/DON'T boxes
- ☐ Notes
- ☐ Warnings
- ☐ Tips

Syntax boxes explain some of the more complicated features of Perl, such as the control structures. Each syntax box consists of a formal definition of the feature followed by an explanation of the elements of the feature. Here is an example of a syntax box:

The syntax of the `for` statement is

```
for (expr1; expr2; expr3) {
        statement_block
}
```

expr1 is the loop initializer. It is evaluated only once, before the start of the loop.

expr2 is the conditional expression that terminates the loop. The conditional expression in *expr2* behaves just like the ones in `while` and `if` statements: If its value is zero, the loop is terminated, and if its value is nonzero, the loop is executed.

statement_block is the collection of statements that is executed if (and when) *expr2* has a nonzero value.

expr3 is executed once per iteration of the loop, and is executed after the last statement in *statement_block* is executed.

Don't try to understand this definition yet!

DO/DON'T boxes present the do's and don'ts for a particular task or feature. Here is an example of such a box:

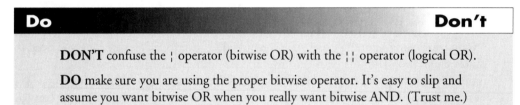

Do	Don't

DON'T confuse the ¦ operator (bitwise OR) with the ¦¦ operator (logical OR).

DO make sure you are using the proper bitwise operator. It's easy to slip and assume you want bitwise OR when you really want bitwise AND. (Trust me.)

Notes are explanations of interesting properties of a particular program feature. Here is an example of a note:

NOTE

In left-justified output, the value being displayed appears at the left end of the value field. In right-justified output, the value being displayed appears at the right end of the value field.

Warnings warn you of programming pitfalls to avoid. Here is a typical warning:

WARNING

You cannot use the last statement inside the do statement. The do statement, although it behaves like the other control structures, is actually implemented differently.

Tips are hints on how to write your Perl programs better. Here is an example of a tip:

TIP

It is a good idea to use all uppercase letters for your file variable names. This makes it easier to distinguish file variable names from other variable names and from reserved words.

Programming Examples

Each feature of Perl is illustrated by examples of its use. In addition, each chapter of this book contains many useful programming examples complete with explanations; these examples show you how you can use Perl features in your own programs.

Each example contains a listing of the program, the input required by and the output generated by the program, and an analysis of how the program works. Special icons are used to point out each part of the example: Type, Input-Output, and Analysis.

In the Input-Output example following Listing IN.1, there are some special typographic conventions. The input you enter is shown in **bold monospace** type, and the output generated by the system or the program is shown in `plain monospace` type. The system prompt (`$` in the examples in this book) is shown so that you know when a command is to be entered on the command line.

TYPE **Listing IN.1. A simple Perl program with comments.**

```
1: #!/usr/local/bin/perl
2: # this program reads a line of input, and writes the line
3: # back out
4: $inputline = <STDIN>;     # read a line of input
5: print( $inputline );      # write the line out
```

OUTPUT
```
$ programIN_1
This is a line of input.
This is a line of input.
$
```

ANALYSIS Line 1 is the header comment. Lines 2 and 3 are comments, not executable lines of code. Line 4 reads a line of input. Line 5 writes the line of input on your screen.

End-of-Day Q&A and Workshop

Each day ends with a Q&A section containing answers to common questions relating to that day's material. There also is a Workshop at the end of each day that consists of quiz questions and programming exercises. The exercises often include BUG BUSTER exercises that help you spot some of the common bugs that crop up in Perl programs. The answers to these quiz questions as well as sample solutions for the exercises are presented in Appendix A, "Answers."

Conventions Used in This Book

This book uses different typefaces to help you differentiate between Perl code and regular English, and also to help you identify important concepts.

- ☐ Actual Perl code is typeset in a special monospace font. You'll see this font used in listings and the Input-Output examples, as well as in code snippets. In the explanations of Perl features, commands, filenames, statements, variables, and any text you see on the screen also are typeset in this font.

- ☐ Command input and anything that you are supposed to enter appears in a **bold monospace** font. You'll see this mainly in the Input-Output examples.

- ☐ Placeholders in syntax descriptions appear in an *italic monospace* font. Replace the placeholder with the actual filename, parameter, or whatever element it represents.

- ☐ *Italics* highlight technical terms when they first appear in the text and are sometimes used to emphasize important points.

What You'll Learn in 21 Days

In your first week of learning Perl, you'll learn enough of the basics of Perl to write many useful Perl programs. Here's a summary of what you'll learn in Week 1:

Day 1, "Getting Started," tells you how to get Perl, how to run Perl programs, and how to read from your keyboard and write to your screen.

Day 2, "Basic Operators and Control Flow," teaches you about simple arithmetic, how to assign a value to a scalar variable, and how to control execution using conditional statements.

Day 3, "Understanding Scalar Values," teaches you about integers, floating-point numbers, and character strings. It also shows you that all three are interchangeable in Perl.

Day 4, "More Operators," tells you all about operators and expressions in Perl and talks about operator associativity and precedence.

Day 5, "Lists and Array Variables," introduces you to lists, which are collections of values, and to array variables, which store lists.

Day 6, "Reading from and Writing to Files," tells you how to interact with your file system by reading from input files, writing to output files, and testing for particular file attributes.

Day 7, "Pattern Matching," describes pattern-matching in Perl and shows how you can substitute values and translate sets of characters in text strings.

By the end of Week 2, you'll have mastered almost all the features of Perl; you'll also have learned about many of the library functions supplied with the language. Here's a summary of what you'll learn:

Day 8, "More Control Structures," discusses the control flow statements not previously covered.

Day 9, "Using Subroutines," shows how you can break your program into smaller, more manageable, chunks.

Day 10, "Associative Arrays," introduces one of the most powerful and useful constructs in Perl—arrays—and it shows how you can use these arrays to simulate other data structures.

Day 11, "Formatting Your Output," shows how you can use Perl to produce tidy reports.

Day 12, "Working with the File System," shows how you can interact with your system's directory structure.

Day 13, "Process, String, and Mathematical Functions," describes the library functions that interact with processes running on the system. It also describes the functions that perform trigonometric and other mathematical operations, and the functions that operate on strings.

Day 14, "Scalar-Conversion and List-Manipulation Functions," describes the library functions that convert values from one form to another and the functions that work with lists and array variables.

By the end of Week 3, you'll know all the features and capabilities of Perl. It covers the rest of the Perl library functions and describes some of the more esoteric concepts of the language. Here's a summary of what you'll learn:

Day 15, "System Functions," describes the functions that manipulate the Berkeley UNIX and UNIX System V environments.

Day 16, "Command-Line Options," describes the options you can supply with Perl to control how your program runs.

Day 17, "System Variables," describes the built-in variables that are included automatically as part of every Perl program.

Day 18, "References in Perl 5," describes the pointer and reference features of Perl 5, including multi-dimensional arrays.

Day 19, "Object-Oriented Programming in Perl," describes the object-oriented capabilities added to Perl 5. These enable you to hide information and divide your program into individual file modules.

Day 20, "Miscellaneous Features of Perl," covers some of the more exotic or obscure features of the language.

Day 21, "The Perl Debugger," shows you how to use the Perl debugger to discover errors quickly.

Week at a Glance

In your first week of teaching yourself Perl, you'll learn enough of the basics to write many useful Perl programs. Although some experience in using a programming language will be an advantage as you read this book, it is not required. In particular, you don't need to know the C programming language before you read this book.

To use this book effectively, you should be able to try out some of the features of Perl as you learn them. To do this, you should have Perl running on your system. If you don't have Perl, Day 1, "Getting Started," tells how you can get it for free.

Each chapter of this book contains quiz and exercise questions that test you on the material covered in the day's lesson. These questions are answered in Appendix A, "Answers."

Where You're Going

The first week covers the essentials of Perl. Here's a summary of what you'll learn.

Day 1, "Getting Started," tells you how to get Perl, how to run Perl programs, and how to read input from your keyboard and write output to your screen.

Day 2, "Basic Operators and Control Flow," teaches you about simple arithmetic, how to assign a value to a scalar variable, and how to control execution using conditional statements.

Day 3, "Understanding Scalar Values," teaches you about integers, floating-point numbers, and character strings. It also shows you that all three are interchangeable in Perl.

Day 4, "More Operators," tells you all about operators and expressions in Perl and talks about operator associativity and precedence.

Day 5, "Lists and Array Variables," introduces you to lists, which are collections of values, and to array variables, which store lists.

Day 6, "Reading from and Writing to Files," tells you how to interact with your file system by reading from input files, writing to output files, and testing for particular file attributes.

Finally, Day 7, "Pattern Matching," describes pattern matching in Perl and shows how you can substitute values and translate sets of characters in text strings.

This is quite a bit of material to learn in one week; however, by the end of the week you'll know most of the essentials of Perl and will be able to write many useful programs.

Day 1

Getting Started

Welcome to *Teach Yourself Perl 5 in 21 Days*. Today you'll learn about the following:

- [ ] What Perl is and why Perl is useful
- [ ] How to get Perl if you do not already have it
- [ ] How to run Perl programs
- [ ] How to write a very simple Perl program
- [ ] The difference between interpretive and compiled programming languages
- [ ] What an algorithm is and how to develop one

What Is Perl?

Perl is an acronym, short for *Practical Extraction and Report Language*. It was designed by Larry Wall as a tool for writing programs in the UNIX environment and is continually being updated and maintained by him.

For its many fans, Perl provides the best of several worlds. For instance:

☐ Perl has the power and flexibility of a high-level programming language such as C. In fact, as you will see, many of the features of the language are borrowed from C.

☐ Like shell script languages, Perl does not require a special compiler and linker to turn the programs you write into working code. Instead, all you have to do is write the program and tell Perl to run it. This means that Perl is ideal for producing quick solutions to small programming problems, or for creating prototypes to test potential solutions to larger problems.

☐ Perl provides all the features of the script languages sed and awk, plus features not found in either of these two languages. Perl also supports a sed-to-Perl translator and an awk-to-Perl translator.

In short, Perl is as powerful as C but as convenient as awk, sed, and shell scripts.

NOTE This book assumes that you are familiar with the basics of using the UNIX operating system.

As you'll see, Perl is very easy to learn. Indeed, if you are familiar with other programming languages, learning Perl is a snap. Even if you have very little programming experience, Perl can have you writing useful programs in a very short time. By the end of Day 2, "Basic Operators and Control Flow," you'll know enough about Perl to be able to solve many problems.

How Do I Find Perl?

To find out whether Perl already is available on your system, do the following:

☐ If you are currently working in a UNIX programming environment, check to see whether the file /usr/local/bin/perl exists.

☐ If you are working in any other environment, check the place where you normally keep your executable programs, or check the directories accessible from your PATH environment variable.

If you do not find Perl in this way, talk to your system administrator and ask whether she or he has Perl running somewhere else. If you don't have Perl running in your environment, don't despair—read on!

Where Do I Get Perl?

One of the reasons Perl is becoming so popular is that it is available free of charge to anyone who wants it. If you are on the Internet, you can obtain a copy of Perl with file-transfer protocol (FTP). The following is a sample FTP session that transfers a copy of the Perl distribution. The items shown in boldface type are what you would enter during the session.

```
$ ftp prep.ai.mit.edu
Connected to prep.ai.mit.edu.
220 aeneas FTP server (Version wu-2.4(1) Thu Apr 14 20:21:35 EDT 1994) ready.
Name (prep.ai.mit.edu:dave): anonymous
331 Guest login ok, send your complete e-mail address as password.
Password:
230-Welcome, archive user!
230-
230-If you have problems downloading and are seeing "Access denied" or
230-"Permission denied", please make sure that you started your FTP
230-client in a directory to which you have write permission.
230-
230-If you have any problems with the GNU software or its downloading,
230-please refer your questions to <gnu@PREP.AI.MIT.EDU>. If you have any
230-other unusual problems, please report them to <root@aeneas.MIT.EDU>.
230-
230-If you do have problems, please try using a dash (-) as the first
230-character of your password — this will turn off the continuation
230-messages that may be confusing your FTP client.
230-
230 Guest login ok, access restrictions apply.
ftp> cd pub/gnu
250-If you have problems downloading and are seeing "Access denied" or
250-"Permission denied", please make sure that you started your FTP
250-client in a directory to which you have write permission.
250-
250-Please note that all files ending in '.gz' are compressed with
250-'gzip', not with the unix 'compress' program.  Get the file README
250- and read it for more information.
250-
250-Please read the file README
250-  it was last modified on Thu Feb 1 15:00:50 1996 - 32 days ago
250-Please read the file README-about-.diff-files
250-  it was last modified on Fri Feb 2 12:57:14 1996 - 31 days ago
250-Please read the file README-about-.gz-files
250-  it was last modified on Wed Jun 14 16:59:43 1995 - 264 days ago
250 CWD command successful.
ftp> binary
200 Type set to I.
ftp> get perl-5.001.tar.gz
200 PORT command successful.
150 Opening ASCII mode data connection for perl-5.001.tar.gz (1130765 bytes).
226 Transfer complete.
1130765 bytes received in 9454 seconds (1.20 Kbytes/s)
ftp> quit
221 Goodbye.
$
```

The commands entered in this session are explained in the following steps. If some of these steps are not familiar to you, ask your system administrator for help.

1. The command

   ```
   $ ftp prep.ai.mit.edu
   ```

   connects you to the main Free Software Foundation source depository at MIT.

2. The user ID `anonymous` tells FTP that you want to perform an anonymous FTP operation.

3. When FTP asks for a password, enter your user ID and network address. This lets the MIT system administrator know who is using the MIT archives. (For security reasons, the password is not actually displayed when you type it.)

4. The command `cd pub/gnu` sets your current working directory to be the directory containing the Perl source.

5. The `binary` command tells FTP that the file you'll be receiving is a file that contains unreadable (non-text) characters.

6. The `get` command copies the file `perl-5.001.tar.gz` from the MIT source depository to your own site. (It's usually best to do this in off-peak hours to make things easier for other Internet users—it takes awhile.) This file is quite large because it contains all the source files for Perl bundled together into a single file.

7. The `quit` command disconnects from the MIT source repository and returns you to your own system.

Once you've retrieved the Perl distribution, do the following:

1. Create a directory and move the file you just received, `perl-5.001.tar.gz`, to this directory. (Or, alternatively, move it to a directory already reserved for this purpose.)

2. The `perl-5.001.tar.gz` file is compressed to save space. To uncompress it, enter the command

   ```
   $ gunzip perl-5.001.tar.gz
   ```

   `gunzip` is the GNU uncompress program. If it's not available on your system, see your system administrator. (You can, in fact, retrieve it from `prep.ai.mit.edu` using anonymous FTP with the same commands you used to retrieve the Perl distribution.)

   When you run `gunzip`, the file `perl-5.001.tar.gz` will be replaced by `perl-5.001.tar`, which is the uncompressed version of the Perl distribution file.

3. The next step is to unpack the Perl distribution. In other words, use the information in the Perl distribution to create the Perl source files. To do this, enter the following command:

```
$ tar xvf - <perl-5.001.tar
```

As this command executes, it creates each source file in turn and displays the name and size of each file as it is created. The tar command also creates subdirectories where appropriate; this ensures that the Perl source files are organized in a logical way.

4. Using your favorite C compiler, compile the Perl source code using the makefile provided. (This makefile should have been created when the source files were unpacked in the last step.)

5. Place the compiled Perl executable into the directory where you normally keep your executables. On UNIX systems, this directory usually is called /usr/local/bin, and Perl usually is named /usr/local/bin/perl.

You might need your system administrator's help to do this because you might not have the necessary permissions.

Other Places to Get Perl

If you cannot access the MIT site from where you are, you can get Perl from the following sites using anonymous FTP:

North America

Site	Location
ftp.netlabs.com	Internet address 192.94.48.152
	Directory /pub/outgoing/perl5.0
ftp.cis.ufl.edu	Internet address 128.227.100.198
	Directory /pub/perl/src/5.0
ftp.uu.net	Internet address 192.48.96.9
	Directory /languages/perl
ftp.khoros.unm.edu	Internet address 198.59.155.28
	Directory /pub/perl
ftp.cbi.tamucc.edu	Internet address 165.95.1.3
	Directory /pub/duff/Perl
ftp.metronet.com	Internet address 192.245.137.1
	Directory /pub/perl/sources
genetics.upenn.edu	Internet address 128.91.200.37
	Directory /perl5

Europe

Site	Location
ftp.cs.ruu.nl	Internet address 131.211.80.17
	Directory /pub/PERL/perl5.0/src
ftp.funet.fi	Internet address 128.214.248.6
	Directory /pub/languages/perl/ports/perl5
ftp.zrz.tu-berlin.de	Internet address 130.149.4.40
	Directory /pub/unix/perl
src.doc.ic.ac.uk	Internet address 146.169.17.5
	Directory /packages/perl5

Australia

Site	Location
sungear.mame.mu.oz.au	Internet address 128.250.209.2
	Directory /pub/perl/src/5.0

South America

Site	Location
ftp.inf.utfsm.cl	Internet address 146.83.198.3
	Directory /pub/gnu

You also can obtain Perl from most sites that store GNU source code, or from any site that archives the Usenet newsgroup comp.sources.unix.

A Sample Perl Program

Now that Perl is available on your system, it's time to show you a simple program that illustrates how easy it is to use Perl. Listing 1.1 is a simple program that asks for a line of input and writes it out.

TYPE
Listing 1.1. A simple Perl program that reads and writes a line of input.

```
1: #!/usr/local/bin/perl
2: $inputline = <STDIN>;
3: print( $inputline );
```

OUTPUT
```
$program1_1
This is my line of input.
This is my line of input.
$
```

ANALYSIS Line 1 is the header comment. Line 2 reads a line of input. Line 3 writes the line of input back to your screen.

The following sections describe how to create and run this program, and they describe it in more detail.

Running a Perl Program

To run the program shown in Listing 1.1, do the following:

1. Using your favorite editor, type the previous program and save it in a file called program1_1.

2. Tell the system that this file contains executable statements. To do this in the UNIX environment, enter the command

   ```
   $ chmod +x program1_1
   ```

3. Run the program by entering the command

   ```
   $ program1_1
   ```

When you run program1_1, it waits for you to enter a line of input. After you enter the line of input, program1_1 prints what you entered, as follows:

```
$ program1_1
This is my line of input.
This is my line of input.
$
```

If Something Goes Wrong

If Listing 1.1 is stored in the file program1_1 and run according to the preceding steps, the program should run successfully. If the program doesn't run, one of two things has likely happened:

☐ The system can't find the file program1_1.

☐ The system can't find Perl.

If you receive the error message

```
program1_1 not found
```

or something similar, your system couldn't find the file program1_1. To tell the system where program1_1 is located, you can do one of two things in a UNIX environment:

- ☐ Enter the command ./program1_1, which gives the system the pathname of program1_1 relative to the current directory.
- ☐ Add the current directory . to your PATH environment variable. This tells the system to search in the current directory when looking for executable programs such as program1_1.

If you receive the message

```
/usr/local/bin/perl not found
```

or something similar, this means that Perl is not installed properly on your machine. See the section "How Do I Find Perl?" earlier today, for more details.

If you don't understand these instructions or are still having trouble running Listing 1.1, talk to your system administrator.

The First Line of Your Perl Program: How Comments Work

Now that you've run your first Perl program, let's look at each line of Listing 1.1 and figure out what it does.

Line 1 of this program is a special line that tells the system that this is a Perl program:

```
#!/usr/local/bin/perl
```

Let's break this line down, one part at a time:

- ☐ The first character in the line, the # character, is the Perl *comment character*. It tells the system that this line is not an executable instruction.
- ☐ The ! character is a special character; it indicates what type of program this is. (You don't need to worry about the details of what the ! character does. All you have to do is remember to include it.)
- ☐ The path /usr/local/bin/perl is the location of the Perl executable on your system. This executable *interprets* your program; in other words, it figures out what you want to do and then does it. Because the Perl executable has the job of interpreting Perl instructions, it usually is called the *Perl interpreter*.

If, after reading this, you still don't understand the meaning of the line #!/usr/local/bin/perl don't worry. The actual specifics of what it does are not important for our purposes in this book. Just remember to include it as the first line of your program, and Perl will take it from there.

1

NOTE

If you are running Perl on a system other than UNIX, you might need to replace the line `#!/usr/local/bin/perl` with some other line indicating the location of the Perl interpreter on your system. Ask your system administrator for details on what you need to include here.

After you have found out what the proper first line is in your environment, include that line as the first line of every Perl program you write, and you're all set.

Comments

As you have just seen, the first character of the line

```
#!/usr/local/bin/perl
```

is the *comment character*, `#`. When the Perl interpreter sees the `#`, it ignores the rest of that line.

Comments can be appended to lines containing code, or they can be lines of their own:

```
$inputline = <STDIN>;    # this line contains an appended comment
# this entire line is a comment
```

You can—and should—use comments to make your programs easier to understand. Listing 1.2 is the simple program you saw earlier, but it has been modified to include comments explaining what the program does.

NOTE

As you work through the lessons in this book and create your own programs—such as the one in Listing 1.2—you can, of course, name them anything you want. For illustration and discussion purposes, I've adopted the convention of using a name that corresponds to the listing number. For example, the program in Listing 1.2 is called `program1_2`.

The program name is used in the Input-Output examples such as the one following this listing, as well as in the Analysis section where the listing is discussed in detail. When you follow the Input-Output example, just remember to substitute your program's name for the one shown in the example.

Listing 1.2. A simple Perl program with comments.

```
1: #!/usr/local/bin/perl
2: # this program reads a line of input, and writes the line
3: # back out
4: $inputline = <STDIN>;      # read a line of input
5: print( $inputline );       # write the line out
```

```
$ program1_2
This is a line of input.
This is a line of input.
$
```

ANALYSIS The behavior of the program in Listing 1.2 is identical to that of Listing 1.1 because the actual code is the same. The only difference is that Listing 1.2 has comments in it.

Note that in an actual program, comments normally are used only to explain complicated code or to indicate that the following lines of code perform a specific task. Because Perl instructions usually are pretty straightforward, Perl programs don't need to have a lot of comments.

Do   Don't

DO use comments whenever you think that a line of code is not easy to understand.

DON'T clutter up your code with unnecessary comments. The goal is readability. If a comment makes a program easier to read, include it. Otherwise, don't bother.

DON'T put anything else after /usr/local/bin/perl in the first line:

```
#!/usr/local/bin/perl
```

This line is a special comment line, and it is not treated like the others.

Line 2: Statements, Tokens, and <STDIN>

Now that you've learned what the first line of Listing 1.1 does, let's take a look at line 2:

```
$inputline = <STDIN>;
```

This is the first line of code that actually does any work. To understand what this line does, you need to know what a Perl statement is and what its components are.

Statements and Tokens

The line of code you have just seen is an example of a Perl *statement*. Basically, a statement is one task for the Perl interpreter to perform. A Perl program can be thought of as a collection of statements performed one at a time.

When the Perl interpreter sees a statement, it breaks the statement down into smaller units of information. In this example, the smaller units of information are $inputline, =, <STDIN>, and ;. Each of these smaller units of information is called a *token*.

Tokens and White Space

Tokens can normally be separated by as many spaces and tabs as you like. For example, the following statements are identical in Perl:

```
$inputline = <STDIN>;
$inputline=<STDIN>;
$inputline      =       <STDIN>;
```

Your statements can take up as many lines of code as you like. For example, the following statement is equivalent to the ones above:

```
$inputline
=
<STDIN>
;
```

The collection of spaces, tabs, and new lines separating one token from another is known as *white space*.

When programming in Perl, you should use white space to make your programs more readable. The examples in this book use white space in the following ways:

☐ New statements always start on a new line.

☐ One blank space is used to separate one token from another (except in special cases, some of which you'll see today).

What the Tokens Do: Reading from Standard Input

As you've seen already, the statement

```
$inputline = <STDIN>;
```

consists of four tokens: $inputline, =, <STDIN>, and ;. The following subsections explain what each of these tokens does.

The $inputline and = Tokens

The first token in line 1, $inputline (at the left of the statement), is an example of a *scalar variable*. In Perl, a scalar variable can store one piece of information.

The = token, called the *assignment operator*, tells the Perl interpreter to store the item specified by the token to the right of the = in the place specified by the token to the left of the =. In this example, the item on the right of the assignment operator is the <STDIN> token, and the item to the left of the assignment operator is the $inputline token. Thus, <STDIN> is stored in the scalar variable $inputline.

Scalar variables and assignment operators are covered in more detail on Day 2, "Basic Operators and Control Flow."

The <STDIN> Token and the Standard Input File

The next token, <STDIN>, represents a line of input from the *standard input file*. The standard input file, or *STDIN* for short, typically contains everything you enter when running a program.

For example, when you run program1_1 and enter

```
This is a line of input.
```

the line you enter is stored in the standard input file.

The <STDIN> token tells the Perl interpreter to read one line from the standard input file, where a *line* is defined to be a set of characters terminated by a new line. In this example, when the Perl interpreter sees <STDIN>, it reads in

```
This is a line of input.
```

If the Perl interpreter then sees another <STDIN> in a different statement, it reads another line of data from the standard input file. The line of data you read earlier is destroyed unless it has been copied somewhere else.

NOTE
> If there are more lines of input than there are <STDIN> tokens, the extra lines of input are ignored.

Because the <STDIN> token is to the right of the assignment operator =, the line

```
This is a line of input.
```

is assigned to the scalar variable $inputline.

The ; Token

The ; token at the end of the statement is a special token that tells Perl the statement is complete. You can think of it as a punctuation mark that is like a period in English.

Line 3: Writing to Standard Output

Now that you understand what statements and tokens are, consider line 3 of Listing 1.1, which is

```
print ($inputline);
```

This statement refers to the *library function* that is called print. Library functions, such as print, are provided as part of the Perl interpreter; each library function performs a useful task.

The print function's task is to send data to the *standard output file*. The standard output file stores data that is to be written to your screen. The standard output file sometimes appears in Perl programs under the name STDOUT.

In this example, print sends $inputline to the standard output file. Because the second line of the Perl program assigns the line

```
This is a line of input.
```

to $inputline, this is what print sends to the standard output file and what appears on your screen.

Function Invocations and Arguments

When a reference to print appears in a Perl program, the Perl interpreter *calls*, or *invokes*, the print library function. This *function invocation* is similar to a function invocation in C, a GOSUB statement in BASIC, or a PERFORM statement in COBOL. When the Perl interpreter sees the print function invocation, it executes the code contained in print and returns to the program when print is finished.

Most library functions require information to tell them what to do. For example, the print function needs to know what you want to print. In Perl, this information is supplied as a sequence of comma-separated items located between the parentheses of the function invocation. For example, the statement you've just seen:

```
print ($inputline);
```

supplies one piece of information that is passed to print: the variable $inputline. This piece of information commonly is called an *argument*.

The following call to print supplies two arguments:

```
print ($inputline, $inputline);
```

You can supply print with as many arguments as you like; it prints each argument starting with the first one (the one on the left). In this case, print writes two copies of $inputline to the standard output file.

You also can tell print to write to any other specified file. You'll learn more about this on Day 6, "Reading From and Writing To Files."

Error Messages

If you incorrectly type a statement when creating a Perl program, the Perl interpreter will detect the error and tell you where the error is located.

For example, look at Listing 1.3. This program is identical to the program you've been seeing all along, except that it contains one small error. Can you spot it?

 TYPE   **Listing 1.3. A program containing an error.**

```
1: #!/usr/local/bin/perl
2: $inputline = <STDIN>
3: print ($inputline);
```

OUTPUT
```
$ program1_3
Syntax error in file program1_3 at line3, next char (
Execution of program1_3 aborted due to compilation errors.
$
```

ANALYSIS   When you try to run this program, an error message appears. The Perl interpreter has detected that line 2 of the program is missing its closing ; character. The error message from the interpreter tells you what the problem is and identifies the line on which the problem is located.

 TIP

> You should fix errors starting from the beginning of your program and working down.
>
> When the Perl interpreter detects an error, it tries to figure out what you meant to say and carries on from there; this feature is known as *error recovery*. Error recovery enables the interpreter to detect as many errors as possible at one time, which speeds up the development process.

Sometimes, however, the Perl interpreter can get confused and think you meant to do one thing when you really meant to do another. In this situation, the interpreter might start trying to detect errors that don't really exist. This problem is known as *error cascading*.

It's usually pretty easy to spot error cascading. If the interpreter is telling you that errors exist on several consecutive lines, it usually means that the interpreter is confused. Fix the first error, and the others might very well go away.

Interpretive Languages Versus Compiled Languages

As you've seen, running a Perl program is easy. All you need to do is create the program, mark it as executable, and run it. The Perl interpreter takes care of the rest. Languages such as Perl that are processed by an interpreter are known as *interpretive languages*.

Some programming languages require more complicated processing. If a language is a *compiled language*, the program you write must be translated into machine-readable code by a special program known as a *compiler*. In addition, library code might need to be added by another special program known as a *linker*. After the compiler and linker have done their jobs, the result is a program that can be executed on your machine—assuming, of course, that you have written the program correctly. If not, you have to compile and link the program all over again.

Interpretive languages and compiled languages both have advantages and disadvantages, as follows:

☐ As you've seen with Perl, it takes very little time to run a program in an interpretive language.

☐ Interpretive languages, however, cannot run unless the interpreter is available. Compiled programs, on the other hand, can be transferred to any machine that understands them.

As you'll see, Perl is as powerful as a compiled language. This means that you can do a lot of work quickly and easily.

Summary

Today you learned that Perl is a programming language that provides many of the capabilities of a high-level programming language such as C. You also learned that Perl is easy to use; basically, you just write the program and run it.

You saw a very simple Perl program that reads a line of input from the standard input file and writes the line to the standard output file. The standard input file stores everything you type from your keyboard, and the standard output file stores everything your Perl program sends to your screen.

You learned that Perl programs contain a header comment, which indicates to the system that your program is written in Perl. Perl programs also can contain other comments, each of which must be preceded by a #.

Perl programs consist of a series of statements, which are executed one at a time. Each statement consists of a collection of tokens, which can be separated by white space.

Perl programs call library functions to perform certain predefined tasks. One example of a library function is print, which writes to the standard output file. Library functions are passed chunks of information called arguments; these arguments tell a function what to do.

The Perl interpreter executes the Perl programs you write. If it detects an error in your program, it displays an error message and uses the error-recovery process to try to continue processing your program. If Perl gets confused, error cascading can occur, and the Perl interpreter might display inappropriate error messages.

Finally, you learned about the differences between interpretive languages and compiled languages, and that Perl is an example of an interpretive language.

Q&A

Q Is there any particular editor I need to use with Perl?

A No. Perl programs are ordinary text files. You can use any text editor you like.

Q Why do I need to enter the chmod +x command before running my program?

A Because Perl programs are ordinary text files, the UNIX operating system does not know that they are executable programs. By default, text files have read and write permissions granted, which means you can look at your file or change it. The chmod +x command adds execute permission to the file; when this permission is granted, the system knows that this is an executable program.

Q Can I use `print` to print other things besides input lines?

A Yes. You'll learn more about how you can use `print` on Day 3, "Understanding Scalar Values."

Q Why is Perl available for free?

A This encourages the dissemination of computer knowledge and capabilities.

It works like this: You can get Perl for free, and you can use it to write interesting and useful programs. If you want, you can then give these programs away and let other people write interesting and useful programs based on your programs. This way, everybody benefits.

You also can modify the source for Perl, provided you tell everybody that your version is a modification of the original. This means that if you think of a clever thing you want Perl to do, you can add it yourself. (However, you can't blame anybody else if your modification breaks something or if it doesn't work.)

Of course, you don't have to give your Perl programs away for free. In fact, you even can sell your Perl programs, provided you don't borrow anything from somebody else's program.

Workshop

The Workshop provides quiz questions to help you solidify your understanding of the material covered and exercises to give you experience in using what you've learned. Try to understand the quiz and exercise answers before continuing to the next day.

Quiz

1. What do Perl's fans appreciate about Perl?
2. What does the Perl interpreter do?
3. Define the following terms:
    a. statement
    b. token
    c. argument
    d. error recovery
    e. standard input file
4. What is a comment, and where can it appear?

5. Where is Perl usually located on a UNIX machine?

6. What is a header comment, and where does it appear in a program?

7. What is a library function?

Exercises

1. Modify program1_1 to print the input line twice.

2. Modify program1_1 to read and print two different input lines.

3. Modify program1_1 to read two input lines and print only the second one.

4. **BUG BUSTER:** What is wrong with the following program?

   ```
   #!/usr/local/bin/perl
   $inputline = <STDIN>;
   print ($inputline)
   print ($inputline);
   ```

5. **BUG BUSTER:** What is wrong with the following program?

   ```
   #!/usr/local/bin/perl
   $inputline = <STDIN>;
   # print my line!    print($inputline);
   ```

6. What does the following program do?

   ```
   #!/usr/local/bin/perl
   $inputline = <STDIN>;
   $inputline2 = <STDIN>;
   print ($inputline2);
   print ($inputline);
   ```

Week 1

Day 2

Basic Operators and Control Flow

Today's lesson gives you the information you need to write some simple Perl programs. You'll learn the following:

- [ ] More about scalar variables and how to assign values to them
- [ ] The basic arithmetic operators and how they work with scalar variables
- [ ] What an expression is
- [ ] How to use the `if` statement and the `==` operator to test for simple conditions
- [ ] How to specify two-way and multi-way branches using `else` and `elsif`
- [ ] How to write simple loops using the `while` and `until` statements

Storing in Scalar Variables Assignment

In yesterday's lesson, you saw the following statement, which assigns a line of input from the keyboard to the variable $inputline:

```
$inputline = <STDIN>;
```

This section tells you more about variables such as $inputline and how to assign values to these variables.

The Definition of a Scalar Variable

The variable $inputline is an example of a *scalar variable*. A scalar variable stores exactly one item—a line of input, a piece of text, or a number, for example. Items that can be stored in scalar variables are called *scalar values*.

You'll learn more about scalar values on Day 3, "Understanding Scalar Values." For today, all you need to remember is that a scalar variable stores exactly one value, which is a scalar value.

Scalar Variable Syntax

The name of a scalar variable consists of the character $ followed by at least one letter, which is followed by any number of letters, digits, or underscore characters (that is, the _ character).

The following are examples of legal scalar variable names:

```
$x
$var
$my_variable
$var2
$a_new_variable
```

These, however, are not legal scalar variable names:

```
variable        # the $ character is missing
$               # there must be at least one letter in the name
$47x            # second character must be a letter
$_var           # again, the second character must be a letter
$variable!      # you can't have a ! in a variable name
$new.var        # you can't have a . in a variable name
```

Perl variables are case-sensitive. This means that the following variables are different:

```
$VAR
$var
$Var
```

Your variable name can be as long as you want.

```
$this_is_a_really_long_but_legal_name
$this_is_a_really_long_but_legal_name_that_is_different
```

The $ character is necessary because it ensures that the Perl interpreter can distinguish scalar variables from other kinds of Perl variables, which you'll see on later days.

TIP	Variable names should be long enough to be self-explanatory but short enough to be easy to read and type.

Assigning a Value to a Scalar Variable

The following statement contains the Perl *assignment operator*, which is the = character:

```
$inputline = <STDIN>;
```

Remember that this statement tells Perl that the line of text read from the standard input file, represented by <STDIN>, is to become the new value of the scalar variable $inputline.

You can use the assignment operator to assign other values to scalar variables as well. For example, in the following statement, the number 42 is assigned to the scalar variable $var:

```
$var = 42;
```

A second assignment to a scalar variable supersedes any previous assignments. In these two statements:

```
$var = 42;
$var = 113;
```

the old value of $var, 42, is destroyed, and the value of $var becomes 113.

Assignment statements can assign text to scalar variables as well. Consider the following statement:

```
$name = "inputdata";
```

In this statement, the text inputdata is assigned to the scalar variable $name.

Note that the quotation marks (the " characters) on either end of the text are not part of the text assigned to $name. This is because the " characters are just there to enclose the text.

Spaces or tabs contained inside the pair of " characters are treated as part of the text:

```
$name = "John Q Hacker";
```

Here, the spaces on either side of the Q are considered part of the text.

In Perl, enclosed text such as John Q Hacker is known as a *character string*, and the surrounding " characters are an example of *string delimiters*. You learn more about character strings on Day 3; for now, all you need to know is that everything inside the " characters is treated as a single unit.

Performing Arithmetic

As you've seen, the assignment operator = takes the value to the right of the = sign and assigns it to the variable on the left of the =:

```
$var = 42;
```

Here, the value 42 is assigned to the scalar variable $var.

In Perl, the assignment operator is just one of many *operators* that perform tasks, or *operations*. Each operation consists of the following components:

- The operator, such as the assignment operator (=)
- One or more *operands*, such as $var and 42

This might sound a little confusing, but it's really quite straightforward. To illustrate, Table 2.1 lists some of the basic arithmetic operators that Perl supports.

Table 2.1. Basic arithmetic operators.

Operator	Operation
+	Addition
–	Subtraction
*	Multiplication
/	Division

You use these operators in the same way you use +, –, and so on when you do arithmetic on paper. For example, the following statement adds 17 and 5 and then assigns the result, 22, to the scalar variable $var:

```
$var = 17 + 5;
```

You can perform more than one arithmetic operation in a single statement like this one, which assigns 19 to $var:

```
$var = 17 + 5 - 3;
```

You can use the value of a variable in an arithmetic operation, as follows:

```
$var1 = 11;
$var2 = $var1 * 6;
```

The second statement takes the value currently stored in $var1, 11, and multiplies it by 6. The result, 66, is assigned to $var2.

Now examine the following statements:

```
$var = 11;
$var = $var * 6;
```

As you can see, $var appears twice in the second statement. What Perl does in this case is straightforward:

1. The first statement assigns the value 11 to $var.
2. In the second statement, the Perl interpreter retrieves the current value of $var, 11, and multiplies it by 6, producing the result 66.
3. This result, 66, is then assigned to $var (destroying the old value, 11).

As you can see, there is no ambiguity. Perl uses the old value of $var in the arithmetic operation, and then it assigns the result of the operation to $var.

NOTE

Perl always performs multiplication and division before addition and subtraction—even if the addition or subtraction operator appears first. Perl does this to conform to the rules of arithmetic. For example, in the following statement:

```
$var = 5 + 6 * 4;
```

$var is assigned 29: 6 is multiplied by 4, and then 5 is added to the result.

Example of Miles-to-Kilometers Conversion

To see how arithmetic operators work, look at Listing 2.1, which performs a simple miles-to-kilometers and kilometers-to-miles conversion.

TYPE **Listing 2.1. Miles-to-kilometers converter.**

```
1:  #!/usr/local/bin/perl
2:
3:  print ("Enter the distance to be converted:\n");
```

continues

Listing 2.1. continued

```
4:  $originaldist = <STDIN>;
5:  chop ($originaldist);
6:  $miles = $originaldist * 0.6214;
7:  $kilometers = $originaldist * 1.609;
8:  print ($originaldist, " kilometers = ", $miles,
9:         " miles\n");
10: print ($originaldist, " miles = ", $kilometers,
11:        " kilometers\n");
```

OUTPUT
```
$ program2_1
Enter the distance to be converted:
10
10 kilometers = 6.2139999999999995 miles
10 miles = 16.09 kilometers
$
```

ANALYSIS Line 3 of this program asks for a distance to convert. To do this, it prints the following text on your screen:

```
Enter the distance to be converted:
```

Note that the \n at the end of the text is not printed. The \n is a special sequence of characters that represents the newline character; when the print library function sees \n, it starts a new line of output on your screen. (You'll learn more about special sequences of characters such as \n on Day 3.)

At this point, you can enter any number you want in response to the program's request for a distance. The input/output example shows an entry of 10.

Line 4 retrieves the line of input you entered and then assigns it to the variable named $originaldist.

Line 5 calls the library function chop, which gets rid of the closing newline character that is part of the input line you entered. The chop library function is described in the following section, "The chop Library Function."

Line 6 determines the number of miles that is equivalent to 10 kilometers and assigns this number to the variable $miles.

Line 7 determines the number of kilometers that is equivalent to 10 miles and assigns this number to the variable $kilometers.

Lines 8–11 print the values of the variables $miles and $kilometers.

NOTE

Different machines handle floating-point numbers (numbers containing a decimal point) in different ways. Because of this, the numbers displayed in your Listing 2.1 output might not be exactly the same as the numbers shown here. These minor differences will appear whenever a floating-point number is printed.

For more information on difficulties with floating-point numbers, refer to the discussion of round-off errors on Day 3, "Understanding Scalar Values."

The chop **Library Function**

The program shown in Listing 2.1 calls a special library function, chop. This function assumes that a line of text is stored in the variable passed to it; chop's job is to delete the character at the right end of the line of text. Consider this example:

```
$line = "This is my line";
chop ($line);
```

After chop is called, the value of $line becomes

```
This is my lin
```

Here's why Listing 2.1 uses chop. The statement

```
$originaldist = <STDIN>;
```

assigns a line of input from the standard input file to the variable $originaldist. When you type 10 and press Enter, the line of input assigned to $originaldist consists of three characters: the 1, the 0, and a newline character. When chop is called, the newline character is removed, and $originaldist now contains the value 10, which can be used in arithmetic operations.

You'll learn more about using lines of input in arithmetic operations and about conversions from lines of input to numbers on Day 3. For now, just remember to call chop after reading a number from the standard input file.

```
$originaldist = <STDIN>;
chop ($originaldist);
```

Expressions

Now that you know a little more about operators, operands, and how they both work, it's time to learn some more terminology as well as the details about exactly what Perl is doing when it evaluates operators such as the arithmetic operators and the assignment operator.

In Perl, a collection of operators and operands is known as an *expression*. Each expression yields a *result*, which is the value you get when the Perl interpreter *evaluates* the expression (that is, when the Perl interpreter performs the specified operations). For example, in the simple expression

```
4 * 5
```

the result is 20, or 4 times 5.

You can think of an expression as a set of subordinate expressions. Consider this example:

```
4 * 5 + 3 * 6
```

When the Perl interpreter evaluates this expression, it first evaluates the subexpressions 4 * 5 and 3 * 6, yielding the results 20 and 18. These results are then (effectively) substituted for the subexpressions, leaving the following:

```
20 + 18
```

The Perl interpreter then performs the addition operation, and the final result of the expression is 38.

Consider the following statement:

```
$var = 4 * 5 + 3;
```

As you can see, the Perl interpreter multiplies 4 by 5, adds 3, and assigns the result, 23, to $var. Here's what the Perl interpreter is doing, more formally, when it evaluates this expression ($var = 4 * 5 + 3):

1. The subexpression 4 * 5 is evaluated, yielding the result 20. The expression being evaluated is now

   ```
   $var = 20 + 3
   ```

   because the multiplication operation has been replaced by its result.

2. The subexpression 20 + 3 is evaluated, yielding 23. The expression is now

   ```
   $var = 23
   ```

3. Finally, the value 23 is assigned to $var.

Here's one more example, this time using the value of a variable in an expression:

```
$var1 = 15;
$var2 = $var1 - 11;
```

When the Perl interpreter evaluates the second expression, it does the following:

1. It retrieves the value currently stored in $var1, which is 15, and replaces the variable with its value. This means the expression is now

   ```
   $var2 = 15 - 11
   ```

   and $var1 is out of the picture.

2. The Perl interpreter performs the subtraction operation, yielding

   ```
   $var2 = 4
   ```

3. $var2 is thus assigned the value 4.

NOTE

An expression and a statement are two different things. A statement, however, can contain a Perl expression. For example, the statement

```
$var2 = 4;
```

contains the Perl expression

```
$var2 = 4
```

and is terminated by a semicolon (;).

The distinction between statements and expressions will become clearer when you encounter other places where Perl statements use expressions. For example, expressions are used in conditional statements, which you'll see later today.

Assignments and Expressions

The assignment operator, like all Perl operators, yields a result. The result of an assignment operation is the value assigned. For example, in the expression

```
$var = 42
```

the result of the expression is 42, which is the value assigned to $var.

Because the assignment operator yields a value, you can use more than one assignment operator in a single expression:

```
$var1 = $var2 = 42;
```

In this example, the subexpression

```
$var2 = 42
```

is performed first. (You'll learn why on Day 4, "More Operators," in the lesson about operator precedence.) The result of this subexpression is 42, and the expression is now

```
$var1 = 42
```

At this point, 42 is assigned to $var1.

Other Perl Operators

So far, you have encountered the following Perl operators, which are just a few of the many operators Perl supports:

- ☐ The assignment operator, =.
- ☐ The arithmetic operators +, -, *, and /.

You'll learn about additional Perl operators on Day 4.

Introduction to Conditional Statements

So far, the Perl programs you've seen have had their statements executed in sequential order. For example, consider the kilometer-to-mile conversion program you saw in Listing 2.1:

```
#!/usr/local/bin/perl

print ("Enter the distance to be converted:\n");
$originaldist = <STDIN>;
chop ($originaldist);
$miles = $originaldist * 0.6214;
$kilometers = $originaldist * 1.609;
print ($originaldist, " kilometers = ", $miles,
        " miles\n");
print ($originaldist, " miles = ", $kilometers,
        " kilometers\n");
```

When the Perl interpreter executes this program, it starts at the top of the program and executes each statement in turn. When the final statement is executed, the program is terminated.

All the statements in this program are *unconditional statements*—that is, they always are executed sequentially, regardless of what is happening in the program. In some situations, however, you might want to have statements that are executed only when certain conditions are true. These statements are known as *conditional statements*.

Perl supports a variety of conditional statements. In the following sections, you'll learn about these conditional statements:

Statement	Description
if	Executes when a specified condition is true.
if-else	Chooses between two alternatives.
if-elsif-else	Chooses between more than two alternatives.
while and until	Repeats a group of statements a specified number of times.

Perl also has other conditional statements, which you'll learn about on Day 8, "More Control Structures."

The `if` Statement

The `if` statement is the simplest conditional statement used in Perl. The easiest way to explain how the `if` statement works is to show you a simple example:

```
if ($number) {
        print ("The number is not zero.\n");
}
```

The `if` statement consists of everything from the word `if` to the closing brace character (}). This statement consists of two parts:

☐ The code between the `if` and the open brace character ({).

☐ The code between the { and the }.

The first part is known as a *conditional expression*; the second part is a set of one or more statements called a *statement block*. Let's look at each part in detail.

The Conditional Expression

The first part of an `if` statement—the part between the parentheses—is the *conditional expression* associated with the `if` statement. This conditional expression is just like any other expression you've seen so far; in fact, you can use any legal Perl expression as a conditional expression.

When the Perl interpreter sees a conditional expression, it evaluates the expression. The result of the expression is then placed in one of two classes:

☐ If the result is a nonzero value, the conditional expression is *true*.

☐ If the result is zero, the conditional expression is *false*.

The Perl interpreter uses the value of the conditional expression to decide whether to execute the statements between the { and } characters. If the conditional expression is true, the statements are executed. If the conditional expression is false, the statements are not executed.

In the example you have just seen,

```
if ($number) {
        print ("The number is not zero.\n");
}
```

the conditional expression consists of the value of the variable $number. If $number contains something other than zero, the conditional expression is true, and the statement

```
print ("The value is not zero.\n");
```

is executed. If $number currently is set to zero, the conditional expression is false, and the print statement is not executed.

Listing 2.2 is a program that contains this simple if statement.

TYPE Listing 2.2. A program containing a simple example of an if statement.

```
1:  #!/usr/local/bin/perl
2:
3:  print ("Enter a number:\n");
4:  $number = <STDIN>;
5:  chop ($number);
6:  if ($number) {
7:          print ("The number is not zero.\n");
8:  }
9:  print ("This is the last line of the program.\n");
```

OUTPUT
```
$ program2_2
Enter a number:
5
The number is not zero.
This is the last line of the program.
$
```

ANALYSIS Lines 3, 4, and 5 of Listing 2.2 are similar to lines you've seen before. Line 3 tells you to enter a number; line 4 assigns the line you've entered to the variable $number; and line 5 throws away the trailing newline character.

Lines 6–8 constitute the if statement itself. As you have seen, this statement evaluates the conditional expression consisting of the variable $number. If $number is not zero, the expression is true, and the call to print is executed. If $number is zero, the expression is false, and the call to print is skipped; the Perl interpreter thus jumps to line 9.

The Perl interpreter executes line 9 and prints the following regardless of whether the conditional expression in line 6 is true or false:

```
This is the last line of the program.
```

Now that you understand how an if statement works, you're ready to see the formal syntax definition for the if statement.

The syntax for the if statement is

```
if (expr) {
        statement_block
}
```

This formal definition doesn't tell you anything you don't already know. *expr* refers to the conditional expression, which evaluates to either true or false. *statement_block* is the group of statements that is executed when *expr* evaluates to true.

WARNING

If you are familiar with the C programming language, you probably have noticed that the if statement in Perl is syntactically similar to the if statement in C. There is one important difference, however: In Perl, the braces ({ and }) must be present.

The following statement is illegal in Perl because the { and } are missing:

```
if ($number)
        print ("The value is not zero.\n");
```

Perl does support a syntax for single-line conditional statements. This is discussed on Day 8.

The Statement Block

The second part of the if statement, the part between the { and the }, is called a *statement block*. A statement block consists of any number of legal Perl statements (including no statements, if you like).

In the following example, the statement block consists of one statement:

```
print ("The value is not zero.\n");
```

NOTE

A statement block can be completely empty. In this statement, for example:

```
if ($number == 21) {
}
```

there is nothing between the { and }, so the statement block is empty. This is perfectly legal Perl code, although it's not particularly useful.

Testing for Equality Using ==

So far, the only conditional expression you've seen is an expression consisting of a single variable. Although you can use any expression you like and any operators you like, Perl provides special operators that are designed for use in conditional expressions. One such operator is the *equality comparison operator*, ==.

The == operator, like the other operators you've seen so far, requires two operands or subexpressions. Unlike the other operators, however, it yields one of two possible results: true or false. (The other operators you've seen yield a numeric value as a result.) The == operator works like this:

☐ If the two subexpressions evaluate to the same numeric value, the == operator yields the result *true*.

☐ If the two subexpressions have different values, the == operator yields the result *false*.

Because the == operator returns either true or false, it is ideal for use in conditional expressions, because conditional expressions are expected to evaluate to either true or false. For an example, look at Listing 2.3, which compares two numbers read in from the standard input file.

Listing 2.3. A program that uses the equality-comparison operator to compare two numbers entered at the keyboard.

TYPE

```
1:  #!/usr/local/bin/perl
2:
3:  print ("Enter a number:\n");
4:  $number1 = <STDIN>;
5:  chop ($number1);
6:  print ("Enter another number:\n");
7:  $number2 = <STDIN>;
8:  chop ($number2);
```

```
9:  if ($number1 == $number2) {
10:         print ("The two numbers are equal.\n");
11: }
12: print ("This is the last line of the program.\n");
```

 OUTPUT

```
$ program2_3
Enter a number:
17
Enter another number:
17
The two numbers are equal.
This is the last line of the program.
$
```

ANALYSIS Lines 3–5 are again similar to statements you've seen before. They print a message on your screen, read a number into the variable $number1, and chop the newline character from the number.

Lines 6–8 repeat the preceding process for a second number, which is stored in $number2.

Lines 9–11 contain the if statement that compares the two numbers. Line 9 contains the conditional expression

```
$number1 == $number2
```

If the two numbers are equal, the conditional expression is true, and the print statement in line 10 is executed. If the two numbers are not equal, the conditional expression is false, so the print statement in line 10 is not executed; in this case, the Perl interpreter skips to the first statement after the if statement, which is line 12.

Line 12 is executed regardless of whether or not the conditional expression in line 9 is true. It prints the following message on the screen:

```
This is the last line of the program.
```

WARNING

Make sure that you don't confuse the = and == operators. Because any expression can be used as a conditional expression, Perl is quite happy to accept statements such as

```
if ($number = 5) {
        print ("The number is five.\n");
}
```

Here, the if statement is evaluated as follows:

1. The number 5 is assigned to $number, and the following expression yields the result 5:

```
$number = 5
```

2. The value 5 is nonzero, so the conditional expression is true.

3. Because the conditional expression is true, this statement is executed:

```
print ("The number is five.\n");
```

Note that the print statement is executed regardless of what the value of $number was before the if statement. This is because the value 5 is assigned to $number by the conditional expression.

To repeat: Be careful when you use the == operator!

Other Comparison Operators

The == operator is just one of many comparison operators that you can use in conditional expressions. For a complete list, refer to Day 4.

Two-Way Branching Using if and else

When you examine Listing 2.3 (shown previously), you might notice a problem. What happens if the two numbers are not equal? In this case, the statement

```
print ("The two numbers are equal.\n");
```

is not printed. In fact, nothing is printed.

Suppose you want to modify Listing 2.3 to print one message if the two numbers are equal and another message if the two numbers are not equal. One convenient way of doing this is with the if-else statement.

Listing 2.4 is a modification of the program in Listing 2.3. It uses the if-else statement to print one of two messages, depending on whether the numbers are equal.

TYPE Listing 2.4. A program that uses the if-else statement.

```
1:  #!/usr/local/bin/perl
2:
3:  print ("Enter a number:\n");
4:  $number1 = <STDIN>;
5:  chop ($number1);
6:  print ("Enter another number:\n");
7:  $number2 = <STDIN>;
```

```
 8:  chop ($number2);
 9:  if ($number1 == $number2) {
10:        print ("The two numbers are equal.\n");
11: } else {
12:        print ("The two numbers are not equal.\n");
13: }
14: print ("This is the last line of the program.\n");
```

OUTPUT

```
$ program2_4
Enter a number:
17
Enter another number:
18
The two numbers are not equal.
This is the last line of the program.
$
```

ANALYSIS Lines 3–8 are identical to those in Listing 2.3. They read in two numbers, assign them to $number1 and $number2, and chop their newline characters.

Line 9 compares the value stored in $number1 to the value stored in $number2. If the two values are equal, line 10 is executed, and the following message is printed:

```
The two numbers are equal.
```

The Perl interpreter then jumps to the first statement after the if-else statement—line 14.

If the two values are not equal, line 12 is executed, and the following message is printed:

```
The two numbers are not equal.
```

The interpreter then continues with the first statement after the if-else—line 14.

In either case, the Perl interpreter executes line 14, which prints the following message:

```
This is the last line of the program.
```

SYNTAX

The syntax for the if-else statement is

```
if (expr) {
       statement_block_1
} else {
       statement_block_2
}
```

As in the if statement, *expr* is any expression (it is usually a conditional expression). *statement_block_1* is the block of statements that the Perl interpreter executes if *expr* is true, and *statement_block_2* is the block of statements that are executed if *expr* is false.

Note that the else part of the if-else statement cannot appear by itself; it must always follow an if.

TIP

In Perl, as you've learned, you can use any amount of white space to separate tokens. This means that you can present conditional statements in a variety of ways.

The examples in this book use what is called the *one true brace* style:

```
if ($number == 0) {
        print ("The number is zero.\n");
} else {
        print ("The number is not zero.\n");
}
```

In this brace style, the opening brace ({) appears on the same line as the if or else, and the closing brace (}) starts a new line.

Other programmers insist on putting the braces on separate lines:

```
if ($number == 0)
{
        print ("The number is zero.\n");
}
else
{
        print ("The number is not zero.\n");
}
```

Still others prefer to indent their braces:

```
if ($number == 0)
    {
        print ("The number is not zero.\n");
    }
```

I prefer the one true brace style because it is both legible and compact. However, it doesn't really matter what brace style you choose, provided that you follow these rules:

- ☐ The brace style is consistent. Every if and else that appears in your program should have its braces displayed in the same way.
- ☐ The brace style is easy to follow.
- ☐ The statement blocks inside the braces always should be indented in the same way.

If you do not follow a consistent style, and you write statements such as

```
if ($number == 0) { print ("The number is zero"); }
```

you'll find that your code is difficult to understand, especially when you start writing longer Perl programs.

Multi-Way Branching Using `elsif`

Listing 2.4 (which you've just seen) shows how to write a program that chooses between two alternatives. Perl also provides a conditional statement, the `if-elsif-else` statement, which selects one of more than two alternatives. Listing 2.5 illustrates the use of `elsif`.

TYPE | **Listing 2.5. A program that uses the `if-elsif-else` statement.**

```
1:  #!/usr/local/bin/perl
2:
3:  print ("Enter a number:\n");
4:  $number1 = <STDIN>;
5:  chop ($number1);
6:  print ("Enter another number:\n");
7:  $number2 = <STDIN>;
8:  chop ($number2);
9:  if ($number1 == $number2) {
10:         print ("The two numbers are equal.\n");
11: } elsif ($number1 == $number2 + 1) {
12:         print ("The first number is greater by one.\n");
13: } elsif ($number1 + 1 == $number2) {
14:         print ("The second number is greater by one.\n");
15: } else {
16:         print ("The two numbers are not equal.\n");
17: }
18: print ("This is the last line of the program.\n");
```

OUTPUT

```
$ program2_5
Enter a number:
17
Enter another number:
18
The second number is greater by one.
This is the last line of the program.
$
```

ANALYSIS You already are familiar with lines 3–8. They obtain two numbers from the standard input file and assign them to $number1 and $number2, chopping the terminating newline character in the process.

Line 9 checks whether the two numbers are equal. If the numbers are equal, line 10 is executed, and the following message is printed:

```
The two numbers are equal.
```

The Perl interpreter then jumps to the first statement after the `if-elsif-else` statement, which is line 18.

If the two numbers are not equal, the Perl interpreter goes to line 11. Line 11 performs another comparison. It adds 1 to the value of $number2 and compares it with the value of $number1. If the two values are equal, the Perl interpreter executes line 12, printing the message

```
The first number is greater by one.
```

The interpreter then jumps to line 18—the statement following the if-elsif-else statement.

If the conditional expression in line 11 is false, the interpreter jumps to line 13. Line 13 adds 1 to the value of $number1 and compares it with the value of $number2. If these two values are equal, the Perl interpreter executes line 14, which prints

```
The second number is greater by one.
```

on the screen. The interpreter then jumps to line 18.

If the conditional expression in line 13 is false, the Perl interpreter jumps to line 15 and executes line 16, which prints

```
The two numbers are not equal.
```

on the screen. The Perl interpreter continues with the next statement, which is line 18.

If you have followed the program logic to this point, you've realized that the Perl interpreter eventually reaches line 18 in every case. Line 18 prints this statement:

```
This is the last line of the program.
```

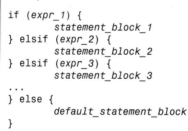

The syntax of the if-elsif-else statement is as follows:

```
if (expr_1) {
        statement_block_1
} elsif (expr_2) {
        statement_block_2
} elsif (expr_3) {
        statement_block_3
...
} else {
        default_statement_block
}
```

Here, expr_1, expr_2, and expr_3 are conditional expressions. statement_block_1, statement_block_2, statement_block_3, and default_statement_block are blocks of statements.

The ... indicates that you can have as many elsif statements as you like. Each elsif statement has the same form:

```
} elsif (expr) {
        statement_block
}
```

Syntactically, an `if-else` statement is just an `if-elsif-else` statement with no `elsif` parts.

If you want, you can leave out the `else` part of the `if-elsif-else` statement, as follows:

```
if (expr_1) {
        statement_block_1
} elsif (expr_2) {
        statement_block_2
} elsif (expr_3) {
        statement_block_3
...
}
```

Here, if none of the expressions—*expr_1*, *expr_2*, *expr_3*, and so on—are true, the Perl interpreter just skips to the first statement following the `if-elsif-else` statement.

NOTE

> The `elsif` parts of the `if-elsif-else` statement must appear between the `if` part and the `else` part.

Writing Loops Using the `while` **Statement**

The conditional statements you've seen so far enable the Perl interpreter to decide between alternatives. However, each statement in the Perl programs that you have seen is either not executed or is executed only once.

Perl also enables you to write conditional statements that tell the Perl interpreter to repeat a block of statements a specified number of times. A block of statements that can be repeated is known as a *loop*.

The simplest way to write a loop in Perl is with the `while` statement. Here is a simple example of a `while` statement:

```
while ($number == 5) {
        print ("The number is still 5!\n");
}
```

The `while` statement is structurally similar to the `if` statement, but it works in a slightly different way. Here's how:

☐ First, the conditional expression located between the parentheses is tested.

☐ If the conditional expression is true, the statement block between the { and } is executed. If the expression is false, the statement block is skipped, and the Perl interpreter jumps to the statement following the while statement. (This is called *exiting the loop*.)

☐ If the statement block is executed, the Perl interpreter jumps back to the start of the while statement and tests the conditional expression over again. (This is the looping part of the while statement, because at this point the Perl interpreter is executing a statement it has executed before.)

The statement block in the while statement is repeated until the conditional expression becomes false. This means that the statement

```
while ($number == 5) {
        print ("The number is still 5!\n");
}
```

loops forever (which is referred to as going into an *infinite loop*) if the value of $number is 5, because the value of $number never changes and the following conditional expression is always true:

```
$number == 5
```

For a more useful example of a while statement—one that does not go into an infinite loop—take a look at Listing 2.6.

Listing 2.6. A program that demonstrates the while statement.

TYPE

```
1:  #!/usr/local/bin/perl
2:
3:  $done = 0;
4:  $count = 1;
5:  print ("This line is printed before the loop starts.\n");
6:  while ($done == 0) {
7:          print ("The value of count is ", $count, "\n");
8:          if ($count == 3) {
9:                  $done = 1;
10:         }
11:         $count = $count + 1;
12: }
13: print ("End of loop.\n");
```

OUTPUT

```
$ program2_6
This line is printed before the loop starts.
The value of count is 1
```

2

```
The value of count is 2
The value of count is 3
End of loop.
$
```

ANALYSIS Lines 3–5 prepare the program for looping. Line 3 assigns the value 0 to the variable $done. (As you'll see, the program uses $done to indicate whether or not to continue looping.) Line 4 assigns the value 1 to the variable $count. Line 5 prints the following line to the screen:

`This line is printed before the loop starts.`

The while statement appears in lines 6–12. Line 6 contains a conditional expression to be tested. If the conditional expression is true, the statement block in lines 7–11 is executed. At this point, the conditional expression is true, so the Perl interpreter continues with line 7.

Line 7 prints the current value of the variable $count. At present, $count is set to 1. This means that line 7 prints the following on the screen:

`The value of count is 1`

Lines 8–10 test whether $count has reached the value 3. Because $count is 1 at the moment, the conditional expression in line 8 is false, and the Perl interpreter skips to line 11.

Line 11 adds 1 to the current value of $count, setting it to 2.

Line 12 is the bottom of the while statement. The Perl interpreter now jumps back to line 6, and the whole process is repeated. Here's how the Perl interpreter continues from here:

- ☐ Line 6: $done == 0 is true, so continue.
- ☐ Line 7: Print The value of count is 2 on the screen.
- ☐ Line 8: $count is 2; $count == 3 is false, so skip to line 11.
- ☐ Line 11: 1 is added to $count; $count is now 3.
- ☐ Line 12: Jump back to the start of the loop, which is line 6.
- ☐ Line 6: $done == 0 is true, so continue.
- ☐ Line 7: Print The value of count is 3 on the screen.
- ☐ Line 8: $count is 3; $count == 3 is true, and the if statement block is executed.
- ☐ Line 9: $done is set to 1. Execution continues with the first statement after the if, which is line 11.
- ☐ Line 11: $count is set to 4.
- ☐ Line 12: Jump back to line 6.
- ☐ Line 6: $done == 0 is now false, because the value of $done is 1. The Perl interpreter exits the loop and continues with the first statement after while, which is line 13.

2

Line 13 prints the following message on the screen:

```
End of loop.
```

At this point, program execution terminates because there are no more statements to execute.

SYNTAX

The syntax for the `while` statement is

```
while (expr) {
        statement_block
}
```

As you can see, the `while` statement is syntactically similar to the `if` statement. *expr* is a conditional expression to be evaluated, and *statement_block* is a block of statements to be executed while *expr* is true.

Nesting Conditional Statements

The `if` statement in Listing 2.6 (shown previously) is an example of a *nested conditional statement*. It is contained inside another conditional statement (the `while` statement). In Perl, you can nest any conditional statement inside another. For example, you can have a `while` statement inside another `while` statement, as follows:

```
while (expr_1) {
        some_statements
        while (expr_2) {
                inner_statement_block
        }
        some_more_statements
}
```

Similarly, you can have an `if` statement inside another `if` statement, or you can have a `while` statement inside an `if` statement.

You can nest conditional statements inside `elsif` and `else` parts of `if` statements as well:

```
if ($number == 0) {
        # some statements go here
} elsif ($number == 1) {
        while ($number2 == 19) {
                # here is a place for a statement block
        }
} else {
        while ($number2 == 33) {
                # here is a place for another statement block
        }
}
```

The braces ({ and }) around the statement block for each conditional statement ensure that the Perl interpreter never gets confused.

TIP

If you plan to nest conditional statements, it's a good idea to indent each statement block to indicate how many levels of nesting you are using. If you write code such as the following, it's easy to get confused:

```
while ($done == 0) {
print ("The value of count is", $count, "\n");
if ($count == 3) {
$done = 1;
}
$count = $count + 1;
}
```

Although this code is correct, it's not easy to see that the statement

```
$done = 1;
```

is actually inside an `if` statement that is inside a `while` statement. Larger and more complicated programs rapidly become unreadable if you do not indent properly.

Looping Using the `until` Statement

Another way to loop in Perl is with the `until` statement. It is similar in appearance to the `while` statement, but it works in a slightly different way.

- ☐ The `while` statement loops *while* its conditional expression is true.
- ☐ The `until` statement loops *until* its conditional expression is true (that is, it loops as long as its conditional expression is *false*).

Listing 2.7 contains an example of the `until` statement.

TYPE **Listing 2.7. A program that uses the `until` statement.**

```
1:  #!/usr/local/bin/perl
2:
3:  print ("What is 17 plus 26?\n");
4:  $correct_answer = 43;      # the correct answer
5:  $input_answer = <STDIN>;
6:  chop ($input_answer);
7:  until ($input_answer == $correct_answer) {
8:          print ("Wrong! Keep trying!\n");
9:          $input_answer = <STDIN>;
10:         chop ($input_answer);
11: }
12: print ("You've got it!\n");
```

OUTPUT
```
$ program2_7
What is 17 plus 26?
39
Wrong! Keep trying!
43
You've got it!
$
```

ANALYSIS Lines 3 and 4 set up the loop. Line 3 prints the following question on the screen:

```
What is 17 plus 26?
```

Line 4 assigns the correct answer, 43, to $correct_answer.

Lines 5 and 6 retrieve the first attempt at the answer. Line 5 reads a line of input and stores it in $input_answer. Line 6 chops off the newline character.

Line 7 tests whether the answer entered is correct by comparing $input_answer with $correct_answer. If the two are not equal, the Perl interpreter continues with lines 8–10; if they are equal, the interpreter skips to line 12.

Line 8 prints the following on the screen:

```
Wrong! Keep trying!
```

Line 9 reads another attempt from the standard input file and stores it in $input_answer. Line 10 chops off the newline character. At this point, the Perl interpreter jumps back to line 7 and tests the new attempt.

The interpreter reaches line 12 when the answer is correct. At this point, the following message appears on the screen, and the program terminates:

```
You've got it!
```

The syntax for the until statement is

```
until (expr) {
        statement_block
}
```

As in the while statement, *expr* is a conditional expression, and *statement_block* is a statement block.

Summary

Today, you learned about scalar variables and how to assign values to them.

Scalar variables and values can be used by the arithmetic operators to perform the basic arithmetic operations of addition, subtraction, multiplication, and division. The chop library function removes the trailing newline character from a line, which enables you to read scalar values from the standard input file.

A collection of operations and their values is known as an expression. The values operated on by a particular operator are called the operands of the operator. Each operator yields a result, which then can be used in other operations.

An expression can be divided into subexpressions, each of which is evaluated in turn.

Today you were introduced to the idea of a conditional statement. A conditional statement consists of two components: a conditional expression, which yields a result of either true or false; and a statement block, which is a group of statements that is executed only when the conditional expression is true.

Some conditional expressions contain the == operator, which returns true if its operands are numerically equal, and returns false if its operands are not.

The following conditional statements were described today:

☐ The `if` statement, which is executed only if its conditional expression is true

☐ The `if-else` statement, which chooses between two alternatives

☐ The `if-elsif-else` statement, which chooses between multiple alternatives

☐ The `while` statement, which loops while a condition is true

☐ The `until` statement, which loops until a condition is true

You also learned about nesting conditional statements, as well as about infinite loops and how to avoid them.

Q&A

Q Which should I use, the `while` statement or the `until` statement?

A It doesn't matter, really; it just depends on which, in your judgment, is easier to read.

Once you learn about the other comparison operators on Day 4, "More Operators," you'll be able to use the `while` statement wherever you can use an `until` statement, and vice versa.

Q In Listing 2.7, you read input from the standard input file in two separate places. Is there any way I can reduce this to one?

A Yes, by using the `do` statement, which you'll encounter on Day 8, "More Control Structures."

Q Do I really need both a `$done` variable and a `$count` variable in Listing 2.6?

A No. On Day 4 you'll learn about comparison operators, which enable you to test whether a variable is less than or greater than a particular value. At that point, you won't need the `$done` variable.

Q How many `elsif` parts can I have in an `if-elsif-else` statement?

A Effectively, as many as you like. (There is an upper limit, but it's so large that you are not likely ever to reach it.)

Q How much nesting of conditional statements does Perl allow? Can I put an `if` inside a `while` that is inside an `if` that is inside an `until`?

A Yes. You can nest as many levels deep as you like. Generally, though, you don't want to go too many levels down because your program will become difficult to read.

The logical operators, which you'll learn about on Day 4, make it possible to produce more complicated conditional expressions. They'll eliminate the need for too much nesting.

Workshop

The Workshop provides quiz questions to help you solidify your understanding of the material covered and exercises to give you experience in using what you've learned. Try and understand the quiz and exercise answers before you go on to tomorrow's lesson.

Quiz

1. Define the following terms:
   a. expression
   b. operand
   c. conditional statement
   d. statement block
   e. infinite loop
2. When does a `while` statement stop looping?
3. When does an `until` statement stop looping?
4. What does the `==` operator do?
5. What is the result when the following expression is evaluated?

   ```
   14 + 6 * 3 - 10 / 2
   ```

6. Which of the following are legal scalar variable names?

   a. `$hello`

   b. `$_test`

   c. `$now_is_the_time_to_come_to_the_aid_of_the_party`

   d. `$fries&gravy`

   e. `$96tears`

   f. `$tea_for_2`

Exercises

1. Write a Perl program that reads in a number, multiplies it by 2, and prints the result.

2. Write a Perl program that reads in two numbers and does the following:

   ☐ It prints `Error: can't divide by zero` if the second number is 0.

   ☐ If the first number is 0 or the second number is 1, it just prints the first number (because no division is necessary).

   ☐ In all other cases, it divides the first number by the second number and prints the result.

3. Write a Perl program that uses the `while` statement to print out the first 10 numbers (1–10) in ascending order.

4. Write a Perl program that uses the `until` statement to print out the first 10 numbers in descending order (10–1).

5. **BUG BUSTER:** What is wrong with the following program? (Hint: there might be more than one bug!)

```
#!/usr/local/bin/perl

$value = <STDIN>;
if ($value = 17) {
        print ("You typed the number 17.\n");
else {
        print ("You did not type the number 17.\n");
}
```

6. **BUG BUSTER:** What is wrong with the following program?

```
#!/usr/local/bin/perl

# program which prints the next five numbers after the
# number typed in
```

```
$input = <STDIN>;
chop ($input);
$input = $input + 1;        # start with the next number;
$input = $terminate + 5;    # we want to loop five times
until ($input == $terminate) {
        print ("The next number is ", $terminate, "\n");
}
```

Day **3**

Understanding Scalar Values

Today's lesson describes everything you need to know about scalar values in Perl. Today, you learn about the following:

- ☐ Scalar values
- ☐ How integers are represented
- ☐ Floating-point values
- ☐ The octal and hexadecimal notations
- ☐ Character strings, and using the double-quote and single-quote characters to enclose them
- ☐ Escape sequences
- ☐ The interchangeability of character strings and numeric values

What Is a Scalar Value?

Basically, a *scalar value* is one unit of data. This unit of data can be either a number or a chunk of text.

There are several types of scalar values that Perl understands. Today's lesson describes each of them in turn and shows you how you can use them.

Integer Scalar Values

The most common scalar values in Perl programs are integer scalar values, also known as *integer constants* or *integer literals*.

An integer scalar value consists of one or more digits, optionally preceded by a plus or minus sign and optionally containing underscores.

Here are a few examples:

```
14
10000000000
-27
1_000_000
```

You can use integer scalar values in expressions or assign them to scalar variables, as follows:

```
$x = 12345;
if (1217 + 116 == 1333) {
        # statement block goes here
}
```

Integer Scalar Value Limitations

In Perl, there is a limit on the size of integers included in a program. To see what this limit is and how it works, take a look at Listing 3.1, which prints out integers of various sizes.

Listing 3.1. A program that displays integers and illustrates their size limitations.

TYPE

```
1:  #!/usr/local/bin/perl
2:
3:  $value = 1234567890;
4:  print ("first value is ", $value, "\n");
5:  $value = 1234567890123456;
6:  print ("second value is ", $value, "\n");
7:  $value = 12345678901234567890;
8:  print ("third value is ", $value, "\n");
```

3

OUTPUT
```
$ program3_1
first value is 1234567890
second value is 1234567890123456
third value is 12345678901234567168
$
```

ANALYSIS This program assigns integer scalar values to the variable `$value`, and then prints `$value`.

Lines 3 and 4 store and print the value 1234567890 without any difficulty. Similarly, lines 5 and 6 successfully store and print the value 1234567890123456.

Line 7 attempts to assign the value 12345678901234567890 to `$value`. Unfortunately, this number is too big for Perl to understand. When line 8 prints out the value assigned to `$value`, it prints out

12345678901234567168

As you can see, the last three digits have been replaced with different values.

Here's what has happened: Perl actually stores integers in the floating-point registers on your machine. In other words, integers are treated as if they are floating-point numbers (numbers containing decimal points).

On most machines, floating-point registers can store approximately 16 digits before running out of space. As the output from line 8 shows, the first 17 digits of the number 12345678901234567890 are remembered and stored by the Perl interpreter, and the rest are thrown away. This means that the value printed by line 8 is not the same as the value assigned in line 7.

This somewhat annoying limitation on the number of digits in an integer can be found in almost all programming languages. In fact, many programming languages have an upper integer limit of 4294967295 (which is equal to 2^{32} minus 1).

The number of digits that can be stored varies from machine to machine. For a more detailed explanation, refer to the discussion of precision in the following section, "Floating-Point Scalar Values."

WARNING

An integer constant that starts with a 0 is a special case:

```
$x = 012345;
```

The 0 at the beginning of the constant (also known as a *leading zero*) tells the Perl interpreter to treat this as an *octal integer constant*. To find out about octal integer constants, refer to the section called "Using Octal and Hexadecimal Notation" later today.

Floating-Point Scalar Values

As you have just seen, integers in Perl actually are represented as floating-point numbers. This means that an integer scalar value is actually a special kind of floating-point scalar value.

In Perl, a floating-point scalar value consists of all of the following:

☐ An optional minus sign (–)

☐ A sequence of digits, optionally containing a decimal point

☐ An optional exponent

Here are some simple examples of floating-point scalar values:

```
11.4
-275
-0.3
.3
3.
```

The optional exponent tells the Perl interpreter to multiply or divide the scalar value by a power of ten. An exponent consists of all of the following:

☐ The letter e (E is also acceptable)

☐ An optional + or –

☐ A one-, two-, or three-digit number

The number in the exponent represents the value by which to multiply or divide, represented as a power of 10. For example, the exponent e+01 tells the Perl interpreter to multiply the scalar value by 10 to the power of 1, or 10. This means that the scalar value 8e+01 is equivalent to 8 multiplied by 10, or 80.

Similarly, the exponent e+02 is equivalent to multiplying by 100, e+03 is equivalent to multiplying by 1,000, and so on. The following scalar values are all equal:

```
541e+01
54.1e+02
5.41e+03
```

A negative exponent tells the Perl interpreter to divide by 10. For example, the value 54e-01 is equivalent to 54 divided by 10, or 5.4. Similarly, e-02 tells the Perl interpreter to divide by 100, e-03 to divide by 1,000, and so on.

The exponent e+00 is equivalent to multiplying by 1, which does nothing. Therefore, the following values are equal:

```
5.12e+00
5.12
```

If you want, you can omit the + when you multiply by a power of ten.

```
5.47e+03
5.47e03
```

Listing 3.2 shows how Perl works with and prints out floating-point scalar values.

Listing 3.2. A program that displays various floating-point
TYPE scalar values.

```
1:  #!/usr/local/bin/perl
2:
3:  $value = 34.0;
4:  print ("first value is ", $value, "\n");
5:  $value = 114.6e-01;
6:  print ("second value is ", $value, "\n");
7:  $value = 178.263e+19;
8:  print ("third value is ", $value, "\n");
9:  $value = 12345678900000000000000000000000;
10: print ("fourth value is ", $value, "\n");
11: $value = 1.23e+999;
12: print ("fifth value is ", $value, "\n");
13: $value = 1.23e-999;
14: print ("sixth value is ", $value, "\n");
```

OUTPUT
```
$ program3_2
first value is 34
second value is 11.460000000000001
third value is 1.7826300000000001e+21
fourth value is 1.2345678899999999e+29
fifth value is Infinity
sixth value is 0
$
```

ANALYSIS As in Listing 3.1, this program stores and prints various scalar values. Line 3 assigns the floating-point value 34.0 to $value. Line 4 then prints this value. Note that because there are no significant digits after the decimal point, the Perl interpreter treats 34.0 as if it is an integer.

Line 5 assigns 114.6e-01 to $value, and line 6 prints this value. Whenever possible, the Perl interpreter removes any exponents, shifting the decimal point appropriately. As a result, line 6 prints out

```
11.460000000000001
```

which is 114.6e-01 with the exponent e-01 removed and the decimal point shifted one place to the left (which is equivalent to dividing by 10).

Note that the number printed by line 6 is not exactly equal to the value assigned in line 5. This is a result of *round-off error*. The floating-point register cannot contain the exact value 11.46, so it comes as close as it can. It comes pretty close—in fact, the first 16 digits are correct.

This number of correct digits is known as the *precision*, and it is a property of the machine on which you are working; the precision of a floating-point number varies from machine to machine. (The machine on which I ran these test examples supports a floating-point precision of 16 or 17 digits. This is about normal.)

NOTE   The size of an integer is roughly equivalent to the supported floating-point precision. If a machine supports a floating-point precision of 16 digits, an integer can be approximately 16 digits long.

Line 6 shows that a floating-point value has its exponent removed whenever possible. Lines 7 and 8 show what happens when a number is too large to be conveniently displayed without the exponent. In this case, the number is displayed in scientific notation.

In *scientific notation*, one digit appears before the decimal point, and all the other significant digits (the rest of the machine's precision) follow the decimal point. The exponent is adjusted to reflect this. In this example, the number

```
178.263e+19
```

is converted into scientific notation and becomes

```
1.7826300000000001e+21
```

As you can see, the decimal point has been shifted two places to the left, and the exponent has, as a consequence, been adjusted from 19 to 21. As before, the 1 at the end is an example of round-off error.

If an integer is too large to be displayed conveniently, the Perl interpreter converts it to scientific notation. Lines 9 and 10 show this. The number

```
123456789000000000000000000000
```

is converted to

```
1.2345678899999999e+29
```

Here, scientific notation becomes useful. At a glance, you can tell approximately how large the number is. (In conventional notation, you can't do this without counting the zeros.)

Lines 11 and 12 show what happens when the Perl interpreter is given a number that is too large to fit into the machine's floating-point register. In this case, Perl just prints the word Infinity.

The maximum size of a floating-point number varies from machine to machine. Generally, the largest possible exponent that can be stored is about e+308.

Lines 13 and 14 illustrate the case of a number having a negative exponent that is too large (that is, it's too small to store). In such cases, Perl either gets as close as it can or just prints 0.

The largest negative exponent that produces reliable values is about e-309. Below that, accuracy diminishes.

Floating-Point Arithmetic and Round-Off Error

The arithmetic operations you saw on Day 2, "Basic Operators and Control Flow," also work on floating-point values. On that day, you saw an example of a miles-to-kilometers conversion program that uses floating-point arithmetic.

When you perform floating-point arithmetic, you must remember the problems with precision and round-off error. Listing 3.3 illustrates what can go wrong and shows you how to attack this problem.

TYPE
Listing 3.3. A program that illustrates round-off error problems in floating-point arithmetic.

```
1:  #!/usr/local/bin/perl
2:
3:  $value = 9.01e+21 + 0.01 - 9.01e+21;
4:  print ("first value is ", $value, "\n");
5:  $value = 9.01e+21 - 9.01e+21 + 0.01;
6:  print ("second value is ", $value, "\n");
```

OUTPUT
```
$ program3_3
first value is 0
second value is 0.01
$
```

ANALYSIS   Line 3 and line 5 both subtract 9.01e+21 from itself and add 0.01. However, as you can see when you examine the output produced by line 4 and line 6, the order in which you perform the addition and subtraction has a significant effect.

In line 3, a very small number, 0.01, is added to a very large number, 9.01e+21. If you work it out yourself, you see that the result is 9.010000000000000000000001e+21.

The final 1 in the preceding number can be retained only on machines that support 24 digits of precision in their floating-point numbers. Most machines, as you've seen, handle only 16 or 17 digits. As a result, the final 1, along with some of the zeros, is lost, and the number instead is stored as 9.0100000000000000e+21.

This is the same as 9.01e+21, which means that subtracting 9.01e+21 yields zero. The 0.01 is lost along the way.

Line 5, however, doesn't have this problem. The two large numbers are operated on first, yielding 0, and then 0.01 is added. The result is what you expect: 0.01.

The moral of the story: Floating-point arithmetic is accurate only when you bunch together operations on large numbers. If the arithmetic operations are on values stored in variables, it might not be as easy to spot this problem.

```
$result = $number1 + $number2 - $number3;
```

If $number1 and $number3 contain large numbers and $number2 is small, $result is likely to contain an incorrect value because of the problem demonstrated in Listing 3.3.

Using Octal and Hexadecimal Notation

So far, all the integer scalar values you've seen have been in what normally is called *base 10* or *decimal notation*. Perl also enables you to use two other notations to represent integer scalar values:

- [ ] Base 8 notation, or *octal*
- [ ] Base 16 notation, or *hexadecimal* (sometimes shortened to *hex*)

To use octal notation, put a zero in front of your integer scalar value:

```
$result = 047;
```

This assigns 47 octal, or 39 decimal, to $result.

To use hexadecimal notation, put 0x in front of your integer scalar value, as follows:

```
$result = 0x1f;
```

This assigns 1f hexadecimal, or 31 decimal, to $result.

Perl accepts either uppercase letters or lowercase letters as representations of the digits a through f:

```
$result = 0xe;
$result = 0xE;
```

Both of the preceding statements assign 14 (decimal) to $result.

If you are not familiar with octal and hexadecimal notations and would like to learn more, read the following sections. These sections explain how to convert numbers to different bases. If you are familiar with this concept, you can skip to the section called "Character Strings."

Decimal Notation

To understand how the octal and hexadecimal notations work, take a closer look at what the standard decimal notation actually represents.

In decimal notation, each digit in a number has one of 10 values: the standard numbers 0 through 9. Each digit in a number in decimal notation corresponds to a power of 10. Mathematically, the value of a digit x in a number is

```
x * 10 to the exponent n,
```

where n is the number of digits you have to skip before reaching x.

This might sound complicated, but it's really straightforward. For example, the number 243 can be expressed as follows:

- ☐ 2 * 10 to the exponent 2 (which is 200), plus
- ☐ 4 * 10 to the exponent 1 (which is 40), plus
- ☐ 3 * 10 to the exponent 0 (which is 3 * 1, which is 3)

Adding the three numbers together yields 243.

Octal Notation

Working through these steps might seem like a waste of time when you are dealing with decimal notation. However, once you understand this method, reading numbers in other notations becomes simple.

For example, in octal notation, each digit x in a number is

```
x * 8 to the exponent n
```

where x is the value of the digit, and n is the number of digits to skip before reaching x. This is the same formula as in decimal notation, but with the 10 replaced by 8.

Using this method, here's how to determine the decimal equivalent of 243 octal:

- ☐ 2 * 8 to the exponent 2, which is 2 * 64, or 128, plus
- ☐ 4 * 8 to the exponent 1, which is 4 * 8, or 32, plus
- ☐ 3 * 8 to the exponent 0, which is 3 * 1, or 3

Adding 128, 32 and 3 yields 163, which is the decimal notation equivalent of 243 octal.

Hexadecimal Notation

Hexadecimal notation works the same way, but with 16 as the base instead of 10 or 8. For example, here's how to convert 243 hexadecimal to decimal notation:

- ☐ 2 * 16 to the exponent 2, which is 2 * 256, or 512, plus
- ☐ 4 * 16 to the exponent 1, which is 4 * 16, or 64, plus
- ☐ 3 * 16 to the exponent 0, which is 3 * 1, or 3

Adding these three numbers together yields 579.

Note that the letters a through f represent the numbers 10 through 15, respectively. For example, here's the hexadecimal number fe in decimal notation:

- ☐ 15 * 16 to the exponent 1, which is 15 * 16, or 240, plus
- ☐ 14 * 16 to the exponent 0, which is 14 * 1, or 14

Adding 240 and 14 yields 254, which is the decimal equivalent of fe.

Why Bother?

You might be wondering why Perl bothers supporting octal and hexadecimal notation. Here's the answer: Computers store numbers in memory in binary (base 2) notation, not decimal (base 10) notation. Because 8 and 16 are multiples of 2, it is easier to represent stored computer memory in base 8 or base 16 than in base 10. (You could use base 2, of course; however, base 2 numbers are clumsy because they are very long.)

> **NOTE**
>
> Perl supports base-2 operations on integer scalar values. These operations, called bit-manipulation operations, are discussed on Day 4, "More Operators."

Character Strings

On previous days, you've seen that Perl enables you to assign text to scalar variables. In the following statement, for instance

```
$var = "This is some text";
```

the text This is some text is an example of what is called a *character string* (frequently shortened to just *string*). A character string is a sequence of one or more letters, digits, spaces, or special characters.

The following subsections show you

☐ How you can substitute for scalar variables in character strings

☐ How to add escape sequences to your character strings

☐ How to tell the Perl interpreter not to substitute for scalar variables

NOTE   C programmers should be advised that character strings in Perl do not contain a hidden null character at the end of the string. In Perl, null characters can appear anywhere in a string. (See the discussion of escape sequences later today for more details.)

Using Double-Quoted Strings

Perl supports *scalar variable substitution* in character strings enclosed by double quotation-mark characters. For example, consider the following assignments:

```
$number = 11;
$text = "This text contains the number $number.";
```

When the Perl interpreter sees $number inside the string in the second statement, it replaces $number with its current value. This means that the string assigned to $text is actually

```
This text contains the number 11.
```

The most immediate practical application of this is in the print statement. So far, many of the print statements you have seen contain several arguments, as in the following:

```
print ("The final result is ", $result, "\n");
```

Because Perl supports scalar variable substitution, you can combine the three arguments to print into a single argument, as in the following:

```
print ("The final result is $result\n");
```

NOTE   From now on, examples and listings that call print use scalar variable substitution because it is easier to read.

Escape Sequences

Character strings that are enclosed in double quotes accept *escape sequences* for special characters. These escape sequences consist of a backslash (\) followed by one or more characters. The most common escape sequence is \n, which represents the newline character as shown in this example:

```
$text = "This is a string terminated by a newline\n";
```

Table 3.1 lists the escape sequences recognized in double-quoted strings.

Table 3.1. Escape sequences in strings.

Escape Sequence	Description
\a	Bell (beep)
\b	Backspace
\c*n*	The Ctrl+*n* character
\e	Escape
\E	Ends the effect of \L, \U or \Q
\f	Form feed
\l	Forces the next letter into lowercase
\L	All following letters are lowercase
\n	Newline
\r	Carriage return
\Q	Do not look for special pattern characters
\t	Tab
\u	Force next letter into uppercase
\U	All following letters are uppercase
\v	Vertical tab

The \Q escape sequence is useful only when the string is used as a pattern. Patterns are described on Day 7, "Pattern Matching."

The escape sequences \L, \U, and \Q can be turned off by \E, as follows:

```
$a = "T\LHIS IS A \ESTRING"; # same as "This is a STRING"
```

To include a backslash or double quote in a double-quoted string, precede the backslash or quote with another backslash:

```
$result = "A quote \" in a string";
$result = "A backslash \\ in a string";
```

A backslash also enables you to include a $ character in a string. For example, the statements

```
$result = 14;
print("The value of \$result is $result.\n");
```

print the following on your screen:

```
The value of $result is 14.
```

You can specify the ASCII value for a character in base 8 or octal notation using \nnn, where each n is an octal digit; for example:

```
$result = "\377";        # this is the character 255, or EOF
```

You can also use hexadecimal notation to specify the ASCII value for a character. To do this, use the sequence \xnn, where each n is a hexadecimal digit.

```
$result = "\xff";        # this is also 255
```

Listing 3.4 is an example of a program that uses escape sequences. This program takes a line of input and converts it to a variety of cases.

TYPE **Listing 3.4. A case-conversion program.**

```
1:  #!/usr/local/bin/perl
2:
3:  print ("Enter a line of input:\n");
4:  $inputline = <STDIN>;
5:  print ("uppercase: \U$inputline\E\n");
6:  print ("lowercase: \L$inputline\E\n");
7:  print ("as a sentence: \L\u$inputline\E\n");
```

OUTPUT
```
$ program3_4
Enter a line of input:
tHis Is My INpUT LiNE.
uppercase: THIS IS MY INPUT LINE.
lowercase: this is my input line.
as a sentence: This is my input line.
$
```

ANALYSIS Line 3 of this program reads a line of input and stores it in the scalar variable $inputline.

Line 5 replaces the string $inputline with the current value of the scalar variable $inputline. The escape character \U tells the Perl interpreter to convert everything in the string into uppercase until it sees a \E character; as a result, line 4 writes the contents of $inputline in uppercase.

Similarly, line 6 writes the input line in all lowercase characters by specifying the escape character \L in the string.

Line 7 combines the escape characters \L and \u. The \L specifies that everything in the string is to be in lowercase; however, the \u special character temporarily overrides this and tells the Perl interpreter that the next character is to be in uppercase. When this character—the first character in the line—is printed, the \L escape character remains in force, and the rest of the line is printed in lowercase. The result is as if the input line is a single sentence in English. The first character is capitalized, and the remainder is in lowercase.

Single-Quoted Strings

Perl also enables you to enclose strings using the ' (single quotation mark) character:

```
$text = 'This is a string in single quotes';
```

There are two differences between double-quoted strings and single-quoted strings. The first difference is that scalar variables are replaced by their values in double-quoted strings but not in single-quoted strings. The following is an example:

```
$string = "a string";
$text = "This is $string";  # becomes "This is a string"
$text = 'This is $string';  # remains 'This is $string'
```

The second difference is that the backslash character, \, does not have a special meaning in single-quoted strings. This means that the statement

```
$text = 'This is a string.\n';
```

assigns the following string to $text:

```
This is a string.\n
```

The \ character is special in only two instances for single-quoted strings. The first is when you want to include a single-quote character ' in a string.

```
$text = 'This string contains \', a quote character';
```

The preceding line of code assigns the following string to $text:

```
This string contains ', a quote character
```

The second instance is to escape the backslash itself.

```
$text = 'This string ends with a backslash \\';
```

The preceding code line assigns the following string to $text:

```
This string ends with a backslash \
```

As you can see, the double backslash makes it possible for the backslash character (\) to be the last character in a string.

WARNING

> Single-quoted strings can be spread over multiple lines. The statement
>
> ```
> $text = 'This is two
>
> lines of text
>
> ';
> ```
>
> is equivalent to the statement
>
> ```
> $text = "This is two\nlines of text\n";
> ```
>
> This means that if you forget the closing ' for a string, the Perl interpreter is likely to get quite confused because it won't detect an error until after it starts processing the next line.

Interchangeability of Strings and Numeric Values

As you've seen, you can use a scalar variable to store a character string, an integer, or a floating-point value. In scalar variables, a value that was assigned as a string can be used as an integer whenever it makes sense to do so, and vice versa. In the following example:

```
$string = "43";
$number = 28;
$result = $string + $number;
```

the value of $string is converted to an integer and added to the value of $number. The result of the addition, 71, is assigned to $result.

Another instance in which strings are converted to integers is when you are reading a number from the standard input file. The following is some code similar to code you've seen before:

```
$number = <STDIN>;
chop ($number);
$result = $number + 1;
```

This is what is happening: When $number is assigned a line of standard input, it really is being assigned a string. For instance, if you enter 22, $number is assigned the string 22\n (the \n represents the newline character). The chop function removes the \n, leaving the string 22, and this string is converted to the number 22 in the arithmetic expression.

WARNING

> If a string contains characters that are not digits, the string is converted to 0 when used in an integer context. For example:
>
> ```
> $result = "hello" * 5;
> # this assigns 0 to $result, since "hello" becomes 0
> ```
>
> This is true even if the string is a valid hexadecimal integer if the quotes are removed, as in the following:
>
> ```
> $result = "0xff" + 1;
> ```
>
> In cases like this, Perl does not tell you that anything has gone wrong, and your results might not be what you expect.
>
> Also, strings containing misprints might not contain what you expect. For example:
>
> ```
> $result = "12O34";        # the letter O, not the number 0
> ```
>
> When converting from a string to an integer, Perl starts at the left and continues until it sees a letter that is not a digit. In the preceding instance, 12O34 is converted to the integer 12, not 12034.

Initial Values of Scalar Variables

In Perl, all scalar variables have an initial value of the null string, "". This means that you do not need to define a value for a scalar variable.

```
#!/usr/local/bin/perl
$result = $undefined + 2;   # $undefined is not defined
print ("The value of \$result is $result.\n");
```

This short program is perfectly legal Perl. The output is

```
The value of $result is 2.
```

Because $undefined is not defined, the Perl interpreter assumes that its value is the null string. This null string is then converted to 0, because it is being used in an addition operation. The result of the addition, 2, is assigned to $result.

TIP

Although you can use uninitialized variables in your Perl programs, you shouldn't. If your Perl program gets to be large (as many complicated programs do), it might be difficult to determine whether a particular variable is supposed to be appearing for the first time or whether it is a spelling mistake that should be fixed. To avoid ambiguity and to make life easier for yourself, initialize every scalar variable before using it.

Summary

Perl supports three kinds of scalar values: integers, floating-point numbers, and character strings.

Integers can be in three notations: standard (decimal) notation, octal notation, and hexadecimal notation. Octal notation is indicated by a leading 0, and hexadecimal notation is indicated by a leading 0x. Integers are stored as floating-point values and can be as long as the machine's floating-point precision (usually 16 digits or so).

Floating-point numbers can consist of a string of digits that contain a decimal point and an optional exponent. The exponent's range can be anywhere from about e-309 to e+308. (This value might be different on some machines.) When possible, floating-point numbers are displayed without the exponent; failing that, they are displayed in scientific notation (one digit before the decimal point).

When you use floating-point arithmetic, be alert for round-off errors. Performing arithmetic operations in the proper order—operating on large numbers first—might yield better results.

You can enclose character strings in either double quotes (") or single quotes ('). If a scalar variable name appears in a character string enclosed in double quotes, the value of the variable is substituted for its name. Escape characters are recognized in strings enclosed in double quotes; these characters are indicated by a backslash (\).

Character strings in single quotes do not support escape characters, with the exception of \\ and \'. Scalar variable names are not replaced by their values.

Strings and integers are freely interchangeable in Perl whenever it is logically possible to do so.

Q&A

Q **If Perl character strings are not terminated by null characters, how does the Perl interpreter know the length of a string?**

A The Perl interpreter keeps track of the length of a string as well as its contents. In Perl, you do not need to use a null character to indicate "end of string."

Q **Why does Perl use floating-point registers for floating-point arithmetic even though they cause round-off errors?**

A Basically, it's a performance issue. It's possible to write routines that store floating-point numbers as strings and convert parts of these strings to numbers as necessary; however, you often don't need more than 16 or so digits of precision anyway.

Applications that need to do high-speed arithmetic calculations of great precision usually run on special computers designed for that purpose.

Q **What happens if I forget to call chop when reading a number from the standard input file?**

A As it happens, nothing. Perl is smart enough to ignore white space at the end of a line that consists only of a number. However, it's a good idea to get into the habit of using chop to get rid of a trailing newline at all times, because the trailing newline becomes significant when you start doing string comparisons. (You'll learn about string comparisons on Day 4, "More Operators.")

Workshop

The Workshop provides quiz questions to help you solidify your understanding of the material covered and exercises to give you experience in using what you've learned. Try and understand the quiz and exercise answers before you go on to tomorrow's lesson.

Quiz

1. Define the following terms:
   a. round-off error
   b. octal notation
   c. precision
   d. scientific notation

2. Convert the following numbers from octal notation to decimal:

   a. 0377

   b. 06

   c. 01131

3. Convert the following numbers from hexadecimal notation to decimal notation:

   a. 0xff

   b. 0x11

   c. 0xbead

4. What does the following line print?

   ```
   print ("I am bored\b\b\b\b\bhappy!\n");
   ```

5. Suppose the value of $num is 21. What string is assigned to $text in each of the following cases?

   a. $text = "This string contains $num.";

   b. $text = "\\$num is my favorite number.";

   c. $text = 'Assign \$num to this string.';

6. Convert the following numbers to scientific notation:

   a. 43.71

   b. 0.000006e-02

   c. 3

   d. −1.04

Exercises

1. Write a program that prints every number from 0 to 1 that has a single digit after the decimal place (that is, 0.1, 0.2, and so on).

2. Write a program that reads a line of input and prints out the following:

   ☐ 1 if the line consists of a non-zero integer

   ☐ 0 if the line consists of 0 or a string

   (Hint: Remember that character strings are converted to 0 when they are converted to integers.)

3. Write a program that asks for a number and keeps trying until you enter the number 47. At that point, it prints Correct! and rings a bell.

4. **BUG BUSTER:** What is wrong with the following program?

   ```
   #!/usr/local/bin/perl

   $inputline = <STDIN>;
   print ('here is the value of \$inputline\', ": $inputline");
   ```

5. **BUG BUSTER:** What is wrong with the following code fragment?

```
$num1 = 6.02e+23;
$num2 = 11.4;
$num3 = 5.171e+22;
$num4 = -2.5;
$result = $num1 + $num2 - $num3 + $num4;
```

6. **BUG BUSTER:** What is wrong with the following statement?

```
$result = "26" + "0xce" + "1";
```

Week 1

Day 4

More Operators

On Day 2, "Basic Operators and Control Flow," you learned about the following operators:

- [ ] The arithmetic operators +, -, *, and /
- [ ] The comparison operator ==
- [ ] The assignment operator =

Today, you learn about the rest of the operators that Perl provides, as well as about operator associativity and precedence. The operators are

- [ ] The arithmetic operators **, %, and - (unary negation)
- [ ] The other integer- and string-comparison operators
- [ ] The logical operators
- [ ] The bit-manipulation operators
- [ ] The assignment operators
- [ ] Autoincrement and autodecrement
- [ ] Concatenating and repeating strings
- [ ] The comma and conditional operators

Using the Arithmetic Operators

The arithmetic operators that you have seen so far—the +, -, *, and / operators—work the way you expect them to: They perform the operations of addition, subtraction, multiplication, and division.

Perl also supports three other arithmetic operations:

☐ Exponentiation

☐ The modulo or remainder operation

☐ Unary negation

Although these operators aren't as intuitively obvious as the ones you've already seen, they are quite easy to use.

Exponentiation

The *exponentiation operator*, **, provides a convenient way to multiply a number by itself repeatedly. For example, here is a simple Perl statement that uses the exponentiation operator:

```
$x = 2 ** 4;
```

The expression 2 ** 4 means "take four copies of two and multiply them." This statement assigns 16 to the scalar variable $x.

Note that the following statements are equivalent, but the first statement is much more concise:

```
$x = 2 ** 7;
$x = 2 * 2 * 2 * 2 * 2 * 2 * 2;
```

When an exponentiation operator is employed, the *base* value (the value to the left of the **) is the number to be repeatedly multiplied. The number to the right, called the *exponent*, is the number of times the multiplication is to be performed. Here are some other simple examples of the exponentiation operator:

```
$x = 9 ** 2;        # 9 squared, or 81
$x = 2 ** 3;        # 2 * 2 * 2, or 8
$x = 43 ** 1;       # this is just 43
```

The ** operator also works on the values stored in variables:

```
$x = $y ** 2;
```

Here, the value stored in $y is multiplied by itself, and the result is stored in $x. $y is not changed by this operation.

```
$x = 2 ** $y;
```

In this case, the value stored in $y becomes the exponent, and $x is assigned 2 multiplied by itself $y times.

You can use the exponent operator with non-integer or negative exponents:

```
2 ** -5          # this is the fraction 1/32
5 ** 2.5         # this is 25 * the square root of 5
```

Listing 4.1 shows an example of a simple program that uses the exponential operator. It prompts for a number, $exponent, and prints out 2 ** $exponent.

TYPE **Listing 4.1. A program that prints out the powers of two.**

```
1:  #!/usr/local/bin/perl
2:
3:  # this program asks for a number, n, and prints 2 to the
4:  # exponent n
5:
6:  print ("Enter the exponent to use:\n");
7:  $exponent = <STDIN>;
8:  chop ($exponent);
9:  print ("Two to the power $exponent is ",
10:       2 ** $exponent, "\n");
```

OUTPUT
```
$ program4_1
Enter the exponent to use:
16
Two to the power 16 is 65536
$
```

ANALYSIS The program shown in Listing 4.1 is useful if you have to use, or be aware of, numbers such as 4,294,967,295 (the largest number that can be stored in a 32-bit unsigned integer) and 2,147,483,647 (the largest number that can be stored in a 32-bit signed integer). The former is equivalent to 2 ** 32 - 1, and the latter is equivalent to 2 ** 31 - 1.

Do	Don't

DON'T use the exponent operator with a negative base and a non-integer exponent:

```
(-5) ** 2.5        # error
```

continues

The result of this expression is a complex (non-real) number (just as, for instance, the square root of –2 is a complex number). Perl does not understand complex numbers.

DON'T produce a result that is larger than the largest floating-point number your machine can understand:

```
10 ** 999999        # error
```

In this example, the exponent is too large to be stored on most machines.

The Remainder Operator

The *remainder operator* retrieves the remainder resulting from the division of one integer by another. Consider the following simple example:

```
$x = 25 % 4;
```

In this case, 25 divided by 4 yields 6, with a remainder of 1. The remainder, 1, is assigned to $x.

The % operator does not work on values that are not integers. Non-integers are converted to integers, as follows:

```
$x = 24.77 % 4.21;   # same as 25 % 4
```

Because division by 0 is impossible, you can't put a 0 to the right of a % operator.

```
$x = 25 % 0;        # error: can't divide by 0
$x = 25 % 0.1;      # error: 0.1 is converted to 0
```

Unary Negation

The *unary negation operator* is a – character in front of a single value. (This distinguishes it from the subtraction operator, which appears between two values.) It is equivalent to multiplying the value by –1, as illustrated by this example:

```
- 5;               # identical to the integer -5
- $y;              # equivalent to $y * -1
```

Using Comparison Operators

On Day 2, "Basic Operators and Control Flow," you learned about the equality comparison operator (==), which compares two values and tests whether they are equal.

```
$x = $a == $b;
```

Recall that the value of $x depends on the values stored in $a and $b:

☐ If $a equals $b, $a == $b is true, and $x is assigned a nonzero value.

☐ If $a is not equal to $b, $a == $b is false, and $x is assigned 0.

The == operator is an example of a *comparison operator*. Comparison operators are most commonly used in control statements such as the if statement, as follows:

```
if ($a == $b) {
        print("$a is equal to $b\n");
}
```

In Perl, the comparison operators are divided into two classes:

☐ Comparison operators that work with numbers

☐ Comparison operators that work with strings

Integer-Comparison Operators

Table 4.1 defines the integer-comparison operators available in Perl.

Table 4.1. Integer-comparison operators.

Operator	Description
<	Less than
>	Greater than
==	Equal to
<=	Less than or equal to
>=	Greater than or equal to
!=	Not equal to
<=>	Comparison returning 1, 0, or –1

Here are simple examples of each of the first six operators in Table 4.1:

```
$x < 10              # true if the value of $x is less than 10
$x > 10              # true if $x is greater than 10
$x == 10             # true if $x is equal to 10
$x <= 10             # true if $x is less than or equal to 10
$x >= 10             # true if $x is greater than or equal to 10
$x != 10             # true if $x is not equal to 10
```

Each of these operators yields one of two values:

- True, or nonzero
- False, or zero

The <=> operator is a special case. Unlike the other integer comparison operators, <=> returns one of three values:

- 0, if the two values being compared are equal
- 1, if the first value is greater
- −1, if the second value is greater

For example, consider the following statement:

```
$y = $x <=> 10;
```

These are the possible results:

- If $x is greater than 10, the first value in the comparison is greater, and $y is assigned 1.
- If $x is less than 10, the second value in the comparison is greater, and $y is assigned −1.
- If $x is equal to 10, $y is assigned 0.

Integer Comparisons and Readability

In any given statement, it's best to use the comparison that can be most easily read. For example, consider the following:

```
if (3.2 < $x) {
        # conditionally executed stuff goes here
}
```

Although the expression 3.2 < $x is perfectly valid, it isn't easy to read because variables usually appear first in comparisons. Instead, it would be better to use

```
if ($x >= 3.2) {
    ...
```

because this is easier to understand. I'm not sure exactly why this is true; I think it's related to the way the English language is spoken. (Normally, we say, "If I had five dollars, I'd buy some milk," instead of, "If five dollars had I, I'd buy some milk," even though both are correct.)

String-Comparison Operators

For every numeric-comparison operator, Perl defines an equivalent string-comparison operator. Table 4.2 displays each string-comparison operator, the comparison it performs, and the equivalent numeric-comparison operator.

Table 4.2. String- and numeric-comparison operators.

String operator	Comparison operation	Equivalent numeric operator
lt	Less than	<
gt	Greater than	>
eq	Equal to	==
le	Less than or equal to	<=
ge	Greater than or equal to	>=
ne	Not equal to	!=
cmp	Compare, returning 1, 0, or –1	<=>

Perl compares strings by determining their places in an alphabetical order. For example, the string aaa is less than the string bbb, because aaa appears before bbb when they are sorted alphabetically.

Here are some examples of string-comparison operators in action:

```
$result = "aaa" lt "bbb";    # result is true
$result = "aaa" gt "bbb";    # result is false
$result = "aaa" eq "bbb";    # result is false
$result = "aaa" le "aaa";    # result is true
$result = "aaa" ge "bbb";    # result is false
$result = "aaa" ne "aaa";    # result is false
$result = "aaa" cmp "bbb";   # result is -1
```

If you are familiar with the C programming language, you might have noticed that the behavior of the cmp operator is identical to that of the C function strcmp().

String Comparison Versus Integer Comparison

You might be thinking: If strings and integers are equivalent in Perl, why do we need two kinds of comparison operators?

To answer this, consider the strings 123 and 45. The result when these two strings are compared depends on whether a string or integer comparison is being performed.

```
$result = "123" < "45";
$result = "123" lt "45";
```

In the first statement, the strings 123 and 45 are converted to integers, and 123 is compared to 45. The result is false and $result is assigned 0, because 123 is not less than 45.

In the second statement, 123 is alphabetically compared to 45. Because 123 is alphabetically less than 45, the result in this case is true, and $result is assigned a nonzero value.

Because these results are different, you must ensure that you are using the proper comparison operator every time. If you don't, your program can contain errors that are not easy to spot. For instance, consider the following:

```
$var1 = "string 1";
$var2 = "string 2";
$result = $var1 == $var2;   # this statement is bad
```

Because == is a numeric-comparison operator, the values string 1 and string 2 are converted to integers before the comparison is performed. Because both strings are non-numeric, they are both converted to the integer 0, and the following comparison becomes true:

```
$var1 == $var2
```

This is probably not what you want.

Comparison and Floating-Point Numbers

There is one thing to keep in mind when you use comparison operators: Floating-point numbers don't always behave properly in comparisons.

Take a look at Listing 4.2.

TYPE

Listing 4.2. A program that contains a floating-point comparison.

```
1:  #!/usr/local/bin/perl
2:
3:  $value1 = 14.3;
4:  $value2 = 100 + 14.3 - 100;
5:  if ($value1 == $value2) {
```

```
6:          print("value 1 equals value 2\n");
7:  } else {
8:          print("value 1 does not equal value 2\n");
9:  }
```

$ program4_2
value 1 does not equal value 2
$

ANALYSIS   At first glance, you might think that $value1 and $value2 are identical. However, when you run this program, you get the following:

value 1 does not equal value 2

What is wrong? To find out, print out the values of $value1 and $value2 before doing the comparison.

```
#!/usr/local/bin/perl
$value1 = 14.3;
$value2 = 100 + 14.3 - 100;
print("value 1 is $value1, value2 is $value2\n");
if ($value1 == $value2) {
        print("value 1 equals value 2\n");
} else {
        print("value 1 does not equal value 2\n");
}
```

When you run this program, you get the following output:

value 1 is 14.300000000000001, value 2 is 14.299999999999997
value 1 does not equal value 2

Well, Perl isn't lying: $value1 and $value2 *are* different. What happened?

To understand what's going on, consider what happens when you take an ordinary calculator and tell it to divide 8 by 3. The actual answer is

2.6666666...

with the number of 6s being infinite. Because your calculator can't display an infinite number of 6s, what it displays is something like the following:

2.6666666667

This is as close to the actual number as your calculator can get. The difference between the actual number and the number displayed is an example of a *round-off error*.

Round-off errors often occur when Perl (or almost any other programming language) stores a floating-point number or adds a number to a floating-point number. The statement

$value1 = 14.3;

actually assigns

```
14.300000000000001
```

to $value1, because 14.3 cannot be exactly represented in the machine's floating-point storage. When 100 is added to this number and subtracted again, the result is

```
14.299999999999997
```

Note that both numbers are very close to 14.3 but aren't exactly 14.3 due to round-off errors. What's worse, each number is affected by a different set of round-off errors, so the two numbers are not identical.

The moral of the story? Be very careful when you use floating-point numbers in comparisons, because round-off errors might affect your results.

Using Logical Operators

The comparison operators you've seen so far are sufficient if you need to test for only one condition before executing a particular code segment, as in this example:

```
if ($value == 26) {
        # the code to execute if the condition is true
}
```

Suppose, however, that a particular section of code is to be executed only when a variety of conditions are true. You can use a sequence of if statements to test for the conditions, as follows:

```
if ($value1 == 26) {
        if ($value2 > 0) {
                if ($string1 eq "ready") {
                        print("all three conditions are true!\n");
                }
        }
}
```

This is tiresome to write and not particularly easy to read.

Fortunately, Perl provides an easier way to deal with multiple conditions: the *logical operators*. The following logical operators are defined:

```
$a ¦¦ $b        # logical or:  true if either is nonzero
$a && $b        # logical and: true only if both are nonzero
! $a            # logical not: true if $a is zero
```

Perl 5 also defines these logical operators:

```
$a or $b        # another form of logical or
$a and $b       # another form of logical and
not $a          # another form of logical not
```

```
$a xor $b        # logical xor: true if either $a or $b is nonzero, but not both
```

The or, and, and not operators listed are identical to ||, &&, and !, except that their precedence is lower. (*Operator precedence* determines the order in which operators are evaluated, and is discussed later today.)

In each case, the result of the operation performed by a logical operator is nonzero if true and 0 if false.

```
$a = 5;
$b = 0;
$a || $b;        # true: $a is not zero
$b || $a;        # also true
$a && $b;        # false: $b is zero
! $a;            # false: $a is nonzero, so ! $a is zero
! $b;            # true: $b is zero, so ! $b is nonzero
```

These logical operators enable you to test for multiple conditions more conveniently. Instead of writing, for example, this code:

```
if ($value1 == 26) {
        if ($value2 > 0) {
                if ($string1 eq "ready") {
                        print("all three conditions are true!\n");
                }
        }
}
```

you now can write this code instead:

```
if ($value == 26 && $value2 > 0 && $string1 eq "ready") {
        print("all three conditions are true!\n");
}
```

In each case, the result is the same: the print operation is performed only when $value is 26, $value2 is greater than 0, and $string1 is "ready."

Evaluation Within Logical Operators

When Perl sees a logical AND operator or a logical OR operator, the expression on the left side of the operator is always evaluated first. For example, consider the following:

```
$a = 0;
$b = 106;
$result = $a && $b;
```

When Perl is evaluating the expression $a && $b, it first checks whether $a is 0. If $a is 0, $a && $b must be false regardless of the value of $b, so Perl doesn't bother checking the value of $b. (This is called *short-circuit evaluation*.)

Similarly, in the following example, Perl doesn't bother checking $b, because $a is nonzero and therefore $a || $b must be true:

```
$a = 43;
$b = 11;
$result = $a || $b;
```

You can take advantage of the order of evaluation of expressions in || or && to safeguard your code.

```
$x == 0 || $y / $x > 5
```

Here is how the preceding statement protects you from division-by-zero errors:

☐ If $x is not 0, $x == 0 is false, so Perl evaluates $y / $x > 5. This cannot produce a division-by-zero error, because $x is guaranteed to be some value other than 0.

☐ If $x is 0, $x == 0 is true. This means that

```
$x == 0 || $y / $x > 5
```

is true, so Perl doesn't bother evaluating the expression to the right of the ||. As a result, the expression

```
$y / $x > 5
```

is not evaluated when $x is 0, and the division-by-zero error is avoided.

Logical Operators as Subexpressions

Expressions that contain logical operators can be contained in larger expressions. The following is an example:

```
$myval = $a || $b || $c;
```

Here, Perl evaluates the expression $a || $b || $c and assigns its value to $myval.

To understand the behavior of this statement, recall that the || operator evaluates its subexpressions in the order given, and evaluates a subexpression only if the previous subexpression is zero. This means that $b is evaluated only if $a is zero.

When the logical OR operator is used in a larger expression, its value is the last subexpression actually evaluated, which is the first subexpression of the logical OR operator that is nonzero. This means that

```
$myval = $a || $b || $c;
```

is equivalent to

```
if ($a != 0) {
        $myvalue = $a;
} elsif ($b != 0) {
```

```
        $myvalue = $b;
} else {
        $myvalue = $c;
}
```

The logical AND operator works in the same way, but isn't as useful. The statement

```
$myval = $a && $b && $c;
```

is equivalent to

```
if ($a == 0) {
        $myvalue = $a;
} elsif ($b == 0) {
        $myvalue = $b;
} else {
        $myvalue = $c;
}
```

This means that `$myval` is set to either `0` or the value of `$c`.

Using Bit-Manipulation Operators

Perl enables you to manipulate the binary digits (or bits) of an integer. To understand how Perl does this, first look at what a bit is and how computers store integers. Once you understand how bits work, you can easily figure out how the bit-manipulation operators work. (If you are familiar with binary notation and the computer representation of an integer, feel free to skip the following section.)

What Bits Are and How They Are Used

On Day 3, "Understanding Scalar Values," you learned that Perl understands three different notations for integers:

☐ Standard notation, or base 10

☐ Octal notation, or base 8

☐ Hexadecimal notation, or base 16

However, when a computer stores an integer, it uses none of these notations; instead, it uses base 2, or *binary notation*.

In binary notation, every number is represented as a series of 0s and 1s. For instance, the number 124 is represented as

```
01111100
```

To understand how to get from base-10 notation to binary notation, recall what the number 124 represents. When we write "124," what we really mean is the following:

- 4 multiplied by 1, plus
- 2 multiplied by 10, plus
- 1 multiplied by 100

In grade school, your teacher probably said these digits represented the "ones place," the "tens place," and the "hundreds place." Each "place" is ten times larger than the place to its right. This means that you also can think of 124 as follows:

- 4 multiplied by 1 (or 10 to the exponent 0), plus
- 2 multiplied by 10 to the exponent 1, plus
- 1 multiplied by 10 to the exponent 2

In binary notation, you can use this same method, but replace the 10s with 2s. Here's how to use this method to figure out that the binary number 01111100 is equivalent to 124 in standard notation. Starting from the right, you have:

- 0 multiplied by 2 to the exponent 0, which is 0
- 0 multiplied by 2 to the exponent 1, which is 0
- 1 multiplied by 2 to the exponent 2, which is 4
- 1 multiplied by 2 to the exponent 3, which is 8
- 1 multiplied by 2 to the exponent 4, which is 16
- 1 multiplied by 2 to the exponent 5, which is 32
- 1 multiplied by 2 to the exponent 6, which is 64
- 0 multiplied by 2 to the exponent 7, which is 0

Adding 2, 8, 16, 32, and 64 gives you 124.

Each of the 0s and 1s in the binary number 01111100 is called a *bit* (which is short for *bi*nary dig*it*). Each bit can have only two possible values: 0 or 1.

In computers, integers are stored as a sequence of bits. This sequence of bits is normally 8, 16, or 32 bits long, depending on the size and configuration of your computer. In the examples in today's lesson, 8-bit integers are assumed; to convert an 8-bit binary number to a 16-bit binary number, just add eight zeros to the left. For example, the following numbers are equivalent:

```
01111100              # 124 as an 8-bit integer
0000000001111100      # 124 as a 16-bit integer
```

The examples in today's lesson use 8-bit integers. The Perl bitwise operators will work on integers of any size.

The Bit-Manipulation Operators

The following bit-manipulation operators are supported in Perl:

- ☐ The & (bitwise AND) operator
- ☐ The ¦ (bitwise OR) operator
- ☐ The ^ (bitwise XOR or "exclusive or") operator
- ☐ The ~ (bitwise NOT) operator
- ☐ The << (left shift) and >> (right shift) operators

The Bitwise AND Operator

In Perl, the & operator represents the bitwise AND operation. This operation works as follows:

- ☐ The value to the left side of the & (also called the *left operand* of the & operation) is converted to an integer, if necessary.
- ☐ The value to the right side of the & (the *right operand*) also is converted to an integer.
- ☐ Each bit of the left operand is compared to the corresponding bit of the right operand.
- ☐ If a pair of corresponding bits both have the value 1, the corresponding bit of the result is set to 1. Otherwise, the corresponding bit of the result is set to 0.

This might sound complicated, but when you take a look at an example, you'll see that it's pretty easy to figure out. For instance, consider the following:

```
$result = 124.3 & 99;
```

First, the left operand, 124.3, is converted to an integer, becoming 124. (The right operand, 99, does not need to be converted.) Next, take a look at the binary representations of 124 and 99:

```
01111100        # this is 124 in binary
01100011        # this is 99 in binary
```

When you examine each pair of bits in turn, you can see that only the second and third pairs (from the left) are both 1. Thus, the & operation yields the following binary result:

```
01100000
```

This is 96 in standard notation. As a consequence, the statement

```
$result = 124.3 & 99;
```

assigns 96 to $result.

DO use the & operator with strings, provided the strings can be converted to numbers, as follows:

```
$result = "124.3" & "99";
```

Remember: Strings and integers are interchangeable in Perl.

DON'T confuse the & operator with the && operator. The && operator performs a logical AND operation, not a bitwise AND operation. For example, the statement

```
$result = 124.3 && 99;
```

assigns a nonzero value to $result (because 124.3 and 99 are both nonzero). This nonzero value is not likely to be the result you want.

DON'T use the & operator with negative integers, because Perl will convert them to unsigned integers, and you won't get the result you want.

The Bitwise OR Operator

The bitwise OR operator, ¦, also compares two integers one bit at a time. However, in the bitwise OR operation, a result bit is 1 if either of the corresponding bits in the operands is 1.

To see how this works, look at another example:

```
$result = 124.3 ¦ 99;
```

Here's how this operation is performed:

☐ As before, the two operands are converted to integers if necessary. The operands become 124 and 99; in binary representation, these are, as before,

```
01111100
01100011
```

☐ Each bit of the left operand is compared with the corresponding bit in the right operand. If either of the corresponding bits is 1, the corresponding result bit is 1.

In this example, every bit becomes 1 except the first one, because at least one of each of the other pairs is a 1. Therefore, the result is

```
01111111
```

which translates to 127. This means that the following statement assigns 127 to `$result`:

```
$result = 124.3 ¦ 99;
```

Do   **Don't**

DO make sure you are using the proper bitwise operator. It's easy to slip and assume you want bitwise OR when you really want bitwise AND. (Trust me.)

DON'T confuse the ¦ operator (bitwise OR) with the ¦¦ operator (logical OR).

The Bitwise XOR Operator

The bitwise XOR ("exclusive or") operator, ^, is similar to the bitwise OR operator, but it's a little more demanding. In the bitwise OR operation, a result bit is 1 if either of the corresponding bits in the operands is 1. In the bitwise XOR operation, a result bit is 1 if *exactly one* of the corresponding bits in the operands is 1.

Here is an example of the bitwise XOR operation:

```
$result = 124.3 ^ 99;
```

This works as follows:

☐ As before, 124.3 is converted to 124, and the binary representations of the two operands are as follows:

```
01111100            # this is 124
01100011            # this is 99
```

☐ Each bit of the left operand is compared with the corresponding bit of the right operand. The corresponding result bit is set to 1 if exactly one of the bits in the operands is 1.

In this case, the result is

```
00011111
```

which is 31. To work through how you get this result, consider the following:

☐ The first bit of the left operand and the first bit of the right operand are both 0. This means the first bit of the result is 0.

☐ The second bit of the left operand and the second bit of the right operand both are 1. Therefore, the second bit of the result is 0, not 1.

- [ ] The same applies for the third bits: Both are 1, so the result bit is 0.
- [ ] The fourth bit of the left operand is 1, and the fourth bit of the right operand is 0. Here, exactly one of the bits is 1, so the result bit becomes 1.
- [ ] Same for the fifth and sixth pairs: The first bit is 1 and the second is 0, so the result is 1.
- [ ] The seventh bit of the left operand is 0, and the seventh bit of the right operand is 1. Again, exactly one of the bits is 1, and the result bit is also 1.
- [ ] Same for the eighth pair: The first bit is 0, the second is 1, so the result is 1.

From this, you can determine that the following statement assigns 31 to $result:

```
$result = 124.3 ^ 99;
```

The Bitwise NOT Operator

Unlike the other bitwise operators you've seen so far, the bitwise NOT operator, ~, is a *unary* operator, meaning it works on only one operand.

The way it works is straightforward, as follows:

- [ ] The operand is converted to an integer, if necessary.
- [ ] Each bit of the operand is examined. If a bit is 0, the corresponding result bit is set to 1, and vice versa.

For example, consider the following:

```
$result = ~99;
```

The binary representation of 99 is

```
01100011
```

Applying the bitwise NOT operation to this number produces

```
10011100
```

This number, in standard notation, is 156. Therefore, the following statement assigns 156 to $result:

```
$result = ~99;
```

Note that the number of bits used to store an integer affects the results produced by the ~ operator. For example, if integers are stored in 16 bits on your computer, the number 99 is represented as

```
0000000001100011
```

This means that applying ~ to this number yields

```
1111111110011100
```

which is 65436 in standard notation. As a consequence, the statement

```
$result = ~99;
```

assigns 65436, not 156, to $result. (On a computer with 32-bit integers, the value assigned is 4294967196.)

The Shift Operators

Perl enables you to shift the bits of an integer using the << (shift left) and >> (shift right) operators. For example, in the statement

```
$result = $x >> 1;
```

every bit of the value stored in $x is shifted one place to the right, and the result is assigned to $result ($x itself is not changed).

To see how this works, consider the following example:

```
$result = 99 >> 1;
```

As you saw earlier, the binary representation of 99 is

```
01100011
```

Shifting every bit right one place yields

```
00110001
```

Note that a 0 is added at the far left, and the bit at the far right disappears.

Because 00110001 in binary notation is the same as 49 in standard notation, the following statement assigns 49 to $result:

```
$result = 99 >> 1;
```

The <<, or shift-left, operator works in the same way:

```
$result = 99 << 1;
```

The shift-left operator works as follows:

```
01100011          # the binary representation of 99
11000110          # after shifting left 1 bit
```

The result of the shift is 198, which is assigned to $result.

Do   **Don't**

DO remember that when you use the >> operator, the bits on the right are lost. For example:

```
$result1 = 17 >> 1;

$result2 = 16 >> 1;
```

In this case, $result1 and $result2 are the same value, 8. This is because the rightmost bit is shifted out in both cases.

DON'T shift left too far, or you might not get the result you want. For example, if you are using 16-bit integers, the statement

```
$result = 35000 << 1;
```

does not assign 70000 to $result as you might think it would because the largest value that can be stored in a 16-bit integer is 65536.

Shifting and Powers of 2

In the following statement, the variable $result is assigned the value 49:

```
$result = 99 / 2;
```

Take a look at the binary representations of 99 and 49:

```
01100011          # 99 in binary form
00110001          # 49 in binary form
```

As you can see, dividing by 2 is identical to shifting right one bit—in each case, every bit is moved one place to the right. Similarly, shifting right two bits is equivalent to dividing by 4:

```
$result = 99 / 4;   # $result is assigned 24
01100011            # 99 in binary
00011000            # 24 in binary
```

Multiplying by 4 is similar to shifting left two bits:

```
$result = 17 * 4;   # $result is assigned 68
00010001            # 17 in binary
01000100            # 68 in binary
```

The general rules are as follows:

☐ Shifting left *n* bits, where *n* is some number greater than 0, is equivalent to multiplying by 2**n*.

☐ Shifting right *n* bits, where *n* is some number greater than 0, is equivalent to dividing by 2**n*.

In the early days of programming, many programmers used shift operators in place of multiplication and division wherever possible, because the shift operations were usually more efficient. (In fact, some compilers would optimize their code by converting multiplication and division to shifts.) Today, it's usually best to use the shift operators when you are manipulating bits, and to use the multiplication and division operators when you're actually doing arithmetic. This will make your programs easier to understand.

Using the Assignment Operators

As you saw on Day 2, the assignment operator = associates, or assigns, a value to a variable. For example, the statement

```
$result = 42;
```

assigns the value 42 to the variable $result.

The = operator can appear more than once in a single statement. For example, in the statement

```
$value1 = $value2 = "a string";
```

the character string a string is assigned to both $value1 and $value2.

Perl also supports other assignment operators, each of which combines an assignment with another operation. For example, suppose that you want to add a value to a scalar variable and assign the result to the following variable:

```
$var = $var + 1;
```

Another way to write this is with the += assignment operator:

```
$var += 1;
```

This statement adds the value 1 to the existing value of $var.

An assignment operator exists for just about every bitwise operator and arithmetic operator that Perl supports. Table 4.3 lists the assignment operators supported in Perl.

4

Table 4.3. The assignment operators.

Operator	Operations performed
=	Assignment only
+=	Addition and assignment
-=	Subtraction and assignment
*=	Multiplication and assignment
/=	Division and assignment
%=	Remainder and assignment
**=	Exponentiation and assignment
&=	Bitwise AND and assignment
¦=	Bitwise OR and assignment
^=	Bitwise XOR and assignment

Table 4.4 shows examples of the assignment operators, along with equivalent statements that use operators you've seen earlier.

Table 4.4. Examples of assignment operators.

Statement using assignment operator	Equivalent Perl statement
$a = 1;	none (basic assignment)
$a -= 1;	$a = $a - 1;
$a *= 2;	$a = $a * 2;
$a /= 2;	$a = $a / 2;
$a %= 2;	$a = $a % 2;
$a **= 2;	$a = $a ** 2;
$a &= 2;	$a = $a & 2;
$a ¦= 2;	$a = $a ¦ 2;
$a ^= 2;	$a = $a ^ 2;

Assignment Operators as Subexpressions

Any expression that contains an assignment operator can appear on the left side of another assignment operator. The following is an example:

```
($a = $b) += 3;
```

In cases such as this, the assignment enclosed in parentheses is performed first. This assignment is then treated as a separate subexpression whose value is the variable to which it is being assigned. For example, $a = $b has the value $a.

This means that the statement shown previously is equivalent to the following two statements:

```
$a = $b;
$a += 3;
```

 TIP

Don't use assignments in this way unless you absolutely have to. At first glance, the statement

```
($a = $b) += 3;
```

appears to add 3 to $b as well as to $a.

Using Autoincrement and Autodecrement

So far, you've seen two ways to add 1 to a scalar variable:

```
$a = $a + 1;
$a += 1;
```

The first method uses the standard assignment operator = and the addition operator +, and the second method uses the addition assignment operator +=.

Perl also supports a third method of adding 1 to a scalar variable: the *autoincrement operator*, or ++. Here are some examples of the ++ operator in action:

```
$a++;
++$a;
$result = $a++;
$result2 = ++$a;
```

In each case, the ++ operator tells Perl to add 1 to the value stored in $a.

In some of the examples, the ++ is in front of the variable it is affecting, whereas in others the ++ follows the variable. If the ++ is first, the operation is a *pre-increment* operation; if the ++ follows, the operation is a *post-increment* operation.

The Autoincrement Operator Pre-Increment

To understand how the pre-increment operation works, first recall that you can use a single statement to assign a value to more than one variable, as follows:

```
$var1 = 43;
$var2 = $var1 += 1;
```

Here, the original value stored in $var1, 43, has 1 added to it. The result, 44, becomes the new value of $var1. This new value of 44 is then assigned to $var2.

The pre-increment operation works in the same way:

```
$var1 = 43;
$var2 = ++$var1;
```

The following code fragment tells Perl to add 1 to $var1 before doing anything else:

```
++$var1
```

As a result, $var1 becomes 44 before the value of $var1 is assigned to $var2. Therefore, $var2 is assigned 44.

The ++ operator is most frequently used in while statements. Listing 4.3 provides an example of a simple program that uses the ++ operator in a while statement.

TYPE Listing 4.3. A program that uses the pre-increment operation.

```
1:  #!/usr/local/bin/perl
2:  $value = 0;
3:  while (++$value <= 5) {
4:          print("value is now $value\n");
5:  }
6:  print("all done\n");
```

OUTPUT

```
$ program4_3
value is now 1
value is now 2
value is now 3
value is now 4
value is now 5
all done
$
```

ANALYSIS Note that the pre-increment operation enables you to add 1 to $value and test it all at the same time. This means that you no longer have to remember to add the following:

```
$value = $value + 1;
```

at the bottom of the while statement, which means that you are less likely to write a while statement that goes on forever.

Now see what happens when you change

```
while (++$value <= 5) {
```

to this:

```
while (++$value <= 0) {
```

and then run the program again. This time, you get the following:

```
all done
```

Because the ++ operator is in front of $value, 1 is added to $value before testing. This means that $value is not less than or equal to 0 when the while statement is executed for the first time; as a result, the code inside the while statement is never executed.

The Autoincrement Operator Post-Increment

The post-increment operator also adds 1 to the variable with which it is associated. However, its behavior is slightly different:

```
$var1 = 43;
$var2 = $var1++;
```

When the ++ operator appears after the variable, the ++ operator is performed *after* everything else is finished. This means that the original value of $var1, 43, is assigned to $var2. After this assignment is completed, 1 is added to $var1 and the new value of $var1 becomes 44.

To see how this works in while statements, examine Listing 4.4. Although it is similar to Listing 4.3, it performs a post-increment operation instead of a pre-increment operation.

Listing 4.4. A program that uses the post-increment operation.

TYPE

```
1:  #!/usr/local/bin/perl
2:  $value = 0;
3:  while ($value++ <= 5) {
4:          print("value is now $value\n");
5:  }
6:  print("all done\n");
```

OUTPUT

```
$ program4_4
value is now 1
value is now 2
value is now 3
value is now 4
value is now 5
value is now 6
all done
$
```

ANALYSIS You are probably wondering why the output of Listing 4.4 contained the following line:

```
value is now 6
```

To figure out what happened, examine the value stored in $value each time the condition in the while statement is tested. Table 4.5 lists the contents of $value when the condition is tested, the result of the test, and $value immediately after the condition is tested (after the ++ operator is applied).

Table 4.5. Condition evaluation.

$value at time of test	Result	$value after test
0	true (0 <= 5)	1
1	true (1 <= 5)	2
2	true (2 <= 5)	3
3	true (3 <= 5)	4
4	true (4 <= 5)	5
5	true (5 <= 5)	6
6	false (6 <= 5)	7 (exit while)

As you know, when the condition at the top of a while statement is true, the code inside the statement is executed, which in this case is

```
print("value is now $value\n");
```

This is why the line

```
value is now 6
```

appears—$value is 5 at the time the condition is tested, so the result is true.

To fix this problem, change the while condition to the following and run the program again:

```
while ($value < 5) {
```

This is the output you get from the changed program:

```
value is now 1
value is now 2
value is now 3
value is now 4
value is now 5
all done
```

Now, when $value is 5, the statement

```
while ($value++ < 5)
```

is false, and the code inside the while is not executed.

The Autodecrement Operator

As you've seen, the ++ operator adds 1 to the value of the variable it is associated with and can appear either before or after the variable. The -- operator, or *autodecrement operator*, works in the same way, but it subtracts 1 from the value of the variable it is associated with, as follows:

```
$a--;
--$a;
$result = $a--;
$result2 = --$a;
```

When the -- operator is in front of the variable, the operation is a *pre-decrement* operation, which means that 1 is subtracted from the variable before anything else happens.

```
$var1 = 56;
$var2 = --$var1;
```

This subtracts 1 from $var1 and assigns the result, 55, back to $var1. The value 55 is then assigned to $var2.

When the -- operator follows the variable, the operation is a *post-decrement* operation, which means that 1 is subtracted from the variable after everything else happens.

```
$var1 = 56;
$var2 = $var1--;
```

This assigns 56 to $var2 and then subtracts 1 from $var1, which means that $var1 now has the value 55.

4

Do	Don't

DO be careful when you use the autoincrement and autodecrement operators. As you've seen, it's easy to get confused and tell your program to loop one too many times or one too few.

I tend not to use these operators in while statements except in very simple cases, because they can get confusing. A better solution is to use the for statement, which you'll learn about on Day 8, "More Control Structures."

continues

DON'T use ++ or -- on both sides of a single variable, as in this statement, because it isn't allowed in Perl:

```
++$var1--;
```

DON'T use autoincrement or autodecrement on a variable and then use the variable again in the same statement.

```
$var1 = 10;
$var2 = $var1 + ++$var1;
```

Is $var2 now 20, 21, or 22? It's impossible to tell. Even different versions of Perl can produce different results!

Using Autoincrement With Strings

If a string value contains only alphabetic characters, the ++ operator can be used to "add one" to a string. In other words, the operator replaces the last character of the string with the next letter of the alphabet. The following is an example:

```
$stringvar = "abc";
$stringvar++;
```

Here, $stringvar now contains abd.

Note that this works only with ++, not --:

```
$stringvar = "abc";
$stringvar--;
```

The -- operator treats abc as a number, which means that it is equivalent to 0. The resulting value of $stringvar is, therefore, −1.

Auto-incrementing strings using ++ also works on capital letters.

```
$stringvar = "aBC";
$stringvar++;
```

The value stored in $stringvar is now aBD.

If the last letter of the string is z or Z, ++ converts this letter to a or A, and then "adds one" to the second-to-last character of the string:

```
$stringvar = "abz";
$stringvar++;             # $stringvar now contains "aca"
$stringvar = "AGZZZ";
$stringvar++;             # $stringvar now contains "AHAAA"
```

This also works if the string contains one or more trailing digits.

```
$stringvar = "ab4";
$stringvar++;              # $stringvar now contains "ab5"
```

As in numeric operations, incrementing a string that ends in 9 carries over to the next character of the string. This works regardless of whether the next character is a digit or alphabetic character.

```
$stringvar = "bc999";
$stringvar++;              # $stringvar now contains "bd000"
```

WARNING

Incrementing string values using ++ works only if the variable has not already been converted to a number.

```
$stringvar = "abc";

$stringvar += 5;

$stringvar++;
```

Here, the value of $stringvar is 6 because abc is converted to 0 by the += operator in the second statement.

Also note that this does not work if the string value contains any character other than a letter or digit, or if a digit is located in the middle of the string.

```
$stringvar = "ab*c";
$stringvar++;
$stringvar = "ab5c";
$stringvar++;
```

In both of these cases, the value stored in $stringvar is converted to its numeric equivalent, 0, before the ++ operation is performed. This means that $stringvar is assigned the value 1.

The String Concatenation and Repetition Operators

So far, the Perl operators you've seen operate only on integers. (To be exact, they can also operate on strings, but they convert the strings to integers first.) Perl also supports the following special operators that manipulate strings:

☐ The . operator, which *concatenates* (joins together) two strings

☐ The x operator, which repeats a string

☐ The .= operator, which combines concatenation and assignment

The String-Concatenation Operator

The string-concatenation operator, ., joins two strings together. For example, the following statement assigns the string potatohead to $newstring:

```
$newstring = "potato" . "head";
```

You can use the . operator with variables as in this example:

```
$string1 = "potato";
$string2 = "head";
$newstring = $string1 . $string2;
```

This also assigns potatohead to $newstring. Note that the values of $string1 and $string2 are not changed by the . operator: $string1 still has the value potato, and $string2 still has the value head.

The String-Repetition Operator

The string-repetition operator, x (literally the letter *x*), makes multiple copies of a string and joins the copies together, as shown in this example:

```
$newstring = "t" x 5;
```

This statement takes five copies of the string t and joins them together, producing the string ttttt. This string is then assigned to the variable $newstring.

You can use variables as operands for the x operator, if you like, as follows:

```
$copystring = "t";
$repeats = 5;
$newstring = $copystring x $repeats;
```

The only restriction is that the variable on the right of the x must contain an integer or a value that can be converted to an integer.

Do   **Don't**

DO make sure you leave a space between the x operator and the values or variables on either side:

```
$newstring = $oldstring x 5;     # this is correct
$newstring = $oldstringx 5;      # incorrect
$newstring = $oldstring x5;      # also incorrect
```

Normally, you don't need to put spaces between an operator and its operands.

```
$x = $x + 1;                     # this is OK
$x=$x+1;                         # this is also OK
```

You need spaces around the x because the letter x can appear in variable names. (For example, $oldstringx is a perfectly valid variable name.)

Concatenation and Assignment

The .= operator combines the operations of string concatenation and assignment. For example, the following statements:

```
$a = "be";
$a .= "witched";             # $a is now "bewitched"
```

are equivalent to these statements:

```
$a = "be";
$a = $a . "witched";
```

You can use the .= operator to write a very simple program that reads multiple lines of input and joins them into a single string. This program is shown in Listing 4.5.

Listing 4.5. A program that reads input lines and concatenates them.

TYPE

```
1:  #!/usr/local/bin/perl
2:  $resultstring = "";
3:  print("Enter your input — type an empty line to quit\n");
4:  $input = <STDIN>;
5:  chop ($input);
6:  while ($input ne "") {
7:          $resultstring .= $input;
8:          $input = <STDIN>;
9:          chop ($input);
10: }
11: print ("Here is the final string:\n");
12: print ("$resultstring\n");
```

OUTPUT

```
$ program4_5
Enter your input — type an empty line to quit
this
is
a
test

Here is the final string:
thisisatest
$
```

ANALYSIS   As you can see from the output of Listing 4.5, the four input lines are joined and have become a single string.

Note that there is a much simpler way to do this in Perl: using the built-in function `join()`. You'll learn about `join()` on Day 5, "Lists and Array Variables."

Other Perl Operators

Perl also supports two other operators that do not fit into any of the preceding categories:

- ☐ The comma operator
- ☐ The conditional operator

The Comma Operator

The *comma operator* (,) is an operator borrowed from the C programming language. It guarantees that a particular part of an expression (the part before the ,) is evaluated first.

Here is an example of a simple statement that uses the , operator:

```
$var1 += 1, $var2 = $var1;
```

Because the , operator indicates that the left operand is to be performed first, 1 is added to $var1 before $var1 is assigned to $var2. In effect, the , operator breaks a statement into two separate statements, as follows:

```
$var1 += 1;
$var2 = $var1;
```

In fact, the only real reason to use the , operator is when two operations are so closely tied together that it is easier to understand the program if they appear as part of the same expression.

The comma operator is often used in conjunction with the = operator, as follows:

```
$val = 26;
$result = (++$val, $val + 5);
```

In this statement, the

```
++$val
```

operation is performed first, because it appears before the , operator. This adds 1 to $val, which means that $val now has the value 27. Then this new value of $val has 5 added to it, and the result, 32, is assigned to $result.

Note that the following expression is enclosed in parentheses:

```
++$val, $val + 5
```

This indicates that this set of operations is to be performed first. Had the parentheses not been present, the statement would have been

```
$result = ++$val, $val + 5;
```

In this case, everything before the comma would be performed first:

```
$result = ++$val
```

This means that $result would be assigned 27, not 32.

You'll learn more about parentheses and the order of operations later today, in the section titled "The Order of Operations."

The Conditional Operator

The conditional operator also is borrowed from the C programming language. Unlike the other operators you've seen, the conditional operator requires three operands, as follows:

- ☐ A condition to test
- ☐ A value that is to be used when the test condition is true (evaluates to a nonzero value)
- ☐ A value that is to be used when the test condition is false (evaluates to zero)

The first two operands are separated by the character ?, and the second and third operands are separated by the character :.

Here is a simple example of an expression that uses the conditional operator:

```
$result = $var == 0 ? 14 : 7;
```

Here, the test condition is the expression

```
$var == 0
```

If this expression is true, the value 14 is assigned to $result. If it is false, the value 7 is assigned to $result.

As you can see, the conditional operator behaves just like the if and else statements. The expression

```
$result = $var == 0 ? 14 : 7;
```

is identical to the following:

```
if ($var == 0) {
        $result = 14;
} else {
        $result = 7;
}
```

The difference between the conditional operator and the if-else construct is that the conditional operator can appear in the middle of expressions. For example, the conditional operator can be used as another way to prevent division by 0, as follows:

```
$result = 43 + ($divisor == 0 ? 0 : $dividend / $divisor);
```

Here, $result is assigned the value 43 plus the result of $dividend divided by $divisor, unless $divisor is 0. If $divisor is 0, the result of the division is assumed to be 0, and $result is assigned 43.

Listing 4.6 is a simple program that reads from the standard input file and compares the input line with a predetermined password.

TYPE **Listing 4.6. A very simple password checker.**

```
1:  #!/usr/local/bin/perl
2:  print ("Enter the secret password:\n");
3:  $password = "bluejays";
4:  $inputline = <STDIN>;
5:  chop ($inputline);
6:  $outputline = $inputline eq $password ?
7:          "Yes, that is the correct password!\n" :
8:          "No, that is not the correct password.\n";
9:  print ($outputline);
```

OUTPUT
```
$ program4_6
Enter the secret password:
orioles
No, that is not the correct password.
$
```

ANALYSIS   When you run program4_6 and type in a random password, you get the results shown in the Input-Output example.

The advantage of using the conditional operator here is that the assignment to $outputline occurs in only one place, and the statement is much more concise. If you use if and else, you need two assignments to $outputline and five lines, as follows:

```
if ($inputline eq $password) {
        $outputline = "Yes, that is the correct password!\n";
} else {
        $outputline = "No, that is not the correct password.\n");
}
```

Of course, the if and else statements are easier to use when things get more complex. Consider the following example:

```
if ($var1 == 47) {
        print("var1 is already 47\n");
        $is_fortyseven = 1;
} else {
        $var1 = 47;
        print("var1 set to 47\n");
        $is_fortyseven = 0;
}
```

You can write this using the conditional operator if you use the comma operator, as follows:

```
$var1 == 47 ? (print("var1 is already 47\n"), $is_fortyseven = 1) :
        ($var1 = 47, print("var1 set to 47\n"), $is_fortyseven = 0);
```

As you can see, this is difficult to understand. The basic rules are as follows:

☐ Use the conditional operator for very simple conditional statements.

☐ Use if and else for everything else.

Conditional Operators on the Left Side of Assignments

In Perl 5, you can use the conditional operator on the left side of an assignment. This enables you to assign a value to either of two variables, depending on the result of a conditional expression.

```
$condvar == 43 ? $var1 : $var2 = 14;
```

This statement checks whether $condvar has the value 43. If it does, $var1 is assigned 14. If it doesn't, $var2 is assigned 14.

Normally, you won't want to use conditional operators in this way because your code will become difficult to follow. Although the following code is a little less efficient, it performs the same task in a way that is easier to understand:

```
$condvar == 43 ? $var1 = 14 : $var2 = 14;
```

The Order of Operations

Perl, like all programming languages, has a clearly defined set of rules that determine which operations are to be performed first in a particular expression. The following three concepts help explain these rules:

4

☐ The concept of *precedence*
☐ The concept of *associativity*
☐ The ability to override precedence and associativity using *parentheses*

Precedence

In grade school, you learned that certain arithmetic operations always are performed before other ones. For example, multiplication and division always are performed before addition and subtraction.

```
4 + 5 * 3
```

Here, the multiplication is performed first, even though the addition is encountered first when the statement is read from left to right. Because multiplication always is performed first, it has higher *precedence* than addition.

Table 4.6 defines the precedence of the operators in Perl. The items at the top of the table have the highest precedence, and the items at the bottom have the lowest.

Table 4.6. Operator precedence.

Operator	Operation Performed
++, --	Autoincrement and autodecrement
-, ~, !	Operators with one operand
**	Exponentiation
=~, !~	Pattern-matching operators
*, /, %, x	Multiplication, division, remainder, repetition
+, -, .	Addition, subtraction, concatenation
<<, >>	Shifting operators
-e, -r, etc.	File-status operators
<, <=, >, >=, lt, le, gt, ge	Inequality-comparison operators
==, !=, <=>, eq, ne, cmp	Equality-comparison operators
&	Bitwise AND
|, ^	Bitwise OR and XOR
&&	Logical AND
||	Logical OR
..	List-range operator
? and :	Conditional operator (together)

Operator	Operation Performed
=, +=, -=, *=, and so on	Assignment operators
,	Comma operator
not	Low-precedence logical NOT
and	Low-precedence logical AND
or, xor	Low-precedence logical OR and XOR

Using this table, you can determine the order of operations in complicated expressions. For example:

```
$result = 11 * 2 + 6 ** 2 << 2;
```

To determine the order of operations in this expression, start at the top of Table 4.6 and work down. The first operator you see is **, which means that it is performed first, leaving

```
$result = 11 * 2 + 36 << 2;
```

The next operation you find in the table is the * operator. Performing the multiplication leaves the following:

```
$result = 22 + 36 << 2;
```

The + operator is next:

```
$result = 58 << 2;
```

Next up is the << operator:

```
$result = 232;
```

The = operator is last on the list and assigns 232 to $result.

You might have noticed that Table 4.6 contains some operators that you've not yet seen and which you'll learn about later:

- [ ] The list-range operator, defined on Day 5
- [ ] The file-status operators, defined on Day 6, "Reading from and Writing to Files"
- [ ] The pattern-matching operators, =~ and !~, defined on Day 7, "Pattern Matching"

4

Associativity

The rules of operator precedence enable you to determine which operation to perform first when an expression contains different operators. But what should you do when an expression contains two or more operators that have the same precedence?

In some cases, it doesn't matter what order you perform the operations in. For example:

```
$result = 4 + 5 + 3;
```

Here, $result gets 12 no matter which addition is performed first. However, for some operations the order of evaluation matters.

```
$result = 2 ** 3 ** 2;
```

If you perform the leftmost exponentiation first, $result is assigned 8 ** 2, or 64. If you perform the rightmost exponentiation first, $result is assigned 2 ** 9, or 512.

Because the order of operations is sometimes important, Perl defines the order in which operations of the same precedence are to be performed. Operations that are performed right-to-left (with the rightmost operation performed first) are said to be *right associative*. Operations that are performed left-to-right (with the leftmost operation performed first) are *left associative*.

Table 4.7 lists the associativity for each of the Perl operators. The operators are sorted according to precedence (in the same order as Table 4.6).

Table 4.7. Operator associativity.

Operator	Associativity
++, --	Not applicable
-, ~, !	Right-to-left
**	Right-to-left
=~, !~	Left-to-right
*, /, %, x	Left-to-right
+, -, .	Left-to-right
<<, >>	Left-to-right
-e, -r, and so on	Not applicable
<, <=, >, >=, lt, le, gt, ge	Left-to-right
==, !=, <=>, eq, ne, cmp	Left-to-right
&	Left-to-right

Operator	Associativity
¦, ^	Left-to-right
&&	Left-to-right
¦ ¦	Left-to-right
..	Left-to-right
? and :	Right-to-left
=, +=, -=, *=, and so on	Right-to-left
,	Left-to-right
not	Left-to-right
and	Left-to-right
or, xor	Left-to-right

From Table 4.7, you see that the exponentiation operator is right associative. This means that in the following:

```
$result = 2 ** 3 ** 2;
```

`$result` is assigned 512, because the rightmost `**` operation is performed first.

Forcing Precedence Using Parentheses

Perl enables you to force the order of evaluation of operations in expressions. To do this, use parentheses as follows:

```
$result = 4 * (5 + 3);
```

In this statement, 5 is added to 3 and then multiplied by 4, yielding 32.

You can use as many sets of parentheses as you like:

```
$result = 4 ** (5 % (8 - 6));
```

Here, the result is 4:

- [ ] 8 - 6 is performed, leaving 4 ** (5 % 2)
- [ ] 5 % 2 is performed, leaving 4 ** 1
- [ ] 4 ** 1 is 4

Do   **Don't**

DO use parentheses whenever you aren't sure whether a particular operation is to be evaluated first. For example, I don't know many programmers who remember that addition operators are evaluated before shifts:

```
$result = 4 << 2 + 3;
```

And virtually no one remembers that && has higher precedence than ¦¦:

```
if ($value == 0 ¦¦ $value == 2 && $value2 == "hello") {
        print("my condition is true\n");
}
```

You can make life a lot easier for people who read your code if you use parentheses when the order of evaluation is not obvious. For example:

```
$result = 4 << (2 + 3);
if ($value == 0 ¦¦ ($value == 2 && $value2 == "hello")) {
        print("my condition is true\n");
}
```

DO use multiple lines, extra spaces, and indentation to make complicated expressions easier to read. For example:

```
if ($value == 0 ¦¦
        ($value == 2 && $value2 == "hello")) {
```

Here, it's obvious that there are two main conditions to be tested and that one of them contains a pair of subconditions.

DON'T leave out closing parentheses by mistake.

```
$result = 4 + (2 << ($value / 2);    # error
```

This statement will be flagged as erroneous because you are missing a closing parenthesis.

A handy way of checking whether you have enough parentheses in complicated expressions is to use this simple trick:

- ☐ Start at the left end of your expression.
- ☐ Starting from 0, add 1 for every left parenthesis you see.
- ☐ Subtract 1 for every closing parenthesis you see.

If your final result is 0, you've got enough opening and closing parentheses. (This doesn't guarantee that you've put the parentheses in the right places, but at least you now know that you have enough of them.)

Summary

Today you learned about the operators that Perl supports. Each operator requires one or more operands, which are the values on which the operator operates. A collection of operands and operators is known as an expression.

The operators you learned how to use are as follows:

- [ ] The arithmetic operators +, -, *, /, %, **, and unary negation
- [ ] The integer-comparison operators ==, !=, <, >, <=, >=, and <=>
- [ ] The string-comparison operators eq, ne, lt, gt, le, ge, and cmp
- [ ] The logical operators ¦¦, &&, and !
- [ ] The bit-manipulation operators ¦, &, ^, ~, <<, and >>
- [ ] The assignment operators =, +=, -=, *=, /=, %=, **=, !=, &=, ^=, and .=
- [ ] The autoincrement operator ++
- [ ] The autodecrement operator --
- [ ] The string-concatenation operator .
- [ ] The string-repetition operator x
- [ ] The comma operator ,
- [ ] The conditional operator (? and : together)

You also learned about operator precedence and associativity, two concepts that tell you which operators in an expression usually are performed first. Operator precedence and associativity can be controlled by putting parentheses around the operations you want to perform first.

Q&A

Q Is there a limit on how large my expressions can be?

A Effectively, no. There is a limit, but it's so large that no one would possibly want to create an expression that long, because it would be impossible to read or understand.

It's easier to understand expressions if they are shorter.

Q Is it better to use += or ++ when adding 1 to a variable?

A It's best to use ++ when using a variable as a counter in a while statement (or in other loops, which you learn about on Day 8, "More Control Structures"). For other addition operations, you should use +=.

Q Why are some operators left associative and others right associative?

A Most operators are left associative, because we normally read from left to right.

Assignment is right associative because it's easier to read. For instance:

```
$var1 = $var2 = 5;
```

If assignment happened to be left associative, $var1 would be assigned the old value of $var2, not 5. This would not be obvious to a casual reader of the program.

Exponentiation is right associative because that's how exponentiation is performed in mathematics.

Other operators that are right associative are easier to read from right to left.

Workshop

The Workshop provides quiz questions to help you solidify your understanding of the material covered and exercises to give you experience in using what you've learned. Try and understand the quiz and exercise answers before you go on to tomorrow's lesson.

Quiz

1. Define the following terms:

    a. operator

    b. operand

    c. expression

    d. precedence

    e. associativity

2. What operations are performed by the following operators?

    a. &&

    b. &

    c. ^

    d. ne

    e. .

3. What operators perform the following operations?

    a. string-equality comparison

    b. remainder

    c. string duplication

    d. bitwise OR

    e. numeric greater-than-or-equal-to

4. What is the binary representation of the following numbers?

    a. 171

    b. 1105

    c. 0

5. What is the standard (base-10) representation of the following numbers?

    a. 01100100

    b. 00001111

    c. 01000001

6. What is the value of the following expressions?

    a. `17 * 2 ** 3 / 9 % 2 << 2`

    b. `0 && (171567 * 98275 / 1174.5 ** 4)`

    c. `1171 ^ 904`

    d. `"abc" . "de" x 2`

Exercises

1. Write a program that uses the << operator to print out the first 16 powers of 2.

2. Rewrite the following statement using the conditional operator:

```
if ($var1 == 5 || $var2 == 7) {
        $result = $var1 * $var2 + 16.5;
} else {
        print("condition is false\n");
        $result = 0;
}
```

3. Rewrite the following expression using the if and else statements:

```
$result = $var1 <= 26 ? ++$var2 : 0;
```

4. Write a program that reads two integers from standard input (one at a time), divides the first one by the second one, and prints out the quotient (the result) and the remainder.

5. Why might the following statement not assign the value 5.1 to $result?

```
$result = 5.1 + 100005.2 - 100005.2;
```

6. Determine the order of operations in the following statement, and add parentheses to the statement to indicate this order:

```
$result = $var1 * 2 << 5 + 3 || $var2 ** 3, $var3;
```

7. What value is assigned to $result by the following code?

```
$var1 = 43;
$var2 = 16;
$result = ++$var2 == 17 ? $var1++ * 2 - 5 : ++$var1 * 3 - 11;
```

8. **BUG BUSTER:** Find and fix the bugs in the following program:

```
#!/usr/local/bin/perl

$num = <STDIN>;
chop ($num);
$x = "";
$x += "hello";
if ($x != "goodbye" ¦ $x == "farewell") {
        $result = $num eq 0 ? 43;
} else {
        $result = ++$num++;
}
print("the result is $result\n");
```

Week 1

Day 5

Lists and Array Variables

The Perl programs you have seen so far deal with *scalar values*, which are single units of data, and *scalar variables*, which can store one piece of information.

Perl also enables you to define an ordered collection of values, known as a *list*; this collection of values can be stored in variables known as *array variables*.

Today's lesson describes lists and array variables, and it shows you what you can do with them. Today, you learn about the following:

☐ What lists are

☐ The relationship between scalar variables and lists

☐ Storing lists in array variables

☐ Accessing an element of an array variable or list

☐ How to use list ranges

☐ Assigning to array variables

☐ Assigning to scalar variables from array variables

☐ Retrieving the length of a list
☐ Using array slices
☐ Using an array to store input
☐ Sorting a list or array variable
☐ Reversing a list or array variable
☐ Creating a string from a list
☐ Creating a list from a string

Introducing Lists

A *list* is a sequence of scalar values enclosed in parentheses. The following is a simple example of a list:

```
(1, 5.3, "hello", 2)
```

This list contains four elements, each of which is a scalar value: the numbers 1 and 5.3, the string hello, and the number 2.

Lists can be as long as needed, and they can contain any scalar value. A list can have no elements at all, as follows:

```
()
```

This list also is called an *empty list*.

NOTE

> A list with one element and a scalar value are different entities. For example, the list
>
> ```
> (43.2)
> ```
>
> and the scalar value
>
> ```
> 43.2
> ```
>
> are not the same thing. This is not a severe limitation because one can be converted to or assigned to the other. See the section titled "Assigning to Scalar Variables from Array Variables" later today.

Scalar Variables and Lists

A scalar variable name can always be included as part of a list. In this case, the current value of the scalar variable becomes the list element value. For example:

```
(17, $var, "a string")
```

If $var has been assigned the value 26, the second element of the list becomes 26. (It remains 26 even if a different value is assigned to $var.)

Similarly, you can use the value of an expression as an element of a list. For example:

```
(17, 26 << 2)
```

This list contains two elements: 17 and 104 (which is 26 left-shifted two places). Expressions in lists, like other expressions, can contain scalar variables.

```
(17, $var1 + $var2)
```

Here, the expression $var1 + $var2 is evaluated and its value becomes the second element of the list.

Lists and String Substitution

Because character strings are scalar values, they can be used in lists, as follows:

```
("my string", 24.3, "another string")
```

You can substitute for scalar variable names in character strings in lists, as follows:

```
($value, "The answer is $value")
```

This list contains two elements: the value of the scalar variable $value, and a string containing the name of $value. If the current value of $value is 26, the two elements of the list are 26 and The answer is 26.

Storing Lists in Array Variables

Perl enables you to store lists in special variables designed for that purpose. These variables are called *array variables* (or *arrays* for short).

The following is an example of a list being assigned to an array variable:

```
@array = (1, 2, 3);
```

Here, the list (1, 2, 3) is assigned to the array variable @array.

Note that the name of the array variable starts with the character @. This enables Perl to distinguish array variables from other kinds of variables—for example, scalar variables, which start with the character $. As with scalar variables, the second character of the variable name must be a letter, while subsequent characters of the name can be letters, numbers, or underscores. Array variable names can be as long as you want.

The following are legal array-variable names:

```
@my_array
@list2
@a_very_long_array_name_with_lots_of_underscores
```

The following are not legal array-variable names:

```
@1array        # can't start with a number
@_array        # can't start with an underscore
@a.new.array   # . is not a legal variable-name character
```

When an array variable is first created (that is, seen for the first time), it is assumed to contain the empty list () unless it is assigned to.

NOTE

> Because Perl uses @ and $ to distinguish array variables from scalar variables, the same name can be used in an array variable and in a scalar variable. For example:
>
> ```
> $var = 1;
> @var = (11, 27.1, "a string");
> ```
>
> Here, the name var is used in both the scalar variable $var and the array variable @var. These are two completely separate variables.
>
> Normally, you won't want to use the same name in both an array and a scalar variable, because this is confusing.

Accessing an Element of an Array Variable

After you have assigned a list to an array variable, you can refer to any element of the array variable as if it is a scalar variable.

For example, to assign the first element of the array variable @array to the scalar variable $scalar, use the following statement:

```
$scalar = $array[0];
```

The character sequence [0] is an example of a *subscript*. A subscript indicates a particular element of an array. In this case, 0 refers to the first element of the array. Similarly, the subscript 1 refers to the second element of the array, as follows:

```
$scalar = $array[1];
```

Here, the second element of the array @array is assigned to $scalar. The general rule is this:

> An array subscript *n*, where *n* is any non-negative integer, always refers to array element *n*+1.

This notation is employed to ensure compatibility with the C programming language, which also starts its array subscripting with 0.

You can assign a scalar value to an individual array element in the same way:

```
@array = (1, 2, 3, 4);
$array[3] = 5;
```

After the second assignment, the value of @array becomes

```
(1, 2, 3, 5)
```

This is because the fourth element of the array has been replaced.

NOTE

If you try to access an array element that does not exist, the Perl interpreter uses the null string (which is equivalent to zero).

```
@array = (1, 2, 3, 4);
$scalar = $array[4];
```

Here, $array[4] refers to the fifth element of @array, which does not exist. In this case, $scalar is assigned the null string.

5

NOTE

The same thing happens when the subscript is a negative number, as follows:

```
$scalar = $array[-1];
```

Once again, the null string is assigned to $scalar.

Note also that arrays automatically grow when a previously unreferenced element is assigned to for the first time:

```
@array = (1, 2, 3, 4);
$array[6] = 17;
```

Because the seventh element of @array is assigned 17, the value of @array is now

```
(1, 2, 3, 4, "", "", 17)
```

The missing fifth and sixth elements now contain the null string.

You can use the value of a scalar variable as a subscript, as follows:

```
$index = 1;
$scalar = $array[$index];
```

Here, the value of $index, 1, becomes the subscript. This means that the second element of @array is assigned to $scalar.

WARNING

When you use a scalar variable as a subscript, make sure that the value stored in the scalar variable corresponds to an array element that exists. For example:

```
@array = (1, 2, 3, 4);
$index = 4;
$scalar = $array[$index];
```

Here, the third statement tries to access the fifth element of @array, which does not exist. In this case, $scalar is assigned the null string, and the Perl interpreter doesn't tell you that anything went wrong.

More Details on Array Element Names

Note that the first character of an array-element variable name is the $ character, not the @ character. For example, to refer to the first element of the array @potato, use

```
$potato[0]
```

and not

```
@potato[0]
```

The basic rule is as follows:

> Things that reference one value—such as scalar variables and array elements—must start with a $.

NOTE

Even though references to elements of array variables start with a $, the Perl interpreter still has no trouble distinguishing scalar variables from array-variable elements. For example, if you have defined a scalar variable $potato and an array variable @potato, the Perl interpreter uses the subscript to distinguish between the scalar variable and the array-variable element.

```
$result = $potato;        # the scalar variable $potato
$result = $potato[0];     # the first element of @potato
```

Using Lists and Arrays in Perl Programs

Now that you have seen how lists and array variables work, it's time to take a look at a simple program that uses them. Listing 5.1 is a simple program that prints the elements of a list.

TYPE **Listing 5.1. A program that prints the elements of a list.**

```
1:  #!/usr/local/bin/perl
2:
3:  @array = (1, "chicken", 1.23, "\"Having fun?\"", 9.33e+23);
4:  $count = 1;
5:  while ($count <= 5) {
6:          print ("element $count is $array[$count-1]\n");
7:          $count++;
8:  }
```

OUTPUT
```
$ program5_1
element 1 is 1
element 2 is chicken
element 3 is 1.23
element 4 is "Having fun?"
element 5 is 9.3300000000000005+e23
$
```

ANALYSIS Line 3 assigns a list containing five elements to the array variable @array.

Line 5 tests whether $count is less than or equal to 5. This conditional expression ensures that the while statement loops five times.

Line 6 prints the current value of $count and the corresponding element of @array. Note that the expression used in the subscript is $count-1, not $count, because subscripting starts from 0. For example, when count is 3, the subscript is 2, which means that the third element of @array is printed.

5

When you examine line 6, you see that Perl lets you substitute for array elements in character strings. When the Perl interpreter sees $array[$count-1] in the character string, it replaces this array element name with its corresponding value.

Listing 5.2 is another example of a program that uses arrays. This one is a little more interesting; it uses the built-in functions rand and int to generate random integers between 1 and 10.

TYPE

Listing 5.2. A program that generates random integers between 1 and 10.

```
1:  #!/usr/local/bin/perl
2:
3:  # collect the random numbers
4:  $count = 1;
5:  while ($count <= 100) {
6:          $randnum = int( rand(10) ) + 1;
7:          $randtotal[$randnum] += 1;
8:          $count++;
9:  }
10:
11: # print the total of each number
12: $count = 1;
13: print ("Total for each number:\n");
14: while ($count <= 10) {
15:         print ("\tnumber $count: $randtotal[$count]\n");
16:         $count++;
17: }
```

OUTPUT

```
$ program5_2
Total for each number:
        number 1: 11
        number 2: 8
        number 3: 13
        number 4: 6
        number 5: 10
        number 6: 9
        number 7: 12
        number 8: 11
        number 9: 11
        number 10: 9
$
```

ANALYSIS This program is divided into two parts: the first part collects the random numbers, and the second part prints them.

Line 5 ensures that the loop *iterates* (is performed) 100 times. You can just as easily have the program generate any other quantity of random numbers just by changing the value in this conditional expression.

Line 6 generates a random number between 1 and 10 and assigns it to the scalar variable $randnum. To see how it does this, first note that the code fragment

```
int ( rand (10) )
```

actually is two function calls, one inside another. When the Perl interpreter sees this, it first calls the inner one, which is rand. The value returned by rand becomes the argument to the library function int.

Here's how line 6 generates a random number:

1. First, it calls the Perl library function rand. This function generates a floating-point random number between 0 and 1 and then multiplies it by the argument it is passed. In this program, rand is passed 10, which means that the random number is multiplied by 10 and is now a floating-point number that is greater than 0 and less than 10.

2. The value returned by rand is then passed to the library function int, which takes a floating-point number and gets rid of the non-integer part. This operation is known as *truncation*. The integer produced by this truncation operation becomes the return value of the function. For example, the following returns 5:

   ```
   int (5.7)
   ```

   In this program, int truncates the random number returned by rand and returns the resulting integer, which is now a random number between 0 and 9.

3. The value 1 is added to the number returned by int, resulting in a random number between 1 and 10.

4. This number is assigned to the scalar variable $randnum.

Line 7 now adds 1 to the element of the array @randtotal corresponding to the number generated. For example, if the random number is 7, the array element $randtotal[7] has 1 added to it.

NOTE
> As you can see, line 7 works even though @randtotal is not initialized. When the program refers to an array element for the first time, the Perl interpreter assumes that the element has an initial value of the null string " ". This null string is converted to 0, which means that adding 1 for the first time produces the result 1, which is what you want.

The second part of the program, which prints the total of each random number, starts with lines 12 and 13. These lines get things started by resetting the counter variable $count to 1 and printing an introductory message.

5

The conditional expression in line 14 ensures that the loop iterates 10 times—once for each possible random number.

Line 15 prints the total for a particular random number.

Using Brackets and Substituting for Variables

As you have just seen, Perl lets you substitute for array-element variable names in strings, as follows:

```
print ("element $count is $array[ $count-1]\n");
```

This might lead to problems if you want to include the characters [and] in character strings. For example, suppose that you have defined the scalar variable $var and the array variable @var. The character string

```
"$var[0]"
```

substitutes the value of the first element of @var in the string. To substitute the value of $var and keep the [0] as it is, you must use one of the following:

```
"${var}[0]"
"$var\[0]"
"$var" . "[0]"
```

The character string

```
"${var}[0]"
```

uses the brace characters { and } to keep var and [separate; this tells the Perl interpreter to substitute for the variable $var, not $var[0]. After the substitution, the brace characters are not included in the string.

> **NOTE**
>
> To include a brace character after a $, use a backslash, as follows:
> ```
> "$\{var}"
> ```
> This character string contains the text ${var}.

The character string

```
"$var\[0]"
```

uses \ to indicate that the [character is to be given a different meaning than normal; in this case, this means that [is to be treated as a printable character and not as part of the variable name to be substituted.

The expression

```
"$var" . "[0]"
```

consists of two character strings joined together by the . operator. Here, the Perl interpreter replaces the first character string with the current value of $var.

Using List Ranges

Suppose that you want to define a list consisting of the numbers 1 through 10, inclusive. You can do this by typing each of the numbers in turn.

```
(1, 2, 3, 4, 5, 6, 7, 8, 9, 10)
```

However, there is a simpler way to do it: Use the *list-range operator*, which is .. (two consecutive period characters). The following is an example of a list created using the list-range operator:

```
(1..10)
```

This tells Perl to define a list that has a first value of 1, a second value of 2, and so on up to 10.

The list-range operator can be used to define part of a list.

```
(2, 5..7, 11)
```

This list consists of five elements: the numbers 2, 5, 6, 7, and 11.

List-range operators can be used with floating-point values. For example:

```
(2.1..5.3)
```

This list consists of four elements: 2.1, 3.1, 4.1, and 5.1. Each element of the list is one greater than the previous element, and the last element of the list is the largest possible number less than or equal to the number to the right of the .. operator. Here, 5.1 is less than 5.3, so it is included in the list; however, 6.1 is greater than 5.3, so it is not included.

NOTE

If the value to the left of the .. operator is greater than the value to the right, an empty list is created.

```
(4.5..1.6)
```

Because 4.5 is greater than 1.6, this list is empty.

If the two values are equal, a one-element list is created.

```
(3..3)
```

This is equivalent to the list (3).

5

List-range operators can specify ranges of strings. For example, the list ("aaa", "aab", "aac", "aad") can be expressed as ("aaa".."aad"). Similarly, the list ("BCY", "BCZ", "BDA", "BDB") is equivalent to ("BCY".."BDB"), and the statement @alphabet = ("a".."z"); creates a list consisting of the 26 lowercase letters of the alphabet and assigns this list to the array variable @alphabet.

List ranges also enable you to use strings to specify numbers that contain leading zeros.

```
@day_of_month = ("01".."31");
```

This statement creates a list consisting of the strings 01, 02, 03 and so on, up to 31, and then assigns this list to @day_of_month. Because each string contains two characters, this array is suitable for use when you are printing a date in a format such as 08-June-1960.

Expressions and List Ranges

The values that define the range of a list-range operator can be expressions, and these expressions can contain scalar variables. For example:

```
($var1..$var2+5)
```

This list consists of all values between the current value of $var1 and the current value of the expression $var2+5.

Listing 5.3 is an example of a program that uses list ranges. This program asks for a start number and an end number, and it prints all the numbers between them.

Listing 5.3. A program that uses list ranges to print a list of
TYPE   **numbers.**

```
1:  #!/usr/local/bin/perl
2:
3:  print ("Enter the start number:\n");
4:  $start = <STDIN>;
5:  chop ($start);
6:  print ("Enter the end number:\n");
7:  $end = <STDIN>;
8:  chop ($end);
9:  @list = ($start..$end);
10: $count = 0;
11: print ("Here is the list:\n");
12: while ($list[$count] != 0 || $list[$count-1] == -1 ||
13:         $list[$count+1] == 1) {
14:         print ("$list[$count]\n");
15:         $count++;
16: }
```

OUTPUT

```
$ program5_3
Enter the start number:
-2
Enter the end number:
2
Here is the list:
-2
-1
0
1
2
$
```

ANALYSIS Lines 3 through 5 retrieve the start of the range to be printed. Line 3 retrieves the number from the standard input file. Line 4 assigns the resulting number to the scalar variable $start. Line 5 chops the trailing newline character.

Lines 6 through 8 repeat the same process for the end of the range, assigning the end of the range to the scalar variable $end.

Line 9 creates a list that consists of the numbers between $start and $end, and stores the list in the array variable @list.

Line 10 initializes the counter variable $count to 0.

Line 11 is a print statement that indicates that the list is about to be printed.

Lines 12 and 13 are the start of the loop that prints the range. The conditional expression to be evaluated consists of three subexpressions that are operands for the logical OR operator ¦¦. If any of these subexpressions are true, the loop continues.

The first subexpression tests for the end of the range. To do this, it takes advantage of the fact that an unidentified list element is equal to the null string and that the null string is equivalent to 0. When the list element $list[$count] is undefined, the following subexpression is false:

```
$list[$count] != 0
```

The second and third subexpressions cover the cases in which 0 is actually a part of the list. If the list to be printed contains 0, one or both of the following conditions must be true:

- ☐ The number 1 must be the next element in the list.
- ☐ The number –1 must be the previous element in the list.

The second and third subexpressions test for these conditions. If either or both of these conditions is true, at least one of the following subexpressions also must be true:

```
$list[$count-1] == -1
$list[$count+1] == 1
```

This ensures that the loop continues. Of course, this doesn't cover the case in which the list consists of just 0; however, that's not a meaningful case. (If you want to be finicky, you can

5

add a special chunk of code that prints 0 if `$start` and `$end` are both 0, but that's not really worth bothering with.)

After this, the rest of the program is straightforward. Line 14 prints a number in the range, line 15 adds one to the counter variable `$count`, and line 16 ends the `while` statement.

TIP

One of the problems with Perl is that it is sometimes difficult to distinguish the following scalar variable or array-element values:

- ☐ The null string `""`, which is converted to 0 in numeric expressions

- ☐ An undefined variable or element, which defaults to the null string, which in turn is converted to 0 in numeric expressions

- ☐ The string `0`, which is converted to the number 0 in numeric expressions

- ☐ A non-numeric string such as `string`, which is converted to 0 in numeric expressions

There are several ways of dealing with this confusion:

1. Retrieve the length of the list stored in an array variable before processing it. This ensures that you don't go past the end of the list. See the section titled "Retrieving the Length of a List" later in today's lesson for more details on how to do this.

2. Compare the value with the string `0` rather than the number 0, as follows:

   ```
   if ($value eq "0") ...
   ```

   This handles the strings that convert to 0 in numeric expressions that are not `0` itself. (It doesn't handle strings such as `0000` or `0.0`, which you might want your program to consider equivalent to 0; to deal with these, see the discussion of the `split` function later in today's lesson.)

3. Initialize the scalar variable or array element to a value other than 0 that you know is not going to appear naturally in your program, such as –99999.

Which particular method is best depends on the program you want to write, the input it expects, and how "bulletproof" the program needs to be.

5

More on Assignment and Array Variables

So far, you've seen that you can assign lists to array variables.

```
@array = (1, 2, 3, 4, 5);
```

You've also seen that you can assign an element of an array to a scalar variable.

```
$scalar = $array[3];
```

The following sections describe the other ways you can use assignment with lists and array variables.

Copying from One Array Variable to Another

You also can assign one array variable to another.

```
@result = @original;
```

Here, the list currently stored in the array variable @original is copied to the array variable @result. Each element of the new array @result is the same as the corresponding element of the array @original. Listing 5.4 shows that this is true.

TYPE **Listing 5.4. A program that copies an array and compares the elements of the two arrays.**

```
1:  #!/usr/local/bin/perl
2:
3:  @array1 = (14, "cheeseburger", 1.23, -7, "toad");
4:  @array2 = @array1;
5:  $count = 1;
6:  while ($count <= 5) {
7:          print("element $count: $array1[$count-1] ");
8:          print("$array2[$count-1]\n");
9:          $count++;
10: }
```

OUTPUT
```
$ program5_4
element 1: 14 14
element 2: cheeseburger cheeseburger
element 3: 1.23 1.23
element 4: -7 -7
element 5: toad toad
$
```

5

ANALYSIS Line 3 assigns the list

```
(14, "cheeseburger", 1.23, -7, "toad")
```

to the array variable @array1. Line 4 then copies this array into a second array variable, @array2.

The rest of the program prints the elements of each array, as follows:

- ☐ Line 5 initializes the counter variable $count to 1.
- ☐ The conditional expression in line 6 ensures that the loop is performed five times.
- ☐ Lines 7 and 8 print the matching element of each array. (Note that the subscript is $count-1, not $count, because the subscript 0 is the first element of the array.)
- ☐ Line 9 adds one to the counter variable $count.

NOTE

You can assign to multiple arrays in one statement. For example:

```
@array1 = @array2 = (1, 2, 3);
```

This assigns a copy of the list (1, 2, 3) to both @array1 and @array2.

Using Array Variables in Lists

As you've already seen, lists can contain scalar variables. For example:

```
@list = (1, $scalar, 3);
```

Here, the value of the scalar variable $scalar becomes the second element of the list assigned to @list.

You also can specify that the value of an array variable is to appear in a list, as follows:

```
@list1 = (2, 3, 4);
@list2 = (1, @list1, 5);
```

Here, the value of the array variable @list1—the list (2, 3, 4)—is substituted for the name @list1, and the resulting list (1, 2, 3, 4, 5) is assigned to @list2.

Listing 5.5 shows an example of a list being contained in another list.

TYPE

Listing 5.5. A program that assigns a list as part of another list.

```
1:  #!/usr/local/bin/perl
2:
3:  @innerlist = " never ";
4:  @outerlist = ("I", @innerlist, "fail!\n");
5:  print @outerlist;
```

OUTPUT

```
$ program5_5
I never fail!
$
```

ANALYSIS Although this program is quite simple, it contains a couple of new tricks. The first of these is in line 3. Here, a scalar value, " never " (note the surrounding spaces), is assigned to the array variable @innerlist. This works because the Perl interpreter automatically converts the scalar value into a one-element list before assigning it to the array variable.

Line 4 assigns a list to the array variable @outerlist. This list is assembled by taking the following list:

```
("I", @innerlist, "fail!\n")
```

and substituting in the current value of the array variable @innerlist. As a result, the list assigned to @outerlist is

```
("I", " never ", "fail!\n")
```

Line 5 prints the list. To do this, it calls the library function print and passes it the array variable @outerlist. When print is given an array variable or a list to print, it prints each element in turn. This means that the following is written to the standard output file:

```
I never fail!
```

Note that print doesn't leave any spaces between the elements of the list when it prints them. The only reason the output is readable is because the character string contains spaces around never. This means that print isn't usually used to print a list of numbers in this way:

```
@list = (1, 2, 3);
print @list;
```

This prints the following, which isn't quite what you want:

5

TIP

In Listing 5.5, the argument passed to the `print` function is not enclosed in parentheses. This is perfectly acceptable. In Perl, the parentheses enclosing arguments to functions are optional. For example, when you call the library function `chop`, instead of writing

```
chop ($number);
```

you can write

```
chop $number;
```

Although this saves a few extra keystrokes, it makes things a little less readable (in this author's opinion).

Besides, eliminating the parentheses can lead to problems. Consider the following example:

```
$fred = "Fred";
print (("Hello, " . $fred . "!\n") x 2);
```

This code prints

```
Hello, Fred!
Hello, Fred!
```

In this case, the parentheses enclosing the arguments to `print` are absolutely necessary. Without them, you have

```
print ("Hello, " . $fred . "!\n") x 2;
```

When the Perl interpreter sees this statement, it assumes that `print` is being called with the following argument, which is not what you want:

```
"Hello, " . $fred . "!\n"
```

As always in programming, the basic rule to follow is this: Do whatever makes your program easier to work with, and use your best judgment.

Substituting for Array Variables in Strings

As you have seen, Perl does not leave spaces if you pass an array variable to `print`:

```
@array = (1, 2, 3);
print (@array, "\n");
```

This prints the following on your screen:

123

To get around this problem, put the array you want to print into a string:

```
print ("@array\n");
```

When the Perl interpreter sees the array variable inside the string, it substitutes the values of the list assigned to the array variables, and leaves a space between each pair of elements. For example:

```
@array = (1, 2, 3);
print ("@array\n");
```

This prints the following on your screen:

```
1 2 3
```

Assigning to Scalar Variables from Array Variables

Consider the following assignment, which you've already seen:

```
@array = ($var1, $var2);
```

Here, the values of the scalar variables $var1 and $var2 are used to form a two-element list that is assigned to the array variable @array.

Perl also enables you to take the current value of an array variable and assign its components to a group of scalar variables. For example:

```
@array = (5, 7);
($var1, $var2) = @array;
```

Here, the first element of the list currently stored in @array, 5, is assigned to $var1. The second element, 7, is assigned to $var2.

Additional elements in an array, if they exist, are ignored. For example:

```
@array = (5, 7, 11);
($var1, $var2) = @array;
```

Here, 5 is assigned to $var1, 7 is assigned to $var2, and 11 is not assigned to anything.

If there are more scalar variables than elements in an array variable, the excess scalar variables are assigned the null string, as follows:

```
@array = (5, 7);
($var1, $var2, $var3) = @array;
```

This assigns 5 to $var1 and 7 to $var2. Because there are not enough elements in @array to assign anything to $var3, $var3 is assigned the null string "".

NOTE

> You also can assign to several scalar variables using a list. For example:
>
> ```
> ($var1, $var2, $var3) = ("one", "two", "three");
> ```
>
> This assigns one to $var1, two to $var2, and three to $var3.
>
> As with array variables, extra values in the list are ignored and extra scalar variables are assigned the null string, as follows:
>
> ```
> ($var1, $var2) = (1, 2, 3);       # 3 is ignored
> ($var1, $var2, $var3) = (1, 2);  # $var3 is now ""
> ```

Retrieving the Length of a List

As you've seen, lists and array variables can be any length you want. As a consequence, Perl provides a way of determining the length of the list assigned to an array variable.

Here's how it works: If an array variable (or list) appears anywhere that a scalar value is expected, the Perl interpreter obtains a scalar value by calculating the length of the list assigned to the array variable.

Consider the following example:

```
@array = (1, 2, 3);
$scalar = @array;
```

In the assignment to $scalar, the Perl interpreter replaces @array with the length of the list currently assigned to @array, which is 3. $scalar, therefore, is assigned the value 3.

WARNING

> Note that the following two statements are not equivalent:
>
> ```
> $scalar = @array;
> ```
>
> ```
> ($scalar) = @array;
> ```
>
> In the first statement, the length of the list in @array is assigned to $scalar. In the second statement, the first element of @array is assigned to $scalar.
>
> It is always important to remember that $scalar and ($scalar) are not the same thing. $scalar is a scalar variable, and ($scalar) is a one-element list containing $scalar.

5

Being able to access the length of an array is useful if you want to write a loop that performs an operation on every element of an array. Listing 5.6 is an example of a program that does just that.

Listing 5.6. A program that prints every element of an array.

TYPE

```
1:  #!/usr/local/bin/perl
2:
3:  @array = (14, "cheeseburger", 1.23, -7, "toad");
4:  $count = 1;
5:  while ($count <= @array) {
6:          print("element $count: $array[$count-1]\n");
7:          $count++;
8:  }
```

OUTPUT

```
$ program5_6
element 1: 14
element 2: cheeseburger
element 3: 1.23
element 4: -7
element 5: toad
$
```

ANALYSIS The only new feature of this program is line 5, which compares the counter variable $count to the length of the array @array. Because the list assigned to @array contains five elements, the conditional expression

```
$count <= @array
```

ensures that the loop iterates five times.

Once again, note that the subscript in line 6 is $count-1, not $count. This caution bears repeating: It is very easy to forget to subtract 1 when you use a value as a subscript.

If you like, you can write your loop in a different way and use $count as a subscript. For example:

```
$count = 0;
while ($count < @array) {
        print ("element $count+1: $array[ $count]\n");
}
```

As you can see, this isn't any easier to follow because you now have to remember these two things:

1. The conditional expression now must use the < operator, not the <= operator. If you use <= here, the loop iterates six times, not five.

5

2. The value of $count is now not the same as the element you are referring to. For example, if you are printing the third element of the array, $count has the value 2. This means that references to $count, such as

```
element $count+1:
```

must add one to the value of $count to get the result you want.

As you can see, there is no intuitive or obvious way of writing programs that loop through arrays. Generally, it's best to pick the way that is easiest for you to remember.

WARNING

> You cannot retrieve the length of a list without first assigning the list to an array variable. For example:
>
> ```
> @array = (10, 20, 30);
> $scalar = @array;
> ```
>
> This assigns 3 to $scalar. Compare this with the following statement:
>
> ```
> $scalar = (10, 20, 30);
> ```
>
> This statement actually assigns 30 to $scalar, not 3. In this statement, the subexpression
>
> ```
> (10, 20, 30)
> ```
>
> is treated as three scalar values separated by comma operators.
>
> For more details on the comma operator, refer to "The Comma Operator" in Day 4.

Using Array Slices

As you've seen, array subscripting enables you to change or access one element of an array. For example:

```
$var = $array[2];
$array[2] = $var;
```

Perl enables you to access more than one element of an array at a time in much the same way. Following is a simple example:

```
@subarray = @array[0,1];
```

Here, the code fragment

```
@array[0,1]
```

refers to the first two elements of the list stored in the array variable. This portion of the array is known as an *array slice*. An array slice is treated just like any other list. In the statement

```
@subarray = @array[0,1];
```

the list consisting of the first two elements of @array is assigned to the array variable @subarray.

Here is another example:

```
@slice = @array[1,2,3];
```

This statement assigns the array slice consisting of the second, third, and fourth elements of @array to the array variable @slice.

WARNING

Although single elements of an array are referenced using the $ character, array slices are referenced using @:

```
$var = $array[0];
@subarray = @array[0,1];
```

The basic rules are as follows:

- ☐ References to single items, such as scalar variables or single array elements, start with a $.

- ☐ References to array variables or array slices, which refer to lists, start with a @.

Listing 5.7 shows a simple example of an array slice.

TYPE

Listing 5.7. A program that demonstrates the use of an array slice.

```
1:  #!/usr/local/bin/perl
2:
3:  @array = (1, 2, 3, 4);
4:  @subarray = @array[1,2];
5:  print ("The first element of subarray is $subarray[0]\n");
6:  print ("The second element of subarray is $subarray[1]\n");
```

5

OUTPUT

```
$ program5_7
The first element of subarray is 2
The second element of subarray is 3
$
```

ANALYSIS Line 3 of this program assigns the following list to the array variable @array:

```
(1, 2, 3, 4)
```

Line 4 assigns a slice of the array variable @array to the array variable @subarray. The array slice

```
@array[1,2]
```

specifies that the second and third elements of the array are to be treated as a list and assigned to @subarray.

NOTE

In array slices, as in references to single elements of an array, subscripts start from zero. For example, the array slice

```
@array[1,2]
```

refers to the second and third elements of an array.

The final two lines of the program print the two elements of the array variable @subarray. As you can see, these elements are identical to the second and third elements of @array.

Using List Ranges in Array-Slice Subscripts

Perl provides a convenient way to refer to large array slices. Instead of writing

```
@array[0,1,2,3,4]
```

to refer to the first five elements of array @array, you can use the list range operator, as follows:

```
@array[0..4]
```

This enables you to assign large array slices easily:

```
@subarray = @array[0..19];
```

This assigns the first 20 elements of @array to @subarray.

Using Variables in Array-Slice Subscripts

You can use the value of a scalar variable in a list range in an array slice subscript. The following is an example:

```
$endrange = 19;
@subarray = @array[0..$endrange];
```

Here, the scalar variable $endrange contains the upper limit of the array slice, which in this case is 19. This means that the array slice to assign is

```
@array[0..19]
```

which assigns the first 20 elements of @array to @subarray.

You can also use the list stored in an array variable to define an array slice. Listing 5.8 shows how this works.

Listing 5.8. A program that uses an array variable as an array-slice subscript.

```
1:  #!/usr/local/bin/perl
2:
3:  @array = ("one", "two", "three", "four", "five");
4:  @range = (1, 2, 3);
5:  @subarray = @array[@range];
6:  print ("The array slice is: @subarray\n");
```

OUTPUT
```
$ program5_8
The array slice is: two three four
$
```

ANALYSIS Line 3 of this program assigns the following list to the array variable @array:

```
("one", "two", "three", "four", "five")
```

Line 4 assigns the list (1, 2, 3) to the array variable @range, which is to serve as the list range.

Line 5 uses the value of @range as the array subscript for an array slice. Because @range contains (1, 2, 3), the slice of @array that is selected consists of the second, third, and fourth elements. These elements are then assigned to the array variable @subarray.

Line 6 prints the selected array slice. When the Perl interpreter sees the variable name @subarray in the character string to be printed, it substitutes the value of @subarray for its name. Because @subarray is inside a character string, the Perl interpreter leaves a space between each pair of elements when printing.

Compare line 6 with the following:

```
print (@subarray, "\n");
```

Here, print leaves no spaces between the elements of @subarray, which means that it prints

```
twothreefour
```

Which outcome you want depends, of course, on what you want your program to do.

Assigning to Array Slices

You can assign to array slices using the notation you have just seen. The following is an example:

```
@array[0,1] = ("string", 46);
```

Here, the first two elements of the array @array become string and 46, respectively.

You can use list-range operators and variables when you assign to array slices as well. The following is an example:

```
@array[0..3] = (1, 2, 3, 4);
@array[0..$endrange] = (1, 2, 3, 4);
```

If there are more items in the array slice than in the list, the extra items in the array slice are assigned the null string, as follows:

```
@array[0..2] = ("string1", "string2");
```

The third element of @array now holds the null string.

If there are fewer items in the array slice than in the list, the extra items in the list are ignored, as in the following:

```
@array[0..2] = (1, 2, 3, 4);
```

In this assignment, the fourth element in the list, 4, is not assigned to anything.

When an array slice is assigned to, the remainder of the array is not changed. Listing 5.9 shows how this works.

TYPE **Listing 5.9. A program that assigns to an array slice.**

```
1:  #!/usr/local/bin/perl
2:
3:  @array = ("old1", "old2", "old3", "old4");
4:  @array[1,2] = ("new2", "new3");
5:  print ("@array\n");
```

OUTPUT
```
$ program5_9
old1 new2 new3 old4
$
```

ANALYSIS In the preceding program, the only statement that did not appear in previous programs is line 4, which assigns the list ("new2", "new3") to the array slice of @array consisting of the second and third elements. This assignment changes the value of @array from

```
("old1", "old2", "old3", "old4")
```

to

```
("old1", "new2", "new3", "old4")
```

Line 5 then prints the changed array.

Overlapping Array Slices

As you've seen, Perl enables you to use array slices on either side of an assignment statement. The following is an example:

```
@newarray = @array[2,3,4];
@array[2,3,4] = @newarray;
```

This means that you can assign from one array slice to another, even if the two slices overlap, as in the following:

```
@array[1,2,3] = @array[2,3,4];
```

The Perl interpreter has no problem with this statement because it copies the list stored in @array[2,3,4] into a temporary location (invisible to you) before assigning it to @array[1,2,3].

Listing 5.10 provides an example of overlapping array slices in use.

TYPE **Listing 5.10. A program containing overlapping array slices.**

```
1:  #!/usr/local/bin/perl
2:
3:  @array = ("one", "two", "three", "four", "five");
4:  @array[1,2,3] = @array[2,3,4];
5:  print ("@array\n");
```

OUTPUT
```
$ program5_10
one three four five five
$
```

ANALYSIS Line 4 is an example of an assignment with overlapping array slices. At the time of assignment, the array slice @array[2,3,4] contains the list

```
("three", "four", "five")
```

This list consists of the last three elements of @array. Assigning this list to @array[1,2,3] means that the list stored in @array changes from

```
("one", "two", "three", "four", "five")
```

to

```
("one", "three", "four", "five", "five")
```

NOTE

Overlapping array slices of varying lengths are dealt with in the same way as other array slice assignments of non-matching lengths. For example:

```
@array = (1, 2, 3, 4, 5);
@array[0..2] = @array[3,4];
```

This assignment assigns the array slice @array[3,4], which is the list (4, 5), to the array slice @array[0..2]. After this assignment, the value of @array is the list

```
(4, 5, "", 4, 5)
```

The third element of @array is now the null string because there are only two elements in the array slice being assigned.

Using the Array-Slice Notation as a Shorthand

So far, I've been using the following array-slice notation to refer to consecutive elements of an array:

```
@array[0,1]
```

In Perl, however, there is no real difference between an array slice and a list containing consecutive elements of the same array. For example, the following statements are equivalent:

```
@subarray = @array[0,1];
@subarray = ($array[0], $array[1]);
```

Because of this, you can use the array-slice notation to refer to any elements of an array, regardless of whether they are in order. For example, the following two statements are equivalent:

```
@subarray = ($array[4], $array[1], $array[3]);
@subarray = @array[4,1,3];
```

In both cases, the array variable @subarray is assigned a list consisting of three elements: the fifth, second, and fourth elements of @array.

You can use this array-slice notation in a variety of ways. For example, you can assign one element of an array multiple times:

```
@subarray = @array[0,0,0];
```

This creates a list consisting of three copies of the first element of @array, and then assigns this list to @subarray.

The array-slice notation provides an easy way to swap elements in a list. The following is an example:

```
@array[1,2] = @array[2,1];
```

This statement swaps the second and third elements of @array. As with the overlapping array slices you saw earlier, the Perl interpreter copies @array[2,1] into a temporary location before assigning it, which ensures that the assignment takes place properly.

For an example of a program that swaps array elements, look at Listing 5.11, which sorts the elements in an array using a simple sort algorithm.

TYPE   **Listing 5.11. A program that sorts an array.**

```
 1:  #!/usr/local/bin/perl
 2:
 3:  # read the array from standard input one item at a time
 4:  print ("Enter the array to sort, one item at a time.\n");
 5:  print ("Enter an empty line to quit.\n");
 6:  $count = 1;
 7:  $inputline = <STDIN>;
 8:  chop ($inputline);
 9:  while ($inputline ne "") {
10:          @array[$count-1] = $inputline;
11:          $count++;
12:          $inputline = <STDIN>;
13:          chop ($inputline);
14:  }
15:
16:  # now sort the array
17:  $count = 1;
18:  while ($count < @array) {
19:          $x = 1;
20:          while ($x < @array) {
21:                  if ($array[$x - 1] gt $array[$x]) {
22:                          @array[$x-1,$x] = @array[$x,$x-1];
23:                  }
24:                  $x++;
25:          }
26:          $count++;
27:  }
28:
29:  # finally, print the sorted array
30:  print ("@array\n");
```

5

OUTPUT
```
$ program5_11
Enter the array to sort, one item at a time.
Enter an empty line to quit.
foo
baz
dip
bar

bar baz dip foo
$
```

ANALYSIS This program is divided into three parts:

☐ Reading the array

☐ Sorting the array

☐ Printing the array

Lines 3–14 read the array into the variable @array. The conditional expression in line 9, $inputline ne "", is true as long as the line is not empty. (Recall that an empty line consists of just the newline character, which the library function chop removes.) In this example, the list foo baz dip bar is read into the array variable @array.

Lines 17–27 perform the sort. The sort consists of two loops, one inside the other. The inner loop works like this:

☐ Line 21 compares the first item in the list with the item next to it. If the first item is greater, line 22 swaps the two items. Otherwise, the two items are left where they are. In this example, foo is greater than baz, so foo becomes the second element in the list. At this point, the list is

```
baz foo dip bar
```

☐ The program then loops back to line 21, which now compares the second pair in the list (the second and third elements). The new second element, foo, is compared to dip. foo is greater, so foo becomes the new third element, and dip becomes the second element:

```
baz dip foo bar
```

☐ Line 20 terminates the loop when the last pair is compared. (Note that the conditional expression compares the inner counting variable $x with the length of the array variable @array. When $x becomes equal to @array, every pair of elements in the list has been compared.)

At this point, the largest element in the list is at the far end of the list:

```
baz dip bar foo
```

The largest value in the list, foo, has been moved to the far right end of the list, where it belongs. The other elements have been displaced to make room.

Lines 17–19 and 26–27 contain the outer loop. This outer loop just makes sure that the inner loop is repeated $n-1$ times, where n is the number of elements in the list. When the inner loop is repeated a second time, the second-largest element moves up to the second position from the right:

```
baz bar dip foo
```

The final pass through the inner loop sorts the final two elements:

```
bar baz dip foo
```

Line 30 then prints the sorted list.

NOTE

> You'll never need to write a program that sorts values in a list because Perl has a library function, sort, that does it for you. See the section "Array Library Functions" later today for more details.

Reading an Array from the Standard Input File

In the programs you have seen so far, single lines of input are read from the standard input file and stored in scalar variables. For example:

```
$var = <STDIN>;
```

In this case, every appearance of <STDIN> means that another line of input is obtained from the standard input file.

Perl also provides a quicker approach: If you assign <STDIN> to an array variable instead of a scalar variable, the Perl interpreter reads in all of the data from the standard input file at once and assigns it. For example, the statement

```
@array = <STDIN>;
```

reads everything typed in and assigns it all to the array variable @array. The variable @array now contains a list; each element of the list is a line of input.

Listing 5.12 is an example of a simple program that reads its input data into an array.

Listing 5.12. A program that reads data into an array and writes the array.

```
1:  #!/usr/local/bin/perl
2:
3:  @array = <STDIN>;
4:  print (@array);
```

OUTPUT

```
$ program5_12
Here is my first line of data.
Here is another line.
Here is the last line.
^D
Here is my first line of data.
Here is another line.
Here is the last line.
$
```

ANALYSIS As you can see, this program is very short. Line 3 reads the input from the standard input file. In this example, the input that is entered consists of the three lines

```
Here is my first line of data.
Here is another line.
Here is the last line.
```

followed by the Ctrl+D key combination. Ctrl+D produces a special character that indicates end of file; when the Perl interpreter sees this, it knows that there is no more input.

NOTE

> A blank line is perfectly acceptable input and does not terminate the reading of input from the standard input file. Only the Ctrl+D character can do that.
>
> Also note that the Ctrl+D character is a non-printing character. When you type it, nothing appears on the screen. In the examples in this book, control characters that are part of the input, such as Ctrl+D, are represented by the ^ character followed by the letter typed. For example, Ctrl+D is represented as
>
> ^D
>
> This representation is the standard one used in the computing world.

After line 3 is executed, the array variable @array contains a list comprising three elements: the three lines of input you just entered. The last character of each input line is the newline character (because you didn't call chop to get rid of it).

Line 4 prints the lines of input you just read. Note that you do not need to separate the lines with spaces or newline characters because each line in @array is terminated by a newline character.

When you use the following statement:

```
@array = <STDIN>;
```

every line of input you enter is stored in @array all at once. If you enter a lot of input, @array can get very large.

Use this statement only when you really need to work with the entire input file at once.

Array Library Functions

Perl provides a number of library functions that work on lists and array variables. You can use them to do the following:

- ☐ Sort array elements in alphabetical order
- ☐ Reverse the elements of an array
- ☐ Remove the last character from all elements of an array
- ☐ Merge the elements of an array into a single string
- ☐ Split a string into array elements

The following sections describe these array library functions.

Sorting a List or Array Variable

The library function sort sorts the elements of an array in alphabetical order and returns the sorted list.

The syntax for the sort library function is

retlist = sort (*array*);

In this syntax, *array* is the list to sort, and *retlist* is the sorted list.

Here are some examples:

```
@array = ("this", "is", "a", "test");
@array2 = sort (@array);
```

After sort is called, the value of @array2 is the list

```
("a", "is", "test", "this")
```

Note that sort does not modify the original list. The statement

```
@array2 = sort (@array);
```

does not change the value of @array. To replace the contents of an array variable with the sorted list, put the array variable on both sides of the assignment, as follows:

```
@array = sort (@array);
```

 Here, the sorted list is put back in @array.

> The sorted list must be assigned to an array variable in order to be used. The statement
>
> ```
> sort (@array);
> ```
>
> doesn't do anything useful because the sorted list is not assigned to anything.

WARNING

Note that sort treats its items as strings, not integers; items are sorted in alphabetical, not numeric, order. For example:

```
@array = (70, 100, 8);
@array = sort (@array);
```

In this case, sort produces

```
(100, 70, 8)
```

not

```
(8, 70, 100)
```

Because sort is treating the elements of the list as strings, the strings to be sorted are 70, 100, and 8. When sorting characters that are not alphabetic, sort looks at the internal representation of the characters to be sorted. If you are not familiar with ASCII (which will be described shortly), this might sound complicated, but it's not too difficult to understand.

Here's how it works: When Perl (or any other programming language) stores a character such as r or 1, what it actually does is store a unique eight-bit number that corresponds to this character. For example, the letter r is represented by the number 114, and 1 is represented by the number 49. Every possible character has its own unique number.

The sort function uses these unique numbers to determine how to sort character strings. When sorting 70, 100, and 8, sort looks at the unique numbers corresponding to 7, 1, and 8, which are the first characters in each of the strings. As it happens, the unique number for 1 is less than that for 7, which is less than that for 8 (which makes sense when you think of it). This means that 100 is "less than" 70, and 70 is "less than" 8.

Of course, if two strings have identical first characters, sort then compares the second characters. For example, when sort sorts 72 and 7$, the first characters are identical; sort then compares the unique number representing 2 with the number representing $. As it happens, the number for $ is smaller, so 7$ is "less than" 72.

NOTE

> The set of unique numbers that correspond to the characters under-stood by the computer is known as the *ASCII character set*.
>
> Most computers today use the ASCII character set, with a couple of exceptions as follows:
>
> ☐ Some IBM computers use an IBM-developed character set called *EBCDIC*. EBCDIC works the same way as ASCII. In both cases, a character such as r or 1 is translated into a number that represents it. The only difference between EBCDIC and ASCII is that the translated numbers are different.
>
> ☐ Computers that print a variety of spoken languages, or which deal with languages such as Japanese or Chinese, use a more complicated 16-bit code to represent the wide variety of characters they understand.
>
> You don't really need to worry about what character set your machine uses, except to take note of the sorting order. A complete listing of the ASCII characters can be found in Appendix B, "ASCII Character Set."

Using Other Sort Keys

Normally, sort sorts in alphabetical order. You can tell the Perl interpreter to sort using any criterion you like. To learn more about sort keys, refer to Day 9, "Using Subroutines."

Reversing a List or Array Variable

The library function reverse reverses the order of the elements of a list or array variable, and returns the reversed list.

The syntax for the reverse library function is

```
retlist = reverse (array);
```

array is the list to reverse, and *retlist* is the reversed list.

Here is an example:

```
@array = ("backwards", "is", "array", "this");
@array2 = reverse(@array);
```

The value assigned to @array2 is the list

```
("this", "array", "is", "backwards")
```

As with sort, reverse does not change the original array.

If you like, you can sort and reverse the same list by passing the list returned by sort to reverse. Listing 5.13 shows an example of this. It reads lines of data from the standard input file and sorts them in reverse order.

Listing 5.13. A program that sorts input lines in reverse order.

TYPE

```
1:  #!/usr/local/bin/perl
2:
3:  @input = <STDIN>;
4:  @input = reverse (sort (@input));
5:  print (@input);
```

OUTPUT

```
$ program5_13
foo
bar
dip
baz
^D
foo
dip
baz
bar
$
```

ANALYSIS Line 3 reads all the input lines from the standard input file into the array variable @input. Each element of input consists of a single line of input terminated with a newline character.

Line 4 sorts and reverses the input line. First, sort is called to sort the input lines in alphabetical order. (Recall that when one library function appears inside another, the innermost one is called first.) The list returned by sort is then passed to reverse, which reverses the order of the elements of the list. The result is a list sorted in reverse order, which is then assigned to @input.

Line 5 prints the sorted lines. Because each line is terminated by a newline character, no extra spaces or newline characters need to be added to make the output readable.

TIP

> If you like, you can omit the parentheses to the call to reverse. This gives you the following statement:
>
> ```
> @input = reverse sort (@input);
> ```
>
> Here is a case where eliminating a set of parentheses actually makes the code more readable; it is obvious that the statement sorts @input in reverse order.

Using chop on Array Variables

As you've seen, the chop library function removes the last character from a character string. The following is an example:

```
$var = "bathe";
chop ($var);      # $var now contains "bath"
```

The chop function also can work on lists in array variables. If you pass an array variable to chop, it removes the last character from every element in the list stored in the array variable. For example:

```
@list = ("rabbit", "12345", "quartz");
chop (@list);
```

After chop is called, the list stored in @list is

```
("rabbi", "1234", "quart")
```

The chop function often is used on arrays read from the standard input file, as shown in the following:

```
@array = <STDIN>;
chop (@array);
```

This call to chop removes the newline character from each input line. In the following section, you will see programs in which this is helpful.

Creating a Single String from a List

The library function `join` creates a single string from a list of strings, which then can be assigned to a scalar variable.

The syntax for the `join` library function is

string = join (*array*);

array is the list to join together, and *string* is the resulting character string.

The following is an example using `join`:

```
$string = join(" ", "this", "is", "a", "string");
```

The first element of the list supplied to `join` contains the characters that are to be used to join the parts of the created string together. In this example, `$string` becomes `this is a string`.

`join` can specify other join strings besides `" "`. For example, the following statement uses a pair of colons to join the strings:

```
$string = join("::", "words", "and", "colons");
```

In this statement, `$string` becomes `words::and::colons`.

You can use any list or array variable as part or all of the argument to `join`. For example:

```
@list = ("here", "is", "a");
$string = join(" ", @list, "string");
```

This assigns `here is a string` to `$string`.

Listing 5.14 is a simple program that uses `join`. It joins together all the input lines from the standard input file.

TYPE **Listing 5.14. A program that takes its input and joins it into a single string.**

```
1:  #!/usr/local/bin/perl
2:
3:  @input = <STDIN>;
4:  chop (@input);
5:  $string = join(" ", @input);
6:  print ("$string\n");
```

OUTPUT
```
$ program5_14
This
is
my
input
```

```
^D
This is my input
$
```

 Line 3 reads all of the input lines into the array variable @input. Each element of @input is a single line of input terminated by a newline character.

Line 4 passes the array variable @input to the library function chop, which removes the last character from each element of the list stored in @input. This removes all of the trailing newline characters.

Line 5 calls join, which joins all the input lines into a single string. The first argument passed to join is " ", which tells join to put one space between each pair of lines. This turns the list

```
("This", "is", "my", "input")
```

into the string

```
This is my input
```

Line 6 prints the string produced by join. Note that the call to print has to specify a newline character because all the newline characters in the input lines have been removed by the call to chop.

Splitting a String into a List

As you've seen, the library function join creates a character string from a list. To undo the effects of join—to split a character string into separate items—call the function split.

The syntax for the library function split is

```
array = split (string);
```

string is the character string to split, and *array* is the resulting array.

The following is a simple example of the use of split:

```
$string = "words::separated::by::colons";
@array = split(/::/, $string);
```

The first argument passed to split tells it where to break the string into separate parts. In this example, the first argument is :: (two colons); because there are three pairs of colons in the string, split breaks the string into four separate parts. The result is the list

```
("words", "separated", "by", "colons")
```

▲ which is assigned to the array variable @array.

5

NOTE

> The / characters surrounding the :: in the call to split indicate that the :: is a *pattern* to be matched. Perl supports a wide variety of special pattern-matching sequences, which you will learn about on Day 7, "Pattern Matching."

The split function is used in a variety of applications. Listing 5.15 uses split to count the number of words in the standard input file.

 TYPE   **Listing 5.15. A simple word-count program.**

```
1:  #!/usr/local/bin/perl
2:
3:  $wordcount = 0;
4:  $line = <STDIN>;
5:  while ($line ne "") {
6:          chop ($line);
7:          @array = split(/ /, $line);
8:          $wordcount += @array;
9:          $line = <STDIN>;
10: }
11: print ("Total number of words: $wordcount\n");
```

OUTPUT
```
$ program5_15
Here is some input.
Here are some more words.
Here is my last line.
^D
Total number of words: 14
$
```

ANALYSIS   When you enter a Ctrl+D (End-of-File) character and read it using <STDIN>, the resulting line is the null string. Line 5 of this program tests for this null string.

Note that line 5 has no problem distinguishing the end of file from a blank input line because a blank input line contains the newline character, and chop has not yet been called. Once the Perl interpreter knows that the program is not at the end of file, line 6 can be called; it chops the newline character off the end of the input line.

Line 7 splits the input line into words. The first argument to split, / /, indicates that the line is to be broken whenever the Perl interpreter sees a space. The resulting list is stored in @array.

Because each element of the list in @array is one word in the input line, the total number of words in the line is equivalent to the number of elements in the array. Line 8 takes advantage of this to count the number of words in the input line. Here's how line 8 works:

☐ When an array variable appears in a place where the Perl interpreter normally expects a scalar value, the number of elements in the list stored in the array variable is substituted for the variable name. In this program, when the Perl interpreter sees @array, it replaces it with the number of elements in @array.

☐ Because the number of elements in the array is the same as the number of words in the input line, the statement

```
$wordcount += @array;
```

actually adds the number of words in the line to $wordcount.

NOTE

Listing 5.15 does not work properly if an input line contains more than one space between words. The following is an example:

```
This  is a line
```

Because there are two spaces between This and is, the split function breaks

```
This  is
```

into three words: This, an empty word "", and is. Because of this, the line

```
This  is a line
```

appears to contain five words when it really contains only four.

To get around this problem, what you need is a pattern that matches one or more spaces. To learn about special patterns such as this, see Day 7.

Listing 5.16 is an example of a program that uses split, join, and reverse to reverse the word order of the input read from the standard input file.

TYPE

Listing 5.16. A program that reverses the word order of the input file.

```
1:  #!/usr/local/bin/perl
2:
3:  @input = <STDIN>;
4:  chop (@input);
5:
6:  # first, reverse the order of the words in each line
```

continues

Listing 5.16. continued

```
7:  $currline = 1;
8:  while ($currline <= @input) {
9:          @words = split(/ /, $input[$currline-1]);
10:         @words = reverse(@words);
11:         $input[$currline-1] = join(" ", @words, "\n");
12:         $currline++;
13: }
14:
15: # now, reverse the order of the input lines and print them
16: @input = reverse(@input);
17: print (@input);
```

OUTPUT
```
$ program5_16
This sentence
is in
reverse order.
^D
order. reverse
in is
sentence This
$
```

ANALYSIS   Line 3 reads all of the standard input file into the array @input. Line 4 then removes the trailing newline characters from the input lines.

Lines 7–13 reverse each individual line. Line 7 compares the current line number, stored in $currline, with the number of lines of input. (Recall that the number of elements in the list is used whenever an array variable appears where a scalar value is expected.)

Line 9 splits a line of input into words. The first argument to split, / /, indicates that a split is to occur every time a space is seen. The list of words is stored in the array variable @words.

Line 10 reverses the order of the list of words stored in @words. After the list has been reversed, line 11 joins the input line back together again. Note that line 11 appends a newline character to the input line.

Now that the words in each individual line have been reversed, all that the program needs to do is reverse the order of the lines themselves. Line 16 accomplishes this.

Line 17 prints the reversed input file. Note that the period character (.) appears at the end of the first word; this is because the reversing program isn't smart enough to detect and get rid of it. (You can use split to get rid of this, too, if you want.)

Other List-Manipulation Functions

Perl provides several other list-manipulation functions also. To learn about these, refer to Day 14, "Scalar-Conversion and List-Manipulation Functions."

Summary

In today's lesson, you learned about lists and array variables. A list is an ordered collection of scalar values. A list can consist of any number of scalar values.

Lists can be stored in array variables, which are variables whose names begin with the character @.

Individual elements of array variables can be accessed using subscripts. The subscript 0 refers to the first element of the list stored in the array variable, the subscript 1 refers to the second element, and so on. If an array element is not defined, it is assumed to hold the null string " ". If a previously undefined array element is assigned to, the array grows appropriately.

The list-range operator provides a convenient way to create a list containing consecutive numbers.

You can copy lists from one array variable to another. In addition, you can include an array variable in a list, which means that the list stored in the array variable is copied into the list containing the array-variable name.

Array-variable names can appear in character strings; in this case, the elements of the list are included in place of the variable name, with a space separating each pair of elements.

You can assign values to scalar variables from array variables, and vice versa.

If an array variable appears in a place where a scalar variable is expected, the length of the list stored in the array variable is used.

You can access any part of a list stored in an array variable by using the array-slice notation. You can assign values to array slices, and they can be used anywhere a list is expected.

The entire contents of the standard input file can be stored in a single array variable.

The library functions sort and reverse sort and reverse lists, respectively. The function chop removes the last character from each element of a list. The function split breaks a single string into a collection of list elements. The function join takes a collection of list elements and joins them into a single string.

Q&A

Q How can I tell whether a reference to an array variable such as @array refers to the stored list or to the length of the list?

A It's usually pretty easy to tell. In a lot of places, using a list makes no sense:

```
$result = $number + @array;
```

For example, it makes no sense here to add a list to $number, so the length of the list stored in @array is used.

Q **Why do array elements use $ for the first character of the element name, and not @? Wouldn't it make more sense to refer to an array element as**

```
@array[2]
```

because we all know that the @ indicates an array variable?

A This relates to the first question. The Perl interpreter needs to know as soon as possible whether a variable reference is a scalar value or a list. The $ indicates right away that the upcoming item is a scalar value.

Eventually, you'll get used to this notation.

Q **Is there a difference between an undefined array variable and an array variable containing the empty list?**

A No. By default, all array variables contain the empty list. Note, however, that the empty list is not the same as a list containing the null string:

```
@array = ("");
```

This list contains one element, which happens to be a null string.

Q **How large an input file can I read in using the following statement?**

```
@array = <STDIN>;
```

A Perl imposes no limit on the size of arrays. Your computer, however, has a finite amount of memory, which limits how large your arrays can be.

Q **Why does Perl add spaces when you substitute for an array variable in a string?**

A The most common use of string substitution is in the print statement. Normally, when you print a list you don't want to have the elements of the list running together, because you want to see where one element stops and the next one starts.

To print the elements of a string without spaces between them, pass the list to print without enclosing it in a string, as follows:

```
print ("Here is my list", @list, "\n");
```

Q **Why does $ appear before 1 in the ASCII character set?**

A The short answer is: Just because. (This reasoning occurs more often in computing than you might think.)

Here's a more detailed explanation: On early machines that used the ASCII character set, performance was more efficient if there was a relationship between, for instance, the location of the uppercase alphabetic characters and the lowercase alphabetic characters. (In fact, if you add 0x20, or 20 hexadecimal, to the ASCII representation of an uppercase letter, you get the corresponding lowercase letter.)

Establishing relationships such as these meant that gaps existed between, for example, the representation of z (which is 90) and the representation of a (which is

97). These gaps are filled by printable non-alphanumeric characters; for example, the representation of [is 91.

As for why $ appears before 1, as opposed to ?, which appears after 1, the explanation is: Just because.

Workshop

The Workshop provides quiz questions to help you solidify your understanding of the material covered and exercises to give you experience in using what you've learned. Try and understand the quiz and exercise answers before you go on to tomorrow's lesson.

Quiz

1. Define the following terms:
   a. list
   b. empty list
   c. array variable
   d. subscript
   e. array slice

2. Assume the following assignments have been performed:
   ```
   @list = (1, 2, 3);
   $scalar1 = "hello";
   $scalar2 = "there";
   ```
   What is assigned to the array variable @newlist in each of the following cases?
   a. @newlist = @list;
   b. @newlist = reverse(@list[1,2]);
   c. @newlist = ($scalar1, @list[1,1]);
   d. ($dummy, @newlist) = @list;
   e. @newlist[2,1,3] = @list[1,2,1];
   f. @newlist = <STDIN>;

3. Assume that the following assignments have been performed:
   ```
   @list1 = (1, 2, 3, 4);
   @list2 = ("one", "two", "three");
   ```
   What is the value of $result in each of the following cases?
   a. ($dummy, $result) = @list1;
   b. $result = @list1;
   c. ($result) = @list2;

      d. `($result) = @list1[1..2];`

      e. `$result = $list2[$list1[$list1[0]]];`

      f. `$result = $list2[3];`

4. What is the difference between a list and an array variable?

5. How does the Perl interpreter distinguish between an array element and a scalar variable?

6. How can you ensure that the @, $, and [characters are not substituted for in strings?

7. How can you obtain the length of a list stored in an array variable?

8. What happens when you refer to an array element that has not yet been defined?

9. What happens when you assign to an array element that is larger than the current length of the array?

Exercises

1. Write a program that counts all occurrences of the word the in the standard input file.

2. Write a program that reads lines of input containing numbers, each of which is separated by exactly one space, and prints out the following:

      a. The total for each line

      b. The grand total

3. Write a program that reads all input from the standard input file and sorts all the words in reverse order, printing out one word per line with duplicates omitted.

4. **BUG BUSTER:** What is wrong with the following statement?

```
$result = @array[4];
```

5. **BUG BUSTER:** What is wrong with the following program? (See if you can figure out what's wrong without checking the listings in today's lesson.)

```
#!/usr/local/bin/perl

@input = <STDIN>;
$currline = 1;
while ($currline < @input) {
        @words = split(/ /, $input[$currline]);
        @words = sort(@words);
        $input[$currline] = join(" ", @words);
        $currline++;
}
print (@input);
```

Day 6

Reading from and Writing to Files

So far, you've learned to read input from the standard input file, which stores data that is entered from the keyboard. You've also learned how to write to the standard output file, which sends data to your screen. In today's lesson, you'll learn the following:

- ☐ How to open a file
- ☐ How to read from and write to an opened file
- ☐ How to redirect standard input and standard output and how to use the standard error file
- ☐ How to close a file
- ☐ About file-test operators, which determine the status of a file
- ☐ How to read from multiple files
- ☐ How to use command-line arguments
- ☐ How to open pipes

Opening a File

Before you can read from or write to a file, you must first open the file. This operation tells the operating system that you are currently accessing the file and that no one else can change it while you are working with it. To open a file, call the library function open.

▼ SYNTAX

The syntax for the open library function is

```
open (filevar, filename);
```

When you call open, you must supply two arguments:

☐ filevar represents the name you want to use in your Perl program to refer to the file.

▲

☐ filename represents the location of the file on your machine.

The File Variable

The first argument passed to open is the name that the Perl interpreter uses to refer to the file. This name is also known as the *file variable* (or the *file handle*).

A file-variable name can be any sequence of letters, digits, and underscores, as long as the first character is a letter.

The following are legal file-variable names:

```
filename
MY_NAME
NAME2
A_REALLY_LONG_FILE_VARIABLE_NAME
```

The following are not legal file-variable names:

```
1NAME
A.FILE.NAME
_ANOTHERNAME
if
```

if is not a valid file-variable name because it has another meaning: as you've seen, it indicates the start of an if statement. Words such as if that have special meanings in Perl are known as *reserved words* and cannot be used as names.

TIP

It's a good idea to use all uppercase letters for your file-variable names. This makes it easier to distinguish file-variable names from other variable names and from reserved words.

6

The Filename

The second item passed to open is the name of the file you want to open. For example, if you are running Perl on a UNIX file system, and your current working directory contains a file named file1 that you would like to open, you can open it as follows:

```
open(FILE1, "file1");
```

This statement tells Perl that you want to open the file file1 and associate it with the file variable FILE1.

If you want to open a file in a different directory, you can specify the complete pathname, as follows:

```
open(FILE1, "/u/jqpublic/file1");
```

This opens the file /u/jqpublic/file1 and associates it with the file variable FILE1.

NOTE If you are running Perl on a file system other than UNIX, use the filename and directory syntax that is appropriate for your system. The Perl interpreter running on that system will be able to figure out where your file is located.

The File Mode

When you open a file, you must decide how you want to access the file. There are three different *file-access modes* (or, simply, *file modes*) available in Perl:

read mode	Enables the program to read the existing contents of the file but does not enable it to write into the file
write mode	Destroys the current contents of the file and overwrites them with the output supplied by the program
append mode	Appends output supplied by the program to the existing contents of the file

By default, open assumes that a file is to be opened in read mode. To specify write mode, put a > character in front of the filename that you pass to open, as follows:

```
open (OUTFILE, ">/u/jqpublic/outfile");
```

This opens the file /u/jqpublic/outfile for writing and associates it with the file variable OUTFILE.

To specify append mode, put two > characters in front of the filename, as follows:

```
open (APPENDFILE, ">>/u/jqpublic/appendfile");
```

This opens the file /u/jqpublic/appendfile in append mode and associates it with the file variable APPENDFILE.

NOTE

Here are a few things to remember when opening files:

☐ When you open a file for writing, any existing contents are destroyed.

☐ You cannot read from and write to the same file at the same time.

☐ When you open a file in append mode, the existing contents are not destroyed, but you cannot read the file while writing to it.

Checking Whether the Open Succeeded

Before you can use a file opened by the open function, you should first check whether the open function actually is giving you access to the file. The open function enables you to do this by returning a value indicating whether the file-opening operation succeeded:

☐ If open returns a nonzero value, the file has been opened successfully.

☐ If open returns 0, an error has occurred.

As you can see, the values returned by open correspond to the values for true and false in conditional expressions. This means that you can use open in if and unless statements. The following is an example:

```
if (open(MYFILE, "/u/jqpublic/myfile")) {
        # here's what to do if the file opened
}
```

The code inside the if statement is executed only if the file has been successfully opened. This ensures that your programs read or write only to files that you can access.

NOTE

If open returns false, you can find out what went wrong by using the file-test operators, which you'll learn about later today.

Reading from a File

Once you have opened a file and determined that the file is available for use, you can read information from it.

To read from a file, enclose the file variable associated with the file in angle brackets (< and >), as follows:

```
$line = <MYFILE>;
```

This statement reads a line of input from the file specified by the file variable MYFILE and stores the line of input in the scalar variable $line.

Listing 6.1 is a simple program that reads input from a file and writes it to the standard output file.

TYPE Listing 6.1. A program that reads lines from a file and prints them.

```
1:  #!/usr/local/bin/perl
2:
3:  if (open(MYFILE, "file1")) {
4:          $line = <MYFILE>;
5:          while ($line ne "") {
6:                  print ($line);
7:                  $line = <MYFILE>;
8:          }
9:  }
```

OUTPUT
```
$ program6_1
Here is a line of input.
Here is another line of input.
Here is the last line of input.
$
```

ANALYSIS
Line 3 opens the file file1 in read mode, which means that the file is to be made available for reading. file1 is assumed to be in the current working directory. The file variable MYFILE is associated with the file file1.

If the call to open returns a nonzero value, the conditional expression

```
open(MYFILE, "file1")
```

is assumed to be true, and the code inside the if statement is executed.

Lines 4–8 print the contents of file1. The sample output shown here assumes that file1 contains the following three lines:

```
Here is a line of input.
Here is another line of input.
Here is the last line of input.
```

Line 4 reads the first line of input from the file specified by the file variable MYFILE, which is file1. This line of input is stored in the scalar variable $line.

Line 5 tests whether the end of the file specified by MYFILE has been reached. If there are no more lines left in MYFILE, $line is assigned the empty string.

Line 6 prints the text stored in $line, which is the line of input read from MYFILE.

Line 7 reads the next line of MYFILE, preparing for the loop to start again.

File Variables and the Standard Input File

Now that you have seen how Perl programs read input from files in read mode, take another look at a statement that reads a line of input from the standard input file.

```
$line = <STDIN>;
```

Here's what is actually happening: The Perl program is referencing the file variable STDIN, which represents the standard input file. The < and > on either side of STDIN tell the Perl interpreter to read a line of input from the standard input file, just as the < and > on either side of MYFILE in

```
$line = <MYFILE>;
```

tell the Perl interpreter to read a line of input from MYFILE.

STDIN is a file variable that behaves like any other file variable representing a file in read mode. The only difference is that STDIN does not need to be opened by the open function because the Perl interpreter does that for you.

Terminating a Program Using die

In Listing 6.1, you saw that the return value from open can be tested to see whether the program actually has access to the file. The code that operates on the opened file is contained in an if statement.

If you are writing a large program, you might not want to put all of the code that affects a file inside an if statement, because the distance between the beginning of the if statement and the closing brace (}) could get very large. For example:

```
if (open(MYFILE, "file1")) {
        # this could be many pages of statements!
}
```

Besides, after a while, you'll probably get tired of typing the spaces or tabs you use to indent the code inside the `if` statement. Perl provides a way around this using the library function `die`.

SYNTAX

The syntax for the `die` library function is

```
die (message);
```

When the Perl interpreter executes the `die` function, the program terminates immediately and prints the message passed to `die`.

For example, the statement

```
die ("Stop this now!\n");
```

prints the following on your screen and terminates the program:

```
Stop this now!
```

Listing 6.2 shows how you can use `die` to smoothly test whether a file has been opened correctly.

Listing 6.2. A program that uses `die` when testing for a successful file open operation.

TYPE

```
1:  #!/usr/local/bin/perl
2:
3:  unless (open(MYFILE, "file1")) {
4:          die ("cannot open input file file1\n");
5:  }
6:
7:  # if the program gets this far, the file was
8:  # opened successfully
9:  $line = <MYFILE>;
10: while ($line ne "") {
11:         print ($line);
12:         $line = <MYFILE>;
13: }
```

OUTPUT

```
$ program6_2
Here is a line of input.
Here is another line of input.
Here is the last line of input.
$
```

ANALYSIS

This program behaves the same way as the one in Listing 6.1, except that it prints out an error message when it can't open the file.

Line 3 opens the file and tests whether the file opened successfully. Because this is an `unless` statement, the code inside the braces (`{` and `}`) is executed unless the file opened successfully.

6

Line 4 is the call to die that is executed if the file does not open successfully. This statement prints the following message on the screen and exits:

```
cannot open input file file1
```

Because line 4 terminates program execution when the file is not open, the program can make it past line 5 only if the file has been opened successfully.

The loop in lines 9–13 is identical to the loop you saw in Listing 6.1. The only difference is that this loop is no longer inside an if statement.

NOTE

Here is another way to write lines 3–5:

```
open (MYFILE, "file1") || die ("Could not open file");
```

Recall that the logical OR operator only evaluates the expression on its right if the expression on its left is false. This means that die is called only if open returns false (if the open operation fails).

Printing Error Information Using die

If you like, you can have die print the name of the Perl program and the line number of the statement containing the call to die. To do this, leave off the trailing newline character in the character string, as follows:

```
die ("Missing input file");
```

If the Perl program containing this statement is called myprog, and this statement is line 14 of myprog, this call to die prints the following and exits:

```
Missing input file at myprog line 14.
```

Compare this with

```
die ("Missing input file\n");
```

which simply prints the following before exiting:

```
Missing input file
```

Specifying the program name and line number is useful in two cases:

☐ If the program contains many similar error messages, you can use die to specify the line number of the message that actually appeared.

☐ If the program is called from within another program, you can use die to indicate that this program generated the error.

Reading into Array Variables

Perl enables you to read an entire file into a single array variable. To do this, assign the file variable to the array variable, as follows:

```
@array = <MYFILE>;
```

This reads the entire file represented by MYFILE into the array variable @array. Each line of the file becomes an element of the list that is stored in @array.

Listing 6.3 is a simple program that reads an entire file into an array.

 Listing 6.3. A program that reads an entire input file into an array.

```
1:  #!/usr/local/bin/perl
2:
3:  unless (open(MYFILE, "file1")) {
4:          die ("cannot open input file file1\n");
5:  }
6:  @input = <MYFILE>;
7:  print (@input);
```

OUTPUT

```
$ program6_3
Here is a line of input.
Here is another line of input.
Here is the last line of input.
$
```

ANALYSIS Lines 3–5 open the file, test whether the file has been opened successfully, and terminate the program if the file cannot be opened.

Line 6 reads the entire contents of the file represented by MYFILE into the array variable @input. @input now contains a list consisting of the following three elements:

```
("Here is a line of input.\n",
 "Here is another line of input.\n",
 "Here is the last line of input.\n")
```

Note that a newline character is included as the last character of each line.

Line 7 uses the print function to print the entire file.

Writing to a File

After you have opened a file in write or append mode, you can write to the file you have opened by specifying the file variable with the print function. For example, if you have opened a file for writing using the statement

```
open(OUTFILE, ">outfile");
```

the following statement:

```
print OUTFILE ("Here is an output line.\n");
```

writes the following line to the file specified by OUTFILE, which is the file called outfile:

```
Here is an output line.
```

Listing 6.4 is a simple program that reads from one file and writes to another.

TYPE

Listing 6.4. A program that opens two files and copies one into another.

```
1:  #!/usr/local/bin/perl
2:
3:  unless (open(INFILE, "file1")) {
4:          die ("cannot open input file file1\n");
5:  }
6:  unless (open(OUTFILE, ">outfile")) {
7:          die ("cannot open output file outfile\n");
8:  }
9:  $line = <INFILE>;
10: while ($line ne "") {
11:         print OUTFILE ($line);
12:         $line = <INFILE>;
13: }
```

OUTPUT

This program writes nothing to the screen because all output is directed to the file called outfile.

ANALYSIS

Lines 3–5 open file1 for reading. If the file cannot be opened, line 4 is executed, which prints the following message on the screen and terminates the program:

```
cannot open input file file1
```

Lines 6–8 open outfile for writing; the > in >outfile indicates that the file is to be opened in write mode. If outfile cannot be opened, line 7 prints the message

```
cannot open output file outfile
```

on the screen and terminates the program.

The only other line in the program that you have not seen in other listings in this lesson is line 11, which writes the contents of the scalar variable $line on the file specified by OUTFILE.

Once this program has completed, the contents of file1 are copied into outfile.

```
Here is a line of input.
Here is another line of input.
Here is the last line of input.
```

WARNING

Make sure that files you open in write mode contain nothing valuable. When the open function opens a file in write mode, any existing contents are destroyed.

The Standard Output File Variable

If you want, your program can reference the standard output file by referring to the file variable associated with the output file. This file variable is named STDOUT.

By default, the print statement sends output to the standard output file, which means that it sends the output to the file associated with STDOUT. As a consequence, the following statements are equivalent:

```
print ("Here is a line of output.\n");
print STDOUT ("Here is a line of output.\n");
```

NOTE

You do not need to open STDOUT because Perl automatically opens it for you.

Merging Two Files into One

In Perl, you can open as many files as you like, provided you define a different file variable for each one. (Actually, there is an upper limit on the number of files you can open, but it's fairly large and also system-dependent.) For an example of a program that has multiple files open at one time, take a look at Listing 6.5. This program merges two files by creating an output file consisting of one line from the first file, one line from the second file, another line from the first file, and so on. For example, if an input file named merge1 contains the lines

```
a1
a2
a3
```

and another file, merge2, contains the lines

```
b1
b2
b3
```

then the resulting output file consists of

```
a1
b1
a2
b2
a3
b3
```

 Listing 6.5. A program that merges two files.

```
 1:  #!/usr/local/bin/perl
 2:
 3:  open (INFILE1, "merge1") ||
 4:          die ("Cannot open input file merge1\n");
 5:  open (INFILE2, "merge2") ||
 6:          die ("Cannot open input file merge2\n");
 7:  $line1 = <INFILE1>;
 8:  $line2 = <INFILE2>;
 9:  while ($line1 ne "" || $line2 ne "") {
10:          if ($line1 ne "") {
11:                  print ($line1);
12:                  $line1 = <INFILE1>;
13:          }
14:          if ($line2 ne "") {
15:                  print ($line2);
16:                  $line2 = <INFILE2>;
17:          }
18:  }
```

OUTPUT

```
$ program6_5
a1
b1
a2
b2
a3
b3
$
```

ANALYSIS   Lines 3 and 4 show another way to write a statement that either opens a file or calls die if the open fails. Recall that the || operator first evaluates its left operand; if the left operand evaluates to true (a nonzero value), the right operand is not evaluated because the result of the expression is true.

Because of this, the right operand, the call to die, is evaluated only when the left operand is false—which happens only when the call to open fails and the file merge1 cannot be opened.

Lines 5 and 6 repeat the preceding process for the file merge2. Again, either the file is opened successfully or the program aborts by calling die.

The program then loops repeatedly, reading a line of input from each file each time. The loop terminates only when both files have been exhausted. If one file is empty but the other is not, the program just copies the line from the non-empty file to the standard output file.

Note that the output from this program is printed on the screen. If you decide that you want to send this output to a file, you can do one of two things:

☐ You can modify the program to write its output to a different file. To do this, open the file in write mode and associate it with a file variable. Then, change the print statements to refer to this file variable.

☐ You can redirect the standard output file on the command line.

For a discussion of the second method, see the following section.

Redirecting Standard Input and Standard Output

When you run programs on UNIX, you can redirect input and output using < and >, respectively, as follows:

```
myprog <input >output
```

Here, when you run the program called myprog, the input for the program is taken from the file specified by *input* instead of from the keyboard, and the output for the program is sent to the file specified by *output* instead of to the screen.

When you run a Perl program and redirect input using <, the standard input file variable STDIN now represents the file specified with <. For example, consider the following simple program:

```
#!/usr/local/bin/perl
$line = <STDIN>;
print ($line);
```

Suppose this program is named myperlprog and is called with the command

```
myperlprog <file1
```

In this case, the statement

```
$line = <STDIN>;
```

reads a line of input from file1 because the file variable STDIN represents file1.

Similarly, specifying > on the command file redirects the standard output file from the screen to the specified file. For example, consider this command:

```
myperlprog <file1 >outfile
```

It redirects output from the standard output file to the file called outfile. Now, the following statement writes a line of data to outfile:

```
print ($line);
```

The Standard Error File

Besides the standard input file and the standard output file, Perl also defines a third built-in file variable, STDERR, which represents the standard error file. By default, text sent to this file is written to the screen. This enables the program to send messages to the screen even when the standard output file has been redirected to write to a file. As with STDIN and STDOUT, you do not need to open STDERR because it automatically is opened for you.

Listing 6.6 provides a simple example of the use of STDERR. The output shown in the input-output example assumes that the standard input file and standard output file have been redirected to files using < and >, as in

```
myprog <infile >outfile
```

Therefore, the only output you see is what is written to STDERR.

Listing 6.6. A program that writes to the standard error file.

```
1:  #!/usr/local/bin/perl
2:
3:  open(MYFILE, "file1") ||
4:          die ("Unable to open input file file1\n");
5:  print STDERR ("File file1 opened successfully.\n");
6:  $line = <MYFILE>;
7:  while ($line ne "") {
8:          chop ($line);
9:          print ("\U$line\E\n");
10:         $line = <MYFILE>;
11: }
```

OUTPUT

```
$ program6_6
File file1 opened successfully.
$
```

This program converts the contents of a file into uppercase and sends the converted contents to the standard output file.

Line 3 tries to open `file1`. If the file cannot be opened, line 4 is executed. This calls `die`, which prints the following message and terminates:

```
Unable to open input file file1
```

NOTE

The function `die` sends its messages to the standard error file, not the standard output file. This means that when a program terminates, the message printed by `die` always appears on your screen, even when you have redirected output to a file.

If the file is opened successfully, line 5 writes a message to the standard error file, which indicates that the file has been opened. As you can see, the standard error file is not reserved solely for errors. You can write anything you want to `STDERR` at any time.

Lines 6–11 read one line of `file1` at a time and write it out in uppercase (using the escape characters `\U` and `\E`, which you learned about on Day 3, "Understanding Scalar Values").

Closing a File

When you are finished reading from or writing to a file, you can tell the Perl interpreter that you are finished by calling the library function `close`.

 The syntax for the `close` library function is

```
close (filevar);
```

`close` requires one argument: the file variable representing the file you want to close. Once you have closed the file, you cannot read from it or write to it without invoking `open` again.

Note that you do not have to call `close` when you are finished with a file: Perl automatically closes the file when the program terminates or when you open another file using a previously defined file variable. For example, consider the following statements:

```
open (MYFILE, ">file1");
print MYFILE ("Here is a line of output.\n");
open (MYFILE, ">file2");
print MYFILE ("Here is another line of output.\n");
```

Here, when file2 is opened for writing, file1 automatically is closed. The file variable MYFILE is now associated with file2. This means that the second print statement sends the following to file2:

```
Here is another line of output.
```

Do	Don't

DO use the <> operator, which is an easy way to read input from several files in succession. See the section titled "Reading from a Sequence of Files," later in this lesson, for more information on the <> operator.

DON'T use the same file variable to represent multiple files unless it is absolutely necessary. It is too easy to lose track of which file variable belongs to which file, especially if your program is large or has many nested conditional statements.

Determining the Status of a File

Many of the example programs in today's lesson call open and test the returned result to see whether the file has been opened successfully. If open fails, it might be useful to find out exactly why the file could not be opened. To do this, use one of the *file-test operators*.

Listing 6.7 provides an example of the use of a file-test operator. This program is a slight modification of Listing 6.6, which is an uppercase conversion program.

TYPE **Listing 6.7. A program that checks whether an unopened file actually exists.**

```
1:  #!/usr/local/bin/perl
2:
3:  unless (open(MYFILE, "file1")) {
4:          if (-e "file1") {
5:                  die ("File file1 exists, but cannot be opened.\n");
6:          } else {
7:                  die ("File file1 does not exist.\n");
8:          }
9:  }
10: $line = <MYFILE>;
11: while ($line ne "") {
12:         chop ($line);
13:         print ("\U$line\E\n");
14:         $line = <MYFILE>;
15: }
```

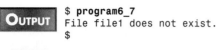

```
$ program6_7
File file1 does not exist.
$
```

ANALYSIS Line 3 attempts to open the file file1 for reading. If file1 cannot be opened, the program executes the if statement starting in line 4.

Line 4 is an example of a file-test operator. This file-test operator, -e, tests whether its operand, a file, actually exists. If the file file1 exists, the expression -e "file1" returns true, the message File file1 exists, but cannot be opened. is displayed, and the program exits. If file1 does not exist, -e "file1" is false, and the library function die prints the following message before exiting:

```
File file1 does not exist.
```

File-Test Operator Syntax

All file-test operators have the same syntax as the -e operator used in Listing 6.7.

The syntax for the file-test operators is

```
-x expr
```

Here, x is an alphabetic character and *expr* is any expression. The value of *expr* is assumed to be a string that contains the name of the file to be tested.

Because the operand for a file-test operator can be any expression, you can use scalar variables and string operators in the expression if you like. For example:

```
$var = "file1";
if (-e $var) {
        print STDERR ("File file1 exists.\n");
}
if (-e $var . "a") {
        print STDERR ("File file1a exists.\n");
}
```

In the first use of -e, the contents of $var, file1, are assumed to be the name of a file, and this file is tested for existence. In the second case, a is appended to the contents of file1, producing the string file1a. The -e operator then tests whether a file named file1a exists.

NOTE The Perl interpreter does not get confused by the expression

```
-e $var . "a"
```

because the . operator has higher precedence than the -e operator. This means that the string concatenation is performed first.

6

> The file-test operators have higher precedence than the comparison operators but lower precedence than the shift operators. To see a complete list of the Perl operators and their precedences, refer to Day 4, "More Operators."

The string can be a complete path name, if you like. The following is an example:

```
if (-e "/u/jqpublic/file1") {
        print ("The file exists.\n");
}
```

This if statement tests for the existence of the file /u/jqpublic/file1.

Available File-Test Operators

Table 6.1 provides a complete list of the file-test operators available in Perl. In this table, *name* is a placeholder for the name of the operand being tested.

Table 6.1. The file-test operators.

Operator	Description
-b	Is *name* a block device?
-c	Is *name* a character device?
-d	Is *name* a directory?
-e	Does *name* exist?
-f	Is *name* an ordinary file?
-g	Does *name* have its setgid bit set?
-k	Does *name* have its "sticky bit" set?
-l	Is *name* a symbolic link?
-o	Is *name* owned by the user?
-p	Is *name* a named pipe?
-r	Is *name* a readable file?
-s	Is *name* a non-empty file?
-t	Does *name* represent a terminal?
-u	Does *name* have its setuid bit set?
-w	Is *name* a writable file?
-x	Is *name* an executable file?

Operator	Description
-z	Is *name* an empty file?
-A	How long since *name* accessed?
-B	Is *name* a binary file?
-C	How long since *name*'s inode accessed?
-M	How long since *name* modified?
-O	Is *name* owned by the "real user" only?*
-R	Is *name* readable by the "real user" only?*
-S	Is *name* a socket?
-T	Is *name* a text file?
-W	Is *name* writable by the "real user" only?*
-X	Is *name* executable by the "real user" only?*

* In this case, the "real user" is the *userid* specified at login, as opposed to the effective user ID, which is the *userid* under which you currently are working. (On some systems, a command such as /user/local/etc/suid enables you to change your effective user ID.)

The following sections describe some of the more common file-test operators and show you how they can be useful. (You'll also learn about more of these operators on Day 12, "Working with the File System.")

More on the -e Operator

When a Perl program opens a file for writing, it destroys anything that already exists in the file. This might not be what you want. Therefore, you might want to make sure that your program opens a file only if the file does not already exist.

You can use the -e file-test operator to test whether or not to open a file for writing. Listing 6.8 is an example of a program that does this.

TYPE

Listing 6.8. A program that tests whether a file exists before opening it for writing.

```
1:  #!/usr/local/bin/perl
2:
3:  unless (open(INFILE, "infile")) {
4:          die ("Input file infile cannot be opened.\n");
5:  }
```

continues

Listing 6.8. continued

```
 6:  if (-e "outfile") {
 7:          die ("Output file outfile already exists.\n");
 8:  }
 9:  unless (open(OUTFILE, ">outfile")) {
10:          die ("Output file outfile cannot be opened.\n");
11:  }
12:  $line = <INFILE>;
13:  while ($line ne "") {
14:          chop ($line);
15:          print OUTFILE ("\U$line\E\n");
16:          $line = <INFILE>;
17:  }
```

OUTPUT
```
$ program6_8
Output file outfile already exists.
$
```

ANALYSIS   This program is the uppercase conversion program again; most of it should be familiar to you.

The only difference is lines 6–8, which use the -e file-test operator to check whether the output file outfile exists. If outfile exists, the program aborts, which ensures that the existing contents of outfile are not lost.

If outfile does not exist, the following expression fails:

```
-e "outfile"
```

and the program knows that it is safe to open outfile because it does not already exist.

Using File-Test Operators in Expressions

If you don't need to know exactly why your program is failing, you can combine all of the tests in Listing 6.8 into a single statement, as follows:

```
open(INFILE, "infile") && !(-e "outfile") &&
    open(OUTFILE, ">outfile") || die("Cannot open files\n");
```

Can you see how this works? Here's what is happening: The && operator, logical AND, is true only if both of its operands are true. In this case, the two && operators indicate that the subexpression up to, but not including, the || is true only if all three of the following are true:

```
open(INFILE, "infile")
!(-e "outfile")
open(OUTFILE, ">outfile")
```

All three are true only when the following conditions are met:

- ☐ The input file infile can be opened.
- ☐ The output file outfile does not already exist.
- ☐ The output file outfile can be opened.

If any of these subexpressions is false, the entire expression up to the ¦¦ is false. This means that the subexpression after the ¦¦ (the call to die) is executed, and the program aborts.

Note that each of the three subexpressions associated with the && operators is evaluated in turn. This means that the subexpression

```
!(-e "outfile")
```

is evaluated only if

```
open(INFILE, "infile")
```

is true, and that the subexpression

```
open(OUTFILE, ">outfile")
```

is evaluated only if

```
!(-e "outfile")
```

is true. This is exactly the same logic that Listing 6.8 uses.

If any of the subexpressions is false, the Perl interpreter doesn't evaluate the rest of them because it knows that the final result of

```
open(INFILE, "infile") && !(-e "outfile") &&
    open(OUTFILE, ">outfile")
```

is going to be false. Instead, it goes on to evaluate the subexpression to the right of the ¦¦, which is the call to die.

This program logic is somewhat complicated, and you shouldn't use it unless you feel really comfortable with it. The if statements in Listing 6.8 do the same thing and are easier to understand; however, it's useful to know how complicated statements such as the following one work because many Perl programmers like to write code that works in this way:

```
open(INFILE, "infile") && !(-e "outfile") &&
    open(OUTFILE, ">outfile") ¦¦ die("Cannot open files\n");
```

In the next few days, you'll see several more examples of code that exploits how expressions work in Perl. "Perl hackers"—experienced Perl programmers—often enjoy compressing multiple statements into shorter ones, and they delight in complexity. Be warned.

6

Testing for Read Permission—the -r Operator

Before you can open a file for reading, you must have permission to read the file. The -r file-test operator tests whether you have permission to read a file.

Listing 6.9 checks whether the person running the program has permission to access a particular file.

Listing 6.9. A program that tests for read permission on a file.

```
1:  #!/usr/local/bin/perl
2:
3:  unless (open(MYFILE, "file1")) {
4:          if (!(-e "file1")) {
5:                  die ("File file1 does not exist.\n");
6:          } elsif (!(-r "file1")) {
7:                  die ("You are not allowed to read file1.\n");
8:          } else {
9:                  die ("File1 cannot be opened\n");
10:         }
11: }
```

OUTPUT

```
$ program6_9
You are not allowed to read file1.
$
```

ANALYSIS Line 3 of this program tries to open file1. If the call to open fails, the program tries to find out why.

First, line 4 tests whether the file actually exists. If the file exists, the Perl interpreter executes line 6, which tests whether the file has the proper read permission. If it does not, die is called; it then prints the following message and exits:

```
You are not allowed to read file1.
```

NOTE

> You do not need to use the -e file-test operator before using the -r file-test operator. If the file does not exist, -r returns false because you can't read a file that isn't there.
>
> The only reason to use both -e and -r is to enable your program to determine exactly what is wrong.

Checking for Other Permissions

You can use file-test operators to test for other permissions as well. To check whether you have write permission on a file, use the -w file-test operator.

```
if (-w "file1") {
        print STDERR ("I can write to file1.\n");
} else {
        print STDERR ("I can't write to file1.\n");
}
```

The -x file-test operator checks whether you have execute permission on the file (in other words, whether the system thinks this is an executable program, and whether you have permission to run it if it is), as illustrated here:

```
if (-x "file1") {
        print STDERR ("I can run file1.\n");
} else {
        print STDERR ("I can't run file1.\n");
}
```

NOTE

If you are the system administrator (for example, you are running as user ID root) and have permission to access any file, the -r and -w file-test operators always return true if the file exists. Also, the -x test operator always returns true if the file is an executable program.

Checking for Empty Files

The -z file-test operator tests whether a file is empty. This provides a more refined test for whether or not to open a file for writing: if the file exists but is empty, no information is lost if you overwrite the existing file.

Listing 6.10 shows how to use -z.

Listing 6.10. A program that tests whether the file is empty before opening it for writing.

```
1:  #!/usr/local/bin/perl
2:
3:  if (-e "outfile") {
4:          if (!(-w "outfile")) {
5:                  die ("Missing write permission for outfile.\n");
```

continues

Listing 6.10. continued

```
6:              }
7:              if (!(-z "outfile")) {
8:                      die ("File outfile is non-empty.\n");
9:              }
10: }
11: # at this point, the file is either empty or doesn't exist,
12: # and we have permission to write to it if it exists
```

```
$ program6_10
File outfile is non-empty.
$
```

 Line 3 checks whether the file outfile exists using -e. If it exists, it can only be opened if the program has permission to write to the file; line 4 checks for this using -w.

Line 7 uses -z to test whether the file is empty. If it is not, line 7 calls die to terminate program execution.

The opposite of -z is the -s file-test operator, which returns a nonzero value if the file is not empty.

```
$size = -s "outfile";
if ($size == 0) {
        print ("The file is empty.\n");
} else {
        print ("The file is $size bytes long.\n");
}
```

The -s file-test operator actually returns the size of the file in bytes. It can still be used in conditional expressions, though, because any nonzero value (indicating that the file is not empty) is treated as true.

Listing 6.11 uses -s to return the size of a file that has a name which is supplied via the standard input file.

TYPE Listing 6.11. A program that prints the size of a file in bytes.

```
1:  #!/usr/local/bin/perl
2:
3:  print ("Enter the name of the file:\n");
4:  $filename = <STDIN>;
5:  chop ($filename);
6:  if (!(-e $filename)) {
7:          print ("File $filename does not exist.\n");
8:  } else {
```

```
9:          $size = -s $filename;
10:         print ("File $filename contains $size bytes.\n");
11: }
```

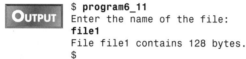

```
$ program6_11
Enter the name of the file:
file1
File file1 contains 128 bytes.
$
```

ANALYSIS Lines 3–5 obtain the name of the file and remove the trailing newline character.

Line 6 tests whether the file exists. If the file doesn't exist, the program indicates this.

Line 9 stores the size of the file in the scalar variable $size. The size is measured in bytes (one byte is equivalent to one character in a character string).

Line 10 prints out the number of bytes in the file.

Using File-Test Operators with File Variables

You can use file-test operators on file variables as well as character strings. In the following example the file-test operator -z tests the file represented by the file variable MYFILE:

```
if (-z MYFILE) {
        print ("This file is empty!\n");
}
```

As before, this file-test operator returns true if the file is empty and false if it is not.

WARNING

> Remember that file variables can be used only after you open the file. If you need to test a particular condition before opening the file (such as whether the file is nonzero), test it using the name of the file.

6

Reading from a Sequence of Files

Many UNIX utility programs are invoked using the following command syntax:

```
programname file1 file2 file3 ...
```

A program that uses this command syntax operates on all of the files specified on the command line in order, starting with *file1*. When *file1* has been processed, the program then proceeds on to *file2*, and so on until all of the files have been exhausted.

In Perl, it's easy to write programs that process an arbitrary number of files because there is a special operator, the <> operator, that does all of the file-handling work for you.

To understand how the <> operator works, recall what happens when you put < and > around a file variable:

```
$list = <MYFILE>;
```

This statement reads a line of input from the file represented by the file variable MYFILE and stores it in the scalar variable $list. Similarly, the statement

```
$list = <>;
```

reads a line of input and stores it in the scalar variable $list; however, the file from which it reads is contained on the command line. Suppose, for example, a program containing a statement using the <> operator, such as the statement

```
$list = <>;
```

is called myprog and is called using the command

```
$ myprog file1 file2 file3
```

In this case, the first occurrence of the <> operator reads the first line of input from file1. Successive occurrences of <> read more lines from file1. When file1 is exhausted, <> reads the first line from file2, and so on. When the last file, file3, is exhausted, <> returns an empty string, which indicates that all the input has been read.

NOTE

If a program containing a <> operator is called with no command-line arguments, the <> operator reads input from the standard input file. In this case, the <> operator is equivalent to <STDIN>.

If a file named in a command-line argument does not exist, the Perl interpreter writes the following message to the standard error file:

```
Can't open name: No such file or directory
```

Here, name is a placeholder for the name of the file that the Perl interpreter cannot find. In this case, the Perl interpreter ignores name and continues on with the next file in the command line.

To see how the <> operator works, look at Listing 6.12, which displays the contents of the files specified on the command line. (If you are familiar with UNIX, you will recognize this as the behavior of the UNIX utility cat.) The output from Listing 6.12 assumes that files file1 and file2 are specified on the command line and that each file contains one line.

6

Listing 6.12. A program that displays the contents of one or more files.

```
1:  #!/usr/local/bin/perl
2:
3:  while ($inputline = <>) {
4:          print ($inputline);
5:  }
```

OUTPUT

```
$ program6_12 file1 file2
This is a line from file1.
This is a line from file2.
$
```

ANALYSIS   Once again, you can see how powerful and useful Perl is. This entire program consists of only five lines, including the header comment and a blank line.

Line 3 both reads a line from a file and tests to see whether the line is the empty string. Because the assignment operator = returns the value assigned, the expression

```
$inputline = <>
```

has the value " " (the null string) if and only if <> returns the null string, which happens only when there are no more lines to read from any of the input files. This is exactly the point at which the program wants to stop looping. (Recall that a "blank line" in a file is not the same as the null string because the blank line contains the newline character.) Because the null string is equivalent to false in a conditional expression, there is no need to use a conditional operator such as ne.

When line 3 is executed for the first time, the first line in the first input file, *file1*, is read and stored in the scalar variable $inputline. Because *file1* contains only one line, the second pass through the loop, and the second execution of line 3, reads the first line of the second input file, *file2*.

After this, there are no more lines in either *file1* or *file2*, so line 3 assigns the null string to $inputline, which terminates the loop.

6

WARNING

When it reaches the end of the last file on the command line, the <> operator returns the empty string. However, if you use the <> operator after it has returned the empty string, the Perl interpreter assumes that you want to start reading input from the standard input file. (Recall that <> reads from the standard input file if there are no files on the command line.)

This means that you have to be a little more careful when you use <> than when you are reading using <MYFILE> (where MYFILE is a file variable). If MYFILE has been exhausted, repeated attempts to read using <MYFILE> continue to return the null string because there isn't anything left to read.

Reading into an Array Variable

As you have seen, if you read from a file using <STDIN> or <MYFILE> in an assignment to an array variable, the Perl interpreter reads the entire contents of the file into the array, as follows:

```
@array = <MYFILE>;
```

This works also with <>. For example, the statement

```
@array = <>;
```

reads all the contents all of the files on the command line into the array variable @array.

As always, be careful when you use this because you might end up with a very large array.

Using Command-Line Arguments as Values

As you've seen, the <> operator assumes that its command-line arguments are files. For example, if you start up the program shown in Listing 6.12 with the command

```
$ program6_12 myfile1 myfile2
```

the Perl interpreter assumes that the command-line arguments myfile1 and myfile2 are files and displays their contents.

Perl enables you to use the command-line arguments any way you want by defining a special array variable called @ARGV. When a Perl program starts up, this variable contains a list consisting of the command-line arguments. For example, the command

```
$ program6_12 myfile1 myfile2
```

sets @ARGV to the list

```
("myfile1", "myfile2")
```

NOTE

The shell you are running (`sh`, `csh`, or whatever you are using) is responsible for turning a command line such as

```
program6_12 myfile1 myfile2
```

into arguments. Normally, any spaces or tab characters are assumed to be separators that indicate where one command-line argument stops and the next begins. For example, the following are identical:

```
program6_12 myfile1 myfile2
program6_12    myfile1    myfile2
```

In each case, the command-line arguments are `myfile1` and `myfile2`.

See your shell documentation for details on how to put blank spaces or tab characters into your command-line arguments.

As with all other array variables, you can access individual elements of `@ARGV`. For example, the statement

```
$var = $ARGV[0];
```

assigns the first element of `@ARGV` to the scalar variable `$var`.

You even can assign to some or all of `@ARGV` if you like. For example:

```
$ARGV[0] = 43;
```

If you assign to any or all of `@ARGV`, you overwrite what was already there, which means that any command-line arguments overwritten are lost.

To determine the number of command-line arguments, assign the array variable to a scalar variable, as follows:

```
$numargs = @ARGV;
```

As with all array variables, using an array variable in a place where the Perl interpreter expects a scalar variable means that the length of the array is used. In this case, `$numargs` is assigned the number of command-line arguments.

6

WARNING

C programmers should take note that the first element of `@ARGV`, unlike `argv[0]` in C, does not contain the name of the program. In Perl, the first element of `@ARGV` is the first command-line argument.

To get the name of the program, use the system variable `$0`, which is discussed on Day 17, "System Variables."

To see how you can use @ARGV in a program, examine Listing 6.13. This program assumes that its first argument is a word to look for. The remaining arguments are assumed to be files in which to look for the word. The program prints out the searched-for word, the number of occurrences in each file, and the total number of occurrences.

This example assumes that the files file1 and file2 are defined and that each file contains the single line

```
This file contains a single line of input.
```

This example is then run with the command

```
$ programname single file1 file2
```

where *programname* is a placeholder for the name of the program. (If you are running the program yourself, you can name the program anything you like.)

TYPE **Listing 6.13. A word-search and counting program.**

```
 1:  #!/usr/local/bin/perl
 2:
 3:  print ("Word to search for: $ARGV[0]\n");
 4:  $filecount = 1;
 5:  $totalwordcount = 0;
 6:  while ($filecount <= @ARGV-1) {
 7:          unless (open (INFILE, $ARGV[$filecount])) {
 8:                  die ("Can't open input file $ARGV[$filecount]\n");
 9:          }
10:          $wordcount = 0;
11:          while ($line = <INFILE>) {
12:                  chop ($line);
13:                  @words = split(/ /, $line);
14:                  $w = 1;
15:                  while ($w <= @words) {
16:                          if ($words[$w-1] eq $ARGV[0]) {
17:                                  $wordcount += 1;
18:                          }
19:                          $w++;
20:                  }
21:          }
22:          print ("occurrences in file $ARGV[$filecount]: ");
23:          print ("$wordcount\n");
24:          $filecount++;
25:          $totalwordcount += $wordcount;
26: }
27: print ("total number of occurrences: $totalwordcount\n");
```

OUTPUT

```
$ program6_13 single file1 file2
Word to search for: single
occurrences in file file1: 1
occurrences in file file2: 1
total number of occurrences: 2
$
```

ANALYSIS Line 3 prints the word to search for. The program assumes that this word is the first argument in the command line and, therefore, is the first element of the array @ARGV.

Lines 7–9 open a file named on the command line. The first time line 7 is executed, the variable $filecount has the value 1, and the file whose name is in $ARGV[1] is opened. The next time through, $filecount is 2 and the file named in $ARGV[2] is opened, and so on. If a file cannot be opened, the program terminates.

Line 11 reads a line from a file. As before, the conditional expression

```
$line = <INFILE>
```

reads a line from the file represented by the file INFILE and assigns it to $line. If the file is empty, $line is assigned the null string, the conditional expression is false, and the loop in lines 11–21 is terminated.

Line 13 splits the line into words, and lines 15–20 compare each word with the search word. If the word matches, the word count for this file is incremented. This word count is reset when a new file is opened.

ARGV **and the** <> **Operator**

In Perl, the <> operator actually contains a hidden reference to the array @ARGV. Here's how it works:

1. When the Perl interpreter sees the <> for the first time, it opens the file whose name is stored in $ARGV[0].

2. After opening the file, the Perl interpreter executes the following library function:

   ```
   shift(@ARGV);
   ```

   This library function gets rid of the first element of @ARGV and moves every other element over one. This means that element *x* of @ARGV becomes element *x-1*.

3. The <> operator then reads all of the lines of the file opened in step 1.

4. When the <> operator exhausts an input file, the Perl interpreter goes back to step 1 and repeats the cycle again.

6

If you like, you can modify your program to retrieve a value from the command line and then fix @ARGV so that the <> operator can work properly. If you modify Listing 6.13 to do this, the result is Listing 6.14.

Listing 6.14. A word-search and counting program that uses <>.

```
1:  #!/usr/local/bin/perl
2:
3:  $searchword = $ARGV[0];
4:  print ("Word to search for: $searchword\n");
5:  shift (@ARGV);
6:  $totalwordcount = $wordcount = 0;
7:  $filename = $ARGV[0];
8:  while ($line = <>) {
9:          chop ($line);
10:         @words = split(/ /, $line);
11:         $w = 1;
12:         while ($w <= @words) {
13:                 if ($words[$w-1] eq $searchword) {
14:                         $wordcount += 1;
15:                 }
16:                 $w++;
17:         }
18:         if (eof) {
19:                 print ("occurrences in file $filename: ");
20:                 print ("$wordcount\n");
21:                 $totalwordcount += $wordcount;
22:                 $wordcount = 0;
23:                 $filename = $ARGV[0];
24:         }
25: }
26: print ("total number of occurrences: $totalwordcount\n");
```

OUTPUT
```
$ program6_14 single file1 file2
Word to search for: single
occurrences in file file1: 1
occurrences in file file2: 1
total number of occurrences: 2
$
```

ANALYSIS Line 3 assigns the first command-line argument, the search word, to the scalar variable $searchword. This is necessary because the call to shift in line 5 destroys the initial value of $ARGV[0].

Line 5 adjusts the array @ARGV so that the <> operator can use it. To do this, it calls the library function shift. This function "shifts" the elements of the list stored in @ARGV. The element in $ARGV[1] is moved to $ARGV[0], the element in $ARGV[2] is moved to $ARGV[1], and so on. After shift is called, @ARGV contains the files to be searched, which is exactly what the <> operator is looking for.

Line 7 assigns the current value of $ARGV[0] to the scalar variable $filename. Because the <> operator in line 8 calls shift, the value of $ARGV[0] is lost unless the program does this.

Line 8 uses the <> operator to open the file named in $ARGV[0] and to read a line from the file. The array variable @ARGV is shifted at this point.

Lines 9–16 behave as in Listing 6.13. The only difference is that the search word is now in $searchword, not in $ARGV[0].

Line 18 introduces the library function eof. This function indicates whether the program has reached the end of the file being read by <>. If eof returns true, the next use of <> opens a new file and shifts @ARGV again.

Lines 19–23 prepare for the opening of a new file. The number of occurrences of the search word is printed, the current word count is added to the total word count, and the word count is reset to 0. Because the new filename to be opened is in $ARGV[0], line 23 preserves this filename by assigning it to $filename.

NOTE

You can use the <> operator to open and read any file you like by setting the value of @ARGV yourself. For example:

```
@ARGV = ("myfile1", "myfile2");
while ($line = <>) {
        ...
}
```

Here, when the statement containing the <> is executed for the first time, the file myfile1 is opened and its first line is read. Subsequent executions of <> each read another line of input from myfile1. When myfile1 is exhausted, myfile2 is opened and read one line at a time.

Opening Pipes

On machines running the UNIX operating system, two commands can be linked using a *pipe*. In this case, the standard output from the first command is linked, or piped, to the standard input to the second command.

Perl enables you to establish a pipe that links a Perl output file to the standard input file of another command. To do this, associate the file with the command by calling open, as follows:

```
open (MYPIPE, "¦ cat >hello");
```

6

The ¦ character tells the Perl interpreter to establish a pipe. When MYPIPE is opened, output sent to MYPIPE becomes input to the command

```
cat >hello
```

Because the cat command displays the contents of the standard input file when called with no arguments, and >hello redirects the standard output file to the file hello, the open statement given here is identical to the statement

```
open (MYPIPE, ">hello");
```

You can use a pipe to send mail from within a Perl program. For example:

```
open (MESSAGE, "¦ mail dave");
print MESSAGE ("Hi, Dave!  Your Perl program sent this!\n");
close (MESSAGE);
```

The call to open establishes a pipe to the command mail dave. The file variable MESSAGE is now associated with this pipe. The call to print adds the line

```
Hi, Dave!  Your Perl program sent this!
```

to the message to be sent to user ID dave.

The call to close closes the pipe referenced by MESSAGE, which tells the system that the message is complete and can be sent. As you can see, the call to close is useful here because you can control exactly when the message is to be sent. (If you do not call close, MESSAGE is closed—and the message is sent—when the program terminates.)

Summary

Perl accesses files by means of file variables. File variables are associated with files by the open statement.

Files can be opened in any of three modes: read mode, write mode, and append mode. A file opened in read mode cannot be written to; a file opened in either of the other modes cannot be read. Opening a file in write mode destroys the existing contents of the file.

To read from an opened file, reference it using <name>, where name is a placeholder for the name of the file variable associated with the file. To write to a file, specify its file variable when calling print.

Perl defines three built-in file variables:

- ☐ STDIN, which represents the standard input file
- ☐ STDOUT, which represents the standard output file
- ☐ STDERR, which represents the standard error file

You can redirect STDIN and STDOUT by specifying < and >, respectively, on the command line. Messages sent to STDERR appear on the screen even if STDOUT is redirected to a file.

The close function closes the file associated with a particular file variable. close never needs to be called unless you want to control exactly when a file is to be made inaccessible.

The file-test operators provide a way of retrieving information on a particular file. The most common file-test operators are

- ☐ -e, which tests whether a file exists
- ☐ -r, -w, and -x, which test whether a file has read, write, and execute permission, respectively
- ☐ -z, which tests whether a file is empty
- ☐ -s, which returns the size of a file

You can use -w and -z to ensure that you do not overwrite a non-empty file.

The <> operator enables you to read data from files specified on the command line. This operator uses the built-in array variable @ARGV, whose elements consist of the items specified on the command line.

Perl enables you to open pipes. A pipe links the output from your Perl program to the input to another program.

Q&A

Q How many files can I have open at one time?

A Basically, as many as you like. The actual limit depends on the limitations of your operating system.

Q Why does adding a closing newline character to the text string affect how die behaves?

A Perl enables you to choose whether you want the filename and line number of the error message to appear. If you add a closing newline character to the string, the Perl interpreter assumes that you want to control how your error message is to appear.

Q Which is better: to use <>, or to use @ARGV and shift when appropriate?

A As is often the case, the answer is "It depends." If your program treats almost all of the command-line arguments as files, it is better to use <> because the mechanics of opening and closing files are taken care of for you. If you are doing a lot of unusual things with @ARGV, it is better not to manipulate it to use <>, because things can get complicated and confusing.

Q Can I open more than one pipe at a time?

A Yes. Your operating system keeps all of the various commands and processes organized and keeps track of which output goes with which input.

Q Can I redirect STDERR?

A Yes, but there is (normally) no reason why you should. STDERR's job is to report extraordinary conditions, and you usually want to see these, not have them buried in a file somewhere.

Q How many command-line arguments can I specify?

A Basically, as many as your command-line shell can handle.

Q Can I write to a file and then read from it later?

A Yes, but you can't do both at the same time. To read from a file you have written to, close the file by calling close and then open the file in read mode.

Workshop

The Workshop provides quiz questions to help you solidify your understanding of the material covered and exercises to give you experience in using what you've learned. Try and understand the quiz and exercise answers before you go on to tomorrow's lesson.

Quiz

1. Define the following terms:
    a. file variable
    b. reserved word
    c. file mode
    d. append mode
    e. pipe

2. From where does the <> operator read its data?

3. What do the following file-test operators do?
    a. -r
    b. -x
    c. -s

4. What are the contents of the array @ARGV when the following Perl program is executed?

```
$ myprog file1    file2 file3
```

5. How do you indicate that a file is to be opened:

    a. In write mode?

    b. In append mode?

    c. In read mode?

    d. As a pipe?

6. What is the relationship between @ARGV and the <> operator?

Exercises

1. Write a program that takes the values on the command line, adds them together, and prints the result.

2. Write a program that takes a list of files from the command line and examines their size. If a file is bigger than 10,000 bytes, print

```
File name is a big file!
```

where *name* is a placeholder for the name of the big file.

3. Write a program that copies a file named `file1` to `file2`, and then appends another copy of `file1` to `file2`.

4. Write a program that counts the total number of words in the files specified on the command line. When it has counted the words, it sends a message to user ID `dave` indicating the total number of words.

5. Write a program that takes a list of files and indicates, for each file, whether the user has read, write, or execute permission.

6. **BUG BUSTER:** What is wrong with the following program?

```
#!/usr/local/bin/perl

open (OUTFILE, "outfile");
print OUTFILE ("This is my message\n");
```

6

Day 7

Pattern Matching

This lesson describes the pattern-matching features of Perl. Today, you learn about the following:

- [ ] How pattern matching works
- [ ] The pattern-matching operators
- [ ] Special characters supported in pattern matching
- [ ] Pattern-matching options
- [ ] Pattern substitution
- [ ] Translation
- [ ] Extended pattern-matching features

Introduction

A *pattern* is a sequence of characters to be searched for in a character string. In Perl, patterns are normally enclosed in slash characters:

```
/def/
```

This represents the pattern def.

If the pattern is found, a match occurs. For example, if you search the string redefine for the pattern /def/, the pattern matches the third, fourth, and fifth characters.

```
redefine
```

You already have seen a simple example of pattern matching in the library function split.

```
@array = split(/ /, $line);
```

Here the pattern / / matches a single space, which splits a line into words.

The Match Operators

Perl defines special operators that test whether a particular pattern appears in a character string.

The =~ operator tests whether a pattern is matched, as shown in the following:

```
$result = $var =~ /abc/;
```

The result of the =~ operation is one of the following:

☐ A nonzero value, or true, if the pattern is found in the string

☐ 0, or false, if the pattern is not matched

In this example, the value stored in the scalar variable $var is searched for the pattern abc. If abc is found, $result is assigned a nonzero value; otherwise, $result is set to zero.

The !~ operator is similar to =~, except that it checks whether a pattern is not matched.

```
$result = $var !~ /abc/;
```

Here, $result is set to 0 if abc appears in the string assigned to $var, and to a nonzero value if abc is not found.

Because =~ and !~ produce either true or false as their result, these operators are ideally suited for use in conditional expressions. Listing 7.1 is a simple program that uses the =~ operator to test whether a particular sequence of characters exists in a character string.

TYPE **Listing 7.1. A program that illustrates the use of the matching operator.**

```
1:  #!/usr/local/bin/perl
2:
3:  print ("Ask me a question politely:\n");
4:  $question = <STDIN>;
```

```
5:  if ($question =~ /please/) {
6:          print ("Thank you for being polite!\n");
7:  } else {
8:          print ("That was not very polite!\n");
9:  }
```

OUTPUT

```
$ program7_1
Ask me a question politely:
May I have a glass of water, please?
Thank you for being polite!
$
```

ANALYSIS Line 5 is an example of the use of the match operator =~ in a conditional expression. The following expression is true if the value stored in $question contains the word please, and it is false if it does not:

```
$question =~ /please/
```

Match-Operator Precedence

Like all operators, the match operators have a defined precedence. By definition, the =~ and !~ operators have higher precedence than multiplication and division, and lower precedence than the exponentiation operator **.

For a complete list of Perl operators and their precedence, see Day 4, "More Operators."

Special Characters in Patterns

Perl supports a variety of special characters inside patterns, which enables you to match any of a number of character strings. These special characters are what make patterns useful.

The + Character

The special character + means "one or more of the preceding characters." For example, the pattern /de+f/ matches any of the following:

```
def
deef
deeef
deeeeeeef
```

NOTE   Patterns containing + always try to match as many characters as possible. For example, if the pattern

/ab+/

is searching in the string

abbc

it matches abb, not ab.

The + special character makes it possible to define a better way to split lines into words. So far, the sample programs you have seen have used

```
@words = split (/ /, $line);
```

to break an input line into words. This works well if there is exactly one space between words. However, if an input line contains more than one space between words, as in

```
Here's  multiple   spaces.
```

the call to split produces the following list:

```
("Here's", "", "multiple", "", "spaces.")
```

The pattern / / tells split to start a new word whenever it sees a space. Because there are two spaces between each word, split starts a word when it sees the first space, and then starts another word when it sees the second space. This means that there are now "empty words" in the line.

The + special character gets around this problem. Suppose the call to split is changed to this:

```
@array = split (/ +/, $line);
```

Because the pattern / +/ tries to match as many blank characters as possible, the line

```
Here's  multiple   spaces.
```

produces the following list:

```
("Here's", "multiple", "spaces")
```

Listing 7.2 shows how you can use the / +/ pattern to produce a count of the number of words in a file.

Listing 7.2. A word-count program that handles multiple spaces between words.

TYPE

```
1:  #!/usr/local/bin/perl
2:
```

```
3:  $wordcount = 0;
4:  $line = <STDIN>;
5:  while ($line ne "") {
6:         chop ($line);
7:         @words = split(/ +/, $line);
8:         $wordcount += @words;
9:         $line = <STDIN>;
10: }
11: print ("Total number of words: $wordcount\n");
```

OUTPUT

```
$ program7_2
Here    is   some input.
Here are    some    more words.
Here        is my  last  line.
^D
Total number of words: 14
$
```

ANALYSIS This is the same word-count program you saw in Listing 5.15, with only one change: The pattern / +/ is being used to break the line into words. As you can see, this handles spaces between words properly.

You might have noticed the following problems with this word-count program:

☐ Spaces at the beginning of a line are counted as a word, because split always starts a new word when it sees a space.

☐ Tab characters are counted as a word.

For an example of the first problem, take a look at the following input line:

```
This line contains leading spaces.
```

The call to split in line 7 breaks the preceding into the following list:

```
("", "This", "line", "contains", "leading", "spaces")
```

This yields a word count of 6, not the expected 5.

There can be at most one empty word produced from a line, no matter how many leading spaces there are, because the pattern / +/ matches as many spaces as possible. Note also that the program can distinguish between lines containing words and lines that are blank or contain just spaces. If a line is blank or contains only spaces, the line

```
@words = split(/ +/, $line);
```

assigns the empty list to @words. Because of this, you can fix the problem of leading spaces in lines by modifying line 8 as follows:

```
$wordcount += (@words > 0 && $words[0] eq "" ?
               @words-1 : @words);
```

7

This checks for lines containing leading spaces; if a line contains leading spaces, the first "word" (which is the empty string) is not added to the word count.

To find out how to modify the program to deal with tab characters as well as spaces, see the following section.

The [] Special Characters

The [] special characters enable you to define patterns that match one of a group of alternatives. For example, the following pattern matches def or dEf:

```
/d[eE]f/
```

You can specify as many alternatives as you like.

```
/a[0123456789]c/
```

This matches a, followed by any digit, followed by c.

You can combine [] with + to match a sequence of characters of any length.

```
/d[eE]+f/
```

This matches all of the following:

```
def
dEf
deef
dEef
dEEEeeeEef
```

Any combination of E and e, in any order, is matched by [eE]+.

You can use [] and + together to modify the word-count program you've just seen to accept either tab characters or spaces. Listing 7.3 shows how you can do this.

Listing 7.3. A word-count program that handles multiple
TYPE **spaces and tabs between words.**

```
 1: #!/usr/local/bin/perl
 2:
 3: $wordcount = 0;
 4: $line = <STDIN>;
 5: while ($line ne "") {
 6:         chop ($line);
 7:         @words = split(/[\t ]+/, $line);
 8:         $wordcount += @words;
 9:         $line = <STDIN>;
10: }
11: print ("Total number of words: $wordcount\n");
```

```
$ program7_3
Here is some input.
Here are some more words.
Here is my last line.
^D
Total number of words: 14
$
```

ANALYSIS This program is identical to Listing 7.2, except that the pattern is now /[\t]+/.

The \t special-character sequence represents the tab character, and this pattern matches any combination or quantity of spaces and tabs.

> **NOTE**
>
> Any escape sequence that is supported in double-quoted strings is supported in patterns. See Day 3, "Understanding Scalar Values," for a list of the escape sequences that are available.

The * and ? Special Characters

As you have seen, the + character matches one or more occurrences of a character. Perl also defines two other special characters that match a varying number of characters: * and ?.

The * special character matches zero or more occurrences of the preceding character. For example, the pattern

```
/de*f/
```

matches df, def, deef, and so on.

This character can also be used with the [] special character.

```
/[eE]*/
```

This matches the empty string as well as any combination of E or e in any order.

> **WARNING**
>
> Be sure not to confuse the * special character with the + special character. If you use the wrong special character, you might not get the results that you want.
>
> For example, suppose that you modify Listing 7.3 to call split as follows:

7

```
@words = split (/[\t ]*/, $list);
```

This matches zero or more occurrences of the space or tab character. When you run this with the input

```
a line
```

here's the list that is assigned to @words:

```
("a", "l", "i", "n", "e")
```

Because the pattern /[\t]*/ matches on zero occurrences of the space or tab character, it matches after every character. This means that split starts a word after every character that is not a space or tab. (It skips spaces and tabs because /[\t]*/ matches them.)

The best way to avoid problems such as this one is to use the * special character only when there is another character appearing in the pattern. Patterns such as

```
/b*[c]/
```

never match the null string, because the matched sequence has to contain at least the character c.

The ? character matches zero or one occurrence of the preceding character. For example, the pattern

```
/de?f/
```

matches either df or def. Note that it does not match deef, because the ? character does not match two occurrences of a character.

Escape Sequences for Special Characters

If you want your pattern to include a character that is normally treated as a special character, precede the character with a backslash \. For example, to check for one or more occurrences of * in a string, use the following pattern:

```
/\*+/
```

The backslash preceding the * tells the Perl interpreter to treat the * as an ordinary character, not as the special character meaning "zero or more occurrences."

To include a backslash in a pattern, specify two backslashes:

```
/\\+/
```

This pattern tests for one or more occurrences of \ in a string.

If you are running Perl 5, another way to tell Perl that a special character is to be treated as a normal character is to precede it with the \Q escape sequence. When the Perl interpreter sees \Q, every character following the \Q is treated as a normal character until \E is seen. This means that the pattern

/\Q^ab*/

matches any occurrence of the string ^ab*, and the pattern

/\Q^ab\E*/

matches ^a followed by zero or more occurrences of b.

For a complete list of special characters in patterns that require \ to be given their natural meaning, see the section titled "Special-Character Precedence," which contains a table that lists them.

Tip

In Perl, any character that is not a letter or a digit can be preceded by a backslash. If the character isn't a special character in Perl, the backslash is ignored.

If you are not sure whether a particular character is a special character, preceding it with a backslash will ensure that your pattern behaves the way you want it to.

Matching Any Letter or Number

As you have seen, the pattern

/a[0123456789]c/

matches a, followed by any digit, followed by c. Another way of writing this is as follows:

/a[0-9]c/

Here, the range [0-9] represents any digit between 0 and 9. This pattern matches a0c, a1c, a2c, and so on up to a9c.

Similarly, the range [a-z] matches any lowercase letter, and the range [A-Z] matches any uppercase letter. For example, the pattern

/[A-Z][A-Z]/

matches any two uppercase letters.

7

To match any uppercase letter, lowercase letter, or digit, use the following range:

`/[0-9a-zA-Z]/`

Listing 7.4 provides an example of the use of ranges with the [ ] special characters. This program checks whether a given input line contains a legal Perl scalar, array, or file-variable name. (Note that this program handles only simple input lines. Later examples will solve this problem in a better way.)

TYPE | **Listing 7.4. A simple variable-name validation program.**

```
1:  #!/usr/local/bin/perl
2:
3:  print ("Enter a variable name:\n");
4:  $varname = <STDIN>;
5:  chop ($varname);
6:  if ($varname =~ /\$[A-Za-z][_0-9a-zA-Z]*/) {
7:          print ("$varname is a legal scalar variable\n");
8:  } elsif ($varname =~ /@[A-Za-z][_0-9a-zA-Z]*/) {
9:          print ("$varname is a legal array variable\n");
10: } elsif ($varname =~ /[A-Za-z][_0-9a-zA-Z]*/) {
11:          print ("$varname is a legal file variable\n");
12: } else {
13:          print ("I don't understand what $varname is.\n");
14: }
```

OUTPUT
```
$ program7_4
Enter a variable name:
$result
$result is a legal scalar variable
$
```

ANALYSIS Line 6 checks whether the input line contains the name of a legal scalar variable. Recall that a legal scalar variable consists of the following:

☐ A $ character

☐ An uppercase or lowercase letter

☐ Zero or more letters, digits, or underscore characters

Each part of the pattern tested in line 6 corresponds to one of the aforementioned conditions given. The first part of the pattern, \$, ensures that the pattern matches only if it begins with a $ character.

NOTE
> The $ is preceded by a backslash, because $ is a special character in patterns. See the following section, "Anchoring Patterns," for more information on the $ special character.

The second part of the pattern,

```
[A-Za-z]
```

matches exactly one uppercase or lowercase letter. The final part of the pattern,

```
[_0-9a-zA-Z]*
```

matches zero or more underscores, digits, or letters in any order.

The patterns in line 8 and line 10 are very similar to the one in line 6. The only difference in line 8 is that the pattern there matches a string whose first character is @, not $. In line 10, this first character is omitted completely.

The pattern in line 8 corresponds to the definition of a legal array-variable name, and the pattern in line 10 corresponds to the definition of a legal file-variable name.

Anchoring Patterns

Although Listing 7.4 can determine whether a line of input contains a legal Perl variable name, it cannot determine whether there is extraneous input on the line. For example, it can't tell the difference between the following three lines of input:

```
$result
junk$result
$result#junk
```

In all three cases, the pattern

```
/\$[a-zA-Z][_0-9a-zA-Z]*/
```

finds the string $result and matches successfully; however, only the first line is a legal Perl variable name.

To fix this problem, you can use *pattern anchors*. Table 7.1 lists the pattern anchors defined in Perl.

Table 7.1. Pattern anchors in Perl.

Anchor	Description
^ or \A	Match at beginning of string only
$ or \Z	Match at end of string only
\b	Match on word boundary
\B	Match inside word

7

These pattern anchors are described in the following sections.

The ^ and $ Pattern Anchors

The pattern anchors ^ and $ ensure that the pattern is matched only at the beginning or the end of a string. For example, the pattern

`/^def/`

matches def only if these are the first three characters in the string. Similarly, the pattern

`/def$/`

matches def only if these are the last three characters in the string.

You can combine ^ and $ to force matching of the entire string, as follows:

`/^def$/`

This matches only if the string is def.

In most cases, the escape sequences \A and \Z (defined in Perl 5) are equivalent to ^ and $, respectively:

`/\Adef\Z/`

This also matches only if the string is def.

NOTE

> \A and \Z behave differently from ^ and $ when the multiple-line pattern-matching option is specified. Pattern-matching options are described later today.

Listing 7.5 shows how you can use pattern anchors to ensure that a line of input is, in fact, a legal Perl scalar-, array-, or file-variable name.

TYPE   **Listing 7.5. A better variable-name validation program.**

```
1:  #!/usr/local/bin/perl
2:
3:  print ("Enter a variable name:\n");
4:  $varname = <STDIN>;
5:  chop ($varname);
6:  if ($varname =~ /^\$[A-Za-z][_0-9a-zA-Z]*$/) {
7:          print ("$varname is a legal scalar variable\n");
8:  } elsif ($varname =~ /^@[A-Za-z][_0-9a-zA-Z]*$/) {
9:          print ("$varname is a legal array variable\n");
```

```
10: } elsif ($varname =~ /^[A-Za-z][_0-9a-zA-Z]*$/) {
11:         print ("$varname is a legal file variable\n");
12: } else {
13:         print ("I don't understand what $varname is.\n");
14: }
```

OUTPUT

```
$ program7_5
Enter a variable name:
x$result
I don't understand what x$result is.
$
```

ANALYSIS The only difference between this program and the one in Listing 7.4 is that this program uses the pattern anchors ^ and $ in the patterns in lines 6, 8, and 10. These anchors ensure that a valid pattern consists of only those characters that make up a legal Perl scalar, array, or file variable.

In the sample output given here, the input

```
x$result
```

is rejected, because the pattern in line 6 is matched only when the $ character appears at the beginning of the line.

Word-Boundary Pattern Anchors

The word-boundary pattern anchors, \b and \B, specify whether a matched pattern must be on a word boundary or inside a word boundary. (A word boundary is the beginning or end of a word.)

The \b pattern anchor specifies that the pattern must be on a word boundary. For example, the pattern

```
/\bdef/
```

matches only if def is the beginning of a word. This means that def and defghi match but abcdef does not.

You can also use \b to indicate the end of a word. For example,

```
/def\b/
```

matches def and abcdef, but not defghi. Finally, the pattern

```
/\bdef\b/
```

matches only the word def, not abcdef or defghi.

7

NOTE

A word is assumed to contain letters, digits, and underscore characters, and nothing else. This means that

```
/\bdef/
```

matches $defghi: because $ is not assumed to be part of a word, def is the beginning of the word defghi, and /\bdef/ matches it.

The \B pattern anchor is the opposite of \b. \B matches only if the pattern is contained in a word. For example, the pattern

```
/\Bdef/
```

matches abcdef, but not def. Similarly, the pattern

```
/def\B/
```

matches defghi, and

```
/\Bdef\B/
```

matches cdefg or abcdefghi, but not def, defghi, or abcdef.

The \b and \B pattern anchors enable you to search for words in an input line without having to break up the line using split. For example, Listing 7.6 uses \b to count the number of lines of an input file that contain the word the.

TYPE

Listing 7.6. A program that counts the number of input lines containing the word the.

```perl
1:  #!/usr/local/bin/perl
2:
3:  $thecount = 0;
4:  print ("Enter the input here:\n");
5:  $line = <STDIN>;
6:  while ($line ne "") {
7:          if ($line =~ /\bthe\b/) {
8:                  $thecount += 1;
9:          }
10:         $line = <STDIN>;
11: }
12:  print ("Number of lines containing 'the': $thecount\n");
```

OUTPUT

```
$ program7_6
Enter the input here:
Now is the time
```

```
for all good men
to come to the aid
of the party.
^D
Number of lines containing 'the': 3
$
```

ANALYSIS This program checks each line in turn to see if it contains the word the, and then prints the total number of lines that contain the word.

Line 7 performs the actual checking by trying to match the pattern

```
/\bthe\b/
```

If this pattern matches, the line contains the word the, because the pattern checks for word boundaries at either end.

Note that this program doesn't check whether the word the appears on a line more than once. It is not difficult to modify the program to do this; in fact, you can do it in several different ways.

The most obvious but most laborious way is to break up lines that you know contain the into words, and then check each word, as follows:

```
if ($line =~ /\bthe\b/) {
        @words = split(/[\t ]+/, $line);
        $count = 1;
        while ($count <= @words) {
                if ($words[$count-1] eq "the") {
                        $thecount += 1;
                }
                $count++;
        }
}
```

A cute way to accomplish the same thing is to use the pattern itself to break the line into words:

```
if ($line =~ /\bthe\b/) {
        @words = split(/\bthe\b/, $line);
        $thecount += @words - 1;
}
```

In fact, you don't even need the if statement.

```
@words = split(/\bthe\b/, $line);
$thecount += @words - 1;
```

Here's why this works: Every time split sees the word the, it starts a new word. Therefore, the number of occurrences of the is equal to one less than the number of elements in @words. If there are no occurrences of the, @words has the length 1, and $thecount is not changed.

WARNING

This trick works only if you know that there is at least one word on the line.

Consider the following code, which tries to use the aforementioned trick on a line that has had its newline character removed using `chop`:

```
$line = <STDIN>;
chop ($line);
@words = split(/\bthe\b/, $line);
$thecount += @words - 1;
```

This code actually subtracts 1 from `$thecount` if the line is blank or consists only of the word `the`, because in these cases `@words` is the empty list and the length of `@words` is 0.

Leaving off the call to `chop` protects against this problem, because there will always be at least one "word" in every line (consisting of the newline character).

Variable Substitution in Patterns

If you like, you can use the value of a scalar variable in a pattern. For example, the following code splits the line `$line` into words:

```
$pattern = "[\\t ]+";
@words = split(/$pattern/, $line);
```

Because you can use a scalar variable in a pattern, there is nothing to stop you from reading the pattern from the standard input file. Listing 7.7 accepts a search pattern from a file and then searches for the pattern in the input files listed on the command line. If it finds the pattern, it prints the filename and line number of the match; at the end, it prints the total number of matches.

This example assumes that two files exist, `file1` and `file2`. Each file contains the following:

```
This is a line of input.
This is another line of input.
```

If you run this program with command-line arguments `file1` and `file2` and search for the pattern `another`, you get the output shown.

TYPE **Listing 7.7. A simple pattern-search program.**

```
1:  #!/usr/local/bin/perl
2:
```

```
3:   print ("Enter the search pattern:\n");
4:   $pattern = <STDIN>;
5:   chop ($pattern);
6:   $filename = $ARGV[0];
7:   $linenum = $matchcount = 0;
8:   print ("Matches found:\n");
9:   while ($line = <>) {
10:          $linenum += 1;
11:          if ($line =~ /$pattern/) {
12:                  print ("$filename, line $linenum\n");
13:                  @words = split(/$pattern/, $line);
14:                  $matchcount += @words - 1;
15:          }
16:          if (eof) {
17:                  $linenum = 0;
18:                  $filename = $ARGV[0];
19:          }
20:  }
21:  if ($matchcount == 0) {
22:          print ("No matches found.\n");
23:  } else {
24:          print ("Total number of matches: $matchcount\n");
25:  }
```

OUTPUT

```
$ program7_7 file1 file2
Enter the search pattern:
another
Matches found:
file1, line 2
file2, line 2
Total number of matches: 2
$
```

ANALYSIS   This program uses the following scalar variables to keep track of information:

☐ $pattern contains the search pattern read in from the standard input file.

☐ $filename contains the file currently being searched.

☐ $linenum contains the line number of the line currently being searched.

☐ $matchcount contains the total number of matches found to this point.

Line 6 sets the current filename, which corresponds to the first element in the built-in array variable @ARGV. This array variable lists the arguments supplied on the command line. (To refresh your memory on how @ARGV works, refer back to Day 6, "Reading from and Writing to Files.") This current filename needs to be stored in a scalar variable, because the <> operator in line 9 shifts @ARGV and destroys this name.

Line 9 reads from each of the files on the command line in turn, one line at a time. The current input line is stored in the scalar variable $line. Once the line is read, line 10 adds 1 to the current line number.

Lines 11–15 handle the matching process. Line 11 checks whether the pattern stored in $pattern is contained in the input line stored in $line. If a match is found, line 12 prints out the current filename and line number. Line 13 then splits the line into "words," using the trick described in the earlier section, "Word-Boundary Pattern Anchors." Because the number of elements of the list stored in @words is one larger than the number of times the pattern is matched, the expression @words - 1 is equivalent to the number of matches; its value is added to $matchcount.

Line 16 checks whether the <> operator has reached the end of the current input file. If it has, line 17 resets the current line number to 0. This ensures that the next pass through the loop will set the current line number to 1 (to indicate that the program is on the first line of the next file). Line 18 sets the filename to the next file mentioned on the command line, which is currently stored in $ARGV[0].

Lines 21–25 either print the total number of matches or indicate that no matches were found.

WARNING

> Make sure that you remember to include the enclosing / characters when you use a scalar-variable name in a pattern. The Perl interpreter does not complain when it sees the following, for example, but the result might not be what you want:
>
> ```
> @words = split($pattern, $line);
> ```

Excluding Alternatives

As you have seen, when the special characters [ ] appear in a pattern, they specify a set of alternatives to choose from. For example, the pattern

```
/d[eE]f/
```

matches def or dEf.

When the ^ character appears as the first character after the [, it indicates that the pattern is to match any character *except* the ones displayed between the [and]. For example, the pattern

```
/d[^eE]f/
```

matches any pattern that satisfies the following criteria:

- ☐ The first character is d.
- ☐ The second character is anything other than e or E.
- ☐ The last character is f.

NOTE

To include a ^ character in a set of alternatives, precede it with a backslash, as follows:

/d[\^eE]f/

This pattern matches d^f, def, or dEf.

Character-Range Escape Sequences

In the section titled "Matching Any Letter or Number" earlier in this chapter, you learned that you can represent consecutive letters or numbers inside the [] special characters by specifying ranges. For example, in the pattern

/a[1-3]c/

the [1-3] matches any of 1, 2, or 3.

Some ranges occur frequently enough that Perl defines special escape sequences for them. For example, instead of writing

/[0-9]/

to indicate that any digit is to be matched, you can write

/\d/

The \d escape sequence means "any digit."

Table 7.2 lists the character-range escape sequences, what they match, and their equivalent character ranges.

Table 7.2. Character-range escape sequences.

Escape sequence	Description	Range
\d	Any digit	[0-9]
\D	Anything other than a digit	[^0-9]
\w	Any word character	[_0-9a-zA-Z]
\W	Anything not a word character	[^_0-9a-zA-Z]
\s	White space	[\r\t\n\f]
\S	Anything other than white space	[^ \r\t\n\f]

7

These escape sequences can be used anywhere ordinary characters are used. For example, the following pattern matches any digit or lowercase letter:

`/[\da-z]/`

> **NOTE**
>
> The definition of word boundary as used by the \b and \B special characters corresponds to the definition of word character used by \w and \W.
>
> If the pattern /\w\W/ matches a particular pair of characters, the first character is part of a word and the second is not; this means that the first character is the end of a word, and that a word boundary exists between the first and second characters matched by the pattern.
>
> Similarly, if /\W\w/ matches a pair of characters, the first character is not part of a word and the second character is. This means that the second character is the beginning of a word. Again, a word boundary exists between the first and second characters matched by the pattern.

Matching Any Character

Another special character supported in patterns is the period (.) character, which matches any character except the newline character. For example, the following pattern matches d, followed by any non-newline character, followed by f:

`/d.f/`

The . character is often used in conjunction with the * character. For example, the following pattern matches any string that contains the character d preceding the character f:

`/d.*f/`

Normally, the .* special-character combination tries to match as much as possible. For example, if the string banana is searched using the following pattern, the pattern matches banana, not ba or bana:

`/b.*a/`

NOTE

There is one exception to the preceding rule: The `.*` character only matches the longest possible string that enables the pattern match as a whole to succeed.

For example, suppose the string `Mississippi` is searched using the pattern

`/M.*i.*pi/`

Here, the first `.*` in `/M.*i.*pi/` matches

`Mississippi`

If it tried to go further and match

`Mississippi`

or even

`Mississippi`

there would be nothing left for the rest of the pattern to match.

When the first `.*` match is limited to

`Mississippi`

the rest of the pattern, `i.*pi`, matches `ippi`, and the pattern as a whole succeeds.

Matching a Specified Number of Occurrences

Several special characters in patterns that you have seen enable you to match a specified number of occurrences of a character. For example, + matches one or more occurrences of a character, and ? matches zero or one occurrences.

Perl enables you to define how many occurrences of a character constitute a match. To do this, use the special characters { and }.

For example, the pattern

`/de{1,3}f/`

matches d, followed by one, two, or three occurrences of e, followed by f. This means that def, deef, and deeef match, but df and deeeef do not.

7

To specify an exact number of occurrences, include only one value between the { and the }.

`/de{3}f/`

This specifies exactly three occurrences of e, which means this pattern only matches deeef.

To specify a minimum number of occurrences, leave off the upper bound.

`/de{3,}f/`

This matches d, followed by at least three es, followed by f.

Finally, to specify a maximum number of occurrences, use 0 as the lower bound.

`/de{0,3}f/`

This matches d, followed by no more than three es, followed by f.

> **NOTE**
>
> You can use { and } with character ranges or any other special character, as follows:
>
> `/[a-z]{1,3}/`
>
> This matches one, two, or three lowercase letters.
>
> `/.{3}/`
>
> This matches any three characters.

Specifying Choices

The special character ¦ enables you to specify two or more alternatives to choose from when matching a pattern. For example, the pattern

`/def¦ghi/`

matches either def or ghi. The pattern

`/[a-z]+¦[0-9]+/`

matches one or more lowercase letters or one or more digits.

Listing 7.8 is a simple example of a program that uses the ¦ special character. It reads a number and checks whether it is a legitimate Perl integer.

TYPE **Listing 7.8. A simple integer-validation program.**

```
 1:  #!/usr/local/bin/perl
 2:
 3:  print ("Enter a number:\n");
 4:  $number = <STDIN>;
 5:  chop ($number);
 6:  if ($number =~ /^-?\d+$|^-?0[xX][\da-fA-F]+$/) {
 7:          print ("$number is a legal integer.\n");
 8:  } else {
 9:          print ("$number is not a legal integer.\n");
10:  }
```

OUTPUT
```
$ program7_8
Enter a number:
0x3ff1
0x3ff1 is a legal integer.
$
```

ANALYSIS Recall that Perl integers can be in any of three forms:

☐ Standard base-10 notation, as in 123

☐ Base-8 (octal) notation, indicated by a leading 0, as in 0123

☐ Base-16 (hexadecimal) notation, indicated by a leading 0x or 0X, as in 0X1ff

Line 6 checks whether a number is a legal Perl integer. The first alternative in the pattern,

`^-?\d+$`

matches a string consisting of one or more digits, optionally preceded by a -. (The ^ and $ characters ensure that this is the only string that matches.) This takes care of integers in standard base-10 notation and integers in octal notation.

The second alternative in the pattern,

`^-?0[xX][\da-fA-F]+$`

matches integers in hexadecimal notation. Take a look at this pattern one piece at a time:

☐ The ^ matches the beginning of the line. This ensures that lines containing leading spaces or extraneous characters are not treated as valid hexadecimal integers.

☐ The -? matches a - if it is present. This ensures that negative numbers are matched.

☐ The 0 matches the leading 0.

☐ The [xX] matches the x or X that follows the leading 0.

7

☐ The [\da-fA-F] matches any digit, any letter between a and f, or any letter between A and F. Recall that these are precisely the characters which are allowed to appear in hexadecimal digits.

☐ The + indicates that the pattern is to match one or more hexadecimal digits.

☐ The closing $ indicates that the pattern is to match only if there are no extraneous characters following the hexadecimal integer.

WARNING

> Beware that the following pattern matches either x *or* one or more of y, not one or more of x or y:
>
> /x¦y+/
>
> See the section called "Special-Character Precedence" later today for details on how to specify special-character precedence in patterns.

Reusing Portions of Patterns

Suppose that you want to write a pattern that matches the following:

☐ One or more digits or lowercase letters

☐ Followed by a colon or semicolon

☐ Followed by another group of one or more digits or lowercase letters

☐ Another colon or semicolon

☐ Yet another group of one or more digits or lowercase letters

One way to indicate this pattern is as follows:

/[\da-z]+[:;][\da-z]+[:;][\da-z]+/

This pattern is somewhat complicated and is quite repetitive.

Perl provides an easier way to specify patterns that contain multiple repetitions of a particular sequence. When you enclose a portion of a pattern in parentheses, as in

([\da-z]+)

Perl stores the matched sequence in memory. To retrieve a sequence from memory, use the special character \n, where n is an integer representing the nth pattern stored in memory.

For example, the aforementioned pattern can be written as

```
/([\da-z]+])[:;]\1[:;]\1/
```

Here, the pattern matched by `[\da-z]+` is stored in memory. When the Perl interpreter sees the escape sequence `\1`, it matches the matched pattern.

You also can store the sequence `[:;]` in memory, and write this pattern as follows:

```
/([\da-z]+)([:;])\1\2\1/
```

Pattern sequences are stored in memory from left to right, so `\1` represents the subpattern matched by `[\da-z]+` and `\2` represents the subpattern matched by `[:;]`.

Pattern-sequence memory is often used when you want to match the same character in more than one place but don't care which character you match. For example, if you are looking for a date in *dd-mm-yy* format, you might want to match

```
/\d{2}([\W])\d{2}\1\d{2}/
```

This matches two digits, a non-word character, two more digits, the same non-word character, and two more digits. This means that the following strings all match:

```
12-05-92
26.11.87
07 04 92
```

However, the following string does not match:

```
21-05.91
```

This is because the pattern is looking for a - between the 05 and the 91, not a period.

WARNING

Beware that the pattern

```
/\d{2}([\W])\d{2}\1\d{2}/
```

is not the same as the pattern

```
/(\d{2})([\W])\1\2\1/
```

In the first pattern, any digit can appear anywhere. The second pattern matches any two digits as the first two characters, but then only matches the same two digits again. This means that

```
17-17-17
```

matches, but the following does not:

```
17-05-91
```

7

Pattern-Sequence Scalar Variables

Note that pattern-sequence memory is preserved only for the length of the pattern. This means that if you define the following pattern (which, incidentally, matches any floating-point number that does not contain an exponent):

```
/-?(\d+)\.?(\d+)/
```

you cannot then define another pattern, such as the following:

```
/\1/
```

and expect the Perl interpreter to remember that \1 refers to the first \d+ (the digits before the decimal point).

To get around this problem, Perl defines special built-in variables that remember the value of patterns matched in parentheses. These special variables are named $n, where n is the nth set of parentheses in the pattern.

For example, consider the following:

```
$string = "This string contains the number 25.11.";
$string =~ /-?(\d+)\.?(\d+)/;
$integerpart = $1;
$decimalpart = $2;
```

In this case, the pattern

```
/-?(\d+)\.?(\d+)/
```

matches 25.11, and the subpattern in the first set of parentheses matches 25. This means that 25 is stored in $1 and is later assigned to $integerpart. Similarly, the second set of parentheses matches 11, which is stored in $2 and later assigned to $decimalpart.

WARNING

> The values stored in $1, $2, and so on, are destroyed when another pattern match is performed. If you need these values, be sure to assign them to other scalar variables.

There is also one other built-in scalar variable, $&, which contains the entire matched pattern, as follows:

```
$string = "This string contains the number 25.11.";
$string =~ /-?(\d+)\.?(\d+)/;
$number = $&;
```

Here, the pattern matched is 25.11, which is stored in $& and then assigned to $number.

Special-Character Precedence

Perl defines rules of precedence to determine the order in which special characters in patterns are interpreted. For example, the pattern

`/x¦y+/`

matches either x or one or more occurrences of y, because + has higher precedence than ¦ and is therefore interpreted first.

Table 7.3 lists the special characters that can appear in patterns in order of precedence (highest to lowest). Special characters with higher precedence are always interpreted before those of lower precedence.

Table 7.3. The precedence of pattern-matching special characters.

Special character	Description
()	Pattern memory
+ * ? {}	Number of occurrences
^ $ \b \B	Pattern anchors
¦	Alternatives

Because the pattern-memory special characters () have the highest precedence, you can use them to force other special characters to be evaluated first. For example, the pattern

`(ab¦cd)+`

matches one or more occurrences of either ab or cd. This matches, for example, abcdab.

WARNING

> Remember that when you use parentheses to force the order of precedence, you also are storing into pattern memory. For example, in the sequence
>
> `/(ab¦cd)+(.)(ef¦gh)+\1/`
>
> the \1 refers to what ab¦cd matched, not to what the . special character matched.

Now that you know all of the special-pattern characters and their precedence, look at a program that does more complex pattern matching. Listing 7.9 uses the various special-pattern characters, including the parentheses, to check whether a given input string is a valid twentieth-century date.

7

TYPE **Listing 7.9. A date-validation program.**

```
1:  #!/usr/local/bin/perl
2:
3:  print ("Enter a date in the format YYYY-MM-DD:\n");
4:  $date = <STDIN>;
5:  chop ($date);
6:
7:  # Because this pattern is complicated, we split it
8:  # into parts, assign the parts to scalar variables,
9:  # then substitute them in later.
10:
11: # handle 31-day months
12: $md1 = "(0[13578]¦1[02])\\2(0[1-9]¦[12]\\d¦3[01])";
13: # handle 30-day months
14: $md2 = "(0[469]¦11)\\2(0[1-9]¦[12]\\d¦30)";
15: # handle February, without worrying about whether it's
16: # supposed to be a leap year or not
17: $md3 = "02\\2(0[1-9]¦[12]\\d)";
18:
19: # check for a twentieth-century date
20: $match = $date =~ /^(19)?\d\d(.)($md1¦$md2¦$md3)$/;
21: # check for a valid but non-20th century date
22: $olddate = $date =~ /^(\d{1,4})(.)($md1¦$md2¦$md3)$/;
23: if ($match) {
24:         print ("$date is a valid date\n");
25: } elsif ($olddate) {
26:         print ("$date is not in the 20th century\n");
27: } else {
28:         print ("$date is not a valid date\n");
29: }
```

OUTPUT
```
$ program7_9
Enter a date in the format YYYY-MM-DD:
1991-04-31
1991-04-31 is not a valid date
$
```

ANALYSIS Don't worry: this program is a lot less complicated than it looks! Basically, this program does the following:

1. It checks whether the date is in the format YYYY-MM-DD. (It allows YY-MM-DD, and also enables you to use a character other than a hyphen to separate the year, month, and date.)

2. It checks whether the year is in the twentieth century or not.

3. It checks whether the month is between 01 and 12.

4. Finally, it checks whether the date field is a legal date for that month. Legal date fields are between 01 and either 29, 30, or 31, depending on the number of days in that month.

If the date is legal, the program tells you so. If the date is not a twentieth-century date but is legal, the program informs you of this also.

Because the pattern to be matched is too long to fit on one line, this program breaks it into pieces and assigns the pieces to scalar variables. This is possible because scalar-variable substitution is supported in patterns.

Line 12 is the pattern to match for months with 31 days. Note that the escape sequences (such as \d) are preceded by another backslash (producing \\d). This is because the program actually wants to store a backslash in the scalar variable. (Recall that backslashes in double-quoted strings are treated as escape sequences.) The pattern

`(0[13578]¦1[02])\2(0[1-9]¦[12]\d¦3[01])`

which is assigned to $md1, consists of the following components:

- [ ] The sequence `(0[13578]¦1[02])`, which matches the month values `01`, `03`, `05`, `07`, `08`, `10`, and `12` (the 31-day months)
- [ ] `\2`, which matches the character that separates the day, month, and year
- [ ] The sequence `(0[1-9]¦[12]\d¦3[01])`, which matches any two-digit number between `01` and `31`

Note that `\2` matches the separator character because the separator character will eventually be the second pattern sequence stored in memory (when the pattern is finally assembled).

Line 14 is similar to line 12 and handles 30-day months. The only differences between this subpattern and the one in line 12 are as follows:

- [ ] The month values accepted are `04`, `06`, `09`, and `11`.
- [ ] The valid date fields are `01` through `30`, not `01` through `31`.

Line 17 is another similar pattern that checks whether the month is `02` (February) and the date field is between `01` and `29`.

Line 20 does the actual pattern match that checks whether the date is a valid twentieth-century date. This pattern is divided into three parts.

- [ ] `^(19)?\d\d`, which matches any two-digit number at the beginning of a line, or any four-digit number starting with `19`
- [ ] The separator character, which is the second item in parentheses—the second item stored in memory—and thus can be retrieved using `\2`
- [ ] `($md1¦$md2¦$md3)$`, which matches any of the valid month-day combinations defined in lines 12, 14, and 17, provided it appears at the end of the line

The result of the pattern match, either true or false, is stored in the scalar variable $match.

Line 22 checks whether the date is a valid date in any century. The only difference between this pattern and the one in line 20 is that the year can be any one-to-four-digit number. The result of the pattern match is stored in $olddate.

Lines 23–29 check whether either $match or $olddate is true and print the appropriate message.

As you can see, the pattern-matching facility in Perl is quite powerful. This program is less than 30 lines long, including comments; the equivalent program in almost any other programming language would be substantially longer and much more difficult to write.

Specifying a Different Pattern Delimiter

So far, all the patterns you have seen have been enclosed by / characters.

```
/de*f/
```

These / characters are known as *pattern delimiters*.

Because / is the pattern-delimiter character, you must use \/ to include a / character in a pattern. This can become awkward if you are searching for a directory such as, for example, /u/jqpublic/perl/prog1.

```
/\/u\/jqpublic\/perl\/prog1/
```

To make it easier to write patterns that include / characters, Perl enables you to use any pattern-delimiter character you like. The following pattern also matches the directory /u/jqpublic/perl/prog1:

```
m!/u/jqpublic/perl/prog1!
```

Here, the m indicates the pattern-matching operation. If you are using a pattern delimiter other than /, you must include the m.

WARNING

There are two things you should watch out for when you use other pattern delimiters.

First, if you use the ' character as a pattern delimiter, the Perl interpreter does not substitute for scalar-variable names.

```
m'$var'
```

This matches the string $var, not the current value of the scalar variable $var.

Second, if you use a pattern delimiter that is normally a special-pattern character, you will not be able to use that special character in your pattern. For example, if you want to match the pattern ab?c (which matches a, optionally followed by b, followed by c) you cannot use the ? character as a pattern delimiter. The pattern

```
m?ab?c?
```

produces a syntax error, because the Perl interpreter assumes that the ? after the b is a pattern delimiter. You can still use

```
m?ab\?c?
```

but this pattern won't match what you want. Because the ? inside the pattern is escaped, the Perl interpreter assumes that you want to match the actual ? character, and the pattern matches the sequence ab?c.

Pattern-Matching Options

When you specify a pattern, you also can supply options that control how the pattern is to be matched. Table 7.4 lists these pattern-matching options.

Table 7.4. Pattern-matching options.

Option	Description
g	Match all possible patterns
i	Ignore case
m	Treat string as multiple lines
o	Only evaluate once
s	Treat string as single line
x	Ignore white space in pattern

All pattern options are included immediately after the pattern. For example, the following pattern uses the i option to ignore case:

```
/ab*c/i
```

You can specify as many of the options as you like, and the options can be in any order.

7

Matching All Possible Patterns

The g operator tells the Perl interpreter to match all the possible patterns in a string. For example, if you search the string balata using the pattern

`/.a/g`

which matches any character followed by a, the pattern matches ba, la, and ta.

If a pattern with the g option specified appears as an assignment to an array variable, the array variable is assigned a list consisting of all the patterns matched. For example,

`@matches = "balata" =~ /.a/g;`

assigns the following list to @matches:

`("ba", "la", "ta")`

Now, consider the following statement:

`$match = "balata" =~ /.a/g;`

The first time this statement is executed, $match is assigned the first pattern matched, which in this case is ba. If this assignment is performed again, $match is assigned the second pattern matched in the string, which is la, and so on until the pattern runs out of matches.

This means that you can use patterns with the g option in loops. Listing 7.10 shows how this works.

 Listing 7.10. A program that loops using a pattern.

```
1:  #!/usr/local/bin/perl
2:
3:  while ("balata" =~ /.a/g) {
4:          $match = $&;
5:          print ("$match\n");
6:  }
```

OUTPUT
```
$ program7_10
ba
la
ta
$
```

ANALYSIS The first time through the loop, $match has the value of the first pattern matched, which is ba. (The system variable $& always contains the last pattern matched; this pattern is assigned to $match in line 4.) When the loop is executed for a second time, $match has the value la. The third time through, $match has the value ta. After this, the loop terminates; because the pattern doesn't match anything else, the conditional expression is now false.

Determining the Match Location

If you need to know how much of a string has been searched by the pattern matcher when the g operator is specified, use the pos function.

```
$offset = pos($string);
```

This returns the position at which the next pattern match will be started.

You can reposition the pattern matcher by putting pos() on the left side of an assignment.

```
pos($string) = $newoffset;
```

This tells the Perl interpreter to start the next pattern match at the position specified by $newoffset.

WARNING

If you change the string being searched, the match position is reset to the beginning of the string.

NOTE

The pos function is not available in Perl version 4.

Ignoring Case

The i option enables you to specify that a matched letter can either be uppercase or lowercase. For example, the following pattern matches de, dE, De, or DE:

```
/de/i
```

Patterns that match either uppercase or lowercase letters are said to be *case-insensitive*.

Treating the String as Multiple Lines

The m option tells the Perl interpreter that the string to be matched contains multiple lines of text. When the m option is specified, the ^ special character matches either the start of the string or the start of any new line. For example, the pattern

```
/^The/m
```

matches the word The in

```
This pattern matches\nThe first word on the second line
```

The m option also specifies that the $ special character is to match the end of any line. This means that the pattern

```
/line.$/m
```

is matched in the following string:

```
This is the end of the first line.\nHere's another line.
```

NOTE

> The m option is defined only in Perl 5. To treat a string as multiple lines when you run Perl 4, set the $* system variable, described on Day 17, "System Variables."

Evaluating a Pattern Only Once

The o option enables you to tell the Perl interpreter that a pattern is to be evaluated only once. For example, consider the following:

```
$var = 1;
$line = <STDIN>;
while ($var < 10) {
        $result = $line =~ /$var/o;
        $line = <STDIN>;
        $var++;
}
```

The first time the Perl interpreter sees the pattern /$var/, it replaces the name $var with the current value of $var, which is 1; this means that the pattern to be matched is /1/.

Because the o option is specified, the pattern to be matched remains /1/ even when the value of $var changes. If the o option had not been specified, the pattern would have been /2/ the next time through the loop.

TIP

> There's no real reason to use the o option for patterns unless you are keen on efficiency. Here's an easier way to do the same thing:

7

```
$var = <STDIN>;
$matchval = $var;
$line = <STDIN>;
while ($var < 10) {
        $result = $line =~ /$matchval/;
        $line = <STDIN>;
        $var++;
}
```

The value of $matchval never changes, so the o option is not necessary.

Treating the String as a Single Line

The s option specifies that the string to be matched is to be treated as a single line of text. In this case, the . special character matches every character in a string, including the newline character. For example, the pattern /a.*bc/s is matched successfully in the following string:

axxxxx \nxxxxbc

If the s option is not specified, this pattern does not match, because the . character does not match the newline.

NOTE | The s option is defined only in Perl 5.

Using White Space in Patterns

One problem with patterns in Perl is that they can become difficult to follow. For example, consider this pattern, which you saw earlier:

/\d{2}([\W])\d{2}\1\d{2}/

Patterns such as this are difficult to follow, because there are a lot of backslashes, braces, and brackets to sort out.

Perl 5 makes life a little easier by supplying the x option. This tells the Perl interpreter to ignore white space in a pattern unless it is preceded by a backslash. This means that the preceding pattern can be rewritten as the following, which is much easier to follow:

/\d{2} ([\W]) \d{2} \1 \d{2}/x

7

Here is an example of a pattern containing an actual blank space:

```
/[A-Z] [a-z]+ \ [A-Z] [a-z]+ /x
```

This matches a name in the standard first-name/last-name format (such as John Smith). Normally, you won't want to use the x option if you're actually trying to match white space, because you wind up with the backslash problem all over again.

NOTE

> The x option is defined only in Perl 5.

The Substitution Operator

Perl enables you to replace part of a string using the substitution operator, which has the following syntax:

```
s/pattern/replacement/
```

The Perl interpreter searches for the pattern specified by the placeholder *pattern*. If it finds *pattern*, it replaces it with the string represented by the placeholder *replacement*. For example:

```
$string = "abc123def";
$string =~ s/123/456/;
```

Here, 123 is replaced by 456, which means that the value stored in $string is now abc456def.

You can use any of the pattern special characters in the substitution operator. For example,

```
s/[abc]+/0/
```

searches for a sequence consisting of one or more occurrences of the letters a, b, and c (in any order) and replaces the sequence with 0.

If you just want to delete a sequence of characters rather than replace it, leave out the replacement string as in the following example, which deletes the first occurrence of the pattern abc:

```
s/abc//
```

Using Pattern-Sequence Variables in Substitutions

You can use pattern-sequence variables to include a matched pattern in the replacement string. The following is an example:

```
s/(\d+)/[$1]/
```

This matches a sequence of one or more digits. Because this sequence is enclosed in parentheses, it is stored in the scalar variable $1. In the replacement string, [$1], the scalar variable name $1 is replaced by its value, which is the matched pattern.

NOTE

Because the replacement string in the substitution operator is a string, not a pattern, the pattern special characters, such as [], *, and +, do not have a special meaning. For example, in the substitution

```
s/abc/[def]/
```

the replacement string is [def] (including the square brackets).

Options for the Substitution Operator

The substitution operator supports several options, which are listed in Table 7.5.

Table 7.5. Options for the substitution operator.

Option	Description
g	Change all occurrences of the pattern
i	Ignore case in pattern
e	Evaluate replacement string as expression
m	Treat string to be matched as multiple lines
o	Evaluate only once
s	Treat string to be matched as single line
x	Ignore white space in pattern

As with pattern matching, options are appended to the end of the operator. For example, to change all occurrences of abc to def, use the following:

```
s/abc/def/g
```

Global Substitution

The g option changes all occurrences of a pattern in a particular string. For example, the following substitution puts parentheses around any number in the string:

7

```
s/(\d+)/($1)/g
```

Listing 7.11 is an example of a program that uses global substitution. It examines each line of its input, removes all extraneous leading spaces and tabs, and replaces multiple spaces and tabs between words with a single space.

TYPE **Listing 7.11. A simple white space cleanup program.**

```
 1:  #!/usr/local/bin/perl
 2:
 3:  @input = <STDIN>;
 4:  $count = 0;
 5:  while ($input[$count] ne "") {
 6:          $input[$count] =~ s/^[ \t]+//;
 7:          $input[$count] =~ s/[ \t]+\n$/\n/;
 8:          $input[$count] =~ s/[ \t]+/ /g;
 9:          $count++;
10:  }
11:  print ("Formatted text:\n");
12:  print (@input);
```

OUTPUT
```
$ program7_11
This is    a  line   of    input.
  Here    is another line.
This      is my  last line of    input.
^D
Formatted text:
This is a line of input.
Here is another line.
This is my last line of input.
$
```

ANALYSIS This program performs three substitutions on each line of its input. The first substitution, in line 6, checks whether there are any spaces or tabs at the beginning of the line. If any exist, they are removed.

Similarly, line 7 checks whether there are any spaces or tabs at the end of the line (before the trailing newline character). If any exist, they are removed. To do this, line 7 replaces the following pattern (one or more spaces and tabs, followed by a newline character, followed by the end of the line) with a newline character:

```
/[ \t]+\n$/
```

Line 8 uses a global substitution to remove extra spaces and tabs between words. The following pattern matches one or more spaces or tabs, in any order; these spaces and tabs are replaced by a single space:

```
/[ \t]+/
```

Ignoring Case

The i option ignores case when substituting. For example, the following substitution replaces all occurrences of the words no, No, NO, and nO with NO. (Recall that the \b escape character specifies a word boundary.)

```
s/\bno\b/NO/gi
```

Replacement Using an Expression

The e option treats the replacement string as an expression, which it evaluates before replacing. For example, consider the following:

```
$string = "0abc1";
$string =~ s/[a-zA-Z]+/$& x 2/e
```

The substitution shown here is a quick way to duplicate part of a string. Here's how it works:

1. The pattern /[a-zA-Z]+/ matches abc, which is stored in the built-in variable $&.

2. The e option indicates that the replacement string, $& x 2, is to be treated as an expression. This expression is evaluated, producing the result abcabc.

3. abcabc is substituted for abc in the string stored in $string. This means that the new value of $string is 0abcabc1.

Listing 7.12 is another example that uses the e option in a substitution. This program takes every integer in a list of input files and multiplies them by 2, leaving the rest of the contents unchanged. (For the sake of simplicity, the program assumes that there are no floating-point numbers in the file.)

TYPE

Listing 7.12. A program that multiplies every integer in a file by 2.

```
 1: #!/usr/local/bin/perl
 2:
 3: $count = 0;
 4: while ($ARGV[$count] ne "") {
 5:         open (FILE, "$ARGV[$count]");
 6:         @file = <FILE>;
 7:         $linenum = 0;
 8:         while ($file[$linenum] ne "") {
 9:                 $file[$linenum] =~ s/\d+/$& * 2/eg;
10:                 $linenum++;
11:         }
12:         close (FILE);
13:         open (FILE, ">$ARGV[$count]");
14:         print FILE (@file);
15:         close (FILE);
16:         $count++;
17: }
```

7

OUTPUT If a file named foo contains the text

```
This contains the number 1.
This contains the number 26.
```

and the name foo is passed as a command-line argument to this program, the file foo becomes

```
This contains the number 2.
This contains the number 52.
```

ANALYSIS This program uses the built-in variable @ARGV to retrieve filenames from the command line. Note that the program cannot use <>, because the following statement reads the entire contents of all the files into a single array:

```
@file = <>;
```

Lines 8–11 read and substitute one line of a file at a time. Line 9 performs the actual substitution as follows:

1. The pattern \d+ matches a sequence of one or more digits, which is automatically assigned to $&.
2. The value of $& is substituted into the replacement string.
3. The e option indicates that this replacement string is to be treated as an expression. This expression multiplies the matched integer by 2.
4. The result of the multiplication is then substituted into the file in place of the original integer.
5. The g option indicates that every integer on the line is to be substituted for.

After all the lines in the file have been read, the file is closed and reopened for writing. The call to print in line 14 takes the list stored in @file—the contents of the current file—and writes them back out to the file, overwriting the original contents.

Evaluating a Pattern Only Once

As with the match operator, the o option to the substitution operator tells the Perl interpreter to replace a scalar variable name with its value only once. For example, the following statement substitutes the current value of $var for its name, producing a replacement string:

```
$string =~ /abc/$var/o;
```

This replacement string then never changes, even if the value of $var changes. For example:

```
$var = 17;
while ($var > 0) {
        $string = <STDIN>;
        $string =~ /abc/$var/o;
        print ($string);
        $var--;  # the replacement string is still "17"
}
```

Again, as with the match operator, there is no real reason to use the o option.

Treating the String as Single or Multiple Lines

As in the pattern-matching operator, the s and m options specify that the string to be matched is to be treated as a single line or as multiple lines, respectively.

The s option ensures that the newline character \n is matched by the . special character.

```
$string = "This is a\ntwo-line string.";
$string =~ s/a.*o/one/s;
# $string now contains "This is a one-line string."
```

If the m option is specified, ^ and $ match the beginning and end of any line.

```
$string = "The The first line\nThe The second line";
$string =~ s/^The//gm;
# $string now contains "The first line\nThe second line"
$string =~ s/e$/k/gm;
# $string now contains "The first link\nThe second link"
```

WARNING

The \A and \Z escape sequences (defined in Perl 5) always match only the beginning and end of the string, respectively. (This is the only case where \A and \Z behave differently from ^ and $.)

NOTE

The m and s options are defined only in Perl 5. To treat a string as multiple lines when you run Perl 4, set the $* system variable, described on Day 17.

Using White Space in Patterns

The x option tells the Perl interpreter to ignore all white space unless preceded by a backslash. As with the pattern-matching operator, ignoring white space makes complicated string patterns easier to read.

```
$string =~ s/\d{2} ([\W]) \d{2} \1 \d{2}/$1-$2-$3/x
```

This converts a day-month-year string to the dd-mm-yy format.

7

NOTE

> Even if the x option is specified, spaces in the replacement string are not ignored. For example, the following replaces 14/04/95 with 14 - 04 - 95, not 14-04-95:
>
> `$string =~ s/\d{2} ([\W]) \d{2} \1 \d{2}/$1 - $2 - $3/x`
>
> Also note that the x option is defined only in Perl 5.

Specifying a Different Delimiter

You can specify a different delimiter to separate the pattern and replacement string in the substitution operator. For example, the following substitution operator replaces /u/bin with /usr/local/bin:

```
s#/u/bin#/usr/local/bin#
```

The search and replacement strings can be enclosed in parentheses or angle brackets.

```
s(/u/bin)(/usr/local/bin)
s</u/bin>/\/usr\/local\/bin/
```

WARNING

> As with the match operator, you cannot use a special character both as a delimiter and in a pattern.
>
> `s.a.c.def.`
>
> This substitution will be flagged as containing an error because the . character is being used as the delimiter. The substitution
>
> `s.a\.c.def.`
>
> does work, but it substitutes def for a.c, where . is an actual period and not the pattern special character.

The Translation Operator

Perl also provides another way to substitute one group of characters for another: the tr translation operator. This operator uses the following syntax:

```
tr/string1/string2/
```

Here, *string1* contains a list of characters to be replaced, and *string2* contains the characters that replace them. The first character in *string1* is replaced by the first character in *string2*, the second character in *string1* is replaced by the second character in *string2*, and so on.

Here is a simple example:

```
$string = "abcdefghicba";
$string =~ tr/abc/def/;
```

Here, the characters a, b, and c are to be replaced as follows:

☐ All occurrences of the character a are to be replaced by the character d.

☐ All occurrences of the character b are to be replaced by the character e.

☐ All occurrences of the character c are to be replaced by the character f.

After the translation, the scalar variable $string contains the value defdefghifed.

NOTE

If the string listing the characters to be replaced is longer than the string containing the replacement characters, the last character of the replacement string is repeated. For example:

```
$string = "abcdefgh";
$string =~ tr/efgh/abc/;
```

Here, there is no character corresponding to d in the replacement list, so c, the last character in the replacement list, replaces h. This translation sets the value of $string to abcdabcc.

Also note that if the same character appears more than once in the list of characters to be replaced, the first replacement is used:

```
$string =~ tr/AAA/XYZ/; replaces A with X
```

The most common use of the translation operator is to convert alphabetic characters from uppercase to lowercase or vice versa. Listing 7.13 provides an example of a program that converts a file to all lowercase characters.

TYPE

Listing 7.13. An uppercase-to-lowercase conversion program.

```
1:  #!/usr/local/bin/perl
2:
3:  while ($line = <STDIN>) {
4:          $line =~ tr/A-Z/a-z/;
5:          print ($line);
6:  }
```

7

```
$ program7_13
THIS LINE IS IN UPPER CASE.
this line is in upper case.
ThiS LiNE Is iN mIxED cASe.
this line is in mixed case.
^D
$
```

ANALYSIS This program reads a line at a time from the standard input file, terminating when it sees a line containing the Ctrl+D (end-of-file) character.

Line 4 performs the translation operation. As in the other pattern-matching operations, the range character (-) indicates a range of characters to be included. Here, the range a-z refers to all the lowercase characters, and the range A-Z refers to all the uppercase characters.

NOTE There are two things you should note about the translation operator:

□ The pattern special characters are not supported by the translation operator.

□ You can use y in place of tr if you want.

```
$string =~ y/a-z/A-Z/;
```

Options for the Translation Operator

The translation operator supports three options, which are listed in Table 7.6.

The c option (c is for "complement") translates all characters that are not specified. For example, the statement

```
$string =~ tr/\d/ /c;
```

replaces everything that is not a digit with a space.

Table 7.6. Options for the translation operator.

Option	Description
c	Translate all characters not specified
d	Delete all specified characters
s	Replace multiple identical output characters with a single character

7

The d option deletes every specified character.

```
$string =~ tr/\t //d;
```

This deletes all the tabs and spaces from $string.

The s option (for "squeeze") checks the output from the translation. If two or more consecutive characters translate to the same output character, only one output character is actually used. For example, the following replaces everything that is not a digit and outputs only one space between digits:

```
$string =~ tr/0-9/ /cs;
```

Listing 7.14 is a simple example of a program that uses some of these translation options. It reads a number from the standard input file, and it gets rid of every input character that is not actually a digit.

TYPE	**Listing 7.14. A program that ensures that a string consists of nothing but digits.**

```
1:  #!/usr/local/bin/perl
2:
3:  $string = <STDIN>;
4:  $string =~ tr/0-9//cd;
5:  print ("$string\n");
```

| OUTPUT | ```
$ program7_14
The number 45 appears in this string.
45
$
``` |
|---|---|

ANALYSIS	Line 4 of this program performs the translation. The d option indicates that the translated characters are to be deleted, and the c option indicates that every character

not in the list is to be deleted. Therefore, this translation deletes every character in the string that is not a digit. Note that the trailing newline character is not a digit, so it is one of the characters deleted.

Extended Pattern-Matching

Perl 5 provides some additional pattern-matching capabilities not found in Perl 4 or in standard UNIX pattern-matching operations.

7
```

Extended pattern-matching capabilities employ the following syntax:

`(?<c>pattern)`

<c> is a single character representing the extended pattern-matching capability being used, and *pattern* is the pattern or subpattern to be affected.

The following extended pattern-matching capabilities are supported by Perl 5:

☐ Parenthesizing subpatterns without saving them in memory

☐ Embedding options in patterns

☐ Positive and negative look-ahead conditions

☐ Comments

Parenthesizing Without Saving in Memory

In Perl, when a subpattern is enclosed in parentheses, the subpattern is also stored in memory. If you want to enclose a subpattern in parentheses without storing it in memory, use the ?: extended pattern-matching feature. For example, consider this pattern:

`/(?:a¦b¦c)(d¦e)f\1/`

This matches the following:

☐ One of a, b, or c

☐ One of d or e

☐ f

☐ Whichever of d or e was matched earlier

Here, \1 matches either d or e, because the subpattern a¦b¦c was not stored in memory. Compare this with the following:

`/(a¦b¦c)(d¦e)f\1/`

Here, the subpattern a¦b¦c is stored in memory, and one of a, b, or c is matched by \1.

Embedding Pattern Options

Perl 5 provides a way of specifying a pattern-matching option within the pattern itself. For example, the following patterns are equivalent:

`/[a-z]+/i`
`/(?i)[a-z]+/`

In both cases, the pattern matches one or more alphabetic characters; the i option indicates that case is to be ignored when matching.

The syntax for embedded pattern options is

`(?option)`

where *option* is one of the options shown in Table 7.7.

Table 7.7. Options for embedded patterns.

Option	Description
i	Ignore case in pattern
m	Treat pattern as multiple lines
s	Treat pattern as single line
x	Ignore white space in pattern

The g and o options are not supported as embedded pattern options.

Embedded pattern options give you more flexibility when you are matching patterns. For example:

```
$pattern1 = "[a-z0-9]+";
$pattern2 = "(?i)[a-z]+";
if ($string =~ /$pattern1¦$pattern2/) {
        ...
}
```

Here, the i option is specified for some, but not all, of a pattern. (This pattern matches either any collection of lowercase letters mixed with digits, or any collection of letters.)

Positive and Negative Look-Ahead

Perl 5 enables you to use the ?= feature to define a boundary condition that must be matched in order for the pattern to match. For example, the following pattern matches abc only if it is followed by def:

`/abc(?=def)/`

This is known as *a positive look-ahead condition.*

7

NOTE

> The positive look-ahead condition is not part of the pattern matched. For example, consider these statements:
>
> ```
> $string = "25abc8";
> $string =~ /abc(?=[0-9])/;
> $matched = $&;
> ```
>
> Here, as always, `$&` contains the matched pattern, which in this case is abc, not abc8.

Similarly, the `?!` feature defines a *negative look-ahead condition*, which is a boundary condition that must not be present if the pattern is to match. For example, the pattern `/abc(?!def)/` matches any occurrence of abc unless it is followed by def.

Pattern Comments

Perl 5 enables you to add comments to a pattern using the `?#` feature. For example:

```
if ($string =~ /(?i)[a-z]{2,3}(?# match two or three alphabetic characters)/ {
    ...
}
```

Adding comments makes it easier to follow complicated patterns.

Summary

Perl enables you to search for sequences of characters using *patterns*. If a pattern is found in a string, the pattern is said to be *matched*.

Patterns often are used in conjunction with the pattern-match operators, `=~` and `!~`. The `=~` operator returns true if the pattern matches, and the `!~` operator returns true if the pattern does not match.

Special-pattern characters enable you to search for a string that meets one of a variety of conditions.

- ☐ The + character matches one or more occurrences of a character.
- ☐ The * character matches zero or more occurrences of a character.
- ☐ The [ ] characters enclose a set of characters, any one of which matches.
- ☐ The ? character matches zero or one occurrences of a character.

- The ^ and $ characters match the beginning and end of a line, respectively. The \b and \B characters match a word boundary or somewhere other than a word boundary, respectively.
- The {} characters specify the number of occurrences of a character.
- The ¦ character specifies alternatives, either of which match.

To give a special character its natural meaning in a pattern, precede it with a backslash \.

Enclosing a part of a pattern in parentheses stores the matched subpattern in memory; this stored subpattern can be recalled using the character sequence \n, and stored in a scalar variable using the built-in scalar variable $n. The built-in scalar variable $& stores the entire matched pattern.

You can substitute for scalar-variable names in patterns, specify different pattern delimiters, or supply options that match every possible pattern, ignore case, or perform scalar-variable substitution only once.

The substitution operator, s, enables you to replace a matched pattern with a specified string. Options to the substitution operator enable you to replace every matched pattern, ignore case, treat the replacing string as an expression, or perform scalar-variable substitution only once.

The translation operator, tr, enables you to translate one set of characters into another set. Options exist that enable you to perform translation on everything not in the list, to delete characters in the list, or to ignore multiple identical output characters.

Perl 5 provides extended pattern-matching capabilities not provided in Perl 4. To use one of these extended pattern features on a subpattern, put (? at the beginning of the subpattern and) at the end of the subpattern.

Q&A

Q How many subpatterns can be stored in memory using *1*, *2*, and so on?

A Basically, as many as you like. After you store more than nine patterns, you can retrieve the later patterns using two-digit numbers preceded by a backslash, such as \10.

Q Why does pattern-memory variable numbering start with 1, whereas subscript numbering starts with 0?

A Subscript numbering starts with 0 to remain compatible with the C programming language. There is no such thing as pattern memory in C, so there is no need to be compatible with it.

Q **What happens when the replacement string in the translate command is left out, as in tr/abc//?**

A If the replacement string is omitted, a copy of the first string is used. This means that

```
tr/abc//
```

does not do anything, because it is the same as

```
tr/abc/abc/
```

If the replacement string is omitted in the substitute command, as in

```
s/abc//
```

the pattern matched—in this case, abc—is deleted.

Q **Why does Perl use characters such as +, *, and ? as pattern special characters?**

A These special characters usually correspond to special characters used in other UNIX applications, such as vi and csh. Some of the special characters, such as +, are used in formal syntax description languages.

Q **Why does Perl use both \1 and $1 to store pattern memory?**

A To enable you to distinguish between a subpattern matched in the current pattern (which is stored in \1) and a subpattern matched in the previous statement (which is stored in $1).

Workshop

The Workshop provides quiz questions to help you solidify your understanding of the material covered and exercises to give you experience in using what you've learned. Try and understand the quiz and exercise answers before you go on to tomorrow's lesson.

Quiz

1. What do the following patterns match?

    a. `/a¦bc*/`

    b. `/[\d]{1,3}/`

    c. `/\bc[aou]t\b/`

    d. `/(xy+z)\.\1/`

    e. `/^$/`

2. Write patterns that match the following:

    a. Five or more lowercase letters (a-z).

    b. Either the number 1 or the string one.

    c. A string of digits optionally containing a decimal point.

    d. Any letter, followed by any vowel, followed by the same letter again.

    e. One or more + characters.

3. Suppose the variable $var has the value abc123. Indicate whether the following conditional expressions return true or false.

    a. `$var =~ /./`

    b. `$var =~ /[A-Z]*/`

    c. `$var =~ /\w{4-6}/`

    d. `$var =~ /(\d)2(\1)/`

    e. `$var =~ /abc$/`

    f. `$var =~ /1234?/`

4. Suppose the variable $var has the value abc123abc. What is the value of $var after the following substitutions?

    a. `$var =~ s/abc/def/;`

    b. `$var =~ s/[a-z]+/X/g;`

    c. `$var =~ s/B/W/i;`

    d. `$var =~ s/(.)\d.*\1/d/;`

    e. `$var =~ s/(\d+)/$1*2/e;`

5. Suppose the variable $var has the value abc123abc. What is the value of $var after the following translations?

    a. `$var =~ tr/a-z/A-Z/;`

    b. `$var =~ tr/123/456/;`

    c. `$var =~ tr/231/564/;`

    d. `$var =~ tr/123/ /s;`

    e. `$var =~ tr/123//cd;`

Exercises

1. Write a program that reads all the input from the standard input file, converts all the vowels (except *y*) to uppercase, and prints the result on the standard output file.

2. Write a program that counts the number of times each digit appears in the standard input file. Print the total for each digit and the sum of all the totals.

3. Write a program that reverses the order of the first three words of each input line (from the standard input file) using the substitution operator. Leave the spacing unchanged, and print each resulting line.

4. Write a program that adds 1 to every number in the standard input file. Print the results.

5. **BUG BUSTER:** What is wrong with the following program?

```perl
#!/usr/local/bin/perl

while ($line = <STDIN>) {
        # put quotes around each line of input
        $line =~ /^.*$/"\1"/;
        print ($line);
}
```

6. **BUG BUSTER:** What is wrong with the following program?

```perl
#!/usr/local/bin/perl

while ($line = <STDIN>) {
        if ($line =~ /[\d]*/) {
                print ("This line contains the digits '$&'\n");
        }
}
```

Week 1 in Review

By now, you know enough about programming in Perl to write programs that perform many useful tasks. The program in Listing R1.1, which takes a number and prints out its English equivalent, illustrates some of the concepts you've learned during your first week.

1

2

3

4

5

6

7

Listing R1.1. Printing the English equivalent of numeric input.

`TYPE`

```perl
 1: #!/usr/local/bin/perl
 2:
 3: # define the strings used in printing
 4: @digitword = ("", "one", "two", "three", "four", "five",
 5:     "six", "seven", "eight", "nine");
 6: @digit10word = ("", "ten", "twenty", "thirty", "forty",
 7:     "fifty", "sixty", "seventy", "eighty", "ninety");
 8: @teenword = ("ten", "eleven", "twelve", "thirteen", "fourteen",
 9:     "fifteen", "sixteen", "seventeen", "eighteen", "nineteen");
10: @groupword = ("", "thousand", "million", "billion", "trillion",
11:     "quadrillion", "quintillion", "sextillion", "septillion",
12:     "octillion", "novillion", "decillion");
13:
14: # read a line of input and remove all blanks, commas and tabs;
15: # complain about anything else
16: $inputline = <STDIN>;
17: chop ($inputline);
18: $inputline =~ s/[, \t]+//g;
19: if ($inputline =~ /[^\d]/) {
20:         die ("Input must be a number.\n");
21: }
22:
23: # remove leading zeroes
24: $inputline =~ s/^0+//;
25: $inputline =~ s/^$/0/;   # put one back if they're all zero
26:
27: # split into digits: $grouping contains the number of groups
28: # of digits, and $oddlot contains the number of digits in the
29: # first group, which may be only 1 or 2 (e.g., the 1 in 1,000)
30: @digits = split(//, $inputline);
31: if (@digits > 36) {
32:         die ("Number too large for program to handle.\n");
33: }
34: $oddlot = @digits % 3;
35: $grouping = (@digits-1) / 3;
36:
37: # this loop iterates once for each grouping
38: $count = 0;
39: while ($grouping >= 0) {
40:         if ($oddlot == 2) {
41:                 $digit1 = 0;
42:                 $digit2 = $digits[0];
43:                 $digit3 = $digits[1];
44:                 $count += 2;
45:         } elsif ($oddlot == 1) {
46:                 $digit1 = 0;
47:                 $digit2 = 0;
48:                 $digits = $digits[0];
49:                 $count += 1;
50:         } else {        # regular group of three digits
51:                 $digit1 = $digits[$count];
52:                 $digit2 = $digits[$count+1];
```

```
53:                         $digit3 = $digits[$count+2];
54:                         $count += 3;
55:             }
56:             $oddlot = 0;
57:             if ($digit1 != 0) {
58:                     print ("$digitword[$digit1] hundred ");
59:             }
60:             if (($digit1 != 0 ¦¦ ($grouping == 0 && $count > 3)) &&
61:                 ($digit2 != 0 ¦¦ $digit3 != 0)) {
62:                     print ("and ");
63:             }
64:             if ($digit2 == 1) {
65:                     print ("$teenword[$digit3] ");
66:             } elsif ($digit2 != 0 && $digit3 != 0) {
67:                     print ("$digit10word[$digit2]-$digitword[$digit3] ");
68:             } elsif ($digit2 != 0 ¦¦ $digit3 != 0) {
69:                     print ("$digit10word[$digit2]$digitword[$digit3] ");
70:             }
71:             if ($digit1 != 0 ¦¦ $digit2 != 0 ¦¦ $digit3 != 0) {
72:                     print ("$groupword[$grouping]\n");
73:             } elsif ($count <= 3 && $grouping == 0) {
74:                     print ("zero\n");
75:             }
76:             $grouping—;
77: }
```

OUTPUT

```
$ programR1_1
11,683
eleven thousand
six hundred and eighty-three
$
```

ANALYSIS This program reads in a number up to 36 digits long and prints out its English equivalent, using one line for each group of three digits.

Lines 4–12 define array variables whose lists are the possible words that can be in a number. The variable @digitword lists the digits; @digit10word lists the words that indicate multiples of ten; @teenword lists the words that represent the values from 11 to 19; and @groupword lists the names for each group of digits. Note that some of these lists have an empty first element; this ensures that the array subscripts refer to the correct value. (For example, without the empty word at the beginning of @digitword, $digitword[5] would refer to four, not five.)

Lines 14–21 read the input and check whether it is valid. Valid numbers consist of digits optionally separated by spaces, tabs, or commas. The substitution operator in line 18 removes these valid separators; the conditional expression in line 19 checks whether any invalid separators exist.

If the program reaches line 24, the input number is valid. Line 24 gets rid of any leading zeros (to ensure that, for example, 000071 is converted to 71). If a number consists entirely of zeros, line 24 converts $inputline to the empty string; line 25 tests for this empty string and adds a zero if necessary.

Lines 30–35 split the number into individual digits and create a list consisting of these digits. This list is assigned to the array variable @digits. Line 34 determines whether the first group of digits contains fewer than three digits; an example of this is the number 45,771, whose first group of digits consists of only two digits. The scalar variable $oddlot is assigned the number of digits in the first group if the group is an odd lot of one or two; it is assigned 0 if the first group of digits contains all three digits.

Line 35 calculates the number of groups of digits (including the initial odd lot). This determines the number of times that the upcoming printing loop is to be iterated.

Lines 38–79 actually print the English value for this number. Each group of three digits is printed on its own line. The scalar variable $count contains the number of digits printed so far and is used as a subscript for the array variable @digits.

To actually print the English value corresponding to a group of three digits, this loop first executes lines 40–57, which assign the values of the digits in the group to three scalar variables: $digit1, $digit2, and $digit3. If the group being handled is the first group, lines 40 and 46 check whether the group is an odd lot. For example, if the first group contains only two digits, the condition in line 40 becomes true, and the variable $digit1, which represents the first digit of the group, is assigned 0. Using $digit1, $digit2, and $digit3 reduces the complexity of the program because no code following line 57 has to check for the value of $oddlot.

The number of digits actually handled is added to the scalar variable $count at this point.

Line 58 assigns 0 to $oddlot. Subsequent groups of digits always contain three digits.

Lines 59–77 print the English value associated with this particular group of digits as follows:

1. Lines 59–61 print the value of the hundreds place in this group (the first of the three digits).

2. Lines 62–64 check whether the word and needs to appear here. The word and is required in the following cases:

   ☐ $digit1 is nonzero and one of the other digits is nonzero (as in three hundred and four)

   ☐ $digit1 is zero, one of the other digits is nonzero, and this is the last group to be handled (as in the and four part of the number 11,004)

3. If the second digit is a 1 (as in 317), one of the "teen words" (such as eleven, twelve, and thirteen) must be used. Line 66 checks for this condition, and line 67 prints the appropriate word.

4. If both of the last two digits are defined, they both must be printed, and a dash must separate them (as in forty-two). Line 69 prints this pair of words and the dash.

5. If only one of the last two digits is defined, it is printed using line 71. (Note that line 71 actually specifies that both digits are printed; however, because only one is actually nonzero, it is the only one that appears. The digit that is zero appears in the output as the empty string because zero is equivalent to the empty string in Perl.)

6. Lines 73–74 print the word associated with this group of digits. For example, if this group is the second-last group of digits, the word thousand is printed.

7. Line 75 handles the special case of the number 0. In this case, the word zero is printed.

Once the English value for a particular group of digits is printed, the scalar variable $grouping has its value decreased by one, and the program continues with the next group of digits. If there are no more digits to print, the program terminates.

Week 2 at a Glance

By now, you know enough about Perl to write many useful programs. You've discovered that Perl is powerful enough to enable you to perform complicated tasks, and simple enough to accomplish them quickly.

Where You're Going

The second week covers most of the features of the language not covered in the first week and describes some of the many library functions supplied with Perl. Here's a summary of what you'll learn.

Day 8, "More Control Structures," discusses the control flow statements not previously covered.

Day 9, "Using Subroutines," shows how you can break down your program into more manageable chunks.

Day 10, "Associative Arrays," introduces one of the most powerful and useful constructs in Perl, associative arrays, and it shows how you can use these arrays to simulate other data structures.

Day 11, "Formatting Your Output," shows how you can use Perl to produce tidy reports.

Day 12, "Working with the File System," shows how you can interact with your system's directory structure.

Day 13, "Process, String, and Mathematical Functions," describes the library functions that interact with processes running on the system, operate on text strings, and perform mathematical operations.

Day 14, "Scalar-Conversion and List-Manipulation Functions," describes the library functions that convert values from one form to another and work with lists and array variables.

By the end of the second week, you'll have mastered almost all of the features of Perl and you'll have learned about many of the library functions supplied with the language.

Day 8

More Control Structures

On Day 2, "Basic Operators and Control Flow," you learned about some of the simpler conditional statements in Perl, including the following:

- [ ] The `if` statement, which defines statements that are executed only when a certain condition is true
- [ ] The `if-else` statement, which chooses between two alternatives
- [ ] The `if-elsif-else` statement, which chooses between multiple alternatives
- [ ] The `unless` statement, which defines statements that are executed unless a specified condition is true
- [ ] The `while` statement, which executes a group of statements while a specified condition is true
- [ ] The `until` statement, which executes a group of statements until a specified condition is true

Today's lesson talks about the other control structures in Perl; these control structures give you a great deal of flexibility when you are determining the order of execution of your program statement.

Today you learn the following control structures:

- ☐ Single-line conditional statements
- ☐ The `for` statement
- ☐ The `foreach` statement
- ☐ The `do` statement
- ☐ The `last` statement
- ☐ The `next` statement
- ☐ The `redo` statement
- ☐ The `continue` statement
- ☐ Labeled blocks
- ☐ The `goto` statement

Using Single-Line Conditional Statements

On Day 2 you saw the `if` statement, which works as follows:

```
if ($var == 0) {
        print ("This is zero.\n");
}
```

If the statement block inside the `if` statement consists of only one statement, Perl enables you to write this in a more convenient way using a *single-line conditional statement*. This is a conditional statement whose statement block contains only one line of code.

The following single-line conditional statement is identical to the `if` statement defined previously:

```
print ("This is zero.\n") if ($var == 0);
```

Single-line conditional statements also work with `unless`, `while`, and `until`:

```
print ("This is zero.\n") unless ($var != 0);
print ("Not zero yet.\n") while ($var-- > 0);
print ("Not zero yet.\n") until ($var-- == 0);
```

In all four cases, the syntax of the single-line conditional statement is the same.

The syntax for the single-line conditional statement is

statement keyword condexpr

Here, *statement* is any Perl statement. *keyword* is either `if`, `unless`, `while`, or `until`. *condexpr* is the conditional expression that is evaluated.

statement is executed in the following cases:

☐ If keyword is if, statement is executed if condexpr is true.

☐ If keyword is unless, statement is executed unless condexpr is true.

☐ If keyword is while, statement is executed while condexpr is true.

☐ If keyword is until, statement is executed until condexpr is true.

To see how single-line conditional expressions can be useful, look at the following examples, starting with Listing 8.1. This is a simple program that copies one file to another. Single-line conditional statements are used to check whether the files opened successfully, and another single-line conditional statement actually copies the file.

Listing 8.1. A program that uses single-line conditional statements to copy one file to another.

TYPE

```
1:  #!/usr/local/bin/perl
2:
3:  die ("Can't open input\n") unless (open(INFILE, "infile"));
4:  die ("Can't open output\n") unless (open(OUTFILE, ">outfile"));
5:  print OUTFILE ($line) while ($line = <INFILE>);
6:  close (INFILE);
7:  close (OUTFILE);
```

OUTPUT There is no output; this program writes to a file.

ANALYSIS As you can see, this program is clear and concise. Instead of using three lines to open a file and check it, as in

```
unless (open (INFILE, "infile")) {
        die ("Can't open input\n");
    }
```

you can now use just one:

```
die ("Can't open input\n") unless (open(INFILE, "infile"));
```

Line 3 opens the input file. If the open is not successful, the program terminates by calling die.

Line 4 is similar to line 3. It opens the output file and checks whether the file actually is open; if the file is not open, the program terminates.

Line 5 actually copies the file. The conditional expression

```
$line = <INFILE>
```

reads a line from the file represented by the file variable INFILE and assigns it to $line. If the line is empty, the conditional expression is false, and the while statement stops executing. If the line is not empty, it is written to OUTFILE.

NOTE

> The conditional expression in a single-line conditional statement is always executed first, even though it appears at the end of the statement. For example:
>
> ```
> print OUTFILE ($line) while ($line = <INFILE>);
> ```
>
> Here, the conditional expression that reads a line of input and assigns it to $line is always executed first. This means that print is not called until $line contains something to print. This also means that the call to print is never executed if INFILE is an empty file (which is what you want).
>
> Because single-line conditional expressions are "backward," be careful when you use them with anything more complicated than what you see here.

You can use the single-line conditional statement in conjunction with the autoincrement operator ++ to write a loop in a single line. For example, examine Listing 8.2, which prints the numbers from 1 to 5 using a single-line conditional statement.

Listing 8.2. A program that loops using a single-line conditional statement.

TYPE

```
1:  #!/usr/local/bin/perl
2:
3:  $count = 0;
4:  print ("$count\n") while ($count++ < 5);
```

OUTPUT

```
$ program8_2
1
2
3
4
5
$
```

ANALYSIS When the Perl interpreter executes line 3, it first evaluates the conditional expression

```
$count++ < 5
```

8

Because the ++ appears after $count, 1 is added to the value of $count after the conditional expression is evaluated. This means that $count has the value 0, not 1, the first time the expression is evaluated. Similarly, $count has the value 1 the second time, 2 the third time, 3 the fourth time, and 4 the fifth time. In each of these five cases, the conditional expression evaluates to true, which means that the loop iterates five times.

After the conditional expression has been evaluated, the ++ operator adds 1 to the value of $count. This new value of $count is then printed. This means that when the loop is first executed, the call to print prints 1, even though the value of $count was 0 when the conditional expression was evaluated.

Problems with Single-Line Conditional Statements

Although single-line conditional statements that contain loops are useful, there are problems. Consider Listing 8.2, which you've just seen. It is easy to forget that $count has to be initialized to one less than the first value you want to use in the loop, and that the conditional expression has to use the < operator, not the <= operator.

For example, take a look at the following:

```
$count = 1;
print ("$count\n") while ($count++ < 5);
```

Here, you have to look closely to see that the first value printed is 2, not 1.

Here is another loop containing a mistake:

```
$count = 0;
print ("$count\n") while ($count++ <= 5);
```

This loop iterates six times, not five; the sixth time through the loop, $count has the value 5 when the conditional expression is evaluated. The expression evaluates to true, $count is incremented to 6, and print therefore prints the value 6.

Here is a related but slightly more subtle problem:

```
$count = 0;
print ("$count\n") while ($count++ < 5);
print ("The total number of iterations is $count.\n");
```

This loop iterates five times, which is what you want. However, after the conditional expression is evaluated for the final time, the value of $count becomes 6, as follows:

☐ Before the conditional expression is evaluated, $count has the value 5.

☐ Because the value of $count is not less than 5, the conditional expression evaluates to false, which terminates the loop.

☐ After the conditional expression is evaluated, the ++ operator adds one to $count, giving it the value 6.

This means that the final `print` statement prints the following, which is probably not what you want:

```
The total number of iterations is 6.
```

Do   **Don't**

DO use the `for` statement as a convenient way to write a concise, compact loop. It is discussed in the next section.

DON'T use the ++ operator to produce a loop in a single-line conditional statement unless it's absolutely necessary. It's just too easy to go wrong with it.

Looping Using the `for` Statement

Many of the programs that you've seen so far use the `while` statement to create a program loop. Here is a simple example:

```
$count = 1;
while ($count <= 5) {
        # statements inside the loop go here
        $count++;
}
```

This loop contains three items that control it:

1. A statement that sets the initial value of the loop. In this loop, the scalar variable `$count` is used to control the number of iterations of the loop, and the statement

   ```
   $count = 1;
   ```

   sets the initial value of `$count` to 1. Statements such as this are called *loop initializers.*

2. A conditional expression that checks to see whether to continue iterating the loop. In this case, the conditional expression

   ```
   $count <= 5
   ```

   is evaluated; if it is false, the loop is terminated.

3. A statement that changes the value of the variable which is tested in the conditional expression. In this loop, the statement

   ```
   count++;
   ```

   adds 1 to the value of `$count`, which is the scalar variable being tested in the conditional expression. Statements such as this are called *loop iterators.*

8

Perl enables you to put the three components that control a loop together on a single line using a for statement. For example, the following statement is equivalent to the loop you've been looking at:

```
for ($count=1; $count <= 5; $count++) {
        # statements inside the loop go here
}
```

Here, the three controlling components—the loop initializer, the conditional expression, and the loop iterator—appear together, and are separated by semicolons.

The syntax of the for statement is

```
for (expr1; expr2; expr3) {
        statement_block
}
```

expr1 is the loop initializer. It is evaluated only once, before the start of the loop.

expr2 is the conditional expression that terminates the loop. The conditional expression in *expr2* behaves just like the ones in while and if statements. If its value is 0 (false), the loop is terminated, and if its value is nonzero, the loop is executed.

statement_block is the collection of statements that is executed if (and when) *expr2* has a nonzero value.

expr3 is executed once per iteration of the loop and is executed after the last statement in *statement_block* is executed.

NOTE

If you know the C programming language, the for statement will be familiar to you. The for statement in Perl is syntactically identical to the for statement in C.

Listing 8.3 is a program based on the example for statement you've just seen.

Listing 8.3. A program that prints the numbers from 1 to 5 using the for statement.

TYPE

```
1:  #!/usr/local/bin/perl
2:
3:  for ($count=1; $count <= 5; $count++) {
4:          print ("$count\n");
5:  }
```

OUTPUT
```
$ program8_3
1
2
3
4
5
$
```

 ANALYSIS Line 3 of the program is the start of the for statement. The first expression defined in the for statement, $count = 1, is the loop initializer; it is executed before the loop is iterated.

The second expression defined in the for statement, $count <= 5, tests whether to continue iterating the loop.

The third expression defined in the for statement, $count++, is evaluated after the last statement in the loop, line 4, is executed.

As you can see from the output, the loop is iterated five times.

💡 **TIP**

Use the for statement instead of while or until whenever possible; when you use the for statement, it is easier to avoid infinite loops.

For example, when you use a while statement, it's easy to forget to iterate the loop. The following is an example:

```
$count = 1;

while ($count <= 5) {
        print ("$count\n");
}
```

The equivalent statement using for is

```
for ($count = 1; $count <= 5; ) {
        print ("$count\n");
}
```

When you use the for statement, it is easier to notice that the loop iterator is missing.

Using the Comma Operator in a for Statement

Some loops need to perform more than one action before iterating. For example, consider the following loop, which reads four lines of input from the standard input file and prints three of them:

```
$line = <STDIN>;
$count = 1;
while ($count <= 3) {
        print ($line);
        $line = <STDIN>;
        $count++;
}
```

This loop needs two loop initializers and two loop iterators: one of each for the variable $count, and one of each to read another line of input from STDIN.

At first glance, you might think that you can't write this loop using the for statement. However, you can use the comma operator to combine the two loop initializers and the two loop iterators into single expressions. Listing 8.4 does this.

TYPE

Listing 8.4. A program that uses the for statement to read four input lines and write three of them.

```
1:  #!/usr/local/bin/perl
2:
3:  for ($line = <STDIN>, $count = 1; $count <= 3;
4:       $line = <STDIN>, $count++) {
5:          print ($line);
6:  }
```

OUTPUT

```
$ program8_4
This is my first line.
This is my first line.
This is my second line.
This is my second line.
This is my last line.
This is my last line.
This input line is not written out.
$
```

ANALYSIS

The loop initializer in this for statement is the expression

```
$line = <STDIN>, $count = 1
```

The comma operator in this expression tells the Perl interpreter to evaluate the first half of the expression—the part to the left of the comma—and then evaluate the second half. The first half of this expression reads a line from the standard input file and assigns it to $line; the second half of the expression assigns 1 to $count.

The loop iterator also consists of two parts:

```
$line = <STDIN>, $count++
```

This expression reads a line from the standard input file and adds 1 to the variable keeping track of when to terminate the loop, which is $count.

> Don't use the for statement if you have a large number of loop
> initializers or loop iterators, because statements that contain a large
> number of comma operators are difficult to read.

Looping Through a List: The foreach Statement

One common use of loops is to perform an operation on every element of a list stored in an
array variable. For example, the following loop checks whether any element of the list stored
in the array variable @words is the word the:

```
$count = 1;
while ($count <= @words) {
        if ($words[$count-1] eq "the") {
                print ("found the word 'the'\n");
        }
        $count++;
}
```

As you've seen, you can use the for statement to simplify this loop, as follows:

```
for ($count = 1; $count <= @words; $count++) {
        if ($words[$count-1] eq "the") {
                print ("found the word 'the'\n");
        }
}
```

Perl provides an even simpler way to do the same thing, using the foreach statement. The
following loop, which uses foreach, is identical to the preceding one:

```
foreach $word (@words) {
        if ($word eq "the") {
                print ("found the word 'the'\n");
        }
}
```

The syntax for the foreach statement is

```
foreach localvar (listexpr) {
        statement_block;
}
```

Here, listexpr is any list or array variable, and statement_block is a collection of statements
that is executed every time the loop iterates.

localvar is a scalar variable that is defined only for the duration of the foreach statement.
The first time the loop is executed, localvar is assigned the value of the first element of the

list in *listexpr*. Each subsequent time the loop is executed, *localvar* is assigned the value of the next element of *listexpr*.

Listing 8.5 shows how this works.

 Listing 8.5. A demonstration of the foreach statement.

```
1:  #!/usr/local/bin/perl
2:
3:  @words = ("Here", "is", "a", "list.");
4:  foreach $word (@words) {
5:          print ("$word\n");
6:  }
```

OUTPUT
```
$ program8_5
Here
is
a
list.
$
```

ANALYSIS The foreach statement in line 4 assigns a word from @list to the local variable $word. The first time the loop is executed, the value stored in $word is the string Here. The second time the loop is executed, the value stored in $word is is. Subsequent iterations assign a and list. to $word.

The loop defined by the foreach statement terminates after all of the words in the list have been assigned to $word.

 NOTE

In Perl, the for statement and the foreach statement are actually synonymous: you can use for wherever foreach is expected, and vice versa.

The foreach **Local Variable**

Note that the scalar variable defined in the foreach statement is defined only for the duration of the loop. If a value is assigned to the scalar variable prior to the execution of the foreach statement, this value is restored after the foreach is executed. Listing 8.6 shows how this works.

TYPE

Listing 8.6. A program that uses the same name inside and outside a `foreach` statement.

```
1:  #!/usr/local/bin/perl
2:
3:  $temp = 1;
4:  @list = ("This", "is", "a", "list", "of", "words");
5:  print ("Here are the words in the list: \n");
6:  foreach $temp (@list) {
7:          print ("$temp ");
8:  }
9:  print("\n");
10: print("The value of temp is now $temp\n");
```

OUTPUT

```
$ program8_6
Here are the words in the list:
This is a list of words
The value of temp is now 1
$
```

ANALYSIS   Line 3 assigns 1 to the scalar variable $temp.

The `foreach` statement that prints the words in the list is defined in lines 6–8. This statement assigns the elements of @list to $temp, one per iteration of the loop.

After the loop is terminated, the original value of $temp is restored, which is 1. This value is printed by line 10.

Variables (such as $temp in lines 6–8) that are only defined for part of a program are known as *local variables*; variables that are defined throughout a program are known as *global variables*. You'll see more examples of local variables on Day 9, "Using Subroutines."

TIP

> It is not a good idea to use $temp the way it is used in Listing 8.6, namely, as both a local and a global variable. You might forget that the value of the global variable—in the case of $temp, the value 1—is overwritten by the value assigned in the `foreach` statement.
>
> Conversely, you might forget that the value assigned to $temp in the `foreach` statement is lost when the `foreach` is finished.
>
> It is better to define a new scalar variable name for the local variable, to avoid confusion.

8

Changing the Value of the Local Variable

Note that changing the value of the local variable inside a `foreach` statement also changes the value of the corresponding element of the list. For example:

```
@list = (1, 2, 3, 4, 5);
foreach $temp (@list) {
        if ($temp == 2) {
                $temp = 20;
        }
}
```

In this loop, when `$temp` is equal to 2, `$temp` is reset to 20. Therefore, the list stored in the array variable `@list` becomes `(1, 20, 3, 4, 5)`.

Use this feature with caution, because it is not obvious that the value of `@list` has changed.

Using Returned Lists in the `foreach` Statement

So far, all of the examples of the `foreach` statement that you've seen have iterated using the contents of an array variable. For example, consider the following:

```
@list = ("This", "is", "a", "list");
foreach $temp (@list) {
        print ("$temp ");
}
```

This loop assigns `This` to `$temp` the first time through the loop, and then assigns `is`, `a`, and `list` to `$temp` on subsequent iterations.

You also can use list constants or the return values from functions in `foreach` statements. For example, the preceding statements can be written as follows:

```
foreach $temp ("This", "is", "a", "list") {
        print("$temp ");
}
```

As before, `$temp` is assigned `This`, `is`, `a`, and `list` in successive iterations of the `foreach` loop.

Listing 8.7 shows how you can use the return value from a function as a loop iterator.

TYPE Listing 8.7. A program that prints out the words in a line in reverse-sorted order.

```
1:  #!/usr/local/bin/perl
2:
3:  $line = <STDIN>;
4:  $line =~ s/^\s+//;
```

continues

Listing 8.7. continued

```
5:  $line =~ s/\s+$//;
6:  foreach $word (reverse sort split(/[\t ]+/, $line)) {
7:          print ("$word ");
8:  }
9:  print ("\n");
```

```
$ program8_7
here is my test line
test my line is here
$
```

ANALYSIS Before splitting the input line into words using split, this program first removes the leading and trailing white space. (If leading and trailing space is not removed, split creates an empty word.) Line 4 removes leading spaces and tabs from the input line. Line 5 removes any trailing spaces and tabs as well as the closing newline character.

Lines 6–8 contain the foreach loop. The list used in this loop is created as follows:

1. First, split breaks the input line into words. The list returned by split is ("here", "is", "my", "test", "line").
2. The list returned by split is passed to the built-in function sort, which sorts the list. The list returned by sort is ("here", "is", "line", "my", "test").
3. The list returned by sort is passed to another built-in function, reverse. This reverses the sorted list, producing the list ("test", "my", "line", "is", "here").
4. Each element of the list returned by reverse is assigned, in turn, to the local scalar variable $word, starting with "test" and proceeding from there.

Line 7 prints the current value stored in $word. Each time the foreach loop iterates, a different value in the list is printed.

NOTE

The code fragment

```
foreach $word (reverse sort split(/[\t ]+/, $line))
```

shows why omitting parentheses when calling built-in functions can sometimes be useful. If all the parentheses are included, this becomes

```
foreach $word (reverse(sort(split(/[\t ]+/, $line))))
```

which is not as readable.

The do **Statement**

So far, all of the loops you've seen test the conditional expression before executing the loop. Perl enables you to write loops that always execute at least once using the do statement.

The syntax for the do statement is

```
do {
        statement_block
} while_or_until (condexpr);
```

As in other conditional statements, such as the if statement and the while statement, *statement_block* is a block of statements to be executed, and *condexpr* is a conditional expression.

while_or_until is either the while keyword or the until keyword. If you use while, *statement_block* loops while *condexpr* is true. For example:

```
do {
        $line = <STDIN>;
} while ($line ne "");
```

This loops while $line is non-empty (in other words, while the program has not reached the end of file).

If you use until, *statement_block* loops until *condexpr* is true. For example:

```
do {
        $line = <STDIN>;
} until ($line eq "");
```

▲ This reads from the standard input file until $line is empty (again, until end of file is reached).

Listing 8.8 is a simple example of a program that uses a do statement.

Type **Listing 8.8. A simple example of a do statement.**

```
1:  #!/usr/local/bin/perl
2:
3:  $count = 1;
4:  do {
5:          print ("$count\n");
6:          $count++;
7:  } until ($count > 5);
```

Output
```
$ program8_8
1
2
3
4
5
$
```

ANALYSIS   Lines 4–7 contain the do statement, which loops five times. Line 7 tests whether the counting variable $count is greater than 5.

 NOTE   The do statement can also be used to call subroutines. See Day 9, "Using Subroutines," for more information.

Exiting a Loop Using the last Statement

Normally, you exit a loop by testing the conditional expression that is part of the loop. For example, if a loop is defined by the while statement, as in the following, the program exits the loop when the conditional expression at the top of the loop, $count <= 10, is false:

```
while ($count <= 10) {
        # statements go here
}
```

In the preceding case, the program can exit the loop only after executing all of the statements in it. Perl enables you to define an exit point anywhere in the loop using a special last statement.

SYNTAX

The syntax for the last statement is simple:

```
last;
```

To see how the last statement works, take a look at Listing 8.9, which adds a list of numbers supplied by means of the standard input file.

TYPE   Listing 8.9. A program that exits using the last statement.

```
1:  #!/usr/local/bin/perl
2:
3:  $total = 0;
4:  while (1) {
5:          $line = <STDIN>;
6:          if ($line eq "") {
7:                  last;
8:          }
9:          chop ($line);
10:         @numbers = split (/[\t ]+/, $line);
11:         foreach $number (@numbers) {
12:                 if ($number =~ /[^0-9]/) {
13:                     print STDERR ("$number is not a number\n");
14:                 }
15:                 $total += $number;
16:         }
```

```
17: }
18: print ("The total is $total.\n");
```

OUTPUT

```
$ program8_9
4 5 7
2 11 6
^D
The total is 35.
$
```

ANALYSIS The loop that reads and adds numbers starts on line 4. The conditional expression at the top of this loop is the number 1. Because this is a nonzero number, this conditional expression always evaluates to true. Normally, this means that the `while` statement loops forever; however, because this program contains a `last` statement, the loop eventually terminates.

Line 6 checks whether the program has reached the end of the standard input file. To do this, it checks whether the line read from the standard input file, now stored in `$line`, is empty. (Recall that the Ctrl+D character, written here as `^D`, marks the standard input file as empty.)

If the line is empty, line 7, the `last` statement, is executed. This statement tells the Perl interpreter to terminate executing the loop and to continue with the first statement after the loop, which is line 18.

Lines 10–16 add the numbers on the input line to the total stored in the scalar variable `$total`. Line 10 breaks the line into individual numbers, and lines 11–16 add each number, in turn, to `$total`.

Line 12 checks whether each number actually consists of the digits 0–9. The pattern `[^0-9]` matches anything that is not a digit; if the program finds such a character, it flags the number as erroneous. (The program can produce empty words if leading or trailing spaces or tabs exist in the line; this is not a problem, because `[^0-9]` doesn't match an empty word.)

NOTE You can use the `last` statement with a single-line conditional statement. For example,

```
last if ($count == 5);
```

terminates the loop if the value of `$count` is 5.

WARNING You cannot use the `last` statement inside the `do` statement. Although the `do` statement behaves like the other control structures, it is actually implemented differently.

Using next to Start the Next Iteration of a Loop

In Perl, the last statement terminates the execution of a loop. To terminate a particular iteration of a loop, use the next statement.

Like last, the syntax for the next statement is simple:

```
next;
```

Listing 8.10 is an example that uses the next statement. It sums up the numbers from 1 to a user-specified upper limit and also produces a separate sum of the numbers divisible by 2.

Listing 8.10. A program that sums the numbers from 1 to a specified number and also sums the even numbers.

```
1:  #!/usr/local/bin/perl
2:
3:  print ("Enter the last number in the sum:\n");
4:  $limit = <STDIN>;
5:  chop ($limit);
6:  $count = 1;
7:  $total = $eventotal = 0;
8:  for ($count = 1; $count <= $limit; $count++) {
9:          $total += $count;
10:         if ($count % 2 == 1) {
11:                 # start the next iteration if the number is odd
12:                 next;
13:         }
14:         $eventotal += $count;
15: }
16: print("The sum of the numbers 1 to $limit is $total\n");
17: print("The sum of the even numbers is $eventotal\n");
```

OUTPUT

```
$ program8_10
Enter the last number in the sum:
7
The sum of the numbers 1 to 7 is 28
The sum of the even numbers is 12
$
```

ANALYSIS The loop in lines 8–15 adds the numbers together. The start of the for statement in line 8 loops five times; the counter variable, $count, is assigned the values 1, 2, 3, 4, and 5 in successive iterations.

Line 9 adds to the total of all the numbers. This statement is always executed.

Line 10 tests whether the current number—the current value of $count—is even or odd. If $count is even, the conditional expression

```
$count % 2 == 1
```

is false, and program execution continues with line 14. If the current value of $count is odd, the Perl interpreter executes line 12, the next statement. This statement tells the Perl interpreter to start the next iteration of the loop.

Note that the loop iterator in the for statement, $count++, is still executed, even though the next statement skips over part of the loop. This ensures that the program does not go into an infinite loop.

Because the next statement is executed when the value of $count is odd, line 14 is skipped in this case. This means that the value of $count is added only when it is even.

WARNING

Be careful when you use next in a while or until loop. The following example goes into an infinite loop:
```
$count = 0;
while ($count <= 10) {
        if ($count == 5) {
                next;
        }
        $count++;
}
```

When $count is 5, the program tells Perl to start the next iteration of the loop. However, the value of $count is not changed, which means that the expression $count == 5 is still true.

To get rid of this problem, you need to increment $count before using next, as in the following:
```
$count = 0;
while ($count <= 10) {
        if ($count == 5) {
                $count++;
                next;
        }
        $count++;
}
```

This, by the way, is why many programming purists dislike statements such as next and last—it's too easy to lose track of where you are and what needs to be updated.

The next statement enables you to check for and ignore unusual conditions when reading input. For example, Listing 8.11 counts the number of words in the input read from the standard input file. It uses the next statement to skip blank lines.

Listing 8.11. A word-counting program that uses the next statement.

```
 1:  #!/usr/local/bin/perl
 2:
 3:  $total = 0;
 4:  while ($line = <STDIN>) {
 5:          $line =~ s/^[\t ]*//;
 6:          $line =~ s/[\t ]*\n$//;
 7:          next if ($line eq "");
 8:          @words = split(/[\t ]+/, $line);
 9:          $total += @words;
10:  }
11:  print ("The total number of words is $total\n");
```

OUTPUT
```
$ program8_11
 Here is my test input.

It contains some words.
^D
The total number of words is 9
$
```

ANALYSIS After line 4 has read a line of input and checked that it is not empty (which means that the end of file has not been reached), the program then gets rid of leading spaces and tabs (line 5) and trailing spaces, tabs, and the trailing newline (line 6). If a line is blank, lines 5 and 6 turn it into the empty string, for which line 7 tests.

Line 7 contains the next statement as part of a single-line conditional statement. If the line is now empty, the next statement tells the program to go to the beginning of the loop and read in the next line of input.

WARNING

> You cannot use the next statement inside the do statement. Although the do statement behaves like the other control structures, it is actually implemented differently.

8

The redo **Statement**

Perl enables you to tell the Perl interpreter to restart an iteration of a loop using the redo statement.

SYNTAX

Like last and next, the syntax for the redo statement is simple:

```
redo;
```

For an example, look at Listing 8.12, which counts the number of words in three non-blank input lines.

Listing 8.12. A word-counting program that uses the redo statement.

TYPE

```
1:  #!/usr/local/bin/perl
2:
3:  $total = 0;
4:  for ($count = 1; $count <= 3; $count++) {
5:          $line = <STDIN>;
6:          last if ($line eq "");
7:          $line =~ s/^[\t ]*//;
8:          $line =~ s/[\t ]*\n$//;
9:          redo if ($line eq "");
10:         @words = split(/[\t ]+/, $line);
11:         $total += @words;
12: }
13: print ("The total number of words is $total\n");
```

OUTPUT

```
$ program8_12
 Here is my test input.

It contains some words.
^D
The total number of words is 9
$
```

ANALYSIS Line 5 reads a line of input from the standard input file. If this line is empty, the conditional expression in line 6 is true, and the last statement exits the loop. (This ensures that the program behaves properly when there are less than three lines of input.)

Line 7 removes the leading blanks and tabs from this line of input, and line 8 removes the trailing white space. If the resulting line is now empty, the line must originally have been blank. Because this program does not want to include a blank line as one of the three lines in which to count words, line 9 invokes the redo statement, which tells the program to start this loop over. The program returns to line 4, the for statement, but does not increment the value of $count.

WARNING

> You cannot use the redo statement inside the do statement. Although the do statement behaves like the other control structures, it is actually implemented differently.

Note that the redo statement is not recommended, because it is too easy to lose track of how many times a program goes through a loop. For example, in Listing 8.12, a quick glance at the for statement in line 4 seems to indicate that the program only loops three times; however, the redo statement might change that.

Listing 8.13 shows an alternative way to solve this problem.

TYPE

Listing 8.13. A program that counts the words in three non-blank lines of input without using the redo statement.

```
1:  #!/usr/local/bin/perl
2:
3:  $nonblanklines = 0;
4:  while (1) {
5:          $line = <STDIN>;
6:          last if ($line eq "");
7:          $line =~ s/^[\t ]*//;
8:          $line =~ s/[\t ]*\n$//;
9:          if ($line ne "") {
10:                 $nonblanklines += 1;
11:                 @words = split(/[\t ]+/, $line);
12:                 $total += @words;
13:         }
14:         last if ($nonblanklines == 3);
15: };
16: print ("The total number of words is $total\n");
```

OUTPUT

```
$ program8_13
 Here is my test input.

It contains some words.
^D
The total number of words is 9.
$
```

ANALYSIS   This program is identical to the previous one, but it is much easier to understand. It uses a more meaningful variable name—$nonblanklines—which implies that blank lines are a special case.

As in Listing 8.12, if the line is a blank line, lines 7 and 8 turn it into an empty line by removing all white space. When this happens, the condition in line 10 fails, and $nonblanklines is not incremented.

Using Labeled Blocks for Multilevel Jumps

As you've seen, the last, next, and redo statements enable you to exit a loop from anywhere inside its statement block, as follows:

```
while (1) {
        $line = <STDIN>;
        last if ($line eq "");
}
```

If the loop is inside another loop, the last, next, and redo statements quit the inner loop only; for example:

```
while ($line1 = <FILE1>) {
        while ($line2 = <FILE2>) {
                last if ($line2 eq "") {
        }
}
```

Here, the last statement only quits the inner while loop. The outer while loop, which reads from the file represented by FILE1, continues executing.

To quit from more than one loop at once, do the following:

1. Assign a label to the outer loop (the one from which you want to quit).
2. When you use last, next, or redo, specify the label you just assigned.

Listing 8.14 shows an example of a last statement that specifies a label.

TYPE **Listing 8.14. A program that uses a label.**

```
 1:  #!/usr/local/bin/perl
 2:
 3:  $total = 0;
 4:  $firstcounter = 0;
 5:  DONE: while ($firstcounter < 10) {
 6:          $secondcounter = 1;
 7:          while ($secondcounter <= 10) {
 8:                  $total++;
 9:                  if ($firstcounter == 4 && $secondcounter == 7) {
10:                          last DONE;
11:                  }
12:                  $secondcounter++;
13:          }
14:          $firstcounter++;
15: }
16: print ("$total\n");
```

$ program8_14
47
$

 ANALYSIS   The outer `while` loop starting in line 5 has the label DONE assigned to it. This label consists of an alphabetic character followed by one or more alphanumeric characters or underscores. The colon (:) character following the label indicates that the label is assigned to the following statement (in this case, the `while` statement).

When the conditional expression in line 9 is true, line 10 is executed. This statement tells the Perl interpreter to jump out of the loop labeled DONE and continue execution with the first statement after this loop. (By the way, this code fragment is just a rather complicated way of assigning 47 to $total.)

WARNING

Make sure that you do not use a label which has another meaning in Perl. For example, the statement

```
if: while ($x == 0) {     # this is an error in Perl
}
```

is flagged as erroneous, because the Perl interpreter doesn't realize that the `if` is not the start of an `if` statement.

You can avoid this problem by using uppercase letters for label names (such as DONE).

Note that labels can be identical to file variable names:

```
FILE1: while ($line = <FILE1>) {
...
}
```

The Perl interpreter has no problem distinguishing the label FILE1 from the file variable FILE1, because it is always possible to determine which is which from the context.

Using next and redo with Labels

You can use `next` and `redo` with labels as well, as shown in the following example:

```
next LABEL;
redo LABEL;
```

This `next` statement indicates that the next iteration of the loop labeled LABEL is to be executed. This `redo` statement indicates that the current iteration of the loop labeled LABEL is to be restarted.

The `continue` **Block**

In a `for` statement, the expression following the second semicolon is executed each time the end of the loop is reached or whenever a `next` statement is executed. For example:

```
for ($i = 1; $i <= 10; $i++) {
        print ("$i\n");
}
```

In this example, the expression `$i++`, which adds 1 to `$i`, is executed after the `print` function is called.

Similarly, you can define statements that are to be executed whenever the end of a `while` loop or an `until` loop is reached. To carry out this task, specify a `continue` statement after the loop.

```
$i = 1;
while ($i <= 10) {
        print ("$i\n");
}
continue {
        $i++;
}
```

A `continue` statement must be followed by a statement block, which is a collection of zero or more statements enclosed in brace characters. This statement block contains the statements to be executed at the bottom of each loop. In this example, the statement

```
$i++;
```

is executed after each call to `print`. This `while` loop therefore behaves like the `for` loop you've just seen.

The `continue` statement is executed even if a pass through the loop is prematurely ended by a `next` statement. It is not executed, however, if the loop is terminated by a `last` statement.

TIP Usually, it is better to use a `for` statement than to use `continue` with a `while` or an `until` statement, because the `for` statement is easier to follow.

The `goto` **Statement**

For the sake of completeness, Perl provides a `goto` statement.

The syntax of the goto statement is

```
goto label;
```

label is a label associated with a statement, as defined in the earlier section, "Using Labeled Blocks for Multilevel Jumps." The statement to which *label* is assigned cannot be in the middle of a do statement or inside a subroutine. (You'll learn about subroutines on Day 9.)

Listing 8.15 is an example of a simple program that uses goto.

 Listing 8.15. A program that uses the goto statement.

```
1:  #!/usr/local/bin/perl
2:
3:  NEXTLINE: $line = <STDIN>;
4:  if ($line ne "") {
5:          print ($line);
6:          goto NEXTLINE;
7:  }
```

OUTPUT

```
$ program8_15
Here is a line of input.
Here is a line of input.
^D
$
```

ANALYSIS This program just reads and writes lines of input until the standard input file is exhausted. If the line read into $line is not empty, line 6 tells the Perl interpreter to jump back to the line to which the NEXTLINE label is assigned, which is line 3.

Note that lines 3–7 are equivalent to the following statement:

```
print ($line) while ($line = <STDIN>);
```

 TIP There is almost never any need to use the goto statement. In fact, using goto often makes it more difficult to follow the logic of the program. For this reason, using goto is not recommended.

Summary

Today you learned about the more complex control structures supported in Perl.

Single-line conditional statements enable you to put a conditional expression on the same line as the statement to be executed if the condition is satisfied. This enables you to write more concise programs.

The `for` statement enables you to put the loop initializer, the loop iterator, and the conditional expression together on the same line. This makes it more difficult to write code that goes into an infinite loop.

The `foreach` statement enables a program to loop based on the contents of a list. When the loop is first executed, the first element in the list is assigned to a local scalar variable that is only defined for the duration of the loop. Subsequent iterations of the loop assign subsequent elements of the list to this local scalar variable.

The `do` statement enables you to write a loop that executes at least once. Its terminating conditional expression appears at the bottom of the loop, not the top.

The `last` statement tells the Perl interpreter to exit the loop and continue execution with the first statement after the loop. The `next` statement tells the Perl interpreter to skip the rest of this iteration of a loop and start with the next one. The `redo` statement tells the Perl interpreter to restart this iteration of a loop. `last`, `next`, and `redo` cannot be used with the `do` statement.

You can assign a label to a statement, which enables you to use `last`, `next`, and `redo` to exit or restart an outer loop from inside an inner loop.

The `continue` statement enables you to define code to be executed each time a loop iterates.

The `goto` statement enables you to jump to any labeled statement in your program.

Q&A

Q **Which control structure is the best one to use as a loop?**

A It depends on what you want to do.

☐ The `foreach` structure is the best way to perform operations on every element of a list.

☐ The `for` statement is the best way to perform an operation a set number of times.

☐ The `while` statement is the best way to perform a loop until a particular condition occurs.

☐ The `do` statement is useful if you want to perform a loop at least once. (However, it is not as useful as the others, because you cannot use `last`, `next`, or `redo` with it.)

Q **Why does Perl bother with the *next*, *last*, and *redo* statements, when the *if-elsif-else* structure can do the job just as well?**

A The `last` and `next` statements are ideal for loops that check for exceptional conditions. For example:

```
for ($count = 1; $count <= 3; $count++) {
        $line = <STDIN>;
        last if ($line eq "");
```

```
$line =~ s/^[\t ]+//;
$line =~ s/[\t ]+\n$//;
@words = split(/[\t ]+/, $line);
$total += @words;
}
```

If the last statement did not exist, the only way to implement this would be with another level of nesting and another condition in the for statement, as follows:

```
for ($count = 1; $count <= 3 && $line ne ""; $count++) {
        $line = <STDIN>;
        if ($line ne "") {
                $line =~ s/^[\t ]+//;
                $line =~ s/[\t ]+\n$//;
                @words = split(/[\t ]+/, $line);
                $total += @words;
        }
}
```

If your program has to check for several exceptional conditions, you might need several levels of if statements to handle them unless you use next or last.

On the other hand, the redo statement should be avoided whenever possible, because it is difficult to follow program logic when it is used.

Q Is the goto statement ever the best way to solve a problem?

A Almost never. Avoid using the goto statement if at all possible.

Q Why is the conditional expression last in single-line conditional statements?

A This is to avoid a problem found in the C programming language. In C, you don't need to put braces around the statement block in a conditional statement if the block consists of only one line. For example, the following is legal:

```
if (x == 0)
        printf ("x is zero\n");
```

With this syntax, it is easy to accidentally forget to add the braces when you add another statement to the statement block, as follows:

```
if (x == 0)
        printf ("x is zero\n");
        printf ("this statement is always printed\n");
```

If you glance at this code quickly, you might think that the second call to printf is executed only if x is 0. However, this code is really

```
if (x == 0)
        printf ("x is zero\n");
printf ("this statement is always printed\n");
```

In Perl, this problem does not exist because the only way to write the first statement is

```
print ("x is zero\n") if (x == 0);
```

Q Is a `continue` block executed if a `redo` statement restarts the loop?

A No. The `continue` block is executed only when an iteration of a loop is successfully completed (by reaching the bottom of a loop or a `next` statement).

Workshop

The Workshop provides quiz questions to help you solidify your understanding of the material covered and exercises to give you experience in using what you've learned. Try and understand the quiz and exercise answers before you go on to tomorrow's lesson.

Quiz

1. How many times does the following loop iterate?

```
for ($count = 0; $count < 7; $count++) {
        print ("$count\n");
}
```

2. How many times does the following loop iterate?

```
$count = 1;
do {
        print ("$count\n");
} until ($count++ > 10);
```

3. How many times does the following loop iterate?

```
for ($count = 1; $count <= 10; $count++) {
        last if ($count == 5);
}
```

4. How many times does the following loop iterate?

```
$restart = 0;
for ($count = 1; $count <= 5; $count++) {
        redo if ($restart++ == 1);
}
```

5. Write a single-line conditional statement that quits a loop if $x equals `done`.

6. Write a single-line conditional statement that restarts a loop if the first element of the list @list is 26.

7. Write a single-line conditional statement that goes to the next iteration of the loop labeled LABEL if $scalar equals #.

8. Write a single-line conditional statement that prints the digits from 1 to 10. (Use a scalar variable, and assume that it has not been previously defined.)

9. What does the `continue` statement do?

Exercises

1. Write a program that uses the do statement to print the numbers from 1 to 10.

2. Write a program that uses the for statement to print the numbers from 1 to 10.

3. Write a program that uses a loop to read and write five lines of input. Use the last statement to exit the loop if there are less than five lines to read.

4. Write a program that loops through the numbers 1 to 20, printing the even-numbered values. Use the next statement to skip over the odd-numbered values.

5. Write a program that uses the foreach statement to check each word in the standard input file. Print the line numbers of all occurrences of the word the (in uppercase, lowercase, or mixed case).

6. Write a program that uses a while loop and a continue statement to print the integers from 10 down to 1.

7. **BUG BUSTER:** What is wrong with the following code?

```
$count = 1;
do {
        print ("$count\n");
        last if ($count == 10);
        $count++;
} while (1);
```

8

Day 9

Using Subroutines

Today's lesson shows you how to use subroutines to divide your program into smaller, more manageable modules. Today, you learn about the following:

- [ ] What a subroutine is
- [ ] How to define subroutines
- [ ] How to invoke subroutines
- [ ] How to return a value from a subroutine
- [ ] How to use the return statement
- [ ] How to use local variables in subroutines
- [ ] How to pass arguments to subroutines
- [ ] How to call subroutines from other subroutines
- [ ] The meaning of recursive subroutines
- [ ] How to pass arrays by name in subroutines using aliasing
- [ ] How to use the do statement with subroutines
- [ ] How to use subroutines to change the sort order used by sort

☐ How to provide startup and termination code using BEGIN and END

☐ How to use AUTOLOAD

What Is a Subroutine?

In Perl, a *subroutine* is a separate body of code designed to perform a particular task. A Perl program executes this body of code by calling or invoking the subroutine; the act of invoking a subroutine is called a *subroutine invocation*.

Subroutines serve two useful purposes:

☐ They break down your program into smaller parts, making it easier to read and understand.

☐ They enable you to use one piece of code to perform the same task multiple times, eliminating needless duplication.

Defining and Invoking a Subroutine

Listing 9.1 shows how a subroutine works. This program calls a subroutine that reads a line from the standard input file and breaks it into numbers. The program then adds the numbers together.

 Listing 9.1. A program that uses a subroutine.

```
1:  #!/usr/local/bin/perl
2:
3:  $total = 0;
4:  &getnumbers;
5:  foreach $number (@numbers) {
6:          $total += $number;
7:  }
8:  print ("the total is $total\n");
9:
10: sub getnumbers {
11:          $line = <STDIN>;
12:          $line =~ s/^\s+|\s*\n$//g;
13:          @numbers = split(/\s+/, $line);
14: }
```

OUTPUT
```
$ program9_1
11 8 16 4
the total is 39
$
```

ANALYSIS Lines 10–14 are an example of a subroutine. The keyword `sub` tells the Perl interpreter that this is a subroutine definition. The `getnumbers` immediately following `sub` is the name of the subroutine; the Perl program uses this name when invoking the subroutine.

The program starts execution in the normal way, beginning with line 3. Line 4 invokes the subroutine `getnumbers`; the `&` character tells the Perl interpreter that the following name is the name of a subroutine. (This ensures that the Perl interpreter does not confuse subroutine names with the names of scalar or array variables.)

The Perl interpreter executes line 4 by jumping to the first executable statement inside the subroutine, which is line 11. The interpreter then executes lines 11–13.

Lines 11–13 create the array `@numbers` as follows:

☐ Line 11 reads a line of input from the standard input file.

☐ Line 12 removes the leading and trailing white space (including the trailing newline) from the input line.

☐ Line 13 then breaks the input line into numbers and assigns the resulting list of numbers to `@numbers`.

After line 13 is finished, the Perl interpreter jumps back to the main program and executes the line immediately following the subroutine call, which is line 5.

Lines 5–7 add the numbers together by using the `foreach` statement to loop through the list stored in `@numbers`. (Note that this program does not check whether a particular element of `@numbers` actually consists of digits. Because character strings that are not digits are converted to 0 in expressions, this isn't a significant problem.)

SYNTAX The syntax for a subroutine definition is

```
sub subname {
        statement_block
}
```

`subname` is a placeholder for the name of the subroutine. Like all Perl names, `subname` consists of an alphabetic character followed by one or more letters, digits, or underscores.

`statement_block` is the body of the subroutine and consists of one or more Perl statements. Any statement that can appear in the main part of a Perl program can appear in a subroutine.

NOTE The Perl interpreter never confuses a subroutine name with a scalar variable name or any other name, because it can always tell from the context which name you are referring to. This means that you can have a subroutine and a scalar variable with the same name. For example:

```
$word = 0;
&word;
```

Here, when the Perl interpreter sees the & character in the second statement, it realizes that the second statement is calling the subroutine named word.

WARNING

When you are defining names for your subroutines, it's best not to use a name belonging to a built-in Perl function that you plan to use.

For example, you could, if you want, define a subroutine named split. The Perl interpreter can always distinguish an invocation of the subroutine split from an invocation of the library function split, because the name of the subroutine is preceded by an & when it is invoked, as follows:

```
@words = &split(1, 2);      # subroutine
@words = split(/\s+/, $line); # library function
```

However, it's easy to leave off the & by mistake (especially if you are used to programming in C, where subroutine calls do not start with an &). To avoid such problems, use subroutine names that don't correspond to the names of library functions.

Perl subroutines can appear anywhere in a program, even in the middle of a conditional statement. For example, Listing 9.2 is a perfectly legal Perl program.

TYPE

Listing 9.2. A program containing a subroutine in the middle of the main program.

```
1:  #!/usr/local/bin/perl
2:
3:  while (1) {
4:          &readaline;
5:          last if ($line eq "");
6:          sub readaline {
7:                  $line = <STDIN>;
8:          }
9:          print ($line);
```

```
10: }
11: print ("done\n");
```

OUTPUT
```
$ program9_2
Here is a line of input.
Here is a line of input.
^D
done
$
```

ANALYSIS This program just reads lines of input from the standard input file and writes them straight back out to the standard output file.

Line 4 calls the subroutine `readaline`. When you examine this subroutine, which is contained in lines 6–8, you can see that it reads a line of input and assigns it to the scalar variable `$line`.

When `readaline` is finished, program execution continues with line 5. When line 5 is executed, the program skips over the subroutine definition and continues with line 9. The code inside the subroutine is never directly executed, even if it appears in the middle of a program; lines 6–8 can be executed only by a subroutine invocation, such as that found in line 4.

TIP | Although subroutines can appear anywhere in a program, it usually is best to put all your subroutines at either the beginning of the program or the end. Following this practice makes your programs easier to read.

Forward References to Subroutines

As you have seen, the Perl interpreter uses the `&` character to indicate that a subroutine is being specified in a statement. In Perl 5, you do not need to supply an `&` character when calling a subroutine if you have already defined the subroutine.

```
sub readaline {
        $line = <STDIN>;
}
...
readaline;
```

Because the Perl interpreter already knows that `readaline` is a subroutine, you don't need to specify the `&` when calling it.

If you prefer to list all your subroutines at the end of your program, you can still omit the &
character provided you supply a forward reference for your subroutine, as shown in the
following:

```
sub readaline;   # forward reference
...
readaline;
...
sub readaline {
        $line = <STDIN>;
}
```

The forward reference tells the Perl interpreter that readaline is the name of a subroutine.
This means that you no longer need to supply the & when you call readaline.

WARNING

> Occasionally, calling a subroutine without specifying the & character
> might not behave the way you expect. If your program is behaving
> strangely, or you are not sure whether or not to use the & character,
> supply the & character with your call.

Returning a Value from a Subroutine

Take another look at the getnumbers subroutine from Listing 9.1.

```
sub getnumbers {
        $line = <STDIN>;
        $line =~ s/^\s+¦\s*\n$//g;
        @numbers = split(/\s+/, $temp);
}
```

Although this subroutine is useful, it suffers from one serious limitation: it overwrites any
existing list stored in the array variable @numbers (as well as any value stored in $line or $temp).
This overwriting can lead to problems. For example, consider the following:

```
@numbers = ("the", "a", "an");
&getnumbers;
print ("The value of \@numbers is: @numbers\n");
```

When the subroutine getnumbers is invoked, the value of @numbers is overwritten. If you just
examine this portion of the program, it is not obvious that this is what is happening.

To get around this problem, you can employ a useful property of subroutines in Perl: The
value of the last expression evaluated by the subroutine is automatically considered to be the
subroutine's *return value*.

For example, in the subroutine getnumbers from Listing 9.1, the last expression evaluated is

```
@numbers = split(/\s+/, $temp);
```

The value of this expression is the list of numbers obtained by splitting the line of input. This means that this list of numbers is the return value for the subroutine.

To see how to use a subroutine return value, look at Listing 9.3, which modifies the word-counting program to use the return value from the subroutine getnumbers.

TYPE **Listing 9.3. A program that uses a subroutine return value.**

```
 1:  #!/usr/local/bin/perl
 2:
 3:  $total = 0;
 4:  @numbers = &getnumbers;
 5:  foreach $number (@numbers) {
 6:          $total += $number;
 7:  }
 8:  print ("the total is $total\n");
 9:
10:  sub getnumbers {
11:          $line = <STDIN>;
12:          $line =~ s/^\s+¦\s*\n$//g;
13:          split(/\s+/, $line);     # this is the return value
14:  }
```

OUTPUT
```
$ program9_3
11 8 16 4
the total is 39
$
```

ANALYSIS Line 4, once again, calls the subroutine getnumbers. As before, the array variable @numbers is assigned the list of numbers read from the standard input file; however, in this program, the assignment is in the main body of the program, not in the subroutine. This makes the program easier to read.

The only other difference between this program and Listing 9.1 is that the call to split in line 13 no longer assigns anything to @numbers. In fact, it doesn't assign the list returned by split to any variable at all, because it does not need to. Line 13 is the last expression evaluated in getnumbers, so it automatically becomes the return value from getnumbers. Therefore, when line 4 calls getnumbers, the list returned by split is assigned to the array variable @numbers.

NOTE

If the idea of evaluating an expression without assigning it confuses you, there's nothing wrong with creating a variable inside the subroutine just for the purpose of containing the return value. For example:

```
sub getnumbers {
        $line = <STDIN>;
```

```
$line =~ s/^\s+¦\s*\n$//g;
@retval = split(/\s+/, $temp); # the return value
}
```

Here, it is obvious that the return value is the contents of @retval.

The only drawback to doing this is that assigning the list returned by split to @retval is slightly less efficient. In larger programs, such efficiency costs are worth it, because subroutines become much more comprehensible.

Using a special return variable also eliminates an entire class of errors, which you will see in "Return Values and Conditional Expressions," later today.

You can use a return value of a subroutine any place an expression is expected. For example:

```
foreach $number (&getnumbers) {
        print ("$number\n");
}
```

This foreach statement iterates on the list of numbers returned by getnumbers. Each element of the list is assigned to $number in turn, which means that this loop prints all the numbers in the list, each on its own line.

Listing 9.4 shows another example that uses the return value of a subroutine in an expression. This time, the return value is used as an array subscript.

Listing 9.4. A program that uses a return value as an array subscript.

TYPE

```
 1:  #!/usr/local/bin/perl
 2:
 3:  srand();
 4:  print ("Random number tester.\n");
 5:  for ($count = 1; $count <= 100; $count++) {
 6:          $randnum[&intrand] += 1;
 7:  }
 8:  print ("Totals for the digits 0 through 9:\n");
 9:  print ("@randnum\n");
10:
11:  sub intrand {
12:          $num = int(rand(10));
13:  }
```

OUTPUT

```
$ progam9_4
Random number tester.
Totals for the digits 0 through 9:
10 9 11 10 8 8 12 11 9 12
$
```

ANALYSIS This program uses the following three built-in functions:

srand Initializes the built-in random-number generator

rand   Generates a random (non-integral) number greater than zero and less than
       the value passed to it

int   Gets rid of the non-integer portion of a number

The subroutine intrand first calls rand to get a random number greater than 0 and less than
10. The return value from rand is passed to int to remove the fractional portion of the
number; this means, for example, that 4.77135 becomes 4. This number becomes the return
value returned by intrand.

Line 6 calls intrand. The return value from intrand, an integer between 0 and 9, serves as
the subscript into the array variable randnum. If the return value from intrand is 7,
$randnum[7] has its value increased by one.

As a consequence, at any given time, the *n*th value of @randnum contains the number of
occurrences of *n* as a random number.

Line 9 prints out the number of occurrences of each of the 10 numbers. Each number should
occur approximately the same number of times (although not necessarily exactly the same
number of times).

Return Values and Conditional Expressions

Because the return value of a subroutine is always the last expression evaluated, the return
value might not always be what you expect.

Consider the simple program in Listing 9.5. This program, like the one in Listing 9.3, reads
an input line, breaks it into numbers, and adds the numbers. This program, however,
attempts to do all the work inside the subroutine get_total.

TYPE

**Listing 9.5. A program illustrating a potential problem with
return values from subroutines.**

```
1:  #!/usr/local/bin/perl
2:
```

continues

Listing 9.5. continued

```
 3:  $total = &get_total;
 4:  print("The total is $total\n");
 5:
 6:  sub get_total {
 7:          $value = 0;
 8:          $inputline = <STDIN>;
 9:          $inputline =~ s/^\s+¦\s*\n$//g;
10:          @subwords = split(/\s+/, $inputline);
11:          $index = 0;
12:          while ($subwords[$index] ne "") {
13:                  $value += $subwords[$index++];
14:          }
15:  }
```

```
$ program9_5
11 8 16 4
the total is
$
```

 ANALYSIS   Clearly, this program is supposed to assign the contents of the scalar variable $value to the scalar variable $total. However, when line 4 tries to print the total, you see that the value of $total is actually the empty string. What has happened?

The problem is in the subroutine get_total. In get_total, as in all other subroutines, the return value is the value of the last expression evaluated. However, in get_total, the last expression evaluated is not the last expression in the program.

The last expression to be evaluated in get_total is the conditional expression in line 12, which is

```
$subwords[$index] ne ""
```

The loop in lines 12–14 iterates until the value of this expression is 0. When the value of this expression is 0, the loop terminates and the subroutine terminates. This means that the value of the last expression evaluated in the subroutine is 0 and that the return value of the subroutine is 0. Because 0 is treated as the null string by print (0 and the null string are equivalent in Perl), line 4 prints the following, which isn't what the program is supposed to do:

```
the total is
```

Listing 9.6 shows how you can get around this problem.

TYPE

Listing 9.6. A program that corrects the problem that occurs in Listing 9.5.

```perl
1:  #!/usr/local/bin/perl
2:
3:  $total = &get_total;
4:  print("The total is $total.\n");
5:  sub get_total {
6:          $value = 0;
7:          $inputline = <STDIN>;
8:          $inputline =~ s/^\s+|\s*\n$//g;
9:          @subwords = split(/\s+/, $inputline);
10:         $index = 0;
11:         while ($subwords[$index] ne "") {
12:                 $value += $subwords[$index++];
13:         }
14:         $retval = $value;
15: }
```

9

OUTPUT

```
$ program9_6
11 8 16 4
the total is 39.
$
```

ANALYSIS   This program is identical to Listing 9.5 except for one difference: line 15 has been added. This line assigns the total stored in $value to the scalar variable $retval.

Line 15 ensures that the value of the last expression evaluated in the subroutine get_total is, in fact, the total which is supposed to become the return value. This means that line 3 now assigns the correct total to $total, which in turn means that line 4 now prints the correct result.

Note that you don't really need to assign to $retval. The subroutine get_total can just as easily be the following:

```perl
sub get_total {
        $value = 0;
        $inputline = <STDIN>;
        $inputline =~ s/^\s+|\s*\n$//g;
        @subwords = split(/\s+/, $inputline);
        $index = 0;
        while ($subwords[$index] ne "") {
                $value += $subwords[$index++];
        }
        $value;
}
```

Here, the final expression evaluated by the subroutine is simply $value. The value of this expression is the current value stored in $value, which is the sum of the numbers in the line.

TIP Subroutines, such as get_total in Listing 9.6, which assign their return value at the very end are known as *single-exit modules*.

Single-exit modules avoid problems like those you saw in Listing 9.5, and they usually are much easier to read. For these reasons, it is a good idea to assign to the return value at the very end of the subroutine, unless there are overwhelming reasons not to do so.

The return **Statement**

Another way to ensure that the return value from a subroutine is the value you want is to use the return statement.

The syntax for the return statement is

```
return (retval);
```

retval is the value you want your subroutine to return. It can be either a scalar value (including the result of an expression) or a list.

Listing 9.7 provides an example of the use of the return statement.

TYPE **Listing 9.7. A program that uses the return statement.**

```
1:  #!/usr/local/bin/perl
2:
3:  $total = &get_total;
4:  if ($total eq "error") {
5:          print ("No input supplied.\n");
6:  } else {
7:          print("The total is $total.\n");
8:  }
9:
10: sub get_total {
11:         $value = 0;
12:         $inputline = <STDIN>;
13:         $inputline =~ s/^\s+|\s*\n$//g;
14:         if ($inputline eq "") {
15:                 return ("error");
16:         }
17:         @subwords = split(/\s+/, $inputline);
18:         $index = 0;
19:         while ($subwords[$index] ne "") {
20:                 $value += $subwords[$index++];
21:         }
22:         $retval = $value;
23: }
```

OUTPUT

```
$ program9_7
^D
No input supplied.
$
```

ANALYSIS This program is similar to the one in Listing 9.6. The only difference is that this program checks whether an input line exists.

If the input line does not exist, the conditional expression in line 14 becomes true, and line 15 is executed. Line 15 exits the subroutine with the return value error; this means that error is assigned to $total in line 3.

This program shows why allowing scalar variables to store either numbers or character strings is useful. When the subroutine get_total detects the error, it can assign a value that is not an integer to $total, which makes it easier to determine that something has gone wrong. Other programming languages, which only enable you to assign either a number or a character string to a particular variable, do not offer this flexibility.

Using Local Variables in Subroutines

The subroutine get_total in Listing 9.7 defines several variables that are used only inside the subroutine: the array variable @subwords, and the four scalar variables $inputline, $value, $index, and $retval.

If you know for certain that these variables are going to be used only inside the subroutine, you can tell Perl to define these variables as *local variables*.

In Perl 5, there are two statements used to define local variables:

- [ ] The my statement, which defines variables that exist only inside a subroutine.
- [ ] The local statement, which defines variables that do not exist inside the main program, but inside the subroutine and any subroutines called by the subroutine. (Calling subroutines from other subroutines is discussed later today.)

In Perl 4, the my statement is not defined, so you must use local to define a variable that is not known to the main program.

Listing 9.8 shows how you can use my to define a variable that exists only inside a subroutine.

NOTE

If you are using Perl 4, replace my with local in all the remaining examples in this chapter. For example, in Listing 9.8, replace my with local in lines 13 and 14, which produces

```
local ($total, $inputline, @subwords);
local ($index, $retval);
```

In Perl, my and local behave identically and use the same syntax. The
only difference between them is that variables created using my are not
known outside the subroutine.

Listing 9.8. A program that uses local variables.

```
 1:  #!/usr/local/bin/perl
 2:
 3:  $total = 0;
 4:  while (1) {
 5:          $linetotal = &get_total;
 6:          last if ($linetotal eq "done");
 7:          print ("Total for this line: $linetotal\n");
 8:          $total += $linetotal;
 9:  }
10:  print ("Total for all lines: $total\n");
11:
12:  sub get_total {
13:          my ($total, $inputline, @subwords);
14:          my ($index, $retval);
15:          $total = 0;
16:          $inputline = <STDIN>;
17:          if ($inputline eq "") {
18:                  return ("done");
19:          }
20:          $inputline =~ s/^\s+¦\s*\n$//g;
21:          @subwords = split(/\s+/, $inputline);
22:          $index = 0;
23:          while ($subwords[$index] ne "") {
24:                  $total += $subwords[$index++];
25:          }
26:          $retval = $total;
27:  }
```

 OUTPUT
```
$ program9_8
11 8 16 4
Total for this line: 39
7 20 6 1
Total for this line: 34
^D
Total for all lines: 73
$
```

ANALYSIS   This program uses two copies of the scalar variable $total. One copy of $total is
defined in the main program and keeps a running total of all of the numbers in all
of the lines.

The scalar variable $total is also defined in the subroutine get_total; in this subroutine, $total refers to the total for a particular line, and line 13 defines it as a local variable. Because this copy of $total is only defined inside the subroutine, the copy of $total defined in the main program is not affected by line 15 (which assigns 0 to $total).

WARNING

Because a local variable is not known outside the subroutine, the local variable is destroyed when the subroutine is completed. If the subroutine is called again, a new copy of the local variable is defined.

This means that the following code does not work:

```
sub subroutine_count {
        my($number_of_calls);
        $number_of_calls += 1;
}
```

This subroutine does not return the number of times subroutine_count has been called. Because a new copy of $number_of_calls is defined every time the subroutine is called, $number_of_calls is always assigned the value 1.

Local variables can appear anywhere in a program, provided they are defined before they are used. It is good programming practice to put all your local definitions at the beginning of your subroutine.

Initializing Local Variables

If you want, you can assign a value to a local variable when you declare it. For example:

```
sub my_sub {
        my($scalar) = 43;
        my(@array) = ("here's", "a", "list");
        # code goes here
}
```

Here, the local scalar variable $scalar is given an initial value of 43, and the local array variable @array is initialized to contain the list ("here's", "a", "list").

Passing Values to a Subroutine

You can make your subroutines more flexible by allowing them to accept values passed from the main program; these values passed from the main program are known as *arguments*.

Listing 9.9 provides a very simple example of a subroutine that accepts three arguments.

Listing 9.9. A program that uses a subroutine to print three numbers and their total.

TYPE

```
 1:  #!/usr/local/bin/perl
 2:
 3:  print ("Enter three numbers, one at a time:\n");
 4:  $number1 = <STDIN>;
 5:  chop ($number1);
 6:  $number2 = <STDIN>;
 7:  chop ($number2);
 8:  $number3 = <STDIN>;
 9:  chop ($number3);
10:  &printnum ($number1, $number2, $number3);
11:
12:  sub printnum {
13:          my($number1, $number2, $number3) = @_;
14:          my($total);
15:          print ("The numbers you entered: ");
16:          print ("$number1 $number2 $number3\n");
17:          $total = $number1 + $number2 + $number3;
18:          print ("The total: $total\n");
19:  }
```

OUTPUT

```
$ program9_9
Enter three numbers, one at a time:
5
11
4
The numbers you entered: 5 11 4
The total: 20
$
```

ANALYSIS Line 10 calls the subroutine printnum. Three arguments are passed to printnum: the value stored in $number1, the value stored in $number2, and the value stored in $number3. Note that arguments are passed to subroutines in the same way they are passed to built-in library functions.

Line 13 defines local copies of the scalar variables $number1, $number2, and $number3. It then assigns the contents of the system variable @_ to these scalar variables. @_ is created whenever a subroutine is called with arguments; it contains a list consisting of the arguments in the order in which they are passed. In this case, printnum is called with arguments 5, 11, and 4, which means that @_ contains the list (5, 11, 4).

The assignment in line 13 assigns the list to the local scalar variables that have just been defined. This assignment works just like any other assignment of a list to a set of scalar variables. The first element of the list, 5, is assigned to the first variable, $number1; the second element of the list, 11, is assigned to $number2; and the final element, 4, is assigned to $number3.

NOTE

After the array variable @_ has been created, it can be used anywhere any other array variable can be used. This means that you do not need to assign its contents to local variables.

The following subroutine is equivalent to the subroutine in lines 12–19 of Listing 9.9:

```
sub printnum {
        my($total);
        print ("The numbers you entered: ");
        print ("$_[0] $_[1] $_[2]\n");
        $total = $_[0] + $_[1] + $_[2];
        print ("The total: $total\n");
}
```

Here, $_[0] refers to the first element of the array variable @_, $_[1] refers to the second element, and $_[2] refers to the third element.

This subroutine is a little more efficient, but it is harder to read.

TIP

It usually is better to define local variables and assign @_ to them because then your subroutines will be easier to understand.

Listing 9.10 is another example of a program that passes arguments to a subroutine. This program uses the same subroutine to count the number of words and the number of characters in a file.

TYPE **Listing 9.10. Another example of a subroutine with arguments passed to it.**

```
1:  #!/usr/local/bin/perl
2:
3:  $wordcount = $charcount = 0;
4:  $charpattern = "";
5:  $wordpattern = "\\s+";
6:  while ($line = <STDIN>) {
7:          $charcount += &count($line, $charpattern);
8:          $line =~ s/^\s+|\s+$//g;
9:          $wordcount += &count($line, $wordpattern);
10: }
11: print ("Totals: $wordcount words, $charcount characters\n");
12:
13: sub count {
14:         my ($line, $pattern) = @_;
```

continues

Listing 9.10. continued

```
15:         my ($count);
16:         if ($pattern eq "") {
17:                 @items = split (//, $line);
18:         } else {
19:                 @items = split (/$pattern/, $line);
20:         }
21:         $count = @items;
22: }
```

OUTPUT

```
$ program9_10
This is a line of input.
Here is another line.
^D
Totals: 10 words, 47 characters
$
```

ANALYSIS   This program reads lines from the standard input file until the file is exhausted. Each line has its characters counted and its words counted.

Line 7 determines the number of characters in a line by calling the subroutine count. This subroutine is passed the line of input and the string stored in $charpattern, which is the empty string. Inside the subroutine count, the local variable $pattern receives the pattern passed to it by the call in line 7. This means that the value stored in $pattern is also the empty string.

Lines 16–20 split the input line. The pattern specified in the call to split has the value stored in $pattern substituted into it. Because $pattern currently contains the empty string, the pattern used to split the line is //, which splits the input line into individual characters. As a result, each element of the resulting list stored in @items is a character in the input line.

The total number of elements in the list—in other words, the total number of characters in the input line—is assigned to $count by line 17. Because this is the last expression evaluated in the subroutine, the resulting total number of characters is returned by the subroutine. Line 8 adds this total to the scalar variable $charcount.

Line 8 then removes the leading and trailing white space; this white space is included in the total number of characters—because spaces, tabs, and the trailing newline character count as characters—but is not included when the line is broken into words.

Line 9 calls the subroutine count again, this time with the pattern stored in $wordpattern, which is \s+. (Recall that you need to use two backslashes in a string to represent a single backslash, because the \ character is the escape character in strings.) This value, representing one or more whitespace characters, is assigned to $pattern inside the subroutine, and the pattern passed to split therefore becomes /\s+/.

When split is called with this pattern, @items is assigned a list of words. The total number of words in the list is assigned to $count and is returned; line 11 adds this returned value to the total number of words.

Passing a List to a Subroutine

If you want, you can pass a list to a subroutine. For example, the following subroutine adds the elements of a list together and prints the result:

```
sub addlist {
        my (@list) = @_;
        $total = 0;
        foreach $item (@list) {
                $total += $item;
        }
        print ("The total is $total\n");
}
```

To invoke this subroutine, pass it an array variable, a list, or any combination of lists and scalar values.

```
&addlist (@mylist);
&addlist ("14", "6", "11");
&addlist ($value1, @sublist, $value2);
```

In each case, the values and lists supplied in the call to addlist are merged into a single list and then passed to the subroutine.

Because values are merged into a single list when a list is passed to a subroutine, you can only define one list as an argument for a subroutine. The subroutine

```
sub twolists {
        my (@list1, @list2) = @_;
}
```

isn't useful because it always assigns the empty list to @list2, and because @list1 absorbs all of the contents of @_.

This means that if you want to have both scalar variables and a list as arguments to a subroutine, the list must appear last, as follows:

```
sub twoargs {
        my ($scalar, @list) = @_;
}
```

If you call this subroutine using

```
&twoargs(47, @mylist);
```

the value 47 is assigned to $scalar, and @mylist is assigned to @list.

If you want, you can call `twoargs` with a single list, as follows:

```
&twoargs(@mylist);
```

Here, the first element of `@mylist` is assigned to `$scalar`, and the rest of `@mylist` is assigned to `@list`.

NOTE

> If you find this confusing, it might help to realize that passing arguments to a subroutine follows the same rules as assignment does. For example, you can have
>
> ```
> ($scalar, @list1) = @list2;
> ```
>
> because `$scalar` is assigned the first element of `@list2`. However, you can't have this:
>
> ```
> (@list1, $scalar) = @list2;
> ```
>
> because all of `@list1` would be assigned to `@list2` and `$scalar` would be assigned the null string.

Calling Subroutines from Other Subroutines

In Perl, you can call subroutines from other subroutines. To call a subroutine from another subroutine, use the same subroutine-invocation syntax you've been using all along. Subroutines that are called by other subroutines are known as *nested subroutines* (because one call is "nested" inside the other).

Listing 9.11 is an example of a program that contains a nested subroutine. It is a fairly simple modification of Listing 9.10 and counts the number of words and characters in three lines of standard input. It also demonstrates how to return multiple values from a subroutine.

TYPE   **Listing 9.11. An example of a nested subroutine.**

```
1:  #!/usr/local/bin/perl
2:
3:  ($wordcount, $charcount) = &getcounts(3);
4:  print ("Totals for three lines: ");
5:  print ("$wordcount words, $charcount characters\n");
6:
7:  sub getcounts {
```

```
 8:         my ($numlines) = @_;
 9:         my ($charpattern, $wordpattern);
10:         my ($charcount, $wordcount);
11:         my ($line, $linecount);
12:         my (@retval);
13:         $charpattern = "";
14:         $wordpattern = "\\s+";
15:         $linecount = $charcount = $wordcount = 0;
16:         while (1) {
17:                 $line = <STDIN>;
18:                 last if ($line eq "");
19:                 $linecount++;
20:                 $charcount += &count($line, $charpattern);
21:                 $line =~ s/^\s+|\s+$//g;
22:                 $wordcount += &count($line, $wordpattern);
23:                 last if ($linecount == $numlines);
24:         };
25:         @retval = ($wordcount, $charcount);
26: }
27:
28: sub count {
29:         my ($line, $pattern) = @_;
30:         my ($count);
31:         if ($pattern eq "") {
32:                 @items = split (//, $line);
33:         } else {
34:                 @items = split (/$pattern/, $line);
35:         }
36:         $count = @items;
37: }
```

OUTPUT

```
$ program9_11
This is a line of input.
Here is another line.
Here is the last line.
Totals for three lines: 15 words, 70 characters
$
```

ANALYSIS The main body of this program now consists of only five lines of code, including the special header comment and a blank line. This is because most of the actual work is being done inside the subroutines. (This is common in large programs. Most of these programs call a few main subroutines, which in turn call other subroutines. This approach makes programs easier to read, because each subroutine is compact and concise.)

Line 3 calls the subroutine getcounts, which retrieves the line and character count for the three lines from the standard input file. Because a list containing two elements is returned by getcounts, a standard "list to scalar variable" assignment can be used to assign the returned list directly to $wordcount and $charcount.

The subroutine getcounts is similar to the main body of the program in Listing 9.10. The only difference is that the while loop has been modified to loop only the number of times specified by the argument passed to getcounts, which is stored in the local variable $numlines.

The subroutine getcounts actually does the word and character counting by calling a nested subroutine, count. This subroutine is identical to the subroutine of the same name in Listing 9.10.

NOTE

> The @_ variable is a local variable that is defined inside the subroutine. When a subroutine calls a nested subroutine, a new copy of @_ is created for the nested subroutine.
>
> For example, in Listing 9.11, when getcounts calls count, a new copy of @_ is created for count, and the @_ variable in getcounts is not changed.

Recursive Subroutines

In Perl, not only can subroutines call other subroutines, but subroutines actually can call themselves. A subroutine that calls itself is known as a *recursive subroutine*.

You can use a subroutine as a recursive subroutine if the following two conditions are true:

☐ All variables the subroutine uses are local (except those which are not changed by the subroutine).

☐ The subroutine contains code that, one way or another, determines when it should stop calling itself.

When all the variables that a subroutine uses are local, the subroutine creates a new copy of the variables each time it calls itself. This ensures that there is no confusion or overlap.

Listing 9.12 is an example of a program that contains a recursive subroutine. This program accepts a list of numbers and operands that is to be evaluated from right to left, as if the list is a stack whose top is the left end of the list. For example, if the input is

```
-   955   *   26   +   11    8
```

this program adds 11 and 8, multiplies the result by 26, and subtracts that result from 955. This is equivalent to the following Perl expression:

```
955 - 26 * (11 + 8)
```

Listing 9.12. A program that uses a recursive subroutine to perform arithmetic.

TYPE

```
 1:  #!/usr/local/bin/perl
 2:
 3:  $inputline = <STDIN>;
 4:  $inputline =~ s/^\s+|\s+$//g;
 5:  @list = split (/\s+/, $inputline);
 6:  $result = &rightcalc (0);
 7:  print ("The result is $result.\n");
 8:
 9:  sub rightcalc {
10:          my ($index) = @_;
11:          my ($result, $operand1, $operand2);
12:
13:          if ($index+3 == @list) {
14:                  $operand2 = $list[$index+2];
15:          } else {
16:                  $operand2 = &rightcalc ($index+2);
17:          }
18:          $operand1 = $list[$index+1];
19:          if ($list[$index] eq "+") {
20:                  $result = $operand1 + $operand2;
21:          } elsif ($list[$index] eq "*") {
22:                  $result = $operand1 * $operand2;
23:          } elsif ($list[$index] eq "-") {
24:                  $result = $operand1 - $operand2;
25:          } else {
26:                  $result = $operand1 / $operand2;
27:          }
28: }
```

OUTPUT

```
$ program9_12
-    98 *   4 +   12   11
The result is 6.
$
```

ANALYSIS This program starts off by reading a line of input from the standard input file and breaking it into its components, which are stored as a list in the array variable @list.

When given the input

```
-    98 *   4 +   12   11
```

lines 3–5 produce the following list, which is assigned to @list:

```
("-", "98", "*", "4", "+", "12", "11")
```

Line 6 calls the subroutine rightcalc for the first time. rightcalc requires one argument, an index value that tells the subroutine what part of the list to work on. Because the first argument here is zero, rightcalc starts with the first element in the list.

Line 10 assigns the argument passed to `rightcalc` to the local variable `$index`. When `rightcalc` is called for the first time, `$index` is `0`.

Lines 13–17 are the heart of this subroutine, because they control whether to call `rightcalc` recursively. The basic logic is that a list such as

```
("-", "98", "*", "4", "+", "12", "11")
```

can be broken into three parts: the first operator, `-`; the first operand, `98`; and a sublist (the rest of the list). Note that the sublist

```
("*", "4", "+", "12", "11")
```

is itself a complete set of operators and operands; because this program is required to perform its arithmetic starting from the right, this sublist must be calculated first.

Line 13 checks whether there is a sublist that needs to be evaluated first. To do this, it checks whether there are more than three elements in the list. If there are only three elements in the list, the list consists of only one operator and two operands, and the arithmetic can be performed right away. If there are more than three elements in the list, a sublist exists.

To evaluate the sublist when it exists, line 16 calls `rightcalc` recursively. The index value passed to this second copy of `rightcalc` is `2`; this ensures that the first element of the list examined by the second copy of `rightcalc` is the element with subscript 2, which is `*`.

At this point, the following is the chain of subroutine invocations, their arguments, and the part of the list on which they are working:

        Level 1   Main program
        Level 2   `rightcalc(0)` — list `("-", "98", "*", "4", "+", "12", "11")`
        Level 3   `rightcalc(2)` — list `("*", "4", "+", "12", "11")`

When this copy of `rightcalc` reaches line 13, it checks whether the sublist being worked on has just three elements. Because this sublist has five elements, line 16 calls yet another copy of `rightcalc`, this time setting the value of `$index` to `4`. The following is the chain of subroutine invocations after this third call:

        Level 1   Main program
        Level 2   `rightcalc(0)` — list `("-", "98", "*", "4", "+", "12", "11")`
        Level 3   `rightcalc(2)` — list `("*", "4", "+", "12", "11")`
        Level 4   `rightcalc(4)` — list `("+", "12", "11")`

When the third copy of this subroutine reaches line 13, it checks whether this portion of the list contains only three elements. Because it does, the conditional expression in line 13 is true. At this point, line 14 is executed for the first time (by any copy of `rightcalc`); it takes the value stored in $index—in this case, 4, adds 2 to it, and uses the result as the subscript into @list. This assigns 11, the seventh element of @list, to $operand2.

Lines 18–27 perform an arithmetic operation. Line 18 adds one to the value in $index to retrieve the location of the first operand; this operand is assigned to $operand1. In this copy of rightcalc, the subscript is 5 (4+1), and the sixth element of @list, 12, is assigned to $operand1.

Line 19 uses $index as the subscript into the list to access the arithmetic operator for this operation. In this case, the fifth element of $index (subscript 4) is +, and the expression in line 19 is true. Line 20 then adds $operand1 to $operand2, yielding $result, which is 23. This value is returned by this copy of rightcalc.

When the third copy of rightcalc returns, execution continues with the second copy of rightcalc because the second copy called the third copy. Line 16 of the second copy assigns the return value of the third copy, 23, to $operand2. The following is the state of the program after line 16 has finished executing:

Level 1   Main program
Level 2   rightcalc(0) — list ("-", "98", "*", "4", "+", "12", "11")
Level 3   rightcalc(2) — list ("*", "4", "+", "12", "11"), $operand2 is 23

The Perl interpreter now executes lines 18–27. Because $index is 2 in this copy of rightcalc, line 18 assigns the fourth element of @list, 4, to $operand1. Line 21 is true in this case because the operator is *; this means that line 22 multiplies $operand1 (4) by $operand2 (23), yielding 92, which is assigned to $result.

At this point, the second copy of rightcalc is finished, and program execution returns to line 16. This assigns the return value from the second copy, 92, to $operand2.

The following is the state of the program after the second copy of rightcalc is finished:

Level 1   Main program
Level 2   rightcalc(0) — list ("-", "98", "*", "4", "+", "12", "11"), $operand2 is 92

Now you're almost finished; the program is executing only one copy of rightcalc. Because $index is 0 in this copy of rightcalc, line 18 assigns 98 to $operand1. Line 23 is true in this case because the operator here is -; line 24 then takes 98 and subtracts 92 from it, yielding a final result of 6.

This final result of 6 is passed to the main program and is assigned to $result. (Note that there is no conflict between $result in the main program and the various copies of $result in rightcalc because $result is defined as a local variable in rightcalc.) Line 7, finally, prints this result.

NOTE   Recursive subroutines are useful when handling complicated data
            structures such as trees. You will see examples of such complicated data
            structures on Day 10, "Associative Arrays."

Passing Arrays by Name Using Aliases

As you have seen, Perl enables you to pass an array as an argument to a subroutine.

```
&my_sub(@array);
```

When the subroutine my_sub is called, the list stored in the array variable @array is copied to
the variable @_ defined in the subroutine.

```
sub my_sub {
        local (@subarray) = @_;
        $arraylength = @subarray;
}
```

If the array being passed is large, it might take some time (and considerable space) to create
a copy of the array. If your application is operating under time or space limitations, or you
just want to make it more efficient, you can specify that the array is to be passed by name.

The following is an example of a similar subroutine that refers to an array by name:

```
sub my_sub {
        local (*subarray) = @_;
        $arraylength = @subarray;
}
```

The *subarray definition tells the Perl interpreter to operate on the actual list passed to
my_sub instead of making a copy.

To call this subroutine, specify * instead of @ with the array variable name, as in the following:

```
@myarray = (1, 2, 3, 4, 5);
&my_sub(*myarray);
```

Specifying *myarray instead of @myarray indicates that the actual contents of @myarray are to
be used (and modified if desired) in my_sub. In fact, while the subroutine is being executed,
the name @subarray becomes identical to the name @myarray. This process of creating another
name to refer to the same variable is known as *aliasing*. @subarray is now an alias of @myarray.

When my_sub terminates, @subarray stops being an alias of @myarray. When my_sub is called
again with a different argument, as in

```
&my_sub(*anotherarray);
```

the variable @subarray in my_sub becomes an alias for @anotherarray, which means that you can use the array variable @subarray to access the storage in @anotherarray.

Aliasing arrays in this manner has one distinct advantage and one distinct drawback. The advantage is that your program becomes more efficient. You don't need to copy the entire list from your main program to the subroutine. The disadvantage is that your program becomes more difficult to follow. You have to remember, for example, that changing the contents of @subarray in the subroutine my_sub also changes the contents of @myarray and @anotherarray. It is easy to lose track of which name refers to which variable.

There is also another problem with aliasing: aliasing affects all variables with the same name, not just array variables.

For example, consider Listing 9.13, which defines a scalar variable named $foo and an array named @foo, and then aliases @foo. As you'll see, the program aliases $foo as well.

TYPE **Listing 9.13. A program that demonstrates aliasing.**

```
 1:  #!/usr/local/bin/perl
 2:
 3:  $foo = 26;
 4:  @foo = ("here's", "a", "list");
 5:  &testsub (*foo);
 6:  print ("The value of \$foo is now $foo\n");
 7:
 8:  sub testsub {
 9:          local (*printarray) = @_;
10:          foreach $element (@printarray) {
11:                  print ("$element\n");
12:          }
13:          $printarray = 61;
14:  }
```

OUTPUT
```
$ program9_13
here's
a
list
The value of $foo is now 61
$
```

ANALYSIS Line 5 calls the subroutine testsub. The argument, *foo, indicates that the array @foo is to be passed to testsub and aliased.

The local variable definition in line 9 indicates that the array variable @printarray is to become an alias of the array variable @foo. This means that the name printarray is defined to be equivalent to the name foo.

9

As a consequence, the scalar variable $printarray becomes an alias of the scalar variable $foo. Because of this, line 13, which seems to assign 61 to $printarray, actually assigns 61 to $foo. This modified value is printed by line 6 of the main program.

NOTE

Aliasing enables you to pass more than one list to a subroutine.

```
@array1 = (1, 2, 3);
@array2 = (4, 5, 6);
&two_array_sub (*array1, *array2);
sub two_array_sub {
        my (*subarray1, *subarray2) = @_;
}
```

In this case, the names array1 and array2 are passed to two_array_sub. subarray1 becomes an alias for array1, and subarray2 becomes an alias for array2.

Using the do Statement with Subroutines

Perl enables you to use the do statement to invoke a subroutine. For example, the following statements are identical:

```
&my_sub(1, 2, 3);
do my_sub(1, 2, 3);
```

There is no real reason to use the do statement in this context.

Specifying the Sort Order

By default, the built-in function sort sorts in alphabetical order. The following is an example:

```
@list = ("words", "to", "sort");
@list2 = sort (@list);
```

Here, @list2 is assigned ("sort", "to", "words").

If you want, you can write a subroutine that defines how sorting is to be accomplished. To understand how to do this, first you need to know a little about how sorting works.

When sort is given a list to sort, it determines the sort order of the elements of the list by repeatedly comparing pairs of elements. To compare a pair of elements, sort calls a special internal subroutine and passes it a pair of arguments. Although the subroutine is not accessible from a Perl program, it basically behaves as follows:

```
sub sort_criteria {
        if ($a gt $b) {
                retval = -1;
        } elsif ($a eq $b) {
                retval = 0;
        } else
                retval = 1;
        }
        $retval;
}
```

This subroutine compares two values, which are stored in $a and $b. It returns -1 if the first value is greater, 0 if the values are equal, and 1 if the second value is greater. (This, by the way, is how the cmp operator works; in fact, the preceding subroutine could compare the two values using a single cmp operator.)

To define your own sorting rules, you must write a subroutine whose behavior is identical to the preceding subroutine. This subroutine must use two global variables named $a and $b to represent the two items in the list currently being compared, and the subroutine must return one of the following values:

-1   If $a is to appear before $b in the resulting sorted list

0   If $a is to be treated as equal to $b

1   If $a is to appear after $b in the resulting sorted list

NOTE

Even though $a and $b are global variables that are used by the sorting subroutine, you still can define global variables of your own named $a and $b without risking their being overwritten.

The built-in function sort saves any existing values of $a and $b before sorting, and then it restores them when sorting is completed.

After you have written the subroutine, you must specify the subroutine name when calling the function sort. For example, if you define a function named foo that provides a set of sorting rules, the following statement sorts a list using the rules defined in foo:

```
@list2 = sort foo (@list1);
```

Listing 9.14 shows how you can define your own sort criteria. This program sorts a list in the normal order, except that it puts strings starting with a digit last. (By default, strings starting with a number appear before strings starting with a letter, and before some—but not all—special characters.) Strings that begin with a digit are assumed to be numbers and are sorted in numerical order.

TYPE **Listing 9.14. A program that defines sort criteria.**

```
1:  #!/usr/local/bin/perl
2:
3:  @list1 = ("test", "14", "26", "test2");
4:  @list2 = sort num_last (@list1);
5:  print ("@list2\n");
6:
7:  sub num_last {
8:          my ($num_a, $num_b);
9:
10:         $num_a = $a =~ /^[0-9]/;
11:         $num_b = $b =~ /^[0-9]/;
12:         if ($num_a && $num_b) {
13:                 $retval = $a <=> $b;
14:         } elsif ($num_a) {
15:                 $retval = 1;
16:         } elsif ($num_b) {
17:                 $retval = -1;
18:         } else {
19:                 $retval = $a cmp $b;
20:         }
21:         $retval;
22: }
```

OUTPUT
```
$ program9_14
test test2 14 26
$
```

ANALYSIS   Line 4 sorts the program according to the sort criteria defined in the subroutine num_last. This subroutine is defined in lines 7–22.

This subroutine first determines whether the items are strings that begin with a digit. Line 10 sets the local variable $num_a to a nonzero value if the value stored in $a starts with a digit; similarly, line 11 sets $num_b to a nonzero value if the value of $b starts with a digit.

Lines 12 and 13 handle the case in which both $num_a and $num_b are true. In this case, the two strings are assumed to be digits, and the numeric comparison operator <=> compares their values. The result of the <=> operation is -1 if the first number is larger, 0 if they are equal, and 1 if the second number is larger.

If $num_a is true but $num_b is false, line 15 sets the return value for this subroutine to 1, indicating that the string that does not start with a digit, $b, is to be treated as greater. Similarly, line 17 sets the return value to -1 if $b starts with a digit and $a does not.

If neither string starts with a digit, line 19 uses the normal sort criterion—alphabetical order—to determine which value is larger. Here, the cmp operator is useful. It returns -1 if the first string is alphabetically greater, 0 if the strings are equal, and 1 if the second string is alphabetically greater.

Predefined Subroutines

Perl 5 defines three special subroutines that are executed at specific times.

☐ The BEGIN subroutine, which is called when your program starts running

☐ The END subroutine, which is called when your program terminates

☐ The AUTOLOAD subroutine, which is called when your program can't find a subroutine it is supposed to execute

NOTE

> These subroutines are not supported in Perl 4.

Creating Startup Code Using BEGIN

Perl 5 enables you to create code that is executed when your program is started. To do this, create a special subroutine named BEGIN. For example:

```
BEGIN {
        print("Hi! Welcome to Perl!\n");
}
```

When your program begins execution, the following line appears on your screen:

```
Hi! Welcome to Perl!
```

The BEGIN subroutine behaves just like any other Perl subroutine. For example, you can define local variables for it or call other subroutines from it.

NOTE

> If you like, you can define multiple BEGIN subroutines. These subroutines are called in the order in which they appear in the program.

Creating Termination Code Using END

Perl 5 enables you to create code to be executed when your program terminates execution. To do this, define an END subroutine, as in the following example:

```
END {
        print("Thank you for using Perl!\n");
}
```

The code contained in the END subroutine is always executed by your program, even if the program is terminated using die. For example, the code

```
die("Prepare to die!\n");
END {
        print("Ha! You can't kill me!\n");
}
```

displays the following on your screen:

```
Prepare to die!
Ha! You can't kill me!
```

NOTE

> You can define multiple END subroutines in your program. In this case, the subroutines are executed in reverse order of appearance, with the last one executed first.

Handling Non-Existent Subroutines Using AUTOLOAD

Perl 5 enables you to define a special subroutine named AUTOLOAD that is called whenever the Perl interpreter is told to call a subroutine that does not exist. Listing 9.15 illustrates the use of AUTOLOAD.

TYPE **Listing 9.15. A program that uses AUTOLOAD.**

```
1: #!/usr/local/bin/perl
2:
3: &nothere("hi", 46);
4:
5: AUTOLOAD {
6:         print("subroutine $AUTOLOAD not found\n");
7:         print("arguments passed: @_\n");
8: }
```

OUTPUT
```
$ program9_15
subroutine main::nothere not found
arguments passed: hi 46
$
```

ANALYSIS This program tries to call the non-existent subroutine nothere. When the Perl interpreter discovers that nothere does not exist, it calls the AUTOLOAD subroutine.

Line 6 uses a special scalar variable, $AUTOLOAD, which contains the name of the subroutine you tried to call. (The main:: text that appears before the subroutine name, nothere, is the name of the package in which the subroutine is found. By default, all your code is placed in one package, called main, so you normally won't need to worry about packages.

When AUTOLOAD is called, the arguments that were to be passed to the non-existent subroutine are passed to AUTOLOAD instead. This means that the @ array variable contains the list ("hi", 46), because these are the arguments that were to be passed to nothere.

TIP

> AUTOLOAD is useful if you plan to organize your Perl program into modules, because you can use it to ensure that crucial subroutines from other files actually exist when you need them. For more information on organizing Perl programs into modules, see Day 19.

9

Summary

Today, you learned about subroutines, which are separated chunks of code intended to perform specific tasks. A subroutine can appear anywhere in your program.

To invoke a subroutine, specify its name preceded by the & character. In Perl 5, the & character is not required if the subroutine exists, or if a forward reference is defined.

A subroutine can return a value (either a scalar value or a list). This return value is the value of the last expression evaluated inside the subroutine. If this last expression is at the end of the subroutine, the subroutine is a single-exit module.

You can define local variables for use inside subroutines. These local variables exist only while the subroutine is being executed. When a subroutine finishes, its local variables are destroyed; if it is invoked again, new copies of the local variables are defined.

You can pass values to subroutines; these values are called arguments. You can pass as many arguments as you like, but only one of these arguments can be a list. If a list is passed to a subroutine, it must be the last argument passed.

The arguments passed to a subroutine are converted into a list and assigned to a special system variable, @_. One copy of @_ exists for each list of arguments passed to a subroutine (that is, @_ is a local variable).

Subroutines can call other subroutines (nested subroutines) and even can call themselves (recursive subroutines).

You can pass an array variable to a subroutine by name by defining an alias for the variable name. This alias affects all variables of that name.

You can use the do statement to invoke a subroutine, although there is no real reason to do so.

You can define a subroutine that specifies the order in which the elements of a list are to be sorted. To use the sort criteria defined by a subroutine, include its name with the call to sort.

The BEGIN subroutine is always executed before your program begins execution. The END subroutine is always executed when your program terminates, even if it was killed off using die. The AUTOLOAD subroutine is executed if your program tries to call a subroutine that does not exist.

Q&A

Q How many levels of nested subroutines can a program have?

A This depends on the amount of memory in your machine. Normally, it is large enough to only be an issue when you are using recursive subroutines.

Q Which is better: passing entire lists or passing array variables by name?

A As with so many issues in programming, this depends on the situation. If your program needs to be space-efficient or to run as quickly as possible, passing array variables by name might be the best choice.

Another option is to use the global array variable both inside and outside the subroutine. This works well if the array variable is the central repository for program data.

Q When are global variables a good idea? When is it better to pass the contents of a variable to a subroutine?

A If your subroutine is a general-purpose subroutine that performs a task such as breaking a scalar value into words, it's a good idea to pass the value as an argument. For example:

```
sub breakline {
        local ($line) = @_;
        @words = split(/\s+/, $line);
}
```

If you do not pass the line as an argument, breakline will be able to work only with the line stored in a particular scalar variable, which makes it less useful.

On the other hand, if your program stores information in a central array, there's no reason to pass the array or the array name to a subroutine that processes the array. For example, if you are using the array @occurs to count all the occurrences of the digits 0 through 9 in a file, there's no reason to pass @occurs to a subroutine. For example:

```
sub printcount {
        for ($count = 0; $count <= 9; $count++) {
                print ("$occurs[$count]\n");
        }
}
```

Because printcount is not likely to be used with any array except @occurs, there's no need to pass it as an argument.

Q **When Perl defines an alias for an array-variable name in a subroutine, such as @localname for @name in a subroutine, why does it also define the alias $localname for $name?**

A Strictly speaking, the * character in an alias represents any character that precedes a variable name (such as @ or $).

For example, consider the following subroutine and the corresponding statement that calls it:

```
sub arraybyname {
        local (*localname) = @_;
}
arraybyname (*name);
```

When the Perl interpreter sees the reference to *localname in the subroutine, it replaces the alias following the * with the name for which the alias is defined. In this case, the Perl interpreter replaces *localname with *name.

The Perl interpreter then determines, from context, whether *name is an array variable, a scalar variable, or something else. In this case, *name is intended to be an array variable, which means that *name becomes @name.

Workshop

The Workshop provides quiz questions to help you solidify your understanding of the material covered and exercises to give you experience in using what you've learned. Try and understand the quiz and exercise answers before you go on to tomorrow's lesson.

Quiz

1. Define the following terms:
    a. subroutine
    b. invocation
    c. argument
    d. single-exit module
    e. aliasing

2. Consider the following program:

```
#!/usr/local/bin/perl

$total = 0;
@list = (1, 2, 3);
@list2 = &my_sub;
sub my_sub {
        local ($total);
        $total = 1;
        @list = (4, 5, 6);
}
```

What are the values stored in the following variables at the end of this program?

   a. $total

   b. @list

   c. @list2

3. What does the following subroutine return?

```
sub sub1 {
        $count = $sum = 0;
        while ($count <= 10) {
                $sum += $count;
                $count++;
        }
}
```

4. What is the value of @list at the end of the following program?

```
#!/usr/local/bin/perl

@list = (1, 2, 3);
&testsub(*list);
sub testsub {
        local (*sublist) = @_;
        $sublist[1] = 5;
}
```

Exercises

1. Write a subroutine that takes two arguments, adds them together, and returns the result.

2. Write a subroutine that counts the number of occurrences of the letter t in a string (which is passed to the subroutine). The subroutine must return the number of occurrences.

3. Write a subroutine that takes two filenames as its arguments and returns a nonzero value if the two files have identical contents. Return 0 if the files differ.

4. Write a subroutine that simulates the roll of a die (that is, it generates a random number between 1 and 6) and returns the number.

5. Write a subroutine that uses recursion to print a list in reverse order. The subroutine must recursively call itself to print the entire list; each invocation must print one word of the list. (Assume that the first call to your subroutine passes the value 0 and the list to be printed.)

6. **BUG BUSTER:** What is wrong with the following program?

```
#!/usr/local/bin/perl

for ($count = 1; $count <= 10; $count++) {
        &print_ten ($count);
}

sub print_ten {
        local ($multiplier) = @_;
        for ($count = 1; $count <= 10; $count++) {
                $printval = $multiplier * 10 + $count;
                print ("$printval\n");
        }
}
```

7. **BUG BUSTER:** What is wrong with the following program?

```
#!/usr/local/bin/perl

$line = <STDIN>;
@words = split(/\s+/, $line);
$searchword = <STDIN>;
&search_for_word (@words, $searchword);

sub search_for_word {
        local (@searchlist, $searchword) = @_;
        foreach $word (@searchlist) {
                return (1) if ($word eq $searchword);
        }
        $retval = 0;
}
```

8. **BUG BUSTER:** What is wrong with the following program?

```
#!/usr/local/bin/perl

$line = <STDIN>;
@words = &split_line($line);
print ("@words\n");

sub split_line {
        local ($line) = @_;
        local (@words);
        @words = split(/\s+/, $line);
        if (@words == 0) {
                @words = ("empty list");
        }
}
```

Day 10

Associative Arrays

Today's lesson shows you how to use associative arrays. You'll learn the following:

- [ ] What an associative array is
- [ ] How to access and create an associative array
- [ ] How to copy to and from an associative array
- [ ] How to add and delete associative array elements
- [ ] How to list array indexes and values
- [ ] How to loop using an associative array
- [ ] How to build data structures using associative arrays

To start, take a look at some of the problems that using array variables creates. Once you have seen some of the difficulties created by array variables in certain contexts, you'll see how associative arrays can eliminate these difficulties.

Limitations of Array Variables

In the array variables you've seen so far, you can access an element of a stored list by specifying a subscript. For example, the following statement accesses the third element of the list stored in the array variable @array:

```
$scalar = $array[2];
```

The subscript 2 indicates that the third element of the array is to be referenced.

Although array variables are useful, they have one significant drawback: it's often difficult to remember which element of an array stores what. For example, suppose you want to write a program that counts the number of occurrences of each capitalized word in an input file. You can do this using array variables, but it's very difficult. Listing 10.1 shows you what you have to go through to do this.

TYPE

Listing 10.1. A program that uses array variables to keep track of capitalized words in an input file.

```
 1:  #!/usr/local/bin/perl
 2:
 3:  while ($inputline = <STDIN>) {
 4:          while ($inputline =~ /\b[A-Z]\S+/g) {
 5:                  $word = $&;
 6:                  $word =~ s/[;.,:-]$//;  # remove punctuation
 7:                  for ($count = 1; $count <= @wordlist;
 8:                                   $count++) {
 9:                          $found = 0;
10:                          if ($wordlist[$count-1] eq $word) {
11:                                  $found = 1;
12:                                  $wordcount[$count-1] += 1;
13:                                  last;
14:                          }
15:                  }
16:                  if ($found == 0) {
17:                          $oldlength = @wordlist;
18:                          $wordlist[$oldlength] = $word;
19:                          $wordcount[$oldlength] = 1;
20:                  }
21:          }
22:  }
23:  print ("Capitalized words and number of occurrences:\n");
24:  for ($count = 1; $count <= @wordlist; $count++) {
25:          print ("$wordlist[$count-1]: $wordcount[$count-1]\n");
26:  }
```

10

```
$ program10_1
Here is a line of Input.
This Input contains some Capitalized words.
^D
Capitalized words and number of occurrences:
Here: 1
Input: 2
This: 1
Capitalized: 1
$
```

ANALYSIS   This program reads one line of input at a time from the standard input file. The loop starting on line 4 matches each capitalized word in the line; the loop iterates once for each match, and it assigns the match being examined in this particular iteration to the scalar variable $word.

Once any closing punctuation has been removed by line 6, the program must then check whether this word has been seen before. Lines 7–15 do this by examining each element of the list @wordlist in turn. If an element of @wordlist is identical to the word stored in $word, the corresponding element of @wordcount is incremented.

If no element of @wordlist matches $word, lines 16–20 add a new element to @wordlist and @wordcount.

Definition

As you can see, using array variables creates several problems. First, it's not obvious which element of @wordlist in Listing 10.1 corresponds to which capitalized word. In the example shown, $wordlist[0] contains Here because this is the first capitalized word in the input file, but this is not obvious to the reader.

Worse still, the program has no way of knowing which element of @wordlist contains which word. This means that every time the program reads a new word, it has to check the entire list to see if the word has already been found. This becomes time-consuming as the list grows larger.

All of these problems with array variables exist because elements of array variables are accessed by numeric subscripts. To get around these problems, Perl defines another kind of array, which enables you to access array variables using any scalar value you like. These arrays are called *associative arrays*.

To distinguish an associative array variable from an ordinary array variable, Perl uses the % character as the first character of an associative array-variable name, instead of the @ character. As with other variable names, the first character following the % must be a letter, and subsequent characters can be letters, digits, or underscores.

The following are examples of associative array-variable names:

```
%assocarray
%a1
%my_really_long_but_legal_array_variable_name
```

 NOTE

> Use the same name for an associative array variable and an ordinary array variable. For example, you can define an array variable named @arrayname and an associative array variable named %arrayname.
>
> The @ and % characters ensure that the Perl interpreter can tell one variable name from another.

Referring to Associative Array Elements

The main difference between associative arrays and ordinary arrays is that associative array subscripts can be any scalar value. For example, the following statement refers to an element of the associative array %fruit:

```
$fruit{"bananas"} = 1;
```

The subscript for this array element is bananas. Any scalar value can be a subscript. For example:

```
$fruit{"black_currant"}
$number{3.14159}
$integer{-7}
```

A scalar variable can be used as a subscript, as follows:

```
$fruit{$my_fruit}
```

Here, the contents of $my_fruit become the subscript into the associative array %fruit.

When an array element is referenced, as in the previous example, the name of the array element is preceded by a $ character, not the % character. As with array variables, this tells the Perl interpreter that this is a single scalar item and is to be treated as such.

 NOTE

> Subscripts for associative array elements are always enclosed in brace brackets ({}), not square brackets ([]). This ensures that the Perl interpreter is always able to distinguish associative array elements from other array elements.

Adding Elements to an Associative Array

The easiest way to create an associative array item is just to assign to it. For example, the statement

```
$fruit{"bananas"} = 1;
```

assigns 1 to the element bananas of the associative array %fruit. If this element does not exist, it is created. If the array %fruit has not been referred to before, it also is created.

This feature makes it easy to use associative arrays to count occurrences of items. For example, Listing 10.2 shows how you can use associative arrays to count the number of capitalized words in an input file. Note how much simpler this program is than the one in Listing 10.1, which accomplishes the same task.

10

TYPE **Listing 10.2. A program that uses an associative array to count the number of capitalized words in a file.**

```
1:  #!/usr/local/bin/perl
2:
3:  while ($inputline = <STDIN>) {
4:          while ($inputline =~ /\b[A-Z]\S+/g) {
5:                  $word = $&;
6:                  $word =~ s/[;.,:-]$//;  # remove punctuation
7:                  $wordlist{$word} += 1;
8:          }
9:  }
10: print ("Capitalized words and number of occurrences:\n");
11: foreach $capword (keys(%wordlist)) {
12:         print ("$capword: $wordlist{$capword}\n");
13: }
```

OUTPUT
```
$ program10_2
Here is a line of Input.
This Input contains some Capitalized words.
^D
Capitalized words and number of occurrences:
This: 1
Input: 2
Here: 1
Capitalized: 1
$
```

ANALYSIS As you can see, this program is much simpler than the one in Listing 10.1. The previous program required 20 lines of code to read input and store the counts for each word; this program requires only seven.

As before, this program reads one line of input at a time from the standard input file. The loop starting in line 4 iterates once for each capitalized word found in the input line; each match is assigned, in turn, to the scalar variable $word.

Line 7 uses the associative array %wordlist to keep track of the capitalized words. Because associative arrays can use any value as a subscript for an element, this line uses the word itself as a subscript. Then, the element of the array corresponding to the word has 1 added to its value.

For example, when the word Here is read in, the associative array element $wordlist{"Here"} has 1 added to its value.

Lines 11–13 print the elements of the associative array. Line 11 contains a call to a special built-in function, keys. This function returns a list consisting of the subscripts of the associative array; the foreach statement then loops through this list, iterating once for each element of the associative array. Each subscript of the associative array is assigned, in turn, to the local variable $capword; in this example, this means that $capword is assigned Here, Input, Capitalized, and This—one per each iteration of the for each loop.

WARNING

An important fact to remember is that associative arrays *always* are stored in "random" order. (Actually, it's the order that ensures fastest access, but, effectively, it is random.) This means that if you use keys to access all of the elements of an associative array, there is no guarantee that the elements will appear in any given order. In particular, the elements do not always appear in the order in which they are created.

To control the order in which the associative array elements appear, use sort to sort the elements returned by keys.

```
foreach $capword (sort keys(%wordlist)) {
        print ("$capword: $wordlist{$capword}\n");
}
```

When line 10 of Listing 10.2 is modified to include a call to sort, the associative array elements appear in sorted order.

Creating Associative Arrays

You can create an associative array with a single assignment. To do this, alternate the array subscripts and their values. For example:

```
%fruit = ("apples", 17, "bananas", 9, "oranges", "none");
```

This assignment creates an associative array of three elements:

- [ ] An element with subscript `apples`, whose value is 17
- [ ] An element with subscript `bananas`, whose value is 9
- [ ] An element with subscript `oranges`, whose value is `none`

WARNING

> Again, it is important to remember that the elements of associative arrays are not guaranteed to be in any particular order, even if you create the entire array at once.

NOTE

> Perl version 5 enables you to use either `=>` or `,` to separate array subscripts and values when you assign a list to an associative array. For example:
>
> `%fruit = ("apples" => 17, "bananas" => 9, "oranges" => "none");`
>
> This statement is identical to the previous one, but is easier to understand; the use of `=>` makes it easier to see which subscript is associated with which value.

As with any associative array, you always can add more elements to the array later on. For example:

```
$fruit{"cherries"} = 5;
```

This adds a fourth element, `cherries`, to the associative array `%fruit`, and gives it the value `5`.

Copying Associative Arrays from Array Variables

The list of subscripts and values assigned to `%fruit` in the previous example is an ordinary list like any other. This means that you can create an associative array from the contents of an array variable. For example:

```
@fruit = ("apples", 6, "cherries", 8, "oranges", 11);
%fruit = @fruit;
```

The second statement creates an associative array of three elements—`apples`, `cherries`, and `oranges`—and assigns it to `%fruit`.

WARNING

If you are assigning a list or the contents of an array variable to an associative array, make sure that the list contains an even number of elements, because each pair of elements corresponds to the subscript and the value of an associative array element.

Similarly, you can copy one associative array into another. For example:

```
%fruit1 = ("apples", 6, "cherries", 8, "oranges", 11);
%fruit2 = %fruit1;
```

You can assign an associative array to an ordinary array variable in the same way. For example:

```
%fruit = ("grapes", 11, "lemons", 27);
@fruit = %fruit;
```

However, this might not be as useful, because the order of the array elements is not defined. Here, the array variable @fruit is assigned either the four-element list

```
("grapes", 11, "lemons", 27)
```

or the list

```
("lemons", 27, "grapes", 11)
```

depending on how the associative array is sorted.

You can also assign to several scalar variables and an associative array at the same time.

```
($var1, $var2, %myarray) = @list;
```

Here, the first element of @list is assigned to $var1, the second to $var2, and the rest to %myarray.

Finally, an associative array can be created from the return value of a built-in function or user-defined subroutine that returns a list. Listing 10.3 is an example of a simple program that does just that. It takes the return value from split, which is a list, and assigns it to an associative array variable.

TYPE **Listing 10.3. A program that uses the return value from a built-in function to create an associative array.**

```
1:  #!/usr/local/bin/perl
2:
3:  $inputline = <STDIN>;
4:  $inputline =~ s/^\s+|\s+\n$//g;
5:  %fruit = split(/\s+/, $inputline);
6:  print ("Number of bananas: $fruit{\"bananas\"}\n");
```

OUTPUT
```
$ program10_3
oranges 5 apples 7 bananas 11 cherries 6
Number of bananas: 11
$
```

ANALYSIS This program reads a line of input from the standard input file and eliminates the leading and trailing white space. Line 5 then calls `split`, which breaks the line into words. In this example, `split` returns the following list:

```
("oranges", 5, "apples", 7, "bananas", 11, "cherries", 6)
```

This list is then assigned to the associative array `%fruit`. This assignment creates an associative array with four elements:

Element	Value
oranges	5
apples	7
bananas	11
cherries	6

Line 6 then prints the value of the element `bananas`, which is `11`.

Adding and Deleting Array Elements

As you've seen, you can add an element to an associative array by assigning to an element not previously seen, as follows:

```
$fruit{"lime"} = 1;
```

This statement creates a new element of `%fruit` with index `lime` and gives it the value `1`.

To delete an element, use the built-in function `delete`. For example, the following statement deletes the element `orange` from the array `%fruit`:

```
delete($fruit{"orange"});
```

Do	**Don't**

DO use the `delete` function to delete an element of an associative array; it's the only way to delete elements.

DON'T use the built-in functions `push`, `pop`, `shift`, or `splice` with associative arrays because the position of any particular element in the array is not guaranteed.

10

Listing Array Indexes and Values

As you saw in Listing 10.2, the keys function retrieves a list of the subscripts used in an associative array. The following is an example:

```
%fruit = ("apples", 9,
          "bananas", 23,
          "cherries", 11);
@fruitsubs = keys(%fruits);
```

Here, @fruitsubs is assigned the list consisting of the elements apples, bananas, and cherries. Note once again that this list is in no particular order. To retrieve the list in alphabetical order, use sort on the list.

```
@fruitindexes = sort keys(%fruits));
```

This produces the list ("apples", "bananas", "cherries").

To retrieve a list of the values stored in an associative array, use the built-in function values. The following is an example:

```
%fruit = ("apples", 9,
          "bananas", 23,
          "cherries", 11);
@fruitvalues = values(%fruits);
```

Here, @fruitvalues contains the list (9, 23, 11), not necessarily in this order.

Looping Using an Associative Array

As you've seen, you can use the built-in function keys with the foreach statement to loop through an associative array. The following is an example:

```
%records = ("Maris", 61, "Aaron", 755, "Young", 511);
foreach $holder (keys(%records)) {
        # stuff goes here
}
```

The variable $holder is assigned Aaron, Maris, and Young on successive iterations of the loop (although not necessarily in that order).

This method of looping is useful, but it is inefficient. To retrieve the value associated with a subscript, the program must look it up in the array again, as follows:

```
foreach $holder (keys(%records)) {
        $record = %records{$holder};
}
```

Perl provides a more efficient way to work with associative array subscripts and their values, using the built-in function each, as follows:

```
%records = ("Maris", 61, "Aaron", 755, "Young", 511);
while (($holder, $record) = each(%records)) {
        # stuff goes here
}
```

Every time the each function is called, it returns a two-element list. The first element of the list is the subscript for a particular element of the associative array. The second element is the value associated with that particular subscript.

For example, the first time each is called in the preceding code fragment, the pair of scalar variables ($holder, $record) is assigned one of the lists ("Maris", 61), ("Aaron", 755), or ("Young", 511). (Because associative arrays are not stored in any particular order, any of these lists could be assigned first.) If ("Maris", 61) is returned by the first call to each, Maris is assigned to $holder and 61 is assigned to $record.

When each is called again, it assigns a different list to the pair of scalar variables specified. Subsequent calls to each assign further lists, and so on until the associative array is exhausted. When there are no more elements left in the associative array, each returns the empty list.

WARNING

Don't add a new element to an associative array or delete an element from it if you are using the each statement on it. For example, suppose you are looping through the associative array %records using the following loop:

```
while (($holder, $record) = each(%records)) {

        # code goes here

}
```

Adding a new record to %records, such as

```
$records{"Rose"} = 4256;
```

or deleting a record, as in

```
delete $records{"Cobb"};
```

makes the behavior of each unpredictable. This should be avoided.

Creating Data Structures Using Associative Arrays

You can use associative arrays to simulate a wide variety of data structures found in high-level programming languages. This section describes how you can implement the following data structures in Perl using associative arrays:

☐ Linked lists

☐ Structures

☐ Trees

☐ Databases

NOTE

The remainder of today's lesson describes applications of associative arrays but does not introduce any new features of Perl. If you are not interested in applications of associative arrays, you can skip to the next chapter without suffering any loss of general instruction.

Linked Lists

A *linked list* is a simple data structure that enables you to store items in a particular order. Each element of the linked list contains two fields:

☐ The value associated with this element

☐ A reference, or *pointer*, to the next element in the list

Also, a special *header variable* points to the first element in the list.

Pictorially, a linked list can be represented as in Figure 10.1. As you can see, each element of the list points to the next.

Figure 10.1.
A linked list.

In Perl, a linked list can easily be implemented using an associative array because the value of one associative array element can be the subscript for the next. For example, the following associative array is actually a linked list of words in alphabetical order:

```
%words = ("abel", "baker",
          "baker", "charlie",
          "charlie", "delta",
          "delta", "");
$header = "abel";
```

In this example, the scalar variable $header contains the first word in the list. This word, abel, is also the subscript of the first element of the associative array. The value of the first element of this array, baker, is the subscript for the second element, and so on, as illustrated in Figure 10.2.

Figure 10.2.
A linked list of words in alphabetical order.

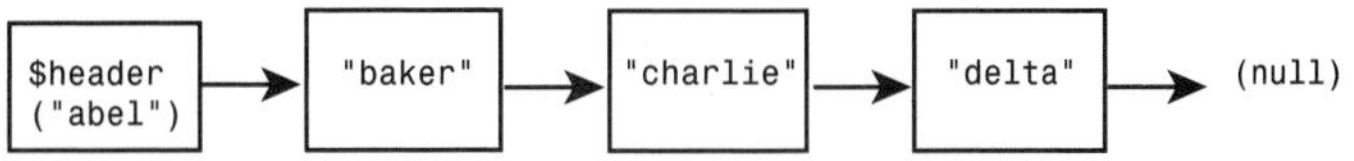

The value of the last element of the subscript, delta, is the null string. This indicates the end of the list.

Linked lists are most useful in applications where the amount of data to be processed is not known, or grows as the program is executed. Listing 10.4 is an example of one such application. It uses a linked list to print the words of a file in alphabetical order.

TYPE

Listing 10.4. A program that uses an associative array to build a linked list.

```
1:  #!/usr/local/bin/perl
2:
3:  # initialize list to empty
4:  $header = "";
5:  while ($line = <STDIN>) {
6:          # remove leading and trailing spaces
7:          $line =~ s/^\s+|\s+$//g;
8:          @words = split(/\s+/, $line);
9:          foreach $word (@words) {
10:                 # remove closing punctuation, if any
11:                 $word =~ s/[.,;:-]$//;
12:                 # convert all words to lower case
13:                 $word =~ tr/A-Z/a-z/;
14:                 &add_word_to_list($word);
15:         }
16: }
17: &print_list;
18:
19: sub add_word_to_list {
```

continues

Listing 10.4. continued

```
20:          local($word) = @_;
21:          local($pointer);
22:
23:          # if list is empty, add first item
24:          if ($header eq "") {
25:                  $header = $word;
26:                  $wordlist{$word} = "";
27:                  return;
28:          }
29:          # if word identical to first element in list,
30:          # do nothing
31:          return if ($header eq $word);
32:          # see whether word should be the new
33:          # first word in the list
34:          if ($header gt $word) {
35:                  $wordlist{$word} = $header;
36:                  $header = $word;
37:                  return;
38:          }
39:          # find place where word belongs
40:          $pointer = $header;
41:          while ($wordlist{$pointer} ne "" &&
42:                  $wordlist{$pointer} lt $word) {
43:                  $pointer = $wordlist{$pointer};
44:          }
45:          # if word already seen, do nothing
46:          return if ($word eq $wordlist{$pointer});
47:          $wordlist{$word} = $wordlist{$pointer};
48:          $wordlist{$pointer} = $word;
49: }
50:
51: sub print_list {
52:          local ($pointer);
53:          print ("Words in this file:\n");
54:          $pointer = $header;
55:          while ($pointer ne "") {
56:                  print ("$pointer\n");
57:                  $pointer = $wordlist{$pointer};
58:          }
59: }
```

OUTPUT

```
$ program10_4
Here are some words.
Here are more words.
Here are still more words.
^D
Words in this file:
are
here
more
some
still
words
$
```

ANALYSIS The logic of this program is a little complicated, but don't despair. Once you understand how this works, you have all the information you need to build any data structure you like, no matter how complicated.

This program is divided into three parts, as follows:

- [ ] The main program, which reads input and transforms it into the desired format
- [ ] The subroutine add_word_to_list, which builds the linked list of sorted words
- [ ] The subroutine print_list, which prints the list of words

Lines 3–17 contain the main program. Line 4 initializes the list of words by setting the header variable $header to the null string. The loop beginning in line 5 reads one line of input at a time. Line 7 removes leading and trailing spaces from the line, and line 8 splits the line into words.

The inner foreach loop in lines 9–15 processes one word of the input line at a time. If the final character of a word is a punctuation character, line 11 removes it; this ensures that, for example, word. (word with a period) is considered identical to word (without a period). Line 13 converts the word to all lowercase characters, and line 14 passes the word to the subroutine add_word_to_list.

This subroutine first executes line 24, which checks whether the linked list of words is empty. If it is, line 25 assigns this word to $header, and line 26 creates the first element of the list, which is stored in the associative array %wordlist. In this example, the first word read in is here (Here converted to lowercase), and the list looks like Figure 10.3.

Figure 10.3.

The linked list with one element in it.

```
┌─────────┐
│ $header │ ───────▶   (null)
│ ("here")│
└─────────┘
```

At this point, the header variable $header contains the value here, which is also the subscript for the element of %wordlist that has just been created. This means that the program can reference %wordlist by using $header as a subscript, as follows:

```
$wordlist{$header}
```

Variables such as $header that contain a reference to another data item are called *pointers*. Here, $header points to the first element of %wordlist.

If the list is not empty, line 31 checks whether the first item of the list is identical to the word currently being checked. To do this, it compares the current word to the contents of $header, which is the first item in the list. If the two are identical, there is no need to add the new word to the list, because it is already there; therefore, the subroutine returns without doing anything.

The next step is to check whether the new word should be the first word in the list, which is the case if the new word is alphabetically ahead of the existing first word. Line 34 checks this.

If the new word is to go first, the list is adjusted as follows:

1. A new list element is created. The subscript of this element is the new word, and its value is the existing first word.
2. The new word is assigned to the header variable.

To see how this adjustment works, consider the sample input provided. In this example, the second word to be processed is are. Because are belongs before here, the array element $wordlist{"are"} is created, and is given the value here. The header variable $header is assigned the value are. This means the list now looks like Figure 10.4.

Figure 10.4.

The linked list with two elements in it.

The header variable $header now points to the list element with the subscript are, which is $wordlist{"are"}. The value of $wordlist{"are"} is here, which means that the program can access $wordlist{"here"} from $wordlist{"are"}. For example:

```
$reference = $wordlist{"are"};
print ("$wordlist{$reference}\n");
```

The value here is assigned to $reference, and print prints $wordlist{$reference}, which is $wordlist{"here"}.

Because you can access $wordlist{"here"} from $wordlist{"are"}, $wordlist{"are"} is a pointer to $wordlist{"here"}.

If the word does not belong at the front of the list, lines 40–44 search for the place in the list where the word does belong, using a local variable, $pointer. Lines 41–44 loop until the value stored in $wordlist{$pointer} is greater than or equal to $word. For example, Figure 10.5 illustrates where line 42 is true when the subroutine processes more.

Figure 10.5.

The linked list when more is processed.

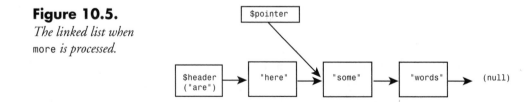

Note that because the list is in alphabetical order, the value stored in $pointer is always less than the value stored in $word.

If the word being added is greater than any word in the list, the conditional expression in line 41 eventually becomes true. This occurs, for example, when the subroutine processes some, as in Figure 10.6.

Figure 10.6.

The linked list when some is processed.

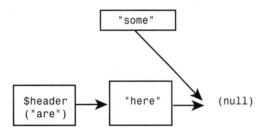

Once the location of the new word has been determined, line 46 checks whether the word already is in the list. If it is, there is no need to do anything.

If the word does not exist, lines 47 and 48 add the word to the list. First, line 47 creates a new element of %wordlist, which is $wordlist{$word}; its value is the value of $wordlist{$pointer}. This means that $wordlist{$word} and $wordlist{$pointer} now point to the same word, as in Figure 10.7.

Figure 10.7.

The linked list as a new word is being added.

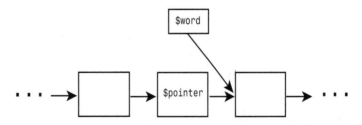

Next, line 48 sets the value of $wordlist{$pointer} to the value stored in $word. This means that $wordlist{$pointer} now points to the new element, $wordlist{$word}, that was just created, as in Figure 10.8.

Figure 10.8.

The linked list after the new word is added.

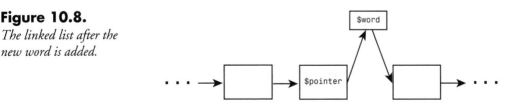

Once the input file has been completely processed, the subroutine `print_list` prints the list, one element at a time. The local variable `$pointer` contains the current value being printed, and `$wordlist{$pointer}` contains the next value to be printed.

NOTE

Normally, you won't want to use a linked list in a program. It's easier just to use `sort` and `keys` to loop through an associative array in alphabetical order, as follows:

```
foreach $word (sort keys(%wordlist)) {
        # print the sorted list, or whatever
}
```

However, the basic idea of a pointer, which is introduced here, is useful in other data structures, such as trees, which are described later on.

Structures

Many programming languages enable you to define collections of data called *structures*. Like lists, structures are collections of values; each element of a structure, however, has its own name and can be accessed by that name.

Perl does not provide a way of defining structures directly. However, you can simulate a structure using an associative array. For example, suppose you want to simulate the following variable definition written in the C programming language:

```
struct {
        int field1;
        int field2;
        int field3;
} mystructvar;
```

This C statement defines a variable named `mystructvar`, which contains three elements, named `field1`, `field2`, and `field3`.

To simulate this using an associative array, all you need to do is define an associative array with three elements, and set the subscripts for these elements to `field1`, `field2`, and `field3`. The following is an example:

```
%mystructvar = ("field1", "",
                "field2", "",
                "field3", "");
```

Like the preceding C definition, this associative array, named `%mystructvar`, has three elements. The subscripts for these elements are `field1`, `field2`, and `field3`. The definition sets the initial values for these elements to the null string.

As with any associative array, you can reference or assign the value of an element by specifying its subscript, as follows:

```
$mystructvar{"field1"} = 17;
```

To define other variables that use the same "structure," all you need to do is create other arrays that use the same subscript names.

Trees

Another data structure that is often used in programs is a *tree*. A tree is similar to a linked list, except that each element of a tree points to more than one other element.

The simplest example of a tree is a *binary tree*. Each element of a binary tree, called a *node*, points to two other elements, called the *left child* and the *right child*. Each of these children points to two children of its own, and so on, as illustrated in Figure 10.9.

Figure 10.9.

A binary tree.

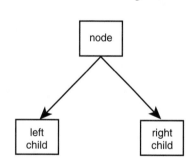

Note that the tree, like a linked list, is a one-way structure. Nodes point to children, but children don't point to their parents.

The following terminology is used when describing trees:

- ☐ Because each of the children of a node is a tree of its own, the left child and the right child are often called the *left subtree* and the *right subtree* of the node. (The terms *left branch* and *right branch* are also used.)
- ☐ The "first" node of the tree (the node that is not a child of another node), is called the *root* of the tree.
- ☐ Nodes that have no children are called *leaf nodes*.

There are several ways of implementing a tree structure using associative arrays. To illustrate one way of doing so, suppose that you wish to create a tree whose root has the value alpha and whose children have the values beta and gamma, as in Figure 10.10.

Figure 10.10.

A binary tree with three nodes.

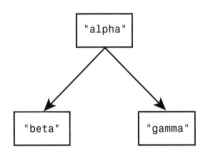

Here, the left child of alpha is beta, and the right child of alpha is gamma.

The problem to be solved is this: How can a program associate both beta and gamma with alpha? If the associative array that is to represent the tree is named %tree, do you assign the value of $tree{"alpha"} to be beta, or gamma, or both? How do you show that an element points to two other elements?

There are several solutions to this problem, but one of the most elegant is as follows: Append the character strings left and right, respectively, to the name of a node in order to retrieve its children. For example, define alphaleft to point to beta and alpharight to point to gamma. In this scheme, if beta has children, betaleft and betaright point to their locations; similarly, gammaleft and gammaright point to the locations of the children of gamma, and so on.

Listing 10.5 is an example of a program that creates a binary tree using this method and then *traverses* it (accesses every node in the tree).

Listing 10.5. A program that uses an associative array to

`TYPE` **represent a binary tree.**

```
 1:  #!/usr/local/bin/perl
 2:
 3:  $rootname = "parent";
 4:  %tree = ("parentleft", "child1",
 5:          "parentright", "child2",
 6:          "child1left", "grandchild1",
 7:          "child1right", "grandchild2",
 8:          "child2left", "grandchild3",
 9:          "child2right", "grandchild4");
10:  # traverse tree, printing its elements
11:  &print_tree($rootname);
```

```
12:
13: sub print_tree {
14:         local ($nodename) = @_;
15:         local ($leftchildname, $rightchildname);
16:
17:         $leftchildname = $nodename . "left";
18:         $rightchildname = $nodename . "right";
19:         if ($tree{$leftchildname} ne "") {
20:                 &print_tree($tree{$leftchildname});
21:         }
22:         print ("$nodename\n");
23:         if ($tree{$rightchildname} ne "") {
24:                 &print_tree($tree{$rightchildname});
25:         }
26: }
```

OUTPUT

```
$ program10_5
grandchild1
child1
grandchild2
parent
grandchild3
child2
grandchild4
$
```

ANALYSIS This program creates the tree depicted in Figure 10.11.

Figure 10.11.

The tree created by Listing 10.5.

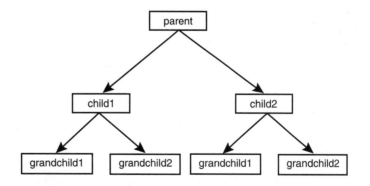

The associative array %tree stores the tree, and the scalar variable $rootname holds the name of the root of the tree. (Note that the grandchild nodes, such as grandchild1, are leaf nodes. There is no need to explicitly create grandchild1left, grandchild1right, and so on because the value of any undefined associative array element is, by default, the null string.)

After the tree has been created, the program calls the subroutine print_tree to traverse it and print its values. print_tree does this as follows:

1. Line 17 appends left to the name of the node being examined to produce the name of the left child, which is stored in $leftchildname. For example, if the root node, parent, is being examined, the value stored in $leftchildname is parentleft.

2. Similarly, line 18 appends right to the node name and stores the result in $rightchildname.

3. Line 19 checks whether the current node has a left child, which is true if $tree{$leftchildname} is defined. (For example, parent has a left child, because $tree{"parentleft"} is defined.) If the current node has a left child, line 20 recursively calls print_tree to print the left subtree (the left child and its children).

4. Line 22 prints the name of the current node.

5. Line 23 checks whether the current node has a right child. If it does, line 24 recursively calls print_tree to print the right subtree.

Note that print_tree prints the names of the nodes of the tree in the following order: left subtree, node, right subtree. This order of traversal is called *infix mode* or *infix traversal*. If you move line 22 to precede line 19, the node is printed first, followed by the left subtree and the right subtree; this order of traversal is called *prefix mode*. If you move line 22 to follow line 25, the node is printed after the subtrees are printed; this is called *postfix mode*.

Databases

As you have seen, you can build a tree using an associative array. To do this, you build the associative array subscripts by joining character strings together (such as joining the node name and "left"). You can use this technique of joining strings together to use associative arrays to build other data structures.

For example, suppose you want to create a database that contains the lifetime records of baseball players. Each record is to consist of the following:

☐ For non-pitchers, a record consists of games played (GP), home runs (HR), runs batted in (RBI) and batting average (AVG). For example, the record on Lou Gehrig would read as follows:

```
Gehrig: 2164 GP, 493 HR, 1991 RBI, .340 BA
```

☐ For pitchers, a record consists of games pitched (GP), wins (W), and earned run average (ERA). For example, the record on Lefty Grove would read as follows:

```
Grove: 616 GP, 300 W, 3.05 ERA
```

To create a database containing player and pitcher records, you need the following fields:

- ☐ A name field, for the player's name
- ☐ A key indicating whether the player was a pitcher
- ☐ The fields defined above

You can use an associative array to simulate this in Perl. To do this, build the subscripts for the associative array by concatenating the name of the player with the name of the field being stored by this element of the array. For example, if the associative array is named %playerbase, $playerbase{"GehrigRBI"}, it contains the career RBI total for Lou Gehrig.

Listing 10.6 shows how to build a player database and how to sequentially print fields from each of the player records.

TYPE **Listing 10.6. A program that builds and prints a database.**

```
1:  #!/usr/local/bin/perl
2:
3:  @pitcherfields = ("NAME", "KEY", "GP", "W", "ERA");
4:  @playerfields = ("NAME", "KEY", "GP", "HR", "RBI", "BA");
5:
6:  # Build the player database by reading from standard input.
7:  # %playerbase contains the database, @playerlist the list of
8:  # players (for later sequential access).
9:  $playercount = 0;
10: while ($input = <STDIN>) {
11:         $input =~ s/^\s+|\s+$//g;
12:         @words = split (/\s+/, $input);
13:         $playerlist[$playercount++] = $words[0];
14:         if ($words[1] eq "player") {
15:                 @fields = @playerfields;
16:         } else {
17:                 @fields = @pitcherfields;
18:         }
19:         for ($count = 1; $count <= @words; $count++) {
20:                 $playerbase{$words[0].$fields[$count-1]} =
21:                         $words[$count-1];
22:         }
23: }
24:
25: # now, print out pitcher win totals and player home run totals
26: foreach $player (@playerlist) {
27:         print ("$player: ");
28:         if ($playerbase{$player."KEY"} eq "player") {
29:                 $value = $playerbase{$player."HR"};
30:                 print ("$value home runs\n");
31:         } else {
32:                 $value = $playerbase{$player."W"};
33:                 print ("$value wins\n");
34:         }
35: }
```

10

```
$ program10_6
Gehrig          player          2164    493     1991    .340
Ruth            player          2503    714     2217    .342
Grove           pitcher         616     300     3.05
Williams        player          2292    521     1839    .344
Koufax          pitcher         397     165     2.76
^D
Gehrig: 493 home runs
Ruth: 714 home runs
Grove: 300 wins
Williams: 521 home runs
Koufax: 165 wins
$
```

ANALYSIS This program has been designed so that it is easy to add new fields to the database. With this in mind, lines 3 and 4 define the fields that are to be used when building the player and pitcher records.

Lines 9–23 build the database. First, line 9 initializes $playercount to 0; this global variable keeps track of the number of players in the database.

Lines 10–12 read a line from the standard input file, check whether the file is empty, remove leading and trailing white space from the line, and split the line into words.

Line 13 adds the player name (the first word in the input line) to the list of player names stored in @playerlist. The counter $playercount then has 1 added to it; this reflects the new total number of players stored in the database.

Lines 14–18 determine whether the new player is a pitcher or not. If the player is a pitcher, the names of the fields to be stored in this player record are to be taken from @pitcherfields; otherwise, the names are to be taken from @playerfields. To simplify processing later on, another array variable, @fields, is used to store the list of fields actually being used for this player.

Lines 19–22 copy the fields into the associative array, one at a time. Each array subscript is made up of two parts: the name of the player and the name of the field being stored. For example, Sandy Koufax's pitching wins are stored in the array element KoufaxW. Note that neither the player name nor the field names appear in this loop; this means that you can add new fields to the list of fields without having to change this code.

Lines 26–35 now search the database for all the win and home run totals just read in. Each iteration of the foreach loop assigns a different player name to the local variable $player. Line 28 examines the contents of the array element named $player."KEY" to determine whether the player is a pitcher.

If the player is not a pitcher, lines 29–30 print out the player's home-run total by accessing the array element $player."HR". If the player is a pitcher, the pitcher's win total is printed out by lines 32–33; these lines access the array element $player."W".

10

Note that the database can be accessed randomly as well as sequentially. To retrieve, for example, Babe Ruth's lifetime batting average, you would access the array element $playerbase{"RuthAVG"}. If the record for a particular player is not stored in the database, attempting to access it will return the null string. For example, the following assigns the null string to $cobbavg because Ty Cobb is not in the player database:

```
$cobbavg = $playerbase{"CobbAVG"};
```

As you can see, associative arrays enable you to define databases with variable record lengths, accessible either sequentially or randomly. This gives you all the flexibility you need to use Perl as a database language.

Example: A Calculator Program

Listing 10.7 provides an example of what you can do with associative arrays and recursive subroutines. This program reads in an arithmetic expression, possibly spread over several lines, and builds a tree from it. The program then evaluates the tree and prints the result. The operators supported are +, -, *, /, and parentheses (to force precedence).

This program is longer and more complicated than the programs you have seen so far, but stick with it. Once you understand this program, you will know enough to be able to write an entire compiler in Perl!

TYPE   **Listing 10.7. A calculator program that uses trees.**

```
 1:  #!/usr/local/bin/perl
 2:  # statements which initialize the program
 3:  $nextnodenum = 1;  # initialize node name generator
 4:  &get_next_item;    # read first value from file
 5:  $treeroot = &build_expr;
 6:  $result = &get_result ($treeroot);
 7:  print ("the result is $result\n");
 8:  # Build an expression.
 9:  sub build_expr {
10:        local ($currnode, $leftchild, $rightchild);
11:        local ($operator);
12:        $leftchild = &build_add_operand;
13:        if (&is_next_item("+") || &is_next_item("-")) {
14:                $operator = &get_next_item;
15:                $rightchild = &build_expr;
16:                $currnode = &get_new_node ($operator,
17:                        $leftchild, $rightchild);
18:        } else {
19:                $currnode = $leftchild;
20:        }
21: }
22: # Build an operand for a + or — operator.
23: sub build_add_operand {
```

continues

Listing 10.7. continued

```
24:         local ($currnode, $leftchild, $rightchild);
25:         local ($operator);
26:         $leftchild = &build_mult_operand;
27:         if (&is_next_item("*") || &is_next_item("/")) {
28:                 $operator = &get_next_item;
29:                 $rightchild = &build_add_operand;
30:                 $currnode = &get_new_node ($operator,
31:                         $leftchild, $rightchild);
32:         } else {
33:                 $currnode = $leftchild;
34:         }
35: }
36: # Build an operand for the * or / operator.
37: sub build_mult_operand {
38:         local ($currnode);
39:         if (&is_next_item("(")) {
40:                 # handle parentheses
41:                 &get_next_item;  # get rid of "("
42:                 $currnode = &build_expr;
43:                 if (! &is_next_item(")")) {
44:                         die ("Invalid expression");
45:                 }
46:                 &get_next_item;  # get rid of ")"
47:         } else {
48:                 $currnode = &get_new_node(&get_next_item,
49:                         "", "");
50:         }
51:         $currnode;  # ensure correct return value
52: }
53: # Check whether the last item read matches
54: # a particular operator.
55: sub is_next_item {
56:         local ($expected) = @_;
57:         $curritem eq $expected;
58: }
59: # Return the last item read; read another item.
60: sub get_next_item {
61:         local ($retitem);
62:         $retitem = $curritem;
63:         $curritem = &read_item;
64:         $retitem;
65: }
66: # This routine actually handles reading from the standard
67: # input file.
68: sub read_item {
69:         local ($line);
70:         if ($curritem eq "EOF") {
71:                 # we are already at end of file; do nothing
72:                 return;
73:         }
74:         while ($wordsread == @words) {
75:                 $line = <STDIN>;
76:                 if ($line eq "") {
77:                         $curritem = "EOF";
78:                         return;
```

```
79:                   }
80:                   $line =~ s/\(/ ( /g;
81:                   $line =~ s/\)/ ) /g;
82:                   $line =~ s/^\s+|\s+$//g;
83:                   @words = split(/\s+/, $line);
84:                   $wordsread = 0;
85:          }
86:          $curritem = $words[$wordsread++];
87: }
88: # Create a tree node.
89: sub get_new_node {
90:          local ($value, $leftchild, $rightchild) = @_;
91:          local ($nodenum);
92:          $nodenum = $nextnodenum++;
93:          $tree{$nodenum} = $value;
94:          $tree{$nodenum . "left"} = $leftchild;
95:          $tree{$nodenum . "right"} = $rightchild;
96:          $nodenum;   # return value
97: }
98: # Calculate the result.
99: sub get_result {
100:          local ($node) = @_;
101:          local ($nodevalue, $result);
102:          $nodevalue = $tree{$node};
103:          if ($nodevalue eq "") {
104:                  die ("Bad tree");
105:          } elsif ($nodevalue eq "+") {
106:                  $result = &get_result($tree{$node . "left"}) +
107:                            &get_result($tree{$node . "right"});
108:          } elsif ($nodevalue eq "-") {
109:                  $result = &get_result($tree{$node . "left"}) -
110:                            &get_result($tree{$node . "right"});
111:          } elsif ($nodevalue eq "*") {
112:                  $result = &get_result($tree{$node . "left"}) *
113:                            &get_result($tree{$node . "right"});
114:          } elsif ($nodevalue eq "/") {
115:                  $result = &get_result($tree{$node . "left"}) /
116:                            &get_result($tree{$node . "right"});
117:          } elsif ($nodevalue =~ /^[0-9]+$/) {
118:                  $result = $nodevalue;
119:          } else {
120:                  die ("Bad tree");
121:          }
122:}
```

OUTPUT

```
$ program10_7
11 + 5 *
(4 - 3)
^D
the result is 16
$
```

ANALYSIS This program is divided into two main parts: a part that reads the input and produces a tree, and a part that calculates the result by traversing the tree.

Figure 10.12.

The tree for the example in Listing 10.7.

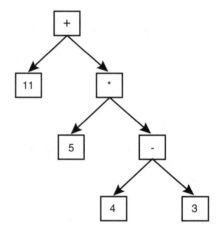

The subroutines `build_expr`, `build_add_operand`, and `build_mult_operand` build the tree. To see how they do this, first look at Figure 10.12 to see what the tree for the example, 11 + 5 * (4 − 3), should look like.

When this tree is evaluated, the nodes are searched in postfix order. First, the left subtree of the root is evaluated, then the right subtree, and finally the operation at the root.

The rules followed by the three subroutines are spelled out in the following description:

1. An *expression* consists of one of the following:
   a. An *add_operand*
   b. An *add_operand*, a + or - operator, and an *expression*

2. An *add_operand* consists of one of the following:
   a. A *mult_operand*
   b. A *mult_operand*, a * or / operator, and an *add_operand*

3. A *mult_operand* consists of one of the following:
   a. A *number* (a group of digits)
   b. An *expression* enclosed in parentheses

The subroutine `build_expr` handles all occurrences of condition 1; it is called (possibly recursively) whenever an *expression* is processed. Condition 1a covers the case in which the expression contains no + or - operators (unless they are enclosed in parentheses). Condition 1b handles expressions that contain one or more + or - operators.

The subroutine `build_add_operand` handles condition 2; it is called whenever an *add_operand* is processed. Condition 2a covers the case in which the add operand contains no * or / operators (except possibly in parentheses). Condition 2b handles add operands that contain one or more * or / operators.

The subroutine `build_mult_operand` handles condition 3 and is called whenever a *mult_operand* is processed. Condition 3a handles multiplication operands that consist of a number. Condition 3b handles multiplication operators that consist of an expression in parentheses; to obtain the subtree for this expression, `build_mult_operand` calls `build_expr` recursively and then treats the returned subtree as a child of the node currently being built.

Note that the tree built by `build_expr`, `build_mult_operand`, and `build_add_operand` is slightly different from the tree you saw in Listing 10.5. In that tree, the value of the node could also be used as the subscript into the associative array. In this tree, the value of the node might not be unique. To get around this problem, a separate counter creates numbers for each node, which are used when building the subscripts. For each node numbered *n* (where *n* is an integer), the following are true:

- [ ] `$tree{n}` contains the value of the node, which is the number or operator associated with the node.
- [ ] `$tree{n."left"}` contains the number of the left child of the node.
- [ ] `$tree{n."right"}` contains the number of the right child of the node.

The subroutines `is_next_item`, `get_next_item`, and `read_item` read the input from the standard input file and break it into numbers and operators. The subroutine `get_next_item` "pre-reads" the next item and stores it in the global variable `$curritem`; this lets `is_next_item` check whether the next item to be read matches a particular operator. To read an item, `get_next_item` calls `read_item`, which reads lines of input, breaks them into words, and returns the next word to be read.

The subroutine `get_new_node` creates a tree node. To do this, it uses the contents of the global variable `$nextnodenum` to build the associative array subscripts associated with the node. `$nextnodenum` always contains a positive integer *n*, which means that the value associated with this node (which is a number or operator) is stored in `$tree{n}`. The location of the left and right children, if any, are stored in `$tree{n."left"}` and `$tree {n."right"}`.

The subroutine `get_result` traverses the tree built by `build_expr` in postfix order (subtrees first), performing the arithmetic operations as it does so. `get_result` returns the final result, which is then printed.

Note that the main part of this program is only eight lines long! This often happens in more complex programs. The main part of the program just calls subroutines, and the subroutines do the actual work.

NOTE

This program is just the tip of the iceberg: you can use associative arrays to simulate any data structure in any programming language.

Summary

In today's lesson, you learned about associative arrays, which are arrays whose subscripts can be any scalar value.

You can copy a list to an associative array, provided there is an even number of elements in the list. Each pair of elements in the list is treated as an associated array subscript and its value. You also can copy an associative array to an ordinary array variable.

To add an element to an associative array, just assign a value to an element whose subscript has not been previously seen. To delete an element, call the built-in function `delete`.

The following three built-in functions enable you to use associative arrays with `foreach` loops:

- [ ] The built-in function `keys` retrieves each associative array subscript in turn.
- [ ] The built-in function `values` retrieves each associative array value in turn.
- [ ] The built-in function `each` retrieves each subscript-value pair in turn (as a two-element list).

Associative arrays are not guaranteed to be stored in any particular order. To guarantee a particular order, use `sort` with `keys`, `values`, or `each`.

Associative arrays can be used to simulate a wide variety of data structures, including linked lists, structures, trees, and databases.

Q&A

Q Are pointers implemented in Perl?

A Yes, if you are using Perl 5; they are discussed on Day 18, "References in Perl 5." Perl 4 does not support pointers.

Q How can I implement more complicated data structures using associative arrays?

A All you need to do is design the structure you want to implement, name each of the fields in the structure, and use the name-concatenation trick to build your associative array subscript names.

Q What do I do if I want to build a tree that has multiple values at each node?

A There are many ways to do this. One way is to append `value1`, `value2`, and so on, to the name of each node; for example, if the node is named `n7`, `n7value1` could be the associative array subscript for the first value associated with the node, `n7value2` could be the subscript for the second, and so on.

Q What do I do if I want to build a tree that has more than two children per node?

A Again, there are many ways to do this. A possible solution is to use `child1`, `child2`, `child3`, and so on, instead of `left` and `right`.

Q How do I destroy a tree that I have created?

A To destroy a tree, write a subroutine that traverses the tree in postfix order (subtrees first). Destroy each subtree (by recursively calling your subroutine), and then destroy the node you are looking at by calling `delete`.

Note that you shouldn't use `keys` or `each` to access each element of the loop before deleting it. Deleting an element affects how the associative array is stored, which means that `keys` and `each` might not behave the way you want them to.

If you want to destroy the entire associative array in which the tree is stored, you can use the `undef` function, which is described on Day 14, "Scalar-Conversion and List-Manipulation Functions."

Workshop

The Workshop provides quiz questions to help you solidify your understanding of the material covered and exercises to give you experience in using what you've learned. Try and understand the quiz and exercise answers before you go on to tomorrow's lesson.

Quiz

1. Define the following terms:
   a. associative array
   b. pointer
   c. linked list
   d. binary tree
   e. node
   f. child

2. What are the elements of the associative array created by the following assignment?

   ```
   %list = ("17.2", "hello", "there", "46", "e+6", "88");
   ```

3. What happens when you assign an associative array to an ordinary array variable?

4. How can you create a linked list using an associative array?

5. How many times does the following loop iterate?

```
%list = ("first", "1", "second", "2", "third", "3");
foreach $word (keys(%list)) {
        last if ($word == "second");
}
```

Exercises

1. Write a program that reads lines of input consisting of two words per line, such as

   bananas 16

   and creates an associative array from these lines. (The first word is to be the subscript and the second word the value.)

2. Write a program that reads a file and searches for lines of the form

   index *word*

   where *word* is a word to be indexed. Each indexed word is to be stored in an associative array, along with the line number on which it first occurs. (Subsequent occurrences can be ignored.) Print the resulting index.

3. Modify the program created in Exercise 2 to store every occurrence of each index line. (Hint: Try building the associative array subscripts using the indexed word, a non-printable character, and a number.) Print the resulting index.

4. Write a program that reads input lines consisting of a student name and five numbers representing the student's marks in English, history, mathematics, science, and geography, as follows:

   Jones 61 67 75 80 72

   Use an associative array to store these numbers in a database, and then print out the names of all students with failing grades (less than 50) along with the subjects they failed.

5. **BUG BUSTER:** What is wrong with the following code?

```
%list = ("Fred", 61, "John", 72,
        "Jack", 59, "Mary", 80);
$surname = "Smith";
foreach $firstname (keys (%list)) {
        %list{$firstname." ".$surname} = %list{$firstname};
}
```

Day 11

Formatting Your Output

The Perl programs you've seen so far produce output using the print function, which writes raw, unformatted text to a file.

Perl also enables you to produce formatted output, using print formats and the built-in function write. Today's lesson describes how to produce formatted output. You'll learn the following:

- ☐ How to define a print format (also sometimes known as a "picture format")
- ☐ How to use the write function
- ☐ How to add formatted values to a print format
- ☐ Which value-field formats are available
- ☐ How to write to other output files
- ☐ How to specify page headers and the page length
- ☐ How to format long character strings
- ☐ How to use the built-in function printf

Defining a Print Format

The following is an example of a simple print format:

```
format MYFORMAT =
==================================
Here is the text I want to display.
==================================
.
```

This defines the print format MYFORMAT.

▼Syntax

The syntax for print formats is

```
format formatname =
lines_of_output
.
```

The special keyword format tells the Perl interpreter that the following lines are a print-format definition. The *formatname* is a placeholder for the name of the print format being defined (for example, MYFORMAT). This name must start with an alphabetic character and can consist of any sequence of letters, digits, or underscores.

The *lines_of_output* consists of one or more lines of text that are to be printed when the print format is utilized; these lines are sometimes called *picture lines*. In the MYFORMAT example, there are three lines of text printed: two lines containing = characters, and the line

▲ Here is the text I want to display.

A print-format definition is terminated with a line containing a period character. This line can contain nothing else; there can be no white space, and the period must be the first character on the line.

Like subroutines, print-format definitions can appear anywhere in program code (even, for example, in the middle of a conditional statement). However, it usually is best to cluster them either at the beginning or the end of the program.

Displaying a Print Format

To display output using a print format, you need to do two things:

- ☐ Set the system variable $- to the format you want to use
- ☐ Call the built-in function write

Listing 11.1 is an example of a simple program that displays output using a print format.

TYPE **Listing 11.1. A program that uses a print format.**

```
 1:  #!/usr/local/bin/perl
 2:
 3:  $~ = "MYFORMAT";
 4:  write;
 5:
 6:  format MYFORMAT =
 7:  ===================================
 8:  Here is the text I want to display.
 9:  ===================================
10:  .
```

OUTPUT
```
$ program11_1
===================================
Here is the text I want to display.
===================================
$
```

ANALYSIS Line 3 of this program assigns the character string MYFORMAT to the system variable $~. This tells the Perl interpreter that MYFORMAT is the print format to use when calling write.

Line 4 calls write, which sends the text defined in MYFORMAT to the standard output file.

Lines 6–10 contain the definition of the print format MYFORMAT.

NOTE

If you don't specify a print format by assigning to $~, the Perl interpreter assumes that the print format to use has the same name as the file variable being written to. In this example program, if line 3 had not specified MYFORMAT as the print format to use, the Perl interpreter would have tried to use a print format named STDOUT when executing the call to write in line 4, because the call to write is writing to the standard output file.

Displaying Values in a Print Format

Of course, the main reason to use print formats is to format values stored in scalar variables or array variables to produce readable output. Perl enables you to do this by specifying *value fields* as part of a format definition.

Each value field specifies a value: the name of a scalar variable, for example, or an expression. When the write statement is invoked, the value is displayed in the format specified by the value field.

Listing 11.2 shows how value fields work. This program keeps track of the number of occurrences of the letters a, e, i, o, and u in a text file.

Listing 11.2. A program that uses value fields to print output.

```
1:  #!/usr/local/bin/perl
2:
3:  while ($line = <STDIN>) {
4:          $line =~ s/[^aeiou]//g;
5:          @vowels = split(//, $line);
6:          foreach $vowel (@vowels) {
7:                  $vowelcount{$vowel} += 1;
8:          }
9:  }
10: $~ = "VOWELFORMAT";
11: write;
12:
13: format VOWELFORMAT =
14: ============================================================
15: Number of vowels found in text file:
16:         a: @<<<<<   e: @<<<<<
17:         $vowelcount{"a"}, $vowelcount{"e"}
18:         i: @<<<<<   o: @<<<<<
19:         $vowelcount{"i"}, $vowelcount{"o"}
20:         u: @<<<<<
21:         $vowelcount{"u"}
22: ============================================================
23: .
```

OUTPUT

```
$ program11_2
This is a test file.
This test file contains some vowels.
The quick brown fox jumped over the lazy dog.
^D
============================================================
Number of vowels found in text file:
        a: 3       e: 10
        i: 7       o: 7
        u: 2
============================================================
$
```

ANALYSIS   This program reads one line of input at a time. Line 4 removes everything that is not a, e, i, o, or u from the input line, and line 5 splits the remaining characters into the array @vowels. Each element of @vowels is one character of the input line.

Lines 6–8 count the vowels in the input line by examining the elements of @vowels and adding to the associative array %vowelcount.

Line 10 sets the current print format to VOWELFORMAT; line 11 prints using VOWELFORMAT.

The print format VOWELFORMAT is defined in lines 13–23. Line 16 is an example of a print format line that contains value fields; in this case, two value fields are defined. Each value field has the format @<<<<<, which indicates six left-justified characters. (For a complete description of the possible value fields, see the section called "Choosing a Value-Field Format," later today.)

When one or more value fields appear in a print-format line, the next line must define the value or values to be printed in this value field. Because line 16 defines two value fields, line 17 defines the two values to be printed. These values are $vowelcount{"a"} and $vowelcount{"e"}, which are the number of occurrences of a and e, respectively.

Similarly, line 18 defines two more value fields to be printed, and line 19 indicates that the values to be printed in these fields are $vowelcount{"i"} and $vowelcount{"o"}. Finally, line 20 defines a fifth value field, and line 21 specifies that $vowelcount{"u"} is to be printed in this field.

NOTE Three things to note about the values that are specified for value-field formats:

- The lines containing values to be printed are not themselves printed. For example, in Listing 11.2, lines 16, 18, and 20 are printed, but lines 17, 19, and 21 are not.

- The Perl interpreter ignores spacing when it looks for values corresponding to value fields. Many people prefer to line up their values with the corresponding value fields on the previous line, but there is no need to do so.

- The number of values specified must match the number of value fields defined on the previous line.

11

Creating a General-Purpose Print Format

One disadvantage of print formats as defined in Perl is that scalar-variable names are included as part of the definition. For example, in the following definition, the scalar variable $winnum is built into the print format definition MYFORMAT:

```
format MYFORMAT =
=========================================================
The winning number is @<<<<<<!
$winnum
=========================================================
.
```

When write is called with this print format, as in the following, you have to remember that $winnum is being used by MYFORMAT.

```
$~ = "MYFORMAT";
write;
```

If, later on, you accidentally delete all references to $winnum in the program, the call to write will stop working properly.

One way to get around this problem is to call write from within a subroutine, and to use variables local to the subroutine in the print format that write uses. Listing 11.3 is a program that does this. It reads a file from the standard input file and prints out the number of occurrences of the five most frequently occurring letters.

Listing 11.3. A program that calls write from within a subroutine.

TYPE

```
1:  #!/usr/local/bin/perl
2:
3:  while ($line = <STDIN>) {
4:          $line =~ tr/A-Z/a-z/;
5:          $line =~ s/[^a-z]//g;
6:          @letters = split(//, $line);
7:          foreach $letter (@letters) {
8:                  $lettercount{$letter} += 1;
9:          }
10: }
11:
12: $~ = "WRITEHEADER";
13: write;
14: $count = 0;
15: foreach $letter (reverse sort occurrences
16:                 (keys(%lettercount))) {
17:         &write_letter($letter, $lettercount{$letter});
18:         last if (++$count == 5);
19: }
20:
21: sub occurrences {
22:         $lettercount{$a} <=> $lettercount{$b};
23: }
24: sub write_letter {
25:         local($letter, $value) = @_;
26:
27:         $~ = "WRITELETTER";
28:         write;
29: }
30: format WRITEHEADER =
31: The five most frequently occurring letters are:
32: .
33: format WRITELETTER =
34:         @:  @<<<<<<
35:         $letter, $value
36: .
```

OUTPUT

```
$ program11_3
This is a test file.
This test file contains some input.
The quick brown fox jumped over the lazy dog.
^D
The five most frequently occurring letters are:
        t: 10
        e: 9
        i: 8
        s: 7
        o: 6
$
```

ANALYSIS   Like the vowel-counting program in Listing 11.2, this program processes one line of input at a time. Line 4 translates all uppercase alphabetic characters into lowercase, so that they can be included in the letter count. Line 5 gets rid of all characters that are not letters, including any white space.

Line 6 splits the line into its individual letters; lines 7–9 examine each letter and increment the appropriate letter counters, which are stored in the associative array `%lettercount`.

Lines 12 and 13 print the following line by setting the current print format to `WRITEHEADER` and calling `write`:

```
The five most frequently occurring letters are:
```

WARNING

> Except in very special cases, never mix calls to `write` with calls to `print`. Your program should use one printing function or the other, not both.

Lines 15–19 sort the array `%lettercount` in order of occurrence. The first letter to appear in the `foreach` loop is the letter that appears most often in the file. To sort the array in order of occurrence, lines 15 and 16 specify that sorting is to be performed according to the rules defined in the subroutine `occurrences`. This subroutine tells the Perl interpreter to use the values of the associative array elements as the sort criterion.

Line 17 passes the letter and its occurrence count to the subroutine `write_letter`. This subroutine sets the current print format to `WRITELETTER`; this print format refers to the local scalar variables `$letter` and `$value`, which contain the values passed to `write_letter` by line 17. This means that each call to `write_letter` prints the letter and value currently being examined by the `foreach` loop.

Note that the first value field in the print format `WRITELETTER` contains only a single character, `@`. This indicates that the write field is only one character long (which makes sense, because this is a single letter).

11

Line 18 ensures that the foreach loop quits after the five most frequently used letters have been examined and printed.

TIP

Some programs, such as the one in Listing 11.3, use more than one print-format definition. To make it easier to see which print format is being used by a particular call to write, always keep the print format specification statement and the write call together. For example:

```
$~ = "WRITEFORMAT";

write;
```

Here, it is obvious that the call to write is using the print format WRITEFORMAT.

Formats and Local Variables

In Listing 11.3, you might have noticed that the subroutine write_letter calls a subroutine to write out a letter and its value:

```
sub write_letter {
        local($letter, $value) = @_;

        $~ = "WRITELETTER";
        write;
}
```

This subroutine works properly even though the WRITELETTER print format is defined outside the subroutine.

Note, however, that local variables defined using my cannot be written out using a print format unless the format is defined inside the subroutine. (To see this for yourself, change line 25 of Listing 11.3 to the following and run the program again:

```
my($letter,$value) = @_;
```

You will notice that the letter counts do not appear.) This limitation is a result of the way local variables defined using my are stored by the Perl interpreter. To avoid this difficulty, use local instead of my when you define local variables that are to be written out using write. (For a discussion of local and my, see Day 9, "Using Subroutines.")

Perl 4 users will not run into this problem, because my is not defined for that version of the language.

11

NOTE In versions of Perl 5 earlier than version 5.001, local variables defined using my cannot be written out at all. Even in version 5.001, variables defined using my might not behave in the way you expect them to. As a consequence, it is best to avoid using my with print formats.

Choosing a Value-Field Format

Now that you know how print formats and write work, it's time to look at the value-field formats that are available. Table 11.1 lists these formats.

Table 11.1. Valid value-field formats.

Field	Value-field format
@<<<	Left-justified output
@>>>	Right-justified output
@¦¦¦	Centered output
@##.##	Fixed-precision numeric
@*	Multiline text

NOTE In *left-justified* output, the value being displayed appears at the left end of the value field. In *right-justified* output, the value being displayed appears at the right end of the value field.

In each of the field formats, the first character is a *line-fill character*. It indicates whether text formatting is required. If the @ character is specified as the line fill character, text formatting is not performed. (For a discussion of text formatting, see the section titled "Formatting Long Character Strings," later today.)

In all cases, except for the multiline value field @*, the width of the field is equal to the number of characters specified. The @ character is included when counting the number of characters in the value field. For example, the following field is five characters wide—one @ character and four > characters:

@>>>>

Similarly, the following field is seven characters wide—four before the decimal point, two after the decimal point, and the decimal point itself:

```
@###.##
```

Listing 11.4 illustrates how you can use the value field formats to produce a neatly printed report. The report is redirected to a file for later printing.

Listing 11.4. A program that uses the various value-field formats.

TYPE

```
 1:  #!/usr/local/bin/perl
 2:
 3:  $company = <STDIN>;
 4:  $~ = "COMPANY";
 5:  write;
 6:
 7:  $grandtotal = 0;
 8:  $custline = <STDIN>;
 9:  while ($custline ne "") {
10:          $total = 0;
11:          ($customer, $date) = split(/#/, $custline);
12:          $~ = "CUSTOMER";
13:          write;
14:          while (1) {
15:                  $orderline = <STDIN>;
16:                  if ($orderline eq "" || $orderline =~ /#/) {
17:                          $custline = $orderline;
18:                          last;
19:                  }
20:                  ($item, $cost) = split(/:/, $orderline);
21:                  $~ = "ORDERLINE";
22:                  write;
23:                  $total += $cost;
24:          }
25:          &write_total ("Total:", $total);
26:          $grandtotal += $total;
27: }
28: &write_total ("Grand total:", $grandtotal);
29:
30: sub write_total {
31:          local ($totalstring, $total) = @_;
32:          $~ = "TOTAL";
33:          write;
34: }
35:
36: format COMPANY =
37: ************* @||||||||||||||||||||||||||||||||||||| *************
38: $company
39: .
40: format CUSTOMER =
41: @<<<<<<<<<<<<<<<<<<<<<<<<<<<<<<         @>>>>>>>>>>>>
42: $customer, $date
```

```
43: .
44: format ORDERLINE =
45:        @<<<<<<<<<<<<<<<<<<<<<<<<<<<<        @####.##
46: $item, $cost
47: .
48: format TOTAL =
49: @<<<<<<<<<<<<<                              @#####.##
50: $totalstring, $total
51:
52: .
```

OUTPUT

```
$ program11_4 >report
Consolidated Widgets, Inc.
John Doe#Feb 11, 1994
1 flying widget:171.42
1 crawling widget:89.99
Mary Smith#May 4, 1994
2 swimming widgets:203.43
^D
$
```

The following report is written to the report file:

```
*************    Consolidated Widgets, Inc.    *************
John Doe                                        Feb 11, 1994
                1 flying widget                       171.42
                1 crawling widget                      89.99
Total:                                                261.41

Mary Smith                                       May 4, 1994
                2 swimming widgets                    203.43
Total:                                                203.43

Grand total:                                          464.84
```

ANALYSIS
This program starts off by reading the company name from the standard input file and then writing it out. Line 5 writes the company name using the print format COMPANY, which uses a centered output field to display the company name in the center of the line.

After the company name has been printed, the program starts processing data for one customer at a time. Each customer record is assumed to consist of a customer name and date followed by lines of orders. The customer name record uses a # character as the field separator, and the order records use : characters as the separator; this enables the program to distinguish one type of record from the other.

Line 13 prints the customer information using the CUSTOMER print format. This format contains two fields: a left-justified output field for the customer name, and a right-justified output field for the date of the transaction.

Line 22 prints an order line using the ORDERLINE print format. This print format also contains two fields: a left-justified output field indicating the item ordered, and a numeric field to display the cost of the item.

The value field format @####.## indicates that the cost is to be displayed as a floating-point number. This number is defined as containing at most five digits before the decimal point, and two digits after.

Finally, the print format TOTAL prints the customer total and the grand total. Because this print format is used inside a subroutine, the same print format can be used to print both totals.

WARNING

Normally, any floating-point number you print is rounded up when necessary. For example, when you print 43.999 in the value field @#.##, it appears as 44.00.

However, a floating-point number whose last decimal place is 5 might or might not round correctly. For example, if you are writing using the value field @#.##, some numbers whose third and last decimal place is 5 will round and others will not. This happens because some floating-point numbers cannot be stored exactly, and the nearest equivalent number that can be stored is a slightly smaller number (which rounds down, not up).

Printing Value-Field Characters

As you have seen, certain characters such as @, <, and > are treated as value fields when they are encountered in print formats. Listing 11.5 shows how to actually print one of these special characters using write.

TYPE **Listing 11.5. A program that prints a value-field character.**

```
1:  #!/usr/local/bin/perl
2:
3:  format SPECIAL =
4:  This line contains the special character @.
5:  "@"
6:  .
7:
8:  $~ = "SPECIAL";
9:  write;
```

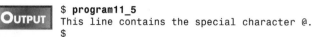

OUTPUT

```
$ program11_5
This line contains the special character @.
$
```

ANALYSIS

The print format line in line 4 contains the special character @, which is a one-character value field. Line 5 specifies that the string @ is to be displayed in this value field when the line is printed.

Using the Multiline Field Format

Listing 11.6 uses the multiline field format @* to write a character string over several lines.

TYPE

Listing 11.6. A program that writes a string using the multiline field format.

```
1:  #!/usr/local/bin/perl
2:
3:  @input = <STDIN>;
4:  $string = join("", @input);
5:  $~ = "MULTILINE";
6:  write;
7:
8:  format MULTILINE =
9:  ****** contents of the input file: ******
10: @*
11: $string
12: *****************************************
13: .
```

OUTPUT

```
$ program11_6
Here is a line of input.
Here is another line.
Here is the last line.
^D
****** contents of the input file: ******
Here is a line of input.
Here is another line.
Here is the last line.
*****************************************
$
```

ANALYSIS

Line 3 reads the entire input file into the array variable @input. Each element of the list stored in @input is one line of the input file.

Line 4 joins the input lines into a single character string, stored in $string. This character string still contains the newline characters that end each line.

Line 6 calls write using the print format MULTILINE. The @* value field in this print-format definition indicates that the value stored in $string is to be written out using as many lines as necessary. This ensures that the entire string stored in $string is written out.

WARNING

If a character string contains a newline character, the only way to display the entire string using `write` is to use the `@*` multiline value field. If you use any other value field, only the part of the string preceding the first newline character is displayed.

Writing to Other Output Files

So far, all of the examples that have used the function `write` have written to the standard output file. However, you can use `write` also to send output to other files.

The simplest way to do this is to pass the file to write to as an argument to `write`. For example, to write to the file represented by the file variable `MYFILE` using the print format `MYFILE`, you can use the following statement:

```
write (MYFILE);
```

Here, `write` writes to the file named `MYFILE` using the default print format, which is also `MYFILE`. This is tidy and efficient, but somewhat restricting because, in this case, you can't use `$~` to choose the print format to use.

The `$~` system variable only works with the *default file variable*, which is the file variable to which `write` sends output. To change the default file variable, and therefore change the file that `$~` affects, call the built-in function `select`, as follows:

```
select (MYFILE);
```

`select` sets the default file variable to use when writing. For example, to write to the file represented by the file variable `MYFILE` using the print format `MYFORMAT`, you can use the following statements:

```
select(MYFILE);
$~ = "MYFORMAT";
write;
```

Here, the built-in function `select` indicates that the file to be written to is the file represented by the file variable `MYFILE`. The statement

```
$~ = "MYFORMAT";
```

selects the print format to be associated with this particular file handle; in this case, the print format `MYFORMAT` is now associated with the file variable `MYFILE`.

NOTE

This is worth repeating: Each file variable has its own current print format. An assignment to $~ only changes the print format for the current file variable (the last one passed to select).

Because select has changed the file to be written to, the call to write no longer writes to the standard output file. Instead, it writes to MYFILE. Calls to write continue to write to MYFILE until the following statement is seen:

```
select(STDOUT);
```

This statement resets the write file to be the standard output file.

WARNING

Changing the write file using select not only affects write; it also affects print. For example, consider the following:

```
select (MYFILE);

print ("Here is a line of text.\n");
```

This call to print writes to MYFILE, not to the standard output file. As with write, calls to print continue to write to MYFILE until another call to select is seen.

11

The select function is useful if you want to be able to use the same subroutine to write to more than one file at a time. Listing 11.7 is an example of a simple program that does this.

TYPE **Listing 11.7. A program that uses the select function.**

```
 1:  #!/usr/local/bin/perl
 2:
 3:  open (FILE1, ">file1");
 4:  $string = "junk";
 5:  select (FILE1);
 6:  &writeline;
 7:  select (STDOUT);
 8:  &writeline;
 9:  close (FILE1);
10:
11:  sub writeline {
12:          $~ = "WRITELINE";
13:          write;
14:  }
15:
```

continues

Listing 11.7. continued

```
16: format WRITELINE =
17:          I am writing @<<<<< to my output files.
18:                       $string
19: .
```

OUTPUT

```
$ program11_7
          I am writing junk    to my output files.
$
```

ANALYSIS Line 5 of this program calls `select`, which sets the default file variable to FILE1. Now, all calls to `write` or `print` write to FILE, not the standard output file.

Line 6 calls `writeline` to write a line. This subroutine sets the current print format for the default file variable to WRITELINE. This means that the file FILE1 now is using the print format WRITELINE, and, therefore, the subroutine writes the following line to the file FILE1 (which is file1):

```
I am writing junk    to my output files.
```

Line 7 sets the default file variable back to the standard output file variable, STDOUT. This means that `write` and `print` now send output to the standard output file. Note that the current print format for the standard output file is STDOUT (the default), not WRITELINE; the assignment to `$~` in the subroutine WRITELINE affects only FILE1, not STDOUT.

Line 8 calls `writeline` again; this time, the subroutine writes a line to the standard output file. The assignment

```
$~ = "WRITELINE";
```

in line 12 associates the print format WRITELINE with the standard output file. This means that WRITELINE is now associated with both STDOUT and FILE1.

At this point, the call to `write` in line 13 writes the line of output that you see on the standard output file.

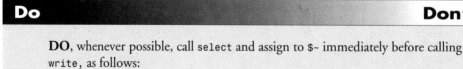

Do   **Don't**

DO, whenever possible, call `select` and assign to `$~` immediately before calling `write`, as follows:

```
select (MYFILE);
$~ = "MYFORMAT";
write;
```

Keeping these statements together makes it clear which file is being written to and which print format is being used.

DON'T use select and $- indiscriminately, because you might lose track of which print format goes with which file variable, and you might forget which file variable is the default for printing.

Saving the Default File Variable

When select changes the default file variable, it returns an internal representation of the file variable that was last selected. For example:

```
$oldfile = select(NEWFILE);
```

This call to select is setting the current file variable to NEWFILE. The old file variable is now stored in $oldfile. To restore the previous default file variable, you can call select as follows:

```
select ($oldfile);
```

At this point, the default file variable reverts back to its original value (what it was before NEWFILE was selected).

WARNING

> The internal representation of the file variable returned by select is not necessarily the name of the file variable.

You can use the return value from select to create subroutines that write to the file you want to write with, using the print format you want to use, without affecting the rest of the program. For example:

```
sub write_to_stdout {
        local ($savefile, $saveformat);
        $savefile = select(STDOUT);
        $saveformat = $~;
        $~ = "MYFORMAT";
        write;
        $~ = $saveformat;
        select($savefile);
}
```

This subroutine calls select to set the default output file to STDOUT, the standard output file. The return value from select, the previous default file, is saved in $savefile.

Now that the default output file is STDOUT, the next step is to save the current print format being used to write to STDOUT. The subroutine does this by saving the present value of $~ in another local variable, $saveformat. After this is saved, the subroutine can set the current print format to MYFORMAT. The call to write now writes to the standard output file using MYFORMAT.

After the call to write is complete, the subroutine puts things back the way they were. The first step is to reset $~ to the value stored in $saveformat. The final step is to set the default output file back to the file variable whose representation is saved in $savefile.

Note that the call to select must appear after the assignment to $~. If the call to select had been first, the assignment to $~ would change the print format associated with the original default file variable, not STDOUT.

As you can see, this subroutine doesn't need to know what the default values outside the subroutine are. Also, it does not affect the default values outside the subroutine.

Specifying a Page Header

If you are sending your output to a printer, you can make your output look smarter by supplying text to appear at the top of every page in your output. This special text is called a *page header.*

If a page header is defined for a particular output file, write automatically paginates the output to that file. When the number of lines printed is greater than the length of a page, write starts a new page.

To define a page header for a file, create a print format definition with the name of *filename*_TOP, where *filename* is a placeholder for the name of the file variable corresponding to the file to which you are writing. For example, to define a header for writing to standard output, define a print format named STDOUT_TOP, as follows:

```
format STDOUT_TOP =
Consolidated Widgets Inc. 1994 Annual Report
.
```

In this case, when the Perl interpreter starts a new page of standard output, the contents of the print format STDOUT_TOP are printed automatically.

Print formats that generate headers can contain value fields which are replaced by scalar values, just like any other print format. One particular value that is often used in page headers is the current page number, which is stored in the system variable $%. For example:

```
format STDOUT_TOP =
Page @<<.
$%
.
```

In this case, when the first page is printed, the program prints the following header at the top of the page:

```
Page 1.
```

NOTE

By default, `$%` is initially set to zero and is incremented every time a new page begins.

To change the pagination, change the value of `$%` before (or during) printing.

Changing the Header Print Format

To change the name of the print format that prints a page header for a particular file, change the value stored in the special system variable `$^`.

As with `$~`, only the value for the current default file can be changed. For example, to use the print format MYHEADER as the header file for the file MYFILE, add the following statements:

```
$oldfile = select(MYFILE);
$^ = "MYHEADER";
select($oldfile);
.
```

These statements set MYFILE to be the current default file, change the header for MYFILE to be the print format MYHEADER, and then reset the current default file to its original value.

Setting the Page Length

By default, the page length is 60 lines. To specify a different page length, change the value stored in the system variable `$=`:

```
$= = 66;     # set the page length to 66 lines
```

This assignment must appear before the first `write` statement.

WARNING

If the page length is changed in the middle of the program, the new page length will not be used until a new page is started.

Listing 11.8 shows how you can set the page length and define a page-header print format for your output file.

Listing 11.8. A program that sets the length and print format for a page.

TYPE

```
 1:  #!/usr/local/bin/perl
 2:
 3:  open (OUTFILE, ">file1");
 4:  select (OUTFILE);
 5:  $~ = "WRITELINE";
 6:  $^ = "TOP_OF_PAGE";
 7:  $= = 60;
 8:  while ($line = <STDIN>) {
 9:          write;
10:  }
11:  close (OUTFILE);
12:
13:  format TOP_OF_PAGE =
14:                                          — page @<
15:                                                  $%
16:  .
17:  format WRITELINE =
18:  @>>>>>>>>>>>>>>>>>>>>>>>>>>>>>>
19:  $line
20:  .
```

OUTPUT

Suppose that you supply the following input:

```
$ program11_8
Here is a line of input.
Here is another line.
Here is the last line.
^D
$
```

The following output is written to the file file1:

```
                          — page 1
               Here is a line of input.
                Here is another line.
                Here is the last line.
```

ANALYSIS

Line 3 opens the file file1 for output and associates it with the file variable OUTFILE.

Line 4 sets the current default file to OUTFILE. Now, when write or print is called with no file variable supplied, the output is sent to OUTFILE.

Line 5 indicates that WRITELINE is the print format to be used when writing to the file OUTFILE. To do this, it assigns WRITELINE to the system variable $~. This assignment does not affect the page header.

Line 6 indicates that TOP_OF_PAGE is the print format to be used when printing the page headers for the file OUTFILE. This assignment does not affect the print format used to write to the body of the page.

Line 7 sets the page length to 60 lines. This page length takes effect immediately, because no output has been written to OUTFILE.

Using print with Pagination

Normally, you won't want to use print if you are using pagination, because the Perl interpreter keeps track of the current line number on the page by monitoring the calls to write. If you must use a call to print in your program and you want to ensure that the page counter includes the call in its line count, adjust the system variable $-. This system variable indicates the number of lines between the current line and the bottom of the page. When $- reaches 0, a top-of-form character is generated, which starts a new page.

The following is a code fragment that calls print and then adjusts the $- variable:

```
print ("Here is a line of output\n");
$- -= 1;
```

When $- has 1 subtracted from its value, the page counter becomes correct.

Formatting Long Character Strings

As you've seen, the @* value field prints multiple lines of text. However, this field prints the output exactly as it is stored in the character string. For example, consider Listing 11.9, which uses @* to write a multiline character string.

TYPE

Listing 11.9. A program that illustrates the limitations of the @* value field.

```
1:  #!/usr/local/bin/perl
2:
3:  $string = "Here\nis an unbalanced line of\ntext.\n";
4:  $~ = "OUTLINE";
5:  write;
6:
7:  format OUTLINE =
8:  @*
9:  $string
10: .
```

OUTPUT

```
$ program11_9
Here
is an unbalanced line of
text.
$
```

ANALYSIS This call to write displays the character string stored in $string exactly as is. Perl enables you to define value fields in print-format definitions that format text. To do this, replace the initial @ character in the value field with a ^ character. When text formatting is specified, the Perl interpreter tries to fit as many words as possible into the output line.

Listing 11.10 is an example of a simple program that does this.

 TYPE

Listing 11.10. A program that uses a value field that does formatting.

```
 1:  #!/usr/local/bin/perl
 2:
 3:  $string = "Here\nis an unbalanced line of\ntext.\n";
 4:  $~ = "OUTLINE";
 5:  write;
 6:
 7:  format OUTLINE =
 8:  ^<<<<<<<<<<<<<<<<<<<<<<<<<<<
 9:  $string
10:  .
```

 OUTPUT
```
$ program11_10
Here is an unbalanced line
$
```

ANALYSIS Line 5 calls write using the print format OUTLINE. This print format contains a value field that specifies that formatting is to take place; this means that the Perl interpreter tries to fit as many words as possible into the line of output. In this case, the first line Here and the four-word string is an unbalanced line fit into the output line.

Note that there are two characters left over in the output line after the four words have been filled in. These characters are not filled, because the next word is not short enough to fit into the space remaining. Only entire words are filled.

One other feature of the line-filling operation is that the substring printed out is actually deleted from the scalar variable $string. This means that the value of $string is now of\ntext.\n. This happens because subsequent lines of output in the same print-format definition can be used to print the rest of the string.

NOTE

> Because the line-filling write operation updates the value used, the value must be contained in a scalar variable and cannot be the result of an expression.

 11

To see how multiple lines of formatted output work, look at Listing 11.11. This program reads a quotation from the standard input file and writes it out on three formatted lines of output.

TYPE

Listing 11.11. A program that writes out multiple formatted lines of output.

```
1:  #!/usr/local/bin/perl
2:
3:  @quotation = <STDIN>;
4:  $quotation = join("", @quotation);
5:  $~ = "QUOTATION";
6:  write;
7:
8:  format QUOTATION =
9:  Quotation for the day:
10: _ _ _ _ _ _ _ _ _ _ _ _ _ _ _ _ _ _ _ _ _ _ _ _ _ _
11:     ^<<<<<<<<<<<<<<<<<<<<<<<<<<<<<<<<<<<<<<<<<<<<<
12:     $quotation
13:     ^<<<<<<<<<<<<<<<<<<<<<<<<<<<<<<<<<<<<<<<<<<<<<
14:     $quotation
15:     ^<<<<<<<<<<<<<<<<<<<<<<<<<<<<<<<<<<<<<<<<<<<<<
16:     $quotation
17: _ _ _ _ _ _ _ _ _ _ _ _ _ _ _ _ _ _ _ _ _ _ _ _ _ _
18: .
```

OUTPUT

```
$ program11_11
Any sufficiently advanced programming
language is indistinguishable from magic.
^D
Quotation for the day:
_ _ _ _ _ _ _ _ _ _ _ _ _ _ _ _ _ _ _ _ _ _ _ _ _
    Any sufficiently advanced programming language is
    indistinguishable from magic.


_ _ _ _ _ _ _ _ _ _ _ _ _ _ _ _ _ _ _ _ _ _ _ _ _
$
```

ANALYSIS The print format QUOTATION defines three value fields on which formatting is to be employed. Each of the three value fields uses the value of the scalar variable $quotation.

Before write is called, $quotation contains the entire quotation with newline characters appearing at the end of each input line. When write is called, the first value field in the print format uses as much of the quotation as possible. This means that the following substring is written to the standard output file:

```
Any sufficiently advanced programming language is
```

After the substring is written, it is removed from $quotation, which now contains the following:

```
indistinguishable from magic.
```

Because the written substring has been removed from $quotation, the remainder of the string can be used in subsequent output lines. Because the next value field in the print format also wants to use $quotation, the remainder of the string appears on the second output line and is deleted. $quotation is now the empty string.

This means that the third value field, which also refers to $quotation, is replaced by the empty string, and a blank line is written out.

WARNING

> The scalar variable containing the output to be printed is changed by a write operation. If you need to preserve the information, copy it to another scalar variable before calling write.

Eliminating Blank Lines When Formatting

You can eliminate blank lines such as the one generated by Listing 11.11. To do this, put a ~ character at the beginning of any output line that is to be printed only when needed.

Listing 11.12 modifies the quotation-printing program to print lines only when they are not blank.

TYPE **Listing 11.12. A program that writes out multiple formatted lines of output and suppresses blank lines.**

```
1:  #!/usr/local/bin/perl
2:
3:  @quotation = <STDIN>;
4:  $quotation = join("", @quotation);
5:  $~ = "QUOTATION";
6:  write;
7:
8:  format QUOTATION =
9:  Quotation for the day:
10: - - - - - - - - - - - - - - - - - - - - - - - - -
11: ~   ^<<<<<<<<<<<<<<<<<<<<<<<<<<<<<<<<<<<<<<<<<<<<<<
12:     $quotation
13: ~   ^<<<<<<<<<<<<<<<<<<<<<<<<<<<<<<<<<<<<<<<<<<<<<<
14:     $quotation
15: ~   ^<<<<<<<<<<<<<<<<<<<<<<<<<<<<<<<<<<<<<<<<<<<<<<
```

```
16:    $quotation
17: — — — — — — — — — — — — — — — — — — — — — — — — — — — — —
18: .
```

```
$ program11_12
Any sufficiently advanced programming
language is indistinguishable from magic.
^D
Quotation for the day:
— — — — — — — — — — — — — — — — — — — — — — — — — — — —
    Any sufficiently advanced programming language is
    indistinguishable from magic.
— — — — — — — — — — — — — — — — — — — — — — — — — — — —
$
```

ANALYSIS If the quotation is too short to require all the lines, remaining lines are left blank. In this case, the quotation requires only two lines of output, so the third isn't printed.

The program is identical to the one in Listing 11.11 in all other respects. In particular, the value of $quotation after the call to write is still the empty string.

Supplying an Indefinite Number of Lines

While Listing 11.12 suppresses blank lines, it imposes an upper limit of three lines. Quotations longer than three lines are not printed in their entirety. To indicate that the formatted output is to use as many lines as necessary, specify two ~ characters at the beginning of the output line containing the value field. Listing 11.13 modifies the quotation program to allow quotations of any length.

TYPE

Listing 11.13. A program that writes out as many formatted lines of output as necessary.

```
1:  #!/usr/local/bin/perl
2:
3:  @quotation = <STDIN>;
4:  $quotation = join("", @quotation);
5:  $~ = "QUOTATION";
6:  write;
7:
8:  format QUOTATION =
9:  Quotation for the day:
10: — — — — — — — — — — — — — — — — — — — — — — — — — — —
11: ~~ ^<<<<<<<<<<<<<<<<<<<<<<<<<<<<<<<<<<<<<<<<<<<<<<<<<
12:     $quotation
13: — — — — — — — — — — — — — — — — — — — — — — — — — — —
14: .
```

```
$ program11_13
Any sufficiently advanced programming
language is indistinguishable from magic.
^D
Quotation for the day:
_ _ _ _ _ _ _ _ _ _ _ _ _ _ _ _ _ _ _ _ _ _ _ _ _ _ _ _ _ _ _
    Any sufficiently advanced programming language is
    indistinguishable from magic.
_ _ _ _ _ _ _ _ _ _ _ _ _ _ _ _ _ _ _ _ _ _ _ _ _ _ _ _ _
$
```

ANALYSIS   The ~~ characters at the beginning of the output field indicate that multiple copies of the output line are to be supplied. The output line is to be printed until there is nothing more to print.

In Listing 11.13, two copies of the line are needed.

Formatting Output Using `printf`

If you want to write output that looks reasonable without going to all the trouble of using `write` and `print` formats, Perl provides a built-in function, `printf`, that prints formatted output.

NOTE
> If you are familiar with the C programming language, the behavior of `printf` in Perl will be familiar; the Perl `printf` and the C `printf` are basically the same.

The arguments passed to the `printf` function are as follows:

☐ The string to be printed, which can contain one or more *field specifiers*

☐ One value for each field specifier appearing in the string to be printed

When `printf` sees a field specifier, it substitutes the corresponding value in the `printf` argument list. The representation of the substituted value in the string depends on the field specifier that is supplied.

Field specifiers consist of the `%` character followed by a single character that represents the format to use when printing. Table 11.2 lists the field-specifier formats and the field-specifier character that represents each.

Table 11.2. Field specifiers for `printf`.

Specifier	Description
%c	Single character
%d	Integer in decimal (base-10) format
%e	Floating-point number in scientific notation
%f	Floating-point number in "normal" (fixed-point) notation
%g	Floating-point number in compact format
%o	Integer in octal (base-8) format
%s	Character string
%u	Unsigned integer
%x	Integer in hexadecimal (base-16) format

Here is a simple example of a call to `printf`:

```
printf("The number I want to print is %d.\n", $number);
```

The string to be printed contains one field specifier, %d, which represents an integer. The value stored in $number is substituted for the field specifier and printed.

Field specifiers also support a variety of options, as follows:

☐ If you are printing an integer using the d, o, u, or x format, you can put an l character in front of the field-specifier character (as in, for example, %ld). This character specifies that the number is a decimal integer in the machine's "long integer" format (corresponding to the C type long). This is useful if your integer is large or might be.

☐ A positive integer following the % character indicates the minimum width of the field. For example, %20s prints a character string in a field of 20 characters. If the string is not large enough to fill the entire field, it is right justified (placed at the right end of the field) and padded with blanks. (If the integer starts with a leading 0, as in %08d, the field is padded with zeros, not blanks.)

☐ A negative integer following the % character indicates the width of the field and requests left justification. For example, %-15s prints a character string in a field of 15 characters, and it fills the right end of the field with blanks if the string is not large enough.

☐ If you are using a field specifier that prints a floating-point number (%e, %f, or %g), you can specify the number of digits that are to appear after the decimal point. To do this, specify a floating-point number after the % character. For example:

```
%8.3f
```

Here, the number preceding the decimal point is the field width (as before), and the number after the decimal point is the number of decimal places to print.

WARNING

If a floating-point number contains more digits than the field specifier wants, the number is rounded to the number of decimal places needed. For example, if `43.499` is being printed using the field `%5.2f`, the number actually printed is `43.50`.

As with the write value field `@##.##`, printf might not always round up when it is handling numbers whose last decimal place is 5. This happens because some floating-point numbers cannot be stored exactly, and the nearest equivalent number that can be stored is a slightly smaller number (which rounds down, not up). For example, `43.495` when printed by `%5.2f` might print `43.49`, depending on how `43.495` is stored.

☐ If you are using a field specifier that prints an integer, character, or string, supplying a floating-point number after the `%` character specifies the maximum length of the value to be printed. In the following example a character string is printed in a 15-character field, but the string itself can be at most 10 characters long:

`%15.10s`

This guarantees that at least five spaces will appear in the printed line.

NOTE

You can use `printf` to print to other files. To do this, specify the file variable corresponding to the file to which you want to print, just as you would with `print` or `write`:

`printf MYFILE ("I am printing %d.\n", $value);`

This means that changing the current default file using `select` affects `printf`.

Summary

Perl enables you to format your output using print-format definitions and the built-in function write. In print-format definitions, you can specify value fields that are to be replaced by either the contents of scalar variables or the values of expressions.

Value fields indicate how to print the contents of a scalar variable or the value of an expression. With a value field, you can specify that the value is to be left justified (blanks added on the right), right justified (blanks added on the left), centered, or displayed as a floating-point number.

You also can define value fields that format a multiline character string. Blank lines can be suppressed, and the field can be defined to use as many output lines as necessary.

The built-in function select enables you to change the default file to which write and print send output.

You can break your output into pages by defining a special header print format that prints header information at the top of each page.

The following system variables enable you to control how write sends output to a file:

- ☐ The system variable $~ contains the name of the print format being used by the current default file.
- ☐ The system variable $^ contains the name of the print format being used as a page header by the current default file.
- ☐ The system variable $= contains the number of lines per printed page.
- ☐ The system variable $- contains the number of lines left on the current page.

The built-in function printf enables you to format an individual line of text using format specifiers.

Q&A

Q Which is better, write or printf?

A It depends on what you want to do. If you want to print reports or control pagination, you'll need to use write. If you just want individual lines of output to look neat, printf might be what you need.

Q How do I generate a page break?

A To do this, set $- to zero. This generates a top-of-form character.

Q **Why do value fields that format text modify the contents of the scalar variable containing the text?**

A When formatted text is printed, the printed text is removed from the scalar variable, and the part of the string that is not printed is retained. This enables you to use other calls to `write` to print the remainder of the text. In fact, you can print the rest of the text in the scalar variable using a completely different print format.

Q **How many print formats can I define?**

A Basically, as many as you like, provided the resulting Perl program can still fit in your machine.

Workshop

The Workshop provides quiz questions to help you solidify your understanding of the material covered and exercises to give you experience in using what you've learned. Try to understand the quiz and exercise answers before you go on to tomorrow's lesson.

Quiz

1. Define value fields that print the following:

    a. Ten left-justified characters

    b. Five right-justified characters

    c. Two centered characters

    d. A floating-point number with five digits before the decimal point and three after it

    e. A field that prints as many formatted lines of 30 left-justified characters as necessary

2. What do these fields print?

    a. `@<<<<`

    b. `@|||||||`

    c. `@`

    d. `@*`

    e. `~  ^>>>>>>>>>`

3. What do these `printf` field specifiers print?

    a. `%5d`

    b. `%11.4f`

    c. `%010d`

    d. `%-12s`

    e. `%x`

4. Why do certain floating-point numbers have round-off problems?

5. How do you create a page header for an output file?

Exercises

1. Write a program that prints the powers of 2 from `2**1` to `2**10`. Use `write` and a print format to print them three to a line. Align the lines so that the right end of each number is lined up with the right end of the corresponding number on the previous line.

2. Repeat Exercise 1 using `printf`.

3. Write a program that reads text and formats it into 40-character lines, left-justified. Put lines of asterisks above and below the text.

4. Write a program that reads a set of dollar values such as `71.43` (one per line). Write out two values per line (the first and second on the first line, and so on). Total each of the resulting columns, and produce a grand total.

5. **BUG BUSTER:** What is wrong with the following program?

```perl
#!/usr/local/bin/perl

format STDOUT =
@*
.
while ($line = <STDIN>) {
        chop ($line);
        if ($line eq "") {
                print ("<blank line>\n");
                next;
        }
        write;
}
```

11

Day 12

Working with the File System

Today's lesson teaches you how to manipulate your machine's file system using some of Perl's built-in library functions. Today, you learn about the following:

- [ ] The file input and output functions
- [ ] The directory-manipulation functions
- [ ] The file-attribute manipulation functions
- [ ] The DBM file functions

WARNING

Many of the functions described in today's lesson use features of the UNIX operating system. If you are using Perl on a machine that is not running UNIX, some of these functions might not be defined or might behave differently.

Check the documentation supplied with your version of Perl for details on which functions are supported or emulated on your machine.

File Input and Output Functions

The following sections describe the built-in library functions that read information from files and write information to files. These library functions perform the following tasks:

- [ ] Basic input and output
- [ ] Skipping or re-reading data from a file
- [ ] Reading individual characters from a file
- [ ] Indicating that a file is a binary file

Basic Input and Output Functions

Some of the input and output functions supplied by Perl have been discussed in earlier chapters. These are

- [ ] open, which lets a program access a file
- [ ] close, which terminates file access
- [ ] print, which writes a string to a file
- [ ] write, which writes information to a file using a print format
- [ ] printf, which formats a string and sends it to a file

The following sections briefly describe these functions again, along with some features of these functions that have not been discussed previously.

The open **Function**

The open function enables a Perl program to access a file. It associates a special file variable with each accessed file. The following is an example:

```
open (MYVAR, "/u/jqpublic/file");
```

Here, open requests access to the file /u/jqpublic/file, and it associates the file MYVAR with this file after it is open. open returns a nonzero value if the open succeeds, and zero if the open fails.

By default, open opens a file for reading only. To open a file for writing, put a > character in front of the filename, as follows:

```
open (MYVAR, ">/u/jqpublic/file");
```

To append information to an existing file, put two > characters in front of the filename, as follows:

```
open (MYVAR, ">>/u/jqpublic/file");
```

To treat the open file as a command to which to pipe data, put a pipe (¦) character in front of the filename, as follows:

```
open (MAIL, "¦mail dave");
```

(For more information, refer to Day 6, "Reading from and Writing to Files.")

Piping Input Using open

The open function enables you to open files in several other ways not previously discussed. For example, to treat the open file as a command that is piping data to this program, put a ¦ character after the filename. For example:

```
open (CAT, "cat file*¦");
```

This call to open executes the command cat file*. This command creates a temporary file consisting of the contents of all files whose name starts with file; these contents are joined (concatenated) into a single file. This file is treated as an input file that is accessible using the file variable CAT.

```
$input = <CAT>;
```

Listing 12.1 is another example of a program that uses piped input. This program uses the output from the w command to list the users who are currently logged on to the machine.

Listing 12.1. A program that receives input from a piped command.

```
1:  #!/usr/local/bin/perl
2:
3:  open (WOUT, "w¦");
4:  $time = <WOUT>;
5:  $time =~ s/^ *//;
6:  $time =~ s/ .*//;
7:  <WOUT>;    # skip headings line
8:  @users = <WOUT>;
9:  close (WOUT);
10: foreach $user (@users) {
11:         $user =~ s/ .*//;
12: }
13: print ("Current time:  $time");
14: print ("Users logged on:\n");
15: $prevuser = "";
16: foreach $user (sort @users) {
17:         if ($user ne $prevuser) {
18:                 print ("\t$user");
19:                 $prevuser = $user;
20:         }
21: }
```

OUTPUT

```
$ program12_1
Current time: 4:25pm
Users logged on:
        dave
        kilroy
        root
        zarquon
$
```

ANALYSIS
The w command lists the current time, the machine load, and the users logged onto the machine. It also lists the job time and the currently executing command for each user.

Here is sample output for the w command:

```
  4:25pm  up 1 day,  6:37,  6 users,  load average: 0.79, 0.36, 0.28
User     tty      login@  idle   JCPU   PCPU what
dave     ttyp0    2:26pm           27      3 w
kilroy   ttyp1    9:01am  2:27   1:04     11 -csh
kilroy   ttyp2    9:02am    43   1:46     27 rn
root     ttyp3    4:22pm     2            -csh
zarquon  ttyp4    1:26pm     4     43     16 cc myprog.c
```

12

```
kilroy    ttyp5     9:03am          2:14     48 /usr/games/hack
```

This Perl program takes the output from the w command and massages it to retrieve only the information needed: the current time and the users who are currently logged on.

Line 3 starts the w command. The call to open specifies that the output from w is to be treated as input to this program, and that the file variable WOUT is to be used to access this input.

Line 4 reads the first line of the input piped from WOUT. This is the line read:

```
4:25pm  up 1 day,  6:37,  6 users,  load average: 0.79, 0.36, 0.28
```

The following two lines extract the current time from this line. First, line 5 removes the leading spaces. Then, line 6 removes everything after the first word, except for the trailing newline character. This leaves the time, 4:25pm, along with the trailing newline, stored in $time.

Line 7 reads the second line from WOUT. Because this line contains no useful information, there is no need to assign it to any scalar variable.

Line 8 reads the rest of the output from w to the array variable @users. After this output has been read, line 9 closes WOUT, which terminates the process that is running the w command.

Each element of the list stored in @users contains one line of user information. Because this program needs only the first word of each line, lines 10–12 get rid of everything else (except, again, for the trailing newline character). After this loop is complete, the array in @users contains a list of users logged on.

Line 13 prints the current time, as stored in $time. Note that print does not need to specify a trailing newline character, because $time contains one.

Lines 16–21 sort the list of users in @users and prints them. Because a user can be logged on more than once, $prevuser stores the last user name printed. The value stored in $user is not printed unless it is not the same as the value stored in $prevuser.

Redirecting One File to Another

Many UNIX shells enable you to direct both the standard output file and the standard error file to the same output file. For example, in the Bourne shell sh, the command

```
$ foo >file1 2>&1
```

runs the command foo and stores the output from the standard output file and the standard error file in file1.

Listing 12.2 shows how you can do this in Perl.

12

TYPE

Listing 12.2. A program that redirects the standard output and standard error files.

```
1:  #!/usr/local/bin/perl
2:
3:  open (STDOUT, ">file1") || die ("open STDOUT failed");
4:  open (STDERR, ">&STDOUT") || die ("open STDERR failed");
5:  print STDOUT ("line 1\n");
6:  print STDERR ("line 2\n");
7:  close (STDOUT);
8:  close (STDERR);
```

OUTPUT   This program produces no output.

ANALYSIS   The following are the contents of the output file file1:

```
line 2
line 1
```

As you can see, these lines aren't in the order intended. To understand what is happening, let's examine this program in more detail.

Line 3 redirects the standard output file. To do this, it opens the output file file1 and associates it with the file variable STDOUT; this closes the standard output file.

Line 4 redirects the standard error file. The argument >&STDOUT tells the Perl interpreter to use the file already opened and associated with STDOUT. This means that the file variable STDERR refers to the same file as STDOUT.

Lines 5 and 6 write to STDOUT and STDERR, respectively. Because these file variables refer to the same file, both lines are written to file1. Unfortunately, they are written in the wrong order. What has happened?

The problem arises because of how UNIX handles the writing of output. When you use print (or any other function) to write to a file such as the standard output file, what the UNIX operating system really does is copy the output to a special internal storage area called a *buffer*. (You can think of a buffer as a giant character string or as an array of characters.) Subsequent output operations continue writing to the buffer until it is full; when the buffer is full, the entire buffer is written out. Copying to a buffer and then writing out the entire buffer takes much less time than writing individual lines of text. (This is because, on most machines, input-output operations are slower than memory-access operations.)

When a program ends, any non-empty buffers are written out. However, the system maintains separate buffers for STDERR and STDOUT, and it writes out the buffer for STDERR first. This means that line 2, which is stored in the STDERR buffer, appears before line 1, which is stored in the STDOUT buffer.

To get around this problem, you can tell the Perl interpreter not to use a buffer for a particular file. To do this, do the following:

1. Select the file using the select function.
2. Assign 1 to the system variable $|.

The system variable $| indicates whether a particular file is to be buffered (in other words, whether it should use a buffer or not). If $| is assigned a nonzero value, no buffer is used. As with $~ and $^, assigning to $| affects the current default file, which is the file last specified in a call to select (or STDOUT, if select has not been called).

Listing 12.3 shows how you can use $| to ensure that your output lines appear in the correct order.

Listing 12.3. A program that redirects standard input and output and turns off buffering.

`TYPE`

```
 1: #!/usr/local/bin/perl
 2:
 3: open (STDOUT, ">file1") || die ("open STDOUT failed");
 4: open (STDERR, ">&STDOUT") || die ("open STDERR failed");
 5: $| = 1;
 6: select (STDERR);
 7: $| = 1;
 8: print STDOUT ("line 1\n");
 9: print STDERR ("line 2\n");
10: close (STDOUT);
11: close (STDERR);
```

`OUTPUT` This program produces no output.

`ANALYSIS` The contents of the output file file1 are now the following:

```
line 1
line 2
```

Line 5 sets $| to 1, which tells the Perl interpreter that the current default file does not need to be buffered. Because select has not yet been called, the current default file is STDOUT, which means that line 5 turns off buffering for the standard output file (which has been redirected to file1).

Line 6 sets the current default file to STDERR, and line 7 once again sets $| to 1. This turns off buffering for the standard error file (which has also been redirected to file1).

Because buffering has been turned off for both STDERR and STDOUT, lines 8 and 9 write to file1 right away. This means that the output lines appear in file1 in the order in which they are printed.

12

Specifying Read and Write Access

To open a file for both read and write access, specify +> before the filename, as follows:

```
open (READWRITE, "+>file1");
```

This opens the file named file1 for both reading and writing. This enables you to overwrite portions of a file.

Opening a file for reading and writing works best in conjunction with the library functions seek and tell, which enable you to skip to the middle of a file. (For more information on seek and tell, refer to the section called "Skipping and Rereading Data," later in today's lesson.)

NOTE

> You also can use +< as the prefix to specify both reading and writing, as follows:
>
> ```
> open (READWRITE, "+<file1");
> ```
>
> The prefix <, by itself, specifies that the file is to be opened for reading. This means that the following two statements are identical:
>
> ```
> open (READONLY, "<read");
> open (READONLY, "read");
> ```

The close Function

The library function close was discussed on Day 6, "Reading from and Writing to Files." It closes a file opened by open, as follows:

```
close (MYFILE);
```

Here, MYFILE is the file variable (passed to open) that is associated with the open file.

NOTE

> If you use close to close a pipe, the program will wait for the piped program to terminate. For example:
>
> ```
> open (MYPIPE, "cat file*¦");
> close (MYPIPE);
> ```
>
> When close is called, the program suspends execution until the command cat file* is terminated.

The `print`, `printf`, **and** `write` **Functions**

The `print`, `printf`, and `write` functions have been covered also in previous chapters, but I'll briefly recap them here.

The `print` function is the simplest function. It writes to the file specified, or to the current default file if no file is specified. For example:

```
print ("Hello, there!\n");
print OUTFILE ("Hello, there!\n");
```

The first statement writes to the current default file (which is STDOUT unless `select` has been called). The second statement writes to the file specified by OUTFILE.

The `printf` function formats a string and sends it to either the file specified or the current default file. For example, the statement

```
printf OUTFILE ("You owe me %8.2f", $owing);
```

takes the value stored in `$owing` and substitutes it for `%8.2f` in the specified string. `%8.2f` is an example of a *field specifier* and indicates that the value stored in `$owing` is to be treated as a floating-point number.

The `write` function uses a print format to send formatted output to the file that is specified or to the current default file. For example:

```
select (OUTFILE);
$~ = "MYFORMAT";
write;
```

This call to `write` uses the print format MYFORMAT to send output to the file OUTFILE.

For more information on `printf` or `write`, refer to Day 11, "Formatting Your Output."

The `select` **Function**

The `select` function also is covered on Day 11. This function is passed a file variable, which becomes the new current default file. For example:

```
select (MYFILE);
```

In this case, MYFILE is now the current default file, which means that calls to `print`, `write`, and `printf` write to MYFILE unless a file variable is explicitly specified.

The `eof` **Function**

The library function `eof` checks whether the last input file read has been exhausted. If all of the input has been read, `eof` returns a nonzero value. If there is input remaining, `eof` returns zero.

12

The eof function was first introduced on Day 6. You might have noticed that, on that day, the examples that use eof use it without parentheses. This is because the behavior of eof is a little tricky if you are using it in conjunction with the <> operator; in this case, eof and eof() behave differently.

Listing 12.4 shows how eof interacts with <>. It prints the contents of one or more input files whose names are supplied on the command line. A line of dashes is printed after each input file is completed.

To run this program yourself, create two files named file1 and file2. Put the following in file1:

```
This is a line from the first file.
Here is the last line of the first file.
```

Then, put the following in file2:

```
This is a line from the second and last file.
Here is the last line of the last file.
```

Finally, specify file1 and file2 on the command line when you run this program. For example, if you have called this program program 12_4, run it as follows:

```
$ program12_4 file1 file2
```

This will give you the output shown in the input-output example.

 Listing 12.4. A program that uses eof and <> together.

```perl
1:  #!/usr/local/bin/perl
2:
3:  while ($line = <>) {
4:          print ($line);
5:          if (eof) {
6:                  print ("— — end of current file — —\n");
7:          }
8:  }
```

OUTPUT
```
$ program12_4 file1 file2
This is a line from the first file.
Here is the last line of the first file.
— — end of current file — —
This is a line from the second and last file.
Here is the last line of the last file.
— — end of current file — —
$
```

ANALYSIS   The <> operator in line 3 tells the program to read the next line of input from the input files supplied on the command line. Line 4 then prints the line.

Line 5 calls eof without parentheses. This is the form of eof that you are familiar with. It returns true if the current input file has been completely read.

WARNING

When you test for end-of-file, use either eof or eof() but not both.

Compare the program in Listing 12.4 with Listing 12.5, which uses eof() instead of eof.

 TYPE **Listing 12.5. A program that uses eof() and <> together.**

```
1:   #!/usr/local/bin/perl
2:
3:   while ($line = <>) {
4:           print ($line);
5:           if (eof()) {
6:                   print ("— — end of output — —\n");
7:           }
8:   }
```

 OUTPUT
```
$ program12_5 file1 file2
This is a line from the first file.
Here is the last line of the first file.
This is a line from the second and last file.
Here is the last line of the last file.
— — end of output — —
$
```

 ANALYSIS Line 5 of this program calls eof with parentheses. Calls to eof with parentheses only return true when all of the files have been read. If the program is at the end of the first input file, eof() returns false because there is still input to be read.

NOTE

If you like, you can use eof with a particular file. For example:

```
if (eof(MYFILE)) {
        # do end-of-file stuff
}
```

Here, the conditional expression returns true if all of MYFILE has been read.

Also, note that the distinction between eof and eof() is only meaningful when you are using the <> operator. If you are just reading from a
single file, it doesn't matter whether you supply parentheses or not. For
example:

```
while ($line = <STDIN>) {
        # stuff goes here
        if (eof) {     # you can also use eof() here
                 # more stuff here
        }
}
```

Indirect File Variables

When you call any of the functions described so far in today's lesson, you can indicate which
file to use by specifying a file variable. However, these functions also enable you to supply a
scalar variable in place of a file variable; when you do, the Perl interpreter treats the value
stored in the scalar variable as the name of the file variable. For example, consider the
following:

```
$filename = "MYFILENAME";
open ($filename, ">file1");
```

This call to open takes the value stored in $filename—MYFILENAME—and uses it as the file-
variable name. This means that the file variable MYFILENAME is now associated with the output
file file1.

Listing 12.6 is an example of a program that stores a file-variable name in a scalar variable and
passes the library variable to Perl input and output functions.

TYPE Listing 12.6. A program that uses a scalar variable to store a file variable name.

```
1:  #!/usr/local/bin/perl
2:
3:  &open_file("INFILE", "", "file1");
4:  &open_file("OUTFILE", ">", "file2");
5:  while ($line = &read_from_file("INFILE")) {
6:          &print_to_file("OUTFILE", $line);
7:  }
8:
9:  sub open_file {
10:         local ($filevar, $filemode, $filename) = @_;
11:
12:         open ($filevar, $filemode . $filename) ||
13:                 die ("Can't open $filename");
14: }
```

```
15: sub read_from_file {
16:         local ($filevar) = @_;
17:
18:         <$filevar>;
19: }
20: sub print_to_file {
21:         local ($filevar, $line) = @_;
22:
23:         print $filevar ($line);
24: }
```

OUTPUT This program produces no output.

ANALYSIS This program is just a fancy way of copying the contents of file1 to file2. Line 3 opens the input file, file1, for reading by calling the subroutine open_file. This subroutine is passed the name of the file variable to use, which is INFILE.

Line 4 uses the same subroutine, open_file, to open the output file, file2, for writing. The file variable OUTFILE is used in this open operation.

Line 5 calls read_from_file to read a line of input and passes it the file variable name INFILE. Line 18 substitutes the value of $filevar, INFILE, into <$filevar>, yielding the result <INFILE>; then, it reads a line from this input file. Because this line-reading operation is the last expression evaluated in the subroutine, the line read is returned by the subroutine and assigned to $line.

Line 6 then passes OUTFILE and the input line just read to the subroutine print_to_file.

12

NOTE

> All of the functions you've seen so far in this chapter—open, close, print, printf, write, select, and eof—enable you to use a scalar variable in place of a file variable.
>
> The functions open, close, write, select, and eof also enable you to use an expression in place of a file variable. The value of the expression must be a character string that can be used as a file variable.

Skipping and Rereading Data

In the programs you've seen so far, input files have always been read in order, starting with the first line of input and continuing on to the end. Perl provides two special functions, seek and tell, which enable you to skip forward or backward in a file so that you can skip or re-read data.

The seek **Function**

The seek function moves backward or forward in a file.

The syntax for the seek function is

```
seek (filevar, distance, relative_to);
```

As you can see, seek requires three arguments:

- ☐ *filevar*, which is the file variable representing the file in which to skip
- ☐ *distance*, which is an integer representing the number of bytes (characters) to skip
- ☐ *relative_to*, which is either 0, 1, or 2

If *relative_to* is 0, the number of bytes to skip is relative to the beginning of the file. If *relative_to* is 1, the skip is relative to the current position in the file (the current position is the location of the next line to be read). If *relative_to* is 2, the skip is relative to the end of the file.

For example, to skip back to the beginning of the file MYFILE, use the following:

```
seek(MYFILE, 0, 0);
```

The following statement skips forward 80 bytes:

```
seek(MYFILE, 80, 1);
```

The following statement skips backward 80 bytes:

```
seek(MYFILE, -80, 1);
```

And the following statement skips to the end of the file (which is useful when the file has been opened for reading and writing):

```
seek(MYFILE, 0, 2);
```

The seek function returns true (nonzero) if the skip was successful, and 0 if it failed. It is often used in conjunction with the tell function, described in the next section.

The tell **Function**

The tell function returns the distance, in bytes, between the beginning of the file and the current position of the file (the location of the next line to be read).

SYNTAX

The syntax for the `tell` function is

```
tell (filevar);
```

filevar, which is required, represents the file whose current position is needed.

For example, the following statement retrieves the current position of the file MYFILE:

```
$offset = tell (MYFILE);
```

NOTE

> `tell` and `seek` accept an expression in place of a file variable, provided the value of the expression is the name of a file variable.

You can use `tell` and `seek` to skip to a particular position in a file. For example, Listing 12.7 uses these functions to print pairs of lines twice each. (This is, of course, not the fastest way to do this.)

TYPE **Listing 12.7. A program that demonstrates** seek **and** tell.

```
 1:  #!/usr/local/bin/perl
 2:
 3:  @array = ("This", "is", "a", "test");
 4:  open (TEMPFILE, ">file1");
 5:  foreach $element (@array) {
 6:          print TEMPFILE ("$element\n");
 7:  }
 8:  close (TEMPFILE);
 9:  open (TEMPFILE, "file1");
10:  while (1) {
11:          $skipback = tell(TEMPFILE);
12:          $line = <TEMPFILE>;
13:          last if ($line eq "");
14:          print ($line);
15:          $line = <TEMPFILE>;  # assume the second line exists
16:          print ($line);
17:          seek (TEMPFILE, $skipback, 0);
18:          $line = <TEMPFILE>;
19:          print ($line);
20:          $line = <TEMPFILE>;
21:          print ($line);
22:  }
```

12

OUTPUT

```
$ program12_7
This
is
This
is
a
test
a
test
$
```

ANALYSIS Lines 3–8 of this program create a temporary file named file1 consisting of four lines: This, is, a, and test. Line 9 opens this temporary file for reading.

Lines 10–22 loop through the test file. Line 11 calls tell to obtain the current position of the file before reading the pair of lines. Lines 12–16 read the lines and print them (first testing whether the end of the file has been reached).

Line 17 then calls seek, which positions the file at the point returned by tell in line 11. This means that the pair of lines read by lines 12 and 15 are read again by lines 18 and 20. Therefore, lines 19 and 21 print a second copy of the input lines.

WARNING

> You cannot use seek and tell if the file variable actually refers to a pipe. For example, if you open a pipe using the statement
>
> ```
> open (MYPIPE, "cat file*¦");
> ```
>
> then the following statement makes no sense:
>
> ```
> $illegal = tell (MYPIPE);
> ```

System Read and Write Functions

In Perl, the easiest way to read input from a file is to use the <*filevar*> operator, where *filevar* is the file variable representing the file to read. Perl also provides two other functions that read from an input file:

☐ read, which is equivalent to the UNIX fread function

☐ sysread, which is equivalent to the read function

Perl also enables you to write output using the built-in function syswrite, which calls the UNIX write function.

These functions are described in the following sections.

The read **Function**

The read function is designed to be equivalent to the UNIX function fread. It enables you to read an arbitrary number of characters (bytes) into a scalar variable.

The syntax for the read function is

```
read (filevar, result, length, skipval);
```

Here, *filevar* is the file variable representing the file to read, *result* is the scalar variable (or array variable element) into which the bytes are to be stored, and *length* is the number of bytes to read.

skipval is an optional argument which specifies the number of bytes to skip before reading.

For example:

```
read (MYFILE, $scalar, 80);
```

This call to read tries to read 80 bytes from the file represented by the file variable MYFILE, storing the resulting character string in $scalar. It returns the number of bytes actually read; if MYFILE is at end-of-file, it returns 0 (read returns the null string if an error occurs).

You can use read to append to an existing scalar variable by specifying a fourth argument, which indicates the number of bytes to skip in the scalar variable.

```
read (MYFILE, $scalar, 40, 80);
```

This call to read reads another 40 bytes from MYFILE. When copying these bytes into $scalar, read first skips the first 80 bytes already stored there.

The sysread **and** syswrite **Functions**

If you want to read data as quickly as possible, you can call sysread instead of read.

The syntax for the sysread function is

```
sysread (filevar, result, length, skipval);
```

These arguments are the same as for read.

For example:

```
sysread (MYFILE, $scalar, 80);
sysread (MYFILE, $scalar, 40, 80);
```

sysread is equivalent to the UNIX function read. The arguments to sysread are the same as those for the Perl read function.

To write as quickly as possible, call the syswrite function, which is equivalent to the UNIX function write.

12

The syntax of the syswrite function is

```
syswrite (filevar, data, length, skipval);
```

Here, *filevar* is the file to write to, *data* is the place where the data is located, *length* is the number of bytes to write, and *skipval* is the number of bytes to skip before writing.

For instance, the following call writes the first 80 bytes of $scalar to the file specified by MYFILE:

```
syswrite (MYFILE, $scalar, 80);
```

Similarly, the following statement skips the first 80 bytes stored in $scalar, and then writes the next 40 bytes to the file specified by MYFILE:

```
syswrite (MYFILE, $scalar, 40, 80);
```

WARNING

Don't use sysread and syswrite unless you know what you are doing. For more information on these functions, refer to the UNIX system manual pages for the read and write functions.

Reading Characters Using getc

Perl provides one other built-in function, getc, which reads a single character of input from a file.

The syntax for calls to the getc function is

```
char = getc (infile);
```

infile is the file from which to read, and *char* is the character returned.

For example:

```
$singlechar = getc(INFILE);
```

This statement reads a character from the file represented by INFILE and stores it (as a character string) in the scalar variable $singlechar.

The getc is useful for "hot key" applications. These applications accept and process input one character at a time rather than one line at a time. Listing 12.8 is an example of such a program. It reads one character at a time and checks whether the character is alphanumeric. If it is, it writes out the next higher letter or number. For example, when you enter a, the program prints out b, and so on. In this example, the alphabetic letters a through z and the digits 0 through 9 are typed in.

TYPE **Listing 12.8. A program that demonstrates the use of `getc`.**

```
1:  #!/usr/local/bin/perl
2:
3:  &start_hot_keys;
4:  while (1) {
5:          $char = getc(STDIN);
6:          last if ($char eq "\\");
7:          $char =~ tr/a-zA-Z0-9/b-zaB-ZA1-90/;
8:          print ($char);
9:  }
10: &end_hot_keys;
11: print ("\n");
12:
13: sub start_hot_keys {
14:         system ("stty cbreak");
15:         system ("stty -echo");
16: }
17:
18: sub end_hot_keys {
19:         system ("stty -cbreak");
20:         system ("stty echo");
21: }
```

OUTPUT
```
$ program12_8
bcdefghijklmnopqrstuvwxyza1234567890
$
```

ANALYSIS The subroutine `start_hot_keys` modifies the runtime environment to support hot-key input. To do this, it uses two calls to the built-in function `system`, which simply takes its argument and executes it. The command `stty cbreak` tells the system to process input one character at a time, and the command `stty -echo` tells the system not to display characters typed at the keyboard.

NOTE

Some machines might not support hot keys or might use different commands to establish the hot-key environment. If you are on a machine that uses different commands to establish the environment, you still can run this program; just change the `stty` commands to whatever works on your machine.

The loop in lines 4–9 reads and writes one character per loop iteration. Line 5 starts off by reading a character from the standard input file using `getc`.

Line 6 tests whether the character read is a backslash. If it is, the loop terminates. If the character is not a backslash, the program continues with line 7. This line translates all alphanumeric characters to the next-highest letter or number; for example, it translates g to h, E to F, and 7 to 8. The characters z, Z, and 9 are translated to a, A, and 0, respectively.

12

Line 8 prints out the translated character. Because the characters you type at the keyboard are not displayed, the program makes it look like your keyboard is malfunctioning. (It's quite disorienting!)

The subroutine end_hot_keys restores the normal working environment by undoing the system calls that are performed by start_hot_keys.

WARNING

> If you are using hot keys, when you clean up make sure you call stty -cbreak *before* calling stty echo. If you call stty echo first, your terminal might wind up not printing newline characters properly.

Reading a Binary File Using `binmode`

If your machine distinguishes between text files and binary files (files that contain unprintable characters), your Perl program can tell the system that a particular file is a binary file. To do this, call the built-in function binmode.

SYNTAX

The syntax for calling the binmode function is

```
binmode (filevar);
```

filevar is a file variable.

binmode expects a file variable (or an expression whose value is the name of a file variable). It must be called after the file is opened, but before the file is read.

The following is an example of a call to binmode:

```
binmode (MYFILE);
```

NOTE

> Normally, you won't need to use this function unless you are running in a DOS-like environment.

Directory-Manipulation Functions

The input and output functions that you have seen earlier read and write data to files. Perl also provides a group of functions that enable you to manipulate UNIX directories. Functions exist that enable you to create, read, open, close, delete, and skip around in directories. The following sections describe these functions.

The `mkdir` **Function**

To create a new directory, call the function `mkdir`.

SYNTAX

The syntax for the `mkdir` function is

```
mkdir (dirname, permissions);
```

`mkdir` requires two arguments:

☐ `dirname`, which is the name of the directory to be created (which can be a character string or an expression whose value is a directory name)

☐ `permissions`, which is an octal (base-8) number specifying the access permissions for the new directory

For example, to create a directory named /u/jqpublic/newdir, you can use the following statement:

```
mkdir ("/u/jqpublic/newdir", 0777);
```

To create a subdirectory of the current working directory, just specify the new directory name, as follows:

```
mkdir ("newdir", 0777);
```

If the current working directory is /u/janedoe/mydir, this creates a subdirectory named /u/janedoe/mydir/newdir.

The permissions value of 0777 in both these examples grants read, write, and execute permissions to everybody. Table 12.1 lists each possible access permission and the octal number associated with it.

Table 12.1. Access permissions for the `mkdir` function.

Value	Permission
4000	Set user ID on execution
2000	Set group ID on execution
1000	Sticky bit (see the UNIX `chmod` manual page)
0400	Read permission for file owner
0200	Write permission for file owner
0100	Execute permission for file owner
0040	Read permission for owner's group
0020	Write permission for owner's group
0010	Execute permission for owner's group

continues

Table 12.1. continued

Value	Permission
0004	Read permission for world
0002	Write permission for world
0001	Execute permission for world

You can combine access permissions by adding (or doing a logical OR operation on) the appropriate octal values in the table. For example, to grant read, write, and execute permission to the owner but only read permission to everybody else, specify 0744 as the permission value.

NOTE

All of the permission values shown here are in octal notation, because a leading zero is specified. If you like, you can use decimal or hexadecimal here, but it won't be as easy to read.

Also note that the permission value set here is affected by the current value of umask. See the description of the umask function later today for more information.

mkdir returns true (nonzero) if the directory is successfully created. It returns false (0) if the directory is not.

The chdir Function

To set a directory to be the current working directory, use the function chdir.

SYNTAX

The syntax for the chdir function is

```
chdir (dirname);
```

dirname is the name of the new current working directory.

chdir returns true if the current directory is set properly, false if an error occurs.

For example, to set the current working directory to /u/jqpublic/newdir, use the following statement:

```
chdir ("/u/jqpublic/newdir");
```

NOTE As with `mkdir`, the directory name passed to `chdir` can be either a character string or an expression whose value is a directory name. For example, the following sets the current directory to be `/u/jqpublic/newdir`:

```
$dir = "/u/jqpublic/";
chdir ($dir . "newdir");
```

The `opendir` Function

You can have your program examine a list of the files contained in a directory. To do this, the first step is to call the built-in function `opendir`.

The syntax for the `opendir` function is

```
opendir (dirvar, dirname);
```

dirvar is the name the program is to use to represent the directory, also known as a *directory variable*, and *dirname* is the name of the directory to open (which can be a character string or the value of an expression).

`opendir` returns true if the open operation is successful, and it returns false otherwise.

For example, to open the directory named `/u/janedoe/mydir`, you can use the following statement:

```
opendir (DIR, "/u/janedoe/mydir");
```

This associates the directory variable `DIR` with the opened directory.

12

NOTE If you like, you can use the same name as both a directory variable and a file variable.

```
opendir (MYNAME, "/u/jqpublic/dir");
open (MYNAME, "/u/jqpublic/dir/file");
```

The Perl interpreter always can tell from context whether a name is being used as a directory variable or as a file variable. (However, there is no real reason to do so. Your programs will be easier to read if you use different names to represent files and directories.)

The `closedir` Function

To close an opened directory, call the `closedir` function.

The syntax for the `closedir` function is

```
closedir (mydir);
```

`closedir` expects one argument: the directory variable associated with the directory to be closed.

The `readdir` Function

After `opendir` has opened a directory, you can access the name of each file or subdirectory stored in the directory by calling the function `readdir`.

The syntax for the `readdir` function is

```
readdir (mydir);
```

Like `closedir`, `readdir` is passed the directory variable that is associated with the open directory.

If the value returned from `readdir` is assigned to a scalar variable, `readdir` returns the name of the first file or subdirectory stored in the directory. For example:

```
$filename = readdir(MYDIR);
```

The first name is returned also if the return value from `readdir` is assigned to an element of an array variable. For example:

```
$filearray[3] = readdir(MYDIR);
$filearray{"foo"} = readdir(MYDIR);
```

If `readdir` is called again, it returns the next name in the directory; subsequent calls return other names, continuing until the directory is exhausted. Listing 12.9 uses `readdir` to list the files and subdirectories in a directory.

Listing 12.9. A program that lists the files and subdirectories in a directory.

```
1:  #!/usr/local/bin/perl
2:
3:  opendir(HOMEDIR, "/u/jqpublic") ||
4:          die ("Unable to open directory");
5:  while ($filename = readdir(HOMEDIR)) {
6:          print ("$filename\n");
7:  }
8:  closedir(HOMEDIR);
```

OUTPUT

```
$ program12_9
.
..
.cshrc
.Xresources
.xsession
test
bin
letter
file1
$
```

ANALYSIS Line 3 opens the directory /u/jqpublic, which is the home directory for user jqpublic. The opendir function associates the directory variable HOMEDIR with /u /jqpublic.

Lines 5–7 read the name of each file in the directory in turn. Line 6 prints each filename as it is read in.

Note that, on a UNIX system, the list of names includes two special files:

☐ The name . (a single period), which represents the current directory

☐ The name .. (two periods), which represents the parent directory

As you can see, readdir reads the names in the order in which they appear in the directory.

Listing 12.10 shows how you can display the names in alphabetical order.

TYPE
Listing 12.10. A program that lists the files and subdirectories in a directory in alphabetical order.

```
1:  #!/usr/local/bin/perl
2:
3:  opendir(HOMEDIR, "/u/jqpublic") ||
4:          die ("Unable to open directory");
5:  @files = readdir(HOMEDIR);
6:  closedir(HOMEDIR);
7:  foreach $file (sort @files) {
8:          print ("$file\n");
9:  }
```

OUTPUT

```
$ program12_10
.
..
.Xresources
.cshrc
.xsession
bin
file1
letter
test
$
```

12

ANALYSIS The readdir function behaves differently when its return value is assigned to an array; in this case, the entire list of files and subdirectories in the directory is assigned to the array variable @files by line 5.

After the entire list is stored, sort can be called to sort the list into alphabetical order. The foreach loop in lines 7–9 then prints the sorted list one name at a time.

The telldir and seekdir Functions

As you've seen, the library functions tell and seek enable you to skip backward and forward in a file. Similarly, the library functions telldir and seekdir enable you to skip backward and forward in a list of directories.

To use telldir, pass it the directory variable defined by opendir. telldir returns the current directory location (where you are in the list of files).

The syntax for the telldir function is

```
location = telldir (mydir);
```

Here, *mydir* is the directory variable corresponding to the directory whose file list you are examining, and *location* is assigned the current directory location.

To skip to the directory location returned by telldir, call seekdir.

The syntax for the seekdir function is

```
seekdir(mydir, location);
```

This call to seekdir sets the current directory location to the location specified by *location*.

> seekdir works only with directory locations returned by telldir.

WARNING

The rewinddir Function

Although being able to skip anywhere you like in a directory list is useful, the most common skipping operation in directory lists is *rewinding* the directory list, or starting over again. Because of this, Perl provides a special function, rewinddir, that handles the rewind operation.

The syntax for the `rewinddir` function is

```
rewinddir (mydir);
```

`rewinddir` sets the current directory location to the beginning of the list of files, which lets you read the entire list of files again. As with the other directory functions, *mydir* is the directory variable defined by `opendir`.

The `rmdir` Function

The final directory function supplied by Perl is `rmdir`, which deletes an empty directory.

The syntax for calling the `rmdir` function is

```
rmdir (dirname);
```

`rmdir` returns true (nonzero) if the directory *dirname* is deleted successfully, and false if the directory is not empty or cannot be deleted.

File-Attribute Functions

Perl provides several library functions that modify the attributes or behavior of files. These functions can be divided into the following groups:

- ☐ Functions that relocate (rename or delete) files
- ☐ Functions that establish links or symbolic links
- ☐ Functions that modify file permissions
- ☐ Other file-attribute functions

These groups of functions are described in the following sections.

File-Relocation Functions

Perl provides the following file-relocation functions:

- ☐ `rename`, which moves or renames a file
- ☐ `unlink`, which deletes a file

The `rename` Function

The built-in function `rename` changes the name of a file.

The syntax for the `rename` function is

```
rename (oldname, newname);
```

oldname is the old filename, and *newname* is the new filename.

The `rename` function returns true if the rename succeeds, and false if an error occurs.

For example, to change a file named name1 to name2, use the following:

```
rename ("name1", "name2");
```

You can use the value stored in a scalar variable as an argument to `rename`, or any variable or expression whose value is a character string, as follows:

```
rename ($oldname, &get_new_name);
```

You can also use `rename` to move a file from one directory to another (provided both directories are in the same file system). For example:

```
rename ("/u/jqpublic/name1", "/u/janedoe/name2");
```

WARNING

When `rename` moves a file, as in

```
rename ("name1", "name2");
```

it does not check whether a file named name2 already exists. Any existing name2 is destroyed by the `rename` operation.

To get around this problem, use the `-e` file-test operator, which checks whether a named file exists, as follows:

```
-e "name2" ¦¦ rename (name1, name2);
```

Here, the ¦¦ operator ensures that `rename` is called only when no file named name2 already exists.

The `unlink` Function

To delete a file, use the `unlink` function.

The syntax for the `unlink` function is

```
num = unlink (filelist);
```

This function takes a list as its argument and deletes all the files named in that list.

`unlink` returns the number of files actually deleted.

The following is an example of a call to unlink:

```
@deletelist = ("file1", "file2");
unlink (@deletelist);
```

The function is called unlink, instead of delete, because what it is actually doing is removing a reference, or *link*, to the particular file. See the following section for more details on links in Perl.

Link and Symbolic Link Functions

In the UNIX environment, files can be "contained" in more than one directory at a time. Each directory contains a reference, or *link*, to the file.

The following sections describe how to create and access links.

NOTE   If a file is referenced by multiple links, unlink removes only one of the links, and the file can still be referenced.

The link Function

To create a link to an existing file, use the built-in function link.

The syntax for the link function is

```
link (newlink, file);
```

newlink is the link being created, and file is the file being linked to.

link returns true if the link is created, and false if an error occurs.

For example:

```
link ("/u/jqpublic/file", "/u/janedoe/newfile");
```

After link has been called, the file /u/jqpublic/file also can be thought of as the file /u /janedoe/newfile. If unlink is called using /u/jqpublic/file, as in

```
unlink ("/u/jqpublic/file");
```

you can still reference the file by specifying the name /u/janedoe/newfile.

12

The `symlink` Function

The link created by the `link` function is called a *hard link*, which means that it actually references the file itself. Many operating systems also support *symbolic links*, which are references to the filename, not to the file itself.

To create a symbolic link, use the function `symlink`.

The syntax for the `symlink` function is

```
symlink (newlink, file);
```

newlink is the link being created, and *file* is the file being linked to.

`symlink`, like `link` returns true if the link is created, and false if an error occurs.

The following is an example of `symlink`:

```
symlink("/u/jqpublic/file", "/u/janedoe/newfile");
```

Here, `/u/janedoe/newfile` is symbolically linked to `/u/jqpublic/file`. Now, when the following statement is executed, the file is actually deleted:

```
unlink ("/u/jqpublic/file");
```

`/u/janedoe/newfile` now references nothing at all. (In this case, `/u/janedoe/newfile` is an example of an *unresolved symbolic link*.) When `/u/jqpublic/file` is created again, you will be able to access the new file using `/u/janedoe/newfile`.

The `readlink` Function

If a filename, such as `/u/janedoe/newfile`, is actually a symbolic link to another filename, the function `readlink` returns the filename to which it is linked.

The syntax for the `readlink` function is

```
filename = readlink (linkname);
```

linkname is the symbolic link, and *filename* is the equivalent filename.

`readlink` returns an empty string if the filename is not a symbolic link. (In particular, `readlink` fails if the filename is actually a hard link.)

For example:

```
$linkname = readlink("/u/janedoe/newfile");
# $linkname now contains "/u/jqpublic/file"
```

Listing 12.11 is an example of a program that prints all the symbolic links in a particular directory.

TYPE | **Listing 12.11. A program that prints symbolic links.**

```
1:  #!/usr/local/bin/perl
2:
3:  $dir = "/u/janedoe";
4:  opendir(MYDIR, $dir);
5:  while ($name = readdir(MYDIR)) {
6:          if (-l $dir . "/" . $name) {
7:                  print ("$name is linked to ");
8:                  print (readlink($dir . "/". $name) . "\n");
9:          }
10: }
11: closedir(MYDIR);
```

OUTPUT
```
$ program12_11
newfile is linked to /u/jqpublic/file
$
```

ANALYSIS This program uses opendir and readdir to examine each file in the directory in turn. Line 6 uses the -l file-test operator to determine whether the filename is actually a symbolic link. If the filename is a symbolic link, the following expression becomes true, and the program executes the calls to print in lines 7 and 8:

```
-l $dir . "/" . $name
```

Line 8 calls readlink, passing it the directory name and the filename stored in $name. Because readlink is called only if the expression in line 6 is true, $name is always a symbolic link.

File-Permission Functions

As you've seen, the built-in function mkdir requires you to specify the access permissions for the directory you are creating. These permissions indicate, for example, whether particular users are allowed to read files from the directory or write into the directory.

In the UNIX environment, each individual file has its own set of access permissions. The set of possible permissions is the same as for directories. (Refer to Table 12.1 in the section titled "The mkdir Function" earlier in today's lesson for a complete list of the possible functions.)

In Perl, three functions are defined that deal with access permissions.

☐ chmod, which changes the access permissions for a file

☐ chown, which changes the owner of a file

☐ umask, which sets the default access permissions for a file

12

The chmod **Function**

To change the access permissions for a list of files, call the chmod function.

The syntax for the chmod function is

```
chmod (permissions, filelist);
```

permissions is the set of access permissions you want to give, and is a standard UNIX file permissions mask. (For example, setting permissions to 0777 gives read, write, and execute permission to everybody. See the section called "The mkdir Function" for a description of the set of permissions.) filelist is the list of files whose permissions you want to change.

The chmod function returns the number of files whose permissions were successfully set.

The following is an example of a call to chmod:

```
@filelist = ("file1", "file2");
chmod (0777, @filelist);
```

In this example, the files file1 and file2 are assigned global read, write, and execute permissions.

NOTE

You cannot change access permissions using chmod unless you have permission to do so. You need to have been granted write permission on a file before you can change its permissions.

The chown **Function**

Normally, the owner of a file is the person who created it. To change the owner of a file, use the function chown.

The syntax for the chown function is

```
chown (userid, groupid, filelist);
```

The chown function requires three arguments:

- ☐ userid, which is the (numerical) user ID of the new owner of the file
- ☐ groupid, which is the new numerical group ID to be assigned to the file (or –1 if the existing group ID is to be preserved)
- ☐ filelist, which is a list of files to change

The chown function returns the number of files changed.

The following is an example of a call to chown:

```
@filelist = ("file1", "file2");
chown (17, -1, @filelist);
```

NOTE

On most UNIX systems, you can retrieve a user ID or group ID from the /etc/passwd file. You can use the Perl function getpwnam to retrieve information from this file. For more information on getpwnam, refer to Day 15, "System Functions."

Also, the superuser (system administrator) is usually the only user allowed to change the owner of a file.

The umask Function

As you've seen, you can change the access permissions for a file using chmod. To specify access permissions you cannot use when you create a file, use the umask function.

The syntax for calls to umask is

```
oldmaskval = umask (maskval);
```

maskval is the current umask value, and umask returns the previous (superseded) umask value in oldmaskval. Each umask value is a file creation mask, and is used to set the default permissions for files and directories. (See the umask manual page for more details on file creation masks.)

For example, the following statement disables group and world access permissions for the newly created file:

```
$oldperms = umask(0022);
```

NOTE

You can determine the current umask value by passing no arguments to umask, as follows:

```
$currperms = umask();
```

This statement assigns the current umask value to $currperms.

Permission File-Test Operators

Some file-test operators in Perl are designed to test for various permissions. Table 12.2 lists these file-test operators; in each case, *filename* is the name of the file being tested.

Table 12.2. File-test operators that test for permissions.

Operator	Description
-g	Does *filename* have its set group ID bit set?
-k	Does *filename* have its "sticky bit" set?
-r	Is *filename* a readable file?
-u	Does *filename* have its set user ID bit set?
-w	Is *filename* a writable file?
-x	Is *filename* an executable file?
-R	Is *filename* readable only if the real user ID can read it?
-W	Is *filename* writable only if the real user ID can write?
-X	Is *filename* executable only if the real user ID can execute it?

In this case, the real user ID is the user ID specified at login, as opposed to the effective user ID, which is the user ID under which you are currently running. (On some machines, a command such as /usr/local/etc/suid enables you to change your effective user ID.)

(See Day 6 for more information on how to use file-test operators.)

Miscellaneous Attribute Functions

The following sections describe other Perl functions that manipulate files.

The truncate Function

The truncate function enables you to reduce the size of a specified file to a particular length.

The syntax for the truncate function is

```
truncate (filename, length);
```

filename is the name of the file to reduce, and *length* is the new length of the file.

For example, the statement

```
truncate ("/u/jqpublic/longfile", 5000);
```

reduces the size of /u/jqpublic/longfile to 5000 bytes in length. (If the file is already smaller than 5000 bytes, truncate does nothing.)

Note

> You can use a file variable in place of the filename.
>
> ```
> truncate (MYFILE, 5000);
> ```
>
> The file variable must refer to a file opened for writing by the open function.

The stat Function

The stat function retrieves information about a particular file when given its name or a file variable representing its name.

The syntax for the stat function is

```
stat (file);
```

Here, *file* is either a filename or a file variable.

stat returns a list containing the following elements, in this order:

- ☐ The device on which the file resides
- ☐ The internal reference number (inode number) for this file
- ☐ The permissions for the file
- ☐ The number of hard links to the file
- ☐ The numerical user ID of the file owner
- ☐ The numerical group ID of the file owner
- ☐ The device type, if this "file" is actually a device
- ☐ The size of the file (in bytes)
- ☐ When the file was last accessed
- ☐ When the file was last modified
- ☐ When the file status last changed
- ☐ The optimal block size for input-output operations on the file system containing the file
- ☐ The number of blocks allocated for this file

Some of the items returned by stat can be obtained using file test operators. Table 12.3 lists these items.

12

Table 12.3. File-test operators that check information returned by `stat`.

Operator	Description
-b	Is *filename* a mountable disk (block device)?
-c	Is *filename* an I/O device (character device)?
-s	Is *filename* a non-empty file?
-t	Does *filename* represent a terminal?
-A	How long since *filename* accessed?
-C	How long since *filename*'s inode accessed?
-M	How long since *filename* modified?
-S	Is *filename* a socket?

For more information on `stat` or the information it returns, see the UNIX manual page for the `stat` command on your machine.

The `lstat` Function

The `lstat` function returns the same information as `stat`, but it assumes that the name being passed as an argument is a symbolic link.

The syntax for `lstat` is the same as that for `stat`.

```
lstat (file);
file is either a filename or a file variable.
```

The `time` Function

The access and modification times returned by `stat` and by the `-A` and `-M` file-test operators are integers representing the number of elapsed seconds from January 1, 1970, to the time the file was accessed or modified.

To obtain the number of elapsed seconds from January 1, 1970, to the present time, call the built-in function `time`.

The syntax for calls to the `time` function is

```
currtime = time ();
```

currtime is the returned elapsed-seconds value.

The `gmtime` and `localtime` Functions

The value returned by `time` can be converted to either Greenwich Mean Time or your computer's local time.

To convert to Greenwich Mean Time, call the `gmtime` function. To convert to local time, call the `localtime` function.

The syntax for the `gmtime` and `localtime` functions is identical:

```
timelist = gmtime (timeval);
timelist = localtime (timeval);
```

Both functions accept the time value returned by `time`, `stat`, or the `-A` and `-M` file-test operators.

Both functions return a list consisting of the following nine elements:

- ☐ Seconds
- ☐ Minutes
- ☐ The hour of the day, which is a value between 0 and 23
- ☐ The day of the month
- ☐ The month, which is a value between 0 (January) and 11 (December)
- ☐ The year
- ☐ The day of the week, which is a value between 0 (Sunday) and 6 (Saturday)
- ☐ The day of the year, which is a value between 0 and 364
- ☐ A flag indicating whether daylight saving time is in effect

For more information on the list returned by `gmtime` or `localtime`, refer to the UNIX manual pages for the system functions with the same names.

The `utime` Function

The time values returned by `stat`, `time`, and the `-A` and `-M` file-test operators can be used to set the access and modification times of other files. To do this, use the `utime` function.

The syntax for the `utime` function is

```
utime (acctime, modtime, filelist);
```

`acctime` is the new access time, `modtime` is the new modification time, and `filelist` is the list of files.

`utime` returns the number of files whose access and modification times have been successfully changed.

The following is an example of a call to utime:

```
$acctime = -A "file1";
$modtime = -M "file1";
@filelist = ("file2", "file3");
utime ($acctime, $modtime, @filelist);
```

Here, the files file2 and file3 have their access and modification times changed to those of file1.

The fileno Function

The fileno function returns the internal UNIX file descriptor associated with a particular file variable.

The syntax for the fileno function is

```
filedesc = fileno (filevar);
```

Here, filevar is the file variable whose descriptor is to be retrieved.

The file descriptor returned by fileno is used in various UNIX system calls; these calls can be accessed using the system function (as described on Day 15).

The flock and fcntl Functions

The flock and fcntl functions call the UNIX system commands of the same name.

The syntax for the flock and fcntl functions is

```
fcntl (filevar, fcntlrtn, value);
flock (filevar, flockop);
```

Here, filevar is a file variable representing an open file. fcntlrtn is a fcntl function as defined in the UNIX fcntl manual page, and value is the value passed to the function, if appropriate. Similarly, flockop is a file-locking operation, as defined in the UNIX flock manual page.

For more information on these functions, refer to the manual pages or to a book about UNIX. (You won't really be able to use these functions effectively unless you know a fair bit about how your operating system works.)

Using DBM Files

Many systems on which Perl is available support files that are created using the Data Base Management (DBM) library. Perl enables you to use an associative array to access a particular DBM file.

The following sections describe how to access DBM files from Perl programs using the dbmopen and dbmclose functions. If you are running Perl 5, these functions have been superseded by the tie and untie functions; see Day 19, "Object-Oriented Programming in Perl," for more details.

For more information on DBM, refer to your system's appropriate manual pages.

The dbmopen **Function**

To associate an associative array with a DBM file, use the dbmopen function.

The syntax for the dbmopen function is

```
dbmopen (array, dbmfilename, permissions);
```

This function requires three arguments:

- ☐ *array*, which is the associative array to use

- ☐ *dbmfilename*, which is the name of the DBM file to open

- ☐ *permissions*, which are the access permissions to use (See the section called "The mkdir Function" for more information on access permissions.)

After the DBM file has been opened, the subscripts for the associative array represent the DBM file keys, and the values of the array represent the values associated with the keys.

Calling dbmopen destroys any existing values in the associative array.

WARNING

12

The dbmclose **Function**

To close a DBM file opened by dbmopen, use dbmclose.

The syntax for the dbmclose function is

```
dbmclose (array);
```

Here, *array* is the associative array specified in the call to dbmopen.

Summary

Today, you learned how to open a pipe that directs input to the program, how to open a file for both reading and writing, and how to associate multiple file variables with a single file. You also learned how to test for the end of a particular input file or for the end of the last input file.

You also learned how to skip backward and forward in files and how to read single characters from a file using getc. You can use getc to build hot-key applications, which act as soon as they read a single character from the keyboard.

Perl provides several functions for manipulating directories. They enable you to create, open, read, close, delete, and skip around in directories. Other Perl functions enable you to move a file from one directory to another, create hard and symbolic links from one location to another, and delete a hard link (or a file).

You learned about the Perl functions that enable you to change the file owner or file permissions, truncate a file, retrieve file information, set file access and modification times, retrieve the file descriptor, and call the flock and fcntl system commands.

Finally, Perl provides an interface to the DBM library that enables you to associate DBM files with associative arrays.

Q&A

Q How can I determine whether a particular Perl function that manipulates the UNIX file system is defined on my machine?

A A Perl function that manipulates the UNIX file system normally has the same name as the UNIX command or C library function that performs the same task. If the UNIX command or C library function is defined, the Perl function is usually defined as well.

To check whether a UNIX command or C library function is defined, enter the command man *name*, where *name* is the name of the Perl library function for which you are checking.

Q Why does a list of files in a directory appear in unsorted order?

A The list appears in the order in which the files are stored in the directory. This varies, depending on the machine; usually, however, newer files appear at the end of the list.

Q Which is better to use: the file-test operators or the built-in function stat?

A Whenever possible, use the file-test operators. They are easier to use and are often more efficient.

Q Why are both `read` and `sysread` defined, when they are so similar?

A `read`, like the UNIX function `fread`, uses the standard UNIX input-output (I/O) environment. `sysread` and `syswrite`, on the other hand, bypass the standard I/O environment and perform low-level system calls.

Q Why are `eof` and `eof()` different?

A The short answer is: Just because. The long answer is that an empty list as an argument (as in `eof()`) refers to the list of files on the command line, as does the `<>` in

```
while ($line = <>) ...
```

`eof`, on the other hand, refers only to the file currently being read.

Workshop

The Workshop provides quiz questions to help you solidify your understanding of the material covered and exercises to give you experience in using what you've learned. Try and understand the quiz and exercise answers before you go on to tomorrow's lesson.

Quiz

1. What do these functions do?

   a. `tell`

   b. `mkdir`

   c. `link`

   d. `unlink`

   e. `truncate`

2. What is the difference between `stat` and `lstat`?

3. What is the difference between `tell` and `telldir`?

4. How are the following files being opened?

   a. `open (MYFILE, "<file1");`

   b. `open (MYFILE, "file2¦");`

   c. `open (MYFILE, "+>file3");`

   d. `open (MYFILE, ">&STDOUT");`

12

5. What permissions are granted by the following values?

    a. `0666`

    b. `0777`

    c. `0700`

    d. `0644`

Exercises

1. Write a program that reads the directory `/u/jqpublic` and prints out all file and directory names that start with a period. Ignore the special files . (one period) and .. (two periods).

2. Write a program that lists all the files (*not* the subdirectories) in the directory `/u/jqpublic` and then lists the contents of any subdirectories, their subdirectories, and so on. (Hint: Use a recursive subroutine.)

3. Write a program that uses `readdir` and `rewinddir` to read a directory named `/u/jqpublic` and print a sorted list of the files and directories in alphabetical order. Ignore all names beginning with a period. (Of course, this is not the most efficient way to do this.)

4. Write a program that uses hot keys and does the following:

    ☐ Reads single digits and prints out their English-language equivalents (for example, `zero` for 0, `one` for 1, and so on)

    ☐ Terminates if it reads the Esc (escape) character

    ☐ Ignores all other input

    ☐ Prints out one English word per line

5. Write a program that reads the directory `/u/jqpublic` and grants global execute permissions for all files ending in `.pl`. Take away all other permissions, except user read, for every other file in the directory. Skip over all subdirectories.

6. **BUG BUSTER:** What is wrong with the following program?

```
#!/usr/local/bin/perl

while ($line = <>) {
        print ($line);
        if (eof()) {
                print ("-- end of current file --\n");
        }
}
```

Day 13

Process, String, and Mathematical Functions

Today's lesson describes three groups of built-in Perl functions:

- [ ] The functions that manipulate processes and programs that are currently running
- [ ] The functions that perform mathematical operations
- [ ] The functions that manipulate character strings

WARNING

Many of the functions described today use features of the UNIX operating system. If you are using Perl on a machine that is not running UNIX, some of these functions might not be defined or might behave differently.

Check the documentation supplied with your version of Perl for details on which functions are supported or emulated on your machine.

Process- and Program-Manipulation Functions

Perl provides a wide range of functions that manipulate both the program currently being executed and other programs (also called processes) running on your machine. These functions are divided into four groups:

- ☐ Functions that start additional processes
- ☐ Functions that stop the current program or another process
- ☐ Functions that control the execution of a program or process
- ☐ Functions that manipulate processes or programs but don't fit into any of the preceding categories

The following sections describe these four groups of process- and program-manipulation functions.

Starting a Process

Several built-in functions provide different ways of creating processes: `eval`, `system`, `fork`, `pipe`, `exec`, and `syscall`. These functions are described in the following subsections.

The `eval` Function

The eval function treats a character string as an executable Perl program.

The syntax for the eval function is

```
eval (string);
```

Here, *string* is the character string that is to become a Perl program.

For example, these two lines of code:

```
$print = "print (\"hello, world\\n\");";
eval ($print);
```

print the following message on your screen:

```
hello, world
```

The character string passed to eval can be a character-string constant or any expression that has a value which is a character string. In this example, the following string is assigned to $print, which is then passed to eval:

```
print ("hello, world\n");
```

The eval function uses the special system variable $@ to indicate whether the Perl program contained in the character string has executed properly. If no error has occurred, $@ contains the null string. If an error has been detected, $@ contains the text of the message.

The subprogram executed by eval affects the program that called it; for example, any variables that are changed by the subprogram remain changed in the main program. Listing 13.1 provides a simple example of this.

TYPE **Listing 13.1. A program that illustrates the behavior of eval.**

```
1:  #!/usr/local/bin/perl
2:
3:  $myvar = 1;
4:  eval ("print (\"hi!\\n\"); \$myvar = 2;");
5:  print ("the value of \$myvar is $myvar\n");
```

OUTPUT
```
$ program13_1
hi!
the value of $myvar is 2
$
```

ANALYSIS The call to eval in line 4 first executes the statement

```
print ("hi!\n");
```

Then it executes the following assignment, which assigns 2 to $myvar:

```
$myvar = 2;
```

The value of $myvar remains 2 in the main program, which means that line 5 prints the value 2. (The backslash preceding the $ in $myvar ensures that the Perl interpreter does not substitute the value of $myvar for the name before passing it to eval.)

NOTE

If you like, you can leave off the final semicolon in the character string passed to eval, as follows:

```
eval ("print (\"hi!\\n\"); \$myvar = 2");
```

As before, this prints hi! and assigns 2 to $myvar.

The eval function has one very useful property: If the subprogram executed by eval encounters a fatal error, the main program does not halt. Instead, the subprogram terminates, copies the error message into the system variable $@, and returns to the main program.

This feature is very useful if you are moving a Perl program from one machine to another and you are not sure whether the new machine contains a built-in function you need. For example, Listing 13.2 tests whether the tell function is implemented.

TYPE

Listing 13.2. A program that uses eval to test whether a function is implemented.

```
1:  #!/usr/local/bin/perl
2:
3:  open (MYFILE, "file1") || die ("Can't open file1");
4:  eval ("\$start = tell(MYFILE);");
5:  if ($@ eq "") {
6:          print ("The tell function is defined.\n");
7:  } else {
8:          print ("The tell function is not defined!\n");
9:  }
```

OUTPUT

```
$ program13_2
The tell function is defined.
$
```

ANALYSIS   The call to eval in line 4 creates a subprogram that calls the function tell. If tell is defined, the subprogram assigns the location of the next line (which, in this case, is the first line) to read to the scalar variable $start. If tell is not defined, the subprogram places the error message in $@.

Line 5 checks whether $@ is the null string. If $@ is empty, the subprogram in line 4 executed without generating an error, which means that the tell function is implemented. (Because assignments performed in the subprogram remain in effect in the main program, the main program can call seek using the value in $start, if desired.) If $@ is not empty, the program assumes that tell is not defined, and it prints a message proclaiming that fact. (This program is assuming that the only reason the subprogram could fail is because tell is not defined. This is a reasonable assumption, because you know that the file referenced by MYFILE has been successfully opened.)

13

WARNING

Although eval is very useful, it is best to use it only for small programs. If you need to generate a larger program, it might be better to write the program to a file and call system to execute it. (The system function is described in the following section.)

Because statements executed by eval affect the program that calls it, the behavior of complicated programs might become difficult to track if eval is used to excess.

The system **Function**

You have seen examples of the system function in earlier lessons.

The syntax for the system function is

```
system (list);
```

This function is passed a list as follows: The first element of the list contains the name of a program to execute, and the other elements are arguments to be passed to the program.

When system is called, it starts a process that runs the program and waits until the process terminates. When the process terminates, the error code is shifted left eight bits, and the resulting value becomes system's return value. Listing 13.3 is a simple example of a program that calls system.

 Listing 13.3. A program that calls system.

```
1:  #!/usr/local/bin/perl
2:
3:  @proglist = ("echo", "hello, world!");
4:  system(@proglist);
```

```
$ program13_3
hello, world!
$
```

ANALYSIS In this program, the call to system executes the UNIX program echo, which displays its arguments. The argument passed to echo is hello, world!.

TIP

When you start another program using system, output data might be mixed, out of sequence, or duplicated.

13

To get around this problem, set the system variable $|, defined for each
file, to 1. The following is an example:

```
select (STDOUT);
$| = 1;
select (STDERR);
$| = 1;
```

When $| is set to 1, no buffer is defined for that file, and output is
written out right away. This ensures that the output behaves properly
when system is called.

See "Redirecting One File to Another" on Day 12, "Working with the
File System," for more information on select and $|.

The fork Function

SYNTAX

The fork function creates two copies of your program: the parent process and the child
process. These copies execute simultaneously.

The syntax for the fork function is

```
procid = fork();
```

fork returns zero to the child process and a nonzero value to the parent process. This nonzero
value is the *process ID* of the child process. (A process ID is an integer that enables the system
to distinguish this process from the other processes currently running on the machine.)

The return value from fork enables you to determine which process is the child process and
which is the parent. For example:

```
$retval = fork();
if ($retval == 0) {
        # this is the child process
        exit;   # this terminates the child process
} else {
        # this is the parent process
}
```

If fork is unable to execute, the return value is a special undefined value for which you can
test by using the defined function. (For more information on defined, see Day 14, "Scalar-
Conversion and List-Manipulation Functions.")

To terminate a child process created by fork, use the built-in function exit, which is
described later in today's lesson.

WARNING

Be careful when you use the `fork` function. The following are a few examples of what can go wrong:

☐ If both copies of the program execute calls to `print` or any other output-generating function, the output from one copy might be mixed with the output from the other copy. There is no way to guarantee that output from one copy will appear before output from the other, unless you force one process to wait for the other.

☐ If you use `fork` in a loop, the program might wind up generating many copies of itself. This can affect the performance of your system (or crash it completely).

☐ Your child process might wind up executing code that your parent process is supposed to execute, or vice versa.

The `pipe` **Function**

The `pipe` function is designed to be used in conjunction with the `fork` function. It provides a way for the child and parent processes to communicate.

The syntax for the `pipe` function is

SYNTAX

```
pipe (infile, outfile);
```

`pipe` requires two arguments, each of which is a file variable that is not currently in use—in this case, *infile* and *outfile*. After `pipe` has been called, information sent via the *outfile* file variable can be read using the *infile* file variable. In effect, the output from *outfile* is piped to *infile*.

To use `pipe` with `fork`, do the following:

1. Call `pipe`.
2. Call `fork` to split the program into parent and child processes.
3. Have one of the processes close *infile*, and have the other close *outfile*.

The process in which *outfile* is still open can now send data to the process in which *infile* is still open. (The child can send data to the parent, or vice versa, depending on which process closes input and which closes output.)

Listing 13.4 shows how `pipe` works. It uses `fork` to create a parent and child process. The parent process reads a line of input, which it passes to the child process. The child process then prints it.

13

TYPE   **Listing 13.4. A program that uses** fork **and** pipe.

```
 1:  #!/usr/local/bin/perl
 2:
 3:  pipe (INPUT, OUTPUT);
 4:  $retval = fork();
 5:  if ($retval != 0) {
 6:          # this is the parent process
 7:          close (INPUT);
 8:          print ("Enter a line of input:\n");
 9:          $line = <STDIN>;
10:          print OUTPUT ($line);
11: } else {
12:          # this is the child process
13:          close (OUTPUT);
14:          $line = <INPUT>;
15:          print ($line);
16:          exit (0);
17: }
```

OUTPUT
```
$ program13_4
Enter a line of input:
Here is a test line
Here is a test line
$
```

ANALYSIS   Line 3 defines the file variables INPUT and OUTPUT. Data sent to OUTPUT can be now read from INPUT.

Line 4 splits the program into a parent process and a child process. Line 5 then determines which process is which.

The parent process executes lines 7–10. Because the parent process is sending data through OUTPUT, it has no need to access INPUT; therefore, line 7 closes INPUT.

Lines 8 and 9 obtain a line of data from the standard input file. Line 10 then sends this line of data to the child process via the file variable OUTPUT.

The child process executes lines 13–16. Because the child process is receiving data through INPUT, it does not need access to OUTPUT; therefore, line 13 closes OUTPUT.

Line 14 reads data from INPUT. Because data from OUTPUT is piped to INPUT, the program waits until the data is actually sent before continuing with line 15.

Line 16 uses exit to terminate the child process. This also automatically closes INPUT.

Note that the <INPUT> operator behaves like any other operator that reads input (such as, for instance, <STDIN>). If there is no more data to read, INPUT is assumed to be at the "end of file," and <INPUT> returns the null string.

Traffic through the file variables specified by `pipe` can flow in only one direction. You cannot have a process both send and receive on the same `pipe`.

If you need to establish two-way communication, you can open two pipes, one in each direction.

The `exec` Function

The `exec` function is similar to the `system` function, except that it terminates the current program before starting the new one.

SYNTAX

The syntax for the `exec` function is

```
exec (list);
```

This function is passed a list as follows: The first element of the list contains the name of a program to execute, and the other elements are arguments to be passed to the program.

For example, the following statement terminates the Perl program and starts the command `mail dave`:

```
exec ("mail dave");
```

Like `system`, `exec` accepts additional arguments that are assumed to be passed to the command being invoked. For example, the following statement executes the command `vi file1`:

```
exec ("vi", "file1");
```

You can specify the name that the system is to use as the program name, as follows:

```
exec "maildave" ("mail dave");
```

Here, the command `mail dave` is invoked, but the program name is set to `maildave`. (This affects the value of the system variable `$0`, which contains the name of the running program. It also affects the value of `argv[0]` if the program to be invoked was originally written in C.)

`exec` often is used in conjunction with `fork`: when `fork` splits into two processes, the child process starts another program using `exec`.

`exec` has the same output-buffering problems as `system`. See the description of `system`, earlier in today's lesson, for a description of these problems and how to deal with them.

13

The `syscall` Function

The `syscall` function calls a system function.

The syntax for the `syscall` function is

```
syscall (list);
```

`syscall` expects a list as its argument. The first element of the `list` is the name of the system call to invoke, and the remaining elements are arguments to be passed to the call.

If an argument in the list passed to `syscall` is a numeric value, it is converted to a C integer (type `int`). Otherwise, a pointer to the string value is passed. See the `syscall` UNIX manual page or the Perl documentation for more details.

NOTE

The Perl header file `syscall.ph` must be included in order to use `syscall`:

```
require ("syscall.ph")
```

For more information on `require`, see Day 20, "Miscellaneous Features of Perl."

Terminating a Program or Process

The following sections describe the functions that terminate either the currently executing program or a process running elsewhere on the system: `die`, `warn`, `exit`, and `kill`.

The `die` and `warn` Functions

The `die` and `warn` functions provide a way for programs to pass urgent messages back to the user who is running them.

The `die` function terminates the program and prints an error message on the standard error file.

The syntax for the `die` function is

```
die (message);
```

`message` is the error message to be displayed.

For example, the call

```
die ("Cannot open input file\n");
```

prints the following message and then exits:

```
Cannot open input file
```

die can accept a list as its argument, in which case all elements of the list are printed.

```
@diemsg = ("I'm about ", "to die\n");
die (@diemsg);
```

This prints out the following message and then exits:

```
I'm about to die
```

If the last argument passed to die ends with a newline character, the error message is printed as is. If the last argument to die does not end with a newline character, the program filename and line number are printed, along with the line number of the input file (if applicable). For example, if line 6 of the file myprog is

```
die ("Cannot open input file");
```

the message it prints is

```
Cannot open input file at myprog line 6.
```

The warn function, like die, prints a message on the standard error file.

The syntax for the warn function is

```
warn (message);
```

As with die, message is the message to be displayed.

warn, unlike die, does not terminate. For example, the statement

```
warn ("Input file is empty");
```

sends the following message to the standard error file, and then continues executing:

```
Input file is empty at myprog line 76.
```

If the string passed to warn is terminated by a newline character, the warning message is printed as is. For example, the statement

```
warn("Danger! Danger!\n");
```

sends

```
Danger! Danger!
```

to the standard error file.

NOTE If eval is used to invoke a program that calls die, the error message printed by die is not printed; instead, the error message is assigned to the system variable $@.

13

The `exit` **Function**

The `exit` function terminates a program.

If you like, you can specify a return code to be passed to the system by passing `exit` an argument using the following syntax:

```
exit (retcode);
```

retcode is the return code you want to pass.

For example, the following statement terminates the program with a return code of 2:

```
exit(2);
```

The `kill` **Function**

The `kill` function enables you to send a signal to a group of processes.

The syntax for invoking the `kill` function is

```
kill (signal, proclist);
```

In this case, *signal* is the numeric signal to send. (For example, a *signal* of 9 kills the listed processes.) *proclist* is a list of process IDs (such as the child process ID returned by `fork`).

signal also can be a signal name enclosed in quotes, as in `"INT"`.

For more details on the signals you can send, refer to the `kill` UNIX manual page.

Execution Control Functions

The `sleep`, `wait`, and `waitpid` functions delay the execution of a particular program or process.

The `sleep` **Function**

The `sleep` function suspends the program for a specified number of seconds.

The syntax for the `sleep` function is

```
sleep (time);
```

time is the number of seconds to suspend program execution.

The function returns the number of seconds that the program was actually stopped.

For example, the following statement puts the program to sleep for five seconds:

```
sleep (5);
```

The `wait` **and** `waitpid` **Functions**

The `wait` function suspends execution and waits for a child process to terminate (such as a process created by `fork`).

The `wait` function requires no arguments:

```
procid = wait();
```

When a child process terminates, `wait` returns the process ID, *procid*, of the process that has terminated. If no child processes exist, `wait` returns -1.

The `waitpid` function waits for a particular child process.

The syntax for the `waitpid` function is

```
waitpid (procid, waitflag);
```

procid is the process ID of the process to wait for, and *waitflag* is a special wait flag (as defined by the `waitpid` or `wait4` manual page). By default, *waitflag* is 0 (a normal wait). `waitpid` returns 1 if the process is found and has terminated, and it returns -1 if the child process does not exist.

Listing 13.5 shows how `waitpid` can be used to control process execution.

| TYPE | **Listing 13.5. A program that uses** `waitpid`. |

```
 1:  #!/usr/local/bin/perl
 2:
 3:  $procid = fork();
 4:  if ($procid == 0) {
 5:          # this is the child process
 6:          print ("this line is printed first\n");
 7:          exit(0);
 8:  } else {
 9:          # this is the parent process
10:          waitpid ($procid, 0);
11:          print ("this line is printed last\n");
12: }
```

| OUTPUT |
```
$ program13_5
this line is printed first
this line is printed last
$
```

| ANALYSIS | Line 3 splits the program into a parent process and a child process. The parent process is returned the process ID of the child process, which is stored in `$procid`.

Lines 6 and 7 are executed by the child process. Line 6 prints the following line:

```
this line is printed first
```

13

Line 7 then calls `exit`, which terminates the child process.

Lines 10 and 11 are executed by the parent process. Line 10 calls `waitpid` and passes it the ID of the child process; therefore, the parent process waits until the child process terminates before continuing. This means that line 11, which prints the second line, is guaranteed to be executed after the first line is printed.

As you can see, `wait` can be used to force the order of execution of processes.

 NOTE

> For more information on the possible values that can be passed as `waitflag`, examine the file `wait.ph`, which is available from the same place you retrieved your copy of Perl. (It might already be on your system.) You can find out more also by investigating the `waitpid` and `wait4` manual pages.

Miscellaneous Control Functions

The `caller`, `chroot`, `local`, and `times` functions perform various process and program-related actions.

The `caller` Function

The `caller` function returns the name and the line number of the program that called the currently executing subroutine.

 SYNTAX

The syntax for the `caller` function is

```
subinfo = caller();
```

`caller` returns a three-element list, *subinfo*, consisting of the following:

☐ The name of the package from which the subroutine was called

☐ The name of the file from which the subroutine was called

☐ The line number of the subroutine call

This routine is used by the Perl debugger, which you'll learn about on Day 21, "The Perl Debugger." For more information on packages, refer to Day 20, "Miscellaneous Features of Perl."

 13

The `chroot` **Function**

The `chroot` function duplicates the functionality of the `chroot` function call.

The syntax for the `chroot` function is

```
chroot (dir);
```

dir is the new root directory.

In the following example, the specified directory becomes the root directory for the program:

```
chroot ("/u/jqpublic");
```

For more information, refer to the `chroot` manual page.

The `local` **Function**

The `local` function was introduced on Day 9, "Using Subroutines." It declares that a copy of a named variable is to be defined for a subroutine. (Refer to that day for examples that use `local` inside a subroutine.)

`local` can be used also to define a copy of a variable for use inside a *statement block* (a collection of statements enclosed in brace brackets), as follows:

```
if ($var == 14) {
        local ($localvar);
        # stuff goes here
}
```

This defines a local copy of the variable `$localvar` for use inside the statement block. Any other copies of `$localvar` that exist are not affected by the changes to this local copy.

Do	Don't

DON'T use `local` inside a loop, as in this example:

```
while ($var <= 14) {
        local ($myvar);
        # stuff goes here
}
```

Here, a new copy of `$myvar` is defined each time the loop iterates. This is probably not what you want.

13

The `times` Function

The `times` function returns the amount of job time consumed by this program and any child processes of this program.

SYNTAX

The syntax for the `times` function is

```
timelist = times
```

As you can see, `times` accepts no arguments. It returns *timelist*, a list consisting of the following four floating-point numbers:

- [ ] The user time consumed by this program
- [ ] The system time consumed by this program
- [ ] The user time consumed by the child processes, if they exist
- [ ] The system time consumed by the child processes, if they exist

Mathematical Functions

Perl provides functions that perform the standard trigonometric operations, plus some other useful mathematical operations. The following sections describe these functions: `sin`, `cos`, `atan2`, `sqrt`, `exp`, `log`, `abs`, `rand`, and `srand`.

The `sin` and `cos` Functions

The `sin` and `cos` functions are passed a scalar value and return the sine and cosine, respectively, of the value.

The syntax of the `sin` and `cos` functions is

```
retval = sin (value);
retval = cos (value);
```

value is a placeholder here. It can be the value stored in a scalar variable or the result of an expression; it is assumed to be in radians. See the following section, "The `atan2` Function," to find out how to convert from radians to degrees.

The `atan2` Function

The `atan2` function calculates and returns the arctangent of one value divided by another, in the range $-\pi$ to π.

The syntax of the `atan2` function is

```
retval = atan2 (value1, value2);
```

If *value1* and *value2* are equal, *retval* is the value of π divided by 4.

Listing 13.6 shows how you can use this to convert from degrees to radians.

Listing 13.6. A program that contains a subroutine that converts from degrees to radians.

```
1:  #!/usr/local/bin/perl
2:
3:  $rad90 = &degrees_to_radians(90);
4:  $sin90 = sin($rad90);
5:  $cos90 = cos($rad90);
6:  print ("90 degrees:\nsine is $sin90\ncosine is $cos90\n");
7:
8:  sub degrees_to_radians {
9:          local ($degrees) = @_;
10:         local ($radians);
11:
12:         $radians = atan2(1,1) * $degrees / 45;
13: }
```

OUTPUT

```
$ program13_6
90 degrees:
sine is 1
cosine is 6.12303176911189629111e-17
$
```

ANALYSIS The subroutine `degrees_to_radians` converts from degrees to radians by multiplying by π divided by 180. Because `atan2(1,1)` returns π divided by 4, all the subroutine needs to do after that is divide by 45 to obtain the number of radians.

In the main body of the program, line 3 converts 90 degrees to the equivalent value in radians (π divided by 2). Line 4 then passes this value to `sin`, and line 5 passes it to `cos`.

NOTE

> The trigonometric operations provided here are sufficient to enable you to perform the other important trigonometric operations. For example, to obtain the tangent of a value, obtain the sine and cosine of the value by calling `sin` and `cos`, and then divide the sine by the cosine.

The sqrt Function

The sqrt function returns the square root of the value it is passed.

The syntax for the sqrt function is

```
retval = sqrt (value);
```

value can be any positive number.

The exp **Function**

The exp function returns the number e `**` *value*, where e is the standard mathematical constant (the base for the natural logarithm) and *value* is the argument passed to exp.

The syntax for the exp function is

```
retval = exp (value);
```

To retrieve e itself, pass exp the value 1.

The log **Function**

The log function takes a value and returns the natural (base e) logarithm of the value.

The syntax for the log function is

```
retval = log (value);
```

The log function undoes exp; the expression

```
$var = log (exp ($var));
```

always leaves $var with the value it started with (if you factor in round-off error).

The abs **Function**

The abs function returns the absolute value of a number. This is defined as follows: if a value is less than zero, abs negates it and returns the result.

```
$result = $abs(-3.5);    # returns 3.5
```

Otherwise, the result is identical to the value:

```
$result = $abs(3.5);     # returns 3.5
$result = $abs(0);       # returns 0
```

The syntax for the abs function is

```
retval = abs (value);
```

value can be any number.

 NOTE

abs is not defined in Perl 4.

The rand **and** srand **Functions**

The rand and srand functions enable Perl programs to generate random numbers.

The rand function is passed an integer value and generates a random floating-point number between 0 and the value.

The syntax for the rand function is

```
retval = rand (num);
```

num is the integer value passed to rand, and *retval* is a random floating-point number between 0 and the *num*.

For example, the following statement generates a number between 0 and 10 and returns it in $retval:

```
$retval = rand (10);
```

srand initializes the random-number generator used by rand. This ensures that the random numbers generated are, in fact, random. (If you do not use srand, you'll get the same set of random numbers each time.)

The syntax for the srand function is

```
srand (value);
```

srand accepts an integer value as an argument; if no argument is supplied, srand calls the time function and uses its return value as the random-number seed.

For an example that uses rand and srand, see the section titled "Returning a Value from a Subroutine" on Day 9.

TIP

The following values and functions return numbers that can make useful random-number seeds:

- ☐ The system variable $$ contains the process ID of the current program. (See Day 17, "System Variables," for more information on $$.)
- ☐ time returns the current time value.
- ☐ Many of the functions described on Day 15, "System Functions," return useful values. For example, getppid returns the process ID of the program's parent process.

For best results, combine two or more of these using the ¦ (bitwise OR) operator.

13

String-Manipulation Functions

This section describes the built-in Perl functions that manipulate character strings. These functions enable you to do the following:

- ☐ Search for a substring in a character string
- ☐ Create a string
- ☐ Replace a substring within a string

The index Function

The index function provides a way of indicating the location of a substring in a string.

The syntax for the index function is

```
position = index (string, substring);
```

string is the character string to search in, and *substring* is the character string being searched for. *position* returns the number of characters skipped before *substring* is located; if *substring* is not found, *position* is set to -1.

Listing 13.7 is a program that uses index to locate a substring in a string.

 Listing 13.7. A program that uses the index function.

```
1:  #!/usr/local/bin/perl
2:
3:  $input = <STDIN>;
4:  $position = index($input, "the");
5:  if ($position >= 0) {
6:          print ("pattern found at position $position\n");
7:  } else {
8:          print ("pattern not found\n");
9:  }
```

OUTPUT

```
$ program13 7
Here is the input line I have typed.
pattern found at position 8
$
```

ANALYSIS This program searches for the first occurrence of the word the. If it is found, the program prints the location of the pattern; if it is not found, the program prints `pattern not found`.

You can use the index function to find more than one copy of a substring in a string. To do this, pass a third argument to index, which tells it how many characters to skip before starting to search. For example:

```
$position = index($line, "foo", 5);
```

This call to index skips five characters before starting to search for foo in the string stored in $line. As before, if index finds the substring, it returns the total number of characters skipped (including the number specified by the third argument to index). If index does not find the substring in the portion of the string that it searches, it returns -1.

This feature of index enables you to find all occurrences of a substring in a string. Listing 13.8 is a modified version of Listing 13.7 that searches for all occurrences of the in an input line.

TYPE **Listing 13.8. A program that uses index to search a line repeatedly.**

```
 1:  #!/usr/local/bin/perl
 2:
 3:  $input = <STDIN>;
 4:  $position = $found = 0;
 5:  while (1) {
 6:          $position = index($input, "the", $position);
 7:          last if ($position == -1);
 8:          if ($found == 0) {
 9:                  $found = 1;
10:                  print ("pattern found — characters skipped:");
11:          }
12:          print (" $position");
13:          $position++;
14:  }
15:  if ($found == 0) {
16:          print ("pattern not found\n");
17:  } else {
18:          print ("\n");
19:  }
```

OUTPUT
```
$ program13 8
Here is the test line containing the words.
pattern found — characters skipped: 8 33
$
```

ANALYSIS Line 6 of this program calls index. Because the initial value of $position is 0, the first call to index starts searching from the beginning of the string. Eight characters are skipped before the first occurrence of the is found; this means that $position is assigned 8.

Line 7 tests whether a match has been found by comparing $position with -1, which is the value index returns when it does not find the string for which it is looking. Because a match has been found, the loop continues to execute.

13

When the loop iterates again, line 6 calls `index` again. This time, `index` skips nine characters before beginning the search again, which ensures that the previously found occurrence of `the` is skipped. A total of 33 bytes are skipped before `the` is found again. Once again, the loop continues, because the conditional expression in line 7 is false.

On the final iteration of the loop, line 6 calls `index` and skips 34 characters before starting the search. This time, `the` is not found, `index` returns -1, and the conditional expression in line 7 is true. At this point, the loop terminates.

 NOTE   To extract a substring found by `index`, use the `substr` function, which is described later in today's lesson.

The `rindex` Function

The `rindex` function is similar to the `index` function. The only difference is that `rindex` starts searching from the right end of the string, not the left.

The syntax for the `rindex` function is

```
position = rindex (string, substring);
```

This syntax is identical to the syntax for `index`. *string* is the character string to search in, and *substring* is the character string being searched for. *position* returns the number of characters skipped before *substring* is located; if *substring* is not found, *position* is set to -1.

The following is an example:

```
$string = "Here is the test line containing the words.";
$position = rindex($string, "the");
```

In this example, `rindex` finds the second occurrence of `the`. As with `index`, `rindex` returns the number of characters between the left end of the string and the location of the found substring. In this case, 33 characters are skipped, and `$position` is assigned 33.

You can specify a third argument to `rindex`, indicating the maximum number of characters that can be skipped. For example, if you want `rindex` to find the first occurrence of `the` in the preceding example, you can call it as follows:

```
$string = "Here is the test line containing the words.";
$position = rindex($string, "the", 32);
```

Here, the second occurrence of `the` cannot be matched, because it is to the right of the specified limit of 32 skipped characters. `rindex`, therefore, finds the first occurrence of `the`.

Because there are eight characters between the beginning of the string and the occurrence, $position is assigned 8.

Like index, rindex returns -1 if it cannot find the string it is looking for.

The length Function

The length function returns the number of characters contained in a character string.

The syntax for the length function is

```
num = length (string);
```

string is the character string for which you want to determine the length, and *num* is the returned length.

Here is an example using length:

```
$string = "Here is a string";
$strlen = length($string);
```

In this example, length determines that the string in $string is 16 characters long, and it assigns 16 to $strlen.

Listing 13.9 is a program that calculates the average word length used in an input file. (This is sometimes used to determine the "complexity" of the text.) Numbers are skipped.

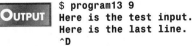

Listing 13.9. A program that demonstrates the use of length.

```
1:  #!/usr/local/bin/perl
2:
3:  $wordcount = $charcount = 0;
4:  while ($line = <STDIN>) {
5:          @words = split(/\s+/, $line);
6:          foreach $word (@words) {
7:                  next if ($word =~ /^\d+\.?\d+$/);
8:                  $word =~ s/[,.;:]$//;
9:                  $wordcount += 1;
10:                 $charcount += length($word);
11:         }
12: }
13: print ("Average word length: ", $charcount / $wordcount, "\n");
```

OUTPUT
```
$ program13 9
Here is the test input.
Here is the last line.
^D
Average word length: 3.5
$
```

13

ANALYSIS This program reads a line of input at a time from the standard input file, breaking the input line into words. Line 7 tests whether the word is a number, and skips it if it is. Line 8 strips any trailing punctuation character from the word, which ensures that the punctuation is not counted as part of the word length.

Line 10 calls length to retrieve the number of characters in the word. This number is added to $charcount, which contains the total number of characters in all of the words that have been read so far. To determine the average word length of the file, line 13 takes this value and divides it by the number of words in the file, which is stored in $wordcount.

Retrieving String Length Using tr

The tr function provides another way of determining the length of a character string, in conjunction with the built-in system variable $_.

SYNTAX

The syntax for the tr function is

```
tr/sourcelist/replacelist/
```

sourcelist is the list of characters to replace, and replacelist is the list of characters to replace with. (For details, see the following listing and the explanation provided with it.)

Listing 13.10 shows how tr works.

TYPE **Listing 13.10. A program that uses tr to retrieve the length of a string.**

```
1:  #!/usr/local/bin/perl
2:
3:  $string = "here is a string";
4:  $_ = $string;
5:  $length = tr/a-zA-Z /a-zA-Z /;
6:  print ("the string is $length characters long\n");
```

OUTPUT
```
$ program13 10
the string is 16 characters long
$
```

ANALYSIS Line 3 of this program creates a string named here is a string and assigns it to the scalar variable $string. Line 4 copies this string into a built-in scalar variable, $_.

Line 5 exploits two features of the tr operator that have not yet been discussed:

☐ If the value to be translated is not explicitly specified by means of the =~ operator, tr assumes that the value is stored in $_.

☐ tr returns the number of characters translated.

In line 5, both the search pattern (the set of characters to look for) and the replacement pattern (the characters to replace them with) are the same. This pattern, `/a-zA-Z /`, tells `tr` to search for all lowercase letters, uppercase letters, and blank spaces, and then replace them with themselves. This pattern matches every character in the string, which means that every character is being translated.

Because every character is being translated, the number of characters translated is equivalent to the length of the string. This string length is assigned to the scalar variable `$length`.

`tr` can be used also to count the number of occurrences of a specific character, as shown in Listing 13.11.

Listing 13.11. A program that uses `tr` to count the occurrences of specific characters.

TYPE

```
 1: #!/usr/local/bin/perl
 2:
 3: $punctuation = $blanks = $total = 0;
 4: while ($input = <STDIN>) {
 5:         chop ($input);
 6:         $total += length($input);
 7:         $_ = $input;
 8:         $punctuation += tr/,:;.-/,:;.-/;
 9:         $blanks += tr/ / /;
10: }
11: print ("In this file, there are:\n");
12: print ("\t$punctuation punctuation characters,\n");
13: print ("\t$blanks blank characters,\n");
14: print ("\t", $total - $punctuation - $blanks);
15: print (" other characters.\n");
```

OUTPUT

```
$ program13 11
Here is a line of input.
This line, another line, contains punctuation.
^D
In this file, there are:
        4 punctuation characters,
        10 blank characters,
        56 other characters.
$
```

ANALYSIS This program uses the scalar variable `$total` and the built-in function `length` to count the total number of characters in the input file (excluding the trailing newline characters, which are removed by the call to `chop` in line 5).

Lines 8 and 9 use `tr` to count the number of occurrences of particular characters. Line 8 replaces all punctuation characters with themselves; the number of replacements performed, and hence the number of punctuation characters found, is added to the total stored in `$punctuation`. Similarly, line 9 replaces all blanks with themselves and adds the number of

13

blanks found to the total stored in $blanks. In both cases, tr operates on the contents of the scalar variable $_, because the =~ operator has not been used to specify another value to translate.

Line 14 uses $total, $punctuation, and $blanks to calculate the total number of characters that are not blank and not punctuation.

NOTE

> Many other functions and operators accept $_ as the default variable on which to work. For example, lines 4–7 of this program also can be written as follows:
>
> ```
> while (<STDIN>) {
>         chop();
>         $total += length();
> ```
>
> For more information on $_, refer to Day 17, "System Variables."

The pos **Function**

The pos function, defined only in Perl 5, returns the location of the last pattern match in a string. It is ideal for use when repeated pattern matches are specified using the g (global) pattern-matching operator.

The syntax for the pos function is

```
offset = pos(string);
```

string is the string whose pattern is being matched. offset is the number of characters already matched or skipped.

Listing 13.12 illustrates the use of pos.

TYPE
Listing 13.12. A program that uses pos to display pattern match positions.

```
1: #!/usr/local/bin/perl
2:
3: $string = "Mississippi";
4: while ($string =~ /i/g) {
5:         $position = pos($string);
6:         print("matched at position $position\n");
7: }
```

13

```
$ program13 12
matched at position 2
matched at position 5
matched at position 8
matched at position 11
```

This program loops every time an i in Mississippi is matched. The number displayed by line 6 is the number of characters to skip to reach the point at which pattern matching resumes. For example, the first i is the second character in the string, so the second pattern search starts at position 2.

NOTE

> You can also use pos to change the position at which pattern matching is to resume. To do this, put the call to pos on the left side of an assignment:
>
> ```
> pos($string) = 5;
> ```
>
> This tells the Perl interpreter to start the next pattern search with the sixth character in the string. (To restart searching from the beginning, use 0.)

The substr **Function**

The substr function lets you assign a part of a character string to a scalar variable (or to a component of an array variable).

The syntax for calls to the substr function is

```
substr (expr, skipchars, length)
```

expr is the character string from which a substring is to be copied; this character string can be the value stored in a variable or the value resulting from the evaluation of an expression. *skipchars* is the number of characters to skip before starting copying. *length* is the number of characters to copy; *length* can be omitted, in which case the rest of the string is copied.

Listing 13.13 provides a simple example of substr.

13

Listing 13.13. A program that demonstrates the use of

substr.

```
1:  #!/usr/local/bin/perl
2:
3:  $string = "This is a sample character string";
```

continues

Listing 13.13. continued

```
4:   $sub1 = substr ($string, 10, 6);
5:   $sub2 = substr ($string, 17);
6:   print ("\$sub1 is \"$sub1\"\n\$sub2 is \"$sub2\"\n");
```

OUTPUT
```
$ program13 13
$sub1 is "sample"
$sub2 is "character string"
$
```

ANALYSIS Line 4 calls `substr`, which copies a portion of the string stored in `$string`. This call specifies that ten characters are to be skipped before copying starts, and that a total of six characters are to be copied. This means that the substring `sample` is copied and stored in `$sub1`.

Line 5 is another call to `substr`. Here, 17 characters are skipped. Because the length field is omitted, `substr` copies the remaining characters in the string. This means that the substring `character string` is copied and stored in `$sub2`.

Note that lines 4 and 5 do not change the contents of `$string`.

String Insertion Using `substr`

In Listing 13.13, which you've just seen, calls to `substr` appear to the right of the assignment operator `=`. This means that the return value from `substr`—the extracted substring—is assigned to the variable appearing to the left of the `=`.

Calls to `substr` can appear also on the left of the assignment operator `=`. In this case, the portion of the string specified by `substr` is *replaced* by the value appearing to the right of the assignment operator.

SYNTAX

The syntax for these calls to `substr` is basically the same as before:

```
substr (expr, skipchars, length) = newval;
```

Here, *expr* must be something that can be assigned to—for example, a scalar variable or an element of an array variable. *skipchars* represents the number of characters to skip before beginning the overwriting operation, which cannot be greater than the length of the string. *length* is the number of characters to be replaced by the overwriting operation. If *length* is not specified, the remainder of the string is replaced.

newval is the string that replaces the substring specified by *skipchars* and *length*. If *newval* is larger than *length*, the character string automatically grows to hold it, and the rest of the string is pushed aside (but *not* overwritten). If *newval* is smaller than *length*, the character string automatically shrinks. Basically, everything appears where it is supposed to without you having to worry about it.

NOTE

By the way, things that can be assigned to are sometimes known as *lvalues*, because they appear to the left of assignment statements (the *l* in *lvalue* stands for "left"). Things that appear to the right of assignment statements are, similarly, called *rvalues*.

This book does not use the terms *lvalue* and *rvalue*, but you might find that knowing them will prove useful when you read other books on programming languages.

Listing 13.14 is an example of a program that uses substr to replace portions of a string.

TYPE

Listing 13.14. A program that replaces parts of a string using substr.

```
1:  #!/usr/local/bin/perl
2:
3:  $string = "Here is a sample character string";
4:  substr($string, 0, 4) = "This";
5:  substr($string, 8, 1) = "the";
6:  substr($string, 19) = "string";
7:  substr($string, -1, 1) = "g.";
8:  substr($string, 0, 0) = "Behold! ";
9:  print ("$string\n");
```

OUTPUT

```
$ program13 14
Behold! This is the sample string.
$
```

ANALYSIS

This program illustrates the many ways you can use substr to replace portions of a string.

The call to substr in line 4 specifies that no characters are to be skipped before overwriting, and that four characters in the original string are to be overwritten. This means that the substring Here is replaced by This, and that the following is the new value of the string stored in $string:

```
This is a sample character string
```

Similarly, the call to substr in line 5 specifies that eight characters are to be skipped and one character is to be replaced. This means that the word a is replaced by the. Now, $string contains the following:

```
This is the sample character string
```

13

Note that the character string is now larger than the original, because the new substring, the, is larger than the substring it replaced.

Line 6 is an example of a call to substr that shrinks the string. Here, 19 characters are skipped, and the rest of the string is replaced by the substring string (because no *length* field has been specified). Now, the following is the value stored in $string:

```
This is the sample string
```

In line 7, the call to substr is passed -1 in the *skipchars* field and is passed 1 in the *length* field. This tells substr to replace the last character of the string with the substring g. (g followed by a period). $string now contains

```
This is the sample string.
```

NOTE
If substr is passed a *skipchars* value of -*n*, where *n* is a positive integer, substr skips to *n* characters from the right end of the string. For example, the following call replaces the last two characters in $string with the string hello:

```
substr($string, -2, 2) = "hello";
```

Finally, line 8 specifies that no characters are to be skipped and no characters are to be replaced. This means that the substring "Behold! " (including a trailing space) is added to the front of the existing string and that $string now contains the following:

```
Behold! This is the sample string.
```

Line 9 prints this final value of $string.

TIP
If you are a C programmer and are used to manipulating strings using pointers, note that substr with a length field of 1 can be used to simulate pointer-like behavior in Perl.

For example, you can simulate the C statement

```
char = *str++;
```

as follows in Perl:

```
$char = substr($str, $offset++, 1);
```

You'll need to define a counter variable (such as $offset) to keep track of where you are in the string. However, this is no more of a chore than remembering to initialize your C pointer variable.

13

You can simulate the following C statement:

```
*str++ = char;
```

by assigning values using substr in the same way:

```
substr($str, $offset++, 1) = $char;
```

You shouldn't use substr in this way unless you really have to. Perl supplies more powerful and useful tools, such as pattern matching and substitution, to get the job done more efficiently.

The study **Function**

The study function is a special function that tells the Perl interpreter that the specified scalar variable is about to be searched many times.

The syntax for the study function is

```
study (scalar);
```

scalar is the scalar variable to be "studied." The Perl interpreter takes the value stored in the specified scalar variable and represents it in an internal format that allows faster access.

For example:

```
study ($myvar);
```

Here, the value stored in the scalar variable $myvar is about to be repeatedly searched.

You can call study for only one scalar variable at a time. Previous calls to study are superseded if study is called again.

 TIP
To check whether study actually makes your program more efficient, use the function times, which displays the user and CPU times for a program or program fragment. (times is discussed earlier today.)

Case Conversion Functions

Perl 5 provides functions that perform case conversion on strings. These are

☐ The lc function, which converts a string to lowercase

☐ The uc function, which converts a string to uppercase

☐ The `lcfirst` function, which converts the first character of a string to lowercase

☐ The `ucfirst` function, which converts the first character of a string to uppercase

The `lc` and `uc` Functions

The syntax for the `lc` and `uc` functions is

```
retval = lc(string);
retval = uc(string);
```

`string` is the string to be converted. `retval` is a copy of the string, converted to either lowercase or uppercase:

```
$lower = lc("aBcDe");  # $lower is assigned "abcde"
$upper = uc("aBcDe");  # $upper is assigned "ABCDE"
```

The `lcfirst` and `ucfirst` Functions

The syntax for the `lcfirst` and `ucfirst` functions is

```
retval = lcfirst(string);
retval = ucfirst(string);
```

`string` is the string whose first character is to be converted. `retval` is a copy of the string, with the first character converted to either lowercase or uppercase:

```
$lower = lcfirst("HELLO");  # $lower is assigned "hELLO"
$upper = ucfirst("hello");  # $upper is assigned "Hello"
```

The `quotemeta` Function

The `quotemeta` function, defined only in Perl 5, places a backslash character in front of any non-word character in a string. The following statements are equivalent:

```
$string = quotemeta($string);
$string =~ s/(\W)/\\$1/g;
```

The syntax for `quotemeta` is

```
newstring = quotemeta(oldstring);
```

`oldstring` is the string to be converted. `newstring` is the string with backslashes added.

`quotemeta` is useful when a string is to be used in a subsequent pattern-matching operation. It ensures that there are no characters in the string which are to be treated as special pattern-matching characters.

The `join` Function

The `join` function has been used many times in this book. It takes the elements of a list and converts them into a single character string.

The syntax for the `join` function is

```
join (joinstr, list);
```

joinstr is the character string that is to be used to glue the elements of *list* together.

For example:

```
@list = ("Here", "is", "a", "list");
$newstr = join ("::", @list);
```

After `join` is called, the value stored in `$newstr` becomes the following string:

```
Here::is::a::list
```

The join string, `::` in this case, appears between each pair of joined elements. The most common join string is a single blank space; however, you can use any value as the join string, including the value resulting from an expression.

The `sprintf` Function

The `sprintf` function behaves like the `printf` function defined on Day 11, "Formatting Your Output," except that the formatted string is returned by the function instead of being written to a file. This enables you to assign the string to another variable.

The syntax for the `sprintf` function is

```
sprintf (string, fields);
```

`string` is the character string to print, and `fields` is a list of values to substitute into the string.

Listing 13.15 is an example that uses `sprintf` to build a string.

TYPE **Listing 13.15. A program that uses `sprintf`.**

```
1:  #!/usr/local/bin/perl
2:
3:  $num = 26;
4:  $outstr = sprintf("%d = %x hexadecimal or %o octal\n",
5:          $num, $num, $num);
6:  print ($outstr);
```

OUTPUT

```
$ program14_9
26 = 1a hexadecimal or 32 octal
$
```

ANALYSIS Lines 4 and 5 take three copies of the value stored in $num and include them as part of a string. The field specifiers %d, %x, and %o indicate how the values are to be formatted.

%d   Indicates an integer displayed in the usual decimal (base-10) format

%x   Indicates an integer displayed in hexadecimal (base-16) format

%o   Indicates an integer displayed in octal (base-8) format

The created string is returned by sprintf. Once it has been created, it behaves just like any other Perl character string; in particular, it can be assigned to a scalar variable, as in this example. Here, the string containing the three copies of $num is assigned to the scalar variable $outstr. Line 6 then prints this string.

NOTE

> For more information on field specifiers or on how printf works, refer to Day 11, which lists the field specifiers defined and provides a description of the syntax of printf.

Summary

Today, you learned about three types of built-in Perl functions: functions that handle process and program control, functions that perform mathematical operations, and functions that manipulate strings.

With the process- and program-control functions, you can start new processes, stop the current program or other processes, or temporarily halt the current program. You also can create a pipe that sends data from one of your created processes to another.

With the functions that perform mathematical operations, you can obtain the sine, cosine, and arctangent of a value. You also can calculate the natural logarithm and square root of a value, or use the value as an exponent of base e.

You also can generate random numbers and define the seed to use when generating the numbers.

Functions that search character strings include index, which searches for a substring starting from the left of a string, and rindex, which searches for a substring starting from the right of a string. You can retrieve the length of a character string using length. By using the translate operator tr in conjunction with the system variable $_, you can count the number of

13

occurrences of a particular character or set of characters in a string. The pos function enables you to determine or set the current pattern-matching location in a string.

The function substr enables you to extract a substring from a string and use it in an expression or assignment statement. substr also can be used to replace a portion of a string or append to the front or back end of the string.

The lc and uc functions convert strings to lowercase or uppercase. To convert the first letter of a string to lowercase or uppercase, use lcfirst or ucfirst.

quotemeta places a backslash in front of every non-word character in a string.

You can create new character strings using join and sprintf. join creates a string by joining elements of a list, and sprintf builds a string using field specifiers that specify the string format.

Q&A

Q How does Perl generate random numbers?

A Basically, by performing arithmetic operations using very large numbers. If the numbers for these arithmetic operations are carefully chosen, a sequence of "pseudo-random" numbers can be generated by repeating the set of arithmetic operations and returning their results.

The random-number seed provided by srand supplies the initial value for one of the numbers used in the set of arithmetic operations. This ensures that the sequence of pseudo-random numbers starts with a different result each time.

Q What programs can be called using system?

A Any program that you can run from your terminal can be run using system.

Q How many processes can a program create using fork?

A Perl provides no limit on how many processes can be created at a time. However, the performance of your system will be adversely affected if you generate too many processes at once.

In particular, programs that call fork and wind up in an infinite loop are sometimes called fork bombs, because they generate thousands of processes and grind your machine to an effective halt. (Your system administrator will not be pleased with you if you do this!)

Q How can I send signals to a process without killing it?

A The kill function actually can send any signal supported by your machine to any running process (that you can access).

Refer to the UNIX system documentation for details on the signals you can send and what their names are.

13

Q What is the difference between the %d and %ld format specifiers in sprintf?

A %ld defines a "long integer." It refers to the largest number of bits that your local machine can use to store an integer. (This is often 32 bits.) %d, on the other hand, is equivalent to your machine's standard integer format. On some machines, %ld and %d are equivalent.

If you are not sure how many bits your machine uses to store integers, or you know you are going to be dealing with large numbers, it's safer to use %ld. (The same holds true for all other integer formats, such as %lx and %lo.)

Q What is the difference between the %c and %s format specifiers in sprintf?

A %c undoes the effect of the ord function. It converts a scalar value into the equivalent ASCII character. (Its behavior is similar to that of the chr function in Pascal.)

%s treats a scalar value as a character string and inserts it into the string at the place specified.

Workshop

The Workshop provides quiz questions to help you solidify your understanding of the material covered and exercises to give you experience in using what you've learned. Try and understand the quiz and exercise answers before you go on to tomorrow's lesson.

Quiz

1. What do these functions do?

    a. srand

    b. pipe

    c. atan2

    d. sleep

    e. gmtime

2. Explain the differences between fork, system, and exec.

3. Explain the differences between wait and waitpid.

4. How can you obtain the value of *p*?

5. How can you obtain the value of the mathematical constant e?

6. What sprintf specifiers produce the following?

    a. A hexadecimal number

    b. An octal number

    c. A floating-point number in exponential format

    d. A floating-point number in standard (fixed) format

7. If the scalar variable `$string` contains `abcdefgh`, what do the following calls return?

    a. `substr ($string, 0, 3);`

    b. `substr ($string, 4);`

    c. `substr ($string, -2, 2);`

    d. `substr ($string, 2, 0);`

8. Assume `$string` contains the value `abcdabcd`. What value is returned by each of the following calls?

    a. `index ($string, "bc");`

    b. `index ($string, "bcde");`

    c. `index ($string, "bc", 1);`

    d. `index ($string, "cd", 3);`

    e. `rindex ($string, "bc");`

9. Assume `$string` contains the value `abcdabcd\n` (the last character being a trailing newline character). What is returned in `$retval` by the following?

    a. `$_ = $string; $retval = tr/ab/ab/;`

    b. `$retval = length ($string);`

Exercises

1. Write a program that uses `fork` and `waitpid` to generate a total of three processes (including the program). Have each process print a line, and have the lines appear in a specified order.

2. Write a program that reads input from a file named `temp` and writes it to the standard output file. Write another program that reads input from the standard output file, writes it to `temp`, and uses `exec` to call the first program.

3. Write a program that prints the natural logarithm of the integers between 1 and 100.

4. Write a program that computes the sum of the numbers from 1 to `10 ** n` for values of `n` from 1 to 6. For each computed value, use `times` to calculate the amount of time each computation takes. Print these calculation times.

5. Write a program that reads an integer value and prints the sine, cosine, and tangent of the value. Assume that the input value is in degrees.

13

6. **BUG BUSTER:** What is wrong with the following program?

```
#!/usr/local/bin/perl

print ("Here is a line of output.   ");
system ("w");
print ("Here is the rest of the line.\n");
```

7. Write a program that uses index to print out the locations of the letters a, e, i, o, and u in an input line.

8. Write a program that uses rindex to do the same thing as the one in Exercise 1.

9. Write a program that uses substr to do the same thing as the one in Exercise 1. (Hint: This will require many calls to substr!)

10. Write a program that uses tr to count all the occurrences of a, e, i, o, and u in an input line.

11. Write a program that reads a number. If the number is a floating-point value, print it in exponential and fixed-point form. If the number is an integer, print it in decimal, octal, and hexadecimal form. (Hint: Recall that printf and sprintf use the same field specifiers.)

12. **BUG BUSTER:** What is wrong with the following program?

```
#!/usr/local/bin/perl

$mystring = <STDIN>;
$lastfound = length ($mystring);
while ($lastfound != -1) {
        $lastfound = index($mystring, "xyz", $lastfound);
}
```

13

Day 14

Scalar-Conversion and List-Manipulation Functions

Today, you learn about the built-in Perl functions that convert scalar values from one form to another, and the Perl functions that deal with variables that have not had values defined for them.

You also learn about the built-in Perl functions that manipulate lists and array variables. These functions are divided into two groups:

☐ The functions that manipulate standard array variables and their lists
☐ The functions that manipulate associative arrays

WARNING

Many of the functions described in today's lesson use features of the UNIX operating system. If you are using Perl on a machine that is not running UNIX, some of these functions might not be defined or might behave differently.

Check the documentation supplied with your version of Perl for details on which functions are supported or emulated on your machine.

The chop **Function**

The chop function was first discussed on Day 3, "Understanding Scalar Values." It removes the last character from a scalar value.

The syntax for the chop function is

```
chop (var);
```

var can be either a scalar value or a list, as described in the following paragraphs.

For example:

```
$mystring = "This is a string";
chop ($mystring);
# $mystring now contains "This is a strin";
```

chop is used most frequently to remove the trailing newline character from an input line, as follows:

```
$input = <STDIN>;
chop ($input);
```

The argument passed to chop can also be a list. In this case, chop removes the last character from every element of the list. For example, to read an entire input file into an array variable and remove all of the trailing newline characters, use the following statements:

```
@input = <STDIN>;
chop (@input);
```

chop returns the character chopped. For example:

```
$input = "12345";
$lastchar = chop ($input);
```

This call to chop assigns 5 to the scalar variable $lastchar.

If chop is passed a list, the last character from the last element of the list is returned:

```
@array = ("ab", "cd", "ef");
$lastchar = chop(@array);
```

This assigns f, the last character of the last element of @array, to $lastchar.

The chomp **Function**

The chomp function, defined only in Perl 5, checks whether the last characters of a string or list of strings match the input line separator defined by the $/ system variable. If they do, chomp removes them.

The syntax for the chomp function is

```
result = chomp(var)
```

As in the chop function, *var* can be either a scalar variable or a list. If *var* is a list, each element of the list is checked for the input end-of-line string. *result* is the total number of characters removed by chomp.

Listing 14.1 shows how chomp works.

TYPE **Listing 14.1. A program that uses the** chomp **function.**

```
1:  #!/usr/local/bin/perl
2:
3:  $/ = "::";    # set input line separator
4:  $scalar = "testing::";
5:  $num = chomp($scalar);
6:  print ("$scalar $num\n");
7:  @list = ("test1::", "test2", "test3::");
8:  $num = chomp(@list);
9:  print ("@list $num\n");
```

OUTPUT
```
$ program14_1
testing 2
test1 test2 test3 4
$
```

ANALYSIS This program uses chomp to remove the input line separator from both a scalar variable and an array variable. The call to chomp in line 5 converts the value of $scalar from testing:: to testing. The number of characters removed, 2, is returned by chomp and assigned to $num.

The call to chomp in line 8 checks each element of @list. The first element is converted from test1:: to test1, and the last element is converted from test3:: to test3. (The second element is ignored, because it is not terminated by the end-of-line specifier.) The total number of characters removed, 4 (two from the first element and two from the last), is returned by chomp and assigned to $num.

NOTE

For more information on the $/ system variable, refer to Day 17, "System Variables."

14

The crypt **Function**

The crypt function encrypts a string using the NBS Data Encryption Standard (DES) algorithm.

The syntax for the crypt function is

```
result = crypt (original, salt);
```

original is the string to be encrypted, and *salt* is a character string of two characters that defines how to change the DES algorithm (to make it more difficult to decode). These two characters can be any letter or digit, or one of the . and / characters. After the algorithm is changed, the string is encrypted using the resulting key.

result is the encrypted string. The first two characters of *result* are the two characters specified in *salt*.

You can use crypt to set up a password checker similar to those used by the UNIX login. Listing 14.2 is an example of a program that prompts the user for a password and compares it with a password stored in a special file.

Listing 14.2. A program that asks for and compares a password.

```
1:  #!/usr/local/bin/perl
2:
3:  open (PASSWD, "/u/jqpublic/passwd") ||
4:          die ("Can't open password file");
5:  $passwd = <PASSWD>;
6:  chop ($passwd);
7:  close (PASSWD);
8:  print ("Enter the password for this program:\n");
9:  system ("stty -echo");
10: $mypasswd = <STDIN>;
11: system ("stty echo");
12: chop ($mypasswd);
13: if (crypt ($mypasswd, substr($passwd, 0, 2)) eq $passwd) {
14:         print ("Correct! Carry on!\n");
15: } else {
16:         die ("Incorrect password: goodbye!\n");
17: }
```

OUTPUT

```
$ program14_2
Enter the password for this program:
bluejays
Correct! Carry on!
$
```

ANALYSIS Note that the password you type is not displayed on the screen.

Lines 3–7 retrieve the correct password from the file /u/jqpublic/passwd. This password can be created by another call to crypt. For example, if the correct password is sludge, the call that creates the string now stored in $passwd could be the following, where $salt contains some two-character string:

```
$retval = crypt ("sludge", $salt);
```

After the correct password has been retrieved, the next step is line 8, which asks the user to type a password. By default, anything typed in at the keyboard is immediately displayed on the screen; this behavior is called *input echoing*. Input echoing is not desirable if a password is being typed in, because someone looking over the user's shoulder can read the password and break into the program.

To make the password-checking process more secure, line 9 calls the UNIX command stty -echo, which turns off input echoing; now the password is not displayed on the screen when the user types it. After the password has been entered, line 11 calls the UNIX command stty echo, which turns input echoing back on.

Line 13 calls crypt to check the password the user has entered. Because the first two characters of the actual encrypted password contain the two-character salt used in encryption, substr is used to retrieve these two characters and use them as the salt when encrypting the user's password. If the value returned by crypt is identical to the encrypted password, the user's password is correct; otherwise, the user has gotten it wrong, and die terminates the program. (A gentler password-checking program usually gives the user two or three chances to type a password before terminating the program.)

This password checker is secure because the actual password does not appear in the program in unencrypted form. (In fact, because the password is in a separate file, it does not appear in the program at all.) This makes it impossible to obtain the password by simply examining the text file.

NOTE The behavior of crypt is identical to that of the UNIX library function crypt. See the crypt(3) manual page for more information on DES encryption.

14

The hex **Function**

The hex function assumes that a character string is a number written in hexadecimal format, and it converts it into a decimal number (a number in standard base-10 format).

SYNTAX

The syntax for the hex function is

```
decnum = hex (hexnum);
```

hexnum is the hexadecimal character string, and *decnum* is the resulting decimal number.

The following is an example:

```
$myhexstring = "1ff";
$num = hex ($myhexstring);
```

This call to hex assigns the decimal equivalent of 1ff to $num, which means that the value of $num is now 511. The value stored in $myhexstring is not changed.

The value passed to the string can contain either uppercase or lowercase letters (provided the letters are between a and f, inclusive). This value can be the result of an expression, as follows:

```
$num = hex ("f" x 2);
```

Here, the expression "f" x 2 is equivalent to ff, which is converted to 255 by hex.

NOTE

> To convert a string from a decimal value to a hexadecimal value, use sprintf and specify either %x (hexadecimal integer) or %lx (long hexadecimal integer).

WARNING

> hex does not handle hexadecimal strings that start with the characters 0x or 0X. To handle these strings, either get rid of these characters using a statement such as
>
> ```
> $myhexstring =~ s/^0[xX]//;
> ```
>
> or call the oct function, which is described later in today's lesson.

The int Function

The int function turns a floating-point number into an integer by getting rid of everything after the decimal point.

The syntax for the `int` function is

```
intnum = int (floatnum);
```

floatnum is the floating-point number, and *intnum* is the resulting integer.

The following is an example:

```
$floatnum = 45.6;
$intnum = int ($floatnum);
```

This call to `int` converts 45.6 to 45 and assigns it to `$intnum`. The value stored in `$floatnum` is not changed.

`int` can be used in expressions as well; for example:

```
$intval = int (68.3 / $divisor) + 1;
```

WARNING

`int` does not round up when you convert from floating point to integer. To round up when you use `int`, add 0.5 first, as follows:

```
$intval = int ($mynum + 0.5);
```

Even then, you still might need to watch out for round-off errors. For example, if 4.5 is actually stored in the machine as, say, 4.499999999, adding 0.5 might still result in a number less than 5, which means that `int` will truncate it to 4.

The oct Function

The `oct` function assumes that a character string is a number written in octal format, and it converts it into a decimal number (a number in standard base-10 format).

The syntax for the `oct` function is

```
decnum = oct (octnum);
```

octnum is the octal character string, and *decnum* is the resulting decimal number.

14

The following is an example:

```
$myoctstring = "177";
$num = oct ($myoctstring);
```

This call to oct assigns the decimal equivalent of 177 to $num, which means that the value of $num is now 127. The value stored in $myoctstring is not changed.

The value passed to oct can be the result of an expression, as shown in the following example:

```
$num = oct ("07" x 2);
```

Here, the expression "07" x 2 is equivalent to 0707, which is converted to 455 by oct.

NOTE   To convert a string from a decimal value to an octal value, use sprintf and specify either %o (octal integer) or %lo (long octal integer).

The oct **Function and Hexadecimal Integers**

The oct function also handles hexadecimal integers whose first two characters start with 0x or 0X:

```
$num = oct ("0xff");
```

This call treats 0xff as the hexadecimal number ff and converts it to 255. This feature of oct can be used to convert any non-standard Perl integer constant.

Listing 14.3 is a program that reads a line of input and checks whether it is a valid Perl integer constant. If it is, it converts it into a standard (base-10) integer.

TYPE   **Listing 14.3. A program that reads any kind of integer.**

```
1:  #!/usr/local/bin/perl
2:
3:  $integer = <STDIN>;
4:  chop ($integer);
5:  if ($integer !~ /^[0-9]+$|^0[xX][0-9a-fA-F]+$/) {
6:          die ("$integer is not a legal integer\n");
7:  }
8:  if ($integer =~ /^0/) {
9:          $integer = oct ($integer);
10: }
11: print ("$integer\n");
```

14

```
$ program14_3
077
63
$
```

ANALYSIS The pattern in line 5 matches one of the following:

☐ One or more digits

☐ A string consisting of 0x or 0X followed by one or more digits or by uppercase or lowercase letters between a and f, inclusive

The first case matches any standard base-10 integer or octal integer (because octal integers start with 0 and consist of the numbers 0 to 7). The second case matches any legal hexadecimal integer. In both cases, the pattern matches only if there are no extraneous characters (blank spaces, or other words or numbers) on the line. Of course, it is easy to use the substitution operator to get rid of these first, if you like.

Line 8 tests whether the integer is either an octal or hexadecimal integer by searching for the pattern /^0/. If this pattern is found, oct converts the integer to decimal, placing the converted integer back in $integer. Note that line 8 does not need to determine which type of integer is contained in $integer because oct processes both octal and hexadecimal integers.

The ord and chr Functions

The ord and chr functions are similar to the Pascal function of the same name. ord converts a single character to its numeric ASCII equivalent, and chr converts a number to its ASCII character equivalent.

The syntax for the ord function is

```
asciival = ord (char);
```

char is the string whose first character is to be converted, and asciival is the resulting ASCII value.

For example, the following statement assigns the ASCII value for the / character, 47, to $ASCIIval:

```
$ASCIIval = ord("/");
```

If the value passed to ord is a character string that is longer than one character in length, ord converts the first character in the string:

```
$mystring = "/ignore the rest of this string";
$charval = ord ($mystring);
```

14

Here, the first character stored in $mystring, /, is converted and assigned to $charval.

The syntax for the chr function is

```
charval = chr (asciival);
```

asciival is the value to be converted, and *charval* is the one-character string representing the character equivalent of *asciival* in the ASCII character set.

For example, the following statement assigns / to $slash, because 47 is the numeric equivalent of / in the ASCII character set:

```
$slash = chr(47);
```

NOTE

The ASCII character set contains 256 characters. As a consequence, if the value passed to chr is greater than 256, only the bottom eight bits of the value are used.

This means, for example, that the following statements are equivalent:

```
$slash = chr(47);
$slash = chr(303);
$slash = chr(559);
```

In each case, the value of $slash is /.

The chr function is defined only in Perl 5. If you are using Perl 4, you will need to call sprintf to convert a number to a character:

```
$slash = sprintf("%c", 47);
```

WARNING

This assigns / to $slash.

The scalar Function

In Perl, some functions or expressions behave differently when their results are assigned to arrays than they do when assigned to scalar variables. For example, the assignment

```
@var = @array;
```

14

copies the list stored in @array to the array variable @var, and the assignment

```
$var = @array;
```

determines the number of elements in the list stored in @array and assigns that number to the scalar variable $var.

As you can see, @array has two different meanings: an "array meaning" and a "scalar meaning." The Perl interpreter determines which meaning to use by examining the rest of the statement in which @array occurs. In the first case, the array meaning is intended, because the statement is assigning to an array variable. Statements in which the array meaning is intended are called *array contexts*.

In the second case, the scalar meaning of @array is intended, because the statement is assigning to a scalar variable. Statements in which the scalar meaning is intended are called *scalar contexts*.

The scalar function enables you to specify the scalar meaning in an array context.

SYNTAX

The syntax for the scalar function is

```
value = scalar (list);
```

list is the list to be used in a scalar context, and *value* is the scalar meaning of the list.

For example, to create a list consisting of the length of an array, you can use the following statement:

```
@array = ("a", "b", "c");
@lengtharray = scalar (@array);
```

Here, the number of elements of @array, 3, is converted into a one-element list and assigned to @lengtharray.

Another useful place to use scalar is in conjunction with the <> operator. Recall that the statement

```
$myline = <MYFILE>;
```

reads one line from the input file MYFILE, and

```
@mylines = <MYFILE>;
```

reads all of MYFILE into the array variable @mylines. To read one line into the array variable @mylines (as a one-element list), use the following:

```
@mylines = scalar (<MYFILE>);
```

Specifying scalar with <MYFILE> ensures that only one line is read from MYFILE.

14

The pack **Function**

The pack function enables you to take a list or the contents of an array variable and convert (pack) it into a scalar value in a format that can be stored in actual machine memory or used in programming languages such as C.

The syntax for the pack function is

```
formatstr = pack(packformat, list);
```

Here, *list* is a list of values; this list of values can, as always, be the contents of an array variable. *formatstr* is the resulting string, which is in the format specified by *packformat*.

packformat consists of one or more *pack-format characters*; these characters determine how the list is to be packed. These pack formats are listed in Table 14.1.

Table 14.1. Format characters for the pack function.

Character	Description
a	ASCII character string padded with null characters
A	ASCII character string padded with spaces
b	String of bits, lowest first
B	String of bits, highest first
c	A signed character (range usually –128 to 127)
C	An unsigned character (usually 8 bits)
d	A double-precision floating-point number
f	A single-precision floating-point number
h	Hexadecimal string, lowest digit first
H	Hexadecimal string, highest digit first
i	A signed integer
I	An unsigned integer
l	A signed long integer
L	An unsigned long integer
n	A short integer in network order
N	A long integer in network order
p	A pointer to a string

14

Character	Description
s	A signed short integer
S	An unsigned short integer
u	Convert to uuencode format
v	A short integer in VAX (little-endian) order
V	A long integer in VAX order
x	A null byte
X	Indicates "go back one byte"
@	Fill with nulls (ASCII 0)

One pack-format character must be supplied for each element in the list. If you like, you can use spaces or tabs to separate pack-format characters, because pack ignores white space.

The following is a simple example that uses pack:

```
$integer = pack("i", 171);
```

This statement takes the number 171, converts it into the format used to store integers on your machine, and returns the converted integer in $integer. This converted integer can now be written out to a file or passed to a program using the system or exec functions.

To repeat a pack-format character multiple times, specify a positive integer after the character. The following is an example:

```
$twoints = pack("i2", 103, 241);
```

Here, the pack format i2 is equivalent to ii.

To use the same pack-format character for all of the remaining elements in the list, use * in place of an integer, as follows:

```
$manyints = pack("i*", 14, 26, 11, 83);
```

Specifying integers or * to repeat pack-format characters works for all formats except a, A, and @. With the a and A formats, the integer is assumed to be the length of the string to create.

```
$mystring = pack("a6", "test");
```

This creates a string of six characters (the four that are supplied, plus two null characters).

14

WARNING

> The a and A formats always use exactly one element of the list, regardless of whether a positive integer is included following the character. For example:
>
> `$mystring = pack("a6", "test1", "test2");`
>
> Here, test1 is packed into a six-character string and assigned to $mystring. test2 is ignored.
>
> To get around this problem, use the x operator to create multiple copies of the a pack-format character, as follows:
>
> `$strings = pack ("a6" x 2, "test1", "test2");`
>
> This packs test1 and test2 into two six-character strings (joined together).

The @ format is a special case. It is used only when a following integer is specified. This integer indicates the number of bytes the string must contain at this point; if the string is smaller, null characters are added. For example:

`$output = pack("a @6 a", "test", "test2");`

Here, the string test is converted to ASCII format. Because this string is only four characters long, and the pack format @6 specifies that the packed scalar value must be six characters long at this point, two null characters are added to the string before test2 is packed.

The pack **Function and C Data Types**

The most frequent use of pack is to create data that can be used by C programs. For example, to create a string terminated by a null character, use the following call to pack:

`$Cstring = pack ("ax", $mystring);`

Here, the a pack-format character converts $mystring into an ASCII string, and the x character appends a null character to the end of the string. This format—a string followed by null—is how C stores strings.

Table 14.2 shows the pack-format characters that have equivalent data types in C.

Table 14.2. Pack-format characters and their C equivalents.

Character	C equivalent
c	char
d	double
f	float
i	int
I	unsigned int (or unsigned)
l	long
L	unsigned long
s	short
S	unsigned short

In each case, pack stores the value in your local machine's internal format.

TIP

You usually won't need to use pack unless you are preparing data for use in other programs.

The unpack **Function**

The unpack function reverses the operation performed by pack. It takes a value stored in machine format and converts it to a list of values understood by Perl.

The syntax for the unpack function is

```
list = unpack (packformat, formatstr);
```

Here, *formatstr* is the value in machine format, and *list* is the created list of values.

As in pack, *packformat* is a set of one or more pack format characters. These characters are basically the same as those understood by pack. Table 14.3 lists these characters.

14

Table 14.3. The pack-format characters, as used by unpack.

Character	Description
a	ASCII character string, unstripped
A	ASCII character string with trailing nulls and spaces stripped
b	String of bits, lowest first
B	String of bits, highest first
c	A signed character (range usually –128 to 127)
C	An unsigned character (usually 8 bits)
d	A double-precision floating-point number
f	A single-precision floating-point number
h	Hexadecimal string, lowest digit first
H	Hexadecimal string, highest digit first
i	A signed integer
I	An unsigned integer
l	A signed long integer
L	An unsigned long integer
n	A short integer in network order
N	A long integer in network order
p	A pointer to a string
s	A signed short integer
S	An unsigned short integer
u	Convert (uudecode) a uuencoded string
v	A short integer in VAX (little-endian) order
V	A long integer in VAX order
x	Skip forward a byte
X	Indicates "go back one byte"
@	Go to specified position

In almost all cases, a call to unpack undoes the effects of an equivalent call to pack. For example, consider Listing 14.4, which packs and unpacks a list of integers.

14

Listing 14.4. A program that demonstrates the relationship between pack and unpack.

```
1:  #!/usr/local/bin/perl
2:
3:  @list_of_integers = (11, 26, 43);
4:  $mystring = pack("i*", @list_of_integers);
5:  @list_of_integers = unpack("i*", $mystring);
6:  print ("@list_of_integers\n");
```

```
$ program14_4
11 26 43
$
```

Line 4 calls pack, which takes all of the elements stored in @list_of_integers, converts them to the machine's integer format, and stores them in $mystring.

Line 5 calls unpack, which assumes that the string stored in $mystring is a list of values stored in the machine's integer format; it takes this string, converts each integer in the string to a Perl value, and stores the resulting list of values in @list_of_integers.

Unpacking Strings

The only unpack operations that do not exactly mirror pack operations are those specified by the a and A formats. The a format converts a machine-format string into a Perl value as is, whereas the A format converts a machine-format string into a Perl value and strips any trailing blanks or null characters.

The A format is useful if you want to convert a C string into the string format understood by Perl. The following is an example:

```
$perlstring = unpack("A", $Cstring);
```

Here, $Cstring is assumed to contain a character string stored in the format used by the C programming language (a sequence of bytes terminated by a null character). unpack strips the trailing null character from the string stored in $Cstring, and stores the resulting string in $perlstring.

Skipping Characters When Unpacking

The @ pack-format character tells unpack to skip to the position specified with the @. For example, the following statement skips four bytes in $packstring, and then unpacks a signed integer and stores it in $skipnum.

```
$skipnum = unpack("@4i", $packstring);
```

14

NOTE

> If unpack is unpacking a single item, it can be stored in either an array variable or a scalar variable. If an array variable is used to store the result of the unpack operation, the resulting list consists of a single element.

If an * character appears after the @ pack-format character, unpack skips to the end of the value being unpacked. This can be used in conjunction with the X pack-format character to unpack the right end of the packed value. For example, the following statement treats the last four bytes of a packed value as a long unsigned integer and unpacks them:

```
$longrightint = unpack("@* X4 L", $packstring);
```

In this example, the @* pack format specifier skips to the end of the value stored in $packstring. Then, the X4 specifier backs up four bytes. Finally, the L specifier treats the last four bytes as a long unsigned integer, which is unpacked and stored in $longrightint.

WARNING

> The number of bytes unpacked by the s, S, i, I, l, and L formats depends on your machine. Many UNIX machines store short integers in two bytes of memory, and integer and long integer values in four bytes. However, other machines might behave differently. In general, you cannot assume that programs that use pack and unpack will behave in the same way on different machines.

The unpack **Function and** uuencode

The unpack function enables you to decode files that have been encoded by the uuencode encoding program. To do this, use the u pack-format specifier.

NOTE

> uuencode, a coding mechanism available on most UNIX systems, converts all characters (including unprintable characters) into printable ASCII characters. This ensures that you can safely transmit files across remote networks.

Listing 14.5 is an example of a program that uses unpack to decode a uuencoded file.

14

TYPE Listing 14.5. A program that decodes a uuencoded file.

```
 1: #!/usr/local/bin/perl
 2:
 3: open (CODEDFILE, "/u/janedoe/codefile") ||
 4:         die ("Can't open input file");
 5: open (OUTFILE, ">outfile") ||
 6:         die ("Can't open output file");
 7: while ($line = <CODEDFILE>) {
 8:         $decoded = unpack("u", $line);
 9:         print OUTFILE ($decoded);
10: }
11: close (OUTFILE);
12: close (CODEDFILE);
```

ANALYSIS The file variable CODEDFILE represents the file that was previously encoded by uuencode. Lines 3 and 4 open the file (or die trying). Lines 5 and 6 open the output file, which is represented by the file variable OUTFILE.

Lines 7–10 read and write one line at a time. Line 7 starts off by reading a line of encoded input into the scalar variable $line. As with any other input file, the null string is returned if CODEDFILE is exhausted.

Line 8 calls unpack to decode the line. If the line is a special line created by uuencode (for example, the first line, which lists the filename and the size, or the last line, which marks the end of the file), unpack detects it and converts it into the null string. This means that the program does not need to contain special code to handle these lines.

Line 9 writes the decoded line to the output file represented by OUTFILE.

NOTE

You can use pack to uuencode lists of elements, as in the following:

```
@encoded = pack ("u", @decoded);
```

Here, the elements in @decoded are encoded and stored in the array variable @encoded. The list in @encoded can then be decoded using unpack, as follows:

```
@decoded = unpack ("u", @encoded);
```

Although pack uses the same uuencode algorithm as the UNIX uuencode utility, you cannot use the UNIX uudecode program on data encoded using pack because pack does not supply the header and footer (beginning and ending) lines expected by uudecode.

14

If you really need to use uudecode with a file created by writing out the output from pack, you'll need to write out the header and footer files as well. (See the UNIX manual page for uuencode for more details.)

The vec **Function**

The vec function enables you to treat a scalar value as a collection of chunks, with each chunk consisting of a specified number of bits; this collection is known as a *vector*. Each call to vec accesses a particular chunk of bits in the vector (known as a *bit vector*).

The syntax for the vec function is

```
retval = vec (vector, index, bits);
```

vector is the scalar value that is to be treated as a vector. It can be any scalar value, including the value of an expression.

index behaves like an array subscript. It indicates which chunk of bits to retrieve. An index of 0 retrieves the first chunk, 1 retrieves the second, and so on. Note that retrieval is from right to left. The first chunk of bits retrieved when the index 0 is specified is the chunk of bits at the right end of the vector.

bits specifies the number of bits in each chunk; it can be 1, 2, 4, 8, 16, or 32.

retval is the value of the chunk of bits. This value is an ordinary Perl scalar value, and it can be used anywhere scalar values can be used.

Listing 14.6 shows how you can use vec to retrieve the value of a particular chunk of bits.

TYPE **Listing 14.6. A program that illustrates the use of** vec**.**

```
1:  #!/usr/local/bin/perl
2:
3:  $vector = pack ("B*", "11010011");
4:  $val1 = vec ($vector, 0, 4);
5:  $val2 = vec ($vector, 1, 4);
6:  print ("high-to-low order values: $val1 and $val2\n");
7:  $vector = pack ("b*", "11010011");
8:  $val1 = vec ($vector, 0, 4);
9:  $val2 = vec ($vector, 1, 4);
10: print ("low-to-high order values: $val1 and $val2\n");
```

14

OUTPUT

```
$ program14_6
high-to-low order values: 3 and 13
low-to-high order values: 11 and 12
$
```

ANALYSIS The call to pack in line 3 assumes that each character in the string 11010011 is a bit to be packed. The bits are packed in high-to-low order (with the highest bit first), which means that the vector stored in $vector consists of the bits 11010011 (from left to right). Grouping these bits into chunks of four produces 1101 0011, which are the binary representations of 13 and 3, respectively.

Line 4 retrieves the first chunk of four bits from $vector and assigns it to $val1. This is the chunk 0011, because vec is retrieving the chunk of bits at the right end of the bit vector. Similarly, line 5 retrieves 1101, because the index 1 specifies the second chunk of bits from the right; this chunk is assigned to $val2. (One way to think of the index is as "the number of chunks to skip." The index 1 indicates that one chunk of bits is to be skipped.)

Line 7 is similar to line 3, but the bits are now stored in low-to-high order, not high-to-low. This means that the string 11010011 is stored as the following (which is 11010011 reversed):

11001011

When this bit vector is grouped into chunks of 4 bits, you get the following, which are the binary representations of 12 and 11, respectively:

1100 1011

Lines 8 and 9, like lines 4 and 5, retrieve the first and second chunk of bits from $vector. This means that $val1 is assigned 11 (the first chunk), and $val2 is assigned 12 (the second chunk).

NOTE

> You can use vec to assign to a chunk of bits by placing the call to vec to the left of an assignment operator. For example:
>
> vec ($vector, 0, 4) = 11;
>
> This statement assigns 11 to the first chunk of bits in $vector. Because the binary representation of 11 is 1011, the last four bits of $vector become 1011.

14

The defined **Function**

By default, all scalar variables and elements of array variables that have not been assigned to are assumed to contain the null string. This ensures that Perl programs don't crash when using uninitialized scalar variables.

In some cases, a program might need to know whether a particular scalar variable or array element has been assigned to or not. The built-in function defined enables you to check for this.

The syntax for the defined function is

```
retval = defined (expr);
```

Here, *expr* is anything that can appear on the left of an assignment statement, such as a scalar variable, array element, or an entire array. (An array is assumed to be defined if at least one of its elements is defined.) *retval* is true (a nonzero value) if *expr* is defined, and false (0) if it is not.

Listing 14.7 is a simple example of a program that uses defined.

TYPE   **Listing 14.7. A program that illustrates the use of defined.**

```
1:  #!/usr/local/bin/perl
2:
3:  $array[2] = 14;
4:  $array[4] = "hello";
5:  for ($i = 0; $i <= 5; $i++) {
6:          if (defined ($array[$i])) {
7:                  print ("element ", $i+1, " is defined\n");
8:          }
9:  }
```

OUTPUT
```
$ program14_7
element 3 is defined
element 5 is defined
$
```

ANALYSIS   This program assigns values to two elements of the array variable @array: the element with subscript 2 (the third element), and the element with subscript 4 (the fifth element).

The loop in lines 5–9 checks each element of @array to see whether it is defined. Because the third and fifth elements—$array[2] and $array[4], respectively—are defined, defined returns true when $i is 2 and when $i is 4.

14

NOTE

Many functions that return the null string actually return a special "undefined" value that is treated as if it is the null string. If this undefined value is passed to defined, defined returns false.

Functions that return undefined include the read function (discussed on Day 12, "Working with the File System") and fork (introduced on Day 13, "Process, String, and Mathematical Functions"). Many functions discussed today and on Day 15, "System Functions," also return the special undefined value when an error occurs.

The general rule is: A function that returns the null string when an error or exceptional condition occurs is usually really returning the undefined value.

The undef Function

The undef function undefines a scalar variable, array element, or an entire array.

SYNTAX

The syntax of the undef function is

```
retval = undef (expr);
```

As in calls to defined, expr can be anything that can appear to the left of a Perl assignment statement. retval is always the special undefined value discussed in the previous section, "The defined Function"; this undefined value is equivalent to the null string.

The following are some examples of undef:

```
undef ($myvar);
undef ($array[3]);
undef (@array);
```

In the first case, the scalar variable $myvar becomes undefined. The Perl interpreter now treats $myvar as if it has never been assigned to. Needless to say, any value previously stored in $myvar is now lost.

In the second example, the fourth element of @array is marked as undefined. Its value, if any, is lost. Other elements of @array are unaffected.

In the third and final example, all the elements of @array are marked as undefined. This lets the Perl interpreter free up any memory used to store the values of @array, which might be

14

useful if your program is working with large arrays. For example, if you have used an array to read in an entire file, as in the following:

```
@bigarray = <STDIN>;
```

you can use the following statement to tell the Perl interpreter that you don't need the contents of the input file and that the interpreter can throw them away:

```
undef (@bigarray);
```

Calls to undef can omit *expr*. In this case, undef does nothing and just returns the undefined value. Listing 14.8 shows how this can be useful.

TYPE

Listing 14.8. A program that illustrates the use of undef to represent an unusual condition.

```
 1:  #!/usr/local/bin/perl
 2:
 3:  print ("Enter the number to divide:\n");
 4:  $value1 = <STDIN>;
 5:  chop ($value1);
 6:  print ("Enter the number to divide by:\n");
 7:  $value2 = <STDIN>;
 8:  chop ($value2);
 9:  $result = &safe_division($value1, $value2);
10:  if (defined($result)) {
11:          print ("The result is $result.\n");
12:  } else {
13:          print ("Can't divide by zero.\n");
14:  }
15:
16:  sub safe_division {
17:          local ($dividend, $divisor) = @_;
18:          local ($result);
19:
20:          $result = ($divisor == 0) ? undef :
21:                  $dividend / $divisor;
22:  }
```

OUTPUT

```
$ program14_8
Enter the number to divide:
26
Enter the number to divide by:
0
Can't divide by zero.
$
```

14

ANALYSIS   Lines 20 and 21 illustrate how you can use `undef`. If `$divisor` is 0, the program is attempting to divide by 0. In this case, the subroutine `safe_division` calls `undef`, which returns the special undefined value. This value is assigned to `$result` and passed back to the main part of the program.

Line 10 tests whether `safe_division` has returned the undefined value by the calling `defined` function. If `defined` returns false, `$result` contains the undefined value, and an attempted division by 0 has been detected.

NOTE

You can use `undef` to undefine an entire subroutine, if you like. The following example:

```
undef (&mysub);
```

frees the memory used to store `mysub`; after this, `mysub` can no longer be called.

You are not likely to need to use this feature of `undef`, but it might prove useful in programs that consume a lot of memory.

Array and List Functions

The following functions manipulate standard array variables and the lists that they store:

- [ ] `grep`
- [ ] `splice`
- [ ] `shift`
- [ ] `unshift`
- [ ] `push`
- [ ] `pop`
- [ ] `split`
- [ ] `sort`
- [ ] `reverse`
- [ ] `map`
- [ ] `wantarray`

14

The grep Function

The grep function provides a convenient way of extracting the elements of a list that match a specified pattern. (It is named after the UNIX search utility of the same name.)

The syntax for the grep function is

```
foundlist = grep (pattern, searchlist);
```

pattern is the pattern to search for. *searchlist* is the list of elements to search in. *foundlist* is the list of elements matched.

Here is an example:

```
@list = ("This", "is", "a", "test");
@foundlist = grep(/^[tT]/, @list);
```

Here, grep examines all the elements of the list stored in @list. If a list element contains the letter t (in either uppercase or lowercase), the element is included as part of @foundlist. As a result, @foundlist consists of two elements: This and test.

Listing 14.9 is an example of a program that uses grep. It searches for all integers on an input line and adds them together.

TYPE   **Listing 14.9. A program that demonstrates the use of grep.**

```
 1:  #!/usr/local/bin/perl
 2:
 3:  $total = 0;
 4:  $line = <STDIN>;
 5:  @words = split(/\s+/, $line);
 6:  @numbers = grep(/^\d+[.,;:]?$/, @words);
 7:  foreach $number (@numbers) {
 8:          $total += $number;
 9:  }
10: print ("The total is $total.\n");
```

OUTPUT
```
$ program14_9
This line of input contains 8, 11 and 26.
The total is 45.
$
```

ANALYSIS   Line 5 splits the input line into words, using the standard pattern /\s+/, which matches one or more tabs or blanks. Some of these words are actually numbers, and some are not.

Line 6 uses grep to match the words that are actually numbers. The pattern /^\d+[.,;:]?$/ matches if a word consists of one or more digits followed by an optional punctuation character. The words that match this pattern are returned by grep and stored in @numbers. After line 6 has been executed, @numbers contains the following list:

```
("8,", "11", "26.")
```

Lines 7–9 use a foreach loop to total the numbers. Note that the totaling operation works properly even if a number being added contains a closing punctuation character: when the Perl interpreter converts a string to an integer, it reads from left to right until it sees a character that is not a digit. This means that the final word, 26., is converted to 26, which is the expected number.

Because split and grep each return a list and foreach expects a list, you can combine lines 5–9 into a single loop if you want to get fancy.

```
foreach $number (grep (/^\d+[.,;:]?$/, split(/\s+/, $line))) {
        $total += $number;
}
```

As always, there is a trade-off of speed versus readability: this code is more concise, but the code in Listing 14.9 is more readable.

Using grep with the File-Test Operators

A useful feature of grep is that it can be used to search for any expression, not just patterns. For example, grep can be used in conjunction with readdir and the file-test operators to search a directory.

Listing 14.10 is an example of a program that searches all the readable files of the current directory for a particular word (which is supplied on the command line). Files whose names begin with a period are ignored.

Listing 14.10. A program that uses grep with the file-test operators.

TYPE

```
1: #!/usr/local/bin/perl
2:
3: opendir(CURRDIR, ".") ||
4:         die("Can't open current directory");
5: @filelist = grep (!/^\./, grep(-r, readdir(CURRDIR)));
6: closedir(CURRDIR);
7: foreach $file (@filelist) {
8:         open (CURRFILE, $file) ||
9:                 die ("Can't open input file $file");
```

continues

14

Listing 14.10. continued

```
10:            while ($line = <CURRFILE>) {
11:                    if ($line =~ /$ARGV[0]/) {
12:                            print ("$file:$line");
13:                    }
14:            }
15:            close (CURRFILE);
16: }
```

```
$ program14_10 pattern
file1:This line of this file contains the word "pattern".
myfile:This file also contains abcpatterndef.
$
```

Line 3 of this program opens the current directory. If it cannot be opened, line 4 calls die, which terminates the program.

Line 5 is actually three function calls in one, as follows:

1. readdir retrieves a list of all of the files in the directory.

2. This list of files is passed to grep, which uses the -r file test operator to search for all files that the user has permission to read.

3. This list of readable files is passed to another call to grep, which uses the expression !/^\./ to match all the files whose names do not begin with a period.

The resulting list—all the files in the current directory that are readable and whose names do not start with a period—is assigned to @filelist.

The rest of the program contains nothing new. Line 6 closes the open directory, and lines 7–16 read each file in turn, searching for the word specified on the command line. (Recall that the built-in array @ARGV lists all the arguments supplied on the command line and that the first word specified on the command line is stored in $ARGV[0].) Line 11 prints any lines containing the word to search for, using the format employed by the UNIX grep command (the filename, followed by :, followed by the line itself).

The splice Function

The splice function enables you to modify the list stored in an array variable. By passing the appropriate arguments to splice, you can add elements to the middle of a list, delete a portion of a list, or replace a portion of a list.

14

The syntax for the `splice` function is

```
retval = splice (array, skipelements, length, newlist)
```

array is the array variable containing the list to be spliced. *skipelements* is the number of elements to skip before splicing. *length* is the number of elements to be replaced. *newlist* is the list to be spliced in; this list can be stored in an array variable or specified explicitly.

If *length* is greater than 0, *retval* is the list of elements replaced by `splice`.

The following sections provide examples of what you can do with `splice`.

Replacing List Elements

You can use `splice` to replace a sublist (a set of elements in a list) with another sublist. The following is an example:

```
@array = ("1", "2", "3", "4");
splice (@array, 1, 2, ("two", "three"));
```

This call to `splice` takes the list stored in `@array`, skips over the first element, and replaces the next two elements with the list (`"two"`, `"three"`). The new value of `@array` is the list

```
("1", "two", "three", "4")
```

If the replacement list is longer than the original list, the elements to the right of the replaced list are pushed to the right. For example:

```
@array = ("1", "2", "3", "4");
splice (@array, 1, 2, ("two", "2.5", "three"));
```

After this call, the new value of `@array` is the following:

```
("1", "two", "2.5", "three", "4")
```

Similarly, if the replacement list is shorter than the original list, the elements to the right of the original list are moved left to fill the resulting gap. For example:

```
@array = ("1", "2", "3", "4");
splice (@array, 1, 2, "twothree");
```

After this call to `splice`, `@array` contains the following list:

```
("1", "twothree", "4")
```

NOTE

> You do not need to put parentheses around the list you pass to `splice`. For example, the following two statements are equivalent:
>
> ```
> splice (@array, 1, 2, ("two", "three"));
> splice (@array, 1, 2, "two", "three");
> ```

14

When the Perl interpreter sees the second form of `splice`, it assumes that the fourth and subsequent arguments are the replacement list.

Listing 14.11 is an example of a program that uses `splice` to replace list elements. It reads a file containing a form letter, and replaces the string <name> with a name read from the standard input file. It then writes out the new letter.

The output shown assumes that the file `form` contains

```
Hello <name>!
This is your lucky day, <name>!
```

Listing 14.11. A program that uses `splice` to replace list elements.

TYPE

```
 1:  #!/usr/local/bin/perl
 2:
 3:  open (FORM, "form") || die ("Can't open form letter");
 4:  @form = <FORM>;
 5:  close (FORM);
 6:  $name = <STDIN>;
 7:  @nameparts = split(/\s+/, $name);
 8:  foreach $line (@form) {
 9:          @words = split(/\s+/, $line);
10:          $i = 0;
11:          while (1) {
12:                  last if (!defined($words[$i]));
13:                  if ($words[$i] eq "<name>") {
14:                          splice (@words, $i, 1, @nameparts);
15:                          $i += @nameparts;
16:                  } elsif ($words[$i] =~ /^<name>/) {
17:                          $punc = $words[$i];
18:                          $punc =~ s/<name>//;
19:                          @temp = @nameparts;
20:                          $temp[@temp-1] .= $punc;
21:                          splice (@words, $i, 1, @temp);
22:                          $i += @temp;
23:                  } else {
24:                          $i++;
25:                  }
26:          }
27:          $line = join (" ", @words);
28:  }
29:  $i = 0;
30:  while (1) {
31:          if (!defined ($form[$i])) {
32:                  $~ = "FLUSH";
33:                  write;
34:                  last;
```

14

```
35:         }
36:         if ($form[$i] =~ /^\s*$/) {
37:             $~ = "FLUSH";
38:             write;
39:             $~ = "BLANK";
40:             write;
41:             $i++;
42:             next;
43:         }
44:         if ($writeline ne "" &&
45:             $writeline !~ / $/) {
46:             $writeline .= " ";
47:         }
48:         $writeline .= $form[$i];
49:         if (length ($writeline) < 60) {
50:             $i++;
51:             next;
52:         }
53:         $~ = "WRITELINE";
54:         write;
55:         $i++;
56: }
57: format WRITELINE =
58: ^<<<<<<<<<<<<<<<<<<<<<<<<<<<<<<<<<<<<<<<<<<<<<<<<<<<<<~
59: $writeline
60: .
61: format FLUSH =
62: ^<<<<<<<<<<<<<<<<<<<<<<<<<<<<<<<<<<<<<<<<<<<<<<<<<<<<<~~
63: $writeline
64: .
65: format BLANK =
66:
67: .
```

OUTPUT

```
$ program14_11
Fred
Hello Fred! This is your lucky day, Fred!
$
```

ANALYSIS This program starts off by reading the entire form letter from the file named `form` into the array variable @form. This makes it possible to format the form letter output later on.

Lines 6 and 7 read the name from the standard input file and break into individual words. This list of words is stored in the array variable @nameparts.

The loop in lines 8–28 reads each line in the form letter and looks for occurrences of the string <name>. First, line 9 breaks the line into individual words. This list of words is stored in the array variable @words.

The while loop starting in line 11 then examines each word of @words in turn. Line 12 checks whether the loop has reached the end of the list by calling defined; if the loop is past the end of the list, defined will return false, indicating that the array element is not defined.

14

Lines 13–15 check whether a word consists entirely of the string <name>. If it does, line 14 calls splice; this call replaces the word <name> with the words in the name list @nameparts.

If a word is not equal to the string <name>, it might still contain <name> followed by a punctuation character. To test for this, line 16 tries to match the pattern /^<name>/. If it matches, lines 17 and 18 isolate the punctuation in a single word. This punctuation is stored in the scalar variable $punc.

Lines 19 and 20 create a copy of the name array @nameparts and append the punctuation to the last element of the array. This ensures that the punctuation will appear in the form letter where it is supposed to—right after the last character of the substituted name. Line 21 then calls splice as in line 14.

After the words in @words have been searched and the name substituted for <name>, line 27 joins the words back into a single line. As an additional benefit, the multiple spaces and tabs in the original line have now been replaced by a single space, which will make the eventual formatted output look nicer.

Lines 30–56 write out the output. The string to be written is stored in the scalar variable $writeline. The program ensures that the form-letter output is formatted by doing the following:

1. First, the print format WRITELINE is defined to use the ^<<<< value-field format. This format fits as much of the contents of $writeline into the line as possible and then deletes the part of $writeline that has been written out.

2. Lines 36–43 enable you to add paragraphs to your form letter. Line 36 tests whether an input line is blank. If it is, the FLUSH print format is used to write out any output from previous lines that has not yet been printed. (Because the output line specified by FLUSH starts with ~~, the line is printed only if it is not blank—in other words, if $writeline actually contains some leftover text.) Then, the BLANK print format writes a blank line.

3. Lines 44–47 check whether a space needs to be placed between the end of one input line and the beginning of the next when formatting.

4. Lines 49–52 ensure that $writeline is always long enough to fill the value field specified by WRITELINE. This guarantees that there will be no unnecessary space in any of the output lines.

5. When @form has been completely read, lines 32–34 ensure that all of the output from previous lines has been written by using the FLUSH print format.

(For more information on the print formats used in this example, refer to Day 11, "Formatting Your Output.")

NOTE

You can use `splice` to splice the contents of a scalar variable into an array. For example:

```
splice (@array, 8, 1, $name);
```

This creates a one-element list consisting of the contents of $name and adds it to the list stored in @array (as the eighth element).

Appending List Elements

You can use `splice` to add a sublist anywhere in a list. To do this, specify a length field of 0. For example:

```
splice (@array, 5, 0, "Hello", "there");
```

This call to `splice` adds the list (`"Hello"`, `"there"`) to the list stored in @array. `Hello` becomes the new sixth element of $list, and `there` becomes the new seventh element; the existing sixth and seventh elements, if they exist, become the new eighth and ninth elements, and every other element is also pushed to the right.

To add a new element to the end of an existing array, specify a `skipelements` value of `-1`, as shown in the following:

```
splice (@array, -1, 0, "Hello");
```

This adds `Hello` as the last element of the list stored in @array.

Listing 14.12 is an example of a program that uses `splice` to insert an element into a list. This program inserts a word count after every tenth word in a file.

Type **Listing 14.12. A program that uses `splice` to insert array elements.**

```
1:  #!/usr/local/bin/perl
2:
3:  $count = 0;
4:  while ($line = <STDIN>) {
5:          chop ($line);
6:          @words = split(/\s+/, $line);
7:          $added = 0;
8:          for ($i = 0; $i+$added < @words; $i++) {
9:                  if ($count > 0 && ($count + $i) % 10 == 0) {
10:                         splice (@words, $i+$added, 0,
11:                                 $count + $i);
```

14

continues

Listing 14.12. continued

```
12:                          $added += 1;
13:                  }
14:          }
15:          $count += @words - $added;
16:          $line = join (" ", @words);
17:          print ("$line\n");
18: }
```

```
$ program14_12
Here is a line with some words on it.
Here are some more test words to count.
A B C D E F G H I J K L M N O P
^D
Here is a line with some words on it.
Here 10 are some more test words to count.
A B C 20 D E F G H I J K L M 30 N O P
$
```

ANALYSIS   This program, like many of the others you have seen, reads one line at a time and breaks the line into words; the array variable @words contains the list of words for a particular line.

The scalar variable $count contains the number of words in the lines previously read. Lines 8 through 14 read each word in the current input line in turn; at any given point, the counting variable $i lists the number of words read in the line, and the sum of $count and $i lists the total number of words read in all input lines.

Line 9 adds the value stored in $count to the value stored in $i; if this value, the current word number, is a multiple of ten, lines 10 and 11 call splice and insert the current word number into the list. As a result, every tenth word is followed by its word number.

The scalar variable $added counts the number of elements added to the list; this ensures that the word numbers added by lines 10 and 11 are not included as part of the word count.

After the word numbers have been inserted into the list, line 16 rebuilds the input line by joining the elements of @words; this new input line includes the word numbers. Line 17 then prints the rebuilt line.

Deleting List Elements

You can use splice to delete list elements without replacing them. To do this, call splice and omit the newlist argument. For example:

```
@deleted = splice (@array, 8, 2);
```

This call to splice deletes the ninth and tenth elements of the list stored in @array. If @array contains subsequent elements, these elements are shifted left to fill the gap. The list of deleted elements is returned and stored in @deleted.

Listing 14.13 reads an input file, uses splice to delete all words greater than five characters long, and writes out the result.

TYPE **Listing 14.13. A program that uses `splice` to delete words.**

```
1:  #!/usr/local/bin/perl
2:
3:  while ($line = <STDIN>) {
4:          @words = split(/\s+/, $line);
5:          $i = 0;
6:          while (defined($words[$i])) {
7:                  if (length($words[$i]) > 5) {
8:                          splice(@words, $i, 1);
9:                  } else {
10:                         $i++;
11:                 }
12:         }
13:         $line = join (" ", @words);
14:         print ("$line\n");
15: }
```

OUTPUT
```
$ program14_13
this is a test of the program which removes long words
^D
this is a test of the which long words
$
```

ANALYSIS This program reads one line of input at a time and breaks each input line into words. Line 7 calls length to determine the length of a particular word. If the word is greater than five characters in length, line 8 calls splice to remove the word from the list.

NOTE You also can omit the length argument when you call splice. If you do, splice deletes everything after the element specified by skipelements:

`splice (@array, 7);`

This deletes the seventh and all subsequent elements of the list stored in @array.

To delete the last element of a list, specify -1 as the skipelements argument.

14

```
splice (@array, -1);
```

In all cases, `splice` returns the list of deleted elements.

The `shift` Function

One list operation that is frequently needed in a program is to remove an element from the front of a list. Because this operation is often performed, Perl provides a special function, `shift`, that handles it.

`shift` removes the first element of the list and moves (or "shifts") every remaining element of the list to the left to cover the gap. `shift` then returns the removed element.

The syntax for the `shift` function is

```
element = shift (arrayvar);
```

`shift` is passed one argument: an array variable that contains a list. `element` is the returned element.

NOTE   `shift` returns the undefined value (equivalent to the null string) if the list is empty.

Here is a simple example using `shift`:

```
@mylist = ("1", "2", "3");
$firstval = shift(@mylist);
```

This call to `shift` removes the first element, 1, from the list stored in `@mylist`. This element is assigned to `$firstval`. `@mylist` now contains the list `("2", "3")`.

If you do not specify an array variable when you call `shift`, the Perl interpreter assumes that `shift` is to remove the first element from the system array variable `@ARGV`. This variable lists the arguments supplied on the command line when the program is started up. For example, if you call a Perl program named `foo` with the following command:

```
foo arg1 arg2 arg3
```

`@ARGV` contains the list `("arg1", "arg2", "arg3")`.

14

This default feature of shift makes it handy for processing command-line arguments. Listing 14.14 is a simple program that prints out its arguments.

Listing 14.14. A program that uses shift to process the command-line arguments.

TYPE

```
1:  #!/usr/local/bin/perl
2:
3:  while (1) {
4:          $currarg = shift;
5:          last if (!defined($currarg));
6:          print ("$currarg\n");
7:  }
```

OUTPUT

```
$ program14_14 arg1 arg2 arg3
arg1
arg2
arg3
$
```

ANALYSIS When this program is called, the array variable @ARGV contains a list of the values supplied as arguments to the program. Line 4 calls shift to remove the first argument from the list and assign it to $currarg.

If there are no elements (or none remaining), shift returns the undefined value, and the call to defined in line 5 returns false. This ensures that the loop terminates when there are no more arguments to read.

NOTE

The shift function is equivalent to the following call to splice:

```
splice (@array, 0, 1);
```

The unshift Function

To undo the effect of a shift function, call unshift.

SYNTAX

The syntax for the unshift function is

```
count = unshift (arrayvar, elements);
```

arrayvar is the list (usually stored in an array variable) to add to, and elements is the element or list of elements to add. count is the number of elements in the resulting list.

14

The following is an example of a call to `unshift`:

```
unshift (@array, "newitem");
```

This adds the element `newitem` to the front of the list stored in `@array`. The other elements of the list are moved to the right to accommodate the new item.

You can use `unshift` to add more than one element to the front of an array. For example:

```
unshift (@array, @sublist1, "newitem", @sublist2);
```

This adds a list consisting of the list stored in `@sublist1`, the element `newitem`, and the list stored in `@sublist2` to the front of the list stored in `@array`.

`unshift` returns the number of elements in the new list, as shown in the following:

```
@array = (1, 2, 3);
$num = unshift (@array, "newitem");
```

This assigns 4 to `$num`.

NOTE

The `unshift` function is equivalent to calling `splice` with a skipelements value of 0 and a length value of 0. For example, the following statements are equivalent:

```
unshift (@array, "item1", "item2");
splice (@array, 0, 0, "item1", "item2");
```

The push **Function**

As you have seen, the `unshift` function adds an element to the front of a list. To add an element to the end of a list, call the `push` function.

SYNTAX

The syntax for the `push` function is

```
push (arrayvar, elements);
```

arrayvar is the list (usually stored in an array variable) to add to, and *elements* is the element or list of elements to add.

The following is an example that uses `push`:

```
push (@array, "newitem");
```

This adds the element `newitem` to the end of the list.

14

The end of the list is always assumed to be the last defined element. For example, consider the following statements:

```
@array = ("one", "two");
$array[3] = "four";
push (@array, "five");
```

Here, the first statement creates a two-element list and assigns it to @array. The second statement assigns four to the fourth element of @array. Because the fourth element is now the last element of @array, the call to push creates a fifth element, even though the third element is undefined. @array now contains the list

```
("one", "two", "", "four", "five");
```

The undefined third element is, as always, equivalent to the null string.

As with unshift, you can use push to add multiple elements to the end of a list, as in this example:

```
push (@array, @sublist1, "newitem", @sublist2);
```

Here, the list consisting of the contents of @sublist1, the element newitem, and the contents of @sublist2 is added to the end of the list stored in @array.

 NOTE

push is equivalent to a call to splice with the skiparguments argument set to the length of the array. This means that the following statements are equivalent:

```
push (@array, "newitem");
splice (@array, @array, 0, "newitem");
```

The pop **Function**

The pop function undoes the effect of push. It removes the last element from the end of a list. The removed element is returned.

The syntax for the pop function is

 SYNTAX

```
element = pop (arrayvar);
```

arrayvar is the array element from which an element is to be removed. element is the returned element.

14

For example, the following statement removes the last element from the list stored in @array and assigns it to the scalar variable $popped:

```
$popped = pop (@array);
```

If the list passed to pop is empty, pop returns the undefined value.

NOTE

> pop is equivalent to a call to splice with a skipelements value of -1 (indicating the last element of the array). This means that the following statements behave in the same way:
>
> ```
> $popped = pop (@array);
> $popped = splice (@array, -1);
> ```

Creating Stacks and Queues

The functions you have just seen are handy for constructing two commonly used data structures: stacks and queues. The following sections provide examples that use a stack and a queue.

Creating a Stack

A *stack* is a data structure that behaves like a stack of plates in a cupboard: the last item added to the stack is always the first item removed. Data items that are added to the stack are said to be pushed onto the stack; items which are removed from the stack are popped off the stack.

As you might have guessed, the functions push and pop enable you to create a stack in a Perl program. Listing 14.15 is an example of a program that uses a stack to perform arithmetic operations. It works as follows:

1. Two numbers are pushed onto the stack.
2. The program reads an arithmetic operator, such as + or −. The two numbers are popped off the stack, and the operation is performed.
3. The result of the operation is pushed onto the stack, enabling it to be used in further arithmetic operations.

After all the arithmetic operations have been performed, the stack should consist of a single element, which is the final result.

The numbers and operators are read from the standard input file.

14

Note that Listing 14.15 is the "inverse" of Listing 9.12. In the latter program, the arithmetic operators appear first, followed by the values.

Listing 14.15. A program that uses a stack to perform arithmetic.

TYPE

```perl
1:  #!/usr/local/bin/perl
2:
3:  while (defined ($value = &read_value)) {
4:          if ($value =~ /^\d+$/) {
5:                  push (@stack, $value);
6:          } else {
7:                  $firstpop = pop (@stack);
8:                  $secondpop = pop (@stack);
9:                  push (@stack,
10:                     &do_math ($firstpop, $secondpop, $value));
11:         }
12: }
13: $result = pop (@stack);
14: if (defined ($result)) {
15:         print ("The result is $result.\n");
16: } else {
17:         die ("Stack empty when printing result.\n");
18: }
19:
20: sub read_value {
21:         local ($retval);
22:         $input =~ s/^\s+//;
23:         while ($input eq "") {
24:                 $input = <STDIN>;
25:                 return if ($input eq "");
26:                 $input =~ s/^\s+//;
27:         }
28:         $input =~ s/^\S+//;
29:         $retval = $&;
30: }
31:
32: sub do_math {
33:         local ($val2, $val1, $operator) = @_;
34:         local ($result);
35:
36:         if (!defined($val1) || !defined($val2)) {
37:                 die ("Missing operand");
38:         }
39:         if ($operator =~ m.^[+-/*]$. ) {
40:                 eval ("\$result = \$val2 $operator \$val1");
41:         } else {
42:                 die ("$operator is not an operator");
43:         }
44:         $result;  # ensure the proper return value
45: }
```

14

```
$ program14_15
11  4 + 26 -
^D
The result is 11.
$
```

ANALYSIS Before going into details, let's first take a look at how the program produces the final result, which is 11:

1. The program starts off by reading the numbers 11 and 4 and pushing them onto the stack. If the stack is listed from the top down, it now looks like this:

    4
    11

    Another way to look at the stack is this: At present, the list stored in @stack is (11, 4).

2. The program then reads the + operator, pops the 4 and 11 off the stack, and performs the addition, pushing the result onto the stack. The stack now contains a single value:

    15

3. The next value, 26, is pushed onto the stack, which now looks like this:

    26
    15

4. The program then reads the − operator, pops 15 and 26 off the stack, and subtracts 15 from 26. The result, 11, is pushed onto the stack.

5. Because there are no more operations to perform, 11 becomes the final result.

This program delegates to the subroutine read_value the task of reading values and operators. This subroutine reads a line of the standard input file and extracts the non-blank items on the line. Each call to read_value extracts one item from an input line; when an input line is exhausted, read_value reads the next one. When the input file is exhausted and there are no more items to return, $input becomes the undefined value, which is equivalent to the null string; the call to defined in line 3 tests for this condition.

If an item returned by read_value is a number, line 5 calls push, which pushes the number onto the stack. If an item is not a number, the program assumes it is an operator. At this point, pop is called twice to remove the last two numbers from the stack, and do_math is called to perform the arithmetic operation.

The do_math subroutine uses a couple of tricks. First, defined is called to see whether there are, in fact, two numbers to add. If one or both of the numbers does not exist, the program terminates.

Next, the subroutine uses the pattern m.^[+-*/]$. to check whether the character string stored in $operator is, in fact, a legal arithmetic operator. (Recall that you can use a pattern delimiter other than / by specifying m followed by the character you want to use as the delimiter. In this case, the period character is the pattern delimiter.)

Finally, the subroutine calls eval to perform the arithmetic operation. eval replaces the name $operator with its current value, and then treats the resulting character string as an executable statement; this performs the arithmetic operation specified by $operator. Using eval here saves space; the only alternative is to use a complicated if-elseif structure.

The result of the operation is returned in $result. Lines 9 and 10 then pass this value to push, which pushes the result onto the stack. This enables you to use the result in subsequent operations.

When the last arithmetic operation has been performed, the final result is stored as the top element of the stack. Line 13 pops this element, and line 15 prints it.

Note that this program always assumes that the last element pushed onto the stack is to be on the left of the arithmetic operation. To reverse this, all you need to do is change the order of $val1 and $val2 in line 33. (Some programs that manipulate stacks also provide an operation which reverses the order of the top two elements of a stack.)

WARNING

The pop function returns the undefined value if the stack is empty. Because the undefined value is equivalent to the null string, and the null string is treated as 0 in arithmetic operations, your program will not complain if you try to pop a number from an empty stack.

To ensure that you get the result you want, always call defined after you call pop to ensure that a value has actually been popped from the stack.

Creating a Queue

A *queue* is a data structure that processes data in the order in which it is entered; such data structures are known as first-in, first-out (or FIFO) structures. (A stack, on the other hand, is an example of a last-in, first-out, or LIFO, structure.)

To create a queue, use the function push to add items to the queue, and call shift to remove elements from it. Because push adds to the right of the list and shift removes from the left, elements are processed in the order in which they appear.

14

Listing 14.16 is an example of a program that uses a queue to add a set of numbers retrieved via a pipe. Each input line can consist of more than one number, and the numbers are added in the order listed.

The input/output example shown for this listing assumes that the numbers retrieved via the pipe are 11, 12, and 13.

TYPE **Listing 14.16. A program that illustrates the use of a queue.**

```
 1:  #!/usr/local/bin/perl
 2:
 3:  open (PIPE, "numbers¦") ||
 4:          die ("Can't open pipe");
 5:  $result = 0;
 6:  while (defined ($value = &readnum)) {
 7:          $result += $value;
 8:  }
 9:  print ("The result is $result.\n");
10:
11:  sub readnum {
12:          local ($line, @numbers, $retval);
13:          while ($queue[0] eq "") {
14:                  $line = <PIPE>;
15:                  last if ($line eq "");
16:                  $line =~ s/^\s+//;
17:                  @numbers = split (/\s+/, $line);
18:                  push (@queue, @numbers);
19:          }
20:          $retval = shift(@queue);
21:  }
```

OUTPUT
```
$ program14_16
The result is 36.
$
```

ANALYSIS This program assumes that a program named numbers exists, and that its output is a stream of numbers. Multiple numbers can appear on a single line of this output. Lines 3 and 4 associate the file variable PIPE with the output from the numbers command.

Lines 6–8 call the subroutine readnum to obtain a number and then add it to the result stored in $result. This subroutine reads input from the pipe, breaks it into individual numbers, and then calls push to add the numbers to the queue stored in @queue. Line 20 then calls shift to retrieve the first element in the queue, which is returned to the main program.

If an input line is blank, the call to `split` in line 17 produces the empty list, which means that nothing is added to `@queue`. This ensures that input is read from the pipe until a non-blank line is read or until the input is exhausted.

The `split` Function

The `split` function was first discussed on Day 5, "Lists and Array Variables." It splits a character string into a list of elements.

The usual syntax for the `split` function is

```
list = split (pattern, value);
```

Here, *value* is the character string to be split. *pattern* is a pattern to be searched for. A new element is started every time *pattern* is matched. (*pattern* is not included as part of any element.) The resulting list of elements is returned in *list*.

For example, the following statement breaks the character string stored in `$line` into elements, which are stored in `@list`:

```
@list = split (/:/, $line);
```

A new element is started every time the pattern `/:/` is matched. If `$line` contains `This:is:a:string`, the resulting list is (`"This"`, `"is"`, `"a"`, `"string"`).

If you like, you can specify the maximum number of elements of the list produced by `split` by specifying the maximum as the third argument. For example:

```
$line = "This:is:a:string";
@list = split (/:/, $line, 3);
```

As before, this breaks the string stored in `$line` into elements. After three elements have been created, no more new elements are created. Any subsequent matches of the pattern are ignored. In this case, the list assigned to `@list` is (`"This"`, `"is"`, `"a:string"`).

TIP

If you use `split` with a limit, you can assign to several scalar variables at once:

```
$line = "11  12  13  14  15";
($var1, $var2, $line) = split (/\s+/, $line, 3);
```

This splits `$line` into the list (`"11"`, `"12"`, `"13  14  15"`). `$var1` is assigned 11, `$var2` is assigned 12, and `$line` is assigned `"13  14  15"`. This enables you to assign the "leftovers" to a single variable, which can then be split again at a later time.

14

The `sort` and `reverse` **Functions**

The `sort` function sorts a list in alphabetical order, as follows:

```
@sorted = sort (@list);
```

The sorted list is returned.

The `reverse` function reverses the order of a list:

```
@reversed = reverse (@list);
```

For more information on the `sort` and `reverse` functions, see Day 5. For information on how you can specify the sort order that `sort` is to use, see Day 9, "Using Subroutines."

The `map` **Function**

The `map` function, defined only in Perl 5, enables you to use each of the elements of a list, in turn, as an operand in an expression.

The syntax for the `map` function is

```
resultlist = map(expr, list);
```

list is the list of elements to be used as operands or arguments; this list is copied by `map`, but is not itself changed. *expr* is the expression to be repeated. The results of the repeated evaluation of the expression are stored in a list, which is returned in *resultlist*.

expr assumes that the system variable $_ contains the element of the list currently being used as an operand. For example:

```
@list = (100, 200, 300);
@results = map($_+1, @list);
```

This evaluates the expression $_+1 for each of 100, 200, and 300 in turn. The results, 101, 201, and 301, respectively, are formed into the list (101, 201, 301). This list is then assigned to @results.

To use `map` with a subroutine, just pass $_ to the subroutine, as in the following:

```
@results = map(&mysub($_), @list);
```

This calls the subroutine `mysub` once for each element of the list stored in @list. The values returned by `mysub` are stored in a list, which is assigned to @results.

This also works with built-in functions:

```
@results = map(chr($_), @list);
@results = map(chr, @list);  # same as above,
➥since $_ is the default argument for chr
```

14

This converts each element of the list in @list to its ASCII character equivalent. The resulting list of characters is stored in @results.

NOTE

For more information on the $_ system variable, refer to Day 17.

The wantarray **Function**

In Perl, the behavior of some built-in functions depends on whether they are dealing with scalar values or lists. For example, the chop function either chops the last character of a single string or chops the last character of every element of a list:

```
chop($scalar);    # chop a single string
chop(@array);     # chop every element of an array
```

Perl 5 enables you to define similar two-way behavior for your subroutines using the wantarray function. (This function is not defined in Perl 4.)

The syntax for the wantarray function is

result = wantarray();

result is a non-zero value if the subroutine is expected to return a list, and is zero if the subroutine is expected to return a scalar value.

Listing 14.17 illustrates how wantarray works.

TYPE   **Listing 14.17. A program that uses the wantarray function.**

```
 1:  #!/usr/local/bin/perl
 2:
 3:  @array = &mysub();
 4:  $scalar = &mysub();
 5:
 6:  sub mysub {
 7:          if (wantarray()) {
 8:                  print ("true\n");
 9:          } else {
10:                  print ("false\n");
11:          }
12:  }
```

14

$ program14_17
true
false
$

  When `mysub` is first called in line 3, the return value is expected to be a list, which means that `wantarray` returns a non-zero (true) value in line 7. The second call to `mysub` in line 4 expects a scalar return value, which means that `wantarray` returns zero (false).

Associative Array Functions

Perl provides a variety of functions that operate on associative arrays. Most of these functions are described in detail on Day 10, "Associative Arrays"; a brief description of each function is presented here.

The keys Function

The keys function returns a list of the subscripts of the elements of an associative array.

 The syntax for `keys` is straightforward:

```
list = keys (assoc_array);
```

`assoc_array` is the associative array from which subscripts are to be extracted, and `list` is the returned list of subscripts.

For example:

```
%array = ("foo", 26, "bar", 17);
@list = keys(%array);
```

This call to keys assigns (`"foo"`, `"bar"`) to `@list`. (The elements of the list might be in a different order. To specify a particular order, sort the list using the `sort` function.)

keys often is used with `foreach`, as in the following example:

```
foreach $subscript (keys (%array)) {
        # stuff goes here
}
```

This loops once for each subscript of the array.

 14

The values **Function**

The values function returns a list consisting of all the values in an associative array.

The syntax for the values function is

```
list = values (assoc_array);
```

assoc_array is the associative array from which values are to be extracted, and list is the returned list of values.

The following is an example that uses values:

```
%array = ("foo", 26, "bar", 17);
@list = values(%array);
```

This assigns the list (26, 17) to @list (not necessarily in this order).

The each **Function**

The each function returns an associative array element as a two-element list. The list consists of the associative array subscript and its associated value. Successive calls to each return another associative array element.

The syntax for the each function is

```
pair = each (assoc_array);
```

assoc_array is the associative array from which pairs are to be returned, and pair is the subscript-element pair returned.

The following is an example:

```
%array = ("foo", 26, "bar", 17);
@list = each(%array);
```

The first call to each assigns either ("foo", 26) or ("bar", 17) to @list. A subsequent call returns the other element, and a third call returns an empty list. (The order in which the elements are returned depends on how the list is stored; no particular order is guaranteed.)

14

The `delete` Function

The `delete` function deletes an associative array element.

The syntax for the `delete` function is

```
element = delete (assoc_array_item);
```

`assoc_array_item` is the associative array element to be deleted, and `element` is the value of the deleted element.

The following is an example:

```
%array = ("foo", 26, "bar", 17);
$retval = delete ($array{"foo"});
```

After `delete` is called, the associative array `%array` contains only one element: the element with the subscript `bar`. `$retval` is assigned the value of the deleted element `foo`, which in this case is 26.

The `exists` Function

The `exists` function, defined only in Perl 5, enables you to determine whether a particular element of an associative array exists.

The syntax for the `exists` function is

```
result = exists(element);
```

`element` is the element of the associative array that is being tested for existence. `result` is nonzero if the element exists, and zero if it does not.

The following is an example:

```
$result = exists($myarray{$mykey});
```

`$result` is nonzero if `$myarray{$mykey}` exists.

Summary

Today, you learned about functions that manipulate scalar values and convert them from one form to another, and about functions that manipulate lists.

The `chop` function removes the last character from a scalar value or from each element of a list.

The `crypt` function encrypts a scalar value, using the same method that the UNIX password encryptor uses.

The `int` function takes a floating-point number and gets rid of everything after the decimal point.

The `defined` function checks whether a scalar variable, array element, or array has been assigned to. The `undef` function enables you to treat a previously defined scalar variable, array element, or array as if it is undefined. `scalar` enables you to treat an array or list as if it is a scalar value.

The other functions described in today's lesson convert values from one form into another. The `hex` and `oct` functions read hexadecimal and octal constants and convert them into decimal form. The `ord` function converts a character into its ASCII decimal equivalent. `pack` and `unpack` convert a scalar value into a format that can be stored in machine memory, and vice versa. `vec` enables you to treat a value as an array of numeric values, each of which is a certain number of bits long.

The `grep` function enables you to extract the elements of a list that match a particular pattern. This function can be used in conjunction with the file-test operators.

The `splice` function enables you to extract a portion of a list or insert a sublist into a list. The `shift` and `pop` functions remove an element from the left and right ends of a list, and the `unshift` and `push` functions add one or more elements to the left and right ends of a list. You can use `push`, `pop`, and `shift` to create stacks and queues.

The `split` function enables you to break a character string into list elements. You can impose an upper limit on the number of list elements to be created.

The `sort` function sorts a list in a specified order. The `reverse` function reverses the order of the elements in a list.

The `map` function copies a list and then performs an operation on every element of the list.

The `wantarray` function enables you to determine whether the statement that called a subroutine is expecting a scalar return value or a list.

Five functions are defined that manipulate associative arrays:

- [ ] `keys`, which returns a list of the array subscripts
- [ ] `values`, which returns a list of the array values
- [ ] `each`, which returns a two-element list consisting of an array subscript and its value
- [ ] `delete`, which deletes an element
- [ ] `exists`, which checks whether a particular element exists

14

Q&A

Q Why is the undefined value equivalent to the null string?

A Basically, to keep Perl programs from blowing up if they try to access a variable that has not yet been assigned to.

Q Why does oct handle hexadecimal constants that start with 0x or 0X?

A There is no particular reason, except that it's a little more convenient. If you find that it bothers you to use oct to convert a hexadecimal constant, get rid of the leading 0x or 0X (using the substitute operator) and call hex instead.

Q I want to put a password check in my program. How can I ensure that it is secure?

A Do two things:

☐ Don't include the unencrypted text of your password in your program source. People can then find out the password just by reading the file.

☐ Use a password that is not a real English-language word or proper name. Include at least one digit. This makes your password harder to "crack."

Q Why does int truncate instead of rounding?

A Some programs might find it useful to just retrieve the integer part of a floating-point number. (For example, in earlier chapters, you have seen int used in conjunction with rand to return a random integer.)

You can always add 0.5 to your number before calling int, which will effectively round it up when necessary.

Q When I pack integers using the s or i pack-format characters, the bits don't appear in the order I was expecting. What is happening?

A Most machines enable you to store integers that are more than one byte long (two- and four-byte integers usually are supported). However, each machine does not store a multibyte integer in the same way. Some machines store the most significant byte of a word at a lower address; these machines are called *big-endian* machines because the big end of a word is first. Other machines, called *little-endian* machines, store the least significant byte of a word at a lower byte address.

If you are not getting the result you expect, you might be expecting big-endian and getting little-endian, or vice versa.

Q The splice function works by shifting elements to the right or left to make room or fill gaps. Is this inefficient?

A No. The Perl interpreter actually stores a list as a sequence of pointers (memory addresses). All splice has to do is rearrange the pointers. This holds true also for sort and reverse.

Q **Can I use** `each` **to work through an associative array in a specified order?**

A No. If you need to access the elements of an associative array in a specified order, use `keys` and `sort` to sort the subscripts, and then retrieve the value associated with each element.

Q **If I am using** `values` **with** `foreach`**, can I retrieve the subscript associated with a particular value if I need it?**

A No. If you are likely to need the subscripts as well as their values, use `each` or `keys`.

Workshop

The Workshop provides quiz questions to help you solidify your understanding of the material covered and exercises to give you experience in using what you've learned. Try and understand the quiz and exercise answers before you go on to tomorrow's lesson.

Quiz

1. What format does each of the following pack-format characters specify?

    a. a

    b. A

    c. d

    d. p

    e. @

2. What do these unpack-format specifiers do?

    a. `"a"`

    b. `"@4A10i*"`

    c. `"@*X4C*"`

    d. `"ix4iX8i"`

    e. `"b*X*B*"`

3. What value is stored in `$value` by the following?

    a. The statements
    ```
    $vector = pack ("b*", "10110110");
    $value = vec ($vector, 3, 1);
    ```

    b. The statements
    ```
    $vector = pack ("b*", "10110110");
    $value = vec ($vector, 1, 2);
    ```

14

4. What's the difference between `defined` and `undef`?

5. Assume `@list` contains (`"1"`, `"2"`, `"3"`, `"4"`, `"5"`). What are the contents of `@list` after the following statement?

    a. `splice (@list, 0, 1, "new");`

    b. `splice (@list, 2, 0, "test1", "test2");`

    c. `splice (@list, -1, 1, "test1", "test2");`

    d. `splice (@list, 2, 1);`

    e. `splice (@list, 3);`

6. What do the following statements return?

    a. `grep (!/^!/, @array);`

    b. `grep (/\b\d+\b/, @array);`

    c. `grep (/./, @array);`

    d. `grep (//, @array);`

7. What is the difference between `shift` and `unshift`?

8. What arguments to `splice` are equivalent to the following function calls?

    a. `shift (@array);`

    b. `pop (@array);`

    c. `push (@array, @sublist);`

    d. `unshift (@array, @sublist);`

9. How can you create a stack using `shift`, `pop`, `push`, or `unshift`?

10. How can you create a queue using `shift`, `pop`, `push`, or `unshift`?

Exercises

1. Write a program that reads two binary strings of *any* length, adds them together, and writes out the binary output. (Hint: This is a really nasty problem. To get this to work, you will need to ensure that your bit strings are a multiple of eight bits by adding zeros at the front.)

2. Write a program that reads two hexadecimal strings of any length, adds them together, and writes out the hexadecimal output. (Hint: This is a straightforward modification of Exercise 1.)

3. Write a program that uses `int` to round a value to two decimal places. (Hint: This is trickier than it seems.)

4. Write a program that encrypts a password and then asks the user to guess it. Give the user three chances to get it right.

14

5. **BUG BUSTER:** What is wrong with the following program?

```perl
#!/usr/local/bin/perl

$bitstring = "00000011";
$packed = pack("b*", $bitstring);
$highbit = vec($packed, 0, 1);
print ("The high-order bit is $highbit\n");
```

6. Write a program that uses splice to sort a list in numeric order.

7. Write a program that "flips" an associative array; that is, the subscripts of the old array become the values of the new, and vice versa. Print an error message if the old array has two subscripts with identical values.

8. Write a program that reads a file from standard input, breaks each line into words, uses grep to get rid of all words longer than five characters, and prints the file.

9. Write a program that reads an input line and uses split to read and print one word of the line at a time.

10. **BUG BUSTER:** What is wrong with the following subroutine?

```perl
sub retrieve_first_element {
        local ($retval);

        $retval = unshift(@array);
}
```

14

Week 2 in Review

By now, you know enough about programming in Perl to write some quite powerful programs. The program in Listing R2.1 illustrates some of the concepts you've learned this week. It prompts you for a directory name, lists the subdirectories for that directory, and stores them in an associative array for later access. It also enables you to move about in the directory hierarchy and print the names of the files in any directory.

Listing R2.1. Browsing directories and printing their contents.

TYPE

```
 1:   #!/usr/local/bin/perl
 2:
 3:   $dircount = 0;
 4:   $curdir = "";
 5:   while (1) {
 6:           # if we don't have a current directory, get one
 7:           if ($curdir eq "") {
 8:                   print ("Enter directory to list:\n");
 9:                   $curdir = <STDIN>;
10:                   $curdir =~ s/^\s+|\s+$//g;
11:                   $curdir = &followlink($curdir);
12:                   &readsubdirs($curdir);
13:           }
14:           $curdir = &menudir($curdir);
15:   }
16:
17:
18:   # Find all subdirectories of the given directory,
19:   # and store them in an associative array.
20:   #
21:   # The associative array subscripts and values are:
22:   # <directory name>:           1
23:   #        (indicates that directory has been read)
24:   # <directory name>.<num>  the <num>th subdirectory
25:
26:   sub readsubdirs {
27:           local ($dirname) = @_;
28:           local ($dirvar, $subdircount, $name, $index);
29:
30:           # open the current directory;
31:           # $dircount ensures that each file variable is unique
32:           $dirvar = "DIR" . ++$dircount;
33:           if (!opendir ($dirvar, $dirname)) {
34:                   warn ("Can't open $dirname\n");
35:                   return;
36:           }
37:
38:           # read all the subdirectories; store in a standard array
39:           chdir ($dirname);
40:           $subdircount = 0;
41:           while ($name = readdir ($dirvar)) {
42:                   next if ($name eq ".");
43:                   if ($dirname eq "/") {
44:                           $name = $dirname . $name;
45:                   } else {
46:                           $name = $dirname . "/" . $name;
47:                   }
48:                   if (-d $name) {
49:                           $dirarray[$subdircount++] = $name;
50:                   }
51:           }
```

```
52:          closedir ($dirvar);
53:
54:          # sort the standard array; assign the sorted array to the
55:          # associative array
56:          @dirarray = sort (@dirarray);
57:          for ($index = 0; $index < $subdircount; $index++) {
58:                  $dirarray {$dirname . $index} = $dirarray[$index];
59:          }
60:          undef (@dirarray);
61:          $dirarray{$dirname} = 1;
62:  }
63:
64:
65:  # Display the subdirectories of the current directory and the
66:  # available menu options.
67:
68:  sub menudir {
69:          local ($curdir) = @_;
70:          local ($base) = 0;
71:          local ($command, $count, $subdir);
72:
73:          while (1) {
74:                  print ("\nCurrent directory is: $curdir\n");
75:                  print ("\nSubdirectories:\n");
76:                  if ($base > 0) {
77:                          print ("<more up>\n");
78:                  }
79:                  for ($count=0; $count<10; $count++) {
80:                          $subdir = $count+$base;
81:                          $subdir = $dirarray{$curdir.$subdir};
82:                          last if ($subdir eq "");
83:                          print ("$count: $subdir\n");
84:                  }
85:                  if ($dirarray{$curdir.($base+10)} ne "") {
86:                          print ("<more down>\n");
87:                  }
88:                  print ("\nEnter a number to move to the ");
89:                  print ("specified directory,\n");
90:                  if ($base > 0) {
91:                          print ("enter < to move up in the list,\n");
92:                  }
93:                  if ($dirarray{$curdir.($base+10)} ne "") {
94:                          print ("enter > to move down in the list,\n");
95:                  }
96:                  print ("enter d to display the files,\n");
97:                  print ("enter e to specify a new directory,\n");
98:                  print ("or enter q to quit entirely.\n");
99:                  print ("> ");
100:                 $command = <STDIN>;
101:                 $command =~ s/^\s+|\s+$//g;
102:                 if ($command eq "q") {
103:                         exit (0);
104:                 } elsif ($command eq ">") {
105:                         if ($dirarray{$curdir.($base+10)} ne "") {
106:                                 $base += 10;
107:                         }
```

continues

Listing R2.1. continued

```
108:                    } elsif ($command eq "<") {
109:                            $base -= 10 if $base > 0;
110:                    } elsif ($command eq "d") {
111:                            &display ($curdir);
112:                    } elsif ($command eq "e") {
113:                            # set the current directory to "" to force
114:                            # the main program to prompt for a name
115:                            return ("");
116:                    } elsif ($command =~ /^\d+$/) {
117:                            $subdir = $dirarray{$curdir.($command+$base)};
118:                            # if subdirectory is the parent directory,
119:                            # remove .. and the last directory name
120:                            # from the path
121:                            if ($subdir =~ /\.\.$/) {
122:                                    $subdir =~ s#(.*)/.*/..#$1#;
123:                            }
124:                            # if subdirectory is defined, it becomes
125:                            # the new current directory
126:                            if ($subdir ne "") {
127:                                    if ($dirarray{$subdir} != 1) {
128:                                            $subdir = &followlink($subdir);
129:                                            &readsubdirs ($subdir);
130:                                    }
131:                                    return ($subdir);
132:                            }
133:                    } else {
134:                            warn ("Invalid command $command\n");
135:                    }
136:            }
137: }
138:
139:
140: # Display the files in a directory, three per line.
141:
142: sub display {
143:         local ($dirname) = @_;
144:         local ($file, $filecount, $printfile);
145:         local (@filelist);
146:
147:         if (!opendir(LOCALDIR, "$dirname")) {
148:                 warn ("Can't open $dirname\n");
149:                 return;
150:         }
151:         chdir ($dirname);
152:         print ("\n\nFiles in directory $dirname:\n");
153:         $filecount = 0;
154:         while ($file = readdir (LOCALDIR)) {
155:                 next if (-d $file);
156:                 $filelist[$filecount++] = $file;
157:         }
158:         closedir ($dirname);
159:         if ($filecount == 0) {
160:                 print ("\tDirectory contains no files.\n");
161:                 return;
162:         }
```

```
163:          @filelist = sort(@filelist);
164:          $filecount = 0;
165:          foreach $printfile (@filelist) {
166:                  if ($filecount == 30) {
167:                          print ("<Press return to continue>");
168:                          <STDIN>;
169:                          $filecount = 0;
170:                  }
171:                  if ($filecount % 3 == 0) {
172:                          print ("\t");
173:                  }
174:                  printf ("%-20s", $printfile);
175:                  $filecount += 1;
176:                  if ($filecount % 3 == 0) {
177:                          print ("\n");
178:                  }
179:          }
180: }
181:
182:
183: # Check whether the directory name is really a symbolic link.
184: # If it is, find the real name and use it.
185:
186: sub followlink {
187:          local ($dirname) = @_;
188:
189:          if (-l $dirname) {
190:                  $dirname = readlink ($dirname);
191:          }
192:          $dirname;          # return value
193: }
```

OUTPUT

```
$ programR2_1
Enter directory to list:
/ag1/dave

Current directory is: /ag1/dave

Subdirectories:
0: /ag1/dave/..
1: /ag1/dave/.elm
2: /ag1/dave/.mosaic
3: /ag1/dave/.nn
4: /ag1/dave/Mail
5: /ag1/dave/News
6: /ag1/dave/bin
7: /ag1/dave/dave
8: /ag1/dave/ems
<more down>

Enter a number to move to the specified directory,
enter > to move down in the list,
enter d to display the files,
enter e to specify a new directory,
or enter q to quit entirely.
```

```
> d
Files in directory /ag1/dave:
            .Xauthority        .Xnormal         .Xresources
            .cshrc             .login           .newsrc
            .xsession          README           calendar
            doclist            foo              ideas
            letter             letter2          sched
Current directory is: /ag1/dave

Subdirectories:
0: /ag1/dave/..
1: /ag1/dave/.elm
2: /ag1/dave/.mosaic
3: /ag1/dave/.nn
4: /ag1/dave/Mail
5: /ag1/dave/News
6: /ag1/dave/bin
7: /ag1/dave/dave
8: /ag1/dave/ems
<more down>

Enter a number to move to the specified directory,
enter > to move down in the list,
enter d to display the files,
enter e to specify a new directory,
or enter q to quit entirely.
> 6
Current directory is: /ag1/dave/bin

Subdirectories:
0: /ag1/dave/bin/..
Enter a number to move to the specified directory,
enter d to display the files,
enter e to specify a new directory,
or enter q to quit entirely.
> q
$
```

ANALYSIS   The program in Listing R2.1 consists of five parts:

☐ A very simple main program

☐ The subroutine &readsubdirs, which reads and stores the subdirectories of a directory

☐ The subroutine &menudir, which displays the subdirectories of the current directory, lists the menu options, and processes the menu choices

☐ The subroutine &display, which lists the files in the current directory

☐ The subroutine &followlink, which checks whether a directory name is really a symbolic link

The main program is quite simple: all it does is prompt for a directory name and call the subroutines &readsubdirs and &menudir. (Many complicated programs are like this: the main portion of the program just calls a few subroutines.)

The subroutine &readsubdirs is passed the name of a directory to examine. Line 33 opens the directory using opendir, and lines 38–51 store the subdirectories in a (standard) array named @dirarray. After this, line 56 sorts the array, and lines 57–59 load the sorted elements into an associative array named %dirarray. (Recall that Perl programs can use the same name for an associative array and for a standard array because the program always can tell them apart.)

The subscripts for the associative array use a simple scheme:

☐ When a directory is read, line 61 defines an associative array element whose subscript is the directory name, and sets its value to 1. (For example, if the directory /ag1/dave is being read, the array element $dirarray{"/ag1/dave"} is set to 1.) This is the way the program indicates that a particular directory has been read.

☐ Line 49 stores the subdirectory names in associative array elements whose subscripts consist of the name of the directory joined with a unique integer. For example, if the first subdirectory of /ag1/dave is named /ag1/dave/foo, the associative array element $dirarray{"/ag1/dave0"} is assigned the value ag1/dave/foo. Similarly, the second subdirectory of /ag1/dave has its name stored in $dirarray{"/ag1/dave1"}, and so on.

Line 60 introduces a function you have not yet seen: undef. This function basically just throws away the contents of @dirarray because the program no longer needs them. (For more details on undef, see Day 14, "Scalar-Conversion and List-Manipulation Functions.")

The subroutine &menudir uses this associative array to display the subdirectories of the current directory. Line 74 prints the name of the current directory, and lines 79–84 print the names of the subdirectories of the directory. If there are more than ten subdirectories, &menudir displays only a "window" of ten subdirectories, and it prints <more down> or <more up> to show that there are more subdirectories available. Each subdirectory is printed with a corresponding number that you can use to select the subdirectory and set it to be the current directory.

After &menudir prints the subdirectory names, lines 88–99 print a list of the available menu commands. These commands are

☐ d, which displays the files stored in the current directory

☐ e, which enables you to enter the name of a directory to display

☐ q, which enables you to quit the program

☐ a number between 0 and 9, which changes the current directory to the specified subdirectory

☐ <, which moves up in the list of subdirectories (if possible)

☐ >, which moves down in the list of subdirectories (again, if possible)

Line 100 reads a command from the standard input file, and line 101 gets rid of any leading or trailing white space. Lines 102–135 determine which command has been entered.

If q has been entered, line 103 calls exit, which terminates the program.

If either > or < has been entered, lines 104–109 move up or down in the directory list. They do this by modifying the value of a variable named $base, which determines how many subdirectory names to skip before lines 79–84 start printing.

If d has been entered, line 111 calls &display, which prints the list of files.

If e has been entered, line 115 exits the subroutine with a return value of the null string. This forces the main program to execute lines 7–13 again, which prompt you for a directory name.

If a number has been entered, line 117 takes the number, joins it to the current directory name, and uses the resulting string as the subscript into the associative array %dirarray. (For example, if the current directory is /ag1/dave and the number 6 has been entered, line 117 accesses the associative array element %dirarray{"/ag1/dave6"}). This is one of the array elements that line 49 of &readsubdirs created; its value is the name of a subdirectory.

Line 127 takes the name of this subdirectory and uses it, in turn, as an associative array subscript. (For example, if the value of %dirarray{"/ag1/dave6"} is "/ag1/dave/bin", line 127 checks the associative array element %dirarray{"/ag1/dave/bin"}.) If the value of this element is 1, &readsubdirs has already read this directory and stored its subdirectory names in the associative array, so the program does not need to do it again. If this element is not defined, the program calls &readsubdirs, which reads and stores the names of the subdirectories of this directory.

The subroutine &display prints the names of the files stored in a particular directory. To save space, it prints the filenames three per line. &display prints only ten lines at a time. If there are more than ten lines (in other words, 30 filenames), line 168 pauses and waits for you to press Enter before continuing to print. This gives you time to read all of the currently displayed names.

The final subroutine is &followlink, which always is called immediately before the subroutine &readsubdirs is called. Its job is to check whether a directory name is really a symbolic link. If it is, line 190 calls readlink, which retrieves the real directory name. This directory name is returned to the calling subroutine or main program and then is passed to &readsubdirs.

As you can see, you now know enough about Perl to write programs that manipulate the file system and use complex data structures. In Week 3, you'll learn about the remainder of Perl's built-in functions and the rest of the features of Perl.

WEEK

3

15

16

17

18

19

20

21

Week 3 at a Glance

You've finished your second week of learning how to program with Perl. By now, you know enough about Perl to consider yourself an accomplished Perl programmer.

Where You're Going

The third week covers the rest of the Perl library functions, describes some of the more esoteric concepts of the language, and introduces some features unique to version 5 of Perl. Here's a summary of what you'll learn.

Day 15, "System Functions," describes the functions that work with lists and array variables.

Day 16, "Command-Line Options," describes the options you can supply with Perl to control how your program runs.

Day 17, "System Variables," describes the built-in variables that are included automatically as part of every Perl program.

Day 18, "References in Perl 5," describes the use of Perl references and the concept of pointers.

Day 19, "Object-Oriented Programming in Perl," covers how to construct objects in Perl and how to use OOP features offered by Perl.

Day 20, "Miscellaneous Features of Perl," covers some of the more exotic or obscure features of the language.

Finally, Day 21, "The Perl Debugger," shows you how to use the Perl debugger to quickly discover errors.

By the end of the third week, you'll know all the features and capabilities of Perl.

Day **15**

System Functions

Today's lesson describes the built-in Perl functions that perform various system-level operations. These functions are divided into three groups:

- ☐ The functions that emulate system library functions
- ☐ The functions that work with Berkeley UNIX sockets
- ☐ The functions that perform UNIX System V IPC operations

WARNING

Many of the functions described in today's lesson use features of the UNIX operating system. If you are using Perl on a machine that is not running UNIX, some of these functions might not be defined or might behave differently.

Check the documentation supplied with your version of Perl for details on which functions are supported or emulated on your machine.

System Library Emulation Functions

Several built-in Perl functions enable you to execute various system library calls from within your Perl program. Each one corresponds to a UNIX system library function.

The following sections briefly describe these system library functions. For more information on a particular system library function, refer to the on-line manual page for that function. For example, to find out more about the getnetent function, refer to your UNIX system's getnetent manual page.

The getgrent Function

In the UNIX environment, each user belongs to a user group. Being in a user group enables you to define files that only certain users—the people in your user group—can read from or write to.

On UNIX systems, the file /etc/group lists the user groups defined for your machine. Each entry in the user group file consists of four components:

☐ The user group name

☐ The user group password, if one exists

☐ The group ID, which is a unique integer that the system uses to identify this particular user group

☐ A list of the user IDs that belong to this group

The Perl function getgrent enables you to retrieve an item from the user group file.

The syntax for the getgrent function is

```
(gname, gpasswd, gid, gmembers) = getgrent;
```

This function returns a four-element list consisting of the four components of a group line entry, as just described. *gname* contains the user group name, *gpasswd* contains the user group password, *gid* is the group ID, and *gmembers* is a character string consisting of a list of the user IDs belonging to this group. The user IDs listed in *gmembers* are separated by spaces.

Each call to getgrent returns another line from the /etc/group file. Therefore, you can put getgrent inside a while loop.

```
while (($gname, $gpasswd, $gid, $gmembers) = getgrent) {
        # do stuff here
}
```

When the /etc/group file is exhausted, getgrent returns the empty list.

Listing 15.1 is an example of a program that uses getgrent to list all the user IDs associated with each group on your system.

TYPE **Listing 15.1. A program that uses getgrent.**

```
1:  #!/usr/local/bin/perl
2:
3:  while (($gname, $gpasswd, $gid, $gmembers) = getgrent) {
4:          $garray{$gname} = $gmembers;
5:  }
6:  foreach $gname (sort keys (%garray)) {
7:          print ("Userids belonging to group $gname:\n");
8:          $gmembers = $garray{$gname};
9:          $userids = 0;
10:         while (1) {
11:                 last if ($gmembers eq "");
12:                 ($userid, $gmembers) =
13:                         split (/\s+/, $gmembers, 2);
14:                 printf ("  %-20s", $userid);
15:                 $userids++;
16:                 if ($userids % 3 == 0) {
17:                         print ("\n");
18:                 }
19:         }
20:         if ($userids % 3 != 0) {
21:                 print ("\n");
22:         }
23: }
```

OUTPUT
```
$ program15_1
Userids belonging to group adm:
  adm                   daemon
Userids belonging to group develop:
  dave                  jqpublic              kilroy
  mpython               ralomar               xyzzy
Userids belonging to group root:
  root
$
```

ANALYSIS Line 3 of this program calls getgrent. This function returns a four-element list whose elements are the components of a group entry stored in the /etc/group file. If /etc/group is exhausted, getgrent returns the empty list.

Line 4 takes the list of group members in $gmembers and stores it in an associative array named %garray. The subscript for this array element is the name of the group, which is contained in $gname.

Lines 6–23 print the list of user IDs for each group. The loop iterates once for each group name, and the call to sort in line 6 ensures that the group names appear in alphabetical order. First, line 7 prints the name of the group. Then, line 8 retrieves the list of user IDs in the group by accessing the associative array %garray. This list is stored, once again, in $gmembers.

Lines 12 and 13 call split to extract the next user ID from the list. split breaks the string into two parts when it sees the first white space. The first part, the substring before the first space, contains one user ID and is assigned to $userid; the rest of the string is reassigned to $gmembers.

The rest of the loop prints the extracted user ID. User IDs are printed three per line to save space.

The setgrent and endgrent Functions

The setgrent function affects the behavior of getgrent: it tells the Perl interpreter to rewind the /etc/group file. After setgrent is called, the next call to getgrent retrieves the first element of the /etc/group file.

The endgrent function tells the Perl interpreter that you no longer need to access the /etc/group file. It frees the memory used to store group information.

Neither setgrent nor endgrent accepts any arguments or returns any values.

The syntax for these functions is

```
setgrent();
endgrent();
```

The getgrnam Function

The getgrnam function enables you to retrieve the group file entry corresponding to a particular group name.

The syntax for the getgrnam function is

```
(gname, gpasswd, gid, gmembers) = getgrnam (name);
```

Here, name is the group name to search for. getgrnam returns the same four-element list that getgrent returns: gname is the group name (which is the same as name), gpasswd is the group password, gid is the group ID, and gmembers is the list of user IDs in the group. If getgrnam does not find a group entry matching name, it returns the empty list.

Listing 15.2 is a modification of Listing 15.1. It asks you for a group name and then prints the user IDs in that group.

TYPE   **Listing 15.2. A program that uses** getgrnam.

```perl
1:  #!/usr/local/bin/perl
2:
3:  print ("Enter the group name to list:\n");
4:  $name = <STDIN>;
5:  chop ($name);
6:  if (!(($gname, $gpasswd, $gid, $gmembers) = getgrnam ($name))) {
7:          die ("Group $name does not exist.\n");
8:  }
9:  $userids = 0;
10: while (1) {
11:         last if ($gmembers eq "");
12:         ($userid, $gmembers) = split (/\s+/, $gmembers, 2);
13:         printf ("  %-20s", $userid);
14:         $userids++;
15:         if ($userids % 3 == 0) {
16:                 print ("\n");
17:         }
18: }
19: if ($userids % 3 != 0) {
20:         print ("\n");
21: }
```

OUTPUT

```
$ program15_2
Enter the group name to list:
develop
  dave                  jqpublic            kilroy
  mpython               ralomar             xyzzy
$
```

ANALYSIS   Line 6 takes the group name stored in $name and passes it to getgrnam. If a group corresponding to that name exists, getgrnam returns the name, password, group ID, and members. If no such group exists, getgrnam returns the empty list, the conditional expression in line 6 fails, and line 7 calls die to terminate the program.

The rest of the program is taken verbatim from Listing 15.1: the while loop in lines 10–18 extracts a user ID from the list of user IDs in $gmembers and prints it, continuing until the list is exhausted.

The getgrid **Function**

The getgrid function is similar to getgrnam, except that it retrieves the group file entry corresponding to a given group ID.

The syntax for the getgrid function is

```
(gname, gpasswd, gid, gmembers) = getgrid (id);
```

Like getgrname, getgrid returns a four-element list consisting of the group name, password, ID, and member list. If the group specified by *id* does not exist, getgrid returns the empty list.

This function often is used to retrieve the associated group name:

```
($gname) = getgrid (11);
```

This line retrieves the group name associated with group ID 11. (The other elements of the list are thrown away.)

WARNING

You must place parentheses around $gname to denote that getgrid is assigning to a list. The statement

```
$gname = getgrid (11);
```

assigns the list returned by getgrid to the scalar variable $gname. In Perl, assigning a list to a scalar variable actually assigns the length of the list to the variable, so this statement assigns 4 to $gname because there are four elements in the list returned by getgrid.

The getnetent Function

The getnetent function enables you to step through the file /etc/networks, which lists the names and addresses of the networks your machine is on.

The syntax for the getnetent function is

```
(name, altnames, addrtype, net) = getnetent();
```

name is the name of a network. *altnames* is a list of alternative names for the network; this list of names is returned as a character string, with spaces separating the individual names. *addrtype* is the address type; at present, this is always whatever value is defined for the system constant AF_INET, which indicates that the address is an Internet address.

15

> **NOTE**
>
> To get the value of AF_INET on your machine, refer to the header file
> /usr/include/netdb.h or /usr/include/bsd/netdb.h, and look for a
> statement similar to the following:
>
> ```
> #define AF_INET    2
> ```
>
> The number that appears after AF_INET is the one you want.

net is the Internet address of this network. This address is represented as a string of four bytes, which can be unpacked into Perl scalar values using the unpack function.

Listing 15.3 shows how you can use getnetent to list the machine names and addresses at your site.

TYPE **Listing 15.3. A program that uses** getnetent.

```
1:  #!/usr/local/bin/perl
2:
3:  print ("Networks this machine is connected to:\n");
4:  while (($name, $altnames, $addrtype, $rawaddr) = getnetent()) {
5:          @addrbytes = unpack ("C4", $rawaddr);
6:          $address = join (".", @addrbytes);
7:          print ("$name, at address $address\n");
8:  }
```

OUTPUT
```
$ program15_3
Networks this machine is connected to:
silver, at address 192.75.236.168
$
```

ANALYSIS
Line 4 calls getnetent, which reads from the file /etc/networks. If the file has been exhausted, getnetent returns the empty list, and the while loop terminates. If /etc/networks still contains an unread entry, getnetent retrieves it and assigns its components to $name, $altnames, $addrtype, and $rawaddr.

$rawaddr contains the Internet address for a particular network. This address is stored as a four-byte integer; each byte contains one component of the address. (This method works because each number in an Internet address has a maximum value of 255, which is the largest value that can fit in a byte.) Line 5 converts this four-byte integer into a list of integers by calling unpack, and it stores the list in @addrbytes.

Line 6 calls join to convert the list of integers into a character string that contains the readable address. Line 7 then prints the network name and the readable address of the network.

The getnetbyaddr Function

The getnetbyaddr function enables you to retrieve the line of input from /etc/networks that matches a particular network number.

The syntax for the getnetbyaddr function is

```
(name, altnames, addrtype, addr) = getnetbyaddr (inaddr, inaddrtype);
```

Here, inaddr is the network number or address for which you want to search. This address must be a packed four-byte integer whose four bytes are the four components of the address. (An example of a network address is 192.75.236.168, which is the machine on which I work.) To build a packed address, use the pack command:

```
@addrbytes = (192, 75, 236, 168);
$packedaddr = pack ("C4", @addrbytes);
```

The packed address in $packedaddr can now be passed to getnetbyaddr.

inaddrtype is the address type, which is always AF_INET (whose value is located in the file /usr/include/netdb.h or /usr/include/bsd/netdb.h).

The getnetbyaddr function returns the same four-element list as getnetent: the name of the network, the list of alternative names, the address type, and the packed address.

The getnetbyname Function

The getnetbyname function is similar to getnetbyaddr, except that it enables you to search in the /etc/networks file for a network of a particular name.

The syntax for the getnetbyname function is

```
(name, altnames, addrtype, net) = getnetbyname (inname);
```

Here, inname is the machine name to search for. Like getnetbyaddr and getnetent, getnetbyname returns a four-element list consisting of the network name, alternative name list, address type, and packed address.

NOTE

You can pass getnetbyname either the principal network name or one of its aliases.

The setnetent **and** endnetent **Functions**

The setnetent function rewinds the /etc/networks file; after setnetent has been called, a call to getnetent returns the first entry in the /etc/networks file.

The syntax for the setnetent function is

```
setnetent (keepopen);
```

keepopen is a scalar value. If keepopen is not zero, the /etc/networks file is not closed after getnetbyname or getnetbyaddr is called; therefore, you can efficiently call these functions repeatedly. If keepopen is zero, the file is closed.

The endnetent function tells the Perl interpreter that your program is finished with the /etc/ networks file. It closes the file and frees any memory used by your program to store related information.

The syntax for the endnetent function is

```
endnetent;
```

It accepts no arguments and returns no values.

The gethostbyaddr **Function**

The gethostbyaddr function searches the file /etc/hosts (or the equivalent name server) for the host name corresponding to a particular Internet address.

The syntax for the gethostbyaddr function is

```
(name, altnames, addrtype, len, addrs) = gethostbyaddr (inaddr, inaddrtype);
```

This function requires two arguments. The first, inaddr, is the Internet address to search for, stored in packed four-byte format (identical to that used by getnetbyaddr). The second argument, inaddrtype, is the address type; at present, only Internet address types are understood, and inaddrtype is always AF_INET. (The value of AF_INET can be found in /usr/include/netdb.h or /usr/include/sys/netdb.h.)

gethostbyaddr returns a five-element list. The first element, name, is the host name corresponding to the Internet address specified by inaddr. altnames is the list of aliases or alternative names by which the host can be referred. addrtype, like inaddrtype, is always AF_INET.

addrs is a list of addresses (main address and alternatives) corresponding to the host node named name. Each address is stored as a four-byte integer. len is the length of the addrs field; this length is always four multiplied by the number of addresses returned in addrs.

Listing 15.4 shows how you can use gethostbyaddr to retrieve the Internet address corresponding to a particular machine name.

 TYPE **Listing 15.4. A program that uses gethostbyaddr.**

```perl
1:  #!/usr/local/bin/perl
2:
3:  print ("Enter an Internet address:\n");
4:  $machine = <STDIN>;
5:  $machine =~ s/^\s+¦\s+$//g;
6:  @bytes = split (/\./, $machine);
7:  $packaddr = pack ("C4", @bytes);
8:  if (!(($name, $altnames, $addrtype, $len, @addrlist) =
9:          gethostbyaddr ($packaddr, 2))) {
10:         die ("Address $machine not found.\n");
11: }
12: print ("Principal name: $name\n");
13: if ($altnames ne "") {
14:         print ("Alternative names:\n");
15:         @altlist = split (/\s+/, $altnames);
16:         for ($i = 0; $i < @altlist; $i++) {
17:                 print ("\t$altlist[$i]\n");
18:         }
19: }
```

OUTPUT

```
$ program15_4
Enter an Internet address:
128.174.5.59
Principal name: ux1.cso.uiuc.edu
$
```

ANALYSIS The program starts by prompting you for an Internet address. (In this example, the Internet address specified is 128.174.5.59, which is the location of a popular public access Gopher site.) Lines 5–7 then convert the address into a four-byte packed integer, which is stored in $packaddr.

Lines 8 and 9 call gethostbyaddr. This function searches the /etc/hosts file for an entry matching the specified machine name. If the entry is not found, the conditional expression becomes false, and line 10 calls die to terminate the program.

NOTE

Line 9 uses the value 2 as the address type to pass to gethostbyaddr. If your machine defines a different value of AF_INET, as defined in the files /usr/include/netdb.h or /usr/include/bsd/netdb.h, replace 2 with that value.

15

15

If the entry is found, line 12 prints the principal machine name, which was returned by gethostbyaddr and is now stored in the scalar variable $name. Line 13 then checks whether the returned entry lists any alternative machine names corresponding to this Internet address.

If alternative machine names exist, lines 14–18 split the alternative name list into individual names and print each name on a separate line.

WARNING

gethostbyaddr and the other functions that access /etc/hosts expect the following format for a host entry:

```
address mainname altname1 altname2 ...
```

Here, address is an Internet address; mainname is the name associated with the address; and altname1, altname2, and so on are the (optional) alternative names for the host.

If your /etc/hosts file is in a different format, gethostbyaddr might not work properly.

The gethostbyname **Function**

The gethostbyname function is similar to gethostbyaddr, except that it searches for an /etc/hosts entry that matches a specified machine name or Internet site name.

The syntax for the gethostbyname function is

```
(name, altnames, addrtype, len, addrs) = gethostbyname (inname);
```

Here, inname is the machine name or Internet site name to search for. gethostbyname, like gethostbyaddr, returns a five-element list consisting of the machine name, a character string containing a list of alternative names, the address type, the length of the address list, and the address list.

Listing 15.5 is a simple program that searches for an Internet address when given the name of a site.

Listing 15.5. A program that uses `gethostbyname`.

```
1:  #!/usr/local/bin/perl
2:
3:  print ("Enter a machine name or Internet site name:\n");
4:  $machine = <STDIN>;
5:  $machine =~ s/^\s+|\s+$//g;
6:  if (!(($name, $altnames, $addrtype, $len, @addrlist) =
7:          gethostbyname ($machine))) {
8:          die ("Machine name $machine not found.\n");
9:  }
10: print ("Equivalent addresses:\n");
11: for ($i = 0; $i < @addrlist; $i++) {
12:         @addrbytes = unpack("C4", $addrlist[$i]);
13:         $realaddr = join (".", @addrbytes);
14:         print ("\t$realaddr\n");
15: }
```

OUTPUT

```
$ program15_5
Enter a machine name or Internet site name:
ux1.cso.uiuc.edu
Equivalent addresses:
128.174.5.59
$
```

ANALYSIS This program prompts for a machine name and then removes the leading and trailing white space from it. After the machine name has been prepared, lines 6 and 7 call `gethostbyname`, which searches for the /etc/hosts entry matching the specified machine name. If `gethostbyname` does not find the entry, it returns the null string, the conditional expression becomes false, and line 8 calls `die` to terminate the program.

If `gethostbyname` finds the entry, the loop in lines 11–15 examines the list of addresses in @addrlist, assembling and printing one address at a time. Line 12 assembles an address by unpacking one element of @addrlist and storing the individual bytes in @addrbytes. Line 13 joins the bytes into a character string, placing a period between each pair of bytes. The resulting string is a readable Internet address, which line 14 prints.

NOTE The machine name passed to `gethostbyname` can be either the principal machine name (as specified in the first element of the returned list) or one of the alternative names (aliases).

15

The gethostent, sethostent, **and** endhostent **Functions**

The gethostent function enables you to read each item of the /etc/hosts file in turn.

15

SYNTAX

The syntax for the gethostent function is

```
(name, altnames, addrtype, len, addrs) = gethostent();
```

The first call to gethostent returns the first element in the /etc/hosts file; subsequent calls to gethostent return successive elements. Each call to gethostent returns a five-element list identical to the list returned by gethostbyaddr or gethostbyname. This list consists of a machine name, a character string listing the alternative machine names, the address type (always AF_INET), the length of the address field, and the address field itself.

WARNING

Many machines simulate an /etc/hosts file using a name server. When a program that is running on a machine using a name server attempts to access /etc/hosts, the server queries various Internet sites for machine names, addresses, and other information.

If a Perl program running on such a machine calls gethostent repeatedly, the program might try to access many Internet sites to obtain machine information. This takes a lot of time and is a strain on Internet resources; do not do it unless you absolutely must, and do it during off-peak hours if possible.

The sethostent function rewinds the /etc/hosts file, which means that the next call to gethostent will return the first entry in the file.

SYNTAX

The syntax for the sethostent function is

```
sethostent (keepopen);
```

keepopen is a scalar value. If keepopen is nonzero, the Perl program keeps /etc/hosts information in memory, which ensures that subsequent calls to gethostent are performed as efficiently as possible. If keepopen is zero, no information is retained after sethostent finishes executing.

The endhostent function closes the /etc/hosts file and indicates that the program is to free any internal memory retaining host-related information.

SYNTAX

The endhostent function expects no arguments and returns no values:

```
endhostent();
```

The `getlogin` Function

The `getlogin` function returns the user ID under which you are logged in. The user ID is retrieved from the file `/etc/utmp`.

The syntax for the `getlogin` function is

```
logname = getlogin();
```

logname is the returned user ID.

The following is a simple example using `getlogin`:

```
$logname = getlogin();
if ($logname == "dave") {
        print ("Hello, dave! How are you?\n");
}
```

The `getpgrp` and `setpgrp` Functions

In the UNIX environment, processes are organized into collections of processes known as process groups. Each process group is identified by a unique integer known as a process group ID.

The `getpgrp` function retrieves the process group ID for a particular process.

The syntax of the `getpgrp` function is

```
pgroup = getpgrp (pid);
```

pid is the process ID whose group you want to retrieve, and *pgroup* is the returned process group ID, which is a scalar value.

If *pid* is not specified or is zero, `getpgrp` assumes that you want the process group ID for the current process (the program you are running).

Listing 15.6 is an example of a program that retrieves its own process group ID.

Type **Listing 15.6. A program that uses `getpgrp`.**

```
1:  #!/usr/local/bin/perl
2:
3:  $pgroup = getpgrp (0);
4:  print ("The process group for this program is $pgroup.\n");
```

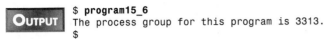

```
$ program15_6
The process group for this program is 3313.
$
```

ANALYSIS Line 3 calls `getpgrp` with the argument **0**, which indicates the current process (the current program). The process group ID for this process is returned in `$pgroup` and then printed.

The `setpgrp` function enables you to set the process group ID for a process.

SYNTAX

The syntax of the `setpgrp` function is

`setpgrp (pid, groupid);`

pid is the ID of the process whose group you want to change, and *groupid* is the process group ID you want your process to be part of. (This group ID is usually returned by a call to `getpgrp`.)

WARNING Not all machines support `setpgrp`, and some machines impose limitations on how you can use it. If your program uses `setpgrp`, you should call `getpgrp` immediately afterward to ensure that the process group ID has been set properly.

The `getppid` Function

On UNIX machines, as you have seen, every running program or other executing process has its own unique process ID. Each program and process also is associated with a parent process, which is the process that started it. For example, when you execute a command that starts a Perl program, the parent process of the Perl program is the shell program from which you entered the command.

To retrieve the process ID for the parent process for your program, call the function `getppid`.

SYNTAX

The syntax of the `getppid` function is

`parentid = getppid();`

Here, *parentid* is the process ID of your program.

You can use `getppid` with `fork` to ensure that each of the two processes produced by `fork` knows the process ID of the other.

Listing 15.7 shows how to do this.

TYPE   **Listing 15.7. A program that calls fork and getppid.**

```
1:  #!/usr/local/bin/perl
2:
3:  $otherid = fork();
4:  if ($otherid == 0) {
5:          # this is the child; retrieve parent ID
6:          $otherid = getppid();
7:  } else {
8:          # this is the parent
9:  }
```

OUTPUT   This program requires no input and generates no output.

ANALYSIS   When line 3 calls fork, the program splits into two separate processes (or running programs, if you want to think of them that way). fork returns 0 to the child process and returns the process ID of the child process to the parent process. At this point, the parent process knows the process ID of the child, but the child does not know the process ID of the parent.

Line 6, which is executed only by the child process, fixes this imbalance by calling getppid and returning the process ID of the parent (the other process created by fork). After the child process executes line 6, both the parent and the child process have stored the process ID of the other process in the scalar variable $otherid.

After each process has the ID of the other, the processes can send signals to one another using the kill function (which is discussed on Day 13, "Process, String, and Mathematical Functions").

The getpwnam **Function**

On UNIX machines, the /etc/passwd file (also known as the password file) contains information on each of the users who are authorized to use the machine. The getpwnam function enables you to retrieve the password file entry for a particular user.

The syntax of the getpwnam function is

```
(username, password, userid, groupid, quota, comment, infofield,
➥_homedir, shell) = getpwnam (name);
```

name is the login user ID of the user whose information you want to retrieve. If an entry in the /etc/passwd file corresponds to this name, getpwnam returns a nine-element list containing the contents of the entry. These contents are

☐   username, which is identical to name

☐   password, which is the user's encrypted password

☐ *userid*, which is the unique numerical ID that represents this user

☐ *groupid*, which is the ID of the group to which this user belongs

☐ *quota* and *comment*, which mean different things on different machines (check your local getpwnam manual page for details)

☐ *infofield*, which is a character string containing personal information about the user (such as the room number of the user's office, or the user's phone number)

☐ *homedir*, which is the user's home directory (the directory that becomes the current directory when the user logs in)

☐ *shell*, which is the command shell that is started when the user logs in

getpwnam returns the empty list if no password file entry for *name* exists.

You can use getpwnam in various ways. The most common way is to retrieve the user ID or group ID corresponding to a particular user name. Listing 15.8 is a program that retrieves and prints the user ID for a particular user.

Listing 15.8. A program that retrieves the user ID for a user.

 TYPE

```
1:  #!/usr/local/bin/perl
2:
3:  print ("Enter a username:\n");
4:  $username = <STDIN>;
5:  $username =~ s/^\s+|\s+$//g;
6:  if (($username, $passwd, $userid) = getpwnam ($username)) {
7:          print ("Username $username has user id $userid.\n");
8:  } else {
9:          print ("Username not found.\n");
10: }
```

OUTPUT

```
$ program15_8
Enter a username:
dave
Username dave has userid 127.
$
```

ANALYSIS
After lines 4 and 5 have retrieved the user name and removed any extraneous white space, line 6 passes the user name to getpwnam. If a password file entry exists for this user name, the nine-element entry is returned, and the first three elements are assigned to $username, $password, and $userid. (The remaining elements are thrown away.) The third element, the user ID, is stored in $userid and is printed by line 7.

The getpwuid **Function**

The getpwuid function is similar to the getpwnam function because it also accesses the /etc/ passwd file. getpwuid, however, searches for the password file entry that matches a particular user ID.

The syntax of the function is

```
(username, password, userid, groupid, quota, comment, infofield,
➥_homedir, shell) = getpwuid (inputuid);
```

inputuid is the user ID that is to be searched for; it must be a nonzero integer. The nine-element list returned by getpwuid is identical to that returned by getpwnam.

NOTE

> The *userid* field in the nine-element list returned by getpwuid is always identical to the *inputuid* field that is passed as an argument.

The getpwent **Function**

The getpwnam and getpwuid functions enable you to retrieve a single entry from the password file. To access each entry of the password file in turn, call getpwent.

The syntax for the getpwent function is

```
(username, password, userid, groupid, quota, comment, infofield,
➥_homedir, shell) = getpwent();
```

When a program calls getpwent for the first time, it retrieves the first entry in the /etc/passwd file. Subsequent calls retrieve further entries; if no more entries remain, the empty list is returned.

The components of the nine-element list returned by getpwent are the same as those in the lists returned by getpwnam and getpwuid.

Listing 15.9 is an example of a program that uses getpwent. It lists the user names known by the machine as well as their user IDs.

TYPE   **Listing 15.9. A program that uses** getpwent.

```
1:  #!/usr/local/bin/perl
2:
3:  while (1) {
4:          last unless (($username, $password, $userid)
5:                          = getpwent());
```

```
6:          $userlist{$username} = $userid;
7:   }
8:   print ("Users known to this machine:\n");
9:   foreach $user (sort keys (%userlist)) {
10:          printf ("%-20s %d\n", $user, $userlist{$user});
11: }
```

OUTPUT

```
$ program15_9
Users known to this machine:
adm                 4
daemon              1
dave                127
ftp                 8
jimmy               711
root                0
$
```

ANALYSIS   The while loop in lines 3–7 uses getpwent to read every entry in the password file. Only the first three elements of the returned list are saved—in the scalar variables $username, $password, and $userid—the rest are thrown away. After the /etc/passwd file has been completely read, line 4 terminates the while loop.

Line 6 creates an associative array element for each user. The subscript for the array element is the user name, and the value of the element is the user ID.

Lines 9–11 print the list of users, sorting them in order by user name and printing the name and user ID for each.

The setpwent **and** endpwent **Functions**

Like getpwent, setpwent and endpwent manipulate the /etc/passwd file.

The setpwent function rewinds the /etc/passwd file.

The syntax of the setpwent function is

```
setpwent (keepopen);
```

If *keepopen* is nonzero, the Perl interpreter assumes that the /etc/passwd file is to be accessed again, and it keeps information about the password file stored in internal memory. If *keepopen* is zero, any information the program has related to the password file is thrown away.

The endpwent function closes the password file and tells the program to throw away any internal memory related to it.

The endpwent function accepts no arguments and returns no values.

```
endpwent();
```

The `getpriority` and `setpriority` **Functions**

In the UNIX environment, each process has a priority, which tells the system which processes are important and which are not. Priorities are integer values that vary from system to system: a typical range is from –20 (most important) to 20 (least important), with a default value of 0.

 NOTE

> Although priority ranges might vary from system to system, the general rule under UNIX is always this: the higher the priority number associated with a process, the less important the process is.

To change the priority for your program, process, process group, or user ID, call the `setpriority` function.

 SYNTAX

The syntax of the `setpriority` function is

`setpriority (category, id, priority);`

category is a scalar value that indicates what processes are to have their priorities altered. To find the value to use, take the following actions:

- ☐ Examine the header file `/usr/include/sys/resource.h`
- ☐ In this file, look up and note the values of the constants `PRIO_PROCESS`, `PRIO_PGRP`, and `PRIO_USER`
- ☐ Pick the appropriate value to use, as described in the remainder of this section

NOTE

> If you are not familiar with the C programming language, the value of a constant is specified by a statement of the following form:
>
> `#define constant value`
>
> Here, *constant* is a constant such as `PRIO_PROCESS`, and *value* is its defined value.

If *category* is the value associated with `PRIO_PROCESS`, only one process has its priority altered. If *category* is the value of `PRIO_PGRP`, every process in a process group has its priority altered. If *category* is the value of `PRIO_USER`, every process belonging to a particular user has its priority altered.

15

The value of *id* depends on *category*. If *category* is the value of PRIO_PROCESS, *id* is the process ID for the process whose priority is to be altered. If *category* is the value of PRIO_PGRP, *id* is the process group ID for the group whose priority is to be altered. If *category* is PRIO_USER, *id* is the user ID for the group whose priority is to be altered.

15

NOTE

> If *category* is the value of PRIO_PROCESS or PRIO_PGRP and *id* is 0, *id* is assumed to be the ID of the current process or process group.

priority is the new priority for the process, group, or user. You can specify a lower priority value for your process or processes (in other words, specify that your processes are "more important") only if you are a privileged user (the superuser).

The function getpriority retrieves the current priority for a process, process group, or user.

SYNTAX

The syntax of the getpriority function is

```
priority = getpriority (category, id);
```

Here, *category* and *id* are identical to the equivalent arguments in setpriority. *priority* is the returned current priority.

Listing 15.10 is a program that lowers the priority of every process you are currently running. It uses several of the functions you have seen in today's lesson.

Listing 15.10. A program that uses setpriority and

getpriority.

```
1:  #!/usr/local/bin/perl
2:
3:  print ("You're not in a hurry today, are you?\n");
4:  $username = getlogin();
5:  ($username, $password, $userid) = getpwnam ($username);
6:  $oldpriority = getpriority (2, $userid);
7:  setpriority (2, $userid, $oldpriority + 1);
```

OUTPUT

```
$ program15_10
You're not in a hurry today, are you?
$
```

ANALYSIS

Line 4 of this program calls getlogin, which retrieves the user's login name. Then, line 5 passes this name to getpwnam, which retrieves the user ID from the /etc/passwd file.

Line 6 calls getpriority. Because the first argument to getpriority is 2 (the value of the system constant PRIO_USER), the current priority for all processes owned by the user specified by the user ID stored in $userid is returned.

Line 7 calls setpriority, adding one to the current priority for the user to obtain the new priority. As in line 6, the first argument to setpriority is 2 (PRIO_USER), which indicates that the current priority for all processes belonging to this user is to be changed.

The getprotoent Function

The getprotoent function enables you to search through the system protocol database, which is stored in the file /etc/protocols.

The syntax of the getprotoent function is

```
(name, aliases, number) = getprotoent();
```

name is the name associated with a particular system protocol. aliases is a scalar value consisting of a list of alternative names for this system protocol, with names being separated by a space. number is the number associated with this particular system protocol.

The first call to getprotoent returns the first element in /etc/protocols. Further calls return subsequent entries; when /etc/protocols is exhausted, getprotoent returns the empty list.

The getprotobyname and getprotobynumber Functions

The getprotobyname and getprotobynumber functions provide ways of searching in the /etc/protocols file.

The getprotobyname function enables you to search for a particular protocol entry in the /etc/protocols file.

The syntax of the getprotobyname function is

```
(name, aliases, number) = getprotobyname (searchname);
```

Here, searchname is the protocol name you are looking for. name, aliases, and number are the same as in getprotoent.

Similarly, getprotobynumber searches for a protocol entry in /etc/protocols that matches a particular protocol number.

The syntax of the getprotobynumber function is

```
(name, aliases, number) = getprotobynumber (searchnum);
```

searchnum is the protocol number to search for. *name*, *aliases*, and *number* are the same as in getprotoent.

Both functions return the empty list if no matching protocol database entry is found.

The setprotoent **and** endprotoent **Functions**

The setprotoent and endprotoent functions provide other ways of manipulating the /etc/protocols file.

The setprotoent function rewinds the /etc/protocols file.

The syntax of the setprotoent function is

```
setprotoent (keepopen);
```

If *keepopen* is a nonzero value, the value indicates that the program should keep /etc/protocols open, because it intends to continue accessing the system protocol database. After setprotoent has been called, the next call to getprotoent reads (or rereads) the first element of the database.

The endprotoent function closes the /etc/protocols file and indicates that the program no longer wants to read any system protocols from the database.

The endprotoent function requires no arguments and returns no values:

```
endprotoent();
```

NOTE

For more information on system protocols, refer to the getprotoent manual page on your system.

The getservent **Function**

The getservent function enables you to search through the system services database, which is stored in the file /etc/services.

EXERCISE

The syntax of the getservent function is

```
(name, aliases, portnum, protoname) = getservent();
```

name is the name associated with a particular system service. *aliases* is a scalar value consisting of a list of alternative names for this system service; the names are separated by a space.

portnum is the port number associated with this particular system protocol, which indicates the location of the port at which the service is residing. This port number is returned as a packed array of integers, which can be unpacked using unpack (with a c* format specifier).

protoname is a protocol name (such as tcp).

The first call to getservent returns the first element in /etc/services. Further calls return subsequent entries; when /etc/services is exhausted, getservent returns the empty list.

The getservbyname **and** getservbyport **Functions**

The getservbyname and getservbyport functions provide ways of searching in the /etc/services file.

The getservbyname function enables you to search the /etc/services file for a particular service name.

SYNTAX

The syntax of the getservbyname function is

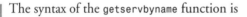

```
(name, aliases, portnum, protoname) = getservbyname (searchname, searchproto);
```

Here, *searchname* and *searchproto* are the service name and service protocol type to be matched. If the name and type are matched, getservbyname returns the system service database entry corresponding to this name and type. This entry is the same four-element list as is returned by getservent. (The empty list is returned if the name and type are not matched.)

Similarly, the getservbyport function searches for a service name that matches a particular service port number.

SYNTAX

The syntax of the getservbyname function is

```
(name, aliases, portnum, protoname) = getservbyname (searchportnum,
➥searchproto);
```

searchportnum and *searchproto* are the port number and protocol type to search for. *name*, *aliases*, *portnum*, and *protoname* are the same as in getservbyname and getservent.

The setservent **and** endservent **Functions**

The setservent and endservent functions provide other ways of manipulating the /etc/services file.

The setservent function rewinds the /etc/services file.

The syntax of the setservent function is

```
setservent (keepopen);
```

After setservent has been called, the next call to getservent retrieves the first element of the /etc/services file. keepopen, if nonzero, specifies that the /etc/services file is still in use and is to remain open.

The function endservent indicates that the /etc/services file can be closed, because it is no longer needed.

The endservent function requires no arguments and returns no values:

```
endservent();
```

The chroot Function

The chroot function enables you to specify the root directory for your program and any subprocesses that it creates.

The syntax of the chroot function is

```
chroot (dirname);
```

dirname is the name of the directory to serve as the root. After chroot has been called, the directory name specified by dirname is appended to every pathname specified by your program and its subprocesses. For example, the statement

```
chroot ("/pub");
```

adds /pub to the front of every directory name. For example, when your program or a subprocess tries to access the directory /u/jqpublic, the directory it accesses is actually /pub/u/jqpublic.

chroot often is used to restrict access to a particular portion of a file system. It can be called only if you have superuser privileges on your machine and execute permission on the specified root directory.

The ioctl Function

The ioctl function enables you to set system-dependent file attributes (such as the special character definitions for your keyboard).

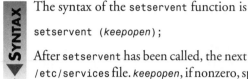

The syntax of the ioctl function is

```
ioctl (filevar, attribute, value);
```

filevar is a file variable representing a previously opened file. *attribute* is a value representing the operation to be performed. Incorporated as part of the *attribute* value is a number indicating whether the operation is retrieving the value of an attribute or setting the value of an attribute.

value holds the attribute value associated with the operation specified by *attribute*. If the operation is setting an attribute, *value* contains the new value of the attribute. If the operation is retrieving the current value of the attribute, *value* is assigned this current value.

ioctl returns a nonzero value if the operation is performed successfully, or zero if the operation fails.

NOTE

For details on what operations can be performed on your machine, refer to the file /usr/include/sys/ioctl.h on your machine. This file is a header file written in the C programming language that contains information on the available ioctl operations.

WARNING

Different machines (and devices) support different ioctl operations. Thus, a program that requests an ioctl operation is not portable if you move it from one machine to another. You therefore should use ioctl operations only when you must.

The alarm **Function**

The alarm function sends a special "alarm" signal, SIGALARM, to your program.

The syntax of the alarm function is

```
alarm (value);
```

value is an expression indicating how many seconds are to pass before the alarm goes off.

15

For more information on signals and their relationship to processes, refer to the description of the kill function on Day 13.

Calling the System select Function

Perl enables you to call the UNIX select function from within your Perl program.

The syntax for a call to the UNIX select function is

```
select (rmask, wmask, emask, timeout);
```

rmask, wmask and emask are bit masks, and timeout is a timeout value in seconds.

For more information on select, refer to the UNIX manual page.

NOTE

> The UNIX select function is different from the Perl select function that you've seen in earlier lessons.
>
> The Perl interpreter determines whether a program is calling the Perl select function or the UNIX select function by counting the number of arguments: the Perl function expects only one, and the UNIX function expects four.

The dump Function

The dump function, which is defined only in Perl 5, enables you to generate a UNIX core dump from within your Perl program.

The syntax for the dump function is

```
dump(label);
```

label is an optional label, specifying where execution is to restart if the UNIX undump command is executed.

WARNING

> If a core dump file created by dump is restarted by the UNIX undump command, files that were open when the program was executing will no longer be open. This means they cannot be read from or written to.

Socket-Manipulation Functions

In Berkeley UNIX environments (version 4.3BSD) and some other environments, processes can communicate with one another using a connection device known as a *socket*. When a socket has been created, one process can write data which can then be read by another process.

Perl supports various functions that create sockets and set up connections with them. The following sections describe these functions.

The socket Function

To create a socket, call the socket function. This function defines a socket and associates it with a Perl file variable.

The syntax of the socket function is

```
socket (socket, domain, type, format);
```

socket is a file variable that is to be associated with the new socket.

domain is the protocol family to use. The legal values for *domain* are listed in the system header file /usr/include/sys/socket.h; these values are represented by the constants PF_UNIX, PF_INET, PF_IMPLINK, and PF_NS.

type is the type of socket to create. The legal values for *type* are also listed in the file /usr/include/sys/socket.h. These legal values are represented by the five constants SOCK_STREAM, SOCK_DGRAM, SOCK_RAW, SOCK_SEQPACKET, and SOCK_RDM.

format is the number of the protocol to be used with the socket. This protocol is normally retrieved by calling getprotobyname. (See the manual page for getprotobyname for details on what protocols are supported on your machine.)

The socket function returns a nonzero value if the socket has been created and zero if an error occurs.

The bind Function

After you create a socket using socket, the next step is to bind the socket to a particular network address. To do this, use the bind function.

The syntax of the bind function is

```
bind (socket, address);
```

Here, *socket* is the file variable corresponding to the socket created by socket.

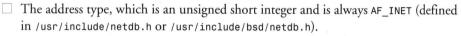

address is the network address to be associated with the socket. This address consists of the following elements:

- ☐ The address type, which is an unsigned short integer and is always AF_INET (defined in /usr/include/netdb.h or /usr/include/bsd/netdb.h).

- ☐ The number of the port to use when connecting, which is a short integer in network order

- ☐ The packed four-byte representation of the Internet address of the machine to which the socket is to be bound

This function returns a nonzero value if the bind operation succeeds and zero if an error occurs.

To create an address suitable for passing to bind, call pack.

```
$address = pack ("Sna4x8", 2, $portnum, $intaddress);
```

Here, the pack format specifier Sna4x8 indicates an unsigned short integer, followed by a short integer in network order (the port number), a four-byte ASCII string (which is the packed address), and eight null bytes. This is the format that bind expects when binding an address to a socket.

The listen **Function**

After an address has been bound to the socket associated with each of the machines that are to communicate, the next step is to define a process that is to be the "listening" process. This process waits for connections to be established with it. (In a client-server architecture, this process corresponds to the server.) To define this listening process, call the listen function.

The syntax of the listen function is

```
listen (socket, number);
```

socket is the socket created using the socket function. *number* is the maximum number of processes that can be queued up to connect to this process.

listen returns a nonzero value if it executes successfully, zero if it does not.

WARNING

The maximum number of processes that can be queued using listen is 5. This limitation is imposed by the Berkeley UNIX operating system.

The accept **Function**

After a process that has been established as the listening process calls listen, the next step is to have this process call the accept function. accept waits until a process wants to connect with it, and then it returns the address of the connecting process.

The syntax of the accept function is

```
accept (procsocket, socket);
```

procsocket is a previously undefined file variable that is to represent the newly created connection. The listening process can then send to or receive from the other process using the file variable specified in *procsocket*. This file variable can be treated like any other file variable: the program can send data through the socket by calling write or print, or can read data using the <> operator.

socket is the socket created by socket and bound to an address by bind.

Listing 15.11 is an example of a program that uses listen and accept to create a simple server. This server just sends the message Hello, world! to any process that connects to it. (A client program that receives this message is listed in the next section, "The connect Function.")

TYPE **Listing 15.11. A simple server program.**

```
1:  #!/usr/local/bin/perl
2:
3:  $line = "Hello, world!\n";
4:
5:  $port = 2000;
6:  while (getservbyport ($port, "tcp")) {
7:          $port++;
8:  }
9:  ($d1, $d2, $prototype) = getprotobyname ("tcp");
10: ($d1, $d2, $d3, $d4, $rawserver) = gethostbyname ("silver");
11: $serveraddr = pack ("Sna4x8", 2, $port, $rawserver);
12: socket (SSOCKET, 2, 1, $prototype) ¦¦ die ("No socket");
13: bind (SSOCKET, $serveraddr) ¦¦ die ("Can't bind");
14: listen (SSOCKET, 1) ¦¦ die ("Can't listen");
15: ($clientaddr = accept (SOCKET, SSOCKET)) ¦¦
16:         die ("Can't accept");
17: select (SOCKET);
18: $¦ = 1;
19: print SOCKET ("$line\n");
20: close (SOCKET);
21: close (SSOCKET);
```

OUTPUT This program requires no input and generates no output.

15

ANALYSIS The first task this server program performs is to search for a port to use when establishing a socket connection. To be on the safe side, the program first checks that the port it is going to use, port 2000, is not reserved for use by another program. If it is reserved, the program checks port 2001, then port 2002, and so on until it finds an unused port.

To do this checking, line 6 calls `getservbyport`. If `getservbyport` returns a non-empty list, the port being checked is listed in the `/etc/services` file, which means that it is being used by some other program. In this case, the port number is increased by one, and `getservbyport` is called again. This process continues until `getservbyport` returns an empty list, which indicates that the port being checked is unused. When lines 5–8 are no longer executing, the scalar variable `$port` contains the number of the port to be used.

Line 9 calls `getprotobyname` to retrieve the `/etc/protocols` entry associated with the TCP protocol. The protocol number associated with the TCP protocol is retrieved from this `/etc/protocols` entry and is stored in the scalar variable `$prototype`. (The other elements of the list are ignored; the convention used by this program is to store element entries that are not going to be used in variables named `$d1`, `$d2`, and so on; the d stands for dummy.)

Line 10 calls `gethostbyname` to retrieve the network address of the machine on which this server is running. This program assumes that the server is running on a local machine named `silver`. To run this program on your own machine, replace `silver` with your machine name.

TIP You can modify this program to run on any machine. To do so, modify line 10 as shown here:

```
($d1, $d2, $d3, $d4, $rawserver) = gethostbyname ('hostname');
```

The string in backquotes, `'hostname'`, tells the Perl interpreter to call the `hostname` program and return its output as a scalar value. The `hostname` program returns the name of the machine on which it is running. Therefore, the call to `gethostbyname` retrieves the address of the machine on which you are running regardless of what the machine is.

This capability enables you to move this program from one machine to another without having to modify it.

Note that enclosing a command in backquotes works for any UNIX command that returns output. For example, the statement

```
$userid = 'whoami';
```

assigns the current login user ID to the scalar variable `$userid` (because the UNIX command `whoami` displays the current login user ID).

After `gethostbyname` has been called, the scalar variable `$rawserver` contains the Internet address of your machine. Line 11 calls `pack` to convert the address type, the port number, and this address into the form understood by the operating system. (The address type parameter, 2, is the local value of `AF_INET`, which is the only address type supported.) This information is stored in the scalar variable `$serveraddr`.

After `pack` is called to build the server address, the program is ready to create a socket. Line 12 does this by calling `socket`. This call to `socket` passes it the file variable `SSOCKET`, the socket domain, the socket type, and the protocol number. After `socket` is called, the file variable `SSOCKET` represents the "master socket" that is to listen for connections. (Note that the values 2 and 1 passed to `socket` are, respectively, the local values of the constants `PF_INET` and `SOCK_STREAM`. `PF_INET` indicates Internet-style protocol, and `SOCK_STREAM` indicates that transmission will be in the form of a stream of bytes. You likely will not need to use any other values for these arguments.)

After the socket has been created, the next step is line 13, which associates the socket with your machine by calling `bind`. This call to `bind` is passed the file variable `SSOCKET` associated with the socket and the server address created by the call to `pack` in line 11.

After the socket is bound to your machine address, you are ready to listen for clients that want to connect to your server. Line 14 does this by calling `listen`. This call to `listen` is passed the file variable `SSOCKET` and the value 1; the latter indicates that only one client is listened for at any particular time.

Line 15 calls `accept`, which waits until a client process wants to connect to this server. When a connection is established, `accept` creates a new socket associated with this connection and uses the file variable `SOCKET` to represent it. (The address of the client connection is returned in `$clientaddr`; if you want to, you can use `unpack` to obtain the address, and then call `gethostbyaddr` to retrieve the name of the machine on which the client process is running.)

When the connection has been established and the file variable `SOCKET` has been associated with it, you can treat `SOCKET` like any other file variable: you can read data from it or write data to it. Lines 17 and 18 turn off buffering for `SOCKET`, which ensures that data sent through the socket is sent right away. (If buffering is left on, the program won't send data until the special internal buffer is full, which means that the client process won't receive the data right away.) After buffering is turned off, line 19 writes the line of data to `SOCKET`, which sends it to the client process. (For more information on buffering and how it works, refer to "Redirecting One File to Another" on Day 12, "Working with the File System.")

WARNING

Although you can both send and receive data through the same socket, doing so is dangerous, because you run the risk of deadlock. *Deadlock* occurs when the client and server processes think that the other is going to send data. Neither can proceed until the other does.

15

> The only way to get out of a deadlock is to send signals to the processes (such as KILL).
>
> To avoid a deadlock, make sure that you understand how data flows between the processes you are running.

The connect **Function**

As you have seen, when two processes communicate using a socket, one process is designated as the listening process. This process calls listen to indicate that it is the listening process, and then it calls accept to wait for a connection from another process. (Listening processes are called *servers*, because they provide service to the processes that connect to them. The processes that connect to servers are called *clients*.)

To connect to a process that has called accept and is now waiting for a connection, use the connect function.

The syntax of the connect function is

connect (*socket*, *address*);

socket is a file variable representing a socket created using socket and bound using bind. *address* is the internal representation of the Internet address to which you want to connect. In the process to which this process is connecting, this address must have been passed to bind to bind it to a socket, and the socket, in turn, must have been specified in calls to listen and accept.

After connect has been called, the program that calls it can send data to or receive data from the other process by means of the file variable specified in socket.

Listing 15.12 is an example of a program that uses connect to obtain data from another process. (The process that sends the data is displayed in Listing 15.11.)

TYPE   **Listing 15.12. A simple client program.**

```
1:  #!/usr/local/bin/perl
2:
3:  $port = 2000;
4:  while (getservbyport ($port, "tcp")) {
5:          $port++;
6:  }
7:  ($d1, $d2, $prototype) = getprotobyname ("tcp");
8:  ($d1, $d2, $d3, $d4, $rawclient) = gethostbyname ("mercury");
9:  ($d1, $d2, $d3, $d4, $rawserver) = gethostbyname ("silver");
10: $clientaddr = pack ("Sna4x8", 2, 0, $rawclient);
```

continues

Listing 15.12. continued

```
11: $serveraddr = pack ("Sna4x8", 2, $port, $rawserver);
12: socket (SOCKET, 2, 1, $prototype) ¦¦ die ("No socket");
13: bind (SOCKET, $clientaddr) ¦¦ die ("Can't bind");
14: connect (SOCKET, $serveraddr);
15:
16: $line = <SOCKET>;
17: print ("$line\n");
18: close (SOCKET);
```

```
$ program15_12
Hello, world!
$
```

 Lines 3–6 obtain the port to use when receiving data by means of a socket connection. As in Listing 15.11, the port number is compared with the list of ports stored in /etc/services by calling getservbyport. The first unused port number greater than or equal to 2000 becomes the number of the port to use. (This program and Listing 15.11 assume that the same /etc/services file is being examined in both cases. If the /etc/services files are different, you will need to choose a port number yourself and specify this port number in both your client program and your server program—in other words, assign a prespecified value to the variable $port.)

Line 7 calls getprotobyname to retrieve the protocol number associated with the TCP protocol. This protocol number is eventually passed to socket.

Lines 8 and 9 retrieve the Internet addresses of the client (this program) and the server (the process to connect to). $rawclient is assigned the Internet address of the client, and $rawserver is assigned the Internet address of the server; each of these addresses is a four-byte scalar value.

Lines 10 and 11 take the addresses stored in $rawclient and $rawserver and convert them to the form used by the socket processing functions. In both cases, the 2 passed to pack is the local value for AF_INET (the only type of address supported in the UNIX environment). Note that line 10 doesn't bother specifying a port value to pass to pack; this is because the connection uses the port specified in the server address in line 11.

Line 12 now calls socket to create a socket for the current program (the client). As in the call to socket in Listing 15.11, the values 2 and 1 passed to socket are the local values of the constants PF_INIT and SOCK_STREAM; if these values are different on your machine, you need to replace the values shown here with the ones defined for your machine. The call to socket in line 12 associates the file variable SOCKET with the newly created socket.

After the socket has been created, line 13 calls bind to associate the socket with the client program. bind requires two arguments: the file variable associated with the socket that has just been created, and the address of the client machine as packed by line 10.

Line 14 now tries to connect to the server process by calling `connect` and passing it the server address created by line 11. If the connection is successful, you can send and receive data through the socket using the SOCKET file variable.

The SOCKET file variable behaves just like any other file variable. This means that line 16 reads a line of data from the server process. Because the server process is sending the character string `Hello, world!` (followed by a newline character), this is the string that is assigned to `$line`. Line 17 then prints `$line`, which means that the following appears on your screen:

```
Hello, world!
```

After the client process is finished with the socket, line 18 calls `close`. This call indicates that the program is finished with the socket. (After the socket is closed by both the server and the client programs, the server program can accept a connection from another client process, if desired.)

The `shutdown` Function

When two processes are communicating using a socket, data can be sent in either direction: the client can receive data from the server, or vice versa. The `shutdown` function enables you to indicate that traffic in one or both directions is no longer needed.

SYNTAX

The syntax for the `shutdown` function is

```
shutdown (socket, direction);
```

Here, `socket` is the file variable associated with the socket whose traffic is to be restricted. `direction` is one of the following values:

☐ 0 indicates that the program can send through the socket but can no longer receive data.

☐ 1 indicates that the program can receive data from the socket but can no longer send.

☐ 2 indicates that both sending and receiving are disallowed.

NOTE

To terminate communication through a socket, call `close` and pass it the file variable associated with the socket:

```
close (SOCKET);
```

This line closes the socket represented by SOCKET.

The `socketpair` Function

The `socketpair` function is similar to `socket`, but it creates a pair of sockets rather than just one socket.

The syntax of the `socketpair` function is

```
socketpair (socket1, socket2, domain, type, format);
```

socket1 is the file variable to be associated with the first newly created socket, and *socket2* is the file variable to be associated with the second socket.

As in `socket`, *domain* is the protocol family to use, *type* is the type of socket to create, and *format* is the number of the protocol to be used with the socket.

`socketpair` often is used to create a bidirectional communication channel between a parent and a child process.

> Some machines that support sockets do not support `socketpair`.

WARNING

The `getsockopt` and `setsockopt` Functions

The `getsockopt` and `setsockopt` functions enable you to obtain and set socket options.

To obtain the current value of a socket option in your environment, call the `getsockopt` function.

The syntax of the `getsockopt` function is

```
retval = getsockopt (socket, opttype, optname);
```

socket is the file variable associated with the socket whose option you want to retrieve.

opttype is the type of option (or option level). The value of the system constant `SOL_SOCKET` specifies a "socket level" option. To find out the other possible values for *opttype*, refer to the system header file `/usr/include/sys/socket.h`.

optname is the name of the option whose value is to be retrieved; *retval* is the value of this option.

To set a socket option, call `setsockopt`.

The syntax of the `setsockopt` function is

```
setsockopt (socket, opttype, optname, value);
```

Here, `socket`, `opttype`, and `optname` are the same as in `getsockopt`, and `value` is the new value of the `optname` option.

 NOTE

> Socket options are system dependent (and a full treatment of them is beyond the scope of this book). For more information on socket options, refer to the `getsockopt` and `setsockopt` manual pages on your machine or to the `/usr/include/sys/socket.h` header file.

The `getsockname` **and** `getpeername` **Functions**

The `getsockname` and `getpeername` functions enable you to retrieve the addresses of the two ends of a socket connection.

The `getsockname` function returns the address of this end of a socket connection (the end created by the currently running program).

The syntax of the `getsockname` function is

```
retval = getsockname (socket);
```

As in the other socket functions, `socket` is the file variable associated with a particular socket. `retval` is the returned address.

The returned address is in packed format as built by the calls to `pack` in Listing 15.11 and Listing 15.12.

The following code retrieves a socket address and converts it into readable form:

```
$rawaddr = getsockname (SOCKET);
($d1, $d2, @addrbytes) = unpack ("SnC4x8", $rawaddr);
$readable = join (".", @addrbytes);
```

 NOTE

> Normally, you already have the address returned by `getsockname` because you need to pass it to `bind` to associate the socket with your machine.

To retrieve the address of the other end of the socket connection, call getpeername.

The syntax of the getpeername function is

```
retval = getpeername (socket);
```

As in getsockname, socket is the file variable associated with the socket, and retval is the returned address.

NOTE

> The address returned by getpeername is normally identical to the address returned by accept.

The UNIX System V IPC Functions

The functions you've just seen describe interprocess communication using sockets. Sockets are supported on machines running the 4.3BSD (Berkeley UNIX) operating system and on some other UNIX operating systems as well.

Some machines that do not support sockets support a set of UNIX System V interprocess communication (IPC) functions. These functions consist of the following:

☐ Functions that send messages from one process to another by means of a message queue

☐ Functions that create and manipulate shared memory

☐ Functions that create and manipulate semaphores

Perl enables you to use these IPC functions by defining Perl functions with the same names as the IPC functions. The following sections provide a brief description of these functions.

For more information on any IPC function, refer to the manual page for that function.

IPC Functions and the require Statement

Before you can use any System V IPC functions, you first must give the program the information it needs to use them.

To do this, add the following statements to your program, immediately following the #!/usr/local/bin/perl header line:

```
require "ipc.ph";
require "msg.ph";
require "sem.ph";
require "shm.ph";
```

The `require` statement is like the `#include` statement in the C preprocessor: it takes the contents of the specified file and includes them as part of your program.

SYNTAX

The syntax for the `require` statement is

```
require "name";
```

Here, *name* is the name of the file to be added to your program.

For example, the following statement includes the file `ipc.ph` as part of your program:

```
require "ipc.ph";
```

NOTE

If the Perl interpreter complains that it cannot find a file that you are trying to include using `require`, one of two things is wrong:

☐ The built-in array variable `@INC` is not defined properly.

☐ The file does not exist.

See the description of `@INC` on Day 17, "System Variables," for more details.

The `msgget` Function

To use the System V message-passing facility, the first step is to create a message queue ID to represent a particular message queue. To do this, call the `msgget` function.

SYNTAX

The syntax of the `msgget` function is

```
msgid = msgget (key, flag);
```

Here, *key* is either `IPC_PRIVATE` or an arbitrary constant. If *key* is `IPC_PRIVATE` or *flag* has `IPC_CREAT` set, the message queue is created, and its queue ID is returned in `msgid`.

If `msgget` is unable to create the message queue, `msgid` is set to the null string.

The `msgsnd` Function

To send a message to a message queue, call the `msgsnd` function.

The syntax of the msgsnd function is

```
msgsnd (msgid, message, flags);
```

msgid is the message queue ID returned by msgget. *message* is the text of the message, and *flags* specifies options that affect the message.

msgsnd returns a nonzero value if the send operation succeeds, zero if an error occurs.

For more information on the format of the message sent by msgsnd, refer to your msgsnd manual page.

The msgrcv Function

To obtain a message from a message queue, call the msgrcv function.

The syntax of the msgrcv function is

```
msgrcv (msgid, message, size, mesgtype, flags);
```

Here, *msgid* is the ID of the message queue, as returned by msgget. *message* is a scalar variable (or array element) in which the message is to be stored. *size* is the size of the message, plus the size of the message type; this message type is specified in mesgtype. *flags* specifies options that affect the message.

msgrcv returns a nonzero value if the send operation succeeds, zero if an error occurs.

The msgctl Function

The msgctl function enables you to set options for message queues and send commands that affect them.

The syntax of the msgctl function is

```
msgctl (msgid, msgcmd, msgarg);
```

msgid is the message queue ID. *msgcmd* is the command to be sent to the message queue; the list of available commands is defined in the file /usr/include/sys/ipc.h.

Some of the commands that can be specified by msgcmd set the values of message queue options. If one of these commands is specified, the new value of the option is specified in *msgarg*.

If an error occurs, msgctl returns the undefined value. msgctl also can return zero or a nonzero value.

The `shmget` **Function**

To use the System V shared memory capability, you must first create the shared memory. To do this, call the `shmget` function.

15

SYNTAX

The syntax of the `shmget` function is

```
shmid = shmget (key, size, flag);
```

Here, *key* is either IPC_PRIVATE or an arbitrary constant. If *key* is IPC_PRIVATE or *flag* has IPC_CREAT set, the shared memory segment is created, and its ID is returned in *shmid*. *size* is the size of the created shared memory (in bytes). If `shmget` is unable to create the message queue, *shmid* is set to the null string.

The `shmwrite` **Function**

To send data to a particular segment of shared memory, call the `shmwrite` function.

SYNTAX

The syntax of the `shmwrite` function is

```
shmwrite (shmid, text, pos, size);
```

shmid is the shared memory ID returned by `shmget`. *text* is the character string to write to the shared memory, *pos* is the number of bytes to skip over in the shared memory before writing to it, and *size* is the number of bytes to write.

This function returns a nonzero value if the write operation succeeds; it returns zero if an error occurs.

NOTE

If the character string specified by *text* is longer than the value specified by *size*, only the first *size* bytes of text are written to the shared memory.

If the character string specified by *text* is shorter than the value specified by *size*, `shmwrite` fills the leftover space with null characters.

The `shmread` **Function**

To obtain data from a segment of shared memory, call the `shmread` function.

The syntax of the shmread function is

```
shmread (shmid, retval, pos, size);
```

Here, *shmid* is the shared memory ID returned by shmget. *retval* is a scalar variable (or array element) in which the returned data is to be stored. *pos* is the number of bytes to skip in the shared memory segment before copying to *retval*, and *size* is the number of bytes to copy.

This function returns a nonzero value if the read operation succeeds, and it returns zero if an error occurs.

The shmctl **Function**

The shmctl function enables you to set options for shared memory segments and send commands that affect them.

The syntax of the shmctl function is

```
shmctl (shmid, shmcmd, shmarg);
```

shmid is the shared memory ID returned by shmget. *shmcmd* is the command that affects the shared memory; the list of available commands is defined in the header file named /usr/include/sys/ipc.h.

Some of the commands that can be specified by shmcmd set the values of shared memory options. If one of these commands is specified, the new value of the option is specified in *shmarg*.

If an error occurs, shmctl returns the undefined value. shmctl also can return zero or a nonzero value.

The semget **Function**

To use the System V semaphore facility, you must first create the semaphore. To do this, call the semget function.

The syntax of the semget function is

```
semid = semget (key, num, flag);
```

Here, *key* is either IPC_PRIVATE or an arbitrary constant. If *key* is IPC_PRIVATE or *flag* has IPC_CREAT set, the shared memory segment is created, and its ID is returned in *semid*. *num* is the number of semaphores created. If semget is unable to create the semaphore, *semid* is set to the null string.

The `semop` **Function**

To perform a semaphore operation, call the `semop` function.

The syntax of the `semop` function is

```
semop (semid, semstructs);
```

Here, `semid` is the semaphore ID returned by `semget`, and `semstructs` is a character string consisting of an array of semaphore structures. Each semaphore structure consists of the following components, each of which is a short integer (as created by the s format character in `pack`):

- ☐ The number of semaphores
- ☐ The semaphore operation
- ☐ The semaphore flags, if any

This function returns a nonzero value if the semaphore operation is successful, zero if an error occurs.

NOTE

> For more information on semaphore operations and the semaphore structure, refer to the `semop` manual page.

The `semctl` **Function**

The `semctl` function enables you to set options for semaphores and send commands that affect them.

The syntax of the `semctl` function is

```
semctl (semid, semcmd, semarg);
```

`semid` is the semaphore ID returned by `semget`. `semcmd` is the command that affects the semaphore; the list of available commands is defined in the file `/usr/include/sys/ipc.h`.

Some of the commands that can be specified by `semcmd` set the values of semaphore options. If one of these commands is specified, the new value of the option is specified in `semarg`.

If an error occurs, `semctl` returns the undefined value. `semctl` also can return zero or a nonzero value.

Summary

Today you learned about Perl functions that emulate system library functions, perform Berkeley UNIX socket operations, and perform System V IPC operations.

Perl functions that emulate system library functions perform the following tasks, among others:

☐ Read the /etc/group file, which lists the user groups for your machine

☐ Read the /etc/networks file, which lists networks to which your machine is connected

☐ Read from the /etc/hosts file, which lists the remote machines accessible from your local network

☐ Obtain the current login user ID

☐ Retrieve the current process group and parent process ID

☐ Read the /etc/passwd file, which lists information about the users who have access to your machine

☐ Obtain the current priority for your program and set it to another value

☐ Read the /etc/protocols file, which lists the types of protocols available for interprocess communication

☐ Read the /etc/services file, which lists the port numbers associated with system services on your machine

Today you also learned about the Berkeley UNIX socket mechanism, which provides interprocess communication using a client-server model. The System V IPC message queue, shared memory, and semaphore capabilities are also briefly covered.

Q&A

Q What is the difference between getnetent and gethostent, and which one accesses /etc/networks?

A On most systems, getnetent accesses the contents of /etc/networks, which lists the names and numbers of the networks for your machine. gethostent, on the other hand, accesses the contents of /etc/hosts, which lists the names and addresses of other machines on local and remote networks.

Q What will happen if I establish a socket connection using a port number listed in /etc/services?

A If the system service is always active, the system likely will not enable you to establish a socket connection using this port. If the system service runs intermittently, you run the risk of disrupting it.

In your programs, it is always best to use a port never used by any other system service.

Q How did sockets get their name?

A A server process that is listening for clients is like an electrical socket on your wall: any client process with the appropriate protocol can "plug into" it.

Q What is the purpose of a semaphore?

A A semaphore is a method of ensuring that only one process can run a particular segment of code or access a particular chunk of shared memory storage at any given time.

A full description of how semaphores work is beyond the scope of this book. Many books on operating systems can give you an introduction to the concepts used in semaphores. Also, the UNIX System V manual pages for the semaphore functions listed in today's lesson provide a brief description of how semaphores work.

Q The machine name I retrieved using gethostbyaddr has a lot of funny characters in it. Why?

A The address you've retrieved is an Internet domain address, which is a list of names separated by periods (.). These domain names ensure that each Internet user and machine can be distinguished from the millions of other users and machines around the world.

For more details on the Internet and how to use it, refer to a book on the subject (many are available).

Workshop

The Workshop provides quiz questions to help you solidify your understanding of the material covered, and exercises to give you experience in using what you've learned. Try and understand the quiz and exercise answers before you go on to tomorrow's lesson.

Quiz

1. Which functions manipulate the following files?

    a. /etc/passwd

    b. /etc/hosts

    c. /etc/networks

    d. /etc/services

2. Which of the following functions are called by client processes and which by server processes when performing socket operations? In what order should these functions be called?

   a. `bind`

   b. `listen`

   c. `socket`

   d. `accept`

   e. `connect`

3. What do the following functions do?

   a. `getpwuid`

   b. `setprotoent`

   c. `gethostbyaddr`

   d. `getgrent`

   e. `getservbyport`

4. How do you send information using a socket?

5. Describe how to list all the (numeric) user IDs on your machine.

Exercises

1. Write a program that lists (by name) all the groups into which user IDs are sorted on your machine. List all the user names in each group. Sort the groups, and the user names in each group, in alphabetical order.

2. Write a program that lists every user name on your machine and prints the home directory for each.

3. Write a program that lists the shells used by users on your machine. List the number of users of each shell, and sort the list in descending order of use.

4. Write a program that splits into two identical processes, and have each process print the process ID of the other.

5. Write a program that sends a specific file, /u/jqpublic/testfile, to clients who request it. The program should send the file by creating a copy of itself using `fork`, and it should be able to send to five clients at once.

6. **BUG BUSTER:** What is wrong with the following program?

```
#!/usr/local/bin/perl

print ("Network names and numbers at your site:\n");
while (($name, $d1, $d2, $address) = getnetent()) {
        print ("$name, at address $address\n");
}
```

Day **16**

Command-Line Options

Today's lesson describes the options you can specify to control how your Perl program operates. These options provide many features, including those that perform the following tasks:

- ☐ Check syntax
- ☐ Print warnings
- ☐ Use preprocessor commands
- ☐ File editing
- ☐ Change the "end of input line" marker

Today's lesson begins with a description of how to supply options to your Perl program.

Specifying Options

There are two ways to supply options to a Perl program:

☐ On the command line, when you enter the command that starts your Perl program
☐ On the first line of your Perl program

The following sections describe these methods of supplying options.

Specifying Options on the Command Line

One way to specify options for a Perl program is to enter them on the command line when you enter the command that starts your program.

The syntax for specifying options on the command line is

```
perl options program
```

Here, *program* is the name of the Perl program you want to run, and *options* is the list of options you want to supply to the program.

For example, the following command runs the Perl program named test1 and passes it the options -s and -w. (You'll learn about these and other options later today.)

```
$ perl -s -w test1
```

Some options need to be specified along with a value. For example, the -0 option requires an integer to be passed with it:

```
$ perl -0 26 test1
```

Here, the integer 26 is associated with the option -0.

If you want, you can omit the space between the option and its associated value, as in the following:

```
$ perl -026 test1
```

As before, this command associates 26 with the -0 option. In either case, the value associated with an option must always immediately follow the option.

NOTE

If an option does not require an associated value, you can put another option immediately after it without specifying an additional — character or space. For example, the following commands are equivalent:

```
$ perl -s -w test1
$ perl -sw test1
```

16

> You can put an option that requires a value as part of a group of
> options, provided that it is last in the group. For example, the following
> commands are equivalent:
>
> ```
> $ perl -s -w -0 26 test1
> $ perl -sw026 test1
> ```

Specifying an Option in the Program

Another way to specify a command option is to include it as part of the header comment for
the program. For example, suppose that the first line of your Perl program is this:

```
#!/usr/local/bin/perl -w
```

In this case, the -w option is automatically specified when you start the program.

WARNING

Perl 4 enables you to specify only one option (or group of options) on
the header comment line. This means that the following line generates
an "unrecognized switch" error message:

```
#!/usr/local/bin/perl -w -s
```

Perl 5 enables as many switches as you like on the command line.
However, some operating systems chop the header line after 32
characters, so be careful if you are planning to use a large number of
switches.

WARNING

Options specified on the command line override options specified in
the header comment. For example, if your header comment is

```
#!/usr/local/bin/perl -w
```

and you start your program with the command

```
$ perl -s test1
```

the program will run with the -s option specified but not the -w
option.

16

The -v Option: Printing the Perl Version Number

The -v option enables you to find out what version of Perl is running on your machine. When the Perl interpreter sees this option, it prints information on itself and then exits without running your program.

This means that if you supply a command such as the following, the file test1 is not executed:

```
$ perl -v test1
```

Here is sample output from the -v command:

```
This is perl, version 5.001

        Unofficial patch level 1m

Copyright (c) 1987-1994, Larry Wall

Perl may be copied only under the terms of either the Artistic License
or the GNU General Public License, which may be found in the Perl 5.0
source kit.
```

The only really useful things here, besides the copyright notice, are the version number of the Perl you are running—in this case, 4.0—and the patch level, which indicates how many repairs, or patches, have been made to this version. Here, the patch level is 36 (which, at this writing, is the latest release of Perl version 4.0).

No other options should be specified if you specify the -v option, because none of them would do anything in this case anyway.

The -c Option: Checking Your Syntax

The -c option tells the Perl interpreter to check whether your Perl program is correct without actually running it. If it is correct, the Perl interpreter prints the following message (in which filename is the name of your program) and then exits without executing your program:

```
filename syntax OK
```

If the Perl interpreter detects errors, it displays them just as it normally does. After printing the error messages, it prints the following message, in which filename is the name of your program:

16

```
filename had compilation errors
```

Again, there is no point in supplying other options if you specify the -c option because the Perl interpreter isn't actually running the program; the only exception is the -w option, which prints warnings. This option is described in the following section.

The -w Option: Printing Warnings

As you have seen on the preceding days, some mistakes are easy to make when you are writing a Perl program, such as accidentally typing the wrong variable name, or using == when you really mean to use eq. Because certain mistakes crop up frequently, the Perl interpreter provides an option that checks for them.

This option, the -w option, prints a warning every time the Perl interpreter sees something that might cause a problem. For example, if the interpreter sees the statement

```
$y = $x;
```

and hasn't seen $x before (which means that $x is undefined), it prints a warning message in the following form if you are running Perl 4:

```
Possible typo: "x" at filename line linenum.
```

Here, *filename* is the name of your Perl program, and *linenum* is the number of the line on which the interpreter has detected a potential problem.

If you are running Perl 5, the message is similar, but also includes the name of the current package:

```
Identifier "main::x" used only once: possible typo at filename line linenum.
```

For more information on packages, see Day 19, "Object-Oriented Programming in Perl."

The following sections provide a partial list of the potential problems detected by the -w option. (If you are running Perl 5, the -w option provides dozens of useful warnings. Consult the Perl manual pages for a complete list.)

NOTE

The -w option can be combined with the -c option to provide a means of checking your syntax for errors and problems before you actually run the program.

Checking for Possible Typos

As you have seen, a statement such as the following one leads to a warning message if $x has not been previously defined:

```
$y = $x;
```

The "possible typo" error message also appears in the following circumstances, among others:

- ☐ If a variable is assigned to but is never used again
- ☐ If a file variable is referred to without being specified in an open statement

Of course, the possible-typo message might flag lines that don't actually contain typos. Following are two of the most common situations in which a possible typo actually is correct code:

- ☐ The Perl 4 interpreter sometimes confuses a print format specifier with a file variable and claims that the name of the print format specifier is a possible typo. For example, the statement

  ```
  format BLANK =
  .
  ```

  (which enables you to print a blank line on a formatted page) might generate the warning message

  ```
  Possible typo: "BLANK" at file1 line 26.
  ```

  This warning message might appear even if the print format is actually used in the program, because it is specified by a statement such as

  ```
  $~ = "BLANK";
  ```

  and the Perl interpreter doesn't realize that the string BLANK refers to the BLANK print format.

- ☐ The Perl 5 interpreter does not generate this warning message.
- ☐ If you call a function that returns a list, and you need only an element of the list, one way to extract that single element is to assign the other elements to dummy variables. For example, if you want to retrieve just the group ID when you call getgrnam, you can do so as shown here:

  ```
  ($d1, $d2, $groupid) = getgrnam ($groupname);
  ```

- ☐ Here, the scalar variables $d1 and $d2 are dummy variables that hold the elements of the group file entry that you do not need. If (as is likely) $d1 and $d2 are not referred to again, the -w option treats $d1 and $d2 as possible typos.

Checking for Redefined Subroutines

One useful feature of the -w option is that it checks whether two subroutines of the same name have been defined in the program. (Normally, if the Perl interpreter sees two subroutines of the same name, it quietly replaces the first subroutine with the second one and carries on.)

If, for example, two subroutines named x are defined in a program, the -w option prints a message similar to the following one:

```
Subroutine x redefined at file1 line 46.
```

The line number specified is the line that starts the second subroutine.

When the -w option has detected this problem, you can decide which subroutine to rename or throw away.

Checking for Incorrect Comparison Operators

Another really helpful feature of the -w option is that it checks whether you are trying to compare a string using the == operator.

In a statement such as the following:

```
if ($x == "humbug") {
        ...
}
```

the conditional expression

```
$x == "humbug"
```

is equivalent to the expression

```
$x == 0
```

because all character strings are converted to 0 when used in a numeric context (a place where a number is expected). This is correct in Perl, but it is not likely to be what you want.

If the -w option is specified and the Perl interpreter sees a statement such as this one, it prints a message similar to the following if you are running Perl 4:

```
Possible use of == on string value at file1 line 26.
```

In Perl 5, the following warning is printed:

```
Argument "humbug" isn't numeric for numeric eq at file1 line 26.
```

In either case, this warning enables you detect these incorrect == operators and replace them with eq operators, which compare strings.

The -w operator doesn't detect the opposite problem, namely:

```
if ($x eq 46) {
        ...
}
```

In this case, the Perl interpreter converts 46 to the string 46 and performs a string comparison.

Because a number and its string equivalent usually mean the same thing, this normally doesn't cause a problem. Watch out, though, for octal numbers in string comparisons, as in the following example:

```
if ($x eq 046) {
        ...
}
```

Here, the octal value 046 is converted to the number 38 before being converted to a string. If you really want to compare $x to 046, this code will not produce the results you expect.

Another thing to watch out for is this: In Perl 4, the -w option does not check for conditional expressions such as the following:

```
if ($x = 0) {
        ...
}
```

because there are many cases in Perl in which the = assignment operator belongs inside a conditional expression. You will have to manually check that you are not specifying = (assignment) when you really mean to use == (equality comparison).

Perl 5 flags this with the following message:

```
Found = in conditional, should be == at filename line filenum.
```

The -e Option: Executing a Single-Line Program

The -e option enables you to execute a Perl program from your shell command line. For example, the command

```
$ perl -e "print ('Hello');"
```

prints the following string on your screen:

```
Hello
```

You can also specify multiple -e options. In this case, the Perl statements are executed left to right. For example, the command

```
$ perl -e "print ('Hello');" -e "print (' there');"
```

prints the following string on your screen:

```
Hello there
```

By itself, the -e option is not all that useful. It becomes useful, however, when you use it in conjunction with some of the other options you'll see in today's lesson.

WARNING

> You can leave off the closing semicolon in a Perl statement passed via the -e option, if you want to:
>
> ```
> $ perl -e "print ('Hello')"
> ```
>
> If you are supplying two or more -e options, however, the Perl interpreter strings them together and treats them as though they are a single Perl program. This means that the following command generates an error because there must be a semicolon after the statement specified with the first -e option:
>
> ```
> $ perl -e "print ('Hello')" -e "print (' there')"
> ```

The -s Option: Supplying Your Own Command-Line Options

As you can see from this chapter, you can control the behavior of Perl by specifying various command-line options. You can control the behavior of your own Perl programs by specifying command-line options for them too. To do this, specify the -s option when you call the program.

Here's an example of a command that passes an option to a Perl program:

```
$ perl -s testfile -q
```

This command starts the Perl program testfile and passes it the -q option.

WARNING

To be able to pass options to your program, you must specify the Perl -s option. The following command does not pass -q as an option:

```
$ perl testfile -q
```

In this case, -q is just an ordinary argument that is passed to your program and stored in the built-in array variable @ARGV.

The easiest way to remember to include -s is to specify it as part of your header comment:

```
#!/usr/local/bin/perl -s
```

This ensures that your program always will check for options. (Unless, of course, you override the option check by providing other Perl options on the command line when you invoke the program.)

If an option is specified when you invoke your Perl program, the scalar variable whose name is the same as the option is automatically set to 1 before program execution begins. For example, if a Perl program named testfile is called with the -q option, as in the following, the scalar variable $q is automatically set to 1:

```
$ perl -s testfile -q
```

You then can use this variable in a conditional expression to test whether the option has been set.

NOTE

If -q is treated as an option, it does not appear in the system variable @ARGV. A command-line argument either sets an option or is added to @ARGV.

Options can be longer than a single character. For example, the following command sets the value of the scalar variable $potato to 1:

```
$ perl -s testfile -potato
```

You also can set an option to a value other than 1 by specifying = and the desired value on the command line:

```
$ perl -s testfile -potato="hot"
```

This line sets the value of $potato to hot.

Listing 16.1 is a simple example of a program that uses command-line options to control its behavior. This program prints information about the user currently logged in.

Listing 16.1. An example of a program that uses command-line options.

TYPE

```
 1: #!/usr/local/bin/perl -s
 2:
 3: # This program prints information as specified by
 4: # the following options:
 5: # -u: print numeric user ID
 6: # -U: print user ID (name)
 7: # -g: print group ID
 8: # -G: print group name
 9: # -d: print home directory
10: # -s: print login shell
11: # -all: print everything (overrides other options)
12:
13: $u = $U = $g = $G = $d = $s = 1 if ($all);
14: $whoami = 'whoami';
15: chop ($whoami);
16: ($name, $d1, $userid, $groupid, $d2, $d3, $d4,
17:        $homedir, $shell) = getpwnam ($whoami);
18: print ("user id: $userid\n") if ($u);
19: print ("user name: $name\n") if ($U);
20: print ("group id: $groupid\n") if ($g);
21: if ($G) {
22:        ($groupname) = getgrgid ($groupid);
23:        print ("group name: $groupname\n");
24: }
25: print ("home directory: $homedir\n") if ($d);
26: print ("login shell: $shell\n") if ($s);
```

OUTPUT

```
$ program16_1 -U -d
user name: dave
home directory: /ag1/dave
$
```

ANALYSIS The header comment in line 1 specifies that the `-s` option is to be automatically specified when this Perl program is invoked. This ensures that options can always be passed to this program (unless, of course, you override the `-s` option on the command line, as described earlier).

The comments in lines 3–11 provide information on what options the program supports. This information is useful when someone is reading or modifying the program because there is no other way to tell which scalar variables are used to test options.

The option `-all` indicates that the program is to print everything; if this option is specified, the scalar variable $all is set to 1. To cut down on the number of comparisons later, line 13 checks whether $all is 1; if it is, the other scalar variables corresponding to command-line options are set to 1. This technique ensures that the following commands are equivalent (assuming that your program is named program16_1):

```
$ program16_1 -all
$ program16_1 -u -U -g -G -d -s
```

The scalar variables listed in line 13 can be assigned to, even though they correspond to possible command-line options, because they behave just like other Perl scalar variables.

Lines 14–17 provide the raw material for the various print operations in this program. To start, when the Perl interpreter sees the string 'whoami', it calls the system command whoami, which returns the name of the user running the program. This name is then passed to getpwnam, which searches the password file /etc/passwd and retrieves the entry for this particular user.

Line 18 checks whether the -u option has been specified. To do this, it checks whether $u has a nonzero value. If it does, the user ID is printed. (The user ID is also printed if -all has been specified because line 13 sets $u to a nonzero value in this case.)

Similarly, line 19 prints the user name if -U has been specified, line 20 prints the group ID if -g has been specified, line 25 prints the home directory if -d has been specified, and line 26 prints the filename of the login shell if -s has been specified.

Lines 21–24 check whether to print the group name. If -g has been specified, $g is nonzero, and line 22 calls getgrid to retrieve the group name.

TIP

Because command-line options can change the initial values of scalar variables, it is a good idea to always assign a value to a scalar variable before you use it. Consider the following example:

```
#!/usr/local/bin/perl

while ($count < 10) {
        print ("$count\n");
        $count++;
}
```

This program normally prints the numbers from 0 to 9 because $count is assumed to have an initial value of 0. However, if this program is called with the -count option, the initial value of $count becomes something other than 0, and the program behaves differently.

If you add the following statement before the while loop, the program always prints the numbers 0 to 9 regardless of what options are specified on the command line:

```
$count = 0;
```

16

The -s **Option and Other Command-Line Arguments**

You can supply both options and command-line arguments to your program (provided that you supply the -s option to Perl). These are the rules that the Perl interpreter follows:

☐ Any arguments immediately following the program name that start with a — are assumed to be options.

☐ Any argument that does not start with a — is assumed to be an ordinary argument and not an option.

☐ When the Perl interpreter sees an argument that is not an option, all subsequent arguments are also treated as ordinary arguments, not options, even if they start with a —.

This means, for example, that the following command treats -w as an option to testfile, and foo and -e as ordinary arguments:

```
$ perl -s testfile -w foo -e
```

The special argument — — also indicates "end of options." For example, the following command treats -w as an option and -e as an ordinary argument. The — — is thrown away.

```
$ perl -s testfile -w — -e
```

The -P **Option: Using the C Preprocessor**

The C preprocessor is a program that takes code written in the C programming language and searches for special preprocessor statements. In Perl, the -P option enables you to use this preprocessor with your Perl program:

```
$ perl -P myprog
```

Here, the Perl program myprog is first run through the C preprocessor. The resulting output is then passed to the Perl interpreter for execution.

NOTE

> Perl provides no way to just run the C preprocessor on a Perl program. To do this, you'll need a C compiler that provides an option which specifies "preprocessor only."
>
> Refer to the documentation for your C compiler for details about how to do this.

The following sections describe some of the most commonly used C preprocessor commands.

The C Preprocessor: A Quick Overview

C preprocessor statements always employ the following syntax:

```
#command value
```

Each C preprocessor statement starts with a # character. *command* is the preprocessor operation to perform, and *value* is the (optional) value associated with this operation.

Macro Substitution: The `#define` Operator

The most common preprocessor statement is `#define`. This statement tells the preprocessor to replace every occurrence of a particular character string with a specified value.

The syntax for `#define` is

```
#define macro     value
```

This statement replaces all occurrences of the character string *macro* with the value specified by *value*. This operation is known as *macro substitution*. *macro* can contain letters, digits, or underscores.

The value specified in a `#define` statement can be any character string or number. For example, the following statement replaces all occurrences of USERNAME with the string "dave" (including the quotation marks):

```
#define USERNAME    "dave"
```

This statement replaces EXPRESSION with the string (14+6), including the parentheses:

```
#define EXPRESSION  (14+6)
```

WARNING

When you are using `#define` with a value that is an expression, it is usually a good idea to enclose the value in parentheses. For example, consider the following Perl statement:

```
$result = EXPRESSION * 5;
```

If your preprocessor command is

```
#define EXPRESSION 14+6
```

the resulting Perl statement becomes

16

```
$result = 14 + 6 * 5;
```

which assigns 44 to $result (because the multiplication is performed first). If you enclose the preprocessor expression in parentheses, as in

```
#define EXPRESSION (14+6)
```

the statement becomes

```
$result = (14 + 6) * 5;
```

which yields the result 100, which is likely what you want.

Also, you always should enclose any parameters (described in the following section) in parentheses, for the same reason.

Passing Arguments Using #define

You can specify one or more parameters with your #define statement. This capability enables you to treat the preprocessor command like a simple function that accepts arguments. For example, the following preprocessor statement takes a specified value and uses it as an exponent:

```
#define POWEROFTWO(val)  (2 ** (val))
```

In the Perl statement

```
$result = POWEROFTWO(1.3 + 2.6) + 4;
```

the preprocessor substitutes the expression 1.3 + 2.6 for val and produces this:

```
$result = (2 ** (1.3 + 2.6)) + 4;
```

You can supply more than one parameter with a #define statement. For example, consider the following statement:

```
#define EXPONENT (base, exp) ((base) ** (exp))
```

Now, the statement

```
$result = EXPONENT(4, 11);
```

yields the following result after preprocessing:

```
$result = ((4) ** (11));
```

The Perl interpreter ignores the extra parentheses.

TIP

> By convention, macros defined using #define normally use all upper-case letters (plus occasional digits and underscores). This makes it easier to distinguish macros from other variable names or character strings.

Listing 16.2 is an example of a Perl program that uses a #define statement to perform macro substitution. This listing is just Listing 15.4 with the preprocessor statement added.

TYPE **Listing 16.2. A program that uses a #define statement.**

```
 1:  #!/usr/local/bin/perl -P
 2:
 3:  #define AF_INET   2
 4:  print ("Enter an Internet address:\n");
 5:  $machine = <STDIN>;
 6:  $machine =~ s/^\s+|\s+$//g;
 7:  @addrbytes = split (/\./, $machine);
 8:  $packaddr = pack ("C4", @addrbytes);
 9:  if (!(($name, $altnames, $addrtype, $len, @addrlist) =
10:          gethostbyaddr ($packaddr, AF_INET))) {
11:          die ("Address $machine not found.\n");
12:  }
13:  print ("Principal name: $name\n");
14:  if ($altnames ne "") {
15:          print ("Alternative names:\n");
16:          @altlist = split (/\s+/, $altnames);
17:          for ($i = 0; $i < @altlist; $i++) {
18:                  print ("\t$altlist[$i]\n");
19:          }
20:  }
```

 OUTPUT

```
$ program16_2
Enter an Internet address:
128.174.5.59
Principal name: ux1.cso.uiuc.edu
$
```

ANALYSIS Line 3 defines the macro AF_INET and assigns it the value 2. When the C preprocessor sees AF_INET in line 10, it replaces it with 2, which is the value of AF_INET on the current machine (as specified in the header file /usr/include/netdb.h or /usr/include/bsd/netdb.h).

If this program is moved to a machine that defines a different value for AF_INET, all you need to do to get this program to work is change line 3 to use the value on that machine.

Using Macros in `#define` Statements

You can use a previously defined macro as the value in another `#define` statement. The following is an example:

```
#define FIRST     1
#define SECOND    FIRST
$result = 43 + SECOND;
```

Here, the macro `FIRST` is defined to be equivalent to the value 1, and `SECOND` is defined to be equivalent to `FIRST`. This means that the statement following the macro definitions is equivalent to the following statement:

```
$result = 43 + 1;
```

Conditional Execution Using `#ifdef` and `#endif`

The `#ifdef` and `#endif` statements control whether a given group of statements is to be included as part of your program.

The syntax for the `#ifdef` and `#endif` statements is

```
#ifdef macro
code
#endif
```

Here, *macro* is any character string that can appear in a `#define` statement. *code* is one or more lines of your Perl program.

When the C preprocessor sees an `#ifdef` statement, it checks whether the macro has been defined using the `#define` statement. If it has, the code specified by *code* is included as part of the program. If it has not, the code specified by *code* is skipped.

NOTE

The code enclosed by `#ifdef` and `#endif` does not have to be a complete Perl statement. For example, the following code is legal:

```
$result = 14 * 2
#ifdef PLUSONE
+ 1
#endif
;
```

Here, `$result` is assigned 17 if `PLUSONE` is defined, 16 if it's not.

Be careful, though: If you abuse `#ifdef`, the resulting program might become difficult to read.

The #ifndef and #else Statements

The #ifndef and #else statements provide additional control over when parts of your program are to be executed.

The #ifndef statement enables you to define code that is to be executed when a particular macro is not defined.

The syntax for #ifndef is the same as for #ifdef:

```
#ifndef macro
code
#endif
```

For example:

```
#ifndef MYMACRO
$result = 26;
#endif
```

The assignment is performed only if MYMACRO has not appeared in a #define statement.

The #else statement enables you to specify code to be executed if a macro is defined and an alternative to choose if the macro is not defined. For example:

```
#ifdef MYMACRO
$result = 47;
#else
print ("Hello, world!\n");
#endif
```

Here, if MYMACRO has been defined by a #define statement, the following statement is executed:

```
$result = 47;
```

If MYMACRO has not been defined, the following statement is executed:

```
print ("Hello, world!\n");
```

You can use #else with #ifndef, as in the following:

```
#ifndef MYMACRO
print ("Hello, world!\n");
#else
$result = 47;
#endif
```

This code is identical to the #ifdef-#else-#endif sequence shown earlier in this section.

The #if Statement

The #if statement enables you to specify that certain lines of your program are to be included only if the expression included with the statement is nonzero.

SYNTAX

The syntax for the `#if` statement is

```
#if expr
code
#endif
```

Here, `expr` is the expression to be evaluated, and `code` is the code to be executed if `expr` is nonzero.

For example, the following statement is executed only if the expression `14 + 3` is nonzero (which it always is, of course):

```
#if 14 + 3
$result = 26;
#endif
```

You can use a macro definition as part of an `#if` statement. If the macro is defined, it has a nonzero value in an `#if` expression; if it is not defined, it has the value zero. Consider the following example:

```
#if MACRO1 ¦¦ MACRO2
$result = 47;
#endif
```

When the preprocessor sees the `#if` statement, it evaluates the expression `MACRO1 ¦¦ MACRO2`. This expression has a nonzero value if either `MACRO1` or `MACRO2` is nonzero. Therefore, the following statement is executed if either `MACRO1` or `MACRO2` is defined:

```
$result = 47;
```

The `#if` statement provides a quick way to remove lines of code from your program temporarily:

```
#if 0
$result = 46;
print ("This line is not printed right now.\n");
#endif
```

Here, the expression included with the `#if` statement is always zero, which means that the statements between `#if` and `#endif` are always skipped.

You can use `#else` with `#if`, as in the following example:

```
#if MACRO1 ¦¦ MACRO2
print ("MACRO1 or MACRO2 is defined.\n");
#else
print ("MACRO1 and MACRO2 are not defined.\n");
#endif
```

This code includes the first print statement if `MACRO1` or `MACRO2` has been defined using `#define`, and it includes the second print statement if neither has been defined.

16

WARNING

> You cannot use the ** (exponentiation) operator in an #if statement because ** is not supported in the C programming language.

Nesting Conditional Execution Statements

You can put one `#ifdef-#else-#endif` construct inside another. For example:

```
#ifdef MACRO1
#ifdef MACRO2
print ("MACRO1 yes, MACRO2 yes\n");
#else
print ("MACRO1 yes, MACRO2 no\n");
#endif
#else
#ifdef MACRO2
print ("MACRO1 no, MACRO2 yes\n");
#else
print ("MACRO1 no, MACRO2 no\n");
#endif
#endif
```

You also can put an `#if-#else-#endif` construct or an `#ifndef-#else-#endif` construct inside an `#ifdef-#else-#endif` construct, or vice versa. The only restriction is that the inner construct must be completely contained in one part of the outer construct.

Including Other Files Using `#include`

Another preprocessor command that is quite useful is the `#include` command. This command tells the C preprocessor to include the contents of the specified file as part of the program.

SYNTAX

The syntax for the `#include` command is

`#include filename`

`filename` is the name of the file to be included.

For example, the following command includes the contents of `myincfile.h` as part of the program:

`#include <myincfile.h>`

When an `#include` statement is found in a Perl program, the C preprocessor searches for the file in the current directory and the `/usr/local/lib/perl` directory. (The `-I` option, described in the following section, enables you to search in other directories.) To instruct the C preprocessor to search only the current directory, enclose the filename in double quotation marks rather than angle brackets.

16

```
#include "myincfile.h"
```

This command limits the search for myincfile.h to the current directory.

You can specify an entire pathname in an #include statement, as in the following example:

```
#include "/u/dave/myincfile.h"
```

This command retrieves the contents of /u/dave/myincfile.h and adds them to the program.

16

NOTE
> Perl also enables you to include other files as part of a program using the require statement. For more information on require, refer to Day 19, "Object-Oriented Programming in Perl."

The -I Option: Searching for C Include Files

You use the -I option with the -P option. It enables you to specify where to look for include files to be processed by the C preprocessor. For example:

```
perl -P -I /u/dave/myincdir testfile
```

This command tells the Perl interpreter to search the directory /u/dave/myincdir for include files (as well as the default directories).

To specify multiple directories to search, repeat the -I option:

```
perl -P -I /u/dave/dir1 -I /u/dave/dir2 testfile
```

This command searches in both /u/dave/dir1 and /u/dave/dir2.

NOTE
> The directories specified in the -I option also are added to the system variable @INC. This technique ensures that the require function can search in the same directories as the C preprocessor.
>
> For more information on @INC, refer to Day 17, "System Variables." For more information on require, refer to Day 19.

The -n Option: Operating on Multiple Files

One of the most common tasks in Perl programs and in UNIX commands is to read the contents of several input files one line at a time and process each input line as it is read. In these programs and commands, the names of the input files are supplied on the command line. A simple example is the UNIX command cat:

```
$ cat file1 file2 file3 ...
```

This command reads one line of input at a time and writes it to the standard output file.

In Perl, one way to read the contents of several input files, one line at a time, is to enclose the <> operator in a while loop:

```
while ($line = <>) {
        # process $line in here
}
```

Another method is to specify the -n option. This option takes your program and executes it once for each line of input in each of the files specified on the command line.

Listing 16.3 is a simple example of a program that uses the -n option. It puts asterisks around each input line and then prints it.

TYPE **Listing 16.3. A simple program that uses the -n option.**

```
1:  #!/usr/local/bin/perl -n
2:
3:  # input line is stored in the system variable $_
4:  $line = $_;
5:  chop ($line);
6:  printf ("* %-52s *\n", $line);
```

OUTPUT
```
$ program16_3 file1
* This test file has only one line in it.              *
$
```

ANALYSIS The -n option encloses the program shown here in an invisible while loop. Each time the program is executed, the next line of input from one of the input files is read and is stored in the system variable $_. Line 4 takes this line and copies it into another scalar variable, $line; line 5 then removes the last character—the trailing newline character—from this line.

Line 6 uses printf to write the input line to the standard output file. Because printf is formatting the input, the asterisks all appear in the same columns (column 1 and column 56) on your screen.

The previous program is equivalent to the following Perl program
(which does not use the -n option):

```
#!/usr/local/bin/perl

while (< >) {
        # input line is stored in the system variable $_
        $line = $_;
        chop ($line);
        printf ("* %-72s *\n", $line);
}
```

The -n and -e options work well together. For example, the following command is equivalent
to the cat command:

```
$ perl -n -e "print $_;" file1 file2 file3
```

The print $_; argument supplied with the -e option is a one-line Perl program. Because the
-n option executes the program once for each input line and reads each input line into the
system variable $_, the statement

```
print $_;
```

prints each input line in turn, which is exactly what the cat command does. (Note that the
parentheses that normally enclose the argument passed to print have been omitted in this
case.)

The previous command can be made even simpler:

```
$ perl -n -e "print" file1 file2 file3
```

By default, if no argument is supplied, print assumes that it is to print the contents of $_.
And, if the program consists of a single statement, there is no need to include the closing
semicolon.

The pattern matching and substitution operators also operate on $_ by default. For example,
the following statement examines the contents of $_ and searches for a digit:

```
$found = /[0-9]/;
```

This default behavior makes it easy to include a search or a substitution in a single-line
command. For example:

```
$ perl -n -e "print if /[0-9]/" file1 file2 file3
```

This command reads each line of the files file1, file2, and file3. If an input line contains
a digit, it is printed.

NOTE

> Several other functions use $_ as the default scalar variable to operate on, which makes those functions ideal for use with the -n and -e options. A full list of these functions is provided in the description of the $_ system variable, which is contained in Day 17.

The -p Option: Operating on Files and Printing

The -p option is similar to the -n option: it reads each line of its input files in turn. However, the -p option also prints each line it reads.

This means, for example, that you can simulate the behavior of the UNIX cat command with the following command:

```
$ perl -p -e ";" file1 file2 file3
```

Here, the ; is a Perl program consisting of one statement that does nothing.

The -p option is designed for use with the -i option, described in the following section.

NOTE

> If both the -p and the -n options are specified, the -n option is ignored.

The -i Option: Editing Files

As you have seen, the -n and -p options read lines from the files specified on the command line. The -i option, when used with the -p option, takes the input lines being read and writes them back out to the files from which they came. This process enables you to edit files using commands similar to those used in the UNIX sed command.

For example, consider the following command:

```
$ perl -p -i -e "s/abc/def/g;" file1 file2 file3
```

This command contains a one-line Perl program that examines the scalar variable $_ and changes all occurrences of abc into def. (Recall that the substitution operator operates on $_ if the =~ operator is not specified.) The -p option ensures that $_ is assigned each line of each input file in turn and that the program is executed once for each input line. Thus, this command changes all occurrences of abc in the files file1, file2, and file3 to def.

WARNING

> Do not use the -i option with the -n option unless you know what you're doing. The following command also changes all occurrences of abc to def, but it doesn't write out the input lines after it changes them:
>
> ```
> $ perl -n -i -e "s/abc/def/g;" file1 file2 file3
> ```
>
> Because the -i option specifies that the input files are to be edited, the result is that the contents of file1, file2, and file3 are completely destroyed.

The -i option also works on programs that do not use the -p option but do contain the <> operator inside a loop. For example, consider the following command:

```
$ perl -i file1 file2 file3
```

In this case, the Perl interpreter copies the first file, file1, to a temporary file and opens the temporary file for reading. Then, it opens file1 for writing and sets the default output file (the file used by calls to print, write, and printf) to be file1.

After the program finishes reading the temporary file to which file1 was copied, it then copies file2 to a temporary file, opens it for reading, opens file2 for writing, and sets the default output file to be file2. This process continues until the program runs out of input files.

Listing 16.4 is a simple example of a program that edits using the -i option and the < > operator. This program evaluates any arithmetic expressions (containing integers) it sees on a single line and replaces them with their results.

TYPE   **Listing 16.4. A program that edits files using the -i option.**

```
1:  #!/usr/local/bin/perl -i
2:
3:  while ($line = <>) {
4:          while ($line =~
5:                  s#\d+\s*[*+-/]\s*\d+(\s*[*+-/]\s*\d+)*#<x>#) {
6:                  eval ("\$result = $&;");
7:                  $line =~ s/<x>/$result/;
8:          }
9:          print ($line);
10: }
```

This program produces no output because output is written to the files specified on the command line.

 The <> operator at the beginning of the while loop (line 3) reads a line at a time from the input file or files. Each line is searched using the pattern shown in line 5. This pattern matches any substring containing the following elements (in the order given):

1. One or more digits

2. Zero or more spaces

3. An *, +, −, or / character

4. Zero or more spaces

5. One or more digits

6. Zero or more of the preceding four subpatterns (which matches the last part of expressions such as 4 + 7 − 3)

This pattern is replaced by a placeholder substring, <x>.

Lines 6 and 7 are executed once for each pattern matched in the input line. The matched pattern, an arithmetic expression, is automatically stored in the system variable $&; line 6 substitutes this expression into a character string and passes this character string to the function eval. The call to eval creates a subprogram that evaluates the expression and returns the result in the scalar variable $result. Line 7 replaces the placeholder, <x>, with the result returned in $result.

When all the arithmetic expressions have been evaluated and substituted for, the inner while loop terminates, and line 9 calls print. Because the -i option has been set, the line is written back to the original input file from which it came.

NOTE

Even though you do not know the name of the file variable that represents the file being edited, you can still set the default output file variable to some other file and change it back later.

To perform this task, recall that the select function returns the file variable associated with the current default file:

```
$editfile = select (MYFILE);  # change default file
# do your write operations here
select ($editfile);           # change default file back
```

After the second select call has been performed, the default output file is, once again, the file being edited.

16

Backing Up Input Files Using the -i Option

By default, the -i option overwrites the existing input files. If you wish, you can save a copy of the original input file or files before overwriting them. To do this, specify a file extension with the -i option:

```
$ perl -i .old file1 file2 file3
```

Here, the .old file extension specified with the -i option tells the Perl interpreter to copy file1 to file1.old before overwriting it. Similarly, the interpreter copies file2 to file2.old, and file3 to file3.old.

The file extension specified with the -i option can be any character string. By convention, file extensions usually begin with a period; this convention makes it easier for you to spot them when you list the files in your directory.

 TIP

If you are using the -i option with a program you are not familiar with, it is a good idea to specify a file extension. Doing so ensures that your files are not damaged if the program does not work the way you expect.

The -a Option: Splitting Lines

The -a option is used with the -n or -p option. If the -a option is set, each input line that is read is automatically split into a list of "words" (sequences of characters that are not white space); this list of words is stored in a special system array variable named @F.

For example, if your input file contains the line

```
This    is    a    test.
```

and if a program that is called with the -a option reads this line, the array @F contains the list

```
("This", "is", "a", "test.")
```

The -a option is useful for extracting information from files. Suppose that your input files contain records of the form

```
company_name        quantity_ordered        total_cost
```

such as, for example,

```
JOHN H. SMITH    10        47.32
```

Listing 16.5 shows how you can use the -a option to easily produce a program that extracts the quantity and total cost fields from these files.

TYPE **Listing 16.5. An example of the -a option.**

```
1:  #!/usr/local/bin/perl
2:
3:  # This program is called with the -a and -n options.
4:  while ($F[0] =~ /[^\d.]/) {
5:          shift (@F);
6:          next if (!defined($F[0]));
7:  }
8:  print ("$F[0] $F[1]\n");
```

OUTPUT
```
$ perl -a -n program16_5
10 47.32
106 11.54
$
```

ANALYSIS Because the program is called with the -a option, the array variable @F contains a list, each element of which is a word from the current input line.

Because the company name in the input file might consist of more than one word (such as JOHN H. SMITH), the while loop in lines 4–7 is needed to get rid of everything that isn't a quantity field or a total cost field. After these fields have been eliminated, line 8 can print the useful fields.

Note that this program just skips over any nonstandard input lines.

The -F Option: Specifying the Split Pattern

The -F option, defined only in Perl 5, is designed to be used in conjunction with the -a option, and specifies the pattern to use when you split input lines into words. For example, suppose Listing 16.5 is called as follows:

```
$ perl -a -n -F:: program16_5
```

In this case, the words in the input file are assumed to be separated by a pair of colons, which means that the program is expecting to read lines such as the following:

```
JOHN H. SMITH::10::47.32
```

NOTE

The -F option ignores opening and closing slashes if they are present because it interprets them as pattern delimiters. This means that the following program invocations are identical:

```
$ perl -a -n -F:: program16_5
$ perl -a -n -F/::/ program16_5
```

16

The -0 Option: Specifying Input End-of-Line

In all the programs you have seen so far, when the Perl interpreter reads a line from an input file or from the keyboard, it reads until it sees a newline character. You can tell Perl that you want the "end-of-line" input character to be something other than the newline character by specifying the -0 option. (The 0 here is the digit zero, not the letter O.)

With the -0 option, you specify which character is to be the end-of-line character for your input file by providing its ASCII representation in base 8 (octal). For example, the command

```
$ perl -0 040 prog1 infile
```

calls the Perl program named prog1 and specifies that it is to use the space character (ASCII 32, or 40 octal) as the end-of-line character when it reads the input file infile (or any other input file).

This means, for example, that if this program reads an input file containing the following:

```
Test input.
Here's another line.
```

it will read a total of four input lines:

- ☐ The first input line consists of the word Test.
- ☐ The second input line consists of input., followed by a newline character, followed by Here's.
- ☐ The third input line consists of the word another.
- ☐ The fourth input line consists of the word line., followed by a newline character.

The -0 option provides a quick way to read an input file one word at a time, assuming that each line ends with at least one blank character. (If it doesn't, you can quickly write a Perl program that uses the -i and -p options to add a space to the end of each line in each file.) Listing 16.6 is an example of a program that uses -0 to read an input file one word at a time.

TYPE **Listing 16.6. A program that uses the -0 option.**

```
1:  #!/usr/local/bin/perl -0040
2:
3:  while ($line = <>) {
4:          $line =~ s/\n//g;
5:          next if ($line eq "");
6:          print ("$line\n");
7:  }
```

OUTPUT

```
$ program16_6 file1
This
line
contains
five
words.
$
```

ANALYSIS The header comment (line 1) specifies that the -0 option is to be used and that the space character is to become the end-of-line character. (Recall that you do not need a space between an option and the value associated with an option.) This means that line 3 reads from the input file until it sees a blank space.

Not everything read by line 3 is a word, of course. There are two types of lines that are not particularly useful that the program must check for:

☐ Empty lines, which are generated when the input file contains two consecutive spaces

☐ Lines containing the newline character (remember, the newline character is no longer an end-of-line character, so now it actually appears in input lines)

Line 4 checks whether any newline characters are contained in the current input line. The substitution in this line is a global substitution, because an input line can contain two or more newline characters. (This occurs when an input file contains a blank line.)

After all the newline characters have been eliminated, line 5 checks whether the resulting input line is empty. If it is, the program continues with the next input line. If the resulting input line is not empty, the input line must be a useful word, and line 6 prints it.

NOTE

If you specify the value 00 (octal zero) with the -0 option, the Perl interpreter reads until it sees two newline characters. This enables you to read an entire paragraph at a time.

If you specify no value with the -0 option, the null character (ASCII 0) is assumed.

The -1 Option: Specifying Output End-of-Line

The -1 option enables you to specify an output end-of-line character for use in print statements.

Like the -0 option, the -1 option accepts a base-8 (octal) integer that indicates the ASCII representation of the character you want to use.

When the -1 option is specified, the Perl interpreter does two things:

☐ If the -n or -p option is specified, each input line read in from the standard input file has its last character (the line terminator) removed. (The Perl interpreter takes this action because it assumes that you want to replace the old end-of-line character with the one specified by the -1 option.)

☐ When you call the print function, the output written by print will be immediately followed by the character specified by the -1 option.

If you do not specify a value with the -1 option, the Perl interpreter uses the character specified by the -0 option, if it is defined. If -0 has not been specified, the end-of-line character is defined to be the newline character.

WARNING

If you are using both the -1 and the -0 option and you do not provide a value with the -1 option, the order of the options becomes significant because the options are processed from left to right.

If the -1 option appears first, the output end-of-line character is set to the newline character. If the -0 option appears first, the output end-of-line character (set by -1) becomes the same as the input end-of-line character (set by -0).

Listing 16.7 is a simple example of a program that uses -1.

TYPE **Listing 16.7. A program that uses the -1 option.**

```
1:  #!/usr/local/bin/perl -1014
2:
3:  print ("Hello!");
4:  print ("This is a very simple test program!");
```

$ `program16_7`
```
Hello!
        This is a very simple test program!
$
```

The -1014 option in the header comment in line 1 sets the output line character to the newline character. This means that every print statement in the program will have a newline character added to it. As a consequence, the output from lines 3 and 4 appear on separate lines.

NOTE

> You can control the input and output end-of-line characters also by using the system variables $/ and $\. For a description of these system variables, refer to Day 17.

The -x Option: Extracting a Program from a Message

The -x option enables you to process a Perl program that appears in the middle of a file (such as a file containing an electronic mail message, which usually contains some mail routing information). When the -x option is specified, the Perl interpreter ignores every line in the program until it sees a header comment (a comment beginning with the #! characters).

WARNING

> If you are using Perl 5, the header comment must also contain the word "perl."

After the Perl interpreter sees the header comment, it then processes the program as usual until one of the following three conditions occurs:

- ☐ The bottom of the program file is reached.
- ☐ The program file contains a line consisting of just the Ctrl+D or Ctrl+Z character.
- ☐ The program file contains a line consisting of the following statement (by itself):

  _ _END_ _

If the Perl interpreter reads one of the end-of-program lines (the second and third conditions listed previously), it ignores everything appearing after that line in the file.

Listing 16.8 is a simple example of a program that works if run with the -x option.

TYPE   **Listing 16.8. A Perl program contained in a file.**

```
 1:  Here is a Perl program that appears in the middle
 2:  of a file.
 3:  The stuff up here is junk, and the Perl interpreter
 4:  will ignore it.
 5:  The next line is the start of the actual program.
 6:  #!/usr/local/bin/perl
 7:
 8:  print ("Hello, world!\n");
 9:  _ _END_ _
10: This line is also ignored, because it is not part
11: of the program.
```

OUTPUT
```
$ program16_8
Hello, world!
$
```

ANALYSIS   If this program is started with the -x option, the Perl interpreter skips over everything until it sees line 6. (Needless to say, if you try to run this program without specifying the -x option, the Perl interpreter will complain.) Line 8 then prints the message Hello, world.

Line 9 is the special end-of-program line. When the Perl interpreter sees this line, it skips the rest of the program.

NOTE

> Of course, you can't specify the -x option in the header comment itself because the Perl interpreter has to know in advance that the program contains lines that must be skipped.

Miscellaneous Options

The following sections describe some of the more exotic options you can pass to the Perl interpreter. You are not likely to need any of these options unless you are doing something unusual (and you really know what you are doing).

The -u Option

The -u option tells the Perl interpreter to generate a core dump file. This file can then be examined and manipulated.

The -U Option

The -U option tells the Perl interpreter to enable you to perform "unsafe" operations in your program. (Basically, you'll know that an operation is considered unsafe when the Perl interpreter doesn't let you perform it without specifying the -U option!)

The -S Option

The -S option tells the Perl interpreter that your program might be contained in any of the directories specified by your PATH environment variable. The Perl interpreter checks each of these directories in turn, in the order in which they are specified, to see whether your program is located there. (This is the normal behavior of the shell for commands in the UNIX environment.)

NOTE

You need to use -S only if you are running your Perl program using the perl command, as in

    $ perl myprog

If you are running the program using a command such as

    $ myprog

your shell (normally) treats it like any other command and searches the directories specified in your PATH environment variable even if you don't specify the -S option.

The -D Option

The -D option sets the Perl interpreter's internal debugging flags. This option is specified with an integer value (for example, -D 256).

For details on this option, refer to the online manual page for Perl.

NOTE

The internal debugging flags specified by -D have nothing to do with the Perl debugger, which is specified by the -d option.

The debugging flags specified by -D provide information on how Perl itself works, not on how your program works.

16

The -T **Option: Writing Secure Programs**

The -T option specifies that data obtained from the outside world cannot be used in any command that modifies your file system. This feature enables you to write secure programs for system administration tasks.

This option is only available in Perl 5. If you are running Perl 4, use a special version of Perl named taintperl. For details on taintperl, see the online documentation supplied with your Perl distribution.

The -d **Option: Using the Perl Debugger**

One final option that is quite useful is -d. This option tells the Perl interpreter to run your program using the Perl debugger. For a complete description of the Perl debugger and how to use it, refer to Day 21, "The Perl Debugger."

NOTE

> If you are specifying the -d option, you still can use other options.

Summary

Today you learned how to specify options when you run your Perl programs. An option is a dash followed by a single letter, and optionally followed by a value to be associated with the option. Options lacking associated values can be grouped together.

You can specify options in two ways: on the command line and in the header comment. Only one option or group of options can be supplied in the header comment.

Available options include those that list the Perl version number, check your syntax, display warnings, allow single-line programs on the command line, invoke the C preprocessor, automatically read from the input files, and edit files in place.

Q&A

Q Why can you specify only one option in the header comment?

A This is a restriction imposed by the UNIX operating system.

Q Why does v display the Perl version number without running the program?

A This option enables you to check whether the version of Perl you are running is capable of running your program. If an old copy of Perl is running on your machine, your program might not work properly.

Q What options enable me to write a program that edits every line of a file?

A Use the -i (edit in place) and -p (print each line) options. (These options are often used with the -e option to perform an editing command similar to those used by the UNIX sed command.)

Q I have a program that needs to run on two or more different machines. Is there a way of writing the program that ensures that I don't have to change the program each time I change machines?

A Here's how to carry out this task:

1. On each machine, define a file that is to be used to store system-dependent constants. Give the file the same name on each machine. For example, you could call the file perldef.h. The location of the file doesn't matter as long as it's a different directory name on each type of machine.

2. In each perldef.h, use #define to define one constant for each type of machine you run. For example, if you are running this program on UNIX 4.3BSD and System V machines, you could define constants named M_BSD and M_SYSV.

3. After you have defined the constants, set the value of each constant to 0, except for the one corresponding to the machine on which you are running. For example, on your 4.3BSD machines, set M_BSD to 1, and set all the other constants to 0.

4. Add the following statement to your program:

    ```
    #include <perldef.h>
    ```

5. In your program, use #if and #endif to enclose any system-dependent information. For example, if a group of statements is to be executed only on 4.3BSD machines, enclose the statements with the statements

    ```
    #if BSD
    #endif
    ```

6. When you run your program, use the -P option to specify C preprocessing, and use the -I option to tell the Perl interpreter to search for the directory corresponding to the perldef.h file for this machine. For example, if you are running your program on a 4.3BSD machine and the perldef.h file for 4.3BSD machines is in the /usr/local/include/bsdperl directory, include the following option when you start your program:

    ```
    -I /usr/local/include/bsdperl
    ```

Q Why does the -p option override the -n option?

A The -p option tells the Perl interpreter that you want to print each input line that you read, and the -n option tells it that you don't want to do so. These options basically contradict one another.

-p overrides -n because -p is safer; if you really want -n, you can throw away the output from -p. If you really want -p and get -n, you won't get the output you want.

Workshop

The Workshop provides quiz questions to help you solidify your understanding of the material covered and exercises to give you experience in using what you've learned. Try and understand the quiz and exercise answers before you go on to tomorrow's lesson.

Quiz

1. What do the following options do?

    a. -0

    b. -s

    c. -w

    d. -x

    e. -n

2. What happens when -l and -0 are both specified, and

    a. -l appears first?

    b. -0 appears first?

3. Why do the -i and -n options destroy input files when included together?

4. How does the C preprocessor distinguish between preprocessor commands and Perl comments?

5. How does the Perl interpreter distinguish options for the interpreter from options for the program itself?

Exercises

1. Write a program that replaces all the newline characters in the file testfile with colons. Use only command-line options to do this.

2. Write a one-line program that prints only the lines containing the word the.

3. Write a one-line program that prints the second word of each input line.

4. Write a program that prints Hello! if you pass the -H switch to it and that prints Goodbye! if you pass the -G switch.

5. Write a one-line program that converts all lowercase letters to uppercase.
6. **BUG BUSTER:** What is wrong with this command line?

    ```
    $ perl -i -n -e "s/abc/def/g";
    ```

7. **BUG BUSTER:** What is wrong with this command line?

    ```
    $ perl -ipe "s/abc/def/g";
    ```

16

Day 17

System Variables

Today's lesson describes the built-in system variables that can be referenced from every Perl program. These system variables are divided into five groups:

- ☐ Global scalar variables
- ☐ Pattern system variables
- ☐ File system variables
- ☐ Array system variables
- ☐ Built-in file variables

The following sections describe these groups of system variables, and also describe how to provide English-language equivalents of their variable names.

Global Scalar Variables

The *global scalar variables* are built-in system variables that behave just like the scalar variables you create in the main body of your program. This means that these variables have the following properties:

☐ Each built-in global scalar variable stores only one scalar value.

☐ Only one copy of a global scalar variable is defined in a program.

Other kinds of built-in scalar variables, which you will see later in this lesson, do not behave in this way.

The following sections describe the global scalar variables your Perl programs can use.

The Default Scalar Variable: $_

The most commonly used global scalar variable is the $_ variable. Many Perl functions and operators modify the contents of $_ if you do not explicitly specify the scalar variable on which they are to operate.

The following functions and operators work with the $_ variable by default:

☐ The pattern-matching operator

☐ The substitution operator

☐ The translation operator

☐ The <> operator, if it appears in a while or for conditional expression

☐ The chop function

☐ The print function

☐ The study function

The Pattern-Matching Operator and $_

Normally, the pattern-matching operator examines the value stored in the variable specified by a corresponding =~ or !~ operator. For example, the following statement prints hi if the string abc is contained in the value stored in $val:

```
print ("hi") if ($val =~ /abc/);
```

By default, the pattern-matching operator examines the value stored in $_. This means that you can leave out the =~ operator if you are searching $_:

```
print ("hi") if ($_ =~ /abc/);
print ("hi") if (/abc/);          # these two are the same
```

NOTE

> If you want to use the !~ (true-if-pattern-not-matched) operator, you will always need to specify it explicitly, even if you are examining $_:
>
> ```
> print ("hi") if ($_ !~ /abc/);
> ```
>
> If the Perl interpreter sees just a pattern enclosed in / characters, it assumes the existence of a =~ operator.

$_ enables you to use pattern-sequence memory to extract subpatterns from a string and assign them to an array variable:

```
$_ = "This string contains the number 25.11.";
@array = /-?(\d+)\.?(\d+)/;
```

In the second statement shown, each subpattern enclosed in parentheses becomes an element of the list assigned to @array. As a consequence, @array is assigned (25,11).

In Perl 5, a statement such as

```
@array = /-?(\d+)\.?(\d+)/;
```

also assigns the extracted subpatterns to the pattern-sequence scalar variables $1, $2, and so on. This means that the statement assigns 25 to $1 and 11 to $2. Perl 4 supports assignment of subpatterns to arrays, but does not assign the subpatterns to the pattern-sequence variables.

The Substitution Operator and $_

The substitution operator, like the pattern-matching operator, normally modifies the contents of the variable specified by the =~ or !~ operator. For example, the following statement searches for abc in the value stored in $val and replaces it with def:

```
$val =~ s/abc/def/;
```

The substitution operator uses the $_ variable if you do not specify a variable using =~. For example, the following statement replaces the first occurrence of abc in $_ with def:

```
s/abc/def/;
```

Similarly, the following statement replaces all white space (spaces, tabs, and newline characters) in $_ with a single space:

```
/\s+/ /g;
```

When you substitute inside $_, the substitution operator returns the number of substitutions performed:

```
$subcount = s/abc/def/g;
```

Here, $subcount contains the number of occurrences of abc that have been replaced by def. If abc is not contained in the value stored in $_, $subcount is assigned 0.

The Translation Operator and $_

The behavior of the translation operator is similar to that of the pattern-matching and substitution operators: it normally operates on the variable specified by =~, and it operates on $_ if no =~ operator is included. For example, the following statement translates all lowercase letters in the value stored in $_ to their uppercase equivalents:

```
tr/a-z/A-Z/;
```

Like the substitution operator, if the translation operator is working with $_, it returns the number of operations performed. For example:

```
$conversions = tr/a-z/A-Z/;
```

Here, $conversions contains the number of lowercase letters converted to uppercase.

You can use this feature of tr to count the number of occurrences of particular characters in a file. Listing 17.1 is an example of a program that performs this operation.

TYPE   **Listing 17.1. A program that counts using tr.**

```
1:  #!/usr/local/bin/perl
2:
3:  print ("Specify the nonblank characters you want to count:\n");
4:  $countstring = <STDIN>;
5:  chop ($countstring);
6:  @chars = split (/\s*/, $countstring);
7:  while ($input = <>) {
8:          $_ = $input;
9:          foreach $char (@chars) {
10:                 eval ("\$count = tr/$char/$char/;");
11:                 $count{$char} += $count;
12:         }
13: }
14: foreach $char (sort (@chars)) {
15:         print ("$char appears $count{$char} times\n");
16: }
```

OUTPUT
```
$ program17_1 file1
Specify the nonblank characters you want to count:
abc
a appears 8 times
c appears 3 times
b appears 2 times
$
```

17

ANALYSIS This program first asks the user for a line of input containing the characters to be counted. These characters can be separated by spaces or jammed into a single word.

Line 5 takes the line of input containing the characters to be counted and removes the trailing newline character. Line 6 then splits the line of input into separate characters, each of which is stored in an element of the array @chars. The pattern /\s*/ splits on zero or more occurrences of a whitespace character; this splits on every nonblank character and skips over the blank characters.

Line 7 reads a line of input from a file whose name is specified on the command line. Line 8 takes this line and stores it in the system variable $_. (In most cases, system variables can be assigned to, just like other variables.)

Lines 9–12 count the number of occurrences of each character in the input string read in line 4. Each character, in turn, is stored in $char, and the value of $char is substituted into the string in line 10. This string is then passed to eval, which executes the translate operation contained in the string.

The translate operation doesn't actually do anything because it is "translating" a character to itself. However, it returns the number of translations performed, which means that it returns the number of occurrences of the character. This count is assigned to $count.

For example, suppose that the variable $char contains the character e and that $_ contains Hi there!. In this case, the string in line 10 becomes the following because e is substituted for $char in the string:

```
$count = tr/e/e/;
```

The call to eval executes this statement, which counts the number of e's in Hi there!. Because there are two e's in Hi there!, $count is assigned 2.

An associative array, %count, keeps track of the number of occurrences of each of the characters being counted. Line 11 adds the count returned by line 10 to the associative array element whose subscript is the character currently being counted. For example, if the program is currently counting the number of e's, this number is added to the element $count{"e"}.

After all input lines have been read and their characters counted, lines 14–16 print the total number of occurrences of each character by examining the elements of %count.

The <> Operator and $_

In Listing 17.1, which you've just seen, the program reads a line of input into a scalar variable named $input and then assigns it to $_. There is a quicker way to carry out this task, however.

17

You can replace

```
while ($input = <>) {
        $_ = $input;
        # more stuff here
}
```

with the following code:

```
while (<>) {
        # more stuff here
}
```

If the <> operator appears in a conditional expression that is part of a loop (an expression that is part of a conditional statement such as `while` or `for`) and it is not to the right of an assignment operator, the Perl interpreter automatically assigns the resulting input line to the scalar variable $_.

For example, Listing 17.2 shows a simple way to print the first character of every input line read from the standard input file.

TYPE

Listing 17.2. A simple program that assigns to $_ using `<STDIN>`.

```
1:  #!/usr/local/bin/perl
2:
3:  while (<STDIN>) {
4:          ($first) = split (//, $_);
5:          print ("$first\n");
6:  }
```

OUTPUT

```
$ program17_2
This is a test.
T
Here is another line.
H
^D
$
```

ANALYSIS

Because `<STDIN>` is inside a conditional expression and is not assigned to a scalar variable, the Perl interpreter assigns the input line to $_. The program then retrieves the first character by passing $_ to `split`.

WARNING

The <> operator assigns to $_ only if it is contained in a conditional expression in a loop. The statement

```
<STDIN>;
```

17

reads a line of input from the standard input file and throws it away
without changing the contents of $_. Similarly, the following statement
does not change the value of $_:

```
if (<>) {
        print ("The input files are not all empty.\n");
}
```

The chop Function and $_

By default, the chop function operates on the value stored in the $_ variable. For example:

```
while (<>) {
        chop;
        # you can do things with $_ here
}
```

Here, the call to chop removes the last character from the value stored in $_. Because the
conditional expression in the while statement has just assigned a line of input to $_, chop gets
rid of the newline character that terminates each input line.

The print Function and $_

The print function also operates on $_ by default. The following statement writes the
contents of $_ to the standard output file:

```
print;
```

Listing 17.3 is an example of a program that simply writes out its input, which it assumes is
stored in $_. This program is an implementation of the UNIX cat command, which reads
input files and displays their contents.

TYPE **Listing 17.3. A simple version of the cat command using $_.**

```
1:  #!/usr/local/bin/perl
2:
3:  print while (<>);
```

OUTPUT
```
$ program17_3 file1
This is the only line in file "file1".
$
```

ANALYSIS This program uses the <> operator to read a line of input at a time and store it in $_.
If the line is nonempty, the print function is called; because no variable is specified
with print, it writes out the contents of $_.

You can use this default version of print only if you are writing to the default output file (which is usually STDOUT but can be changed using the select function). If you are specifying a file variable when you call print, you also must specify the value you are printing.

For example, to send the contents of $_ to the output file MYFILE, use the following command:

```
print MYFILE ($_);
```

The study **Function and** $_

If you do not specify a variable when you call study, this function uses $_ by default:

```
study;
```

The study function increases the efficiency of programs that repeatedly search the same variable. It is described on Day 13, "Process, String, and Mathematical Functions."

Benefits of the $_ **Variable**

The default behavior of the functions listed previously is useful to remember when you are writing one-line Perl programs for use with the -e option. For example, the following command is a quick way to display the contents of the files file1, file2, and file3:

```
$ perl -e "print while <>;" file1 file2 file3
```

Similarly, the following command changes all occurrences of abc in file1, file2, and file3 to def:

```
$ perl -ipe "s/abc/def/g" file1 file2 file3
```

TIP

Although $_ is useful in cases such as the preceding one, don't overuse it. Many Perl programmers write programs that have references to $_ running like an invisible thread through their programs.

Programs that overuse $_ are hard to read and are easier to break than programs that explicitly reference scalar variables you have named yourself.

The Program Name: $0

The $0 variable contains the name of the program you are running. For example, if your program is named perl1, the statement

```
print ("Now executing $0...\n");
```

displays the following on your screen:

```
Now executing perl1...
```

The $0 variable is useful if you are writing programs that call other programs. If an error occurs, you can determine which program detected the error:

```
die ("$0: can't open input file\n");
```

Here, including $0 in the string passed to die enables you to specify the filename in your error message. (Of course, you can always leave off the trailing newline, which tells Perl to print the filename and the line number when printing the error message. However, $0 enables you to print the filename without the line number, if that's what you want.)

NOTE
You can change your program name while it is running by modifying the value stored in $0.

The User ID: $< and $>

The $< and $> variables contain, respectively, the real user ID and effective user ID for the program. The real user ID is the ID under which the user of the program logged in. The effective user ID is the ID associated with this particular program (which is not always the same as the real user ID).

NOTE
If you are not running your Perl program on the UNIX operating system, the $< and $> variables might have no meaning. Consult your local documentation for more details.

Listing 17.4 uses the real user ID to determine the user name of the person running the program.

TYPE **Listing 17.4. A program that uses the `$<` variable.**

```
1:  #!/usr/local/bin/perl
2:
3:  ($username) = getpwuid($<);
4:  print ("Hello, $username!\n");
```

 OUTPUT
```
$ program17_4
Hello, dave!
$
```

ANALYSIS   The `$<` variable contains the real user ID, which is the login ID of the person running this program. Line 3 passes this user ID to `getpwuid`, which retrieves the password file entry corresponding to this user ID. The user name is the first element in this password file, and it is stored in the scalar variable `$username`. Line 4 then prints this user name.

NOTE

> On certain UNIX machines, you can assign `$<` to `$>` (set the effective user ID to be the real user ID) or vice versa. If you have superuser privileges, you can set `$<` or `$>` to any defined user ID.

The Group ID: `$(` and `$)`

The `$(` and `$)` variables define the real group ID and the effective group ID for this program. The real group ID is the group to which the real user ID (stored in the variable `$<`) belongs; the effective group ID is the group to which the effective user ID (stored in the variable `$>`) belongs.

If your system enables users to be in more than one group at a time, `$(` and `$)` contain a list of group IDs, with each pair of group IDs being separated by spaces. You can convert this into an array by calling `split`.

Normally, you can only assign `$(` to `$)`, and vice versa. If you are the superuser, you can set `$(` or `$)` to any defined group ID.

NOTE

> `$(` and `$)` might not have any useful meaning if you are running Perl on a machine running an operating system other than UNIX.

17

The Version Number: $]

The $] system variable contains the current version number. You can use this variable to ensure that the Perl on which you are running this program is the right version of Perl (or is a version that can run your program).

Normally, $] contains a character string similar to this:

```
$RCSfile: perl.c,v $$Revision: 4.0.1.8 $$Date: 1993/02/05 19:39:30 $
Patch level: 36
```

The useful parts of this string are the revision number and the patch level. The first part of the revision number indicates that this is version 4 of Perl. The version number and the patch level are often combined; in this notation, this is version 4.036 of Perl.

You can use the pattern-matching operator to extract the useful information from $]. Listing 17.5 shows one way to do it.

Listing 17.5. A program that extracts information from the
TYPE   **$] variable.**

```
1:  #!/usr/local/bin/perl
2:
3:  $] =~ /Revision: ([0-9.]+)/;
4:  $revision = $1;
5:  $] =~ /Patch level: ([0-9]+)/;
6:  $patchlevel = $1;
7:  print ("revision $revision, patch level $patchlevel\n");
```

OUTPUT
```
$ program17_5
revision 4.0.1.8, patch level 36
$
```

ANALYSIS   This program just extracts the revision and patch level from $] using the pattern-matching operator. The built-in system variable $1, described later today, is defined when a pattern is matched. It contains the substring that appears in the first subpattern enclosed in parentheses. In line 3, the first subpattern enclosed in parentheses is [0-9.]+. This subpattern matches one or more digits mixed with decimal points, and so it matches 4.0.1.8. This means that 4.0.1.8 is assigned to $1 by line 3 and is assigned to $revision by line 4.

Similarly, line 5 assigns 36 to $1 (because the subpattern [0-9]+, which matches one or more digits, is the first subpattern enclosed in parentheses). Line 6 then assigns 36 to $patchlevel.

WARNING

On some machines, the value contained in $] might be completely different from the value used in this example. If you are not sure whether $] has a useful value, write a little program that just prints $]. If this program prints something useful, you'll know that you can run programs that compare $] with an expected value.

The Input Line Separator: $/

When the Perl interpreter is told to read a line of input from a file, it usually reads characters until it reads a newline character. The newline character can be thought of as an input line separator; it indicates the end of a particular line.

The system variable $/ contains the current input line separator. To change the input line separator, change the value of $/. The $/ variable can be more than one character long to handle the case in which lines are separated by more than one character. If you set $/ to the null character, the Perl interpreter assumes that the input line separator is two newline characters.

Listing 17.6 shows how changing $/ can affect your program.

TYPE   **Listing 17.6. A program that changes the value of $/.**

```
1:  #!/usr/local/bin/perl
2:
3:  $/ = ":";
4:  $line = <STDIN>;
5:  print ("$line\n");
```

OUTPUT
```
$ program17_6
Here is some test input: here is the end.
Here is some test input:
$
```

ANALYSIS   Line 3 sets the value of $/ to a colon. This means that when line 4 reads from the standard input file, it reads until it sees a colon. As a consequence, $line contains the following character string:

```
Here is some test input:
```

Note that the colon is included as part of the input line (just as, in the normal case, the trailing newline character is included as part of the line).

17

WARNING

The -0 (zero, not the letter O) switch sets the value of $/. If you change the value of $/ in your program, the value specified by -0 will be thrown away.

To temporarily change the value of $/ and then restore it to the value specified by -0, save the current value of $/ in another variable before changing it.

For more information on -0, refer to Day 16, "Command-Line Options."

The Output Line Separator: $\

The system variable $\ contains the current output line separator. This is a character or sequence of characters that is automatically printed after every call to print.

By default, $\ is the null character, which indicates that no output line separator is to be printed. Listing 17.7 shows how you can set an output line separator.

TYPE **Listing 17.7. A program that uses the $\ variable.**

```
1:  #!/usr/local/bin/perl
2:
3:  $\ = "\n";
4:  print ("Here is one line.");
5:  print ("Here is another line.");
```

OUTPUT
```
$ program17_7
Here is one line.
Here is another line.
$
```

ANALYSIS Line 3 sets the output line separator to the newline character. This means that a list passed to a subsequent print statement always appears on its own output line. Lines 4 and 5 now no longer need to include a newline character as the last character in the line.

WARNING

The -l option sets the value of $\. If you change $\ in your program without saving it first, the value supplied with -l will be lost. See Day 16 for more information on the -l option.

The Output Field Separator: $,

The $, variable contains the character or sequence of characters to be printed between elements when print is called. For example, in the following statement the Perl interpreter first writes the contents of $a:

```
print ($a, $b);
```

It then writes the contents of $, and then finally, the contents of $b.

Normally, the $, variable is initialized to the null character, which means that the elements of a print statement are printed next to one another. Listing 17.8 is a program that sets $, before calling print.

 TYPE   **Listing 17.8. A program that uses the $, variable.**

```
1:  #!/usr/local/bin/perl
2:
3:  $a = "hello";
4:  $b = "there";
5:  $, = " ";
6:  $\ = "\n";
7:  print ($a, $b);
```

 OUTPUT
```
$ program17_8
hello there
$
```

ANALYSIS   Line 5 sets the value of $, to a space. Consequently, line 7 prints a space after printing $a and before printing $b.

Note that $\, the default output separator, is set to the newline character. This setting ensures that the terminating newline character immediately follows $b. By contrast, the following statement prints a space before printing the trailing newline character:

```
print ($a, $b, "\n");
```

NOTE

> Here's another way to print the newline immediately after the final element that doesn't involve setting $\:
>
> ```
> print ($a, $b . "\n");
> ```
>
> Here, the trailing newline character is part of the second element being printed. Because $b and \n are part of the same element, no space is printed between them.

The Array Element Separator: $"

Normally, if an array is printed inside a string, the elements of the array are separated by a single space. For example:

```
@array = ("This", "is", "a", "list");
print ("@array\n");
```

Here, the print statement prints

```
This is a list
```

A space is printed between each pair of array elements.

The built-in system variable that controls this situation is the $" variable. By default, $" contains a space. Listing 17.9 shows how you can control your array output by changing the value of $".

17

TYPE **Listing 17.9. A program that uses the $" variable.**

```
1:  #!/usr/local/bin/perl
2:
3:  $" = "::";
4:  @array = ("This", "is", "a", "list");
5:  print ("@array\n");
```

OUTPUT
```
$ program17_9
This::is::a::list
$
```

ANALYSIS Line 3 sets the array element separator to :: (two colons). Array element separators, like other separators you can define, can be more than one character long.

Line 5 prints the contents of @array. Each pair of elements is separated by the value stored in $", which is two colons.

NOTE

The $" variable affects only entire arrays printed inside strings. If you print two variables together in a string, as in

```
print ("$a$b\n");
```

the contents of the two variables are printed with nothing separating them regardless of the value of $".

To change how arrays are printed outside strings, use $\, described earlier today.

The Number Output Format: $#

By default, when the print function prints a number, it prints it as a 20-digit floating point number in compact format. This means that the following statements are identical if the value stored in $x is a number:

```
print ($x);
printf ("%.20g", $x);
```

To change the default format that print uses to print numbers, change the value of the $# variable. For example, to specify only 15 digits of precision, use this statement:

```
$# = "%.15g";
```

This value must be a floating-point field specifier, as used in printf and sprintf.

NOTE
> The $# variable does not affect values that are not numbers and has no effect on the printf, write, and sprintf functions.

For more information on the field specifiers you can use as the default value in $#, see "Formatting Output Using printf" on Day 11, "Formatting Your Output."

WARNING
> The $# variable is deprecated in Perl 5. This means that although $# is supported, it is not recommended for use and might be removed from future versions of Perl.

The eval Error Message: $@

If a statement executed by the eval function contains an error, or an error occurs during the execution of the statement, the error message is stored in the system variable $@. The program that called eval can decide either to print the error message or to perform some other action.

For example, the statement

```
eval ("This is not a perl statement");
```

assigns the following string to $@:

```
syntax error in file (eval) at line 1, next 2 tokens "This is"
```

The $@ variable also returns the error generated by a call to die inside an eval. The following statement assigns this string to $@:

```
eval ("die (\"nothing happened\")");
nothing happened at (eval) line 1.
```

The $@ variable also returns error messages generated by the require function. See Day 19, "Object-Oriented Programming in Perl," for more information on require.

The System Error Code: $?

The $? variable returns the error status generated by calls to the system function or by calls to functions enclosed in back quotes, as in the following:

```
$username = 'hostname';
```

The error status stored in $? consists of two parts:

☐ The exit value (return code) of the process called by system or specified in back quotes

☐ A status field that indicates how the process was terminated, if it terminated abnormally

The value stored in $? is a 16-bit integer. The upper eight bits are the exit value, and the lower eight bits are the status field. To retrieve the exit value, use the >> operator to shift the eight bits to the right:

```
$retcode = $? >> 8;
```

For more information on the status field, refer to the online manual page for the wait function or to the file /usr/include/sys/wait.h. For more information on commands in back quotes, refer to Day 20, "Miscellaneous Features of Perl."

The System Error Message: $!

Some Perl library functions call system library functions. If a system library function generates an error, the error code generated by the function is assigned to the $! variable. The Perl library functions that call system library functions vary from machine to machine.

NOTE

> The $! variable in Perl is equivalent to the errno variable in the C programming language.

The Current Line Number: $.

The $. variable contains the line number of the last line read from an input file. If more than one input file is being read, $. contains the line number of the last input file read. Listing 17.10 shows how $. works.

TYPE   **Listing 17.10. A program that uses the $. variable.**

```
1:  #!/usr/local/bin/perl
2:
3:  open (FILE1, "file1") ||
4:          die ("Can't open file1\n");
5:  open (FILE2, "file2") ||
6:          die ("Can't open file2\n");
7:  $input = <FILE1>;
8:  $input = <FILE1>;
9:  print ("line number is $.\n");
10: $input = <FILE2>;
11: print ("line number is $.\n");
12: $input = <FILE1>;
13: print ("line number is $.\n");
```

OUTPUT
```
$ program17_10
line number is 2
line number is 1
line number is 3
$
```

ANALYSIS   When line 9 is executed, the input file FILE1 has had two lines read from it. This means that $. contains the value 2. Line 10 then reads from FILE2. Because it reads the first line from this file, $. now has the value 1. When line 12 reads a third line from FILE1, $. is set to the value 3. The Perl interpreter remembers that two lines have already been read from FILE1.

NOTE

> If the program is reading using <>, which reads from the files listed on the command line, $. treats the input files as if they are one continuous file. The line number is not reset when a new input file is opened.

17

> You can use eof to test whether a particular file has ended, and then reset $. yourself (by assigning zero to it) before reading from the next file.

Multiline Matching: $*

Normally, the operators that match patterns (the pattern-matching operator and the substitution operator) assume that the character string being searched is a single line of text. If the character string being searched consists of more than one line of text (in other words, it contains newline characters), set the system variable $* to 1.

NOTE
> By default, $* is set to 0, which indicates that multiline pattern matches are not required.

17

WARNING
> The $* variable is deprecated in Perl 5. If you are running Perl 5, use the m pattern-matching option when matching in a multiple-line string. See Day 7, "Pattern Matching," for more details on this option.

The First Array Subscript: $[

Normally, when a program references the first element of an array, it does so by specifying the subscript 0. For example:

```
@myarray = ("Here", "is", "a", "list");
$here = $myarray[0];
```

The array element $myarray[0] contains the string Here, which is assigned to $here.

If you are not comfortable with using 0 as the subscript for the first element of an array, you can change this setting by changing the value of the $[variable. This variable indicates which value is to be used as the subscript for the first array element.

Here is the preceding example, modified to use 1 as the first array element subscript:

```
$[ = 1;
@myarray = ("Here", "is", "a", "list");
$here = $myarray[1];
```

In this case, the subscript 1 now references the first array element. This means that $here is assigned Here, as before.

TIP

> Don't change the value of $[. It is too easy for a casual reader of your program to forget that the subscript 0 no longer references the first element of the array. Besides, using 0 as the subscript for the first element is standard practice in many programming languages, including C and C++.

NOTE

> $[is deprecated in Perl 5.

Multidimensional Associative Arrays and the $; Variable

So far, all the arrays you've seen have been one-dimensional arrays, which are arrays in which each array element is referenced by only one subscript. For example, the following statement uses the subscript foo to access an element of the associative array named %array:

```
$myvar = $array{"foo"};
```

Perl does not support multidimensional associative arrays directly. The following statement is not a legal Perl statement:

```
$myvar = $array{"foo"}{"bar"};
```

However, Perl enables you to simulate a multidimensional associative array using the built-in system variable $;.

Here is an example of a statement that accesses a (simulated) multidimensional array:

```
$myvar = $array{"foo","bar"};
```

When the Perl interpreter sees this statement, it converts it to this:

```
$myvar = $array{"foo" . $; . "bar"};
```

The system variable $; serves as a subscript separator. It automatically replaces any comma that is separating two array subscripts.

Here is another example of two equivalent statements:

```
$myvar = $array{"s1", 4, "hi there"};
$myvar = $array{"s1".$;.4.$;."hi there"};
```

The second statement shows how the value of the $; variable is inserted into the array subscript.

By default, the value of $; is \034 (the Ctrl+\ character). You can define $; to be any value you want. Listing 17.11 is an example of a program that sets $;.

TYPE **Listing 17.11. A program that uses the $; variable.**

```
1:  #!/usr/local/bin/perl
2:
3:  $; = "::";
4:  $array{"hello","there"} = 46;
5:  $test1 = $array{"hello","there"};
6:  $test2 = $array{"hello::there"};
7:  print ("$test1 $test2\n");
```

OUTPUT
```
$ program17_11
46 46
$
```

ANALYSIS Line 3 sets $; to the string ::. As a consequence, the subscript "hello","there" in lines 4 and 5 is really hello::there because the Perl interpreter replaces the comma with the value of $;.

Line 7 shows that both "hello","there" and hello::there refer to the same element of the associative array.

WARNING

If you set $;, be careful not to set it to a character that you are actually using in a subscript. For example, if you set $; to ::, the following statements reference the same element of the array:

```
$array{"a::b", "c"} = 1;
$array{"a", "b::c"} = 2;
```

In each case, the Perl interpreter replaces the comma with ::, producing the subscript a::b::c.

The Word-Break Specifier: $:

On Day 11 you learned how to format your output using print formats and the write statement. Each print format contains one or more value fields that specify how output is to appear on the page.

If a value field in a print format begins with the ^ character, the Perl interpreter puts a word in the value field only if there is room enough for the entire word. For example, in the following program (a duplicate of Listing 11.9),

```
1:  #!/usr/local/bin/perl
2:
3:  $string = "Here\nis an unbalanced line of\ntext.\n";
4:  $~ = "OUTLINE";
5:  write;
6:
7:  format OUTLINE =
8:  ^<<<<<<<<<<<<<<<<<<<<<<<<<<
9:  $string
10: .
```

the call to write uses the OUTLINE print format to write the following to the screen:

```
Here is an unbalanced line
```

Note that the word of is not printed because it cannot fit into the OUTLINE value field.

To determine whether a word can fit in a value field, the Perl interpreter counts the number of characters between the next character to be formatted and the next word-break character. A *word-break character* is one that denotes either the end of a word or a place where a word can be split into two parts.

By default, the legal word-break characters in Perl are the space character, the newline character, and the — (hyphen) character. The acceptable word break characters are stored in the system variable $:.

To change the list of acceptable word-break characters, change the value of $:. For example, to ensure that all hyphenated words are in the same line of formatted output, define $: as shown here:

```
$: = " \n";
```

Now only the space and newline characters are legal word-break characters.

WARNING

Normally, the tab character is not a word-break character. To allow lines to be broken on tabs, add the tab character to the list specified by the $: variable:

```
$: = " \t\n-";
```

17

The Perl Process ID: $$

The $$ system variable contains the process ID for the Perl interpreter itself. This is also the process ID for your program.

The Current Filename: $ARGV

When you use the <> operator, the Perl interpreter reads input from each file named on the command line. For example, suppose that you are executing the program myprog as shown here:

```
$ myprog test1 test2 test3
```

In myprog, the first occurrence of the <> operator reads from test1. Subsequent occurrences of <> continue reading from test1 until it is exhausted; at this point, <> reads from test2. This process continues until all the input files have been read.

On Day 6, "Reading from and Writing to Files," you learned that the @ARGV array lists the elements of the command line and that the first element of @ARGV is removed when the <> operator reads a line. (@ARGV also is discussed later today.)

When the <> operator reads from a file for the first time, it assigns the name of the file to the $ARGV system variable. This enables you to keep track of what file is currently being read. Listing 17.12 shows how you can use $ARGV.

TYPE **Listing 17.12. A simple file-searching program using $ARGV.**

```
1:  #!/usr/local/bin/perl
2:
3:  print ("Enter the search pattern:\n");
4:  $string = <STDIN>;
5:  chop ($string);
6:  while ($line = <>) {
7:          if ($line =~ /$string/) {
8:                  print ("$ARGV:$line");
9:          }
10: }
```

OUTPUT
```
$ program17_12 file1 file2 file3
Enter the string to search:
the
file1:This line contains the word "the".
$
```

ANALYSIS This program reads each line of the input files supplied on the command line. If a line contains the pattern specified by $string, line 8 prints the name of the file and then the line itself. Note that the pattern in $string can contain special pattern characters.

NOTE

> If <> is reading from the standard input file (which occurs when you have not specified any input files on the command line), $ARGV contains the string — (a single hyphen).

The Write Accumulator: $^A

The $^A variable is used by write to store formatted lines to be printed. The contents of $^A are erased after the line is printed.

This variable is defined only in Perl 5.

The Internal Debugging Value: $^D

The $^D variable displays the current internal debugging value. This variable is defined only when the -D switch has been specified and when your Perl interpreter has been compiled with debugging included.

See your online Perl documentation for more details on debugging Perl. (Unless you are using an experimental version of Perl, you are not likely to need to debug it.)

The System File Flag: $^F

The $^F variable controls whether files are to be treated as system files. Its value is the largest UNIX file descriptor that is treated as a system file.

Normally, only STDIN, STDOUT, and STDERR are treated as system files, and the value assigned to $^F is 2. Unless you are on a UNIX machine, are familiar with file descriptors, and want to do something exotic with them, you are not likely to need to use the $^F system variable.

Controlling File Editing Using $^I

The $^I variable is set to a nonzero value by the Perl interpreter when you specify the -i option (which edits files as they are read by the <> operator).

The following statement turns off the editing of files being read by <>:

```
undef ($^I);
```

When $^I is undefined, the next input file is opened for reading, and the standard output file is no longer changed.

17

Do	Don't

DO open the files for input and output yourself if your program wants to edit some of its input files and not others; this process is easier to follow.

DON'T use $^I if you are reading files using the -n or -p option unless you really know what you are doing, because you are not likely to get the behavior you expect. If -i has modified the default output file, undefining $^I does not automatically set the default output file to STDOUT.

The Format Form-Feed Character: $^L

The $^L variable contains the character or characters written out whenever a print format wants to start a new page. The default value is \f, the form-feed character.

Controlling Debugging: $^P

The $^P variable is used by the Perl debugger. When this variable is set to zero, debugging is turned off.

You normally won't need to use $^P yourself, unless you want to specify that a certain chunk of code does not need to be debugged.

The Program Start Time: $^T

The $^T variable contains the time at which your program began running. This time is in the same format as is returned by the time function: the number of seconds since January 1, 1970.

The following statement sets the file-access and -modification times of the file test1 to the time stored in $^T:

```
utime ($^T, $^T, "test1");
```

For more information on the time and utime functions, refer to Day 12, "Working with the File System."

NOTE

> The time format used by $^T is also the same as that used by the file test operators -A, -C, and -M.

Suppressing Warning Messages: $^W

The $^W system variable controls whether warning messages are to be displayed. Normally, $^W is set to a nonzero value only when the -w option is specified.

You can set $^W to zero to turn off warnings inside your program. This capability is useful if your program contains statements that generate warnings you want to ignore (because you know that your statements are correct). For example:

```
$^W = 0;    # turn off warning messages
# code that generates warnings goes here
$^W = 1;    # turn warning messages back on
```

WARNING

Some warnings are printed before program execution starts (for example, warnings of possible typos). You cannot turn off these warnings by setting $^W to zero.

The $^X Variable

The $^X variable displays the first word of the command line you used to start this program. If you started this program by entering its name, the name of the program appears in $^X. If you used the perl command to start this program, $^X contains perl.

The following statement checks to see whether you started this program with the command perl:

```
if ($^X ne "perl") {
        print ("You did not use the 'perl' command ");
        print ("to start this program.\n");
}
```

Pattern System Variables

The system variables you have seen so far are all defined throughout your program. The following system variables are defined only in the current block of statements you are running. (A *block* of statements is any group of statements enclosed in the brace characters { and }.) These *pattern system variables* are set by the pattern-matching operator and the other operators that use patterns (such as, for example, the substitution operator). Many of these pattern system variables were first introduced on Day 7.

> **TIP**
>
> Even though the pattern system variables are defined only inside a particular block of statements, your programs should not take advantage of that fact. The safest way to use the pattern-matching variables is to assign any variable that you might need to a scalar variable of your own.

Retrieving Matched Subpatterns

When you specify a pattern for the pattern-matching or substitution operator, you can enclose parts of the pattern in parentheses. For example, the following pattern encloses the subpattern \d+ in parentheses. (The parentheses themselves are not part of the pattern.)

```
/(\d+)\./
```

This subpattern matches one or more digits.

After a pattern has been matched, the system variables $1, $2, and so on match the subpatterns enclosed in parentheses. For example, suppose that the following pattern is successfully matched:

```
/(\d+)([a-z]+)/
```

In this case, the match found must consist of one or more digits followed by one or more lowercase letters. After the match has been found, $1 contains the sequence of one or more digits, and $2 contains the sequence of one or more lowercase letters.

Listing 17.13 is an example of a program that uses $1, $2, and $3 to match subpatterns.

Listing 17.13. A program that uses variables containing
TYPE matched subpatterns.

```
 1: #!/usr/local/bin/perl
 2:
 3: while (<>) {
 4:         while (/(-?\d+)\.(\d+)([eE][+-]?\d+)?/g) {
 5:                 print ("integer part $1, decimal part $2");
 6:                 if ($3 ne "") {
 7:                         print (", exponent $3");
 8:                 }
 9:                 print ("\n");
10:         }
11: }
```

```
$ program17_13 file1
integer part 26, decimal part 147, exponent e-02
integer part -8, decimal part 997
$
```

This program reads each input line and searches for floating-point numbers. Line 4 matches if a floating-point number is found. (Line 4 is a `while` statement, not an `if`, to enable the program to detect lines containing more than one floating-point number. The loop starting in line 4 iterates until no more matches are found on the line.)

When a match is found, the first set of parentheses matches the digits before the decimal point; these digits are copied into $1. The second set of parentheses matches the digits after the decimal point; these matched digits are stored in $2. The third set of parentheses matches an optional exponent; if the exponent exists, it is stored in $3.

Line 5 prints the values of $1 and $2 for each match. If $3 is defined, its value is printed by line 7.

Do	Don't

DO use $1, not $0, to retrieve the first matched subpattern. $0 contains the name of the program you are running.

DON'T confuse $1 with \1. \1, \2, and so on are defined only inside a pattern. See Day 7 for more information on \1.

In patterns, parentheses are counted starting from the left. This rule tells the Perl interpreter how to handle nested parentheses:

```
/(\d+(\.)?\d+)/
```

This pattern matches one or more digits optionally containing a decimal point. When this pattern is matched, the outer set of parentheses is considered to be the first set of parentheses; these parentheses contain the entire matched number, which is stored in $1.

The inner set of parentheses is treated as the second set of parentheses because it includes the second left parenthesis seen by the pattern matcher. The variable $2, which contains the subpattern matched by the second set of parentheses, contains . (a period) if a decimal point is matched and the empty string if it is not.

17

Retrieving the Entire Pattern: $&

When a pattern is matched successfully, the matched text string is stored in the system variable $&. This is the only way to retrieve the matched pattern because the pattern matcher returns a true or false value indicating whether the pattern match is successful. (This is not strictly true, because you could enclose the entire pattern in parentheses and then check the value of $1; however, $& is easier to use in this case.) Listing 17.14 is a program that uses $& to count all the digits in a set of input files.

TYPE **Listing 17.14. A program that uses $&.**

```
1:  #!/usr/local/bin/perl
2:
3:  while ($line = <>) {
4:          while ($line =~ /\d/g) {
5:                  $digitcount[$&]++;
6:          }
7:  }
8:  print ("Totals for each digit:\n");
9:  for ($i = 0; $i <= 9; $i++) {
10:         print ("$i: $digitcount[$i]\n");
11: }
```

OUTPUT
```
$ program17_14 file1
Totals for each digit:
0: 11
1: 6
2: 3
3: 1
4: 2
5:
6: 1
7:
8:
9: 1
$
```

ANALYSIS This program reads one line at a time from the files specified on the command line. Line 4 matches each digit in the input line in turn; the matched digit is stored in $&.

Line 5 takes the value of $& and uses it as the subscript for the array @digitcount. This array keeps a count of the number of occurrences of each digit.

When the input files have all been read, lines 9–11 print the totals for each digit.

NOTE   If you need the value of $&, be sure to get it before exiting the while loop or other statement block in which the pattern is matched. (A statement block is exited when the Perl interpreter sees a } character.)

For example, the pattern matched in line 4 cannot be accessed outside of lines 4–6 because this copy of $& is defined only in these lines. (This rule also holds true for all the other pattern system variables defined in today's lesson.)

The best rule to follow is to either use or assign a pattern system variable immediately following the statement that matches the pattern.

Retrieving the Unmatched Text: the $` and $' Variables

When a pattern is matched, the text of the match is stored in the system variable $&. The rest of the string is stored in two other system variables:

☐ The unmatched text preceding the match is stored in the $` variable.

☐ The unmatched text following the match is stored in the $' variable.

For example, if the Perl interpreter searches for the /\d+/ pattern in the string qwerty1234uiop, it matches 1234, which is stored in $&. The substring qwerty, which precedes the match, is stored in $`. The rest of the string, uiop, is stored in $'.

If the beginning of a text string is matched, $` is set to the empty string. Similarly, if the last character in the string is part of the match, $' is set to the empty string.

The $+ Variable

The $+ variable matches the last subpattern enclosed in parentheses. For example, when the following pattern is matched, $+ matches the digits after the decimal point:

`/(\d+)\.(\d+)/`

This variable is useful when the last part of a pattern is the only part you really need to look at.

File System Variables

Several system variables are associated with file variables. One copy of each file system variable is defined for each file that is referenced in your Perl program. Many of these system variables were first introduced on Day 11. The variables mentioned there are redefined here for your convenience.

The Default Print Format: $~

When the write statement sends formatted output to a file, it uses the value of the $~ system variable for that file to determine the print format to use.

When a program starts running, the default value of $~ for each file is the same as the name of the file variable that represents the file. For example, when you write to the file represented by the file variable MYFILE, the default value of $~ is MYFILE. This means that write normally uses the MYFILE print format. (For the standard output file, this default print format is named STDOUT.)

If you want to specify a different print format, change the value of $~ before calling the write function. For example, to use the print format MYFORMAT when writing to the standard output file, use the following code:

```
select (STDOUT);  # making sure you are writing to STDOUT
$~ = "MYFORMAT";
write;
```

This call to write uses MYFORMAT to format its output.

WARNING

Remember that one copy of $~ is defined for each file variable. Therefore, the following code is incorrect:

```
$~ = "MYFORMAT";
select (MYFILE);
write;
```

In this example, the assignment to $~ changes the default print format for whatever the current output file happens to be. This assignment does not affect the default print format for MYFILE because MYFILE is selected after $~ is assigned. To change the default print format for MYFILE, select it first:

```
select (MYFILE);
$~ = "MYFORMAT";
write;
```

This call to write now uses MYFORMAT to write to MYFILE.

17

Specifying Page Length: $=

The $= variable defines the page length (number of lines per page) for a particular output file. $= is normally initialized to 60, which is the value that the Perl interpreter assumes is the page length for every output file. This page length includes the lines left for page headers, and it is the length that works for most printers.

If you are directing a particular output file to a printer with a nonstandard page length, change the value of $= for this file before writing to it:

```
select ("WEIRDLENGTH");
$= = 72;
```

This code sets the page length for the WEIRDLENGTH file to 72.

WARNING

$= is set to 60 by default only if a page header format is defined for the page. If no page header is defined, $= is set to 9999999 because Perl assumes that you want your output to be a continuous stream.

If you want paged output without a page header, define an empty page header for the output file.

Lines Remaining on the Page: $-

The $- variable associated with a particular file variable lists the number of lines left on the current page of that file. Each call to write subtracts the number of lines printed from $-. If write is called when $- is zero, a new page is started. (If $- is greater than zero, but write is printing more lines than the value of $-, write starts a new page in the middle of its printing operation.)

When a new page is started, the initial value of $- is the value stored in $=, which is the number of lines on the page.

The program in Listing 17.15 displays the value of $-.

TYPE   **Listing 17.15. A program that displays $-.**

```
1:  #!/usr/local/bin/perl
2:
3:  open (OUTFILE, ">outfile");
4:  select ("OUTFILE");
5:  write;
```

17

```
 6:  print STDOUT ("lines to go before write: $-\n");
 7:  write;
 8:  print STDOUT ("lines to go after write: $-\n");
 9:  format OUTFILE =
10:   This is a test.
11:  .
12:  format OUTFILE_TOP =
13:  This is a test.
14:  .
```

OUTPUT
```
$ program17_15
lines to go before write: 58
lines to go after write: 57
$
```

ANALYSIS Line 3 opens the output file outfile and associates the file variable OUTFILE with this file. Line 4 then calls select, which sets the default output file to OUTFILE.

Line 5 calls write, which starts a new page. Line 6 then sends the value of $- to the standard output file, STDOUT, by specifying STDOUT in the call to print. Note that the copy of $- printed is the copy associated with OUTFILE, not STDOUT, because OUTFILE is currently the default output file.

Line 7 calls write, which sends a line of output to OUTFILE and decreases the value of $- by one. Line 8 prints this new value of $-.

NOTE

> If you want to force your next output to appear at the beginning of a new page, you can set $- to zero yourself before calling write.
>
> When a file is opened, the copy of $- for this file is given the initial value of zero. This technique ensures that the first call to write always starts a page (and generates the header for the page).

The Page Header Print Format: $^

When write starts a new page, you can specify the page header that is to appear on the page. To do this, define a page header print format for the output file to which the page is to be sent.

The system variable $^ contains the name of the print format to be used for printing page headers. If this format is defined, page headers are printed; if it does not exist, no page headers are printed.

By default, the copy of $^ for a particular file is set equal to the name of the file variable plus the string _TOP. For example, for the file represented by the file variable MYFILE, $^ is given an initial value of MYFILE_TOP.

To change the page header print format for a particular file, set the default output file by calling select, and then set $^ to the print format you want to use. For example:

```
select (MYFILE);
$^ = "MYHEADER";
```

This code changes the default output file to MYFILE and then changes the page header print format for MYFILE to MYHEADER. As always, you must remember to select the file before changing $^ because each file has its own copy of $^.

Buffering Output: $¦

When you send output to a file using print or write, the operating system might not write it right away. Some systems first send the output to a special array known as a *buffer*; when the buffer becomes full, it is written all at once. This process of output buffering is usually a more efficient way to write data.

In some circumstances, you might want to send output straight to your output file without using an intervening buffer. (For example, two processes might be sending output to the standard output file at the same time.)

The $¦ system variable indicates whether a particular file is buffered. By default, the Perl interpreter defines a buffer for each output file, and $¦ is set to 0. To eliminate buffering for a particular file, select the file and then set the $¦ variable to a nonzero value. For example, the following code eliminates buffering for the MYFILE output file:

```
select (MYFILE);
$¦ = 1;
```

These statements set MYFILE as the default output file and then turn off buffering for it.

WARNING

If you want to eliminate buffering for a particular file, you must set $¦ before writing to the file for the first time because the operating system creates the buffer when it performs the first write operation.

17

The Current Page Number: $%

Each output file opened by a Perl program has a copy of the $% variable associated with it. This variable stores the current page number. When write starts a new page, it adds one to the value of $%. Each copy of $% is initialized to 0, which ensures that $% is set to 1 when the first page is printed. $% often is displayed by page header print formats.

Array System Variables

The system variables you've seen so far have all been scalar variables. The following sections describe the array variables that are automatically defined for use in Perl programs. All of these variables, except for the @_ variable, are global variables: their value is the same throughout a program.

The @_ Variable

The @_ variable, which is defined inside each subroutine, is a list of all the arguments passed to the subroutine.

For example, suppose that the subroutine my_sub is called as shown here:

```
&my_sub("hello", 46, $var);
```

The values hello and 46, plus the value stored in $var, are combined into a three-element list. Inside my_sub, this list is stored in @_.

In a subroutine, the @_ array can be referenced or modified, just as with any other array variable. Most subroutines, however, assign @_ to locally defined scalar variables using the local function:

```
sub my_sub {
        local ($arg1, $arg2, $arg3) = @_;
        # more stuff goes here
}
```

Here, the local statement defines three local variables, $arg1, $arg2, and $arg3. $arg1 is assigned the first element of the list stored in @_, $arg2 is assigned the second, and $arg3 is assigned the third.

For more information on subroutines, refer to Day 9, "Using Subroutines."

NOTE If the shift function is called inside a subroutine with no argument specified, the @_ variable is assumed, and its first element is removed.

17

The @ARGV **Variable**

When you run a Perl program, you can specify values that are to be passed to the program by including them on the command line. For example, the following command calls the Perl program myprog and passes it the values hello and 46:

```
$ myprog "hello" 46
```

Inside the Perl program, these values are stored in a special built-in array named @ARGV. In this example, @ARGV contains the list ("hello", 46).

Here is a simple statement that prints the values passed on the command line:

```
print ("@ARGV\n");
```

The @ARGV array also is associated with the <> operator. This operator treats the elements in @ARGV as filenames; each file named in @ARGV is opened and read in turn. Refer to Day 6 for a description of the <> operator.

NOTE

If the shift function is called in the main body of a program (outside a subroutine) and no arguments are passed with it, the Perl interpreter assumes that the @ARGV array is to have its first element removed.

The following loop assigns each element of @ARGV, in turn, to the variable $var:

```
while ($var = shift) {
        # stuff
}
```

The @F **Variable**

In Perl, if you specify the -n or -p option, you can also supply the -a option. This option tells the Perl interpreter to break each input line into individual words (throwing away all tabs and spaces). These words are stored in the built-in array variable @F. After an input line has been (automatically) read, the @F array variable behaves like any other array variable.

For more information on the -a, -n, or -p options, refer to Day 16, "Command-Line Options."

NOTE

> When the -a option is specified and an input line is broken into words, the original input line can still be accessed because it is stored in the $_ system variable.

The @INC Variable

The @INC array variable contains a list of directories to be searched for files requested by the require function. This list consists of the following items, in order from first to last:

- ☐ The directories specified by the -I option
- ☐ The Perl library directory, which is normally /usr/local/bin/perl
- ☐ The current working directory (represented by the . character)

Like any array variable, @INC can be added to or modified.

For more information on the require function, refer to Day 19.

The %INC Variable

The built-in associative array %INC lists the files requested by the require function that have already been found.

When require finds a file, the associative array element $INC{file} is defined, in which file is the name of the file. The value of this associative array element is the location of the actual file.

When require requests a file, the Perl interpreter first looks to see whether an associative array element has already been created for this file. This action ensures that the interpreter does not try to include the same code twice.

The %ENV Variable

The %ENV associative array lists the environment variables defined for this program and their values. The environment variables are the array subscripts, and the values of the variables are the values of the array elements.

For example, the following statement assigns the value of the environment variable TERM to the scalar variable $term:

```
$term = $ENV{"TERM"};
```

The %SIG Variable

In the UNIX environment, processes can send signals to other processes. These signals can, for example, interrupt a running program, trigger an alarm in the program, or kill off the program.

You can control how your program responds to signals it receives. To do this, modify the %SIG associative array. This array contains one element for each available signal, with the signal name serving as the subscript for the element. For example, the INT (interrupt) signal is represented by the $SIG{"INT"} element.

The value of a particular element of %SIG is the action that is to be performed when the signal is received. By default, the value of an array element is DEFAULT, which tells the program to do what it normally does when it receives this signal.

You can override the default action for some of the signals in two ways: you can tell the program to ignore the signal, or you can define your own signal handler. (Some signals, such as KILL, cannot be overridden.)

To tell the program to ignore a particular type of signal, set the value of the associative array element for this signal to IGNORE. For example, the following statement indicates that the program is to ignore any INT signals it receives:

```
$SIG{"INT"} = "IGNORE";
```

If you assign any value other than DEFAULT or IGNORE to a signal array element, this value is assumed to be the name of a function that is to be executed when this signal is received. For example, the following statement tells the program to jump to the subroutine named interrupt when it receives an INT signal:

```
$SIG{"INT"} = "interrupt";
```

Subroutines that can be jumped to when a signal is received are called *interrupt handlers*, because signals interrupt normal program execution. Listing 17.16 is an example of a program that defines an interrupt handler.

TYPE **Listing 17.16. A program containing an interrupt handler.**

```
1:  #!/usr/local/bin/perl
2:
3:  $SIG{"INT"} = "wakeup";
4:  sleep();
5:
6:  sub wakeup {
7:          print ("I have woken up!\n");
8:          exit();
9:  }
```

OUTPUT

```
$ program17_16
I have woken up!
$
```

ANALYSIS Line 3 tells the Perl interpreter that the program is to jump to the wakeup subroutine when it receives the INT signal. Line 4 tells the program to go to sleep. Because no argument is passed to sleep, the program will sleep until a signal wakes it up.

To wake up the process, get the process ID using the ps command, and then send an INT signal to the process using the kill command. (See the manual page for kill, and the related documentation for signal handling, to see how to perform this task in your environment.)

When the program receives the INT signal, it executes the wakeup subroutine. This subroutine prints the following message and then exits:

```
I have woken up!
```

If desired, you can use the same subroutine to handle more than one signal. The signal actually sent is passed as an argument to the called subroutine, which ensures that your subroutine can determine which signal triggered it:

```perl
sub interrupt {
        local ($signal) = @_;

        print ("Interrupted by the $signal signal.\n");
}
```

If a subroutine exits normally, the program returns to where it was executing when it was interrupted. If a subroutine calls exit or die, the program execution is terminated.

NOTE When a program continues executing after being interrupted, the element of %SIG corresponding to the received signal is reset to DEFAULT. To ensure that repeated signals are trapped by your interrupt handler, redefine the appropriate element of %SIG.

Built-In File Variables

Perl provides several built-in file variables, most of which you have previously seen. The only file variables that have not yet been discussed are DATA and _ (underscore). The others are briefly described here for the sake of completeness.

STDIN, STDOUT, **and** STDERR

The file variable STDIN is, by default, associated with the standard input file. Using STDIN with the <> operator, as in <STDIN>, normally reads data from your keyboard. If your shell has used < or some equivalent redirection operator to specify input from a file, <STDIN> reads from that file.

The file variable STDOUT normally writes to the standard output file, which is usually directed to your screen. If your shell has used > or the equivalent to redirect standard output to a file, writing to STDOUT sends output to that file.

STDERR represents the standard error file, which is almost always directed to your screen. Writing to STDERR ensures that you see error messages even when you have redirected the standard output file.

You can associate STDIN, STDOUT, or STDERR with some other file using open:

```
open (STDIN, "myinputfile");
open (STDOUT, "myoutputfile");
open (STDERR, "myerrorfile");
```

Opening a file and associating it with STDIN overrides the default value of STDIN, which means that you can no longer read from the standard input file. Similarly, opening a file and associating it with STDOUT or STDERR means that writing to that particular file variable no longer sends output to the screen.

To associate a file variable with the standard input file after you have redirected STDIN, specify a filename of −:

```
open (MYSTDIN, "-");
```

To associate a file variable with the standard output file, specify a filename of >−:

```
open (MYSTDOUT, ">-");
```

You can, of course, specify STDIN with − or STDOUT with >− to restore the original values of these file variables.

ARGV

ARGV is a special file variable that is associated with the current input file being read by the <> operator. For example, consider the following statement:

```
$line = <>;
```

This statement reads from the current input file. Because ARGV represents the current input file, the preceding statement is equivalent to this:

```
$line = <ARGV>;
```

You normally will not need to access ARGV yourself except via the <> operator.

DATA

The DATA file variable is used with the __END__ special value, which can be used to indicate the end of a program. Reading from DATA reads the line after __END__, which enables you to include a program and its data in the same file.

Listing 17.17 is an example of a program that reads from DATA.

 Listing 17.17. An example of the DATA file variable.

```
1: #!/usr/local/bin/perl
2:
3: $line = <DATA>;
4: print ("$line");
5: __END__
6: This is my line of data.
```

OUTPUT
```
$ program17_17
This is my line of data.
$
```

ANALYSIS The __END__ value in line 5 indicates the end of the program. When line 3 reads from the DATA file variable, the first line after __END__ is read in and is assigned to $line. (Subsequent requests for input from DATA read successive lines, if any exist.) Line 6 then prints this input line.

NOTE For more information on __END__ and methods of indicating the end of the program, refer to Day 20, "Miscellaneous Features of Perl."

The Underscore File Variable

The _ (underscore) file variable represents the file specified by the last call to either the stat function or a file test operator. For example:

```
$readable = -r "/u/jqpublic/myfile";
$writeable = -w _;
```

Here, the _ file variable used in the second statement refers to /u/jqpublic/myfile because this is the filename that was passed to -r.

You can use _ anywhere that a file variable can be used, provided that the file has been opened appropriately:

```
if (-T $myoutfile) {
        print _ ("here is my output\n");
}
```

Here, the file whose name is stored in $myoutfile is associated with _ because this name was passed to -T (which tests whether the file is a text file). The call to print writes output to this file.

The main benefit of _ is that it saves time when you are using several file-test operators at once:

```
if (-r "myfile" || -w _ || -x _) {
        print ("I can read, write, or execute myfile.\n");
}
```

Using _ rather than myfile saves time because file test operators normally call the UNIX system function stat. If you specify _, the Perl interpreter is told to use the results of the preceding call to the UNIX stat function and to not bother calling it again.

Specifying System Variable Names as Words

As you have seen, the system variables defined by Perl normally consist of a $, @ or % followed by a single non-alphanumeric character. This ensures that you cannot define a variable whose name is identical to that of a Perl system variable.

If you find Perl system variable names difficult to remember or type, Perl 5 provides an alternative for most of them. If you add the statement

```
use English;
```

at the top of your program, Perl defines alternative variable names that more closely resemble English words. This makes it easier to understand what your program is doing. Table 17.1 lists these alternative variable names.

Table 17.1. Alternative names for Perl system variables.

Variable	Alternative name(s)
$_	$ARG
$0	$PROGRAM_NAME

Variable	Alternative name(s)
$<	$REAL_USER_ID or $UID
$>	$EFFECTIVE_USER_ID or $EUID
$(	$REAL_GROUP_ID or $GID
$)	$EFFECTIVE_GROUP_ID or $EGID
$]	$PERL_VERSION
$/	$INPUT_RECORD_SEPARATOR or $RS
$\	$OUTPUT_RECORD_SEPARATOR or $ORS
$,	$OUTPUT_FIELD_SEPARATOR or $OFS
$"	$LIST_SEPARATOR
$#	$OFMT
$@	$EVAL_ERROR
$?	$CHILD_ERROR
$!	$OS_ERROR or $ERRNO
$.	$INPUT_LINE_NUMBER or $NR
$*	$MULTILINE_MATCHING
$[	none (deprecated in Perl 5)
$;	$SUBSCRIPT_SEPARATOR or $SUBSEP
$:	$FORMAT_LINE_BREAK_CHARACTERS
$$	$PROCESS_ID or $PID
$^A	$ACCUMULATOR
$^D	$DEBUGGING
$^F	$SYSTEM_FD_MAX
$^I	$INPLACE_EDIT
$^L	$FORMAT_FORMFEED
$^P	$PERLDB
$^T	$BASETIME
$^W	$WARNING
$^X	$EXECUTABLE_NAME
$&	$MATCH
$'	$PREMATCH
$'	$POSTMATCH

17

continues

Table 17.1. continued

Variable	Alternative name(s)
$+	$LAST_PAREN_MATCH
$~	$FORMAT_NAME
$=	$FORMAT_LINES_PER_PAGE
$-	$FORMAT_LINES_LEFT
$^	$FORMAT_TOP_NAME
$¦	$OUTPUT_AUTOFLUSH
$%	$FORMAT_PAGE_NUMBER

Summary

Today you learned about the built-in system variables available within every Perl program. These system variables are divided into five groups:

☐ Global scalar variables, which are defined everywhere in the program and contain a single scalar value

☐ Pattern system variables, which are defined immediately after a pattern-matching or substitution operation has been performed

☐ File system variables, which are defined for each input or output file accessible from the program

☐ Array system variables, each of which contains a list

☐ Built-in file variables, which are associated with files that are automatically open or automatically available

You also learned how to specify English-language equivalents for Perl system variables.

Q&A

Q Why do some system variables use special characters rather than letters in their names?

A To distinguish them from variables that you define and to ensure that the reset function (described in the next chapter) cannot affect them.

Q Why do some functions use $_ as the default, whereas others do not?

A The functions that use $_ as the default are those that are likely to appear in Perl programs specified on the command line using the -e option.

Q What is the current line number when $. is used with the <> operator?

A Effectively, the <> operator treats its input files as if they are a single file. This
means that $. contains the total number of lines seen, not the line number of the
current input file. (If you want $. to contain the line number of the current file, set
$. to zero each time eof returns true.)

Q Are pattern system variables local or global?

A Each pattern system variable is defined only in the current subroutine or block of
statements.

Q Why does Perl define both the $" and the $, system variables?

A Some programs like to treat the following statements differently:

```
print ("@array");
  print (@array);
```

(In fact, by default, the first statement puts a space between each pair of elements
in the array, and the second does not.) The $" and $, variables handle these two
separate cases.

17

Workshop

The Workshop provides quiz questions to help you solidify your understanding of the
material covered, and exercises to provide you with experience in using what you've learned.

Quiz

1. List the functions and operators that use $_ by default.
2. What do the following variables contain?

    a. $=

    b. $/

    c. $?

    d. $!

    e. @_

3. Explain the differences between ARGV, $ARGV, and @ARGV.
4. Explain the difference between @INC and %INC.
5. Explain the difference between $0 and $1.

Exercises

1. Write a program that reads lines of input, replaces multiple blanks and tabs with a single space, converts all uppercase letters to lowercase, and prints the resulting lines. Use no explicit variable names in this program.

2. Write a program that uses $' and $_ to remove all extra spaces from input lines.

3. Write a program that prints the directories in your PATH environment variable, one per line.

4. Write a program that prints numbers, starting with 1 and continuing until interrupted by an INT signal.

5. Write a program whose data consists of one or more numbers per input line. Put the input lines in the program file itself. Add the numbers and print their total.

6. **BUG BUSTER:** What is wrong with the following statement?

```
if ($line =~ /abc/) {
        $' =~ s/ +/ /;
}
```

Day **18**

References in Perl 5

by Kamran Husain

Today's lesson describes the use of Perl references and the concept of pointers. Today's lesson also shows you how to use references to create complex data structures, pass pointers around, and work with subroutines. You learn the following topics:

☐ Hard and symbolic references

☐ Using references to arrays and scalars

☐ Passing arrays to subroutines by reference

☐ References to subroutines

Introduction to References

A *reference* is simply a pointer to something, such as a Perl variable, array, hash (also known as an associative array), or even a subroutine. The concept of a reference is probably familiar to Pascal or C programmers. A reference is simply an address to a value. How you use that value is up to you as the programmer and what the language lets you get away with. In Perl, you can refer to a pointer as a reference; in fact, you can use the terms pointer and reference interchangeably without any loss of meaning.

References are useful in creating complex data structures in Perl. In fact, you cannot really define any complicated structures in Perl without using references.

The two types of references in Perl 5 are *hard* and *symbolic*. A symbolic reference contains the name of a variable. Symbolic references are useful for creating variable names and addressing them at runtime. Basically, a symbolic link is like the name of a file or a soft link on a UNIX system. Hard references are more like hard links in the file system (that is, merely another path to the same underlying item).

Perl 4 permits only symbolic references, which are difficult to use. For example, in Perl 4, you have to use names to index to an associative array called _main{} of symbol names for a package. Perl 5 now lets you have hard references to data.

Hard references keep track of reference counts. When the reference count becomes zero, Perl automatically frees the item referred to. If that item happens to be a Perl object, the object is *destructed*—freed to the memory pool. Perl is object-oriented in itself because everything in Perl is an object. Packages and modules make it much easier to use objects in Perl.

Hard references are easy to use in Perl as long as you use them as scalars. To use hard references as anything but scalars, you have to explicitly de-reference the variable and tell it how you want it to behave. If this sounds confusing, don't worry; references are covered on Day 19, "Object-Oriented Programming in Perl," to help make this concept clearer.

Using References

In today's lesson, a scalar value refers to a variable such as `$pointer`. The variable `$pointer` contains one data item; whether the item is a number, string, or an address is determined by how you use it.

Any scalar can hold a hard reference, and because arrays and hashes do contain scalars, it follows that you can now easily build complex data structures of different combinations of arrays of arrays, arrays of hashes, hashes of functions, and so on. As long as you understand that you are working only with scalars, you should be able to navigate through the most complex structures with proper dereferencing.

Let's cover some of the basics first before we get too deep into the chapter.

To use the value of `$pointer` as the pointer to an array, you reference the items in the array as `@$pointer`. This notation of "`@$pointer`" roughly translates to "take the address in `$pointer` and then use it as an array." Similarly for hashes, you would use `%$pointer` as the reference to the first element in the hash.

Because there are several ways to construct references, you can have references to just about anything, such as arrays, scalar variables, subroutines, file handles, and, yes—to the delight of C programmers—even other references. Perl gives you the power to write enough complicated code to hang yourself.

Now look at some of the ways that you can create and use references in Perl.

Using the Backslash Operator

Using the backslash operator is analogous to using the ampersand (&) operator in C to pass the address of an operator. Usually, you use the backslash operator to create a second, new reference to a variable. The following code shows how to create a reference to a scalar variable:

```
$variable = 22;
$pointer = \$variable;
$ice = "jello"
$iceptr = \$ice;
```

$pointer points to the location that contains the value of $variable. The pointer $iceptr points to "jello". Even if the original reference $variable gets destroyed, you can still access the value from the $pointer reference. There is a hard reference at work here, so you will have to get rid of both $pointer and $variable for the space in which 22 is allocated to be freed back to the memory pool.

In the preceding code, the variable $pointer contains the address of $variable, not the value itself. To get the value, you have to de-reference $pointer with two $$. The following sample script shows how this works:

```
#!/usr/bin/perl

$value = 10;

$pointer = \$value;

printf "\n Pointer Address $pointer of  $value \n";

printf "\n What Pointer *($pointer) points to $$pointer\n";
```

The $value in the script is set to 10. The $pointer is set to point to the address of $value. The two printf statements show how the value of the variable is referenced. If you run the script shown, you see something very close to the following output:

```
Pointer Address SCALAR(0x806c520) of  10

What Pointer *(SCALAR(0x806c520)) points to 10
```

The address in the output from your script will probably be different from what's shown. However, you can see that $pointer gave the address and $$pointer gave the value of the scalar that $variable points to.

18

Pay attention to how the address is shown in the pointer variable. The word SCALAR is followed by a long hexadecimal number. The word SCALAR tells you that the address points to a scalar variable. The number following SCALAR is the address where the actual value of the scalar variable is kept.

NOTE

A pointer is an address. The data at that address is referred to by a pointer. If the pointer happens to point to an invalid address, you can get bad data. Generally, Perl will simply return a NULL value, but you should not rely on this, and should program to initialize all your pointers to refer to valid data items.

References and Arrays

Perhaps the most important point you must remember about Perl is that all Perl @ARRAYs and %HASHes are always one-dimensional. As such, the arrays and hashes hold scalar values only and do not directly contain other arrays or complex data structures. A member of an array is either a number or a reference (including strings).

You can use the backslash operator on arrays and hashes just as you would for scalar variables. You would use something like Listing 18.1 for arrays.

TYPE   **Listing 18.1. Using the backslash operator on arrays.**

```
1   #!/usr/bin/perl
2   #
3   # Using Array references
4   #
5   $pointer = \@ARGV;
6   printf "\n Pointer Address of ARGV = $pointer\n";
7   $i = scalar(@$pointer);
8   printf "\n Number of arguments : $i \n";
9   $i = 0;
10  foreach (@$pointer) {
11      printf "$i : $$pointer[$i++]; \n";
12      }
```

18

```
$ test 1 2 3 4

Pointer Address of ARGV = ARRAY(0x806c378)

Number of arguments : 4
0 : 1;
1 : 2;
2 : 3;
3 : 4;
```

Examine the lines that pertain to references in the shell script shown, which prints the contents of the input argument array @ARGV. Line 5 is where the reference $pointer is set to point to the array @ARGV. Line 6 simply prints the address of ARGV. You probably will never have to use the address of ARGV, but had you been using another array, this is a quick way to get to the address of the first element of the array.

NOTE

> Pointers are referred to as references, and vice versa.

The $pointer returns the address of the first element of an array. In Listing 18.1, the array happened to be @ARGV. A pointer to an array should sound familiar to C programmers because a reference to a one-dimensional array is simply a pointer to the first element of the array.

Line 7 calls the function scalar() (not to be confused with the type of variable scalar) to get the count of the number of elements in an array. The parameter passed in could be @ARGV, but with the pointer $pointer, you must specify the type of parameter that is expected by the scalar() function. Therefore, you specify the type of parameter as an array by using @$pointer.

The type of $pointer in this case is a pointer to the array whose number of elements you must return from the scalar() function. The call to the function has @$pointer as the passed parameter. The $pointer gives the address of the first element, and the @ sign forces the passing of the address of the first element as an array reference.

Line 10 contains the same reference to the array that line 7 contains. Line 11 lists all the elements of the array using the $$pointer[$i] item. How do you interpret this? The $pointer points to the first element in the array. The program then gets the ($i - 1)-th item in the array ($pointer[$i++]) and increments $i. Finally, the value at $$pointer[$i] is returned as a scalar. Because the autoincrement operator is low on the operator precedence priority list, $i is incremented last of all.

18

You can also use the backslash operator with associative arrays. The idea is the same—you are substituting the $pointer for all references to the name of the associative array. The number following the word ARRAY in the pointer address of ARGV in the previous example is the address of ARGV. The address itself won't do you any good, because most programs do not need this information, but just realize that references to arrays and scalars are displayed with the type that they happen to be pointing to.

For pointers to functions, the address is printed with the word CODE, and for a hash, it is printed as HASH. See Listing 18.2 for an example of how to print out an address to a hash.

TYPE   **Listing 18.2. Using references to a hash.**

```perl
#!/usr/bin/perl
1#
2 # Using Associative Array references
3 #
4 %month = (
5      '01', 'Jan',
6      '02', 'Feb',
7      '03', 'Mar',
8      '04', 'Apr',
9      '05', 'May',
10      '06', 'Jun',
11      '07', 'Jul',
12      '08', 'Aug',
13      '09', 'Sep',
14      '10', 'Oct',
15      '11', 'Nov',
16      '12', 'Dec',
17      );
18
19 $pointer = \%month;
20
21 printf "\n Address of hash = $pointer\n ";
22
23 #
24 # The following lines would be used to print out the
25 # contents of the associative array if %month was used.
26 #
27 # foreach $i (sort keys %month) {
28 # printf "\n $i $$pointer{$i} ";
29 # }
30
31 #
32 # The reference to the associative array via $pointer
33 #
34 foreach $i (sort keys %$pointer) {
35      printf "$i is $$pointer{$i} \n";
36 }
```

OUTPUT

```
$ mth

Address of hash = HASH(0x806c52c)

01 is Jan
02 is Feb
03 is Mar
04 is Apr
05 is May
06 is Jun
07 is Jul
08 is Aug
09 is Sep
10 is Oct
11 is Nov
12 is Dec
```

ANALYSIS The reference to the associative array is made with the code in line 19, $pointer = \%month;. As with ordinary arrays, the references to the elements of the array are made with the $$pointer{$index} construct. Of course, because the array is really a hash, the $index is the key into the hash and not a number. See lines 34 and 35 to see how elements in the array are being referenced.

You don't have to construct associative arrays using the comma operator. You can use the => operator instead. In the later Perl module and sample code in this chapter, you will see the => operator, which is the same as the comma operator. Using => makes the code a bit easier to read. See Listing 18.3 for a sample usage of the => operator.

18

TYPE **Listing 18.3. Using the => operator.**

```perl
1 #!/usr/bin/perl
2 #
3 # Using Array references
4 #
5 %weekday = (
6     '01' => 'Mon',
7     '02' => 'Tue',
8     '03' => 'Wed',
9     '04' => 'Thu',
10     '05' => 'Fri',
11     '06' => 'Sat',
12     '07' => 'Sun',
13     );
14 $pointer = \%weekday;
15 $i = '05';
16 printf "\n ================= start test ================= \n";
17 #
18 # These next two lines should show an output
19 #
20     printf '$$pointer{$i} is ';
```

continues

Listing 18.3. continued

```
21    printf "$$pointer{$i} \n";
22    printf '${$pointer}{$i} is ';
23    printf "${$pointer}{$i} \n";
24    printf '$pointer->{$i} is ';
25
26    printf "$pointer->{$i}\n";
27 #
28 # These next two lines should not show anything
29 #
30    printf '${$pointer{$i}} is ';
31    printf "${$pointer{$i}} \n";
32    printf '${$pointer->{$i}} is ';
33    printf "${$pointer->{$i}}";
34 printf "\n ================== end of test ================= \n";
35
```

OUTPUT

```
================== start test =================
$$pointer{$i} is Fri
${$pointer}{$i} is Fri
$pointer->{$i} is Fri
${$pointer{$i}} is
${$pointer->{$i}} is
================== end of test =================
```

ANALYSIS As you can see, the first two lines provided the expected output. The first reference is used in the same way as references to regular arrays. The second line uses the `${pointer}` and then indexes using `{$i}`, and the leftmost `$` de-references (gets) the value at the location reached after the indexing. See Lines 20 through 23.

NOTE

When in doubt, print it out. Always use the print statements in Perl to print out values of suspect code. This way you can be sure of how Perl is interpreting your code. Print statements are a cheap tool to use for learning how the Perl interpreter works.

Then, two lines of the output didn't work as expected. In the third line, `$pointer{$i}` tries to reference an array where there is no first element. Because the first element does not point to a valid string, nothing is printed. Nothing is printed in the fourth line of the output for the same reason. See lines 30 through 33.

Multidimensional Arrays

You create a reference to an array through the statement @array = list. You use square brackets to create a reference to a complex anonymous array. Consider the following statement, which sets the parameters for a three-dimensional drawing program:

```
$line = ['solid', 'black', ['1','2','3'] , ['4', '5', '6']];
```

The preceding statement constructs an array of four elements. The array is referred to by the scalar $line. The first two elements are scalars, indicating the type and color of the line to draw. The next two elements are references to anonymous arrays and contain the starting and ending points of the line.

To get to the elements of the inner array elements, you can use the following multidimensional syntax:

`$arrayReference->[$index]`	single-dimensional array
`$arrayReference->[$index1][$index2]`	two-dimensional array
`$arrayReference->[$index1][$index2][$index3]`	three-dimensional array

You can create as complex a structure as your sanity, design practices, and computer memory allow. Be kind to the person who might have to manage your code—please keep it as simple as possible. On the other hand, if you are just trying to impress someone with your coding ability, Perl gives you a lot of opportunity to mystify yourself and improve your social life.

18

> **TIP**
>
> When you have more than three dimensions for any array, consider using a different data structure to simplify the code.

Let's see how creating arrays within arrays works in practice. See Listing 18.4 to see how to print out the information pointed at by the $list reference.

TYPE   **Listing 18.4. Using multi-dimensional array references.**

```
1   #!/usr/bin/perl
2   #
3   # Using Multi-dimensional Array references
4   #
```

continues

Listing 18.4. continued

```
5    $line = ['solid', 'black', ['1','2','3'] , ['4', '5', '6']];
6    print "\$line->[0] = $line->[0] \n";
7    print "\$line->[1] = $line->[1] \n";
8    print "\$line->[2][0] = $line->[2][0] \n";
9    print "\$line->[2][1] = $line->[2][1] \n";
10   print "\$line->[2][2] = $line->[2][2] \n";
11   print "\$line->[3][0] = $line->[3][0] \n";
12   print "\$line->[3][1] = $line->[3][1] \n";
13   print "\$line->[3][2] = $line->[3][2] \n";
14   print "\n"; # The obligatory output beautifier.
```

OUTPUT

```
$line->[0] = solid
$line->[1] = black
$line->[2][0] = 1
$line->[2][1] = 2
$line->[2][2] = 3
$line->[3][0] = 4
$line->[3][1] = 5
$line->[3][2] = 6
```

What about the third dimension for an array? Look at a modified version of the same program but add a new twist to the list just created. See Listing 18.5.

Listing 18.5. Using multi-dimensional array references again.

```
1    #!/usr/bin/perl
2    #
3    # Using Multi-dimensional Array references again
4    #
5    $line = ['solid', 'black', ['1','2','3', ['4', '5', '6']]];
6    print "\$line->[0] = $line->[0] \n";
7    print "\$line->[1] = $line->[1] \n";
8    print "\$line->[2][0] = $line->[2][0] \n";
9    print "\$line->[2][1] = $line->[2][1] \n";
10   print "\$line->[2][2] = $line->[2][2] \n";
11   print "\$line->[2][3][0] = $line->[2][3][0] \n";
12   print "\$line->[2][3][1] = $line->[2][3][1] \n";
13   print "\$line->[2][3][2] = $line->[2][3][2] \n";
14   print "\n";
```

OUTPUT   There is no output for this listing.

ANALYSIS   In this example of an array that's three deep, you must use a reference such as $line ->[2][3][0]. For a C programmer, this is akin to the statement Array_pointer[2][3][0], where the pointer is pointing to what's declared as an array with three indices.

Can you see how easy it is to set up complex structures of arrays within arrays? The examples shown thus far have used only hard-coded numbers as the indices. There is nothing preventing you from using variables instead.

As with array constructors, you can mix and match hashes and arrays to create as complex a structure as you want.

Let's see how these two hashes and arrays can be combined. Listing 18.6 uses the point numbers and coordinates to define a cube.

TYPE **Listing 18.6. Defining a cube.**

```
1   #!/usr/bin/perl
2   #
3   # Using Multi-dimensional Array and Hash references
4   #
5   %cube = (
6       '0', ['0', '0', '0'],
7       '1', ['0', '0', '1'],
8       '2', ['0', '1', '0'],
9       '3', ['0', '1', '1'],
10      '4', ['1', '0', '0'],
11      '5', ['1', '0', '1'],
12      '6', ['1', '1', '0'],
13      '7', ['1', '1', '1']
14      );
15  $pointer = \%cube;
16  print "\n Da Cube \n";
17  foreach $i (sort keys %$pointer) {
18      $list = $$pointer{$i};
19      $x = $list->[0];
20      $y = $list->[1];
21      $z = $list->[2];
22      printf " Point $i =  $x,$y,$z \n";
23  }
```

OUTPUT There is no output for this listing.

ANALYSIS In Listing 18.6, %cube contains point numbers and coordinates in a hash. Each coordinate itself is an array of three numbers. The $list variable is used to get a reference to each coordinate definition with the following statement:

```
$list = $$pointer{$i};
```

After you get the list, you can reference off of it to get to each element in the list with the following statement:

```
$x = $list->[0];
$y = $list->[1];
```

The same result—assigning values to $x, $y, and $z—could be achieved with the following two lines of code:

```
($x,$y,$z) = @$list;
$x = $list->[0];
```

This works because you are de-referencing what $list points to and using it as an array, which in turn is assigned to the list ($x,$y,$z). The $x is still assigned with the -> operator.

When you're working with hashes or arrays, de-referencing by -> is similar to de-referencing by $. When you are accessing individual array elements, you are often faced with writing statements such as the following:

```
$$names[0] = "Kamran";
$names->[0] = "Kamran";
```

Both lines are equivalent. The $names in the first line has been replaced with the -> operator in the second line. In the case of hashes, the two statements that do the same type of referencing are listed as shown in the following code:

```
$$lastnames{"Kamran"} = "Husain";
$lastnames->{"Kamran"} = "Husain";
```

Array references are created automatically when they are first referenced in the left side of an equation. Using a reference such as $array[$i] creates an array into which you can index with $I. Scalars and even multidimensional arrays are created the same way. The following statement creates the contours array if it did not already exist:

```
$contours[$x][$y][$z] = &xlate($mouseX,$mouseY);
```

Arrays in Perl can be created and grown on demand. Referencing them for the first time creates the array. Referencing them again at different indices creates the referenced elements for you.

References to Subroutines

In the same way you reference individual items such as arrays and scalar variables, you can also point to subroutines. This is similar to pointing to a function in C. To construct such a reference, you use the following type of statement:

```
$pointer_to_sub = sub { ... declaration of sub ... } ;
```

Notice the use of the semicolon at the end of the sub declaration. The subroutine pointed to by $pointer_to_sub points to the same function reference even if this statement is placed in a loop. This feature of Perl enables you to declare anonymous sub() functions in a loop without worrying about whether you are chewing up memory by declaring the same function over and over.

To call a subroutine by reference, you must use the following type of reference:

```
&$pointer_to_sub( parameters );
```

This code works because you are de-referencing the $pointer_to_sub and using it with the ampersand (&) as a pointer to a function. The *parameters* portion might or might not be empty depending on how your function is defined.

The code within a sub is simply a declaration created through a previous statement. The code within the sub is not executed immediately, however. It is compiled and set for each use. Consider Listing 18.7.

TYPE **Listing 18.7. References to subroutines.**

```
1 #!/usr/bin/perl
2 sub print_coor{
3     my ($x,$y,$z) = @_;
4     print "$x $y $z \n";
5     return $x;};
6  $k = 1;
7  $j = 2;
8  $m = 4;
9  $this  = print_coor($k,$j,$m);
10 $that  = print_coor(4,5,6);
```

OUTPUT
```
$ test
1 2 3
4 5 6
```

ANALYSIS This output reflects that the assignment of $x, $y, and $z was done when the first declaration of print_coor was encountered as a call. In Listing 18.7, each reference $this and $that points to a different subroutine, the arguments to which were passed at run-time.

Using Subroutine Templates

Subroutines are not limited to returning data types only; they can also return references to other subroutines. The returned subroutines run in the context of the calling routine but are set up in the original call that created them. This behavior is due to the way closure is handled in Perl. *Closure* means that if you define a function in one context, it runs in that particular context where it was first defined. (See a book on object-oriented programming to get more information on closure.)

18

For an example of how closure works, Listing 18.8 shows code that you could use to set up different types of error messages. Such subroutines are useful in creating templates of all error messages.

 TYPE **Listing 18.8. Using closures.**

```perl
#!/usr/bin/perl


sub errorMsg {
        my $lvl = shift;
        #
        # define the subroutine to run when called.
        #
         return sub {

        my $msg = shift;  # Define the error type now.
        print "Err Level $lvl:$msg\n"; }; # print later.
         }
$severe  = errorMsg("Severe");
$fatal = errorMsg("Fatal");
$annoy = errorMsg("Annoying");

&$severe("Divide by zero");
&$fatal("Did you forget to use a semi-colon?");
&$annoy("Uninitialized variable in use");
```

OUTPUT
```
$severe  = errorMsg("Severe");
$fatal   = errorMsg("Fatal");
$annoy   = errorMsg("Annoying");
```

ANALYSIS The subroutine errorMsg declared here uses a local variable called lvl. After this declaration, errorMsg uses $lvl in the subroutine it returns to the caller. The value of $lvl is therefore set in the context when the subroutine errorMsg is first called, even though the keyword my is used. The three calls that follow set up three different $lvl variable values, each in their own context:

```
$severe  = errorMsg("Severe");
$fatal   = errorMsg("Fatal");
$annoy   = errorMsg("Annoying");
```

When the subroutine, errorMsg, returns, the value of $lvl is retained for each context in which $lvl was declared. The $msg value from the referenced call is used, but the value of $lvl remains what was first set in the actual creation of the function.

Sounds confusing? It is. This is primarily the reason you do not see such code in most Perl programs.

Using Subroutines to Work with Multiple Arrays

Using arrays is great for collecting relevant information in one place. Now let's see how we can work with multiple arrays through subroutines. You pass one or more arrays into Perl subroutines by reference. However, you have to keep in mind a few subtle things about using the @_ symbol when you process these arrays in the subroutine. Look at Listing 18.9, which is an example of a subroutine that expects a list of names and a list of phone numbers.

TYPE **Listing 18.9. Passing multiple arrays.**

```
1  #!/usr/bin/perl
2  @names = (mickey, goofy, daffy );
3  @phones = (5551234, 5554321, 666 );
4  $i = 0;
5  sub listem {
6      my (@a,@b) = @_;
7      foreach (@a) {
8          print "a[$i] = ". $a[$i] . " " . "\tb[$i] = " . $b[$i] ."\n";
9          $i++;
10         }
11     }
12 &listem(@names, @phones);
```

OUTPUT
```
a[0] = mickey    b[0] =
a[1] = goofy     b[1] =
a[2] = daffy     b[2] =
a[3] = 5551234   b[3] =
a[4] = 5554321   b[4] =
a[5] = 666       b[5] =
```

ANALYSIS Whoa! What happened to the @b array, and why is the rest of @a just like the array @b? This result occurs because the array @_ of parameters in a subroutine is one—I repeat, only one—long list of parameters. If you pass in fifty arrays, the @_ is one array of all the elements of the fifty arrays concatenated together.

In the subroutine in Listing 18.9, the assignment my (@a, @b) = @_ gets loosely interpreted by your Perl interpreter as, "Let's see, @a is an array, so assign one array from @_ to @a and then assign everything else to @b." Never mind that the @_ is itself an array and will therefore get assigned to @a, leaving nothing to assign to @b.

To illustrate this point, let's change the script to how it appears in Listing 18.10.

TYPE **Listing 18.10. Passing a scalar and an array.**

```perl
#!/usr/bin/perl
@names = (mickey, goofy, daffy );
@phones = (5551234, 5554321, 666 );
$i = 0;
sub listem {
    my ($a,@b) = @_;
    print " \$a is " . $a . "\n";
    foreach (@b) {
        print "b[$i] = $b[$i] \n";
        $i++;
        }
    # ----------------------------------------------
    # Actually, you could write the for loop as
    # foreach (@b) {
    #    print $_ . "\n" ;
    #    }
    # This your secret answer to Quiz question 18.4.
    # ----------------------------------------------
    }

&listem(@names, @phones);
```

OUTPUT

```
$ testArray

 $a is mickey
b[0] = goofy
b[1] = daffy
b[2] = 5551234
b[3] = 5554321
b[4] = 666
```

ANALYSIS Do you see how $a was assigned the first value and then @b was assigned the rest of the values? In order get around this @_ interpretation feature and pass arrays into subroutines, you have to pass arrays in by reference, which you do by modifying the script to look like the following:

```perl
#!/usr/bin/perl

@names = (mickey, goofy, daffy );
@phones = (5551234, 5554321, 666 );
$i = 0;
sub listem {
    my ($a,$b) = @_;
    foreach (@$a) {
        print "a[$i] = " . @$a[$i] . " " . "\tb[$i] = " . @$b[$i] ."\n";
        $i++;
        }
    }

&listem(\@names, \@phones);
```

18

The following major changes were necessary to bring the original script to this point:

- [ ] The local variables for the sub listem are now scalars, not array references. As a result, $a is the first item on the @_ list, and $b is the second item.

- [ ] The local parameters ($a and $b) are used as array references with the statements @$a and @$b, respectively.

- [ ] The call to the subroutine passes the references to the arrays with the backslash, \@names and \@phones, thus passing only two items to the subroutine.

The following output matches what we expected:

```
$ testArray2
a[0] = mickey    b[0] = 5551234
a[1] = goofy     b[1] = 5554321
a[2] = daffy     b[2] = 666
```

Do	Don't

DO pass by reference whenever possible.

DO pass arrays by reference when you are passing more than one array to a subroutine.

DON'T use (@variable)=@_ in a subroutine unless you want to concatenate all the passed parameters into one long array.

18

Pass By Value or By Reference?

When used in a subroutine argument list, scalar variables are always passed by reference. You do not have a choice here. You can, however, modify the values of these variables if you really want to. To access these variables, you can use the @_ array and index each individual element in it using $_[$index], where $index counts from zero up.

Arrays and hashes are different beasts altogether. You can either pass them as references once or pass references to each element in the array. For long arrays, the choice should be fairly obvious—pass the reference to the array only. In either case, you can use the references to modify what you want in the original array.

The @_ mechanism concatenates all the input arrays in a subroutine into one long array. This feature is nice if you do want to process the incoming arrays as one long array. Usually, you want to keep the arrays separate when you process them in a subroutine, and passing by reference is the best way to do that. Hold that thought: Don't use globals.

In short, pass by reference and respect the value of any global variable unless there is a strong compelling reason not to.

References to File Handles

Sometimes, you have to write the same output to different output files. For example, an application programmer might want the output to go to the screen in one instance, the printer in another, and a file in another—or even all three at the same time. Rather than make separate statements for each handle, it would be nice to write something like the following:

```
spitOut(\*STDIN);
spitOut(\*LPHANDLE);
spitOut(\*LOGHANDLE);
```

Notice that the file handle reference is sent with the *FILEHANDLE syntax because you refer to the symbol table in the current package. In the subroutine that handles the output to the file handle, you would have code that looks something like the following:

```
sub spitOut {
    my $fh = shift;
    print $fh "Gee Wilbur, I like this lettuce\n";
}
```

What Does the *variable Operator Do?

In UNIX (and other operating systems), the asterisk is a sort of wildcard operator. In Perl, you can refer to other variables and so on by using the asterisk operator:

```
*iceCream;
```

When used in this manner, the asterisk is also known as a *typeglob*. The asterisk at the beginning of a term can be thought of as a wildcard match for all the mangled names generated internally by Perl.

You can use a typeglob in the same way you use a reference because the de-reference syntax always indicates the kind of reference you want. ${*iceCream} and ${\$iceCream} both indicate the same scalar variable. Basically, *iceCream refers to the entry in the internal _main associative array of all symbol names for the _main package. *kamran really translates to $_main{'kamran'} if you are in the _main package context. If you are in another package, the _packageName{} hash is used.

When evaluated, a typeglob produces a scalar value that represents the first objects of that name. This includes file handles, format specifiers, and subroutines.

Using Symbolic References... Again

Using brackets around references makes constructing strings easier:

```
    $road = ($w)  ? "free":"high";
print "${road}way";
```

The preceding line prints highway or freeway depending on the value of $w. This syntax will be familiar to you if you write make files or shell scripts. In fact, you can use this ${variable} construct outside of double quotes, as in the following example:

```
print ${road};
print ${road} . "way";
print ${ road } . "way";
```

You can also use reserved words in the ${ } brackets. Check out the following lines:

```
$if = "road";
print "\n ${if} way \n";
```

Using reserved words for anything other than their intended purpose, however, is playing with fire. Be imaginative and make up your own variables. You can use reserved words but will have to remember to force interpretation as a reserved word by adding anything that makes it more than a reference. It's generally not a good idea to use a variable called ${while}, because it is confusing to read.

When you work with hashes, you have to create an extra reference to the index. In other words, you cannot use something like this:

```
$clients { \$credit } = "despicable" ;
```

The \$credit variable will be converted to a string and won't be used correctly as an index in the hash. You have to use a two-step procedure such as this:

```
$chist = \@credit;
$x{ $chist } = "despicable";
```

Declaring Variables with Curly Braces

The preceding section brings up an interesting point about curly braces for a use other than indexing into hashes. In Perl, curly braces are usually reserved for delimiting blocks of code. Assume you were returning the passed list by sorting it in reverse order. The passed list is in @_ of the called subroutine, so the following two statements are equivalent:

```
sub backward {
    { reverse sort @_ ; }
    };
```

18

```
sub backward {
    reverse sort @_ ;
    };
```

When preceded by the @ operator, curly braces enable you to set up small blocks of evaluated code.

```
#!/usr/bin/perl


sub average {
    ($a,$b,$c) = @_;
        $x = $a + $b + $c;
        $x2 = $a*$a + $b*$b + $c*$c;
    return ($x/3, $x2/3 ); }

$x = 1;
$y = 34;
$x = 47;

print "The midpt is @{[&average($x,$y,$z)]} \n";
```

This script prints 27 and 1121.6666. In the last line of code with the @{} in the double-quoted string, the contents of the @{} are evaluated as a block of code. The block creates a reference to an anonymous array that contains the results of the call to the subroutine average($x,$y,$z). The array is constructed because of the brackets around the call. As a result, the [] construct returns a reference to an array, which in turn is converted by @{} into a string and inserted into the double-quoted string.

More on Hard Versus Symbolic References

By now, you should be able to see the difference between hard and symbolic links. Let's look at some of the minor details of the two types of links and how these links are handled in Perl.

When you use a symbolic reference that does not exist, Perl creates the variable for you and uses it. For variables that already exist, the value of the variable is substituted for the $variable string. This substitution is a powerful feature of Perl because you can construct variable names from variable names.

Consider the following example:

```
1 $lang = "java";
2 $java = "coffee";
3 print "${lang}\n";
4 print "hot${lang}\n";
5 print "$$lang \n"
```

Look at line 5. The $$lang is first reduced to $java. Then recognizing that $java can also be re-parsed, the value of $java ("coffee") is used.

The value of the scalar produced by $$lang is taken to be the name of a new variable, and the variable at $name is used. The following is the output from this example:

```
java
hotjava
coffee
```

The difference between a hard reference ($lang) and a symbolic reference ($$lang) is how the variable name is derived. With a hard reference, you are referring to a variable's value directly. Either the variable exists in the symbol table for the package you are in (that is, which lexical context you are in), or the variable does not exist. With a symbolic reference, you are using another level of indirection by constructing or deriving a symbol name from an existing variable.

To force only hard references in a program and protect yourself from accidentally creating symbolic references, you can use the module called strict, which forces Perl to do strict type checking. To use this module, place the following statement at the top of your Perl script:

```
use strict 'refs';
```

From this point on, only hard references are allowed for the rest of the script. You place this use strict ... statement within curly braces to limit the type checking to the code block within the braces. For example, in the following code, the type checking would be limited to the code in the subroutine java():

```
sub java {
   use strict "refs";
   #
   # type  checking here.
}
...
# no type checking here.
```

To turn off the strict type checking at any time within a code block, use this statement:

```
no strict 'refs';
```

One last point: Symbolic references cannot be used on variables declared with the my construct because these variables are not kept in any symbol table. Variables declared with the my construct are valid only for the block in which they are created. Variables declared with the local word are visible to all ensuing lower code blocks because they are in a symbol table.

For More Information

In addition to consulting the obvious documents such as the Perl man pages, look at the Perl source code for more information. The 't/op' directory in the Perl source tree has some regression test routines that should definitely get you thinking. A lot of documents and references are available at the Web sites www.perl.com and www.metronet.com.

Summary

The two types of references in Perl 5 are hard and symbolic. Hard links work like hard links in UNIX file systems. You can have more than one hard link to the same item; Perl keeps a reference count for you. This reference count is incremented or decremented as references to the item are created or destroyed. When the count goes to zero, the link and the object it is pointing to are both destroyed. Symbolic links, which are created through the ${} construct, are useful in providing multiple stages of references to objects.

You can have references to scalars, arrays, hashes, subroutines, and even other references. References themselves are scalars and have to be de-referenced to the context before being used. Use @$pointer for an array, %$pointer for a hash, &$pointer for a subroutine, and so on for dereferencing.

Multidimensional arrays are possible using references in arrays and hashes.

Parameters are passed into a subroutine through references. The @_ array is really all the passed parameters concatenated in one long array. To send separate arrays, use the references to the individual items.

Tomorrow's lesson covers Perl objects and references to objects. We have deliberately not covered Perl objects in this chapter because it requires some knowledge of references. References are used to create and refer to objects, constructors, and packages.

Q&A

Q How do I know what type of address a pointer is pointing to?

A The address printed out with the print statement on a reference has a qualifier word in front of it. For example, a reference to a hash has the word HASH followed by an address value, an array has the word ARRAY, and so on.

Q How are multidimensional arrays possible using Perl?

A References in Perl point to scalars only. References to arrays point to the beginning of the array. Arrays can contain references to other arrays, hashes, and so on. The way to create multidimensional arrays in Perl is by using references to references.

Q **What's the best way to pass more than one array into a subroutine?**

A Pass references to the arrays, using the \@*arrayname* for each array passed—as in the following call:

```
mysub(\@one, \@two);
```

Within the subroutine, take each reference off one at a time.

```
my ($a, $b) = @_;
```

Now use @$a and @$b to get to the arrays passed into the subroutines.

Q **Why is *moo more efficient to use than $_main{'moo'}? Is there a difference in usage?**

A Both *moo and $_main{'moo'} mean the same variable (as long as you aren't using a package). *moo is more efficient because the reference is looked up once at compile time, whereas $_main{'moo'} is evaluated at runtime and evaluated each time it is run.

Workshop

The Workshop provides quiz questions to help you solidify your understanding of the material covered and exercises to give you experience in using what you've learned. Try and understand the quiz and exercise answers before you go on to tomorrow's lesson.

Quiz

1. Given that $pointer is a pointer to a hash, what's wrong with the following line of code?

```
$x= ${$pointer->{$i}};
```

2. Why is $b not being set in the following line of code? What do you have to do to make it okay?

```
sub xxx {
    my ($a, $b) = @_;
}
```

3. What's the difference between these two lines of code?

```
printf "$i : $$pointer[$i++]; ";

printf " and $i : $pointer->[$i++]; \n";
```

4. What do the following lines of code print out?

```
$HelpHelpHelp = \\\"Help";
print $$$$HelpHelpHelp;
```

5. What's the use of the `${variable}` construct? How could the following three lines of code be rewritten?

```
$name = ${$scalarref};
draw(@{$coordinates}, $display);
${$months}[0] = "March";
```

Exercises

1. Write a Perl script to print out address types of different variables and complex structures.

2. Write a Perl code fragment that constructs an array of pointers to functions. How would you use it?

   Strong Hint:

```
$foo = sub foo { print "foo\n"; }
$bar = sub bar { print "bar\n"; }
$yuk = sub yuk { print "yuk\n"; }
$huh = sub huh { print "huh\n"; }
@list = ($foo, $bar, $yuk, $huh);
```

3. Explain the difference between hard and symbolic references.

4. Write a Perl subroutine that takes two arrays as arguments and returns the reverse-sorted copy of each array.

5. Modify the following script to print the value of `$this` and `$that`. Are they the same? If not, why not?

```
#!/usr/bin/perl

sub print_coor{
    my ($x,$y,$z) = @_;
    print "$x $y $z \n";
    return $x;};

$k = 1;
$j = 2;
$m = 4;
$this  = print_coor($k,$j,$m);

$that  = print_coor(4,5,6);
```

Day **19**

Object-Oriented Programming in Perl

by Kamran Husain

Today's lesson teaches you how to use the object-oriented programming (OOP) features of Perl as well as how to construct objects in Perl. The discussion also includes inheritance, overriding methods, and data encapsulation.

An Introduction to Modules

A *module* is a Perl package. Objects in Perl are based on references to data items within a package. An *object* in Perl is simply a reference to something that knows which class it belongs to. (References are covered on Day 18, "References in Perl 5.") For more information, you can consult the perlmod and perlobj text files at http://www.metronet.com. These files are the primary source of information on the Internet about Perl modules.

In object-oriented programming with other languages, you declare a class and then create objects of that class. All objects of a particular class behave in a certain way, which is governed by the methods of that class. You can create new classes by defining new ones or by inheriting properties from an existing class.

Programmers already familiar with object-oriented principles will recognize the terminology used here. Perl is, and pretty much always has been, an object-oriented language. In Perl 4, the use of packages provides different symbol tables from which to choose symbol names. Perl 5 changes the syntax a bit and somewhat formalizes the use of objects.

The Three Important Rules

The next three declarations are extremely important to understanding how objects, classes, and methods work in Perl.

- ☐ A *class* is a Perl package. This package for a class provides the methods for objects.
- ☐ A *method* is simply a Perl subroutine. The only catch with writing such methods is that the name of the class is the first argument.
- ☐ An object in Perl is simply a reference to some data item within the class.

The rest of today's lesson covers each of the preceding items in more detail.

Classes in Perl

One rule is important enough to repeat: A Perl class is simply a package. When you see a Perl document that refers to a "class," think "package." Existing Perl 5 syntax enables you to create a class. If you are already a C programmer, you do not have to know a lot of new syntax. What might be a new concept to Perl 4 programmers is the use of the double colon (::) to signify the base and inherited classes.

One of the key features of OOP is inheritance. The inheritance feature offered by Perl, however, is not the same as you might expect from other object-oriented languages. Perl classes inherit methods only; you must use your own mechanisms to implement data inheritance.

Because each class is a package, it has its own name space with its own associative array of symbol names. Each class can therefore use its own independent set of symbol names. As with package references, you can address the variables in a class with the back quote (') operator. Members of a class are addressed as `$class'$member`. In Perl 5, you can use the double colon instead of the ' to get the reference. For example, `$class'member` is the same as `$class::$member`.

Creating a Class

This section covers the requisite steps to take when you create a new class. The example illustrates the semantics in the creation of a simple class called Cocoa, which is used for printing the required parts of a source code file for a simple Java application. You will not become a Java expert, nor will this package require you to have any experience in Java; the focus is the concept of creating a class. The example could have just as easily used a phone book application, but how many similar examples have you already seen in books?

NOTE

I am currently still developing the package Java.pm. It's named Cocoa.pm in development because it does not have the high caffeine content of a full-featured, or even mildly useful, Java.pm package. Perhaps after reading today's lesson you will be able to contribute to the Java.pm Perl package; if so, send e-mail to khusain@ikra.com.

Time now for a shameless plug for *Perl Unleashed*, which is also by Sams Publishing, due the summer of 1996. It will contain gobs of information about writing and using classes and packages—and track the initial development stages of the Java.pm package. (Hmmm. Maybe the package should be called Bean.pm in its early stages.)

First of all, create a package file called Cocoa.pm. (The .pm extension, which is the default extension for packages, stands for Perl module.) A module is a package, and a package is a class for all practical purposes. Before you do anything else, place a 1; in the file. As you add more lines to the package file, make sure you keep the 1; as the last line. The following code shows the basic structure of the file:

```
package Cocoa;
#
# Put "require" statements in for all required,imported packages
#

#
# Just add code here
#

1;   # terminate the package with the required 1;
```

This requirement is important: Don't forget to always keep the 1; line as the last of the package file. This statement is required for all packages in Perl. If you forget this statement, your package will not be processed by Perl.

Congratulations; you have just created your first package file. Now you are ready to add your methods to this package and make it a class. The first method you should add is the new()

method, which must be called whenever you create a new object. The new() method is the constructor for the object.

Blessing a Constructor

A *constructor* is a Perl subroutine in a class that returns a reference to something that has the class name attached to it. Connecting a class name with a reference is referred to as "blessing" an object because the function to establish the connection is called bless.

The following code segment shows the syntax for the bless function:

```
bless YeReference [,classname]
```

YeReference is the reference to the object being blessed. The classname is optional and specifies the name of the package from which the object will get methods. If the classname is not specified, the name of the current package is used instead.

The way to create a constructor in Perl is to return a reference to an internal structure that has been blessed into this Cocoa class. Listing 19.1 shows the initial Cocoa.pm package.

TYPE **Listing 19.1. The initial Cocoa.pm package.**

```
package Cocoa;

sub new {
    my $this = {};  # Create an anonymous hash, and #self points to it.
    bless $this;       # Connect the hash to the package Cocoa.
    return $this;    # Return the reference to the hash.
    }

1;
```

OUTPUT There is no output for Listing 19.1.

ANALYSIS The {} constructs a reference to a hash that contains no key/value pairs. The returned value to this hash is assigned to the local variable $this. The bless() function takes that reference to $this, tells the object it references that it's now a Cocoa, and returns the reference.

The returned value to the calling function now refers to this anonymous hash. On return from the new() function, the $this reference is destroyed, but the calling function keeps a reference to this hash. Therefore, the reference count to the hash won't be zero and Perl keeps the hash in memory. (You do not have to keep it around, but it's nice to have it around for reference later.)

To create an object, you make a call such as the following:

```
$cup = new Cocoa;
```

Listing 19.2 shows you how to use this package to create the constructor.

TYPE   **Listing 19.2. Creating the constructor.**

```
1   #!/usr/bin/perl
2   push (@INC,'pwd');
3   use Cocoa;
4   $cup = new Cocoa;
```

ANALYSIS   Line 1 refers to the location of the Perl interpreter to use. Your Perl interpreter may be located at /usr/local/bin/perl or wherever you installed it.

In line 2, the local directory is added to the search path in @INC for the list of paths to use when looking for a package. You can create your module in a different directory and specify the path explicitly there. Had I created the package in /home/khusain/test/scripts/, line 2 would read as follows:

```
push (@INC,"/home/khusain/test/scripts");
```

In line 3, you include the package Cocoa.pm to get all the functionality in your script. The use statement asks Perl to look in the @INC path for a file named Cocoa.pm and include it in the copy of the source file being parsed. The use statement is required if you want to work with a class.

Line 4 creates the Cocoa object by calling the new function on it. Now comes the beauty (and confusion and power) of Perl. There is more than one way to do this. You can rewrite line 4 as the following:

```
$cup = Cocoa->new();
```

If you are a C programmer, you can use the double colons (::) to force the function new() from the Cocoa package. As a result, line 4 could also be written as the following:

```
$cup = Cocoa::new();
```

Nothing prevents you from adding more code in the constructor than what is shown here. For the Cocoa.pm module, you can, if you like, print a disclaimer when each object is created. You might want to use the constructor to initialize variables or set up arrays or pointers specific to the module.

19

Do	**Don't**

DO initialize variables in your module in the constructor.

DO use the my construct to create variables in a method.

DON'T use the local construct in a method unless you really do want the variables to be passed down to other subroutines.

DON'T use global variables in the class module.

> **TIP**
>
> When you are working with instance variables, it is sometimes easy to visualize a Perl object as simply an associative array. Then it's easy to see that each index in the associative array is a member of that class and each item at the index of the associative array is a value of that member.

Listing 19.3 shows what the Cocoa constructor looks like.

TYPE **Listing 19.3. Revised constructor for Cocoa.pm.**

```
sub new {
    my $this = {};
    print "\n /* \n ** Created by Cocoa.pm \n ** Use at own risk";
    print "\n ** Did this code even get pass the javac compiler? ";
    print "\n **/ \n";
    bless $this;
    return $this;
    }
```

OUTPUT The following shows the output from running the test script called testme on this bare-bones class:

```
$ testme

/*
** Created by Cocoa.pm
** Use at own risk
** Did this code even get pass the javac compiler?
**/
```

Regardless of which of the three methods shown here you used to create the Cocoa object, you should see the same output.

ANALYSIS Great. Now you've created some comments at the beginning of a file with some print statements. You can just as easily call other functions in or outside of the package to

19

get more initialization functionality. For example, as development progresses, you see the new() function evolve to resemble the following:

```
sub new {
    my $this = {}
    bless $this;
    $this->doInitialization();
    return $this;
}
```

When you create any given class, you should allow it to be inherited. You should be able to call the new operator with the class name as the first parameter. This capability to parse the class name from the first argument causes the class to be inherited. As a result, the new function becomes more or less like the following:

```
sub new {
        my $class = shift;          # Get the request class name
        my $this = {};
        bless $this, $class         # Use class name to bless() reference
        $this->doInitialization();
        return $this;
    }
```

The preceding method forces your class users to make calls in the form of one of three ways:

- [ ] Cocoa::new()

- [ ] Cocoa->new()

- [ ] new Cocoa;

What if you wanted to use a reference to the object instead, such as $obj->new()? The doInitialization() method used will be whatever $class you blessed the object into. The following code uses the function call ref() to determine if the class exists per se. The ref() function returns true if the item passed to it is a reference and null if it is not a reference. With classes, the true value returned from the ref() function is the name of the class.

```
sub new {
    my $this = shift;                # Get the class name
    my $class = ref($this) || $this;
    ➥# If class exists, use it  else use reference.
    my $this = {};

    bless $this, $class
    $this->doInitialization();

    return $this;
}
```

Within the class package, the methods typically treat the reference as an ordinary reference. Outside the class package, the reference is generally treated as an opaque value that can only be accessed through the class's methods. You can access the values within the package directly, but it's not a good idea to do so because such access defeats the whole purpose of object orientation.

19

It's possible to bless a reference object more than once. However, the caveat is that the new class must get rid of the object at the previously blessed reference. For C and Pascal programmers, this is like assigning a pointer to `malloced` memory and then assigning the same pointer to another location without first freeing the previous location. In effect, a Perl object must belong to only one class at a time.

What's the real difference between an object and a reference? Perl objects are blessed to belong to a class. References are not blessed; if they are, they belong to a class and are objects. Objects know to which class they belong. References do not have a class to which they belong.

Instance Variables

The arguments to a `new()` function for a constructor are called *instance variables*. Instance variables are used to do initialization for each instance of an object as it's created. For example, the `new()` function could expect a name for each new instance of the object created. Using instance variables allows you to customize each object as it is created.

You can use either an anonymous array or anonymous hash to hold instance variables. To use a hash to store the parameters coming in, the code would resemble the following:

```
sub new {
        my $type = shift;
        my %parm = @_;
        my $this = {};
        $this->{'Name'} = $parm{'Name'};
        $this->{'x'}  = $parm{'x'};
        $this->{'y'}  = $parm{'y'};
        bless $this, $type;
}
```

You can also use an array instead of a hash to store the instance variables.

```
sub new {
        my $type = shift;
        my %parm = @_;
        my $this = [];
        $this->[0] = $parm{'Name'};
        $this->[1] = $parm{'x'};
        $this->[2] = $parm{'y'};
        bless $this, $type;
}
```

To construct an object, you can pass the parameters with the `new()` function call. For example, the call to create the Cocoa object becomes the following:

```
$mug = Cocoa::new( 'Name' => 'top',
'x' => 10,
'y' => 20 );
```

The => operator has the same function of the comma operator, but => is a bit more readable.

You can write this code with commas instead of the => operator if you prefer.

To access the variables as you would any other data members, you can use the following statements:

```
print "Name=$mug->{'Name'}\n";
print "x=$mug->{'x'}\n";
print "y=$mug->{'y'}\n";
```

Methods

A *method* in a Perl class is simply a Perl subroutine. Perl doesn't provide any special syntax for method definition. A method expects its first argument to be the object or package on which it is invoked. Perl has two types of methods: static and virtual.

A *static* method expects a class name as the first argument. A *virtual* method expects a reference to an object as the first argument. The way each method handles the first argument determines whether the method is static or virtual.

A static method applies functionality to the entire class as a whole because it uses the name of the class. Functionality in static methods is therefore applicable to all objects of the class. Generally, static methods ignore the first argument because they already know which class they are in. Constructors are static methods.

A virtual method expects a reference to an object as its first argument. Typically, the first thing a virtual method does is shift the first argument into a self or this variable and then use that shifted value as an ordinary reference. For example, consider the following code:

```
1. sub nameLister {
2.     my $this = shift;
3.     my ($keys ,$value );
4.     while (($key, $value) = each (%$this)) {
5.         print "\t$key is $value.\n";
6.     }
7. }
```

Line 2 in the listing is where the $this variable is set to point to the object. In line 4, the $this array is de-referenced at every $key location.

TIP

Look at the .pm files in the Perl distribution for sample code that will show you how methods are declared and used.

19

Exporting Methods

If you tried to invoke the Cocoa.pm package right now, you'd get an error message from Perl at compile time about the methods not being found. This error occurs because the Cocoa.pm methods have not been exported. To export these functions, you need the Exporter module. Add the following lines to the beginning of code in the package:

```
require Exporter;
@ISA = qw(Exporter);
```

These two lines force the inclusion of the Exporter.pm module and then set the @ISA array with the name of the Exporter class to look for.

To export your own class's methods, you list them in the @EXPORT array. For example, to export the closeMain and declareMain methods, you use the following statement:

```
@EXPORT(declareMain, closeMain);
```

Inheritance in a Perl class is through the @ISA array. The @ISA array does not have to be defined in every package; however, when it is defined, Perl treats it as a special array of directory names. This array is similar to the @INC array, where directories are searched for files to include. The @ISA array contains the names of the classes (packages) to look for methods in other classes in if a method in the current package is not found. The @ISA array contains the names of the base classes from which the current class inherits. The search is done in the order that the classes are listed in the @ISA arrays.

All methods called by a class must belong to the same class or the base classes defined in the @ISA array. If a method isn't found in the @ISA array, Perl looks for an AUTOLOAD() routine. This optional routine is defined as sub in the current package. To use the AUTOLOAD function, you call the autoload.pm package with the use Autoload; statement. The AUTOLOAD function tries to load the called function from the installed Perl libraries. If the AUTOLOAD call also fails, Perl makes one final try at the UNIVERSAL class, which is the catch-all for all methods not defined elsewhere. Perl generates an error about unresolved functions if this step also fails.

Invoking Methods

There are two ways to invoke a method for an object: by making a reference to an object (virtual) or explicitly referring to the class name (static). You have to export a method to be able to call it. Add a few more methods to the Cocoa class to get the file to resemble the following code:

```
package Cocoa;
require Exporter;

@ISA = qw(Exporter);
```

```
@EXPORT = qw(setImports, declareMain, closeMain);

#
# This routine creates the references for imports in Java functions
#
sub setImports{
    my $class = shift @_;
    my @names = @_;

    foreach (@names) {
    print "import " .  $_ . ";\n";
    }
    }


#
# This routine declares the main function in a Java script
#
sub declareMain{
    my $class = shift @_;
    my ( $name, $extends, $implements) = @_;

    print "\n public class $name";
    if ($extends) {
            print " extends " . $extends;
    }
    if ($implements) {
            print " implements " . $implements;
    }
   print " { \n";
}

#
# This routine declares the main function in a Java script
#
sub closeMain{
   print "} \n";
}

#
#  This subroutine creates the header for the file.
#
sub new {
    my $this = {};
    print "\n /* \n ** Created by Cocoa.pm \n ** Use at own risk \n */ \n";
    bless $this;
    return $this;
    }

1;
```

Now, write a simple Perl script to use the methods for this class. Because you can only start
and close the header, examine the following code for a script to create a skeleton Java applet
source:

```
#!/usr/bin/perl

use Cocoa;
```

```
$cup = new Cocoa;

$cup->setImports( 'java.io.InputStream', 'java.net.*');
$cup->declareMain( "Msg" , "java.applet.Applet", "Runnable");
$cup->closeMain();
```

This script generates code for a Java applet called Msg that extends the java.applet.Applet applet and implements functions that are runnable. You call the function with the $cup->... call. The following three lines of code:

```
$cup->setImports( 'java.io.InputStream', 'java.net.*');3
$cup->declareMain( "Msg" , "java.applet.Applet", "Runnable");
$cup->closeMain();
```

could be rewritten as functions:

```
Cocoa::setImports($cup,  'java.io.InputStream', 'java.net.*');
Cocoa::declareMain($cup, "Msg" , "java.applet.Applet", "Runnable");
Cocoa::closeMain($cup);
```

This type of equivalence was shown in the section "Blessing a Constructor," earlier today. In both cases, the first parameter is the reference to the object itself. Running the test script shown generates the following output:

```
/*
** Created by Cocoa.pm
** Use at own risk
*/
import java.io.InputStream;
import java.net.*;

 public class Msg extends java.applet.Applet implements Runnable {
}
```

An important note about calling the methods: If you have any arguments in a method, use parentheses if you are using the -> (also known as indirect) method. The parentheses are required to include all the arguments with the following statement:

```
$cup->setImports( 'java.io.InputStream', 'java.net.*');
```

However, the following statement:

```
Cocoa::setImports($cup,  'java.io.InputStream', 'java.net.*');
```

can also be rewritten without parentheses as this:

```
Cocoa::setImports $cup,  'java.io.InputStream', 'java.net.*' ;
```

The choice is yours about how you make your code readable to other programmers. Use parentheses if you feel that it will make the code more readable.

Overrides

Sometimes you want to specify which class's method to use, such as when the same named method is specified in two different classes. For example, if the function grind is defined in both Espresso and Qava classes, you can specify which class's function to use by using the :: operator. The following calls would use the call in Espresso:

```
$mess = Espresso::grind("whole","lotta","bags");
Espresso::grind($mess, "whole","lotta","bags");
```

The following calls would use the grind() function in the Qava class:

```
$mess = Qava::grind("whole","lotta","bags");
Qava::grind($mess, "whole","lotta","bags");
```

You might want to call a method based on some action that the program you are writing has already taken. In other words, you want to use the Qava method for a certain condition and the Espresso method for another. In this case, you can use symbolic references to make the call to the required function, as in the following example:

```
$method = $local ? "Qava::" : "Espresso::";
$cup->{$method}grind(@args);
```

Destructors

Perl tracks the number of links to objects. When the last reference to an object is freed to the memory pool, the object is automatically destroyed. This destruction of the object could occur after your code stops and the script is about to exit. For global variables, the destruction happens after the last line in your code executes.

If you want to capture control just before the object is freed, you can define a DESTROY() method in your class. Note the use of all capital letters in the name. The DESTROY() method is called just before the object is released, which enables you to do any necessary cleanup. The DESTROY() function does not call other DESTROY() functions automatically; Perl doesn't do nested destruction for you. If your constructor re-blessed a reference from one of your base classes, your DESTROY() might need to call DESTROY() for any base classes. All object references that are contained in a given object are freed and destroyed automatically when the current object is freed.

Usually, you do not have to define a DESTROY function, but when you do need it, it takes the following form:

```
sub DESTROY {
#
# Add code here.
#
}
```

19

For most purposes, Perl uses a simple, reference-based garbage collection system. The number of references to any given object at the time of garbage collection must be greater than zero, or the memory for that object is freed. When your program exits, an exhaustive search-and-destroy function in Perl does garbage collection. Everything in the process is summarily deleted. In UNIX or UNIX-like systems, this might seem like a waste, but it's actually quite necessary to perform in embedded systems or in a multithreaded environment.

Inheritance

Methods in classes are inherited with the paths in the @ISA array. Variables must be set up explicitly for inheritance. Assume you define a new class called Bean.pm to include some of the functionality that another class Coffee.pm will inherit.

The example in this section demonstrates how to inherit instance variables from one class (also referred to as a "superclass" or "base class"). The steps in inheritance require calling the superclass's constructor and adding one's own instance variables to the new object.

In this example, the Coffee class inherits values from the base class called Bean. The two files are called Coffee.pm and Bean.pm, respectively.

Listing 19.4 is the code for Bean.pm.

TYPE   **Listing 19.4. The code for Bean.pm.**

```
package Bean;
require Exporter;

@ISA = qw(Exporter);
@EXPORT = qw(setBeanType);

sub new {
    my $type = shift;
    my $this = {};
    $this->{'Bean'} = 'Colombian';
    bless $this, $type;
    return $this;
    }

#
# This subroutine sets the class name
sub setBeanType{
    my ($class, $name) =  @_;
    $class->{'Bean'} = $name;
    print "Set bean to $name \n";
    }
1;
```

19

OUTPUT Listing 19.4 has no output.

ANALYSIS In this listing, the $this variable sets a value in the anonymous hash for the 'Bean' type to be 'Colombian'. The setBeanType() method is also declared so that the 'Bean' type can also be changed by a program.

The subroutine for resetting the value of 'Bean' uses the $class reference to get to the anonymous hash for the object. Remember that a reference to this anonymous hash created the reference in the first place with the new() function.

The values in the Bean class will be inherited by the Coffee class. The Coffee.pm file is shown in Listing 19.5.

TYPE **Listing 19.5. The Coffee.pm file.**

```
1  #
2  # The Coffee.pm file to illustrate inheritance.
3  #
4  package Coffee;
5  require Exporter;
6  require Bean;
7  @ISA = qw(Exporter, Bean);
8  @EXPORT = qw(setImports, declareMain, closeMain);
9  #
10 # set item
11 #
12 sub setCoffeeType{
13     my ($class,$name) =  @_;
14     $class->{'Coffee'} = $name;
15     print "Set coffee type to $name \n";
16     }
17 #
18 #  constructor
19 #
20 sub new {
21     my $type  = shift;
22      my $this = Bean->new();      ##### <- LOOK HERE!!! ####
23     $this->{'Coffee'} = 'Instant';  # unless told otherwise
24     bless $this, $type;
25     return $this;
26     }
27  1;
```

OUTPUT Listing 19.5 has no output.

ANALYSIS Note the use of the `require Bean;` statement in line 6. This line forces the inclusion of the `Bean.pm` file and all its related functions. Lines 12 through 16 define a subroutine to use when resetting the value of the local variable in `$class->{'Coffee'}`.

Look at the `new()` constructor for the `Coffee` class in line 20. The `$this` reference points to the anonymous hash returned by `Bean.pm` and not a hash created locally. In other words, the following statement creates an entirely different hash that has nothing to do with the hash created in the `Bean.pm` constructor:

```
my $this = {};  # This is not the way to do it for inheritance.
my $this = $theSuperClass->new();  # this is the way.
```

Listing 19.6 shows how to call these functions.

TYPE **Listing 19.6. Calling inherited methods.**

```
1    #!/usr/bin/perl
2    push (@INC,'pwd');
3    use Coffee;
4    $cup = new Coffee;
5    print "\n ------------------ Initial values ----------- \n";
6    print "Coffee: $cup->{'Coffee'} \n";
7    print "Bean: $cup->{'Bean'} \n";
8    print "\n ------------------ Change Bean Type ---------- \n";
9    $cup->setBeanType('Mixed');
10   print "Bean Type is now $cup->{'Bean'} \n";
11   print "\n ---------------- Change Coffee Type ---------- \n";
12   $cup->setCoffeeType('Instant');
13   print "Type of coffee: $cup->{'Coffee'} \n";
```

OUTPUT
```
------------------ Initial values -----------
Coffee: Instant
Bean: Colombian

------------------ Change Bean Type ----------
Set bean to Mixed
Bean Type is now Mixed

---------------- Change Coffee Type ----------
Set coffee type to Instant
Type of coffee: Instant
```

ANALYSIS The initial values for the `'Bean'` and `'Coffee'` indices in the anonymous hash for the object are printed first. The member functions are called to set the values to different names and then printed.

Methods can have several types of arguments. It's how you process the arguments that counts. For example, you can add the following method to the `Coffee.pm` module:

```
sub makeCup {
    my ($class, $cream, $sugar, $dope) = @_;
    print "\n=================================== \n";
    print "Making a cup \n";
    print "Add cream \n" if ($cream);
    print "Add $sugar sugar cubes\n" if ($sugar);
    print "Making some really addictive coffee ;-) \n" if ($dope);
    print "================================= \n";
}
```

The function makeCup() takes three arguments but processes them only if it sees them. To test this functionality, consider Listing 19.7.

TYPE | **Listing 19.7. Using the makeCup() function.**

```
1    #!/usr/bin/perl
2    push (@INC,'pwd');
3    use Coffee;
4    $cup = new Coffee;
5    #
6    #  With no parameters
7    #
8    print "\n Calling  with no parameters: \n";
9    $cup->makeCup;
10   #
11   #  With one parameter
12   #
13   print "\n Calling  with one parameter: \n";
14   $cup->makeCup('1');
15   #
16   #  With two parameters
17   #
18   print "\n Calling  with two parameters: \n";
19   $cup->makeCup(1,'2');
20   #
21   #  With all three parameters
22   #
23   print "\n Calling  with three parameters: \n";
24   $cup->makeCup('1',3,'1');
```

OUTPUT

```
Calling  with no parameters:

===================================
Making a cup
===================================

 Calling  with one parameter:

===================================
Making a cup
Add cream
===================================
```

```
 Calling  with two parameters:

==================================
Making a cup
Add cream
Add 2 sugar cubes
==================================

 Calling  with three parameters:

==================================
Making a cup
Add cream
Add 3 sugar cubes
Making some really addictive coffee ;-)
==================================
```

ANALYSIS Line 9 calls the function with no parameters. In line 14, the function call has one parameter. The parameters are passed either as strings or integers, something this particular method does not care about. Look at line 19 and line 24, where both strings and numbers are passed in the same function call. However, some methods you write in the future might require this distinction.

In any event, you can have default values set in the function if the expected parameter is not passed. The behavior of the method can be different depending on the number of arguments you pass it.

Overriding Methods

Inheriting functionality from another class is beneficial in that you can get all the exported functionality of the base class in your new class. To see an example of how this works, add a function in the Bean.pm class called printType. Here's the subroutine:

```
sub printType {
    my $class =  shift @_;
    print "The type of Bean is $class->{'Bean'} \n";
}
```

Do not forget to update the @EXPORT array by adding the name of the function to export. The new statement should look like this:

```
@EXPORT = qw(setBeanType, printType, printType);
```

Now call the printType function. The next three lines show three ways to call the function:

```
$cup->Coffee::printType();
$cup->printType();
$cup->Bean::printType();
```

The output from all three lines is the same:

```
The type of Bean is Mixed
The type of Bean is Mixed
The type of Bean is Mixed
```

Why is this so? There is no printType() function in the inheriting class, so the printType() function in the base class is used instead. Naturally, if you want your own class to have its own printType function, you have to define it.

In the Coffee.pm file, add the following lines:

```
#
# This routine prints the type of $class->{'Coffee'}
#
sub printType {
    my $class =  shift @_;
    print "The type of Coffee is $class->{'Coffee'} \n";
}
```

You must also modify the @EXPORT to work with this function:

```
@EXPORT = qw(setImports, declareMain, closeMain, printType);
```

Now the output from the three lines looks like this:

```
The type of Coffee is Instant
The type of Coffee is Instant
The type of Bean is Mixed
```

The base class function is called only when the Bean:: override is given. In the other cases, only the inherited class function is called.

What if you do not know the base class name or even where the name is defined? In this case, you can use the SUPER:: pseudo-class reserved word. Using the SUPER:: override enables you to call an overridden superclass method without actually knowing where that method is defined. The SUPER:: construct is meaningful only within the class.

If you're trying to control where the method search begins and you're executing in the class itself, you can use the SUPER:: pseudo class, which instructs Perl to start looking in your base class's @ISA list without explicitly naming it:

```
$this->SUPER::function( ... argument list ... );
```

Instead of Bean:: we can use SUPER::. The call to the function printType() becomes

```
$cup->SUPER::printType();
```

and the output is the following:

```
The type of Bean is Mixed
```

19

A Few Comments About Classes and Objects in Perl

One advertised strength of object-oriented languages is the ease with which new code can use old code. Packages in Perl let you reuse code through the use of objects and inheritance. OOP languages use data encapsulation to let you hide the inner workings of complicated code. Packages and modules in Perl provide a great deal of data encapsulation with the use of the my construct. Perl, however, does not guarantee that a class inheriting your code will not attempt to access your class variables directly, thereby eliminating the advantage of data encapsulation. They can if they really want to; however, this type of procedure is considered bad practice, and shame on you if you do it.

Do	Don't

DO define methods to access class variables.

DON'T access class variables directly from outside the module.

When writing a package, you should ensure that everything a method needs is available through the object or is passed as a parameter to the method. From within the package, access any global variables only through references passed through methods.

For static or global data to be used by the methods, you have to define the context of the data in the base class using the local() construct. The subclass will then call the base class to get the data for it. On occasion, a subclass might want to override that data and replace it with new data. When this happens, the superclass might not know how to find the new copy of the data. In such cases, it's best to define a reference to the data and then have all base classes and subclasses modify the variable through that reference.

Finally, you will see references to objects and classes such as the following:

```
use Coffee::Bean;
```

This code is interpreted to mean "Look for Bean.pm in the Coffee subdirectory in all the directories in the @INC array." If I were to move Bean.pm into the ./Coffee directory, all the previous examples would work with the new use statement. The advantage to this approach is that you have one subclass class file in one directory and the base class in a lower directory. It helps keep code organized. To have a statement like the following:

```
use Another::Sub::Menu;
```

you would see a directory sub-tree like this:

```
./Another/Sub/Menu.pm
```

Summary

This chapter provides a brief introduction to object-oriented programming in Perl. Perl provides the OOP features of data encapsulation and inheritance using modules and packages. A class in Perl is simply a package. A package for a class provides all the methods for objects created for the class.

An object is simply a reference to data that knows which class it belongs to. A method in a class is simply a subroutine. The only catch about writing such methods is that the name of the class is always the first argument of the method.

The bless() function is used to tie a reference to a class name. The bless() function is called in the constructor function new() to create an object and then connect the reference to the object with the name of the class.

With inheritance, the base class is the class from which methods (and data) are inherited. The base class is also called the superclass. The class that inherits these items from the superclass is called the subclass. Multiple inheritance is allowed in Perl. Data inheritance is the programmer's responsibility and requires using references. The subclass is allowed to know things about its immediate superclass; the superclass is not allowed to know anything about a subclass.

Q&A

Q What does the bless() function do?

A The bless() function takes one or two arguments. The first argument is a reference to an object. The second argument is optional and specifies the name of a class; if the name is not specified, the default is the current class. After the call, the reference uses the name as its class name. As a result, the reference becomes an object of the class whose name was specified.

Q What's the difference between an object and a reference?

A Objects are blessed; references are not. Objects belong to a class, but references do not have to.

Q What's the difference between static and virtual methods?

A Static methods expect a class name as the first argument. Virtual methods expect a reference to an object as the first argument. Static methods are class-wide; virtual methods are object-specific.

19

Q I just added a method to my class file, but it is never called! What's wrong?

A Make sure you are using the `require Exporter;` statement and that the name of the new function is in the `@EXPORTER` array.

Workshop

The Workshop provides quiz questions to help you solidify your understanding of the material covered and exercises to give you experience in using what you've learned. Try and understand the quiz and exercise answers before you go on to tomorrow's lesson.

Quiz

1. Show at least three ways to create a new object of a given class, `Balloon`.

2. What's wrong the following lines of code?

```
{
my $x;          my $y;
$x = \$y;
}
```

3. What are the three most important rules about OOP in Perl?

4. How do you override a call to a method to use the base class instead of the subclass?

Exercises

1. Write a simple class to print out the day of the week using the Zellers congruence formula to get the day of the week given a date. The following shows the formula in Perl code:

```
$zy = $year;
$zm = ($month + 10) % 12;
$zy— if ($m > 10);
$zc = int ( $y / 100 );
$yy = $year % 100;

$zeller =  ( int ( (26*$zm - 2)/10) + $dayOfMonth
        + $yy + int($yy/4)
        + int ($zc/4) - 2* $zc ) % 7;
```

2. Extend the class you just created to allow specifying a date at creation time where the day, month, year, or all three can be optional. Hint: Use the date function to get the current date.

3. Create a class to list the entire directory tree when given a path name.

4. Modify the following function to print black if no parameters are passed to it:

```perl
sub makeCup {
    my ($class, $cream, $sugar, $dope) = @_;
    print "\n================================= \n";
    print "Making a cup \n";
    print "Add cream \n" if ($cream);
    print "Add $sugar sugar cubes\n" if ($sugar);
    print "Making some really nice coffee ;-) \n" if ($dope);
    print "================================= \n";
}
```

19

Day **20**

Miscellaneous Features of Perl

Today's lesson describes the features of Perl that have not been covered in previous chapters:

☐ The `require` function, which retrieves code from other files

☐ The `$#array` variables

☐ Alternative methods of string quoting using q, qq, qw, and <<

☐ The special internal values `__LINE__`, `__FILE__`, and `__END__`

☐ Incorporating output from other commands using back quotes

☐ The ?? pattern-matching construct and the `reset` function

☐ Using <> with indirect file variables and as a filename specifier

☐ Using the *name construct globally

☐ Packages

☐ Modules

Today's lesson also provides a brief overview of the following topics:

- ☐ Using Perl in C programs
- ☐ Using Perl in CGI scripts
- ☐ Translators from other languages to Perl

The require **Function**

The require function provides a way to break your program into separate files and create libraries of functions. For example, if you have stored Perl statements in the file myfile.pl, you can include them as part of your program by adding the following statement:

```
require ("myfile.pl");
```

When the Perl interpreter sees this require statement, it searches the directories specified by the built-in array variable @INC for a file named myfile.pl. If such a file is found, the statements in the file are executed; if no such file exists, the program terminates and prints the error message

```
Can't find myfile.pl in @INC
```

on your screen (by writing it to the standard error file STDERR). (For more details on the @INC array, refer to Day 17, "System Variables.")

As in a subroutine call, the last expression evaluated inside a file included by require becomes the return value. The require function checks whether this value is zero, and terminates if it is. For example, suppose that the file myfile.pl contains the following statements:

```
print ("hello, world!\n");
$var = 14;
```

If the statements in this file are executed by

```
require ("myfile.pl");
```

the return value of myfile.pl is the following expression, which has the value 14:

```
$var = 14
```

Because this value is not zero, the program continues execution with the statement following the require.

If myfile.pl contains the following statements, the return value of myfile.pl is 0:

```
print ("hello, world!\n");
$var = 0;
```

Because this value is zero, the Perl interpreter prints the following error message along with the name and current line number of your program; then it exits:

```
myfile.pl did not return true value
```

TIP

By convention, files containing Perl statements normally have the suffix `.pl`. This makes it easy to determine which files in a directory contain Perl programs or code included in Perl programs using `require`.

You can pass any scalar value to `require`, including those stored in scalar variables or array elements:

```
@reqlist = ("file1.pl", "file2.pl", "file3.pl");

require ($reqlist[$0]);
require ($reqlist[$1]);
require ($reqlist[$2]);
```

Here, the successive calls to `require` include the contents of `file1.pl`, `file2.pl`, and `file3.pl`.

You can also specify no filename, as in the following:

```
require;
```

In this case, the value of the scalar variable `$_` is the filename whose contents are to be executed.

WARNING

One limitation Perl imposes on the `require` statement is that the contents of a particular file can be included only once in a program. To repeat a block of code many times, your only alternative is to put it in a separate program and call it using the `system` function or the `eval` function.

Also, if two directories in `@INC` contain a file named by `require`, only the first one is included.

20

The require **Function and Subroutine Libraries**

The require function enables you to create libraries of subroutines that can be used in all your Perl programs. To create a subroutine library, you need only take the following steps:

1. Decide on a directory in which to store your subroutine library.

2. Move your subroutines to separate files, and move these files to your subroutine directory.

3. To each file, add an executable statement that contains an expression with a nonzero value. This step is necessary because files executed by require must return a nonzero value, and an empty program is assumed to have the value zero. The easiest way to perform this task is to add the following statement to the bottom of each file:

   ```
   1;
   ```

   This statement is just a simple expression (the number 1) with a nonzero value.

4. In your main program, use require to refer to one or more of the files that contain your library subroutines, as needed.

5. When you start your main program, use the -I option to specify the name of the subroutine directory. Alternatively, add the subroutine directory to the @INC array before calling require.

For example, suppose that the directory /u/jqpublic/perldir contains your Perl subroutine library and that the subroutine mysub is stored in the file mysub.pl in that directory. (Naming the file after the subroutine is an easy way to remember where the subroutine is located.) Now, to include mysub as part of your program, add the following statements:

```
unshift (@INC, "/u/jqpublic/perldir");
require ("mysub.pl");
```

The call to unshift adds the directory /u/jqpublic/perldir to the @INC array, which ensures that any subsequent calls to require will search this directory. The call to require then includes the contents of mysub.pl as part of your program, which means that mysub now is included.

 TIP

You should use unshift, not push, to add to the @INC array. The push function adds to the end of the list stored in @INC, which means that your subroutine library directory will be searched last.

As a consequence, if your subroutine file has the same name as a file contained in /usr/local/lib/perl, your file will not be included, because require includes only the first file matching the specified name.

> You can control the search order of @INC by creating or reshuffling it yourself before calling require.

Using require **to Specify a Perl Version**

Perl 5 enables you to use a require statement to specify the version of Perl needed to run your program. When Perl sees a require statement with a numeric associated value, it only runs the program if the version of Perl is greater than or equal to the number. For example, the following statement indicates that the program is to be run only if the Perl interpreter is version 5.001 or higher:

```
require 5.001;
```

If it is not, the program terminates.

This is useful if your program uses a feature of Perl that you know does not work properly in earlier versions of the language.

NOTE

Because Perl 4 does not understand

```
require 5.001;
```

it detects an error and terminates when it sees this statement. This is basically what you want to have happen.

The $#array **Variables**

For each array variable defined in your program, a variable named $#array, in which array is the name of your array, is also defined. This variable contains the subscript of the last element of the array. For example:

```
@myarray = ("goodbye", "cruel", "world");
$lastsub = $#myarray;
```

Here, there are three elements in @myarray, which are referenced by the subscripts 0, 1, and 2. Because the subscript of the last element of the array is 2, $#myarray contains the value 2.

20

NOTE

Because the value of the maximum subscript is affected by the system variable $[, the value of each $#array variable is also affected by $[. For example:

```
$[ = 1;
@myarray = ("goodbye", "cruel", "world");
$lastsub = $#myarray;
```

Here, the first subscript of the array is 1, because $[is set to that value. This means that the maximum subscript is 3 and the value of $#myarray is also 3.

Any $#array variable that does not correspond to a defined array has the value -1. For example:

```
$sublength = $#notdefined;
```

Here, if the array @notdefined does not exist, $sublength is assigned -1.

A $#array variable is also defined for each built-in array variable. This means, for example, that the $#ARGV variable contains the number of elements included on the command line. You can use this variable to check whether files have been specified on the command line:

```
if ($#ARGV == -1) {
        die ("No files specified.\n");
}
```

If there are no "holes" (undefined elements) in the array, you can use a $#array variable in a loop. Listing 20.1 shows how you can carry out this action.

TYPE

Listing 20.1. A program that uses a $#array **variable in a** loop.

```
1:   #!/usr/local/bin/perl
2:
3:   @myarray = ("testing", 98.6, "Olerud", 47);
4:   for ($i = 0; $i <= $#myarray; $i++) {
5:           print ("$myarray[$i]\n");
6:   }
```

OUTPUT

```
$ program20_1
testing
98.599999999999994
Olerud
47
$
```

20

ANALYSIS Line 3 assigns a four-element list to the array variable @myarray. Therefore, the largest subscript used in the array is 3; this value is automatically assigned to the variable $#myarray.

The for statement in line 4 terminates when $i is greater than $#myarray. This technique ensures that each element of @myarray is printed, in turn, by line 5.

WARNING

Using $#myarray to terminate the loop isn't as useful if the array contains undefined elements as in the following:

```
@myarray = ("test1", "test2");
$myarray[5] = "test3";
for ($i = 0; $i <= $#myarray; $i++) {
        print ("$myarray[$i]\n");
}
```

This loop iterates six times, because the largest subscript of the array is 5. Therefore, three blank lines are printed, because the elements of @myarray with the subscripts 2, 3, and 4 have not been defined. (You can get around this by using the defined function.)

Controlling Array Length Using $#array

You can use $#array to control the length of an array variable.

If a $#array variable is assigned a value that is larger than the current largest subscript of the corresponding array, the missing elements are created and initialized to the special internal undefined value (equivalent to the null string). For example:

```
@myarray = ("hi", "there");
$#myarray = 4;
```

This code sets the maximum subscript of $#myarray to 4. Because the subscript of the last defined element is 1, three empty elements are created with subscripts 2, 3, and 4.

You can use this technique to create a large array all at once:

```
$#bigarray = 9999;
```

This statement creates an array large enough to hold 10,000 values (or fails trying). If this statement executes successfully, you know that your machine has enough space to store @bigarray before actually assigning to all or part of it.

20

In Perl 5, if the value you assign to a `$#array` variable is less than the current maximum subscript, the leftover array values are destroyed. For example:

```
@myarray = ("hello", "there", "Dave!");
$#myarray = 1;
```

Here, `@myarray` is originally assigned a three-element list, which means that its maximum subscript is 2. Assigning 1 to `$#myarray` sets the maximum subscript to 1, which means that `@myarray` now contains `("hello", "there")`. The third element, `Dave!`, is destroyed.

NOTE

This is one instance in which Perl 5 and Perl 4 behave differently. In Perl 4, array elements are not destroyed when `$#array` is assigned a value less than the current maximum subscript.

In Perl 4, array elements that have been "removed" by assigning to the `$#array` variable can be restored to existence by resetting `$#array` to its original value.

Alternative String Delimiters

As you've seen, Perl enables you to enclose character strings in either single quotation marks or double quotation marks. Strings in double quotation marks are searched for variable names, which are replaced with their values when found; strings in single quotation marks are not searched.

Consider the following example:

```
$var = 5;
print ("$var\n");
print ('$var\n');
```

The first call to `print` prints 5 followed by a newline character; the second prints the string `$var\n` as is.

Perl enables you to use any delimiter you want in place of either single quotation marks or double quotation marks. To specify a string that—like a single-quoted string—is not searched for variable names, use q followed by the delimiter you want to use. For example, the following strings are equivalent:

```
q!hello $there!
'hello $there'
```

20

A useful trick is to use newline characters as delimiters:

```
q
this is my string
```

This example is equivalent to the following because the newline after the q indicates the beginning of the string, and the newline after string indicates the end of the string:

```
'this is my string'
```

To define a string that is searched for variable names, use qq:

```
qq/This string contains $var./
```

The / characters delimit the string

```
This string contains $var.
```

which is then searched for variable names. This means that $var is replaced by its current value.

NOTE

If you use a left parenthesis as the opening delimiter for a string defined using q or qq, the Perl interpreter expects a right parenthesis as the closing delimiter. This method of operation enables you to treat q and qq as if they were functions:

```
q(Here is a single quoted string);
qq(Here is a double quoted string);
```

These are equivalent to both of the following:

```
'Here is a single quoted string'
"Here is a double quoted string"
```

Be careful not to leave a space between the q or qq and the left parenthesis; if you do, the Perl interpreter will assume that the space character, not the (, is the delimiter.

20

qw, defined in Perl 5, provides a convenient way of breaking a string into words. The following statements are equivalent:

```
@words = qw/this is a list of words/;
@words = split(' ', q/this is a list of words/);
```

In each case, @words is assigned the list

```
("this", "is", "a", "list", "of", "words")
```

qw supports any alternative string delimiter supported by q and qq.

Defining Strings Using <<

You can use << (two left angle brackets) to indicate the beginning of a string. This string continues until the next blank line. The following is an example:

```
$longstring = <<
Here is the first part of the string.
Here is the last part of the string.

# here is the next statement
```

This example defines a string consisting of the two input lines

```
Here is the first part of the string.
Here is the last part of the string.
```

and assigns it to $longstring. The newline characters are included as part of the string.

You can specify the characters that indicate "end of string" by including them after the <<. For example:

```
$longstring = <<END
Here is the first part of the string.
Here is the last part of the string.
END
# here is the next statement.
```

Here, END indicates the end of the string.

You can enclose the end-of-string characters in either single or double quotation marks. Single-quoted end-of-string characters behave like normal end-of-string characters:

```
$longstring = <<'END'
Here is the first part of the string.
Here is the last part of the string.
END
# here is the next statement
```

Double-quoted end-of-string characters are searched for variable names, which are replaced by their values if found.

```
$endchars = "END";
$longstring = <<"$endchars"
Here is the first part of the string.
Here is the last part of the string.
END
# here is the next statement
```

Here, $endchars is replaced by its value, END, which is used to indicate the end of the string.

A string created using << can be used wherever a string is expected. For example, the statement

```
print <<END
Hello there!
This is a test!
END
```

writes the following to the standard output file:

```
Hello there!
This is a test!
```

(This is one place where omitting the parentheses when you pass an argument to a function becomes useful.)

You can use the x operator to write a string more than once:

```
print <<END x 2
Hello there!
END
```

This sends the following to the standard output file:

```
Hello there!
Hello there!
```

You can supply more than one << at a time. If you do, they are processed in the order in which they are received. For example, the statement

```
$longstring = <<END1 <<END2
This is the first part.
END1
This is the second part.
END2
```

assigns the following (including the trailing newlines) to $longstring:

```
This is the first part.
This is the second part.
```

Do	Don't

DON'T leave a space between the << and the end-of-string characters. (If you do, the Perl interpreter will terminate the string when it sees the next blank line.)

DON'T put anything else in the line containing the end-of-string characters.

20

Special Internal Values

Perl defines three special internal values your program can use: __LINE__, __FILE__, and __END__.

__LINE__ and __FILE__ contain, respectively, the current line number and current filename of the program you are running. These are the values that die and warn use when printing the line number and filename on which an error or a warning occurs.

__END__ is a special value that indicates "end of file." Everything after __END__ is treated as data. If the program is contained in a file, you can read the data after __END__ by reading from the DATA file variable:

```
$data = <DATA>;
```

NOTE | __LINE__ and __FILE__ cannot be substituted into double-quoted strings.
You can use the ^D or ^Z character (Ctrl+D or Ctrl+Z) in place of __END__.

WARNING | __END__ does not need to appear on a line by itself as long as some white space separates it from the next item in the file. However, the first line of the file represented by DATA is always the line immediately following the __END__. For example:

```
__END__ Here is some input.
Here is some more input.
```

In this case, the first line read by <DATA> is

```
Here is some more input.
```

The information immediately following the __END__ is lost.

Using Back Quotes to Invoke System Commands

Perl provides a way to treat the value printed by a system command as a string. To do this, enclose the system command in back quote characters (the ` character).

For example, here is a way to include your user name in a Perl program:

```
$myname = `whoami`;
chop ($myname);
```

The first statement calls the system command whoami, which prints the name of the person logged on. This name is assigned to $myname. (The call to chop is necessary because whoami appends a newline character to the name, which enables it to appear on its own line on the screen.)

The Perl interpreter performs variable substitution on the string enclosed in back quotes before treating it as a system command.

```
$command = "whoami";
$myname = `$command`;
chop ($myname);
```

Here, the value of $command, whoami, is substituted into the string enclosed in back quotes, and it becomes the system command that is called.

When a system command is executed, the return code from the command is stored in the system variable $?. To determine whether the system command has executed properly, check this system variable. (Normally, a value of zero indicates successful execution, and any other value indicates an error. The actual error value depends on the command.)

To use a character other than a back quote as a delimiter, use qx:

```
$myname = qx#whoami#;
chop ($myname);
```

As with q and qq, described previously, the first character after qx is treated as the string delimiter. The string continues until another string delimiter—in this case, #—is seen.

NOTE

> If (is used as an opening string delimiter,) becomes the closing string delimiter:
>
> ```
> $myname = qx(whoami);
> ```

Pattern Matching Using ?? and the reset Function

The ?? pattern matching operator is identical to the // pattern-matching operator you have been using all along, except that it matches only once, even if it is inside a loop. For example, the following statement loops only once, because the pattern ?abc? is not matched the second time it is executed:

```
while ($line =~ ?abc?) {
        # stuff goes here
}
```

To make the ?? pattern matching operator match again, call the reset function. This function tells the Perl interpreter that a particular ?? operator can be used to match a pattern again. Listing 20.2 is an example of a program that uses ?? and reset.

Listing 20.2. A demonstration of ?? and the reset function.

```
1:  #!/usr/local/bin/perl
2:
3:  while ($line = <STDIN>) {
4:          last unless ($line =~ ?\bthe\b?);
5:          print ("$`$");
6:          reset;
7:  }
```

```
$ program20_2
this is the first line
this is   first line
the next line of input
 next line of input
last line – not matched
$
```

ANALYSIS   Line 4 of this program uses the ?? pattern matching operator to check whether the word the appears in the current input line. If it does not, the program terminates. If it does, line 5 uses the $` and $_ variables to print the parts of the line not matched.

Line 6 calls reset, which resets the ?? operator in line 4. If reset is not called, line 4 will not match even if the new input line contains the word the.

> The ?? operator is deprecated in Perl version 5. This means that the operator is still supported but is considered obsolete. Future versions of Perl might not support this operator.
>
> **WARNING**

Using reset with Variables

You also can use the reset function to clear all variables whose name begins with a specified character. The following statement assigns the null string to all scalar variables whose names begin with the letter w (such as, for instance, $which) and assigns the empty list to all array variables whose names begin with this letter:

```
reset ("w");
```

The following statement assigns the null string or the empty list to all variables whose names begin with a or e:

```
reset ("ae");
```

You can use ranges of letters with `reset`:

```
reset ("a-d");
```

This example resets all variables whose names begin with a, b, c, or d.

WARNING

> Be careful with `reset` because it resets all variables whose names begin with the specified letters, including built-in variables such as @ARGV.

Other Features of the <> Operator

As you've seen, the <> operator reads from the file specified by the enclosed file variable. For example, the following statement reads a line from the file represented by MYFILE:

```
$line = <MYFILE>;
```

The following sections describe how to use <> with scalar variable substitution and how to use <> to create a list of filenames.

Scalar Variable Substitution and <>

If a scalar variable is contained in the <> operator, the value of the variable is assumed to be the name of a file variable. For example:

```
$filename = "MYFILE";
$line = <$filename>;
```

Here, the value of `$filename`, MYFILE, is assumed to be the file variable associated with the input file to read from. When you change the value of `$filename`, you change the input file.

Creating a List of Filenames

UNIX commands that manipulate files, such as `mv` and `cp`, enable you to supply a pattern to generate a list of filenames. Any filename matching this pattern is included as part of the list. For example, the following command copies every file whose name ends in `.pl` to the directory /u/jqpublic/srcdir:

```
$ cp *.pl /u/jqpublic/srcdir
```

20

In Perl, if the <> operator encloses something other than a file variable or a scalar variable containing a file variable, it is assumed to be a pattern that matches a list of files. For example, the following statement assigns a list of the filenames ending in .pl to the array variable @filelist:

```
@filelist = <*.pl>;
```

You can use filename patterns in loops:

```
while ($line = <*.pl>) {
        print ("$line\n");
}
```

This code prints each filename ending in .pl on a separate line.

Global Indirect References and Aliases

On Day 9, "Using Subroutines," you learned that you can pass the name of an array to a subroutine using an alias. For example:

```
sub my_sub {
        local (*subarray) = @_;
        $arraylength = @subarray;
}
```

The *subarray definition in my_sub tells the Perl interpreter to operate on the actual list instead of making a copy. When this subroutine is called by a statement such as the following, the Perl interpreter realizes that myarray and subarray refer to the same array variable:

```
&my_sub(*myarray);
```

When a name is given an alias, all variables with that name can be referred to using the alias. This means, in this example, that the @subarray variable and the @myarray variable refer to the same array. If the program also defines variables named $subarray and %subarray, you can use $myarray and %myarray, respectively, to refer to these variables.

In the earlier example, the following two statements:

```
my_sub (*myarray);
local (*subarray) = @_;
```

are equivalent to the assignment

```
local (*subarray) = *myarray;
```

In each case, the name subarray is defined to be an alias of the name myarray. Because *subarray is contained inside a local definition in a subroutine, subarray and myarray are equivalent only while the subroutine is being executed.

If desired, you can define an alias for a name that remains in force throughout your program. For example:

```
*subarray = *myarray;
```

If this statement is part of your main program, `subarray` becomes an alias for `myarray` in all parts of your program, including all subroutines. The values of `$subarray`, `@subarray`, and `%subarray`, if they are defined, are lost.

Listing 20.3 is a simple example of a program that defines and uses a global alias.

 Listing 20.3. An example of a global alias.

```
1:  #!/usr/local/bin/perl
2:
3:  *name2 = *name1;
4:  $name1 = 14;
5:  print ("$name2\n");
```

OUTPUT
```
$ program20_3
14
$
```

ANALYSIS Line 3 of this program defines `name2` as an alias for `name1`. Every variable named `name1` can therefore be referred to using the name `name2`. As a result, `$name1` and `$name2` are really the same scalar variable; this means that line 5 prints the value assigned in line 4.

Do   **Don't**

DON'T use aliases unless you absolutely must, because they can become very confusing.

DO, instead, substitute the variable name into a string and then execute it using `eval`. This is a better way to reference a variable indirectly. For example:
```
$name2 = '$name1';
eval ("$name2 = 14;");
```

The string `$name1` is substituted for the variable name `$name2`, yielding the string
```
$name1 = 14;
```

`eval` then executes this statement, which assigns `14` to `$name1`.

20

Packages

A Perl program keeps track of the variables and subroutines defined within it by storing their names in a symbol table. In Perl, the collection of names in a symbol table is called a *package*. The following sections describe packages and how to use them.

Defining a Package

Perl enables you to define more than one package for a program, with each package contained in a separate symbol table. To define a package, use the `package` statement.

```
package mypack;
```

This statement creates a new package named `mypack`. All variable and subroutine names defined from this point on in the program are stored in the symbol table associated with the new package. This process continues until another `package` statement is encountered.

Each symbol table contains its own set of variable and subroutine names, and each set of names is independent. This means that you can use the same variable name in more than one package.

```
$var = 14;
package mypack;
$var = 6;
```

The first statement creates a variable named `$var` and stores it in the main symbol table. The statement following the `package` statement creates another variable named `$var` and stores it in the symbol table for the `mypack` package.

Switching Between Packages

You can switch back and forth between packages at any time. Listing 20.4 shows how you can carry out this action.

> **TYPE** **Listing 20.4. A program that switches between packages.**

```
1:  #!/usr/local/bin/perl
2:
3:  package pack1;
4:  $var = 26;
5:  package pack2;
6:  $var = 34;
7:  package pack1;
8:  print ("$var\n");
```

OUTPUT

```
$ program20_4
26
$
```

ANALYSIS Line 3 defines a package named pack1. Line 4 creates a variable named $var, which is then stored in the symbol table for the pack1 package. Line 5 then defines a new package, pack2. Line 6 creates another variable named $var, which is stored in the symbol table for the pack2 package. Two separate copies of $var now exist, one in each package.

Line 7 specifies the pack1 package again. Because pack1 has already been defined, this statement just sets the current package to be pack1; therefore, all variable and subroutine references and definitions refer to names stored in the symbol table for this package.

As a consequence, when line 8 refers to $var, it refers to the $var stored in the pack1 package. The value stored in this variable, 26, is retrieved and printed.

The main Package

The default symbol table, in which variable and subroutine names are normally stored, is associated with the package named main. If you have defined a package using the package statement and you want to switch back to using the normal default symbol table, specify the main package as shown here:

```
package main;
```

When this statement is executed, your program resumes behaving as though no package statements have ever been seen. Subroutine and variable names are stored as they normally are.

Referring to One Package from Another

To refer to a variable or subroutine defined in one package from inside another package, precede the variable name with the package name followed by a single quotation-mark character. For example:

```
package mypack;
$var = 26;
package main;
print ("$mypack'var\n");
```

20

Here, $mypack'var refers to the variable named $var located in the package mypack.

WARNING

Do not put any spaces between the quotation-mark character and either the package name or the variable name. The following examples are not correct:

```
$mypack ' var
$mypack' var
$mypack 'var
```

NOTE

In Perl 5, the package name and variable name are separated by a pair of colons instead of a quotation mark:

```
$mypack::var
```

The quotation-mark character is supported for now but might not be understood in future versions of Perl.

Specifying No Current Package

Perl 5 enables you to state that there is to be no current package. To do this, specify a package statement without a package name, as in the following:

```
package;
```

This tells the Perl interpreter that all variables must have their package names explicitly specified in order for a statement to be valid.

```
$mypack::var = 21;    # OK
$var = 21;            # error - no current package
```

This restriction remains in effect until a current package is explicitly defined by another package statement.

Packages and Subroutines

A package definition affects all the statements in a program, including subroutine definitions. For example:

```
package mypack;
subroutine mysub {
        local ($myvar);
        # stuff goes here
}
```

Here, the names mysub and myvar are both part of the mypack package. To call the subroutine mysub from outside the package mypack, specify &mypack'mysub.

You can change packages in the middle of a subroutine:

```
package pack1;
subroutine mysub {
        $var1 = 1;
        package pack2;
        $var1 = 2;
}
```

This code creates two copies of $var1, one in pack1 and one in pack2.

NOTE

> Local variables that are part of packages can be referenced only in the subroutine or statement block in which they are defined. (In other words, they behave just like ordinary local variables do.)

Defining Private Data Using Packages

The most common use of packages is in files containing subroutines and global variables that are used in these subroutines. By defining a package for these subroutines, you can ensure that the global variables used in the subroutines are used nowhere else; such variables are called *private data*.

Better still, you can ensure that the package name itself is used nowhere else. Listing 20.5 is an example of a file containing a package name and variable names that are used nowhere else.

20

TYPE   **Listing 20.5. A file that contains private data.**

```
1:  package privpack;
2:  $valtoprint = 46;
3:
4:  package main;
5:  # This function is the link to the outside world.
6:  sub printval {
7:          &privpack'printval();
8:  }
9:
10: package privpack;
11: sub printval {
12:         print ("$valtoprint\n");
13: }
14:
15: package main;
16: 1;   # return value for require
```

OUTPUT   This subroutine, by itself, cannot generate its output until printval is called.

ANALYSIS   This file can be divided into two parts: the part that communicates with the outside world and the part that does the work. The part that communicates is in the main or default package, and the part that does the work is in a special package named privpack. This package is defined only in this file.

The subroutine printval, defined in lines 6–8, is designed to be called from programs and subroutines defined elsewhere. Its only task is to call the version of printval defined in the privpack package.

The version of printval in the privpack package prints the number by retrieving it from the scalar variable $valtoprint. This variable is also part of the privpack package, and it is defined only inside it.

Lines 15 and 16 ensure that this file behaves properly if it is included in a program by require. Line 15 sets the current package to the default package, and line 16 is a nonzero return value to ensure that require does not generate an error.

Packages and System Variables

The following variables are assumed to be in the main package, even when referenced from inside another package:

- ☐ The file variables STDIN, STDOUT, STDERR, and ARGV
- ☐ The %ENV, %INC, @INC, $ARGV, and @ARGV variables
- ☐ Any system variable with a special character in its name (such as, for example, $_ and $%)

Accessing Symbol Tables

To actually look in a symbol table from within a program, use the associative array %_package, in which *package* is the name of the package whose symbol table you want to access. For example, the variable %_main contains the default symbol table.

Normally, you will not need to look in the symbol table yourself.

Modules

Most large programs are divided into components, each of which performs a specific task or set of tasks. Each component normally contains one or more executable functions, plus the variables needed to make these functions work. The collection of functions and variables in a component is known as a *program module*. One module can appear in a variety of programs.

Creating a Module

Perl 5 enables you to use packages to define modules. To define a module in Perl 5, create the package and store it in a file of the same name. For example, a package named Mymodule would be stored in the file Mymodule.pm. (The .pm suffix indicates that the file is a Perl module.)

Listing 20.6 creates a module named Mymodule, containing subroutines myfunc1 and myfunc2, and variables $myvar1 and $myvar2. This code should be stored in the file Mymodule.pm.

TYPE **Listing 20.6. Code that creates a Perl module.**

```
 1:  #/usr/local/bin/perl
 2:
 3:  package Mymodule;
 4:  require Exporter;
 5:  @ISA = qw(Exporter);
 6:  @EXPORT = qw(myfunc1 myfunc2);
 7:  @EXPORT_OK = qw($myvar1 $myvar2);
 8:
 9:  sub myfunc1 {
10:      $myvar1 += 1;
11:  }
12:
13:  sub myfunc2 {
14:      $myvar2 += 2;
15:  }
```

ANALYSIS Lines 3–7 use the standard Perl module definition conventions. Line 3 defines the package. Line 4 includes a built-in Perl module, Exporter, which provides information about these definition conventions. Lines 6 and 7 define the subroutines and variables that are to be made available to the outside world.

20

Line 6 creates a special array named @EXPORT. This array lists the subroutines that can be called by other programs. Here, the subroutines myfunc1 and myfunc2 are accessible. Any subroutine defined inside a module that is not included in the list assigned to @EXPORT is a private subroutine, and can only be called inside the module.

Line 7 creates another special array, called @EXPORT_OK, that lists the variables that can be accessed by other programs. Here, the variables $myvar1 and $myvar2 are accessible from the outside world.

Importing Modules Into Your Program

To import a module into your Perl program, use the use statement. For example, the following statement imports the Mymodule module into a program:

```
use Mymodule;
```

The subroutines and variables in Mymodule can now be used in your program.

To undefine a previously imported module, use the no statement. For example, the following statement undefines the Mymodule module:

```
no Mymodule;
```

Listing 20.7 is an example of a program that imports and undefines a module. The integer module referenced here specifies that all arithmetic operations are to be on integers. Floating-point numbers are converted to integers before the arithmetic operations are performed.

TYPE **Listing 20.7. A program that uses the use and no statements.**

```
1:  #/usr/local/bin/perl
2:
3:  use integer;
4:  $result = 2.4 + 2.4;
5:  print ("$result\n");
6:
7:  no integer;
8:  $result = 2.4 + 2.4;
9:  print ("$result\n");
```

OUTPUT
```
$ program20_7
4
4.8
$
```

ANALYSIS Line 3 of this program imports the integer module. As a consequence, Line 4 converts 2.4 to 2 before performing the addition, yielding the result 4.

20

Line 7 undefines the `integer` module. This tells the Perl interpreter to revert to using floating-point numbers in arithmetic operations.

WARNING

> If a use or no statement appears inside a statement block, it remains in effect only for the duration of that block. For example:
>
> ```
> use integer;
> $result1 = 2.4 + 2.4;
> if ($result1 == 4) {
>     no integer;
>     $result2 = 3.4 + 3.4;
> }
> $result3 = 4.4 + 4.4;
> ```
>
> Here, the no statement is only in effect inside the `if` statement. In the statement after the `if`, the `integer` module is still in use, which means that 4.4 is converted to 4 before the addition is performed.

Using Predefined Modules

Perl 5 provides a variety of predefined modules that perform useful tasks. Each module can be imported by the use statement and removed by the no statement.

The following are some of the most useful modules in this library:

integer	As you have seen, this module tells Perl to use integer arithmetic instead of floating-point arithmetic.
diagnostics	Tells the Perl interpreter to print more diagnostic messages (warnings) when running your program.
English	Allows the use of English names as synonyms for system variables.
Env	A Perl module that imports environment variables.
POSIX	The Perl interface to the POSIX standard (IEEE 1003.1).
Socket	Loads the C programming language's socket handling mechanisms.

A complete list of the predefined modules included with Perl 5 can be found in your Perl documentation.

20

TIP

> Perl 5 users all over the world write useful modules and make them available to the Perl community through the Internet. The Comprehensive Perl Archive Network (CPAN) of Perl archives provides a complete list of these modules. More information on the CPAN network is available at the Web site located at `http://www.perl.com/perl/CPAN/README.html`.

Using Perl in C Programs

Perl 5 enables you to call Perl subroutines from within C programs. To add this capability, you need to do two things: add references to Perl to your program source, and then link the Perl library when you compile your program.

See the Perl documentation for more details on how to use Perl subroutines in C programs.

Perl and CGI Scripts

The Common Gateway Interface (CGI) is a standard for interfacing external applications with information servers (such as those found on the World Wide Web).

For more information on CGI, go to the Web page located at `http://hoohoo.ncsa.uiuc.edu/cgi`. A library of CGI scripts written in Perl can be found at `http://www.bio.cam.ac.uk/web/cgi-lib.pl.txt`.

Translators and Other Supplied Code

The Perl distribution provides programs that translate the following items into Perl:

- ☐ Programs written in the awk programming language
- ☐ Scripts written for the sed command
- ☐ Commands sent to the find command
- ☐ Include files written in the C programming language

For information on these translation programs, refer to the documentation supplied with your Perl distribution.

Summary

Today you learned about features of Perl that were not discussed on previous days.

- ☐ require, which includes code from other files
- ☐ The $#array variable, which returns the largest subscript of an array
- ☐ Alternative methods of enclosing strings using q, qq, qw, <<, and qx
- ☐ The special internal values __LINE__, __FILE__, and __END__, which retrieve the current filename and line number and end the program
- ☐ Using back quotes to treat the output from a command as a scalar value
- ☐ Using ?? to match a pattern once, and using reset to reset ?? and variables
- ☐ Using <> with indirect file variables and file lists
- ☐ Global aliasing using *
- ☐ Packages and modules
- ☐ Using Perl in C programs

Q&A

Q Why does a file included by require need to execute a statement? Why does require check a return code?

A Because files included by require can contain statements that are immediately executed, checking for a return code enables programs to determine whether code included by require generated any errors.

Q Is a $#array variable defined for system array variables such as @ARGV?

A Yes. For example, $#ARGV contains the largest subscript of the @ARGV array; you can test this to determine whether your program was passed enough arguments.

Q Are $#array variables defined for associative arrays?

A No, because there is no concept of a "largest subscript" in associative arrays.

Q What happens to system variables when reset is called? For example, is @ARGV reset when reset is passed "A"?

A The reset function affects all variables, including system variables. For this reason, you should be careful when you use reset.

20

Workshop

The Workshop provides quiz questions to help you solidify your understanding of the material covered, and exercises to give you experience in using what you've learned. Try and understand the quiz and exercise answers before you go on to tomorrow's lesson.

Quiz

1. What do these constants contain?

    a. `__LINE__`

    b. `__FILE__`

    c. `__END__`

2. What is the value of each of the following strings? (Assume that $var has the value `hello`.)

    a. `q(It's time to say $var)`

    b. `qq "It's time to say $var";  # a comment`

    c. `qx/echo $var/`

3. What is stored in @array after the following statements have been executed?
    ```
    @array = ("one", "two", "three", "four");
    $#array = 2;
    $array[4] = "five";
    ```

4. How can you include code from another file in your program?

Exercises

1. Write a program that uses the <> operator to list all the files in a directory in alphabetical order.

2. Write a program that uses a subroutine named sum to add the numbers in a list and return the total. Read the list from standard input (one per line). Assume that the subroutine is contained in the file /u/jqpublic/perlfiles/sum.pl. Print the total returned by sum.

3. Write a program that creates two packages named pack1 and pack2. For each package, read a line from standard input and assign it to the variable $var. Assume that each $var contains a number, add the two numbers together, and print the total.

4. **BUG BUSTER:** What is wrong with the following statements?

```
print ("Perl files in this directory:\n");
$filepattern = "*.pl";
while ($name = <$filepattern>) {
        print ("$name\n");
}
```

5. **BUG BUSTER:** What is wrong with the following statement?

```
print << EOF
Here is part of my string.
Here is the rest of my string.
EOF
```

20

Day 21

The Perl Debugger

Today's lesson describes the Perl debugging facility. You'll learn the following:

- ☐ How to enter and exit the Perl debugger
- ☐ How to list parts of your program
- ☐ How to execute one statement at a time
- ☐ How to set breakpoints and trace program execution
- ☐ How to perform line actions
- ☐ About other useful debugging commands

Entering and Exiting the Perl Debugger

The following sections describe how to start the Perl debugger and how to exit.

Entering the Debugger

To debug a Perl program, specify the -d option when you run the program. For example, to debug a program named debugtest, specify the following command:

```
$ perl -d debugtest
```

You can supply other options along with -d if you want to.

When the Perl interpreter sees the -d option, it starts the Perl debugger. The debugger begins by displaying a message similar to the following one on your screen:

```
Loading DB routines from $RCSfile: perldb.pl,v  $$Revision: 4.0.1.3
$$Date: 92/06/08 13:43:57 $
Emacs support available.

Enter h for help.

main::(debugtest:3):          $dircount = 0;
  DB<1>
```

The first few lines display the date on which this version of the debugger was created. The only lines of interest are the last two.

The second-to-last line in this display lists the line that the debugger is about to execute. When the debugger starts, the first executable line of the program is displayed.

When the debugger displays a line that it is about to execute, it also provides the following information about the line:

- [ ] The package in which the line is contained (in this case, the default package, which is main)
- [ ] The name of the file containing the line (here, the file is named debugtest)
- [ ] The current line number (which, in this example, is 3)

The last line of the display prompts you for a debugging command. The number enclosed in angle brackets indicates the command number; in this case, the number is 1, because you are about to specify the first debugging command.

Later today you will learn how to use the debugging command number to re-enter debugging commands you have previously executed.

NOTE

> To enter the debugger without supplying a program, supply the -e option with the -d option:
>
> ```
> $ perl -d -e "1;"
> ```

> This line starts the debugger with a "program" consisting of the single statement
>
> 1;
>
> (which is an expression that doesn't do anything meaningful).
>
> Starting the debugger without a program enables you to examine the predefined system variables or supply statements to be executed. You will learn how to perform both of these tasks later in today's lesson.

Exiting the Debugger

To exit the debugger, enter the debugging command q:

```
DB<1> q
```

This command halts program execution immediately and returns you to the command shell.

Listing Your Program

You can list any part of your program from within the debugger. The following sections describe debugging commands that perform the display operations.

The l command

The simplest way to list part of your program is with the l command, which lists the next few statements in your program:

```
  DB<1> l
3:        $dircount = 0;
4:        $curdir = "";
5:        while (1) {
6:                # if we don't have a current directory, get one
7:                if ($curdir eq "") {
8:                        print ("Enter directory to list:\n");
9:                        $curdir = <STDIN>;
10:                       $curdir =~ s/^\s+|\s+$//g;
11:                       $curdir = &followlink($curdir);
12:                       &readsubdirs($curdir);
```

The l command lists a window of executable statements, which is a group of statements small enough to be easily displayed on your screen. A window usually consists of about ten statements. The line number of each statement is displayed at the beginning of its line.

21

NOTE   The statements displayed in today's lesson are taken from the program
presented in "Week 2 in Review."

Entering the l command again displays the window of statements immediately following the
last displayed line, which in this example is line 12:

```
DB<1> l
13:                    }
14:                    $curdir = &menudir($curdir);
15:        }
16:
17:
18:        # Find all subdirectories of the given directory,
19:        # and store them in an associative array.
20:        #
21:        # The associative array subscripts and values are:
22:        # <directory name>:        1
```

You can specify the lines displayed by the l command. If you specify a single line number with
the l command, it displays that line:

```
DB<1> l 10
10:                            $curdir =~ s/^\s+|\s+$//g;
```

To display a range of lines, specify the first and last line number, and separate them with a
hyphen:

```
DB<1> l 10-15
10:                            $curdir =~ s/^\s+|\s+$//g;
11:                            $curdir = &followlink($curdir);
12:                            &readsubdirs($curdir);
13:                    }
14:                    $curdir = &menudir($curdir);
15:        }
```

To display a specified number of lines starting at a certain point, supply the starting line
number, a + character, and a number of additional lines to display:

```
DB<1> l 10+5
10:                            $curdir =~ s/^\s+|\s+$//g;
11:                            $curdir = &followlink($curdir);
12:                            &readsubdirs($curdir);
13:                    }
14:                    $curdir = &menudir($curdir);
15:        }
```

You also can use the l command to specify a subroutine to display. To do this, provide the
name of the subroutine to display:

```
DB<1> l readsubdirs
26:        sub readsubdirs {
27:                local ($dirname) = @_;
```

21

```
28:             local ($dirvar, $subdircount, $name, $index);
29:
30:             # open the current directory;
31:             # $dircount ensures that each file variable is unique
32:             $dirvar = "DIR" . ++$dircount;
33:             if (!opendir ($dirvar, $dirname)) {
34:                     warn ("Can't open $dirname\n");
35:                     return;
```

This command lists the statements in the subroutine. If the subroutine is too large to fit in a single window, only the first few statements are listed; you can list subsequent statements by entering l with no arguments.

The - Command

You can display the lines immediately preceding the last displayed line by entering the – command. For example, the following – command lists the window of lines immediately preceding the subroutine readsubdirs.

```
  DB<1> -
16:
17:
18:     # Find all subdirectories of the given directory,
19:     # and store them in an associative array.
20:     #
21:     # The associative array subscripts and values are:
22:     # <directory name>:        1
23:     #        (indicates that directory has been read)
24:     # <directory name>.<num>  the <num>th subdirectory
25:
```

Subsequent – commands go back further in the file.

The w Command

To list a window of lines containinga specified line, use the w command, and specify the number of the line to be included:

```
  DB<1> w 7
4:      $curdir = "";
5:      while (1) {
6:              # if we don't have a current directory, get one
7:              if ($curdir eq "") {
8:                      print ("Enter directory to list:\n");
9:                      $curdir = <STDIN>;
10:                     $curdir =~ s/^\s+|\s+$//g;
11:                     $curdir = &followlink($curdir);
12:                     &readsubdirs($curdir);
13:              }
```

The w command displays the three lines before the specified line and fills the window with the lines following it.

21

The // and ?? Commands

You can search for a line containing a particular pattern by enclosing the pattern in slashes:

```
DB<1> /Find/
18:     # Find all subdirectories of the given directory,
```

The debugger searches forward from the last displayed line for a line matching the specified pattern. If it finds such a line, the line is displayed.

To search backward for a particular pattern, enclose the pattern in question marks:

```
DB<1> ?readsubdirs?
12:                 &readsubdirs($curdir);
```

This command starts with the last displayed line and searches backward until it finds a line matching the specified pattern.

NOTE

> Patterns specified by // and ?? can contain any special character understood by the Perl interpreter.
>
> You optionally can omit the final / or ? character when you match a pattern.

The s Command

The s command lists all the subroutines in the current file, one subroutine per line:

```
DB<> S
main::display
main::followlink
main::menudir
main::readsubdirs
```

Each subroutine name is preceded by the package name and a single quotation mark.

Stepping Through Programs

One of the most useful features of the Perl debugger is the capability to execute a program one statement at a time. The following sections describe the statements that carry out this action.

The s **Command**

To execute a single statement of your program, use the s command:

```
  DB<2> s
main::(debugtest:4):         $curdir = "";
```

This command executes one statement of your program and then displays the next statement to be executed. If the statement executed needs to read from the standard input file, the debugger waits until the input is provided before displaying the next line to execute.

TIP

> If you have forgotten which line is the next line to execute (because, for example, you have displayed lines using the l command), you can list the next line to execute using the L command:
>
> ```
>   DB<2> L
> 3:     $dircount = 0;
> ```
>
> The L command lists the last lines executed by the program. It also lists any breakpoints and line actions that have been defined for particular lines. Breakpoints and line actions are discussed later today.

If the statement executed by the s command calls a subroutine, the Perl debugger enters the subroutine but does not execute any statements in it. Instead, it stops at the first executable statement in the subroutine and displays it. For example, if the following is the current line:

```
main::(debugtest:12):                        &readsubdirs($curdir);
```

specifying the s command tells the Perl debugger to enter readsubdirs and display the following, which is the first executable line of readsubdirs:

```
main::readsubdirs(debugtest:27):     local ($dirname) = @_;
```

The s command assumes that you want to debug the subroutine you have entered. If you know that a particular subroutine works properly and you don't want to step through it one statement at a time, use the n command, described in the following section.

The n **Command**

The n command, like the s command, executes one line of your program and displays the next line to be executed:

```
  DB<2> n
main::(debugtest:5):         while (1) {
```

The n statement, however, does not enter any subroutines. If the statement executed by n contains a subroutine call, the subroutine is executed in its entirety. After the subroutine is executed, the debugger displays the line immediately following the call.

For example, if the current line is

```
main::(debugtest:12):                          &readsubdirs($curdir);
```

the n command tells the debugger to execute readsubdirs and then display the next line in the program, which is

```
main::(debugtest:13:):              }
```

Combining the use of s and n ensures that the debugger examines only the subroutines you want to see.

NOTE The Perl debugger does not enable you to enter any library functions. You can enter only subroutines that you have created yourself or that have been created previously and added to a subroutine library.

The f command

The f command tells the Perl debugger to execute the remainder of the statements in the current subroutine and then display the line immediately after the subroutine call. This is useful when you are looking for a bug and have determined that the current subroutine does not contain the problem.

The Carriage-Return Command

If you are stepping through a program using s or n, you can save yourself some typing by just pressing Enter when you want to execute another statement. When you press Enter, the debugger repeats the last s or n command executed.

For example, to step from line 5 to line 7, you can use the s command as usual:

```
  DB<3> s
main::(debugtest:7):                if ($curdir eq "") {
```

(Line 6 is skipped because it contains no executable statements.) To execute line 7, you can now just press Enter:

```
  DB<2>
main::(debugtest:8):                    print ("Enter directory to list:\n");
```

21

NOTE

Pressing Enter has no effect if you have not specified any s or n commands.

The r Command

If you are inside a subroutine and decide that you no longer need to step through it, you can tell the Perl debugger to finish executing the subroutine and return to the statement after the subroutine call. To do this, use the r command:

```
  DB<4> r
main::(debugtest:13:):                    }
```

The statement displayed by the debugger is the first statement following the call to the subroutine.

Displaying Variable Values

Another powerful feature of the Perl debugger is the capability to display the value of any variable at any time. The following sections describe the commands that perform this action.

The X Command

The X command displays variables in the current package (which is main if no other package has been specified). If the X command is specified by itself, it lists all the variables in the current package, including the system-defined variables and the variables used by the Perl interpreter itself. Usually, you won't want to use the X command by itself, because there are a lot of system-defined and internal variables known to the Perl interpreter.

To print the value of a particular variable or variables, specify the variable name or names with the X command:

```
  DB<5> X dircount
$dircount = '0'
```

This capability often is useful when you are checking for errors in your program.

WARNING

You must not supply the $ character with the variable name when you use the X command. If you supply the $ character (or the @ or % characters for arrays), the debugger displays nothing.

21

You can use X to display the values of array variables and associative array variables.

```
  DB<6> X regarray
@regarray = (
  0      14
  1      'hello'
  2      36
)
  DB<7> X assocarray
%assoc_array = (
  'hi'  1
  'there' 2
)
```

Each command prints the subscripts of the array and their values. Regular arrays are printed in order of subscript; associative arrays are printed in no particular order.

NOTE

If you have an array variable and a scalar variable with the same name, the X command prints both variables:

```
  DB<8> X var
$var = '0'
@var = (
  0        'test1'
  1        'test2'
)
```

There is no way to use X to display one variable but not the other.

The V Command

The V command is identical to the X command except that it prints the values of variables in any package. If you specify just a package name, as in the following, this command displays the values of all variables in the package (including system-defined and internal variables):

```
DB<9> V mypack
```

If you specify a package name and one or more variable names, as in the following, the debugger prints the values of the variables (if they are defined in that package):

```
  DB<10> V main dircount
$dircount = '0'
```

Breakpoints

As you have seen, you can tell the Perl debugger to execute one statement at a time. Another way of controlling program execution is to tell the debugger to execute up to a certain specified point in the program, called a *breakpoint*.

The following sections describe the commands that create breakpoints, and the command that executes until a breakpoint is detected.

The b Command

To set a breakpoint in your program, use the b command. This command tells the debugger to halt program execution whenever it is about to execute the specified line. For example, the following command tells the debugger to halt when it is about to execute line 10:

```
DB<11> b 10
```

(If the line is not breakable, the debugger will return Line 10 is not breakable.)

NOTE

> You can have as many breakpoints in your program as you want. The debugger will halt program execution if it is about to execute any of the statements at which a breakpoint has been defined.

The b command also accepts subroutine names:

```
DB<12> b menudir
```

This sets a breakpoint at the first executable statement of the subroutine menudir.

You can use the b command to tell the program to halt only when a specified condition is true. For example, the following command tells the debugger to halt if it is about to execute line 10 and the variable $curdir is equal to the null string:

```
DB<12> b 10 ($curdir eq "")
```

The condition specified with the b statement can be any legal Perl conditional expression.

21

WARNING

> If a statement is longer than a single line, you can set a breakpoint only
> at the first line of the statement:
>
> ```
> 71:      print ("Test",
> 72:      " here is more output");
> ```
>
> Here, you can set a breakpoint at line 71, but not line 72.

The c Command

After you have set a breakpoint, you can tell the debugger to execute until it reaches either
the breakpoint or the end of the program. To do this, use the c command:

```
  DB<13> c
main::(debugtest:10):                        $curdir =~ s/^\s+|\s+$//g;
  DB<14>
```

When the debugger detects that it is about to execute line 10—the line at which the
breakpoint was set—it halts and displays the line. (Recall that the debugger always displays
the line it is about to execute.)

The debugger now prompts you for another debugging command. This action enables you
to start executing one statement at a time using n or s, continue execution using c, set more
breakpoints using b, or perform any other debugging operation.

You can specify a temporary (one-time-only) breakpoint with the c command by supplying
a line number:

```
  DB<15> c 12
main::(debugtest:12):                        &readsubdirs($curdir);
```

The argument 12 supplied with the c command tells the debugger to define a temporary
breakpoint at line 12 and then resume execution. When the debugger reaches line 12, it halts
execution, displays the line, and deletes the breakpoint. (The line itself still exists, of course.)

Using c to define a temporary breakpoint is useful if you want to skip a few lines without
wasting your time executing the program one statement at a time. Using c also means that
you don't have to bother defining a breakpoint using b and deleting it using d (described in
the following section).

21

TIP

> If you intend to define breakpoints using c or b, it is a good idea to ensure that each line of your program contains at most one statement. If you are in the habit of writing lines that contain more than one statement, such as
>
> ```
> $x++; $y++;
> ```
>
> you won't get as much use out of the debugger, because it can't stop in the middle of a line.

The L Command and Breakpoints

To list all of your breakpoints, use the L command. This command lists the last few lines executed, the current line, the breakpoints you have defined, and the conditions under which the breakpoints go into effect.

```
  DB<16> L
3:      $dircount = 0;
4:      $curdir = "";
5:      while (1) {
7:              if ($curdir eq "") {
10:                     $curdir =~ s/^\s+¦\s+$//g;
  break if (1)
```

Here, the program has executed lines 3–7, and a breakpoint is defined for line 10. (Line 6 is not listed because it is a comment.) You can distinguish breakpoints from executed lines by looking for the breakpoint conditional expression, which immediately follows the breakpoint. Here, the conditional expression is (1), which indicates that the breakpoint is always in effect.

The d and D Commands

When you are finished with a breakpoint, you can delete it using the d command.

```
DB<16> d 10
```

This command tells the debugger to delete the breakpoint at line 10. The line itself remains in the program.

If you do not specify a breakpoint to delete, the debugger assumes that a breakpoint is defined for the next line to be executed, and deletes it.

```
main::(debugtest:12):                        &readsubdirs($curdir);
  DB<17> d
```

21

Here, line 12 is the next line to be executed, so the debugger deletes the breakpoint at line 12.

To delete all your breakpoints, use the D command.

```
DB<18> D
```

This command deletes all the breakpoints you have defined with the b command.

Tracing Program Execution

When you run a program using the Perl debugger, you can tell it to display each line as it is executed. When the debugger is doing this, it is said to be in *trace mode*.

To turn on trace mode, use the T command.

```
  DB<18> t
Trace = on
```

When a statement is executed in trace mode, the statement is displayed. For example, if the current line is line 5 and the command c 10 (which executes up to line 10) is entered, the following is displayed:

```
  DB<18> c 10
main::(debugtest:5):      while (1) {
main::(debugtest:7):            if ($curdir eq "") {
main::(debugtest:10):                $curdir =~ s/^\s+¦\s+$//g;
  DB<19>
```

The debugger prints and executes line 5 and line 7, then displays line 10 and waits for further instructions.

To turn off trace mode, specify the t command again.

```
  DB<19> t
Trace = off
```

At this point, trace mode is turned off until another t command is entered.

Line Actions

The Perl debugger enables you to specify one or more statements to be executed whenever the program reaches a specified line. Such statements are known as line actions. The most common line actions are printing the value of a variable and resetting a variable containing an erroneous value to the value you want.

The following sections describe the debugging commands that define line actions.

21

The a Command

To specify a line action for a particular line, use the a command.

```
DB<19> a 10 print ("curdir is $curdir\n");
```

This command tells the debugger to execute the statement

```
print ("curdir is $curdir\n");
```

whenever it is about to execute line 10 of the program. The debugger performs the action just after it displays the current line and before it asks for the next debugging command.

To create a line action containing more than one statement, just string the statements together. If you need more than one line for the statements, put a backslash at the end of the first line.

```
  DB<20> a 10 print ("curdir is $curdir\n"); print \
("this is a long line action\n");
```

In this case, when the debugger reaches line 10, it executes the following statements:

```
print ("curdir is $curdir\n");
print ("this is a long line action\n");
```

The A Command

To delete the line actions defined using the a command, use the A command.

```
DB<21> A
```

This command deletes all line actions currently defined.

NOTE The A command does not affect the < and > commands, described in the following section.

The < and > Commands

To define a line action that is to be executed before the debugger executes any further statements, use the > command.

```
DB<21> > print ("curdir before execution is $curdir\n");
```

This command tells the debugger to print the value of $curdir before continuing.

21

Similarly, the < command defines a line action that is to be performed after the debugger has finished executing statements and before it asks for another debugging command:

```
DB<22> < print ("curdir after execution is $curdir\n");
```

This command tells the debugger to print the value of $curdir before halting execution again.

The < and > commands are useful when you know that one of your variables has the wrong value, but you don't know which statement assigned the wrong value to the variable. By single-stepping through the program using s or n, and printing the variable either before or after executing each statement, you can determine where the variable was given its incorrect value.

NOTE

> To delete a line action defined by the < command, enter another < command with no line action defined.
>
> ```
> DB<23> <
> ```
>
> Similarly, the following command undoes the effects of a > command:
>
> ```
> DB<24> >
> ```

Displaying Line Actions Using the L Command

The L command prints any line actions you have defined using the a command (as well as breakpoints and executed lines). For example, suppose that you have defined a line action using the following command:

```
DB<25> a 10 print ("curdir is $curdir\n");
```

The L command then displays this line action as shown here:

```
main::(debugtest:10):                          $curdir =~ s/^\s+¦\s+$//g;
  action:  print ("curdir is $curdir\n");
```

The line action is always displayed immediately after the line for which it is defined. This method of display enables you to distinguish lines containing line actions from other lines displayed by the L command.

Other Debugging Commands

The following sections describe the debugging commands not previously covered.

Executing Other Perl Statements

In the debugger, anything that is not a debugging command is assumed to be a Perl statement and is performed right away. For example:

```
DB<4> @array = (1, 2, 3);
```

You can use statements such as this to alter values in your program as it is being executed. This capability is useful when you are testing your code.

NOTE

> If you wish, you can omit the semicolon at the end of the statement.

The H Command: Listing Preceding Commands

The H (for "history") command lists the preceding few commands you have entered.

```
  DB<4> H
3: b 7
2: b 14
1: b 13
```

The commands are listed in reverse order, with the most recently executed command listed first. Each command is preceded by its command number, which is used by the ! command (described in the following section).

NOTE

> The debugger saves only the commands that actually affect the debugging environment. Commands such as l and s, which perform useful work but do not change how the debugger behaves, are not listed by the H command.
>
> This is not a significant limitation because you can enter the letter again if needed.

21

The ! Command: Executing Previous Commands

Each command that is saved by the debugger and can be listed by the H command has a command number. You can use this command number to repeat a previously executed command. For example, to repeat command number 5, make the following entry:

```
  DB <11> !5
b 8
  DB <12>
```

The debugger displays command number 5—in this case, the command b 8—and then executes it.

If you omit the number, the debugger repeats the last command executed.

```
  DB <12> $foo += $bar + 1
  DB <13> !
$foo += $bar + 1
  DB <14>
```

If you specify a negative number with !, the debugger skips back that many commands:

```
  DB <14> $foo += $bar + 1
  DB <15> $foo *= 2
  DB <16> ! -2
$foo += $bar + 1
  DB <17>
```

Here, the ! -2 command refers to the command $foo += $bar + 1.

WARNING

> You can use ! only to repeat commands that are actually repeatable. Use the H command to list the commands that the debugger has saved and that can be repeated.

The T Command: Stack Tracing

The T command enables you to display a stack trace, which is a collection of all the subroutines that have been called, listed in reverse order. Here is an example:

```
  DB <16> T
$ = &main::sub2('hi') from file debug1 line 7
$ = &main::sub1('hi') from file debug1 line 3
```

Here, the T command indicates that the program is currently inside subroutine sub2, which was called from line 7 of your program; this subroutine is part of the main package. The call to sub2 is passed the argument 'hi'.

The $ = preceding the subroutine name indicates that the subroutine call is expecting a scalar return value. If the call is expecting a list to be returned, the characters @ = appear in front of the subroutine name.

The next line of the displayed output tells you that sub2 was called by another subroutine, sub1. This subroutine was also passed the argument 'hi', and it was called by line 3 of the program. Because the stack trace lists no more subroutines, line 3 is part of your main program.

NOTE

> The list of arguments passed to a subroutine that is displayed by the stack trace is the list of actual values after variable substitution and expression evaluation are performed. This procedure enables you to use the stack trace to check whether your subroutines are being passed the values you expect.

The p Command: Printing an Expression

An easy way to print the value of an expression from inside the debugger is to use the p command.

```
  DB <17> p $curdir + 1
1
```

The p command evaluates the expression and displays the result.

NOTE

> The p command writes to the screen even when the program has redirected STDOUT to a file.

The = Command: Defining Aliases

If you find yourself repeatedly entering a long debugging command and you want to save yourself some typing, you can define an alias for the long command by using the = command. For example:

```
  DB <15> = pc print ("curdir is $curdir\n");
= pc print ("curdir is $curdir\n");
```

The = command prints the alias you have just defined and then stores it in the associative array %DB'alias (package DB, array name alias) for future reference. From here on, the command

```
DB <16> pc
```

is equivalent to the command

```
DB <16> print ("curdir is $curdir\n");
```

To list the aliases you have defined so far, enter the = command by itself:

```
  DB <17> =
pc =  print ("curdir is $curdir\n")
```

This command displays your defined aliases and their equivalent values.

Predefining Aliases

You can define aliases that are to be created every time you enter the Perl debugger.

When the debugger starts, it first searches for a file named .perldb in your home directory. If the debugger finds this file, it executes the statements contained there.

To create an alias, add it to the .perldb file. For example, to add the alias

```
= pc print ("curdir is $curdir\n");
```

add the following statement to your .perldb file:

```
$DB'alias{"pc"} = 's/^pc/print ("curdir is $curdir\n");/';
```

Here's how this works: when the Perl debugger creates an alias, it adds an element to the $DB'alias associative array. The subscript for this element is the alias you are defining, and the value is a substitution command that replaces the alias with the actual command you want to use. In the preceding example, the substitution takes any command starting with pc and replaces it with

```
print ("curdir is $curdir\n");
```

WARNING

Be careful when you define aliases in this way. For example, your substitution should match only the beginning of a command, as in /^pc/. Otherwise, the alias will replace any occurrence of the letters pc with your print command, which is not what you want.

The h Command: Debugger Help

The h (for help) command provides a list of each of the debugger commands listed in today's lesson, along with a one-line explanation of each. This is handy if you are in the middle of debugging a program and forget the syntax of a particular command.

Summary

Today, you have learned about the Perl debugger. This debugger enables you to perform the following tasks, among others:

- List any part of your source file
- Step through your program one statement at a time
- Display any variables you have defined
- Set breakpoints, which tell the debugger when to stop and request further commands
- Set line actions, which are statements to be executed when the program reaches a particular line
- Trace program execution as it happens
- Print a stack trace, which lists the current subroutine you are in and the subroutines that called it

Q&A

Q Is it possible to enter more than one debugging command at a time?

A No; however, there's no real need to do so. If you want to perform several single steps at once, use the c command to skip ahead to a specified point. If you want to both step ahead and print the value of a variable, use the < or > command.

Q Is it possible to examine variables in one package while inside another?

A Yes. Use the V command or the standard Perl package/variable syntax.

Q If I discover that my program works and I want to turn off debugging, what do I do?

A You cannot exit the debugger in the middle of a program. However, if you delete all breakpoints and line actions and then enter the c command, the program begins executing normally and is no longer under control of the debugger.

Q How can I convert to a reusable breakpoint a one-time breakpoint created using c?

A By default, the b command sets a breakpoint at the line that is about to be executed. This is the line at which c has set its one-time breakpoint.

21

Q How can I execute other UNIX commands from inside the debugger?

A Enter a statement containing a call to the Perl system function. For example, to display the contents of the current directory, enter the following command:

```
DB <11> system ("ls");
```

To temporarily escape from the debugger to a UNIX shell, enter the following command:

```
DB <12> system ("sh");
```

When you are finished with the shell, enter the command exit, and you will return to the debugger.

Q What special built-in variables can be accessed from inside the debugger?

A All of them.

Workshop

The Workshop provides quiz questions to help you solidify your understanding of the material covered.

Quiz

1. Define the following terms:
    a. trace mode
    b. stack trace
    c. breakpoint
    d. line action
2. Explain the differences between the X and V commands.
3. Explain the differences between the / / and ?? commands.
4. Explain the differences between the < and > commands.
5. Explain the differences between the s and n commands.
6. What do the following commands do?
    a. l
    b. l 26
    c. l 5-7
    d. l 5+7
    e. w

Week 3 in Review

In the final week of teaching yourself how to use Perl, you've learned about the extensive Perl function library and about built-in system variables and options. The pair of programs in Listings R3.1 and R3.2 use some of the features you've learned about during this week.

These programs provide a simple "chat" service. The first program, the chat server, establishes connections with clients and passes messages back and forth. The second program, the chat client, enables users to establish connections to this server and send messages to the other users running the chat program.

Each message that a user enters is sent to all the clients currently running the chat program. To quit chatting, the user enters quit.

The server program can be called with the -m (for monitor) option. When -m is specified, each message sent by a client is displayed by the server as it is sent.

TYPE   **Listing R3.1. The chat server program.**

```
1:   #!/usr/local/bin/perl -s
2:
3:   # get port from command line, or use 2000 as default
4:   if ($#ARGV == -1) {
5:           $port = 2000;
6:   } else {
7:           $port = $ARGV[0];
8:   }
9:   if (getservbyport($port, "tcp")) {
10:          die ("can't access port $port\n");
11:  }
12:
13:  # initialization stuff
14:  $nextport = $port + 1;
15:  $maxclient = 0;
16:
17:  # establish main socket connection:  clients use this to
18:  # get ports for their own connections
19:  ($d1, $d2, $prototype) = getprotobyname ("tcp");
20:  $hostname = 'hostname';
21:  chop ($hostname);
22:  ($d1, $d2, $d3, $d4, $serverraddr) = gethostbyname ($hostname);
23:  $serveraddr = pack ("Sna4x8", 2, $port, $serverraddr);
24:  socket (SSOCKET, 2, 1, $prototype) ¦¦
25:          die ("No main server socket\n");
26:  bind (SSOCKET, $serveraddr) ¦¦
27:          die ("Can't bind main server socket\n");
28:  listen (SSOCKET, 5) ¦¦
29:          die ("Can't listen on main server socket\n");
30:  select (STDOUT);
31:  $¦ = 1;
32:
33:  while (1) {
34:          # listen for clients
35:          ($clientaddr = accept (SOCKET, SSOCKET)) ¦¦
36:                  die ("Can't accept connection to main socket\n");
37:          select (SOCKET);
38:          $¦ = 1;
39:          # find ports for new client
40:          $recvport = $nextport;
41:          while (getservbyport($recvport, "tcp")) {
42:                  $recvport++;
43:          }
44:          $nextport = $recvport + 1;
45:          print SOCKET ("$recvport\n");
46:          $sendport = $nextport;
47:          while (getservbyport($sendport, "tcp")) {
48:                  $sendport++;
49:          }
```

```
50:             $nextport = $sendport + 1;
51:             # send ports to client
52:             print SOCKET ("$sendport\n");
53:             print SOCKET ("$$\n");
54:             close (SOCKET);
55:             # now connect for this client: first receive, then send
56:             socket (C1SOCKET, 2, 1, $prototype) ||
57:                     die ("No receive client socket\n");
58:             $msgaddr = pack ("Sna4x8", 2, $recvport, $serverraddr);
59:             bind (C1SOCKET, $msgaddr) ||
60:                     die ("Can't bind receive client\n");
61:             listen (C1SOCKET, 1) ||
62:                     die ("Can't listen for receive client\n");
63:             $rsockname = "CRSOCKET" . $maxclient;
64:             ($clientaddr = accept ($rsockname, C1SOCKET)) ||
65:                     die ("Can't accept receive client\n");
66:             socket (C2SOCKET, 2, 1, $prototype) ||
67:                     die ("No send client socket\n");
68:             $msgaddr = pack ("Sna4x8", 2, $sendport, $serverraddr);
69:             bind (C2SOCKET, $msgaddr) ||
70:                     die ("Can't bind send client\n");
71:             listen (C2SOCKET, 1) ||
72:                     die ("Can't listen for send client\n");
73:             $ssockname = "CSSOCKET" . $maxclient;
74:             ($clientaddr = accept ($ssockname, C2SOCKET)) ||
75:                     die ("Can't accept send client\n");
76:             select ($ssockname);
77:             $| = 1;
78:             # when a new client is created, we have to kill all the
79:             # existing children and start new ones, so that all
80:             # of the sockets are known to all of the clients
81:             for ($i = 0; $i <= $maxclient-1; $i++) {
82:                     kill (2, $procids[$i]);
83:             }
84:             for ($i = 0; $i <= $maxclient; $i++) {
85:                     if ($child = fork()) {
86:                             # parent: continue forking
87:                             $procids[$i] = $child;
88:                     } else {
89:                             # child: communicate with this client
90:                             &talk_to_client ($i, $maxclient);
91:                             exit(0);
92:                     }
93:             }
94:             # once we're done forking, go back and listen for
95:             # more clients
96:             $maxclient += 1;
97:     }
98:
99: sub talk_to_client {
100:         local ($clientnum, $maxclient) = @_;
101:         local ($msg, $i, $count, $rsockname, $sockname);
102:
103:         # get read socket for this client
104:         $rsockname = "CRSOCKET" . $clientnum;
105:         while (1) {
```

continues

Listing R3.1. continued

```
106:                    $msg = <$rsockname>;
107:                    last if ($msg eq "quit");
108:                    if ($m) {
109:                            select (STDOUT);
110:                            print ("$msg");
111:                    }
112:
113:                    # send message to all other clients
114:                    for ($i = 0; $i <= $maxclient; $i++) {
115:                            $sockname = "CSSOCKET" . $i;
116:                            select ($sockname);
117:                            print ("$msg");
118:                    }
119:            }
120: }
```

ANALYSIS This program starts off by obtaining the number of the port to be used for the main socket connection. This port number is assumed to be the first argument on the command line; if no port number is supplied, 2000 is used. Lines 9–11 call getservbyport to check whether this port number is mentioned in the /etc/services file. If it is, the port number is reserved for use by some other program and can't be used here.

Next, lines 17–29 define a socket using the specified port number. Client programs use this socket to establish connections to the server. Note, in particular, that lines 20–21 read the machine name by calling the UNIX hostname command. This enables you to move this program to another machine without having to edit it.

Once the main socket has been established, the server is ready to listen for clients. When a client establishes a connection, the server finds two unused port numbers and sends them to the client. These ports will be used to establish two new socket connections—one for reading and one for writing—which will be used by the server and this particular client. This leaves the main socket free to establish connections with other clients. Lines 44–54 handle the task of obtaining the ports and sending them to the client; lines 55–77 then establish connections to the client using the sockets. (Note that line 53 also sends the process ID of the chat server to the client. This enables the client to kill off the server if something horrible happens.)

The chat server communicates with a client by spawning a child process that handles the task of receiving a message from that client and sending it to the other clients. One child process is defined for each client. The call to fork in line 85 creates a child process.

When a child process is created, it knows the names of the file variables corresponding to the sockets defined for each of the existing clients. However, if a new client appears, the existing child processes cannot send messages to the new client because they cannot access its sockets (because they are created after the children were spawned). To ensure that the existing clients can send messages to the new clients, the server program does the following:

1. It kills all the child processes that communicate with clients. Lines 81–83 accomplish this task by calling kill.

2. The server creates a new child process for each client. Lines 84–93 perform this task.

At this point, each client can talk to every other client because all of the socket connections are known by each child. (Recall that when a program splits into parent and child processes, each process has a copy of all the variables that have been defined to this point.)

The chat server uses the global variable $maxclient to keep track of how many clients are on the machine. This ensures that the correct number of child processes are created.

Each child process created by fork calls the subroutine talk_to_client, which reads messages from the client and then sends them to all the other clients via the "send" socket connections. Line 106 reads a message from the client. Line 107 checks whether the message is in fact quit; if it is, the subroutine (and the process) terminates. Lines 108–111 then print the message if the -m option is specified. Finally, lines 113–118 send the message to the other clients.

NOTE

The chat server does not make any attempt to clean up after itself or to reuse sockets closed by clients. This means that this particular program can't be used by too many clients at a time, or by too many different clients.

If you are looking for a challenging exercise, try modifying this program to close sockets when clients are finished with them. (This is a challenging exercise because the child process somehow has to tell the main server that the socket can be closed. You can do it, but it's not easy!)

Now that you've seen how the chat server works, Listing R3.2 shows the chat client program. Users run this program to establish a connection with the chat server and to chat with other users.

TYPE | **Listing R3.2. The chat client program.**

```
1:    #!/usr/local/bin/perl
2:
3:    # obtain the server port from the command line;
4:    # use 2000 as the default
5:    if ($#ARGV == -1) {
6:          $servport = 2000;
```

continues

Listing R3.2. continued

```
 7:  } else {
 8:          $servport = $ARGV[0];
 9:  }
10:
11:  # obtain the server machine name from the command line;
12:  # use "silver" as the default
13:  if ($#ARGV < 1) {
14:          $servname = "silver";
15:  } else {
16:          $servname = $ARGV[1];
17:  }
18:  # establish socket connection with server to obtain
19:  # ports for this client
20:  if (getservbyport($servport, "tcp")) {
21:          die ("can't access port $servport\n");
22:  }
23:  ($d1, $d2, $prototype) = getprotobyname ("tcp");
24:  $hostname = 'hostname';
25:  chop ($hostname);
26:  ($d1, $d2, $d3, $d4, $clientraddr) = gethostbyname ($hostname);
27:  ($d1, $d2, $d3, $d4, $serverraddr) = gethostbyname ($servname);
28:  $clientaddr = pack ("Sna4x8", 2, 0, $clientraddr);
29:  $serveraddr = pack ("Sna4x8", 2, $servport, $serverraddr);
30:  socket (SOCKET, 2, 1, $prototype) ||
31:          die ("No server socket\n");
32:  bind (SOCKET, $clientaddr) ||
33:          die ("Can't bind server socket\n");
34:  connect (SOCKET, $serveraddr) ||
35:          die ("Can't connect to server\n");
36:  $sendport = <SOCKET>;
37:  $recvport = <SOCKET>;
38:  $serverid = <SOCKET>;
39:  close (SOCKET);
40:  chop ($sendport);
41:  chop ($recvport);
42:
43:  # use returned ports to create sockets for this client:
44:  # first socket is send, the second is receive
45:  $conncaddr = pack ("Sna4x8", 2, 0, $clientraddr);
46:  $connsaddr = pack ("Sna4x8", 2, $sendport, $serverraddr);
47:  socket (SSOCKET, 2, 1, $prototype) ||
48:          &nuke ("No send socket");
49:  bind (SSOCKET, $conncaddr) ||
50:          &nuke ("Can't bind send socket");
51:  connect (SSOCKET, $connsaddr) ||
52:          &nuke ("Can't connect to send socket");
53:  $connraddr = pack ("Sna4x8", 2, $recvport, $serverraddr);
54:  socket (RSOCKET, 2, 1, $prototype) ||
55:          &nuke ("No receive socket");
56:  bind (RSOCKET, $conncaddr) ||
57:          &nuke ("Can't bind receive socket");
58:  connect (RSOCKET, $connraddr) ||
59:          &nuke ("Can't connect to receive socket");
60:  select (SSOCKET);
61:  $| = 1;
62:  select (STDOUT);
```

```
63:  $| = 1;
64:
65:  # now, we're ready to go:  prompt for user name
66:  select (STDOUT);
67:  print ("Welcome to chat!  Who are you? ");
68:  $username = <STDIN>;
69:  chop ($username);
70:  print ("Type 'quit' to exit chat.\n");
71:  $child = fork();
72:  if ($child == 0) {
73:          # child: receive messages
74:          &receive_msgs();
75:          exit(0);
76:  }
77:  # parent: send messages
78:  while (1) {
79:          # prompt for message
80:          select (STDOUT);
81:          $msg = <STDIN>;
82:          chop ($msg);
83:          # send message to server
84:          select (SSOCKET);
85:          if ($msg eq "quit") {
86:                  print ($msg);
87:                  last;
88:          }
89:          if ($msg !~ /^\s*$/) {
90:                  print ($username . ": " . $msg . "\n");
91:          }
92:  }
93:  kill (9, $child);
94:  close (RSOCKET);
95:  close (SSOCKET);
96:
97:  sub receive_msgs {
98:          local ($msg);
99:
100:         while (1) {
101:                 $msg = <RSOCKET>;
102:                 select (STDOUT);
103:                 print ("$msg");
104:         }
105: }
106:
107: sub nuke {
108:         local ($errmsg) = @_;
109:
110:         kill (-9, $serverid);
111:         die ("$errmsg\n");
112: }
```

ANALYSIS This program starts off by obtaining the port number of the main socket connection employed by the chat server. This port number can be supplied on the command line; if it is not, the chat program uses 2000 as the port number.

The chat program then obtains the name of the machine on which the chat server is running. This name also can be supplied on the command line; if it isn't, the chat program assumes the machine is a local machine named silver.

Lines 23–41 establish a connection to the main server socket and receive the port numbers for the sockets to be used by this particular client-server connection. The client also receives the process ID of the server.

Once the port numbers have been received, the chat program can connect to the chat server by establishing two socket connections with the server: one to send messages and another to receive them. Lines 43–63 accomplish this task.

When these socket connections have been established, the chat program is ready to send messages. Lines 67–68 ask for a name by which you can identify yourself to the other users on the system. Once this name has been read in, the chat program splits itself in two by calling fork. The parent process handles the sending of messages, and the child handles messages received by other clients. This ensures that sending and receiving can take place at the same time.

Lines 77–95 send messages to the chat server. Line 81 prompts for a line of input. If the line of input is the message quit, the client program kills off its child, closes its socket connection, and exits. Otherwise, the message—along with the name of the user sending it—is transmitted to the chat server via the "write" socket. The server then sends it to all of the clients on the system.

The child process calls the subroutine receive_msgs, which handles the task of receiving messages from the other clients. Messages are received via the "read" socket and are printed as they are received.

If something goes radically wrong, the chat program calls the subroutine nuke, which kills both itself and the server program.

Answers

Answers for Day 1, "Getting Started"

Quiz

1. Perl has the power of a high-level programming language such as C, and the ease of use of simple languages such as shell scripts.

2. The Perl interpreter executes your Perl program (starting from the beginning, and continuing one statement at a time).

3. The answers are as follows:

   a. A statement is one particular task or instruction (usually corresponding to a line of code). A statement is terminated by a semicolon (;).

   b. A token is the smallest unit of information understood by the Perl interpreter. A statement consists of several tokens.

   c. An argument is an item passed to a library function (such as $inputline to print).

   d. Error recovery occurs when the Perl interpreter detects an error in your program. The interpreter tries to deduce what you meant to write and attempts to continue detecting errors in the program.

   e. The standard input file is the file that stores the characters you enter at the keyboard.

4. A comment is any text that is preceded by a #. A comment can appear anywhere in your program. Everything after the # character is assumed to be part of the comment.

5. Perl usually is located in the file /usr/local/bin/perl.

6. The header comment is the special comment that tells the system that this is a Perl program. It appears as the first line of every Perl program.

7. A library function is defined as part of the Perl interpreter and performs a specific task.

Exercises

1. The following is one possible solution:

```
#!/usr/local/bin/perl
$inputline = <STDIN>;
print ($inputline, $inputline);
```

2. The following is one possible solution:

```
#!/usr/local/bin/perl
$inputline = <STDIN>;
print ($inputline);
$inputline = <STDIN>;
print ($inputline);
```

3. The following is one possible solution:

```
#!/usr/local/bin/perl
$inputline = <STDIN>;
$inputline = <STDIN>;     # this throws away the previous input line
print( $inputline );
```

4. The third line of the program is missing a semicolon at the end of the statement:

```
#!/usr/local/bin/perl
$inputline = <STDIN>;
print ($inputline);
```

5. The `print($inputline)` line is ignored because the entire third line is being treated as a comment. You want the following instead:

```
#!/usr/local/bin/perl
$inputline = <STDIN>;
print($inputline);   # print my line!
```

6. This program reads two lines of input and prints them in reverse order (second line first).

Answers for Day 2, "Basic Operators and Control Flow"

Quiz

1. The answers are as follows:

   a. An expression is a collection of operators and the values on which they operate.

   b. An operand is a value associated with an operator.

   c. A conditional statement is a statement that is executed only when its conditional expression is true.

   d. A statement block is a collection of statements contained inside the braces of a conditional statement. The statement block is executed only when the conditional expression associated with its conditional statement is true.

   e. An infinite loop is a conditional statement whose conditional expression is always true.

2. A `while` statement stops looping when its conditional expression is false.

3. An `until` statement stops looping when its conditional expression is true.

4. The `==` operator compares its two operands. If they are numerically equal, the `==` operator yields a result of true; otherwise, it yields false.

5. 27.

6. The legal ones are a, c, and f.

Exercises

1. Here is one possible solution:

```perl
#!/usr/local/bin/perl

print ("Enter a number to be multiplied by 2:\n");
$number = <STDIN>;
chop ($number);
$number = $number * 2;
print ("The result is ", $number, "\n");
```

2. Here is one possible solution:

```perl
#!/usr/local/bin/perl

print ("Enter the dividend (number to divide):\n");
$dividend = <STDIN>;
chop ($dividend);
print ("Enter the divisor (number to divide by):\n");
$divisor = <STDIN>;
chop ($divisor);
if ($divisor == 0) {
        print ("Error: can't divide by zero!\n");
} elsif ($dividend == 0) {
        $result = $dividend;
} elsif ($divisor == 1) {
        $result = $dividend;
} else {
        $result = $divisor / $dividend;
}
if ($divisor == 0) {
        # skip the print, since we detected an error
} else {
        print ("The result is ", $result, "\n");
}
```

3. Here is one possible solution:

```perl
#!/usr/local/bin/perl

$count = 1;
$done = 0;
while ($done == 0) {
        print ($count, "\n");
        if ($count == 10) {
```

```
                $done = 1;
        }
        $count = $count + 1;
}
```

4. Here is one possible solution:

```
#!/usr/local/bin/perl

$count = 10;
until ($count == 0) {
        print ($count, "\n");
        $count = $count - 1;
}
```

5. There are, in fact, three separate bugs in this program:

   a. You must call chop to get rid of the trailing newline character in $value before comparing it to 17.

   b. The conditional expression should read $value == 17, not $value = 17.

   c. There should be a closing brace } before the else.

6. This program contains an infinite loop. To fix it, add the following statement just before the closing brace }:

```
$input = $input + 1;
```

Also, the statement

```
$input = $terminate + 5;
```

should read

```
$terminate = $input + 5;
```

Answers for Day 3, "Understanding Scalar Values"

Quiz

1. The answers are as follows:

   a. A round-off error is the difference between the floating-point number that appears in a program and the number as it is represented in the machine.

   b. Octal notation is another way of referring to base-8 notation: Each digit can be a number from 0 to 7 and is multiplied by 8 to the exponent n, where n is the number of digits to skip.

c. The precision of a floating-point representation on a machine is the number of significant digits it can hold.

d. Scientific notation is a way of writing floating-point numbers. It consists of one digit before the decimal point, as many digits as required after the decimal point, and an exponent.

2. The answers are as follows:

a. 255 (the ASCII end-of-file character)

b. 6

c. 601

3. The answers are as follows:

a. 255

b. 17

c. 48813

4. This line prints I am bored, and then backspaces over bored and replaces it with happy!. (I don't know a lot of practical uses for the \b escape character, but it's fun to watch.)

5. The answers are as follows:

a. `This string contains 21.`

b. `\21 is my favorite number.`

c. `Assign \$num to this string.`

6. The answers are as follows:

a. `4.371e01`

b. `6.0e-08` (the .0 is optional)

c. `3.0e+00` (actually, 3 by itself is acceptable)

d. `-1.04e+00`

Exercises

1. Here is one possible solution:

```
#!/usr/local/bin/perl

$count = 1;
$number = 0.1;
until ($count == 10) {
        print ("$number\n");
        $number = $number + 0.1;
        $count = $count + 1;
}
```

2. Here is one possible solution:

```
#!/usr/local/bin/perl

$inputline = <STDIN>;
chop ($inputline);
if ($inputline == 0) {
        print ("0\n");
} else {
        print ("1\n");
}
```

3. Here is one possible solution:

```
#!/usr/local/bin/perl

print ("Enter a number:\n");
$number = <STDIN>;
chop ($number);
until ($number == 47) {
        print ("Wrong! Try again!\n");
        $number = <STDIN>;
        chop ($number);
}
print ("\aCorrect!\n");
```

4. The first string in the `print` statement is not terminated properly, because there is a backslash \ before the final '. To fix this, add another quote:

```
print ('here is the value of \$inputline\'', ": $inputline");
```

5. This code fragment does not produce the expected result because of a round-off error. Try subtracting $num3 from $num1 before adding $num2 and $num4.

6. `"0xce"` converts to 0, not to the hexadecimal constant 0xce. To fix this, leave off the quotes.

Answers for Day 4, "More Operators"

Quiz

1. The answers are as follows:

   a. An operator is a character or string of characters that represents a particular Perl operation.

   b. An operand is a value used by an operator. In Perl, operators require one, two, or three operands.

   c. An expression is a collection of operators and operands, yielding a final result.

   d. Operator precedence is the order in which different types of operations are performed.

   e. Operator associativity is the order in which operations of the same precedence are performed.

2. The answers are as follows:

    a. logical AND

    b. bitwise AND

    c. bitwise XOR

    d. string inequality

    e. string concatenation

3. The answers are as follows:

    a. `eq`

    b. `%`

    c. `x`

    d. `¦`

    e. `>=`

4. The answers are as follows:

    a. 0000000010101011

    b. 0000010001010001

    c. 0 (or 00000000)

5. The answers are as follows:

    a. 100

    b. 15

    c. 65

6. The answers are as follows:

    a. 4

    b. 0 (I hope you didn't calculate all of the expression! Once you see the first 0, you should know that the result is 0.)

    c. 1819

    d. `"abcdede"`

Exercises

1. The following is just one of many possible answers:

```
#!/usr/local/bin/perl

$value = 1;
$counter = 0;
while ($counter < 16) {
        print ("2 to the power $counter is $value\n");
```

A

```
        $value = $value << 1;
        $counter++;
}
```

2. The answer is as follows:

```
$result = $var1 == 5 || $var2 == 7 ?
        $var1 * $var2 + 16.5 :
        (print("condition is false\n"), 0);
```

3. The answer is as follows:

```
if ($var1 <= 26) {
        $result = ++$var2;
} else {
        $result = 0;
}
```

4. The following is just one of many possible answers:

```
#!/usr/local/bin/perl

print("Enter the integer to be divided:\n");
$dividend = <STDIN>;
print("Enter the integer to divide by:\n");
$divisor = <STDIN>;
# check for division by zero
if ($divisor == 0) {
        print("error: can't divide by zero\n");
} else {
        $quotient = $dividend / $divisor;
        $remainder = $dividend % $divisor;
        print("The result is $quotient\n");
        print("The remainder is $remainder\n");
}
```

5. Adding 100005.2 and then subtracting it causes round-off errors, which means that the final value isn't exactly the same as 5.1.

6. ($result = ((($var1 * 2) << (5 + 3)) || ($var2 ** 3))), $var3;

7. 81

8. Here is the corrected program, with the fixed errors listed:

```
#!/usr/local/bin/perl

$num = <STDIN>;
chop ($num);
$x = "";
$x .= "hello";       # += is for integers
if ($x ne "goodbye" || $x eq "farewell") {
        # the previous line had two problems:
        #    the operators were numeric, not string;
        #    the or operator was bitwise, not logical.
        $result = $num == 0 ? 43 : 0;
        # the : and third operand were missing in the previous
        # line; eq replaced by ==
} else {
        $result = ++$num;   # can't have ++ on both sides
}
print("the result is $result\n");
```

Answers for Day 5, "Lists and Array Variables"

Quiz

1. The answers are as follows:

    a. A list is an ordered collection of scalar values.

    b. An empty list is a list with zero elements in it.

    c. An array variable is a variable that can store a list.

    d. A subscript is a scalar value that refers to an element of a list. The subscript 0 refers to the first element, the subscript 1 refers to the second, and so on.

    e. An array slice is a list consisting of some elements of an array variable. (Notice that the elements do not have to be in order.)

2. The answers are as follows:

    a. `(1, 2, 3)`

    b. `(3, 2)`

    c. `("hello", 2, 2)`

    d. `(2, 3)`

    e. `("", 3, 2, 2)`

    f. The contents of the standard input file, one line per list element.

3. The answers are as follows:

    a. `2`

    b. `4`

    c. `"one"`

    d. `2`

    e. `"three"`

    f. `""` (Only three elements in the list are stored in `@list2`.)

4. A list is a collection of scalar values. An array variable is a place where you can store a list.

5. The brackets `[]` enclosing the subscript distinguish an array element from a scalar variable.

A

6. You can do this in many ways. The two easiest are

☐ Use single-quoted strings, which do not allow substitutions.

☐ Put a backslash \ before the character that you want left as is.

7. You can obtain the length of a list stored in an array variable by assigning the array variable to a scalar variable.

8. All undefined array elements are assumed to contain the null string " ".

9. When you assign to an array element that is larger than the current length of the array, the array grows to include the new element.

Exercises

1. Here is one possible solution:

```perl
#!/usr/local/bin/perl

$thecount = 0;
$line = <STDIN>;
while ($line ne "") {
        chop ($line);
        @words = split(/ /, $line);
        $wordindex = 1;
        while ($wordindex <= @words) {
                if ($words[$wordindex-1] eq "the") {
                        $thecount += 1;
                }
                $wordindex++;
        }
        $line = <STDIN>;
}
print ("Total occurrences of \"the\": $thecount\n");
```

2. Here is one possible solution:

```perl
#!/usr/local/bin/perl

$grandtotal = 0;
$line = <STDIN>;
while ($line ne "") {
        $linetotal = 0;
        @numbers = split(/ /, $line);
        $numbercount = 1;
        while ($numbercount <= @numbers) {
                $linetotal += $numbers[$numbercount-1];
                $numbercount++;
        }
        print("line total: $linetotal\n");
        $grandtotal += $linetotal;
        $line = <STDIN>;
}
print("grand total: $grandtotal\n");
```

3. Here is one possible solution:

```perl
#!/usr/local/bin/perl

@lines = <STDIN>;
chop (@lines);
$longlongline = join(" ", @lines);
@words = split(/ /, $longlongline);
@words = reverse sort (@words);
$index = 0;
print("Words sorted in reverse order:\n");
while ($index < @words) {
        # note that the first time through, the following
        # comparison references $words[-1]. This is all
        # right, as $words[-1] is replaced by the null
        # string, and we want the first word to be printed
        if ($words[$index] ne $words[$index-1]) {
                print ("$words[$index]\n");
        }
        $index++;
}
```

4. The array element reference should be $array[4], not @array[4].

5. There are four separate bugs in this program:

   a. You must call chop to remove the newline characters from the input lines stored in @input. Otherwise, they make your output unreadable.

   b. Similarly, you have to append a newline when calling join:

      ```perl
      $input[$currline] = join(" ", @words, "\n");
      ```

   c. The conditional expression should read

      ```perl
      $currline <= @input
      ```

      instead of

      ```perl
      $currline < @input
      ```

      to make sure that the last line of the input file is read.

   d. Your subscripts should read [$currline-1], not [$currline]. (This bug will keep coming up in your programs because it's easy to forget that subscripts start with zero.)

Answers for Day 6, "Reading from and Writing to Files"

Quiz

1. The answers are as follows:

    a. A file variable is a name that represents an open file.

    b. A reserved word is a word that can't be used as a variable name because it has a special meaning in Perl (such as if).

    c. The file mode specifies how you want to access a file when you open it (read, write, or append).

    d. Append mode indicates that you want to open the file for writing and append anything you write to the existing contents of the file.

    e. A pipe is a connection between output from one program and input to another.

2. The <> operator reads its data from the files specified on the command line.

3. The answers are as follows:

    a. -r tests whether you have permission to read a file.

    b. -x tests whether you have permission to execute a file (and whether the file is executable).

    c. -s indicates the size of a file in bytes.

4. @ARGV contains the following list:

    ```
    ("file1", "file2", "file3")
    ```

5. The answers are as follows:

    a. To open a file in write mode, put a > character in front of the filename.

    b. To open a file in append mode, put two > characters (>>) in front of the filename.

    c. To open a file in read mode, just specify the filename. By default, files are opened in read mode.

    d. To open a pipe, put a ¦ character in front of the command to be piped to.

6. The <> operator reads data from the files whose names are stored in the array variable @ARGV. When the <> operator runs out of data in one file, it opens the file named in $ARGV[0] and then calls shift to move the elements of @ARGV over.

Exercises

1. Here is one possible solution:

```perl
#!/usr/local/bin/perl

$total = 0;
$count = 1;
while ($count <= @ARGV) {
        $total += $ARGV[$count-1];
        $count++;
}
print ("The total is $total.\n");
```

2. Here is one possible solution:

```perl
#!/usr/local/bin/perl

$count = 1;
while ($count <= @ARGV) {
        if (-e $ARGV[$count-1] && -s $ARGV[$count-1] > 10000) {
                print ("File $ARGV[$count-1] is a big file!\n");
        }
        $count++;
}
```

3. Here is one possible solution:

```perl
#!/usr/local/bin/perl
open (INFILE, "file1") ||
        die ("Can't open file1 for reading\n");
open (OUTFILE, ">file2") ||
        die ("Can't open file2 for writing\n");
# the following only works if file1 isn't too big
@contents = <INFILE>;
print OUTFILE (@contents);
# we don't really need the call to close, but they
# make things a little clearer
close (OUTFILE);
open (OUTFILE, ">>file2") ||
        die ("Can't append to file2\n");
print OUTFILE (@contents);
```

4. Here is one possible solution:

```perl
#!/usr/local/bin/perl

$wordcount = 0;
while ($line = <>) {
        # this isn't the best possible pattern to split with,
        # but it'll do until you've finished Day 7
        @words = split(/ /, $line);
        $wordcount += @words;
}
open (MESSAGE, "| mail dave") ||
        die ("Can't mail to userid dave.\n");
print MESSAGE ("Total number of words: $wordcount\n");
close (MESSAGE);
```

5. Here is one possible solution:

```perl
#!/usr/local/bin/perl

$count = 1;
while ($count <= @ARGV) {
        print ("File $ARGV[$count-1]:");
        if (!(-e $ARGV[$count-1])) {
                print (" does not exist\n");
        } else {
                if (-r $ARGV[$count-1]) {
                        print (" read");
                }
                if (-w $ARGV[$count-1]) {
                        print (" write");
                }
                if (-x $ARGV[$count-1]) {
                        print (" execute");
                }
                print ("\n");
        }
        $count++;
}
```

6. This program is opening outfile in read mode, not write mode. To open in write mode, change the call to open to

```perl
open (OUTFILE, ">outfile");
```

Answers for Day 7, "Pattern Matching"

Quiz

1. The answers are as follows:

   a. Either the letter a or b, followed by zero or more occurrences of c.

   b. One, two, or three digits.

   c. The words cat, cot, and cut. (This pattern does not match these letters if they are in the middle of a word.)

   d. The first part of this pattern matches a subpattern consisting of x, one or more of y, and z. The rest of the pattern then matches a period, followed by the subpattern first matched.

   e. This matches an empty line (the null string).

2. The answers are as follows:

   a. `/[a-z]{5,}/`

   b. `/1¦one/`

   c. `/\d+\.?\d+/`

   d. `/([A-Za-z])[aeiou]\1/`

   e. `/\++/`

3. Items a, b, c, and f are true; d and e are false.

4. The answers are as follows:

   a. `"def123abc"`

   b. `"X123X"`

   c. `"aWc123abc"`

   d. `"abd"`

   e. `"abc246abc"`

5. The answers are as follows:

   a. `"ABC123ABC"`

   b. `"abc456abc"`

   c. `"abc456abc"`

   d. `"abc abc"`

   e. `"123"`

Exercises

1. Here is one possible solution:

```
#!/usr/local/bin/perl

while ($line = <STDIN>) {
        $line =~ tr/aeiou/AEIOU/;
        print ($line);
}
```

2. Here is one possible solution:

```
#!/usr/local/bin/perl

while ($inputline = <STDIN>) {
        $inputline =~ tr/0-9/ /c;
        $inputline =~ s/ +//g;
        @digits = split(//, $inputline);
```

A

```
                $total += @digits;
                $count = 1;
                while ($count <= @digits) {
                        $dtotal[$digits[$count-1]] += 1;
                        $count++;
                }
        }
        print ("Total number of digits found: $total\n");
        print ("Breakdown:\n");
        $count = 0;
        while ($count <= 9) {
                if ($dtotal[$count] > 0) {
                        print ("\tdigit $count: $dtotal[$count]\n");
                }
                $count++;
        }
```

3. Here is one possible solution:

```
#!/usr/local/bin/perl

while ($line = <STDIN>) {
        $line =~ s/(\w+)(\s+)(\w+)(\s+)(\w+)/$5$2$3$4$1/;
        print ($line);
}
```

4. Here is one possible solution:

```
#!/usr/local/bin/perl

while ($line = <STDIN>) {
        $line =~ s/\d+/$&+1/eg;
        print ($line);
}
```

5. There are two problems. The first is that the pattern matches the entire line, including the closing newline. You do not want to put a quotation mark after the closing newline of each line. In this case, it causes the program to omit the s operator, which specifies substitution.

    The second problem is that the replacement string should contain $1, not \1. \1 is defined only inside the search pattern.

6. The pattern uses the * special character, which matches zero or more occurrences of any digit. This means the pattern always matches.

    The pattern should use the + special character, which matches one or more occurrences of any digit.

Answers for Day 8, "More Control Structures"

Quiz

1. 7
2. 11
3. 5
4. 6
5. `last if ($x eq "done");`
6. `redo if ($list[0] == 26);`
7. `next LABEL if ($scalar eq "#");`
8. `print ("$count\n") while ($count++ < 10);`
9. The `continue` statement defines a block of code to be executed each time a `while` or `until` statement loops.

Exercises

1. Here is one possible solution:

```
#!/usr/local/bin/perl

$count = 1;
do {
        print ("$count\n");
        $count++;
} while ($count <= 10);
```

2. Here is one possible solution:

```
#!/usr/local/bin/perl

for ($count = 1; $count <= 10; $count++) {
        print ("$count\n");
}
```

3. Here is one possible solution:

```
#!/usr/local/bin/perl

for ($count = 1; $count <= 5; $count++) {
        $line = <STDIN>;
        last if ($line eq "");
        print ($line);
}
```

4. Here is one possible solution:

```
#!/usr/local/bin/perl

for ($count = 1; $count <= 20; $count++) {
        next if ($count % 2 == 1);
        print ("$count\n");
}
```

5. Here is one possible solution:

```
#!/usr/local/bin/perl

$linenum = 0;
while ($line = <STDIN>) {
        $linenum += 1;
        $occurs = 0;
        $line =~ tr/A-Z/a-z/;
        @words = split(/\s+/, $line);
        foreach $word (@words) {
                $occurs += 1 if ($word eq "the");
        }
        if ($occurs > 0) {
                print ("line $linenum: $occurs occurrences\n");
        }
}
```

6. Here is one possible solution:

```
#!/usr/local/bin/perl

$count = 10;
while ($count >= 1) {
        print ("$count\n");
}
continue {
        $count--;
}
```

7. You can't use the `last` statement inside a `do` statement. To get around this problem, use another loop construct such as `while` or `for`, or put the conditional expression in the `while` statement at the bottom.

Answers for Day 9, "Using Subroutines"

Quiz

1. The answers are as follows:

   a. A subroutine is a separate body of code designed to perform a particular task.

   b. An invocation is a statement that tells the Perl interpreter to execute a particular subroutine.

c. An argument is a value that is passed to a subroutine when it is invoked.

d. A single-exit module is a subroutine whose return value is calculated by the final statement in the subroutine.

e. Aliasing occurs when one name is defined to be equivalent to another.

2. The answers are as follows:

a. 0

b. (4, 5, 6)

c. (4, 5, 6)

3. False (or zero), because the conditional expression $count <= 10 is the last expression evaluated in the subroutine.

4. (1, 5, 3)

Exercises

1. Here is one possible solution:

```
sub add_two {
        local ($arg1, $arg2) = @_;

        $result = $arg1 + $arg2;
}
```

2. Here is one possible solution:

```
sub count_t {
        local ($string) = @_;

        # There are a couple of tricks you can use to do this.
        # This one splits the string into words using "t" as
        # the split pattern. The number of occurrences of "t"
        # is one less than the number of words resulting from
        # the split.
        @dummy = split(/t/, $string);
        $retval = @dummy - 1;
}
```

3. Here is one possible solution:

```
sub diff {
        local ($file1, $file2) = @_;

        # return false if we can't open a file
        return (0) unless open (FILE1, "$file1");
        return (0) unless open (FILE2, "$file2");
        while (1) {
                $line1 = <FILE1>;
                $line2 = <FILE2>;
                if ($line1 eq "") {
                        $retval = ($line2 eq "");
                        last;
```

A

```
                    }
                    if ($line2 eq "" || $line1 ne $line2) {
                            $retval = 0;
                            last;
                    }
            }
            # you should use close here, as this subroutine may
            # be called many times
            close (FILE1);
            close (FILE2);
            # ensure that the return value is the last evaluated
            # expression
            $retval;
    }
```

4. Here is one possible solution:

```
sub dieroll {
        $retval = int (rand(6)) + 1;
}
```

5. Here is one possible solution:

```
# assume that the first call to printlist passes the argument
# 0 as the value for $index
sub printlist {
        local ($index, @list) = @_;

        if ($index + 1 < @list) {
                &printlist ($index+1, @list);
        }
        # the conditional handles the case of an empty list
        print ("$list[$index]\n") if (@list > 0);
}
```

6. The subroutine print_ten overwrites the value stored in the global variable $count. To fix this problem, define $count as a local variable. (You also should define $printval as a local variable, in case someone adds this variable to the main program at a later time.)

7. The local statement in the subroutine assigns both the list and the search word to @searchlist, which means that $searchword is assigned the empty string. To fix this problem, switch the order of the arguments, putting the search word first.

8. If split produces a nonempty list, the last expression evaluated in the subroutine is the conditional expression, which has the value 0 (false):

```
@words == 0
```

Therefore, the return value of this subroutine is 0, not the list of words.

To get around this problem, put the following statement after the if statement:

```
@words;
```

This ensures that the list of words is always the return value.

Answers for Day 10, "Associative Arrays"

Quiz

1. The answers are as follows:

   a. An associative array is an array whose subscripts can be any scalar value.

   b. A pointer is an associative array element whose value is the subscript of another associative array element.

   c. A linked list is an associative array in which each element of the array points to the next.

   d. A binary tree is a data structure in which each element points to (at most) two other elements.

   e. A node is an element of a binary tree.

   f. A child is an element of a binary tree that is pointed to by another element.

2. This statement creates an associative array containing three elements:

   ☐ An element with subscript 17.2 whose value is hello

   ☐ An element with subscript there whose value is 46

   ☐ An element with subscript e+6 whose value is 88

3. When you assign an associative array to an ordinary array variable, the value of the array variable becomes a list consisting of all of the subscript/value pairs of the associative array (in the order in which they were stored in the associative array, which is random).

4. Define a scalar variable containing the value of the list's first element. Then, use the value of one associative array element as the subscript for the next.

5. This is a trick question: Because the associative array %list stores its elements in random order, it is not clear how many times the foreach loop iterates. It could be one, two, or three.

Exercises

1. Here is one possible solution:

```
#!/usr/local/bin/perl

while ($line = <STDIN>) {
        $line =~ s/^\s+¦\s+$//g;
        ($subscript, $value) = split(/\s+/, $line);
        $array{$subscript} = $value;
}
```

2. Here is one possible solution:

```perl
#!/usr/local/bin/perl

$linenum = 0;
while ($line = <STDIN>) {
        $linenum += 1;
        $line =~ s/^\s+|\s+$//g;
        @words = split(/\s+/, $line);
        if ($words[0] eq "index" &&
                $index{$words[1]} eq "") {
                $index{$words[1]} = $linenum;
        }
}
foreach $item (sort keys (%index)) {
        print ("$item: $index{$item}\n");
}
```

3. Here is one possible solution:

```perl
#!/usr/local/bin/perl

$linenum = 0;
while ($line = <STDIN>) {
        $linenum += 1;
        $line =~ s/^\s+|\s+$//g;
        @words = split(/\s+/, $line);
        # This program uses a trick: for each word, the array
        # item $index{"word"} stores the number of occurrences
        # of that word. Each occurrence is stored in the
        # element $index{"word#n"}, where[]is a
        # positive integer.
        if ($words[0] eq "index") {
                if ($index{$words[1]} eq "") {
                        $index{$words[1]} = 1;
                        $occurrence = 1;
                } else {
                        $index{$words[1]} += 1;
                        $occurrence = $index{$words[1]};
                }
                $index{$words[1]."#".$occurrence} = $linenum;
        }
}

# The loop that prints the index takes advantage of the fact
# that, when the list is sorted, the elements that count
# occurrences are always processed just before the
# corresponding elements that store occurrences. For example:
# $index{word}
# $index{word#1}
# $index{word#2}
foreach $item (sort keys (%index)) {
        if ($item =~ /#/) {
                print ("\n$item:");
        } else {
                print (" $index{$item}");
        }
}
print ("\n");
```

4. Here is one possible solution:

```perl
#!/usr/local/bin/perl

$student = 0;
@subjects = ("English", "history", "mathematics",
             "science", "geography");
while ($line = <STDIN>) {
        $line =~ s/^\s+|\s+$//g;
        @words = split (/\s+/, $line);
        @students[$student++] = $words[0];
for ($count = 1; $count <= 5; $count++) {
                $marks{$words[0].$subjects[$count-1]} =
                        $words[$count];
        }
}

# now print the failing grades, one student per line
foreach $student (sort (@students)) {
        $has_failed = 0;
        foreach $subject (sort (@subjects)) {
                if ($marks{$student.$subject} < 50) {
                        if ($has_failed == 0) {
                                $has_failed = 1;
                                print ("$student failed:");
                        }
                        print (" $subject");
                }
        }
        if ($has_failed == 1) {
                print ("\n");
        }
}
```

5. This program has one problem and one unwanted feature.

The problem: Adding a new element to %list in the middle of a foreach loop that uses the function keys yields unpredictable results.

The unwanted feature: The foreach loop doubles the size of the associative array because the original elements Fred, John, Jack, and Mary are not deleted.

Answers for Day 11, "Formatting Your Output"

Quiz

1. The answers are as follows:

    a. @<<<<<<<<<

    b. @>>>>

A

   c. @¦

   d. @####.###

   e. -- ^<<<<<<<<<<<<<<<<<<<<<<<<<<<<<

2. The answers are as follows:

   a. Five left-justified characters.

   b. Seven centered characters.

   c. One character.

   d. Multiple (unformatted) lines of text.

   e. Ten right-justified characters, with the line being printed only if the line is not blank.

3. The answers are as follows:

   a. An integer (base 10) in a field of at least five digits.

   b. A floating-point number with a total field width of 11 characters, four of which are to the right of the decimal point.

   c. A base-10 integer in a field of at least 10 digits. Empty characters in the field are filled with zeroes.

   d. A character string of at least 12 characters, left-justified.

   e. An integer in hexadecimal (base-16) form.

4. Numbers with rounding problems are numbers that normally round up but cannot be exactly stored on the machine. The closest equivalent that can be stored rounds down.

5. To create a page header for an output file, define a print format named `filename_TOP`, where `filename` is the file variable associated with the file. (Or, you can create a print format of any name and assign the name to the system variable `$^`.)

Exercises

1. Here is one possible solution:

```
#!/usr/local/bin/perl

for ($count = 1; $count <= 9; $count += 3) {
        $num1 = 2 ** $count;
        $num2 = 2 ** ($count + 1);
        $num3 = 2 ** ($count + 2);
        write;
}
$num1 = 2 ** 10;
```

```
$num2 = $num3 = "";
write;

format STDOUT =
^>>> ^>>> ^>>>
$num1 $num2 $num3
.
```

2. Here is one possible solution:

```
#!/usr/local/bin/perl

for ($count = 1; $count <= 10; $count++) {
        printf ("%4d", 2 ** $count);
        if ($count % 3 == 0) {
                print ("\n");
        } else {
                print (" ");
        }
}
print ("\n");
```

3. Here is one possible solution:

```
#!/usr/local/bin/perl
@text = <STDIN>;
$line = join("", @text);
write;
format STDOUT =
******************************************
~~^<<<<<<<<<<<<<<<<<<<<<<<<<<<<<<<<<<<<<<<<
$line
******************************************
.
```

4. Here is one possible solution:

```
#!/usr/local/bin/perl
$total1 = $total2 = 0;
while (1) {
        $num1 = <STDIN>;
        last if ($num1 eq "");
        chop ($num1);
        $num2 = <STDIN>;
        last if ($num2 eq "");
        chop ($num2);
        $~ = "LINE";
        write;
        $total1 += $num1;
        $total2 += $num2;
}
$~ = "TOTAL";
write;
$~ = "GRAND_TOTAL";
write;

format LINE =
                    @####.##   @####.##
                    $num1      $num2
```

```
.
format TOTAL =
   column totals:  @#####.##  @#####.##
                     $total1    $total2
.
format GRAND_TOTAL =
grand total:                   @#####.##
                     $total1 + $total2
.
```

5. When print writes a line to the page, the $- variable is not automatically updated. This means that the line count is off. To fix this, subtract one from the $- variable yourself.

Also, you must specify what is to be printed by the STDOUT print format:

```
format STDOUT =
@*
$line
.
```

Answers for Day 12, "Working with the File System"

Quiz

1. The answers are as follows:

   a. The tell function returns the current location in the file being read (the location of the next line to read).

   b. The mkdir function creates a directory.

   c. The link function creates a hard link (defines a second name that refers to a particular file).

   d. The unlink function destroys a hard link (the connection between the filename and the file). If no additional hard links have been defined (using link), unlink deletes the file.

   e. The truncate function reduces the size of a file to the length specified.

2. lstat assumes that the name it is working with is a symbolic link. stat assumes it is working with an actual file.

3. tell retrieves the location of the next line to be read in a file. telldir retrieves the location of the next name to be read in a directory.

4. The answers are as follows:

    a. file1 is open for reading only.

    b. file2 is actually a pipe that is sending the output from a command to this program (where it is treated as input).

    c. file3 is open for reading and writing. (+<file3 is equivalent.)

    d. MYFILE is being treated as identical to STDOUT (the two file variables now refer to the same file).

5. The answers are as follows:

    a. Read and write permissions for everybody.

    b. Read, write, and execute permissions for everybody.

    c. Read, write, and execute permissions for the owner only.

    d. Read and write permissions for the owner; read permissions for everybody else.

Exercises

1. Here is one possible solution:

```
#!/usr/local/bin/perl
opendir (MYDIR, "/u/jqpublic") ||
        die ("Can't open directory");
while ($file = readdir (MYDIR)) {
        next if ($file =~ /^\.{1,2}$|^[^.]/);
        print ("$file\n");
}
closedir (MYDIR);
```

2. Here is one possible solution:

```
#!/usr/local/bin/perl
$filecount = 1;
&print_dir ("/u/jqpublic");

sub print_dir {
        local ($dirname) = @_;
        local ($file, $subdir, $filevar);

        $filevar = "MYFILE" . $filecount++;
        opendir ($filevar, $dirname) ||
                die ("Can't open directory");
        # first pass: read and print file names
        print ("\ndirectory $dirname:\n");
        while ($file = readdir ($filevar)) {
                next if ($file eq "." || $file eq "..");
                next if (-d ($dirname . "/" . $file));
                print ("$file\n");
        }
        # second pass: recursively print subdirectories
```

A

```
                rewinddir ($filevar);
                while ($subdir = readdir ($filevar)) {
                        next unless (-d ($dirname . "/" . $subdir));
                        next if ($subdir eq "." || $subdir eq "..");
                        &print_dir ($dirname . "/" . $subdir);
                }
                closedir ($filevar);
        }
```

3. Here is one possible solution:

```
#!/usr/local/bin/perl
opendir (MYDIR, "/u/jqpublic") ||
        die ("Can't open directory");
# the following is a trick: "." is alphabetically less than
# anything we want to print, so it makes a handy
# initial value
$lastfile = ".";
until (1) {
        rewinddir (MYDIR);
        $currfile = "";
        while ($file = readdir (MYDIR)) {
                next if ($file =~ /^\./);
                if ($file gt $lastfile &&
                    ($currfile eq "" || $file lt $currfile)) {
                        $currfile = $file;
                }
        }
        last if ($currfile eq "");
        print ("$currfile\n");
        $lastfile = $currfile;
}
closedir (MYDIR);
```

4. Here is one possible solution:

```
#!/usr/local/bin/perl

@digits = ("zero", "one", "two", "three",
           "four", "five", "six", "seven",
           "eight", "nine");
&start_hot_keys;
while (1) {
        $char = getc(STDIN);
        last if ($char eq "\033");
        next if ($char =~ /[^0-9]/);
        print ("$digits[$char]\n");
}
&end_hot_keys;

sub start_hot_keys {
        system ("stty cbreak");
        system ("stty -echo");
}

sub end_hot_keys {
        system ("stty -cbreak");
        system ("stty echo");
}
```

5. Here is one possible solution:

```perl
#!/usr/local/bin/perl

$dir = "/u/dave/newperl/testdir";
opendir (MYDIR, $dir) ||
        die ("Can't open directory");
chdir ($dir);
while ($file = readdir (MYDIR)) {
        next if (-d $file);
        next if ($file eq "." || $file eq "..");
        if ($file =~ /\.pl$/) {
                @stat = stat($file);
                chmod (($stat[2] | 0700), $file);
        } else {
                chmod (0400, $file);
        }
}
closedir (MYFILE);
```

6. This program is trying to use eof() to test for the end of a particular input file. In
Perl, eof() tests for the end of the entire set of input files, and eof (with no
parentheses) tests for the end of a particular input file.

Answers for Day 13, "Process, String, and Mathematical Functions"

Quiz

1. The answers are as follows:

    a. srand provides a seed for the random number generator.

    b. pipe creates an input file variable and output file variable that are linked
    together. This is most frequently used by fork to allow processes to commu-
    nicate with one another.

    c. atan2 calculates the arctangent for a particular value (in the range $-\pi$ to π).

    d. sleep suspends the program for a specified number of seconds.

    e. gmtime returns the current Greenwich Mean Time (in machine-readable
    format).

2. fork starts an identical copy of the program currently running. system starts a
completely different program that runs concurrently (at the same time as the
current program). exec terminates the current program and starts a new one.

3. wait waits for any child process to terminate. waitpid waits for a particular child
process to terminate.

4. The easiest way to obtain the value of π is with the following statement:

```
$pi = atan2(1, 1) * 4;
```

This normally produces as close an approximation of π as is possible on your system.

5. You can obtain e with this statement: `$e = exp(1);`

6. The answers are as follows:

   a. `%x`

   b. `%o`

   c. `%e`

   d. `%f`

7. The answers are as follows:

   a. `"abc"`

   b. `"efgh"`

   c. `"gh"`

   d. The null string (a length of 0 is being specified)

8. The answers are as follows:

   a. 1

   b. −1

   c. 1

   d. 6

   e. 5

9. The answers are as follows:

   a. 4

   b. 9

Exercises

1. Here is one possible solution:

```
#!/usr/local/bin/perl

$child = fork();
if ($child == 0) {
        print ("This line goes first\n");
        exit (0);
} else {
        $child2 = fork();
```

```
                    if ($child2 == 0) {
                            waitpid ($child, 0);
                            print ("This line goes second\n");
                            exit (0);
                    } else {
                            waitpid ($child2, 0);
                            print ("This line goes third\n");
                    }
            }
```

2. Here is a program that reads from temp:

```
#!/usr/local/bin/perl

open (INFILE, "temp") ¦¦ die ("Can't open input");
while ($line = <INFILE>) {
        print ($line);
}
close (INFILE);
```

Here is a program that writes to temp and calls the first program (which is assumed to be named ch13.2a):

```
#!/usr/local/bin/perl

open (OUTFILE, ">temp") ¦¦ die ("Can't open output");
while ($line = <STDIN>) {
        print OUTFILE ($line);
}
close (OUTFILE);
exec ("ch13.2a");
```

3. Here is one possible solution:

```
#!/usr/local/bin/perl

for ($val = 1; $val <= 100; $val++) {
        print ("log of $val is ", log($val), "\n");
}
```

4. Here is one possible solution:

```
#!/usr/local/bin/perl

for ($i = 1; $i <= 6; $i++) {
        &sum(10 ** $i);
}

sub sum {
        local($limit) = @_;
        local(@startval, @stopval);
        local($i, $count);

        $count = 0;
        @startval = times();
        for ($i = 1; $i <= $limit; $i++) {
                $count += $i;
        }
        @stopval = times();
        print ("sum $limit: ", $stopval[0]-$startval[0], "\n");
}
```

A

5. Here is one possible solution:

```perl
#!/usr/local/bin/perl

$degrees = <STDIN>;
chop ($degrees);
$radians = $degrees * atan2(1,1) / 45;
$sin = sin ($radians);
$cos = cos ($radians);
print ("sin of $degrees is ", $sin, "\n");
print ("cos of $degrees is ", $cos, "\n");
print ("tan of $degrees is ", $sin/$cos, "\n");
```

6. The output specified by the first call to print might get jumbled because the call to system defines its own standard output buffers. To get around this problem, set the system variable $¦ to 1 before calling system.

7. Here is one possible solution:

```perl
#!/usr/local/bin/perl

@searchletters = ("a", "e", "i", "o", "u");
$inputline = <STDIN>;
foreach $letter (@searchletters) {
        printf("searching for $letter...\n");
        $location = 0;
        while (1) {
                $location = index ($inputline, $letter,
                            $location);
                last if ($location == -1);
                print("\tfound at location $location\n");
                $location += 1;
        }
}
```

8. Here is one possible solution:

```perl
#!/usr/local/bin/perl

@searchletters = ("a", "e", "i", "o", "u");
$inputline = <STDIN>;
foreach $letter (@searchletters) {
        printf("searching for $letter...\n");
        $location = length ($inputline);
        while (1) {
                $location = rindex ($inputline, $letter,
                                $location);
                last if ($location == -1);
                print("\tfound at location $location\n");
                $location -= 1;
        }
}
```

9. Here is one possible solution:

```perl
#!/usr/local/bin/perl

@searchletters = ("a", "e", "i", "o", "u");
$inputline = <STDIN>;
```

```
$len = length ($inputline);
foreach $letter (@searchletters) {
        print ("searching for $letter...\n");
        $currpos = 0;
        while ($currpos < $len) {
                $substring = substr ($inputline, $currpos, 1);
                if ($letter eq $substring) {
                        print("\tfound at location $currpos\n");
                }
                $currpos++;
        }
}
```

10. Here is one possible solution:

```
#!/usr/local/bin/perl

$_ = <STDIN>;    # reads to $_ by default
print ("number of a's found: ", tr/a/a/, "\n");
print ("number of e's found: ", tr/e/e/, "\n");
print ("number of i's found: ", tr/i/i/, "\n");
print ("number of o's found: ", tr/o/o/, "\n");
print ("number of u's found: ", tr/u/u/, "\n");
```

11. Here is one possible solution:

```
#!/usr/local/bin/perl

$number = <STDIN>;
if ($number =~ /\.¦[eE]/) {
        printf ("in exponential form: %e\n", $number);
        printf ("in fixed-point form: %f\n", $number);
} else {
        printf ("in decimal form: %d\n", $number);
        printf ("in octal form: 0%o\n", $number);
        printf ("in hexadecimal form: 0x%x\n", $number);
}
```

12. This program goes into an infinite loop if index actually finds the substring xyz. To get around this problem, increment $lastfound (at the bottom of the loop) before calling index again.

Answers for Day 14, "Scalar-Conversion and List-Manipulation Functions"

Quiz

1. The answers are as follows:

   a. A character string, padded with null characters if necessary.

   b. A character string, padded with blanks if necessary.

A

    c. A floating-point number (double-precision).

    d. A pointer to a string (as in the C programming language).

    e. Skip to the position specified.

2. The answers are as follows:

    a. Unpack a character string (unstripped).

    b. Skip four bytes, unpack a 10-character string (stripping null characters and blanks), and then treat the rest of the packed string as integers.

    c. Skip to the end of the packed string, back up four bytes, and unpack four unsigned characters.

    d. Unpack the first integer, skip four bytes, unpack an integer, skip back eight bytes, and unpack another integer. (This, effectively, unpacks the first, third, and second integers in that order.)

    e. Unpack a string of bits in low-to-high order, back up to the beginning, and unpack the same string of bits in high-to-low order.

3. The answers are as follows:

    a. 1

    b. 3

4. `defined` tests whether a particular value is equivalent to the special "undefined" value. `undef` sets a scalar variable, array element, or array variable to be equal to the special undefined value.

5. The answers are as follows:

    a. `("new", "2", "3", "4", "5")`

    b. `("1", "2", "test1", "test2", "3", "4", "5")`

    c. `("1", "2", "3", "4", "test1", "test2")`

    d. `("1", "2", "4", "5")`

    e. `("1", "2", "3")`

6. The answers are as follows:

    a. This returns every list element that does not start with an exclamation mark.

    b. This returns every list element that contains a word that consists entirely of digits.

    c. This returns every nonempty list element.

    d. This returns every list element.

7. `unshift` adds one or more elements to the left end of a list. `shift` removes an element from the left end of a list.

8. The answers are as follows:

    a. `splice (@array, 0, 1);`

    b. `splice (@array, @array-1, 1);`

    c. `splice (@array, scalar(@array), 0, @sublist);`

    d. `splice (@array, 0, 0, @sublist);`

9. You can create a stack using `push` to add elements and `pop` to remove them (or by using `shift` and `unshift` in the same way).

10. You can create a queue using `push` to add elements and `shift` to remove them (or by using `unshift` and `pop` in the same way).

Exercises

1. Here is one possible solution:

```perl
#!/usr/local/bin/perl
$string1 = <STDIN>;
chop ($string1);
$len1 = length ($string1);
$string2 = <STDIN>;
chop ($string2);
$len2 = length ($string2);
if ($len1 % 8 != 0) {
        $string1 = "0" x (8 - $len1 % 8) . $string1;
        $len1 += 8 - $len1 % 8;
}
if ($len2 % 8 != 0) {
        $string2 = "0" x (8 - $len2 % 8) . $string2;
        $len2 += 8 - $len2 % 8;
}
if ($len1 > $len2) {
        $string2 = "0" x ($len1 - $len2) . $string2;
} else {
        $string1 = "0" x ($len2 - $len1) . $string1;
        $len1 += ($len2 - $len1);
}
$bytes1 = pack ("b*", $string1);
$bytes2 = pack ("b*", $string2);
$carry = 0;
$count = $len1 - 1;
while ($count >= 0) {
        $bit1 = vec ($bytes1, $count, 1);
        $bit2 = vec ($bytes2, $count, 1);
        $result = ($bit1 + $bit2 + $carry) & 1;
        $carry = ($bit1 + $bit2 + $carry) >> 1;
        vec ($bytes1, $count, 1) = $result;
        $count—;
}
$resultstring = unpack ("b*", $bytes1);
$resultstring = $carry . $resultstring if ($carry > 0);
print ("$resultstring\n");
```

2. Here is one possible solution:

```perl
#!/usr/local/bin/perl
$string1 = <STDIN>;
chop ($string1);
$len1 = length ($string1);
$string2 = <STDIN>;
chop ($string2);
$len2 = length ($string2);
if ($len1 % 8 != 0) {
        $string1 = "0" x (8 - $len1 % 8) . $string1;
        $len1 += 8 - $len1 % 8;
}
if ($len2 % 8 != 0) {
        $string2 = "0" x (8 - $len2 % 8) . $string2;
        $len2 += 8 - $len2 % 8;
}
if ($len1 > $len2) {
        $string2 = "0" x ($len1 - $len2) . $string2;
} else {
        $string1 = "0" x ($len2 - $len1) . $string1;
        $len1 += ($len2 - $len1);
}
$bytes1 = pack ("h*", $string1);
$bytes2 = pack ("h*", $string2);
$carry = 0;
$count = $len1 - 1;
while ($count >= 0) {
        $nybble1 = vec ($bytes1, $count, 4);
        $nybble2 = vec ($bytes2, $count, 4);
        $result = ($nybble1 + $nybble2 + $carry) & 15;
        $carry = ($nybble1 + $nybble2 + $carry) >> 4;
        vec ($bytes1, $count, 4) = $result;
        $count--;
}
$resultstring = unpack ("h*", $bytes1);
$resultstring = $carry . $resultstring if ($carry > 0);
print ("$resultstring\n");
```

3. Here is one possible solution:

```perl
#!/usr/local/bin/perl

$value = <STDIN>;
$value *= 100;
$value = int ($value + 0.5);
$value = sprintf ("%.2f", $value / 100);
print ("$value\n");
```

4. Here is one possible solution:

```perl
#!/usr/local/bin/perl

$passwd = crypt ("bluejays", "ez");
$try = 1;
while (1) {
        print ("Enter the secret password:\n");
        system ("stty -echo");
```

```
        $guess = <STDIN>;
        system ("stty echo");
        if (crypt ($guess, substr ($passwd, 0, 2))
                eq $passwd) {
                print ("Correct!\n");
                last;
        }
        if ($try == 3) {
                die ("Sorry! Goodbye!\n");
        }
        print ("Try again — ");
        $try++;
}
```

5. This program is actually reading the low-order bit of the bit vector. To read the high-order bit, use vec ($packed, 7, 1).

6. Here is one possible solution:

```
#!/usr/local/bin/perl

# This program uses a very dumb sorting algorithm.
@list = (41, 26, 11, 9, 8);    # sample list to sort
for ($outer = 0; $outer < @list; $outer++) {
        for ($inner = 0; $inner < @list; $inner++) {
                if ($list[$inner] > $list[$inner+1]) {
                        $x = splice (@list, $inner, 1);
                        splice (@list, $inner+1, 0, $x);
                }
        }
}
```

7. Here is one possible solution:

```
#!/usr/local/bin/perl

# assume %oldarray is assigned here
while (($subscript, $value) = each (%oldarray)) {
        if (defined ($newarray{$value})) {
                print STDERR ("$value already defined\n");
        } else {
                $newarray{$value} = $subscript;
        }
}
```

8. Here is one possible solution:

```
#!/usr/local/bin/perl

while ($line = <STDIN>) {
        @words = split (/\s+/, $line);
        @shortwords = grep (/^.{1,5}$/, @words);
        print ("@shortwords\n");
}
```

9. Here is one possible solution:

```
#!/usr/local/bin/perl

$line = <STDIN>;
```

```
$line =~ s/^\s+//;
while (1) {
        last if ($line eq "");
        ($word, $line) = split (/\s+/, $line, 2);
        print ("$word\n");
}
```

10. This subroutine is trying to remove an element from a list using unshift. The subroutine should use shift, not unshift.

Answers for Day 15, "System Functions"

Quiz

1. The answers are as follows:

    a. endpwent, getpwent, getpwnam, getpwuid, and setpwent.

    b. endhostent, gethostbyaddr, gethostbyname, gethostent, and sethostent.

    c. endnetent, getnetbyaddr, getnetbyname, getnetent, and setnetent.

    d. endservent, getservbyname, getservbyport, getservent, and setservent.

2. Server processes call socket, bind, listen, and accept, in that order. Client processes call socket, bind, and connect, in that order.

3. The answers are as follows:

    a. getpwuid searches for an entry in /etc/passwd that matches a specific user ID.

    b. setprotoent rewinds the /etc/protocols file.

    c. gethostbyaddr searches the /etc/hosts file for a particular network (Internet) address.

    d. getgrent retrieves the next entry from the /etc/group file.

    e. getservbyport searches the /etc/services file for an entry corresponding to a particular port number.

4. To send information using a socket, use an output function such as print or printf, and specify the file variable associated with the socket.

5. You can obtain all the user IDs on your system by using getpwent to read the /etc/passwd file. This file contains one entry per user ID, and the user ID is part of the entry.

Exercises

1. Here is one possible solution:

```perl
#!/usr/local/bin/perl

while (($gname, $password, $groupid, $userids)
        = getgrent()) {
        $garray{$gname} = $userids;
}
foreach $gname (sort keys (%garray)) {
        print ("Group $gname:\n");
        @userids = split (/\s+/, $garray{$gname});
        foreach $userid (sort (@userids)) {
                print ("\t$userid\n");
        }
}
```

2. Here is one possible solution:

```perl
#!/usr/local/bin/perl

while (($name, $d1, $d2, $d3, $d4, $d5, $d6, $homedir) =
        getpwent()) {
        $dirlist{$name} = $homedir;
}
foreach $name (sort keys (%dirlist)) {
        printf ("userid %-15s has home directory %s\n",
                $name, $dirlist{$name});
}
```

3. Here is one possible solution:

```perl
#!/usr/local/bin/perl

while (@retval = getpwent()) {
        $retval[8] = "<null>" if ($retval[8] eq "");
        $shellarray{$retval[8]} += 1;
}
foreach $shell (sort count keys (%shellarray)) {
        printf ("%-25s %5d %s\n", $shell, $shellarray{$shell},
                ($shellarray{$shell} == 1 ?
                "occurrence" : "occurrences"));
}
sub count {
        $shellarray{$b} <=> $shellarray{$a};
}
```

4. Here is one possible solution:

```perl
#!/usr/local/bin/perl

$otherid = fork();
if ($otherid == 0) {
        # child process
        $otherid = getppid();
}
$| = 1;  # eliminate print buffers
print ("The process id of the other process is $otherid.\n");
```

5. Here is one possible solution:

```perl
#!/usr/local/bin/perl

$port = 2000;
while (getservbyport($port, "tcp")) {
        $port++;
}
($d1, $d2, $prototype) = getprotobyname ("tcp");
# in the following, replace "silver" with the name
# of your machine
($d1, $d2, $d3, $d4, $rawaddr) = gethostbyname ("silver");
$serveraddr = pack ("Sna4x8", 2, $port, $rawaddr);
socket (SSOCKET, 2, 1, $prototype) || die ("No socket");
bind (SSOCKET, $serveraddr) || die ("Can't bind");
listen (SSOCKET, 5) || die ("Can't listen");
while (1) {
        ($clientaddr = accept (SOCKET, SSOCKET))
        || die ("Can't accept");
        if (fork() == 0) {
                select (SOCKET);
                $| = 1;
                open (MYFILE, "/u/jqpublic/testfile");
                while ($line = <MYFILE>) {
                        print SOCKET ($line);
                }
                close (MYFILE);
                close (SOCKET);
                exit (0);
        }
}
```

6. getnetent returns an address as an array of four bytes, not as a readable address. To convert the address returned by getnetent to readable form, call unpack.

Answers for Day 16, "Command-Line Options"

Quiz

1. The answers are as follows:

   a. The -0 option specifies the end of file character for the input line.

   b. The -s option enables you to specify options for your program.

   c. The -w option tells the Perl interpreter to warn you if it sees something that it thinks is erroneous.

d. The -x option tells the Perl interpreter that your program is to be extracted from a file.

e. The -n option indicates that each line of the files specified on the command line is to be read.

2. The answers are as follows:

   a. The input end-of-line character becomes either newline or the character specified by -l. The output end-of-line character becomes either null or the character specified by -0.

   b. The input end-of-line character becomes either the character specified by -l or the character specified by -0; if neither option has a value supplied with it, the input line character becomes null. The output end-of-line character becomes either null or the character specified by -0.

3. The -n option tells the Perl interpreter to read each line of the input file, but does not explicitly tell it to write out its input. The -i option copies the input file to a temporary file, and then opens the input file for writing. If you do not explicitly write to the file yourself, nothing gets written to it.

4. This is a trick question: It doesn't. You'll have to make sure that your Perl comments are not C preprocessor commands.

5. The options for the interpreter appear before the Perl program name in the command line, or in the header comment for the program. The options for the program appear after the program name.

Exercises

1. Here is one possible solution:

```
$ perl -i -p -l072 -e ";" testfile
```

Note that -e ";" indicates an empty program. (Otherwise, the Perl interpreter would assume that testfile was the program, not the input file.)

2. Here is one possible solution:

```
$ perl -ne "print if (/\bthe\b/);" file1 file2 ...
```

3. Here is one possible solution:

```
$ perl -nae 'print ("$F[1]\n");' file1 file2 ...
```

4. Here is one possible solution:

```
#!/usr/local/bin/perl -s
print ("Hello\n") if ($H == 1);
print ("Goodbye\n") if ($G == 1);
```

A

5. Here is one possible solution:

```
$ perl -i -pe "tr/a-z/A-Z/;" file1 file2 ...
```

6. This command line wipes out all of your input files. Use the -p option instead of the -n option.

7. The -i option can be specified with a value (for creating a backup version of the file). The Perl interpreter thinks that pe is the suffix to append to the filename, and does not realize that these are supposed to be options. (I get tripped up by this problem all the time.)

Answers for Day 17, "System Variables"

Quiz

1. The pattern-matching operator, the substitution operator, the translation operator, the <> operator (if it appears in a while or for conditional expression), the chop function, the print function, and the study function.

2. The answers are as follows:
   a. The $= variable contains the page length of a particular output file.
   b. The $/ variable contains the input end-of-line character.
   c. The $? variable contains the return code returned by a command called by the system function or enclosed in back quotes.
   d. The $! variable contains the error code generated by a system library routine.
   e. The @_ variable contains the list of arguments passed to a subroutine by the calling program or calling subroutine.

3. ARGV is the file variable used by the <> operator to read from the list of input files specified on the command line. $ARGV is the name of the current file being read by the <> operator. @ARGV is the list of arguments (or files) specified on the command line.

4. @INC contains the directories to search when looking for files to be included. %INC lists the files requested by the require function that have already been found.

5. $0 is the name of the program you are running. $1 is defined when a pattern is matched, and is the first subpattern enclosed in parentheses in the matched pattern.

Exercises

1. Here is one possible solution:

    ```
    #!/usr/local/bin/perl -i

    while (<>) {
            s/[ \t]+/ /g;
            tr/A-Z/a-z/;
            print;
    }
    ```

    All of these statements use the system variable $_ by default.

2. Here is one possible solution:

    ```
    #!/usr/local/bin/perl -i

    while ($line = <>) {
            while ($line =~ /  +/g) {
                    $line = $` . " " . $';
            }
            print ($line);
    }
    ```

3. Here is one possible solution:

    ```
    #!/usr/local/bin/perl

    @dirlist = split (/:/, $ENV{"PATH"});
    foreach $dir (@dirlist) {
            print ("$dir\n");
    }
    ```

    Note that if your machine uses a character other than : to separate entries in the
    value of your PATH environment variable, you should use this character instead.

4. Here is one possible solution:

    ```
    #!/usr/local/bin/perl

    $SIG{"INT"} = stopnum;
    $num = 1;
    while (1) {
            print ("$num\n");
            $num++;
    }

    sub stopnum {
            print ("\nInterrupted.\n");
            exit (0);
    }
    ```

5. Here is one possible solution:

    ```
    #!/usr/local/bin/perl

    $total = 0;
    while ($line = <DATA>) {
            @nums = split (/\s+/, $line);
    ```

```
            foreach $num (@nums) {
                    $total += $num;
            }
    }
    print ("The total is $total.\n");
    __END__
    4  17  26
    11
    9     5
```

6. The substitution operator matches a pattern, so it overwrites the value of $'. To fix this, copy $' into a scalar variable of your own before searching for extra spaces.

Answers for Day 18, "References in Perl 5"

Quiz

1. The correct way to write this is `$pointer->{$i}`. You are dereferencing more than once in the line shown in the question.

2. Make the line

   `my($a,$b)`

   look like this:

   `my (\$a,\$b)`

   Then use `@$a` and `@$b` to access these arrays by reference.

3. There is no difference as far as accessing the variable in `$i` is concerned.

4. The word `Help`.

5. The `${variable}` can be used to create symbolic references. The three lines could be rewritten by eliminating `${}` constructs and using the values instead.

Exercises

1. Here is one possible solution:

```
$p1 = @a;
$p2 = %a;
$p3 = sub { return @_ ; };
printf "\n Array reference = $p1";
printf "\n Hash reference = $p2";
printf "\n Subroutine reference = $p3";
```

2. Use the code in the given hint to construct your function with one exception: you use an array for @list. Then you can call each function by using the index in the @list:

```
&$list[$index]();
```

3. Hard links are maintained by Perl and have to be greater than zero for a variable to exist. Soft links can point to nothing and are created by a user program.

4. Add the following lines to the end of the code:

```
printf "\n Address = $this, $that";
printf "\n Difference of Address = %f \n" $this - $that";
```

The addresses are not different because they point to the same function.

Answers for Day 19, "Object-Oriented Programming in Perl"

Quiz

1. The following is correct:

```
Balloon::new();
Balloon->new();
new Balloon;
```

2. This causes a memory leak. The memory allocated for $y has an extra reference. The reference count for $y is set when $x is set to it. After the block of code ends, the $y reference count remains nonzero. As a result, the memory $y hangs around until the program exits.

3. A class is only a package that provides methods, an object is a reference, and a method is a subroutine with the first argument as the name of the class.

4. Use *BaseClassName*:: explicitly in front of the function name to force Perl to use the base class.

Exercises

1. Create a file called Zeller.pm like this:

```
package Zeller;

require Exporter;
@EXPORT = (Zeller);

sub Zeller {
my ($month,$day,$year) = @_;
```

```
<<< Insert code from sample here>>>
}

1;
```

Then use the file in your Perl script like this:

```
use Zeller;

$z = Zeller(7,21,1962);
print "\n Day of the week = $z";
```

2. Check if the number of incoming parameters is not three. Use the call to `date +\%D`. The answer will return in mm/dd/yy format. Split the response on `/` to get the month.

```
$count = scalar (@_);
if ($count != 3) {
    $dt = 'date +\%D';
    ($month,$day,$year) = split($_,'/');
else {
    my ($month,$day,$year) = @_;
}
$z = Zeller($month,$day,$year);
```

3. Here is one possible solution:

```
#!/usr/bin/perl
print 'find . -depth -print ';
```

4. Add the following lines of code to the beginning of the function:

```
if (scalar(@_) == 0) {
    print "\n ================================= \n";
    print " Making a black cup of coffee. ";
    print "\n ================================= \n";
return;
}
```

Answers for Day 20, "Miscellaneous Features of Perl"

Quiz

1. The answers are as follows:

    a. `__LINE__` contains the current line number of the executing program or subroutine.

    b. `__FILE__` contains the current file being executed.

    c. `__END__` indicates the end of the Perl program.

2. The answers are as follows:

    a. It's time to say $var

    b. "It's time to say hello"; (including the quotes and the semicolon)

    c. hello

3. ("one", "two", "three", "", "five")

4. There are two ways:

    ☐ With the #include preprocessor command.

    ☐ Adding the file's directory to @INC and then passing the filename to require.

Exercises

1. Here is one possible solution:

```
#!/usr/local/bin/perl

@filelist = <*>;
foreach $file (sort (@filelist)) {
        print ("$file\n");
}
```

2. Here is one possible solution:

```
#!/usr/local/bin/perl

unshift (@INC, "/u/jqpublic/perlfiles");
require ("sum.pl");
@numlist = <STDIN>;
chop (@numlist);
$total = &sum (@numlist);
print ("The total is $total.\n");
```

3. Here is one possible solution:

```
#!/usr/local/bin/perl

package pack1;
$var = <STDIN>;
chop ($var);
package pack2;
$var = <STDIN>;
chop ($var);
package main;
$total = $pack1'var + $pack2'var;
print ("The total is $total.\n");
```

4. In this case, <$filepattern> is treated as a scalar variable containing the name of a file variable, not as a scalar variable containing a file list pattern. (To obtain the latter, use <${filepattern}>.)

5. There should be no space between the << and the EOF. The space after the << means that the end-of-string character string is assumed to be null; therefore, print only prints the first of the two lines in the string.

Answers for Day 21, "The Perl Debugger"

Quiz

1. The answers are as follows:

    a. Trace mode controls whether lines are displayed as they are executed. If trace mode is on, lines are displayed; if it is off, they are not.

    b. A stack trace is a display of the current subroutine being executed, plus a listing of the subroutine that called this one, and so on back to the original main program.

    c. A breakpoint is a line in the program before which execution is halted and further debugging commands are requested.

    d. A line action is a statement that is executed whenever a particular line of the program is reached.

2. The X command displays only variables in the current package. The V command can display variables in any package.

3. The // command searches forward in the file for a line matching the specified pattern; the ?? command searches backward.

4. The > command defines a line action that is to be executed before the debugger executes any further statements. The < command defines a line action that is to be performed after the debugger has finished executing the next statement or group of statements.

5. The s command steps into a subroutine when it encounters one; the n command executes the subroutine without stepping into it, stopping at the statement following the subroutine.

6. The answers are as follows:

    a. This displays the next window of statements, continuing where the last l command left off.

    b. This displays just line 26.

    c. This displays lines 5–7.

    d. This displays lines 5–12.

    e. This displays the window of statements surrounding the current line.

APPENDIX

B

ASCII Character Set

Dec	Hex	Char		Dec	Hex	Char
000	00			028	1C	∟
001	01	☺		029	1D	↔
002	02	☻		030	1E	▲
003	03	♥		031	1F	▼
004	04	♦		032	20	
005	05	♣		033	21	!
006	06	♠		034	22	"
007	07	•		035	23	#
008	08	◘		036	24	$
009	09	○		037	25	%
010	0A	◙		038	26	&
011	0B	♂		039	27	'
012	0C	♀		040	28	(
013	0D	♪		041	29	)
014	0E	♫		042	2A	*
015	0F	¤		043	2B	+
016	10	►		044	2C	,
017	11	◄		045	2D	-
018	12	↕		046	2E	.
019	13	‼		047	2F	/
020	14	¶		048	30	0
021	15	§		049	31	1
022	16	▬		050	32	2
023	17	↨		051	33	3
024	18	↑		052	34	4
025	19	↓		053	35	5
026	1A	→		054	36	6
027	1B	←		055	37	7

Dec	Hex	Char		Dec	Hex	Char
056	38	8		084	54	T
057	39	9		085	55	U
058	3A	:		086	56	V
059	3B	;		087	57	W
060	3C	<		088	58	X
061	3D	=		089	59	Y
062	3E	>		090	5A	Z
063	3F	?		091	5B	[
064	40	@		092	5C	\
065	41	A		093	5D	]
066	42	B		094	5E	^
067	43	C		095	5F	_
068	44	D		096	60	`
069	45	E		097	61	a
070	46	F		098	62	b
071	47	G		099	63	c
072	48	H		100	64	d
073	49	I		101	65	e
074	4A	J		102	66	f
075	4B	K		103	67	g
076	4C	L		104	68	h
077	4D	M		105	69	i
078	4E	N		106	6A	j
079	4F	O		107	6B	k
080	50	P		108	6C	l
081	51	Q		109	6D	m
082	52	R		110	6E	n
083	53	S		111	6F	o

B

Dec	Hex	Char		Dec	Hex	Char
112	70	p		140	8C	î
113	71	q		141	8D	ì
114	72	r		142	8E	Ä
115	73	s		143	8F	Å
116	74	t		144	90	É
117	75	u		145	91	æ
118	76	v		146	92	Æ
119	77	w		147	93	ô
120	78	x		148	94	ö
121	79	y		149	95	ò
122	7A	z		150	96	û
123	7B	{		151	97	ù
124	7C	|		152	98	ÿ
125	7D	}		153	99	Ö
126	7E	~		154	9A	Ü
127	7F	Δ		155	9B	¢
128	80	Ç		156	9C	£
129	81	ü		157	9D	¥
130	82	é		158	9E	₧
131	83	â		159	9F	ƒ
132	84	ä		160	A0	á
133	85	à		161	A1	í
134	86	å		162	A2	ó
135	87	ç		163	A3	ú
136	88	ê		164	A4	ñ
137	89	ë		165	A5	Ñ
138	8A	è		166	A6	ª
139	8B	ï		167	A7	º

Dec	Hex	Char		Dec	Hex	Char
168	A8	¿		196	C4	─
169	A9	⌐		197	C5	┼
170	AA	¬		198	C6	╞
171	AB	½		199	C7	╟
172	AC	¼		200	C8	╚
173	AD	¡		201	C9	╔
174	AE	«		202	CA	╩
175	AF	»		203	CB	╦
176	B0	░		204	CC	╠
177	B1	▒		205	CD	═
178	B2	▓		206	CE	╬
179	B3	│		207	CF	╧
180	B4	┤		208	D0	╨
181	B5	╡		209	D1	╤
182	B6	╢		210	D2	╥
183	B7	╖		211	D3	╙
184	B8	╕		212	D4	╘
185	B9	╣		213	D5	╒
186	BA	║		214	D6	╓
187	BB	╗		215	D7	╫
188	BC	╝		216	D8	╪
189	BD	╜		217	D9	┘
190	BE	╛		218	DA	┌
191	BF	┐		219	DB	█
192	C0	└		220	DC	▄
193	C1	┴		221	DD	▌
194	C2	┬		222	DE	▐
195	C3	├		223	DF	▀

B

Dec	Hex	Char		Dec	Hex	Char
224	E0	α		251	FB	$\sqrt{}$
225	E1	β		252	FC	^{n}
226	E2	Γ		253	FD	^{2}
227	E3	π		254	FE	∎
228	E4	Σ		255	FF	
229	E5	σ				
230	E6	μ				
231	E7	γ				
232	E8	Φ				
233	E9	θ				
234	EA	Ω				
235	EB	δ				
236	EC	∞				
237	ED	$\emptyset$				
238	EE	$\in$				
239	EF	$\cap$				
240	F0	$\equiv$				
241	F1	$\pm$				
242	F2	$\geq$				
243	F3	$\leq$				
244	F4	$\lceil$				
245	F5	$\rfloor$				
246	F6	$\div$				
247	F7	$\approx$				
248	F8	$\circ$				
249	F9	$\bullet$				
250	FA	$\cdot$				

INDEX

Symbols

A

X-Y-Z

Add to Your Sams Library Today with the Best Books for Programming, Operating Systems, and New Technologies

The easiest way to order is to pick up the phone and call
1-800-428-5331
between 9:00 a.m. and 5:00 p.m. EST.
For faster service please have your credit card available.

ISBN	Quantity	Description of Item	Unit Cost	Total Cost
0-672-30745-6		HTML and CGI Unleashed (book/CD)	$49.99	
0-672-30402-3		Unix Unleashed (book/CD)	$49.99	
1-57521-009-6		Teach Yourself CGI Programming with Perl in a Week	$39.99	
1-57521-014-2		Teach Yourself Web Publishing with HTML in 14 Days, Premier Edition (book/CD)	$39.99	
1-57521-005-3		Teach Yourself More Web Publishing with HTML in a Week	$29.99	
1-57521-039-8		Presenting Java	$25.00	
1-57521-030-4		Teach Yourself Java in 21 Days (book/CD)	$39.99	
0-672-30474-0		Windows 95 Unleashed (book/CD)	$39.99	
0-672-30602-6		Programming Windows 95 Unleashed (book/CD)	$49.99	
0-672-30819-3		Microsoft Office 95 Unleashed (book/CD)	$45.00	
0-672-30717-0		Tricks of the Doom Programming Gurus (book/CD)	$39.99	
❏ 3 ½" Disk		Shipping and Handling: See information below.		
❏ 5 ¼" Disk		TOTAL		

Shipping and Handling: $4.00 for the first book, and $1.75 for each additional book. Floppy disk: add $1.75 for shipping and handling. If you need to have it NOW, we can ship product to you in 24 hours for an additional charge of approximately $18.00, and you will receive your item overnight or in two days. Overseas shipping and handling adds $2.00 per book and $8.00 for up to three disks. Prices subject to change. Call for availability and pricing information on latest editions.

201 W. 103rd Street, Indianapolis, Indiana 46290

1-800-428-5331 — Orders   1-800-835-3202 — FAX   1-800-858-7674 — Customer Service

Book ISBN 0-672-30894-0

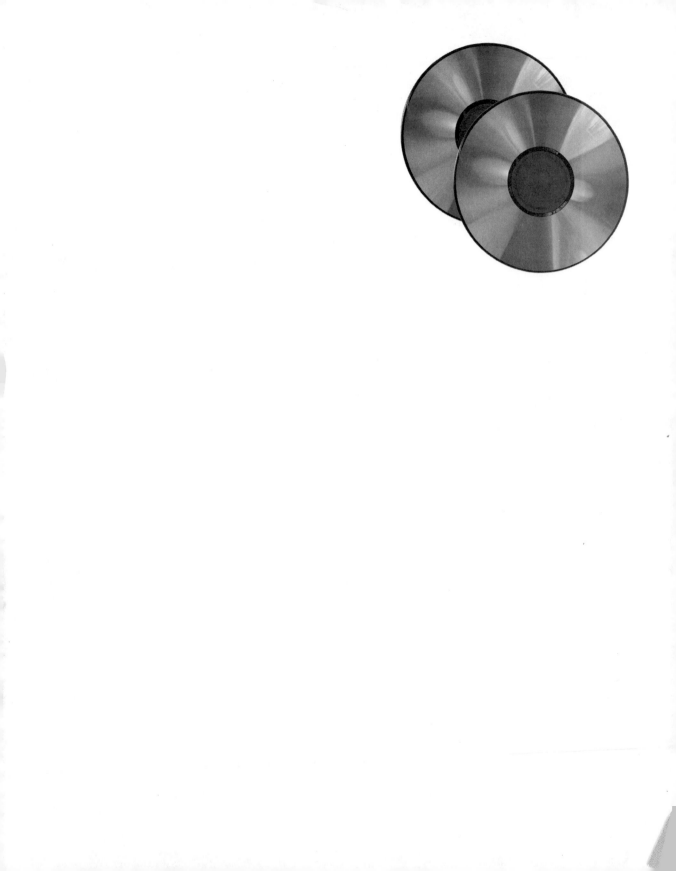

What's On the Disc

The companion CD-ROM contains software distributed under the GNU license, programs mentioned in the book, and many useful examples.

Windows (all Versions) Instructions

Insert the disc into your CD-ROM drive. From File Manager or Program Manager, choose Run from the File menu. Type `<drive>`SETUP and press Enter, where `<drive>` corresponds to the drive letter of your CD-ROM. For example, if your CD-ROM drive is drive D, type `D:`SETUP and press Enter. Follow the on-screen instructions in the installation program. Files will be installed to a directory named `\TYPERL` unless you choose a different directory during installation.

INSTALL creates a Windows program manager group called "Teach Yourself Perl."

DOS or UNIX (ISO 9660) Installation Instructions

Look in the individual directories for software and associated documentation. A README file, both in text and HTML formats, is available in the root directory of the CD-ROM for program descriptions. The README file also contains links to other World Wide Web locations for supplemental software and assistance.

Technical Support

Macmillan Computer Publishing can't help you with Perl difficulties or software from third parties, but we can assist you if a problem arises with the CD-ROM itself.

E-mail Support
Send e-mail to `support@mcp.com`

Telephone
(317) 381-3833

Fax
(317) 581-4773

Mail
Macmillan Computer Publishing
Attention: Support Department
201 West 103rd Street
Indianapolis, IN 46290-1093

World Wide Web
`http://www.mcp.com/samsnet`

Internet FTP
`ftp.mcp.com (/pub/samsnet)`